ALSO BY JUDITH MILLER

Saddam Hussein and the Crisis in the Gulf
(with Laurie Mylroie)

One, by One, by One

Judith Miller

REPORTING FROM
A MILITANT MIDDLE EAST

God Has Ninety-nine Names

A TOUCHSTONE BOOK
Published by Simon & Schuster

FOR JASON

TOUCHSTONE
Rockefeller Center
1230 Avenue of the Americas
New York, NY 10020

First Touchstone Edition 1997

TOUCHSTONE *and colophon are*
registered trademarks of Simon & Schuster Inc.

Designed by Edith Fowler

Manufactured in the United States of America

10 9 8 7 6 5 4 3 2

Library of Congress Cataloging-in-Publication Data
Miller, Judith.
    God has ninety-nine names : reporting from a
militant Middle East / Judith Miller.
        p.   cm.
    Includes index.
    1. Islam and politics — Middle East.
2. Middle East — Politics and government — 1979– .
3. Miller, Judith — Journeys — Middle East.
I. Title.
BP63.A4M53625   1996
322'.1'0917671 — dc20   96-4179   CIP
ISBN 0-684-80973-7
      0-684-83228-3 (Pbk.)

The author and publisher gratefully acknowledge permission to reprint extracts
    from the following works:
Saad Sowayan, *Nabati Poetry: The Oral Poetry of Arabia* (Berkeley: University
    of California Press, 1985). Copyright © 1985 by Saad Abdullah Sowayan.
    Reprinted with the permission of the Regents of the University of California
    and the University of California Press.
Mahmoud Darweesh, *Sand and Other Poems* (London and New York: Kegan
    Paul International, 1986).
Roy Mottahedeh, *The Mantle of the Prophet* (New York: Simon & Schuster,
    1985). Copyright © 1985 by Roy Mottahedeh. Reprinted with the permis-
    sion of Simon & Schuster.

Contents

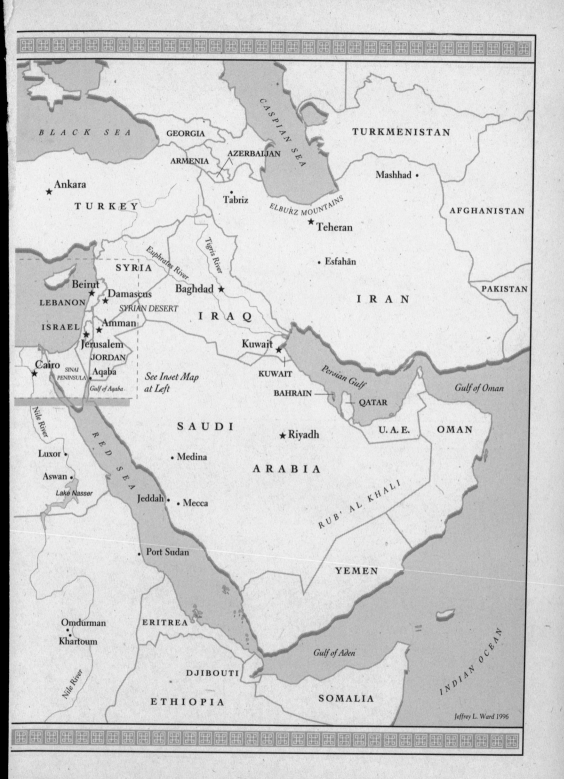

BLACK SEA

GEORGIA

ARMENIA

AZERBAIJAN

CASPIAN SEA

TURKMENISTAN

Mashhad •

★ Ankara

TURKEY

Tabriz •

ELBURZ MOUNTAINS

AFGHANISTAN

★ Teheran

Euphrates River

Tigris River

• Esfahān

PAKISTAN

SYRIA

Beirut ★

Damascus ★

SYRIAN DESERT

LEBANON

★ Baghdad

I R A Q

I R A N

ISRAEL

Amman ★

Jerusalem ★

JORDAN

Cairo ★

SINAI
PENINSULA

Aqaba •

Gulf of Aqaba

See Inset Map
at Left

Kuwait ★

KUWAIT

Persian Gulf

Gulf of Oman

BAHRAIN —

QATAR

Nile River

RED SEA

S A U D I

★ Riyadh

U. A. E.

OMAN

Luxor •

• Medina

A R A B I A

Aswan •

Lake Nasser

Jeddah •

• Mecca

RUB' AL KHALI

• Port Sudan

YEMEN

Omdurman •

Khartoum •

ERITREA

Nile River

DJIBOUTI

Gulf of Aden

INDIAN OCEAN

ETHIOPIA

SOMALIA

Jeffrey L. Ward 1996

Introduction

IT WAS a perfect morning. In only a few hours, Khartoum would be stifling. But at six o'clock on January 18, 1985, the air was clear, the sky already a swimming-pool blue.

In my room at the Hilton, the only sound was the hum of a twenty-year-old air conditioner pumping lukewarm air. I drank my coffee and read the morning paper, trying not to think about what lay ahead. I had seen and done many things as the Cairo bureau chief of *The New York Times* and witnessed many startling events since my first trip to the region in 1971, when I was a young student. But I had never covered an execution.

An hour later, I left for Kobar Prison. The prison's rectangular courtyard, about the size of a football field, was three-quarters full when the *Times's* Egyptian office manager, Gamal Mohieddin, and I arrived. I was wearing a white cloak and head scarf, hoping that the prison guards would not realize that I was a foreigner. The policemen waved us through, into the prison parking lot, without even a second glance at me in the backseat, the correct place to be for a woman in much of the Middle East. I kept my head down as Gamal and I walked slowly through the crowd to the center of the prison yard and found places to sit on the sandy ground.

The scaffolding was at the far end of the courtyard, elevated but still lower than the prison's sandstone walls. The scene at Kobar was gay, nothing like the grim photographs I had seen of prisons where Americans are executed, with friends and relatives of the condemned huddling outside the walls amid protesters holding candles in the night.

I seemed to be the only woman in the yard. Many of the several hundred men appeared to know one another. They greeted each other in the traditional Islamic welcome: *"Assalam Aleykum,"* peace be with you. *"Aleykum Salam,"* and unto you, came the reply again and again. The tall, dark-skinned men in their foot-high turbans and flowing white robes laughed and chatted about the weather, prospects for this year's crops, and the unending civil war in southern Sudan. Gradually, everyone sat down in the sand to wait under the sun that seemed to grow harsher by the minute. The execution was scheduled for ten o'clock.

Shortly before the appointed time, Mahmoud Muhammad Taha was led into the courtyard. The condemned man, his hands tied behind him, was smaller than I expected him to be, and from where I sat, as his guards hustled him along, he looked younger than his seventy-six years. He held his head high and stared silently into the crowd. When they saw him, many in the crowd leaped to their feet, jeering and shaking their fists at him. A few waved their Korans in the air.

I managed to catch only a glimpse of Taha's face before the executioner placed an oatmeal-colored sack over his head and body, but I shall never forget his expression: His eyes were defiant; his mouth firm. He showed no hint of fear.

The crowd began cheering as two Sudanese guards in sand-colored uniforms tightened a noose around the sack where Mahmoud Taha's neck must have been. Though the babble of the crowd drowned out their words, they seemed to be screaming at him. Suddenly, the guards stood back, the platform snapped open, the rope became taut, and the sack that covered Taha wriggled in the air. A few seconds later, the sack merely swayed a bit at the end of the rope. Idiotically, I thought of potatoes.

A roar erupted in the courtyard: *"Allahu Akbar!"* the crowd screamed— God is great! The din intensified as the men began chanting in unison: *"Allahu Akbar! Allahu Akbar! Islam huwa al-hall!"* (Islam is the solution).

The exuberant men hugged and kissed one another. Justice has been done, a man next to me shrieked, falling to his knees, touching his forehead to the sand, uttering a Muslim prayer. Stunned and sickened by the jubilation around me, I pulled at Gamal's sleeve and tried to tell him that we should leave. But I couldn't speak. In my nervousness, I must have tugged at my head scarf, which was now askew. Recognizing the danger, Gamal pulled the scarf down over my exposed bangs and pushed me firmly toward the courtyard door. As we edged our way toward the heavy iron gate, the sand began rising in an orange cloud under the shuffling of hundreds of feet. When we reached the exit, I craned my neck to catch one last look at the scaffolding: The sack, Taha's body, was still dangling from the rope. I wondered when they would cut it down.

To MANY of the Sudanese who applauded his execution that day, Taha had committed the worst possible crime. He had been convicted of sedition and "apostasy," abandoning Islam—a charge that he denied. But Taha insisted to the end that he was not a heretic—a *murtadd*, a Muslim who had abandoned Islam—but an Islamic reformer, a believer whose "crime" was having opposed

President Gaafar al-Nimeiri's cruel interpretation of Islam's sharia, the Muslim holy law. From what I knew of the situation, I, too, felt that Taha was killed not for his lack of religious convictions but because of them.

His execution was my introduction to the Islamic fervor that has shivered Middle Eastern politics ever since 1979, when the Ayatollah Ruholla Khomeini, the glum Muslim puritan from Islam's minority wing, Shiism, ousted the shah of Iran in a popular revolution. While Iranians are Shiites, the smaller of the two great branches of Islam, the Islamic revival, sparked by the ayatollah's revolution, soon took hold in Sunni Muslim lands as well. Now in almost every Arab capital, would-be Khomeinis promise a more "authentic" and "virtuous" government, and in almost every Arab state there is a struggle for power between the autocratic rulers and the Islamic militants who claim to represent millions of the unhappily ruled, the educated-but-unemployable, futureless young, the poor, the dispossessed — those whom Muslims call "the disinherited" and whom they recruit by the tens of thousands. Whereas Taha's execution was exceptional in 1985 in Sudan, thousands of men and women in that country and throughout the region have since been killed for their ideas in the name of Allah, and the killing goes on.

Taha's fate intensified my interest in this growing militancy, which, in 1985, I assumed naively was something new. But contemporary Islamic radicalism, often called "fundamentalism," a word borrowed from nineteenth-century European and American Protestants who also opposed scholarly explication of their scriptures in favor of a "fundamentalist" reading of sacred texts, turned out to be only a new expression of a struggle almost as old as Islam itself — the latest attempt to impose a militant version of the "straight path," the way enjoined by the Prophet Muhammad, who founded Islam in seventh-century Arabia.

Over the succeeding decade, I encountered this movement in many forms in every Middle Eastern country I covered. After the 1991 Gulf war divided the Middle East, it was widely and foolishly predicted that America would introduce a new order in the region based on democracy, capitalism, and human rights. But these militant Islamic movements — committed to establishing Islamic states that in theory will combine economic development with Islamic justice — have endured and in some countries have become vastly more influential and threatening to the prevailing order. Even in countries where there is little prospect that Islamic forces will rule, Islam now provides the vocabulary of everyday life, reshaping the language of politics, fundamental aspects of national culture, and long-standing traditions. In most Arab states, even secular leaders have increasingly relied on Islam to shore up their rule. Thus, the power struggles are no longer between the defenders of the "secular" order and advocates of religious rule but, rather, over who will rule in the name of Islam.

This book is my attempt to understand these militants and their movements as well as the responses to them in the varied and culturally distinct countries where they have emerged as either challengers or rulers. When I started this project soon after the Gulf war, the late Albert Hourani, an eminent British historian of Arab descent, urged me to avoid generalizations about the resurgence of Islam. Of course, militant Islamic movements had some common themes, heroes, and villains, but, he cautioned, they varied dramatically from one country to another and could best be evaluated "within the context of their individual societies and their own distinctive histories, political traditions, and cultures."[1] I have followed his advice and attempted to describe these movements as I have witnessed them in ten Middle Eastern countries, all but two of them Arab.

Though Islam itself is based partly on the principle of *tawhid*, the "oneness" of God—which implies, in addition to monotheism, the inseparability of church and state, or in Islamic terms, of religion and politics—militant Islam takes many forms. And while radical Arab Muslims assert that Islam is the only force that can unify the Arabs, as Arab nationalism promised but failed to do for the previous generation, what I have seen so far suggests the contrary. If anything, militant Islam becomes ever more fragmented and diverse. Just as the Koran gives ninety-nine names for God, Islam—and Islamic militancy, in particular—occurs in many varieties, as distinct from country to country as Catholicism is in France, Italy, Brazil, and America. There is no more an Islamic world than there is an Arab world or a Christian world. This book contains very few predictions, but of this I am sure: There will not be a single, unified Islamic *umma*, or community, any more than there is a single Arab nation, even in the unlikely event that Islamic radicals topple every quasi-secular government in the Middle East.

My reasons for choosing the countries I have written about are obvious, but less so is the order in which I have written about them. I begin with Egypt, the self-proclaimed "mother of the world," for it was, in fact, Arab nationalism's standard-bearer under its former ruler Colonel-turned-President Gamal Abdel Nasser as well as the birthplace of the Muslim Brotherhood, which, though it now claims to be nonviolent, remains the world's largest and most influential militant Islamic organization. The historical center of Arab political and cultural life, Egypt has faced an energetic and violent Islamic challenge in recent years. Given its population, geography, and history, Egypt's political fate will inevitably affect that of the smaller, weaker Arab states around it. Egypt is also the Arab country I love best. It was the first Arab state I visited, and it was in Cairo that I was based for *The New York Times* between 1983 and 1985.

Saudi Arabia, the subject of my second chapter, is the birthplace of the Prophet Muhammad and hence of Islam, the faith of more than a billion Muslims throughout the world, less than a majority of whom are Arab.[2] I have tried to describe how the militants have used the events of the Prophet's life and some of the laws and political traditions he created to justify their own views on how society should be organized. Arabia also produced the region's first modern militant Islamic state—the result of an alliance between a religious leader and a local tribal chief in the eighteenth century.

I turn next to Sudan because it is the only Sunni Arab state in which militant Muslims now rule. The seven-year reign of the National Islamic Front, a branch of Sudan's Muslim Brotherhood that seized power in a military coup in 1989, provides much evidence of the appalling crimes of this ostensibly Islamic state, which should serve as a warning to other Arabs of the dangers they face should they, too, attempt to reconstruct human nature according to religious doctrine.

Then Algeria. A vicious war has raged between the secular government and Islamic radicals since 1992, when the military refused to accept the militants' electoral victory and decided instead to crush the Islamic populist movement. The conflict has already claimed some forty thousand lives, and its outcome remains unclear. I look next at another North African country — Libya, an oil-rich Arab land in which, once again, a military officer, the erratic but durable Colonel Muammar al-Qaddafi, has suppressed religious militants as well as secular dissenters who oppose him. While militant Sunni Muslims despise him for having banned the Muslim Brotherhood in Libya and radical Shiites blame him for the "disappearance" of a leading Lebanese cleric during a visit to Libya in 1978, Qaddafi himself has imposed his own eccentric form of "Islamic" rule on his sparsely populated country.

I then move to what the French once called the Levant, the eastern Mediterranean Arab states, each with its own distinct preoccupations and political traditions. Lebanon is slowly emerging from the seventeen-year civil war that all but destroyed what was once the Arab Middle East's most prosperous and intellectually vital society. But modern Lebanon, whose national boundaries were drawn by Europeans around an uncongenial assembly of heterogeneous ethnic and religious groups, is struggling under a new demographic reality: The state that was created for, and long dominated by, Christians now contains a solidly Muslim majority. Shiite Muslims alone, many of them supporters of Hezbollah and other violent Islamic groups, constitute about 40 percent of the population. I have tried to describe the efforts by Lebanon's political elite, dominated by Syria, to devise a new modus vivendi among its fractious religious sects and clans while responding to growing demands from politicized Muslims for a fairer division of political power and spoils. I have also described the evolution of the violent, Iranian-supported Hezbollah into a more traditional political party, a transformation that has intriguing implications for Lebanon's political future.

In neighboring, politically stagnant Syria, President Hafiz al-Assad has precluded such sectarian warfare by murderous repression of his own militant Muslims. So far, Assad's rule by the threat of renewed state terror holds firm.

Syria's exact opposite is Jordan. Of all the Arab states, Jordan has been among the boldest in offering militant Muslims political rights and participation in government. Its daring experiment offers some tentative lessons for other Arab states confronting radical Islamic pressures.

While most Westerners once associated militancy affecting Israel largely with Hamas, the militant wing of the Muslim Brotherhood in the West Bank and Gaza, the assassination of Israel's Prime Minister Yitzhak Rabin in November 1995 revealed the intensity of Jewish militancy — Islamic radicalism's counterpart. Like their Islamic soul mates, Jewish fundamentalists openly advocate replacing their system, in this case a democracy, with a theocracy in which the word of God, as they interpret it, would be law. They, too, have their *fatwas*, their bitter hatreds, and fanatical clerics who issue death warrants for Arab leaders and their own. They, too, condemn their society and its leaders, portraying their prime minister as "traitorous" and his government's policies as a "betrayal of Judaism." In their world of self-righteous hatred and intolerance, no one — and no idea — is safe. But Jewish militancy is the subject of another book. In my chapter on Israel I have tried to examine not only the evolution of Hamas in the territory that Israel has occupied since the 1967 war and from which it is now partially withdrawing in keeping with its dramatic 1993 peace agreement with the Palestine Liberation Organization, but also the development of what few realize is one of the region's fastest-growing Islamic groups — the homegrown, largely nonviolent Islamic Movement of Israel, which flourishes within Israel's 1948 borders among its Muslim citizens, who now constitute some 18 percent of the population. Democracy has so far proven a boon to Israel's Islamists.

While I have written much about Palestinians, I have not written about Palestine, for it is not yet born, though I expect it soon will be. Nevertheless, Palestinians, united by a common dream, remain geographically dispersed. As such, they face a variety of challenges within their own diaspora. For too many years Palestine has been a cause rather than a place, and Palestinians have suffered from the burden of having been for far too long the issue around which other Arabs have rallied and tried to unify themselves, a symbolic rather than a real people with needs and problems that most Arab states have preferred to ignore. For a people betrayed time and again by Arab leaders, including their own, the militant Islamic promise of justice and territorial redemption through a return to Islam has been a particularly seductive illusion.

I conclude with the Islamic Republic of Iran, which remains among the Middle East's most intellectually dynamic societies. Non-Arab, Shiite Persia was modern militant Islam's first victory. Despite a debilitating eight-year war initiated by Iraq in 1980, an abysmal economic performance, widespread corruption, support for international terrorism that has alienated much of the West and Arab states as well, and intense political repression at home, the Islamic revolution and the republic it spawned retain widespread support among millions of poor Iranians. But within the elite, many have despaired of the Islamic dream and are now trying to flee — to America or to any other country that will have them. A tiny but influential minority, however, chooses to remain, hoping to make Islam succeed as a political framework, in effect, by separating once again the political functions of the state from the ideological and often inept clergy that has dominated Iranian political life since 1979. Whether or not they succeed — and Iranian history and the brutality of Middle Eastern politics make such a victory most unlikely — these Islamic reformers have launched a thrilling debate that has kept Iran a fascinating, if unpredictable, place.

I have not included, for very different reasons, two countries that readers might expect to find in this book: Turkey and Iraq. Until the early twentieth century, Turkey was the seat of a great Islamic empire and the first Islamic state to experience a secular revolution. Yet Turkey remains somewhat isolated from the rest of the region. It is not an Arab country, and recent developments there, unlike those in non-Arab Iran, seem to have had little impact on the Arab-oriented Middle East. I have not written about Iraq because I have not been permitted to go there since 1986. Shortly before the Gulf war, I coauthored a book about Saddam Hussein and his monstrous regime. I could hardly expect a visa in return. Not long ago, an Iraqi diplomat told me that I was on a very short list of writers who are considered the regime's "eternal enemies."

I am not a scholar, and this is not a scholarly book. While I have identified some of my sources in numerous footnotes, this book is based largely on interviews I have conducted and on my travels and adventures during twenty-five years of reporting from the region. Though scholars may wince at my rendering of Arabic terms, I have tried to transliterate them in a form that is most easily recognizable to non-Arab readers; the inconsistencies in spelling result mainly from quotations from sources that have used a different form.

I have also tried to avoid the debate about what to call the movements I have described. Though I have used the term occasionally, I am not comfortable with "fundamentalist" because the militant movements embrace far more than a preference for religious orthodoxy. Moreover, while a great many Muslims are orthodox in their religious practices, by no means are they all politically oriented; fewer still follow a militant line. Many of these Muslim traditionalists shun politics on principle. Others, especially those in such conservative states as Saudi Arabia, where sharia is already the basis of most laws, consider themselves what we would call "fundamentalists," but they, too, do not oppose their governments, however wanting they may be, since their leaders attempt, at least in theory, to apply sharia and abide by what they view as Islamic tradition.

My focus, rather, is the young militants and the men who lead them, those who see Islam as a way of bringing about revolutionary change in their societies. They are deeply political in that they view politics as a way of replacing secular laws and rulers not just with Muslim edicts and Muslim rulers but with what they call "Islam." They are also determined to rid their societies of secular and even traditional "un-Islamic" customs, ethnic and sectarian cleavages, and social injustice, which they blame for having prevented Muslims from developing and prospering. They are, moreover, not traditionalist but "modern" in their outlook; many of them are young and often the products of Western secular training, especially in the sciences.

As Olivier Roy, the French political scientist, has argued, these militants are the product of Muslim cultures that have already been both "modernized" and "Westernized," partly reshaped by Western education, values, and culture

—American films, music, and fashion.[3] The Algerians who write "Islam is the solution" on the Casbah walls do so in French, dressed in blue jeans and leather jackets. They would not be out of place in a Left Bank café. Thus, this militant or radical Islam, or Islamism, which is what I prefer to call this trend, does not represent primarily "hatred of the other," in Roy's words, so much as "hatred of oneself and of one's desires." The militants I write about inhabit a "hybrid world" and promote a cult of nostalgia for an imagined past that they seek to reclaim by securing sufficient political power to "re-Islamize" their societies and produce, if not a more democratic, a more "just" government and "authentic" environment.

Some militants, including those who support Egypt's Muslim Brotherhood, advocate gradual change through nonviolent preaching, education, and pressuring their rulers to make their societies more "Islamic" in law and deed; others, such as adherents of the numerous "Islamic Jihad" groups, endorse ousting or killing "un-Islamic" leaders and their secular elite and even military coups to secure power and impose an Islamic order. Many movements include advocates of both collaboration and confrontation, persuasion and violence, who oscillate pragmatically between these methods. But whether they favor Islamization "from below" or "from above,"[4] their goal is the same—power.

This book is not merely about politics, though politics is at its center. What I've tried to do is convey in a historical context the mood of the countries within the region, the tone of their debates, and the forms taken by the struggle for dominance in each of them. I have paid special attention to three groups: Christians and other non-Muslim minorities; intellectuals; and women. All three are likely to be most dramatically and, I fear, adversely affected should the Islamization under way in the region prevail.

While I have tried to keep an open mind about traditions and cultures that differ from my own, I make no apology for the fact that as a Western woman and an American, I believe firmly in the inherent dignity of the individual and the value of human rights and legal equality for all. In this commitment, I, too, am unapologetically militant.

Apart from this, I have tried to approach the region and its people in a spirit of inquiry. Almost seventy years ago, Freya Stark, another woman writer and traveler with a passion for the Middle East, wrote these words in her diary from Damascus: "Most people seem to want to stagnate when they reach middle age. I hope I shall not become so, resenting ideas that are not my ideas, and seeing the world with all its changes and growth as a series of congealed formulas. To feel, and think, and learn—learn always: surely that is being alive and young in the real sense."[5]

EGYPT

There are some kinds of laughter that make you cry.

AL-MUTANABBI, poet (A.D. 915–965)

ON MY FIRST DAY as Cairo bureau chief of *The New York Times* in August 1983, I saw a donkey drop dead just outside my office on Kasr el Nil, a major commercial street where smart shoppers, young men on motorbikes and bicycles, donkey carts, taxis, and smoke-belching buses jostle for space on the narrow roadway. In 115-degree heat — almost as hot as my office, where the air conditioning had broken down yet again an hour earlier — the donkey probably died of exhaustion.

I was watching from my second-story window as the donkey stood still for a few seconds while his owner beat him across the neck and head. Then, without warning, the donkey fell over dead.

Instantly, a small crowd gathered around the animal, yelling advice at the owner, who by this time understood that further whipping would not revive his poor beast. But he had no idea what to do next. He put his hands on top of his white-turbaned head, the headdress typical of so-called Upper Egypt, which is, in fact, in the southern part of the country, and rocked back and forth in grief.

At this moment, a taxi swerved to avoid hitting the donkey and collided instead with another small black-and-white taxi. The drivers leaped out of their cars, yelling and waving their fists. The crowd grew larger, turning away from the distraught donkey owner and toward the two men on the verge of a brawl.

By this time, traffic was snarled all along Kasr el Nil and the adjoining streets. Normally, Cairo's traffic bleats like herds of goats. That day, however, the bleating was a steady blare as drivers, sweating in their vehicles, leaned on their horns.

The two drivers lunged at each other, but men in the crowd kept them apart. Another group of young men tried to push the two dented taxis off the main road; still others helped the donkey owner drag his dead animal down a side street.

Amid the commotion, a small boy carrying a tray filled with thimble-sized glasses of tea emerged from nowhere and offered a glass to the weeping donkey owner and to the taxi drivers, who were still cursing each other. All three began sipping tea. The traffic slowly started moving again. The donkey owner sat down on a merchant's chair, presumably to discuss the animal he had just lost. It was then that I noticed that the horns had stopped blaring.

It was all over in less than ten minutes. In no time at all, the three men were calm, or calmer, apparently consoled; two of them were actually smiling. The crowd had dispersed, and normal life had resumed on Kasr el Nil.

SOMEWHERE BETWEEN laughter and tears there is Egypt. As a reporter, I had covered Egypt for more than twenty years and never quite knew whether to laugh or weep. No other Arab country tried my patience, broke my heart, or fascinated me as much. For Egypt, despite its problems, was thrilling. Its kind, good-humored, and generous people took quiet pride in being Egyptian, descendants of one of the oldest and greatest civilizations. Cairo's vibrant theater, literature, and cosmopolitan life still had no equal in the Arab world. For me, Egypt inspired a kaleidoscope of emotions — from fury and despair to delight and euphoria, often in a single day, sometimes in a single hour.

The donkey's death was a small thing at the time, nothing I could write about for the *Times*. There had been no riot. No Arab official had said or done anything that merited the world's attention. Yet to this day that scene stays in my mind for what it revealed about the Egyptians and their society.

Anger has a short half-life in Egypt. Frustrations that would push a less benign and lackadaisical people to riot and rebellion tend to be accepted by Egyptians as their fate — Allah's will. The standard Egyptian reply to the setbacks of daily life is *"ma'alesh,"* accompanied by a sigh. The term itself implies submission to fate, conflating "I'm sorry," "It doesn't really matter," "It won't be so bad in the long run," and "You can't do anything about it, anyway" with a simple shrug. A quintessentially Egyptian expression, *"ma'alesh"* is the ultimate acceptance of what life dispenses, no matter how irrational or unjust. *Ma'alesh* is one clue — their history is another — that compared to Iranians or Algerians, for example, Egyptians are not a revolutionary people. In fact, Egypt has been ruled for the past two hundred years by only two regimes: the descendants of Mohammed Ali, the Turko-Circassian commander of mercenary forces who ruled from 1805 in the name of the Ottoman Empire and whose dynasty ended with the deposed King Farouk and the departure of his British protectors in 1952, followed by a succession of Egyptian military-backed governments that began with Muhammed Naguib and Gamal Abdel Nasser and his Free Officers Movement, the first Egyptians to rule their country since the pharaohs. Nasser, the revered symbol of the Arabs' quest for greatness through socialism and Arab unity — the embodiment of pan-Arabism — was himself a modern pharaoh. His impact on Egypt was devastating, but even after Egypt's defeat by Israel in 1967, when the sham of Nasser's revolution became undeniable, Egyptians still worshiped him. After Nasser came Anwar Sadat, who shattered Nasser's pan-Arabist vision by making a shocking and solitary peace with Israel; Sadat risked and lost Egypt's leadership of the Arabs, but he was heir to Nasser's praetorian bureaucracy, and the Egyptian people dutifully followed him. So, too, did they follow Hosni Mubarak, who embarked in the 1980s on ultracautious political and economic reform.

Despite its infatuation with revolutionary slogans and lofty Arab nationalist rhetoric, Egypt has never experienced a true revolution that has overthrown a ruler. Egyptians, of course, have rioted over the centuries, usually against excessive taxation and repressive rule, for food and sometimes for patriotic reasons, but the outbursts were not sustained. While Nasser and Sadat rewrote Egyptian history to portray their 1952 takeover as a revolution, it was, in fact, more of a military coup.

For centuries, Egyptians have suffered, died, and joked about their oppressors — and in this way endured.[1] In the mid–tenth century, for instance, when a black eunuch named Abu al-Misk Kafur ruled Egypt, intense earthquakes, followed by a great fire, were said to have destroyed seventeen hundred houses in the capital. But in the deferential manner still typical of so many Egyptian intellectuals, a leading poet of the day wrote that the earth was "shaking with joy at the blessing of such a ruler as Kafur."[2]

Egypt's tradition has usually been to accept a conqueror's religion and politics — eventually. Egyptians slowly converted to Christianity under the Romans, eager to see the end of the despised Ptolemies. They then embraced Islam to rid Egypt of Byzantine misrule. But Egypt's Islamic conversion was even more gradual. By 725, almost a hundred years after the Muslim conquest, 95 percent of Egyptians were still Christian. It was not until the tenth century that Islam finally triumphed.[3]

Military power, however, not religion, has always been the true basis of legitimacy along the Nile.[4] Religious scholars, the ulema, were the servants and occasional partners of a succession of foreign rulers, but they never ruled. Even when Bonaparte offered the ulema the highest government posts, they spurned the offers of this hated "son of a Christian" but nonetheless urged their fellow Egyptians to obey the French pharaoh.[5] The Egyptian people as a whole, much less the fellaheen — Egypt's long-suffering tillers of the soil — never had much to say about how the country was run.

Most students of Egypt believe that for reasons of history, geography, and national and religious culture, Egypt will never see an Iranian-style revolution involving the masses. Egyptians have expected their leaders to become pharaohs, and so far, at least, anger along the Nile has been quickly spent. But during my recent trips to Cairo I had to wonder: Could this be changing?

Hosni Mubarak, in his grand presidential palace, now in his third six-year term, had grown increasingly stubborn in his isolation. Most Egyptian intellectuals who had once supported him were now cowed or alienated into silence — or worse, from the government's standpoint, seduced into open alliance with the Islamists. Many professionals, normally supporters of the quasi-secular status quo and hostile to radical change, were themselves demanding a more "Islamic" government. Egypt's 6–8 million Coptic Christians, the Islamic movement's traditional foes, were on the defensive after more than a decade of bloody battles against militants in Upper Egypt, often ignored until recently by an indifferent government. Copts by the thousands were emigrating or trying to. The American Coptic Association asserted that at least a million Copts had fled their country, 400,000 of whom were said to live in the United States.[6] Egypt's tired political parties — even the socialist Nasserists — were seeking renewal through alliances with the Muslim Brotherhood. The secular civic groups and associations on which civil society depends were frail and ill funded, lacking real roots or mass appeal. Over the past decade, Islamists had succeeded in penetrating most government institutions — schools, universities, ministries, and most recently, the courts, once respected for their professionalism and relative independence. Only the army and security services were said to be "reliable." But for how long?

Mubarak was combating radical Islam in several ways. His aides were convinced that the government's endurance depends on economic growth — on liberalizing Egypt's creaking command economy so as to keep pace with the country's rapidly growing population, now approaching 60 million people, almost twice its population in 1971, when I first visited Cairo. But prosperity was unlikely unless the government suppressed the Islamic violence that deterred foreign investment and had already cost the country more than $3 billion in tourist revenue since 1992. So the army and security forces were aggressively repressing the militants; some sixty-two Islamists had been sentenced to death in military courts since 1992, and more than twenty-five thousand people were now in prison.

At the same time, the government was promoting its own quiescent brand of Islam in response to growing popular pressures for a more Islamic society. But its efforts to outdo the Islamists in religious purity created the very Islamic atmosphere that put secular individuals and institutions on the defensive. Each time I returned in the mid-1990s, Egypt seemed to have become more decrepit and more "Islamic." The headquarters of Mubarak's ruling National Democratic Party, a discredited shell of an organization, now featured a giant sign spelling out "Allah" in green neon letters. The official television channels were flooded with sheikhs waving their fists, denouncing "un-Islamic" conduct. Preachers, even in some state mosques, denounced the moral degeneracy of Egypt's "enemies" — foreigners, Jews, and, of course, the Coptic Christians, who represent at least 10 percent of the population and whose presence long predates Islam. The audience for these sheikhs was increasing among the multitudes of young, poor, and frustrated middle-class Egyptians for whom the slogans of Islam provide both comfort in their daily misery and hope for a better future. There was now much occasion for this Islamic appeal, especially when it denied responsibility for the bombings and terrorism sponsored by the more violent Islamic groups.

The Islamic trend was also fed by the government's growing alienation from the public — obvious official corruption, an arrogant security apparatus, and an inert bureaucracy whose members, according to a UN study, work an average of twenty-seven minutes per day. Though the militants' organizations were being suppressed, the Islamic culture they were promoting seemed to be steadily gaining ground. The seemingly changeless Egypt I had first encountered only twenty years ago was disappearing. How long could a quasi-secular government rule a society that in its despair was becoming increasingly Islamic?

THE FALL of 1993 was a turning point in the government's war against the militants. That year, during my extended stay in Egypt, Cairo itself had felt on edge, as fragile as its overburdened infrastructure. Mubarak, the traditional brunt of coffeehouse jokes, had just been reelected to another six-year term by 96 percent of the vote. He was, of course, the only candidate.

I could sense the yearning for change; "renewal," my Egyptian friends called it. But Mubarak, comfortable with the men he knew — and all but one were men — seemed impervious to the unmistakable dissatisfaction of people who had once believed in him.

His long-serving cabinet was the object of some of the best jokes. "The only thing unmoved by the earthquake [the tremor in 1992 that killed 550 people, injured 10,000, and left thousands more homeless] was Atef Sidki's chair," Egyptians said of their prime minister, then sixty-three, who had been in office for six years. Amal Osman, the minister of social welfare and the only woman in the cabinet, had served under Sadat and Mubarak for more than fourteen years, so long that even she had asked to be replaced.

But until 1996 Mubarak had refused to make significant changes. Why had Mubarak backed away from his campaign pledge to infuse his third term with new ideas and young blood?

"Because their tombs weren't ready," said my wise friend Tahseen Bashir, a former government official and the unfailing source of Cairo's latest political humor. As always in Cairo, humor hid the frustration. But it could not hide the panic inspired by the assassinations, bombings, and other violence that year.

The president's pharaonic aloofness now suggested impotence. During the earthquake of October 1992, for example, Mubarak was visiting China. Not until he returned almost two days later did official assistance to the dead and injured begin in earnest. In the meantime, Islamic groups were providing tents, food, clothing, and medical aid within hours of the disaster. For its part, the government could do no better than knock the tents down and throw out the homeless on the grounds that the Islamic housing was not government licensed. Ultimately, the government provided massive aid — far more than the Islamic groups. But by then Islamists had made their point.

No leader, of course, could solve Egypt's awesome problems, especially since Nasser's once omnipotent and omnipresent state had diminished as a presence in people's lives under Sadat's *infitah*, the so-called capitalist opening. For far too many Egyptians, especially the poor, the Egyptian government had become simply the army and the police.

GENERAL HASSAN AL-ALFI, Egypt's interior minister, the man in charge of Egypt's war against Islamic militants, wore a well-tailored gray suit, solid, not flashy, and black leather loafers with tassels. He looked like a businessman, not a cop, and he seemed serene for a man who had almost been killed only two months before. Two of his bodyguards and four civilians had been murdered and fifteen others wounded, including the minister himself, when Islamic militants bombed his limousine at 6:00 A.M. in August 1993. A tall, strong man of fifty-seven, with a hesitant smile and a large, nearly bald head, he welcomed me formally but warmly in his downtown office.

The Interior Ministry complex was ringed with armored personnel carriers and police carrying machine guns. Inside were squarish men sweating in ill-made suits who carried their walkie-talkies as if they were pistols. But the minister's office was cool and tranquil. The walls were decorated not with police-academy diplomas but with engraved sayings from the Koran. The upholstery was leather — cool to the touch. Noisy Cairo seemed far away; the only sound was the air conditioner. The lighting was subdued, a relief from the fluorescent blast of the corridors of this and most other Cairo offices.

"I have great respect for your country," Alfi began with what seemed more sincerity than diplomacy required. He told me that in 1976 he had attended a four-month training course in Quantico, the FBI's national academy in Virginia. "I enjoyed it enormously."

Since becoming minister in April 1993 — the sixth man to hold that post under Mubarak — he had implemented a new strategy for combating terrorism as well as many reforms in police procedures, he said. What many officials had once downplayed as isolated incidents of provincial terrorism were now turning up in Cairo and demanded top law enforcement priority, he said. Improving the training and equipment of the police, narrowing the targets of investigations, and enhancing the collection of information in accordance with legal and human-rights standards were now main goals. In addition, he continued, the public would be "made aware that the killers who conduct violence against officials and innocent tourists are not Muslims; that they do not practice any religion. There is nothing in the Koran that justifies such murder. These men are using Islam as a cover for their political goals."

Increasingly, he said, the Egyptian public understood this. Cooperation with law enforcement authorities had increased sharply, especially since February, when Egyptians had been killed in a series of mysterious bombings in cafés frequented by working people. Thanks to tips from "ordinary citizens," he said, arrests were continuing. But so were the murders.

The government had done other things to stop the violence that Alfi did not mention. Another official told me that Egypt had sent military intelligence officials to "the source," Peshāwar, the Pakistani city near the Afghan frontier that throughout the 1980s had been a center for the militant Islamic spies, military planners, guerrilla commanders, and would-be political leaders who had driven the godless Soviet army from Afghanistan. After the Soviet defeat, almost three thousand of the more than six thousand men who registered between 1987 and 1993 with the Pakistani government as volunteers in this jihad, or holy war, were still in Peshāwar looking for ways to continue their campaign.[7] Thousands of other mujahideen, holy warriors who were trained in urban guerrilla warfare and bomb making and who had never bothered to register, had returned to Egypt and other secular Arab states to bring the jihad home. Egyptian officials estimated that eight hundred of the two thousand Egyptian young men who had fought in Afghanistan, "Afghans," as they were known, had returned to Egypt and joined Islamic groups hoping to overthrow the secular government. Other jihad veterans of the anti-Soviet war were still training younger recruits in Jalālābād, the Afghan regional capital where Gulbuddin Hekmatyar, leader of the fundamentalist Hezb-i-Islami guerrilla group who had become Afghanistan's prime minister after Moscow's defeat, had extended sanctuary to five to six thousand radical Arabs. Among them for a time was Sheikh Omar Abdel Rahman, the Egyptian cleric who had blessed the murder of President Sadat and was convicted in late 1995 in New York of conspiracy in the 1993 plot to blow up New York bridges, tunnels, and public buildings. The Egyptian agents sent to Peshāwar in 1993 had returned empty-handed, according to the official who told me about them. The men they were seeking had fled to safety in Afghanistan or Europe.

Alfi's empire was as enormous as the task before it. He was the nominal head of three separate security forces, which, including informants, numbered more then 300,000, rivaling the army's 440,000 men.[8] Yet the violence continued.

In 1992, Islamic assassins had gunned down my good and brave friend Farag Foda, a professor and columnist, a human-rights activist, and an outspoken critic of the Islamic militants. The murder had shocked Cairo and terrified intellectuals. "Keeping your head in such polarized times means keeping your head down," an Egyptian friend had told me. Unlike many of my friends, Farag had refused to do that. On the day of his murder, he had announced the formation of a political group aimed at rallying Egyptians of all religions around the goal of civic tolerance. The radical Gama'at Islamiya, or "Islamic Groups," he said, were actually "Gama'at Zalamiya," a rhyming pun that meant "Groups of Darkness." About two weeks before his murder, he mocked what passed for intellectual discourse among Islamists by citing a recent sermon by Egypt's most popular preacher, Abdel Hamid Kishk, a blind sheikh who constantly attacked both the government and its official religious establishment. Kishk had been telling his audience that Muslims who entered paradise would enjoy eternal erections and the company of young boys draped in earrings and necklaces. Some of the ulema, the religious scholars at al-Azhar University, the government's seat of Islamic learning, had disagreed. Yes, they said, men in paradise would have erections, but merely protracted, not perpetual. Other experts disputed the possibility of pederasty in paradise. "Is this what concerns Muslims at the end of the 20th century?" Foda asked in a column in *October* magazine. "The world around us is busy with the conquest of space, genetic engineering and the wonders of the computer," while Muslim scholars, he wrote in "sadness and pain," were worried about sex in paradise.[9] In a column published just before he was killed, Foda reported that the Tunisian government had videotaped militant Islamic leaders on their prayer rugs, unwilling to await paradise, making love to beautiful women here on earth. Meanwhile, Egyptian militants in Assyut were ordering believers not to eat eggplants and squash because of their resemblance to sexual organs. "The Groups of Darkness are obsessed with sex," he wrote.

While Western and Arab analysts stressed the differences between militant Islamic groups in Egypt and the Muslim Brotherhood, which ostensibly opposed violence, Farag Foda's murder showed that such distinctions were often of little practical consequence in Egypt. The Gama'a Islamiya, inspired by Sheikh Omar Abdel Rahman, had claimed credit for Foda's murder. But the allegedly moderate Muslim Brotherhood and even al-Azhar, the government-supported center of Islamic learning, did not condemn the killing. In fact, al-Azhar's Nadwat al Ulema (Circle of Ulema), an informal group of sheikhs and Muslim scholars, had asked the government shortly before Foda was killed to prevent him from establishing his political group and had complained loudly about his writings. They stopped just short of declaring his essays and him blasphemous.[10] Ma'moun Hodeiby, spokesman for the Muslim Brotherhood, said that his group "regretted" the murder, but he blamed Foda's death on the government for having permitted him and other writers to use the government-run media to "stab Islam in the back."[11] Finally, Sheikh Muhammad al-Ghazali, a former Brotherhood member and a leading Islamic expert who once held important positions at al-Azhar, a man whom officials described as "moderate," had testified at the trial of Foda's murderers that the assailants could not be executed because Islam prescribes no punishment for those who fulfill their religious duties by killing apostates. The defendants were eventually executed.

Foda was only the Islamic militants' latest and most prominent victim. Between March 1992 and the end of September 1993, 202 people had been killed in politically motivated assaults, three of whom were foreign tourists.[12] By mid-October 1993, fifteen of the thirty-one militants sentenced to death, mostly by emergency military courts, had already been sent to the gallows — more than at any other time in Egypt's modern history, even after Sadat's assassination.

Alfi told me that the terrorists were getting weapons and money from networks outside Egypt—from Iran and Sudan, which Cairo had long accused of supporting terrorism in Egypt and elsewhere. "So there is a danger not only for Egypt but also for you and the entire free world," he warned, a reference, I thought, to the 1993 bombing of New York's World Trade Center and efforts to blow up other New York monuments by the Islamic militants encouraged by Sheikh Abdel Rahman, the Egyptian.

Alfi had previously served as governor of Assyut Province, the militants' main stronghold two hundred miles south of Cairo. Egypt's last three interior ministers had all served in this impoverished seat of radical Islamic fervor, Egypt's third-largest city. Unlike his predecessor, Alfi did not favor dialogue with the militants. Cairenes whispered that the previous minister had been fired for exploring a truce with the radicals brokered by the Muslim Brotherhood and other "moderate" al-Azhar sheikhs and preachers, including Muhammad Ghazali, the sheikh who had testified that Farag Foda's murderers should go unpunished. But the government, now embarrassed by its dialogue, denied that negotiations had taken place. The new minister's opposition to any deals or overt accommodation with the state's enemies was undoubtedly reinforced by their assault on him.

This was more than an Egyptian problem, Alfi repeated emphatically. The fanatics were financed from abroad. And the divisions among them that so fascinated scholars, diplomats, and journalists were of little importance. "The Islamic Jihad and the Gama'a Islamiya," he said, referring to Egypt's two leading militant groups, "are just names. The names may differ, but their methods and goals are the same. None of them is Muslim. They are butchers."

The government had stressed the irreligious nature of this "sinful" attack on Alfi in its broadcasts and the press. To assure Egyptians that security had been restored, it announced that 245 "Islamic militants" had been rounded up in Cairo alone—presumably the usual suspects. In an interview from his hospital bed, Alfi attributed his narrow escape to "heavenly providence": Only ten minutes before the attack, he had shifted from the right to the left side of his car, a move that had, in fact, saved his life. The hospital interview lasted less than a minute, but Alfi managed to invoke the name of God nine times. The interviewer, too, attributed Alfi's narrow escape to God.[13] Fearful of government retribution, even the cautious Muslim Brotherhood unconditionally condemned the assault, which it had not done in the case of Farag Foda.

I asked Alfi about Egypt's alleged violations of human rights in its fight against Islamic extremism. In October, Human Rights Watch/Middle East, a private, New York–based human-rights group, had issued yet another report critical of Egypt's record. The document concluded that abuses were increasing and that Mubarak should be held accountable. Although Sadat had substantially reduced torture between 1971 and his death in 1981, Mubarak, projecting himself as the defender of the state against Islamic deviants, had apparently tolerated its reinstitution.[14] Methods included beating men and even women with coiled wires on their bodies and on the soles of their feet while they were held in painful contortions, electric shocks to the genitals, sexual molestation, threats to beat and rape wives and children of male detainees, and forcing victims to stand outdoors for hours, naked, while they were doused with cold water.

Without a trace of indignation, Alfi calmly told me that the charges were untrue. His tone was different from his predecessor's response to similar allegations the previous spring. Not only were such charges "groundless," his predecessor had told me, but human rights were "better served in Egypt than in the United States or the United Kingdom."[15] Nevertheless, he added, Egyptians preferred stability to democracy. He would never permit an Islamist victory at the ballot box, he had admitted during a public debate, a view that reflected that of his boss. "I refuse to allow human rights to become a slogan to protect terrorists," Mubarak had told journalists.

There had been no recent arrests of relatives as hostages, Minister Alfi maintained, daintily sipping his Arabic coffee, his face expressionless. Perhaps a prisoner was occasionally ill treated; it happened under the best of governments. But arrests were not arbitrary, and torture was neither systemic nor officially condoned.

I wanted to believe him, but I did not. I knew that Human Rights Watch pursued its investigations carefully. I hated to imagine men like Mubarak and Alfi sanctioning the torture and degradation of fellow human beings. What, exactly, had we taught Alfi at Quantico?

How did he feel, I asked, about the militants' attempt on his own life? Had the ambush changed his policies or his attitude toward such violence?

I recalled the photos I had seen of the bloody attack. A young man on a motorcycle had driven his bomb-laden vehicle into Alfi's black limousine, shattering the bulletproof windows, destroying an escort jeep, and damaging some twenty-five cars parked on the street.[16] Shards of bomb and glass had slashed the minister's right arm. Mubarak had sent him to Geneva for surgery. Alfi had returned only two weeks earlier with three steel plates in his arm.

"Well, my boxing days are over," he replied, making light of his wounds. "But it didn't change me. Before I took this job, I may have underestimated such people. But now I know them; they are criminals. I am determined to rid Egypt of them.

"If anything, I suppose the attack may have increased my determination to fight them," Alfi continued. "And it bolstered my faith in God. Because I am a Muslim, I know that each of us has a fate, a certain time allowed. I guess my time just hadn't come."

THE GRAY POLICE VAN pulled conspicuously up to the horseshoe entrance of the Nile Hilton. It had no markings, but such vehicles were well known in Cairo. Oh, no, I thought, as I climbed quickly into the back of the van, hoping not to be seen. What an obvious target we were.

Alfi had agreed to let me see the place where the bomb that nearly killed him had been assembled and to interview the State Security Investigation (SSI) officers directly in charge of the investigation of his assailants. If he hadn't agreed, I would never have gotten near the SSI's once-lavish, two-story villa in fashionable Dokki.

The villa seemed innocent enough despite the heavily armed police and oil-barrel barricades. Maj. Ashraf Qadous, the thirty-five-year-old plainclothes officer who had "broken" the case, walked me through the villa, explaining how he had found the "bomb factory." His colleagues greeted him with the deference usually afforded bosses.

Qadous was compactly built. His eyes were expressive; his manner, gentle. He spoke to me in Arabic through my translator. He was dressed that day in a poor Egyptian copy of American blue jeans, an elastic band at the waist, and a turquoise tropical print shirt—the *Miami Vice* look. He had come from humble origins in Cairo and had never been outside Egypt, much less to America. He had been a detective in the SSI for ten years and before that had worked in the criminal division.

"You find the same kinds of criminals in both lines of work," he said. "It's almost never middle-class people who do the killing. The engineer who helped shoot Sadat was an exception. These people are almost always from the lowest levels of society—the real sickos, the crazies, and never women, at least not in Egypt. My criminal work was good training for fighting terrorism."

The police would never have found the militants, he said, without help from ordinary Egyptians. "Egyptians hate this violence, so they help us. That's why I love my work. Because I love my country, I hate terrorism," he added. He seemed sincere, but I suspected that there was more to him than his boyish enthusiasm suggested.

A new group called Vanguards of Conquest, which Qadous said was more commonly known as New Jihad, had claimed responsibility for the attempt on Alfi's life. New Jihad, despite its name, was actually a re-creation of an older group on the Egyptian terrorist scene.

Hisham Mubarak—no relation to the president—a lawyer at Cairo's Center for Human Rights Legal Aid who had recently finished a book about the militants,[17] had warned me earlier that assigning responsibility for the urban terrorism that plagued Egypt was tricky, given the deliberately nebulous nature of these groups, their secretive cellular structure and often overlapping memberships.

Many of the groups had sprung from a handful of radicals who had broken away in the early 1960s from the Muslim Brotherhood, Egypt's oldest, most important, and technically illegal Muslim organization. After years of government repression, the Brotherhood was now ostensibly nonviolent, reformist, and committed to a peaceful transition to an Islamic state. But most intelligence officials—Arab and non-Arab alike—believed that the well-financed Brotherhood, or the Ikhwan, as it is known, maintained contacts with the violent groups and at the very least quietly encouraged them. The semilegal, semibanned Brotherhood, a senior intelligence official told me, was the true historical and spiritual "mother" of all Islamic terrorist organizations, though Hisham Mubarak and other students of the Islamic trend disagreed. The only things I knew for sure were that many radical Islamists had once been Brothers themselves[18] and that based on its official statements, the Brotherhood was, with rare exceptions, reluctant to condemn unconditionally the terrorism that gripped Egypt.[19]

Qadous said that New Jihad had been formed in 1993 by some activists from the old "Jihad," the militant organization founded in 1960 that had assassinated Sadat in 1981.[20] Most of New Jihad's key figures, in fact, were veterans of that murderous assault.[21]

Until the resurrection of New Jihad, the organization known as the Islamic Group, or Gama'a Islamiya, had claimed responsibility for most of the recent Islamic violence.[22] Founded in the early 1970s as an Islamic association at the University of Assyut, the Gama'a, too, had roots in the old Jihad, since some of its founders had been associated with the original Jihad group. In late 1980, according to Hisham Mubarak, the Gama'a and Jihad merged. Together they plotted the assassination of the "pharaoh Sadat" and in 1981 killed him. After Jihad members gunned down Sadat at the parade, Gama'a activists in Assyut tried to provoke an insurrection in Upper Egypt, which the government crushed with massive force.

After the execution of five Islamic militants directly involved in Sadat's assassination, President Mubarak released many militants from prison. Veteran activists began meeting again—some overseas, some surreptitiously within Egypt, and some even in jail. Egypt's Tura Prison in Cairo, where many Islamists were held, became a major militant training and recruitment center. "They even held strategy debates in jail," Hisham Mubarak told me. In 1984 the Gama'a and Jihad activists split again because of personal rivalries and ideological disputes.[23] By 1985 the Gama'a had begun carrying out violent actions aimed at bringing down the state, while Jihad went underground to resume its original goal of infiltrating the military and security services, hoping to seize power.

Between 1985 and 1993, when New Jihad emerged, Gama'a had spearheaded 90 percent of the attacks on intellectuals and other secular "unbelievers" —police officers, government officials, and Coptic Christians. It also began targeting foreign tourists. At the same time, however, another Gama'a branch, the so-called *Da'wa,* or Islamic "call," operated openly in Cairo's slums and throughout rural Egypt, recruiting members and sympathizers in mosques and universities and, like the Muslim Brotherhood, administering social services through charities and affiliated groups in Cairo's fetid slums and in the impoverished villages of the south.

New Jihad, by contrast, was now primarily a paramilitary group that considered building a mass political base and providing social-services distractions from its main task—infiltrating the military, murdering officials, and seizing control of the state to make Egypt truly "Islamic." Hisham Mubarak and Major Qadous agreed that the Jihad group was responsible for most recent assaults on senior officials and that most of the assailants were former "Afghans." Dr. Ayman al-Zawahri, a physician and Jihad leader in exile in Switzerland — of all places — bragged in a fax to an Egyptian newspaper that many more Egyptians would die in the ambitious suicide attacks his New Jihad was planning. "We call it martyrdom," Zawahri told the paper.[24] Such sacrifices, he added, were unavoidable if Egypt was to become an Islamic state.

Qadous told me that he first suspected that the old Jihad had reconstituted itself in the spring of 1993 when several powerful, nail-packed bombs exploded in crowded Cairo coffee shops and squares, killing sixteen and wounding more than sixty bystanders. The Islamic Group had immediately denied responsibility. Soon Cairo was buzzing with rumors about the reemergence of al-Jihad, or New Jihad. The group was not only skilled in urban warfare, thanks to American and Pakistani military training for the war in Afghanistan, but also wealthy because of Saudi and Iranian financial support for the anti-Soviet holy warriors. When New Jihad announced its existence by claiming credit for the attack on Minister Alfi in August 1993, it refused to apologize for the deaths of the civilians it had also killed. Rather, its spokesmen warned, Egyptians should "avoid areas of holy war against the regime, especially where motorcades pass by."

Although Qadous's boss Alfi claimed to be uninterested in the distinctions among the Islamic groups challenging Egypt, those differences were crucial to Qadous. For while the Gama'a and New Jihad both believed in violence to overthrow Mubarak's regime in favor of an Islamic state, their recruits and tactics differed, Qadous told me. The Islamic Group recruited mostly in poor villages, urban slums, and among students. New Jihad, as its parent group had done earlier, tended to recruit within professional classes and among former students, particularly in Alexandria and Cairo. Since it concentrated on killing senior officials — symbols of the regime — its priority was underground infiltration, particularly within the police and the army, which it saw as the only Egyptian group that could change the status quo. A key Jihad strategist, in fact, had argued explicitly that Nasser's "Free Officers" were the only group in modern Egypt that had ever succeeded in seizing power.[25] To topple the government, militant Islamists had to adopt the putschist tactics of the 1950s and conduct themselves, in effect, like Islamic "Free Officers." So while the Gama'a sought publicity, New Jihad demanded disciplined secrecy.

Qadous himself had arrested many militants from the Islamic Group — more than three thousand alleged members were already in prison, he told me. But New Jihad posed a deadlier threat to society, he thought. The bombs that had exploded in coffeehouses and public squares, as well as the one that had nearly killed his minister, were not only packed with nails and shrapnel and, hence, designed to kill and maim people; they were also more sophisticated than those planted so far by the Islamic Group.

Qadous and his fellow detectives hoped to exploit the rivalry between the groups, though the competition was still friendly, he admitted. Both groups, for example, shared many of the same heroes, safe havens, and sympathizers. While the Islamic Group claimed that Sheikh Omar Abdel Rahman, who had encouraged the 1993 bomb plots in New York, was its emir, or leader, New Jihad also paid homage to the notorious preacher's militant piety. Sheikh Abdel Rahman, a Muslim Brother in his younger days, was usually identified as the Gama'a spiritual guide, but Muhammad Islambuli, a Jihad leader, had been Abdel Rahman's host when the sheikh visited Peshāwar in 1988 and 1990.

At least three Jihad members were responsible for the attack on Minister Alfi, Qadous told me. Diya' al-Din Mahmud Hafiz Zaki, a twenty-one-year-old militant from Upper Egypt who had lived in Cairo's Bulak al-Dakrur slum, was killed instantly when he slammed his motorcycle into Alfi's car. The bomb had been placed in a metal box mounted on top of the motorcycle. "The box itself was a bomb," Qadous explained. On one side was TNT; the other side was filled with nails and ball bearings. Jars of jam were loaded on top of the box to disguise its contents. The detonator was attached to the box within easy reach of the rider, who exploded the bomb as he drove into Alfi's vehicle. Parts of the motorcycle were so deeply embedded in Diya's body that it was difficult to identify his remains.[26]

The organizer of the attack was a thirty-three-year-old "Afghan" and veteran of several previous assaults — "a pro," Qadous told me. Nazih Nushi Rashid Ahmad had monitored the assault from behind a refreshment stand — what he assumed was a safe distance. But part of his right leg was blown off in the blast, and he had sought treatment at a nearby hospital. By the time the police tracked him down three hours after the attack, doctors had amputated his leg. The police interrogated Nazih for several hours at the hospital, and he provided preliminary details of the attack, according to a ministry account of the incident. He died that night after losing seven pints of blood.

Trained in Afghanistan, Nazih was among the most wanted Islamists in Egypt, the police said. When they found him in the hospital, Nazih was wearing thick glasses and was unshaved. He only vaguely resembled the Christian whose identity card he had stolen.[27]

Nazih had a long history of militant activism, Qadous's boss, Gen. Salah Salameh, the head of the Giza SSI Directorate, told me at the villa the day after I had first interviewed Qadous. Detained five times by the police since 1981, Nazih was first arrested when still a student in a roundup of Islamic militants after Sadat's death. Released for lack of evidence, he fled to Afghanistan, where he was trained in bomb making, among other lethal skills. "He came back to Egypt in 1985," General Salameh said. "We knew he had been a Jihad member for some time. We finally caught up with him in 1987, imprisoned him for three months for trying to rob a Christian jewelry shop, and then released him."

General Salameh said he did not know why such a dangerous character had been set free. But I knew that the police often released detainees whom it thought it had "turned" in prison, those who agreed to become informers but who then fled.

"In 1990 we started hunting him again after he was implicated in an attack on a tourist bus, but he eluded us," the general said. "In 1991 he tried to murder a prison governor."

Qadous had gone to Nazih's home near the Pyramids after the prison attack in 1991 to look for him. There the police had found three machine guns, stocks of ammunition, and four homemade grenades. The house itself was unusual, Qadous told me. The wooden door that led to the street was reinforced on the interior with sheet metal. Clearly, Nazih had been expecting trouble.

"We learned that he had been using a false passport to travel to and from Saudi Arabia," General Salameh said. "His wife and kids still live there. That, of course, was where his money came from."

The general did not need to elaborate. Egyptian officials accused Saudi Arabia, Egypt's historical rival and, ostensibly, recent ally in the Gulf war, of funding the terrorism that plagued their country. Given their dependence on the Gulf for money and jobs, most Egyptians regarded Saudis with a mixture of frustrated envy, condescension, and loathing. While the Saudi government had supposedly ended its support for potentially violent Islamic groups after most of its Islamic beneficiaries betrayed Riyadh by supporting Saddam Hussein in the 1991 Gulf war, wealthy Saudis and Saudi government-licensed charities had continued financing "Islamic" causes in Egypt and abroad. An Egyptian friend who followed the militants closely told me that Dr. Zawahri, the New Jihad leader who now lived in Switzerland, and Jihad and Gama'a activists throughout Europe were still receiving regular stipends from Abdel Rasoul Sayeef, the leader of a branch of the Afghan mujahideen that was Saudi funded.

While General Salameh had focused on Nazih — the most dangerous militant to be caught in some time — I became interested in the fate of a third man allegedly involved in the August attack on Minister Alfi: Ahmed Farouq, age twenty-two. The police had tracked him down less than two weeks after the bombing, and Ahmed Farouq had supposedly confessed to involvement in three separate bombing attacks in Cairo, including the one on Alfi, General Salameh told me. On September 3, 1993, the day after his arrest, Farouq had died in prison. "A heart attack," the general said. "We had questioned his father and the rest of his family. Ahmed's father told us that his first wife, Ahmed's mother, had died young of the same heart ailment. Apparently, it ran in the family."

I had heard rumors, I told him, that Farouq's family had been detained and mistreated to induce Farouq to surrender. Was that true?

"No," the general snapped. "We questioned the family in their homes. It was normal police procedure, and if I may say so, superb police work." Major Qadous sat quietly in a corner, beaming with pride.

The day of the attack, General Salameh had authorized Qadous to release pictures of Nazih and Diya' to the newspapers. On August 20, the day after their photographs ran, a metalworker in a poor part of Cairo, near the Pyramids, had called Qadous. The man said that someone who resembled Diya' had ordered a metal window cover for his house a few weeks earlier. Diya' had refused to let the metalworker come to the house to measure the window; he had brought him the specifications for the frame himself. When the window was ready, Diya' had hired a taxi to collect the frame and take it home. Qadous and the metalworker began hunting for the driver.

"That's where Diya' made a mistake," Qadous said, recounting the hunt with growing animation. "He used a taxi driver from his local Pyramids taxi station near the shop. Had he used an ordinary taxi driver on the street, we might never have found him."

That same day, Qadous and the taxi driver went to the address to which the frame had been delivered. Yes, the driver told Qadous, this was definitely the house.

The bomb factory that I visited with Major Qadous in October 1993 was a nondescript white-brick shack on an unpaved side road alongside a filthy Nile canal in Kafr el Menfa, half a mile from the Pyramids. The crude structure, with its sand floor and straw-thatched roof, had been built in less than a day on land rented from a local farmer.

Qadous told me that after he and the taxi driver had first located the house, "instinct" told him not to enter it alone that day. On August 21, the following morning, he and a team of well-armed officers, bomb-sniffing dogs, and armored vehicles surrounded the hideout.

"We knew that there had to be a third man involved," Qadous explained as he led me into the house, which was still surrounded by SSI guards, "because terrorist cells almost always have a minimum of three, maximum five, people."

With luck, the third man might still have been in the house, Qadous thought as his men encircled it. The house was empty. But the terrorists had left a gift for unwanted intruders like Qadous: a bomb set to explode on contact buried under the sand, just behind the metal swinging doors to the courtyard. Fortunately for Qadous, the armored vehicle had knocked the metal door down directly over the detonator. When Qadous and his men entered the house, they stepped on the door, not the detonator. Had the door not fallen precisely on that spot, Qadous would have been killed.

I could hardly imagine how three men had spent months in this abysmal dwelling, with its three tiny, dank rooms: a crude kitchen without running water, a living room in which the three of them had slept on metal cots, and a workroom in which they had fashioned metal sheets and spikes into a bomb. Some of the spikes were still lying on the ground. Qadous told me not to touch them. He had also found other bomb ingredients: aluminum powder, remnants of TNT, and oxygen canisters. The only furniture still in the house was an overturned, once-overstuffed ottoman whose insides had been shredded and strewn over the sand floor. "Inside this chair we found their instructions," Qadous said. "All handwritten in Arabic. Do x, y, and z. Beware of this and that." Normally such instructions were faxed from Peshāwar, but the origin of these was unclear. No weapons had been found.

The house's plumbing was a makeshift hole in the ground that the militants had dug. They had carried their own water from a nearby well and stored it in a large rusty barrel that occupied a third of what passed for the kitchen.

"It was a perfect hideout," said Qadous with grudging admiration. Next door was the El Nassera Company, an aluminum factory. "At night they would gather up aluminum fragments, empty oxygen tubes, nails, and other material for bombs—all free."

Abou Bakr Mohammed Rashad, a farmer who had rented the militants the land in April 1993 for a hundred pounds a month (about thirty dollars), told me he was shocked to learn who his tenants were. Rashad had identified the police photos of all three assailants and confirmed that they had all shared the house. "They seemed so nice, so well behaved, and not very religious," he told me as he rocked back and forth on the dusty, garbage-strewn road in obvious distress. "None of them even had a beard. I rented them the land cheaply because they seemed so poor. I invited them to lunch once or twice. But mostly they kept to themselves."

The men had told Rashad they were ironworkers. "I asked them if they needed a guardian to protect the metal and their equipment. Can you imagine! They said no, they would do it themselves."

Qadous tried to console the landowner, apparently still anxious that the police might suspect him of involvement with the assassins. There was no way he could have known who the terrorists were or what they were up to, the detective told him. These guys were pros. No one would have suspected.

As we left the house that chilly October day, Qadous frowned. "There was enough material in this house for several bombs," he told me quietly. "We know what two of the bombs were used for, but we haven't found the others. That's what worries me."

AHMED ALI AHMED FAROUQ once had nine children. Now he had eight. His son Ahmed, allegedly the third terrorist in the attack on Alfi, died in police custody in September. He was the youngest son. A prince of a boy, Farouq said. Never gave him any trouble. Worked hard, always. His son was innocent. He had been tortured to death.

The words came out haltingly at first, then in a torrent of bitter grief.

After my meetings with Major Qadous, I had gone to visit Ahmed Farouq's father with Nadia Tewfik, a fearless Egyptian journalist and my translator. A founder of the Egyptian Organization for Human Rights (EOHR), Baha Eddin Hassan, had urged me to see Ahmed's father but had warned me that the family might be reluctant to talk; the police had terrified them.

The Farouqs lived in Bulak al-Dakrur, where some fifty thousand Egyptians were crammed into an area no bigger than three football fields. Bulak's unpaved, garbage-strewn streets were so narrow and the buildings so close together that the sun was barely visible at noon.

Ahmed's father, a fifty-seven-year-old builder, met us at the entrance to the hundred-year-old apartment house in which he lived with one of his two wives. In the dark, we inched up the narrow spiral staircase to the fifth and top floor of the building. The steps were warped and worn; the dank corridor smelled of urine and rotting citrus.

Despite the deep cracks in the green stucco walls left by the earthquake a year earlier, the family's apartment was spotless. Except for the high bed on which Nadia and I sat, our legs dangling over the side, there was little furniture in the tiny flat. I noticed that there were no Koranic slogans on the wall, a traditional feature of Egyptian apartments.

Zenab Ashmawi, Ahmed's second wife, a small, sturdy woman with large, square bare feet who wore a black peasant dress and matching head scarf, shoved into our hands two bottles of Schweppes orange soda, already opened in our honor.

It was late in the afternoon when Ahmed and his wife began talking. At first he spoke so softly that I couldn't hear his words because a rooster was crowing on the flat rooftop alongside us where I could see lines of laundry drying in the dust and sun. Strains of Arab music accompanied a slight breeze that blew into the tiny room in which we all huddled. Ahmed Ali Ahmed pointed out the window in the direction of a small mosque and a date palm at the edge of the city. His son's grave was over there.

"They said he was a terrorist, but he was the kindest of all my children," Ahmed said as Zenab nodded fervently. "He was not involved in politics; he worked with me in construction. He was rarely out of my sight."

The Farouqs' ordeal began at 2:00 A.M. on August 20, 1993, when they were awakened by banging at the door. Ahmed Farouq opened it and found himself staring at the short muzzles of machine guns. "The officers pushed past me and began searching the house. They told my wife to shut up or they would tie her to the bed," he said. "Then they took me to the house where my other wife and kids live and ransacked that."

From there the police took him and his wife Zenab to the SSI villa that I had visited the previous day. The officials I had interviewed the day before were on the second floor. On the ground floor toward the back of the house, Farouq said, was a large room covered with tiles. "I was naked and blindfolded, standing on the cold floor. They tied my hands and ankles together. Then" — he paused, tears welling in his eyes as he began stroking the remaining strands of his hair and pulling nervously at his cropped mustache — "they started beating me with a thick iron club. I was covered in blood, but they kept yelling insults and beating me. You can't imagine what they called me."

Zenab began weeping, too. "I was on my knees, begging them not to hit me," she said, joining the conversation. "I told them that I didn't know where Ahmed was, that he wasn't even my son; he was my husband's son. I screamed at them: 'Don't hit me. I'll divorce him!' "

Ahmed, Zenab, and her mother were all crying by then. Nadia and I sat on the bed, exchanging helpless glances, our pens in one hand, our now-warm bottles of Schweppes in the other. I shuddered as I recalled the villa and felt a wave of shame. I had never really questioned what the police had told me. But now, right in front of me, sat a family that seemed to me perfectly innocent but claimed to have been terribly abused. I believed them.

Over the next two weeks, Ahmed continued, the police detained and interrogated thirteen members of his family, two at a time. They threatened to bring his wives to the villa and rape them.

"Almost two weeks after they first came for me, they told me I was going home. They had found my son. They were going to interrogate him."

Two days later, Ahmed Farouq was called back to police headquarters. They told him to collect Ahmed's body from the morgue. "I knew they had killed him," he told us.

But didn't his son have a heart condition? Hadn't his wife died of the same disease? I asked, hoping for, but no longer expecting, an innocent explanation for his son's sudden death.

Ahmed and Zenab exchanged bitter smiles. "Ahmed's mother was fat, yes. And she had died ten years ago, when Ahmed was just a boy," the father replied. "But she did not have a heart condition. And neither did Ahmed."

But hadn't he signed a document stating that his son had died of a heart attack?

"I signed nothing. Never," Ahmed insisted. "The police told me to say that Ahmed had heart disease. They told me not to mourn or discuss his death with anyone. They wouldn't even let me see his body when I got to the morgue. I buried him without ever seeing him again. I never gave them a statement. We only got one document. It shows that Ahmed died of torture."

Zenab pulled a large chest out from under the high bed on which Nadia and I were seated and rummaged through it. She extracted a thin white envelope that contained a single sheet of paper. Ahmed Farouq's death certificate, dated September 4, 1993 — a day after Ahmed's death — did not prove that Ahmed had been beaten to death, but it did not mention a heart condition, either. "The corpse had superficial injuries," the certificate stated, attributing the death to "heart failure and loss of breath."

Ahmed's tears now fell on the paper. "A heart condition!" he wailed. "Ahmed was healthy and strong. He worked in construction. He had served in the army! He was recalled last year during the Gulf war. They sent him to Ismailia. If he had heart disease, why would they have accepted him back in the army?"

BARELY OVER five feet tall, Ahmed Farouq's wife looked like a child. She did not seem old enough to be having a second one herself. Even her flowing black dress and matching *hijab*, the Islamic veil covering all but her face and her hands, could not hide her pregnancy.

"Our lives have been shattered," Madiha Fadl said bitterly when we met her in late October at the Farouqs' other family home in another part of Bulak.

She was twenty-three years old. She and Ahmed had been married for three years. Their first child, a daughter, was turning two. She was seven months pregnant with their second.

During the week, she said, Ahmed worked at a construction site in the 10th of Ramadan City, another of the sprawling, dull new towns being built at the edge of Cairo. But he returned home every Thursday night to spend Friday with his family. Ahmed was a devoted husband and father, she told Nadia and me.

"If he had been involved in politics or terrorism, I would have known," she said. "He was kind and affectionate. He worked, ate, prayed, and slept. He feared God."

At his direction, Madiha had worn the *niqaab* after they were married. "He told me it was sinful not to wear it," she said. The *niqaab*, unlike the *hijab*, covered the face as well as the hair and the body. "If it were up to me, I would still wear it," she told us defiantly. "This is protection for women. This is what the Islam that God has given us commands."

At the time of the Prophet Muhammad, she said, women wore the *niqaab* in public so that no one would be able to identify his wives. The *niqaab* had protected them against harassment when Muhammad's new religion still had few adherents and was vulnerable. But in modern Egypt, she said, the *niqaab* made women targets of police harassment. For men it was having a beard.

Ahmed knew that the police were rounding up young bearded men and even veiled women, she said. "So he shaved off his beard and made me take off the *niqaab*. We did it for our daughter. But it did him no good.

"Now I can't wear the *niqaab*. I must find work to earn money for my daughter. Any kind of work. But no shop or office or school would employ me if I wore the *niqaab*. They would be too afraid."

Since her husband's death she had not entered the apartment on the second floor that she and Ahmed had shared in their brief married life. The police had occupied the entire building for two weeks while Ahmed was at large, she said, just in case he returned home to see her. She had fled to her parents' house, which the police also visited three or four times a day. Now she wanted to show us her former home. Her family had just finished cleaning it up, she explained. The police had overturned potted plants, ripped open the sofa, and torn everything up looking for arms and stolen money.

The apartment was small, immaculate, and as quiet as a tomb. On one wall were an electric clock, now stopped, and a plaque with a saying from the Koran. A few small potted plants stood on a shelf near the window, which also held a leather-bound copy of the Koran.

Returning to her apartment brought back memories of Ahmed to Madiha, who showed us first where their daughter had slept and then, choking back a sob, their own bedroom.

A huge wooden bedroom set filled almost the entire room. A large armoire, painted white and decorated with small, pastel-colored, carved flowers, covered a wall, and a matching headboard above the double bed filled another. Tiny Madiha, shrouded in black, seemed lost amid all this white furniture. The bedroom set must have been a wedding present, part of the dowry that her family had provided to launch the young couple on what might have been in different times a happy, uneventful life.

Madiha opened a small drawer in the mantel on the side of the bed and pulled out a passport-sized photo of Ahmed, whose clean-shaven face stared out innocently.

"Was this the face of a terrorist?" she said, sobbing, collapsing on the edge of the bed. "He was my whole life. Now he's gone. I feel his soul more strongly here in our room. My daughter wakes up at night and asks, 'Where's Daddy?' What can I tell her? I haven't even told her he is dead, that he is never coming home. She's too young to understand.

"Calamity has come to this house," she said, growing angry. "When they took me to the police station, I saw my father-in-law — blindfolded, handcuffed, terrified. They released me at four o'clock in the morning. Just set me out onto the street alone, with no money, no transportation home.

"My brother, who is too afraid to talk to you, was also picked up by the police. After they finished with him, his feet were swollen and bleeding. They had pulled out his toenails. They had whipped him, shocked his genitals with electricity. If they hadn't found Ahmed, they would have beaten him to death.

"My brother-in-law Mohammed lost his construction job. He was fired. So was my father-in-law, the man you interviewed. The boss told them to leave, to get out of there. 'Because of you, our workers have been detained, our architects interrogated; don't come back,' he told them.

"Our friends are afraid of us now. You come here, but no one else will. The police told people at the mosque that Ahmed and all his family were members of Jihad. So none of us goes to the mosque anymore. I pray at home.

"The police warned us not to say anything about what had happened. The officer in charge told us that if we talked, no power on earth could protect us. We would disappear and never be found again. That's why my brother and my uncle can't talk to you. My uncle has ten children," she said, looking at Nadia and me accusingly. "Can you promise me that they won't be taken?"

But why was she talking to us? I wondered. Why would her father-in-law risk the government's fury by describing their nightmare to human-rights groups and foreign journalists? The police had warned me that families of victims often invented stories of torture and abuse to arouse popular sentiment against security operations. But Madiha's grief and rage seemed genuine — as genuine as Major Qadous's had been when he insisted that Ahmed Farouq was an assassin.

"I don't care anymore," she cried, leaping to her feet, her small voice rising. "I know I must protect my daughter. But I'm so tired of being afraid. The people who did this to us are not Muslims. Our government is unjust. There is no mercy in Egypt. Everyone is suffering, not just us. We are dogs to them, not human beings. If this state adhered to Islam, things like this wouldn't happen. But there is no Islam or justice here!

"If they had done this to someone guilty, someone who was involved in terrorism," she looked up defiantly, "I would understand. But Ahmed was innocent! And killing innocent people is wrong. Will no one ever pay for the murder of my husband? Will no one kill the dogs who ate his flesh? They are infidels. They are the ones who deserve to be killed."

As we left Madiha's tiny apartment, Nadia frowned and said bitterly: "She's one of them—an Islamist. She was lying to us."

Nadia was probably right. Madiha must have known that her husband had led a clandestine life. His parents, too, must have suspected more than they had let on. After all, the farmer who had rented the bombers their hideout had identified Farouq as one of his three tenants. And the manager of the construction company where Farouq supposedly worked had told me that contrary to what Farouq's father and Madiha had said, Ahmed Farouq had not lived at the site for months, which suggested that he could well have been at the bomb factory. But still, I pitied them all.

Everyone had lied about something—or told me part of the truth: Ahmed's father and stepmother, Madiha, Major Qadous, and Minister Alfi. It was impossible to know exactly who was guilty of what. But this much seemed clear to me: Ahmed Farouq, in his desire to destroy Egypt's unjust, "un-Islamic" government, had killed six fellow Egyptians and wounded fifteen civilians. His family, who had probably done nothing except remain silent about their son's activities, had been abused by the police. While I could not condone what the police had done, neither could I forget the minister's charred car, the bodies, and pieces of them, scattered along Cairo's Sheikh Rihan Street, where Ahmed and his friends had staged their assault. As an Egyptian, Nadia, who had almost wept as she listened to the Farouq family's ordeal, could nonetheless not hide her disgust for people responsible for such violence and for those who condoned it. Moreover, I was in no position to judge what seemed her callous indifference to the police's use of torture to locate the Farouq family's son. Ahmed Farouq and his friends must have known when they tried to kill a minister that this ancient, tough state would do whatever was necessary to preserve its power and that many Egyptians, given their history, would sanction such methods. Though I had always argued that governments had to respect human rights and civil liberties, could I honestly say that Americans would act any differently if the bombings of the World Trade Center and Oklahoma City federal building had not been isolated events?

BAHA EDDIN HASSAN, whose face reminded me of those I had seen on the ancient tombs of Upper Egypt, spoke calmly and deliberately, without apparent indignation, as we discussed the Ahmed Farouq case and human rights in Egypt.

"In the past four months, four people, including Ahmed Farouq, have died under torture," he said. "Our group has filed protests and demands for official investigations in each case—all unanswered, of course."

The government detested the Egyptian Organization for Human Rights, the group that forty-five-year-old Hassan and some colleagues founded in 1985. The EOHR, which ran on a tiny budget, with a core of volunteers of differing political agendas, had complained to the United Nations in mid-1993 that the continuous extension of emergency laws since President Sadat's death had led to "wide transgressions" by Egypt's security apparatus. It also accused the government of encouraging Islamic radicalism by cultivating its own, ostensibly tamed religious establishment, which was now trying to make life more "Islamic" for everyone. For one example, it had permitted the sheikhs of al-Azhar, the state's most important Islamic center, to ban more than 150 books since 1952, as well as movies and songs, although Egyptian law theoretically protected such work.[28] It blamed the government for failing to condemn the assassination of Farag Foda. "When the 'moderate' Sheikh Ghazali defended Foda's assassins in court, the government said nothing," Hassan complained, even after al-Azhar had disassociated itself from Ghazali's *fatwa*, his Islamic ruling. Hassan's impassive demeanor hid his outrage. "This omnipotent government is supposed to be the guardian of civil society!" he said. "But it is contributing to its erosion."

The government's greatest abuse, he added, was its arbitrary mass arrests, its systematic torture, its hostage taking, and the security forces that ran wild in the war against Islamic extremism. Legally, suspects could not be held for more than two months without being charged. But many had been imprisoned for months, some for years. A prisoner would be "released" for a day without leaving jail and then "rearrested" for another two months. Each young suspect had families and friends, or perhaps a young wife like Madiha Fadl, who would despise the government, if they did not hate it already, for abusing their loved ones.

But wasn't Ahmed Farouq, in fact, a terrorist? I asked. I doubted that the police had frightened all of his accusers into lying to me. And if Farouq had been a terrorist, I told Hassan, he might have planted his remaining bombs in Cairo cafés or given them to fellow fanatics to continue murdering Egyptians. Did the police not have a duty to protect society from such threats?

Hassan's face hardened. "If Farouq was a terrorist — and I do not know that he was not," he replied impatiently, "the state should have tried and convicted him in a civilian court of law, as it does in your country. But Ahmed Farouq never had a chance to defend himself even in a military court. He was tortured to death. That should not happen in a civilized society."

We both knew, of course, that such things happened in civilized countries. Even Minister Alfi had acknowledged that suspects were occasionally mistreated in his jails. But how did Hassan know that torture was now systemic?

In 1992 six people died under torture, he replied, but only one was suspected of Islamic violence. That suggested that torture had become routine, no longer reserved for political opponents. In 1993 a security officer had injected a mixture of feces and water into a prisoner's leg to make him confess, Hassan said. The man was accused of stealing cars.

Because of terrorism, Hassan said, the government was now above the law. The only pressure came from the United States, which gave Egypt $2.15 billion in annual aid. Washington, which acknowledged in its 1994 human-rights report that there was "convincing evidence" that police and security forces "systemically practice torture," occasionally expressed polite criticism of documented abuses through diplomatic channels and made discreet inquiries into allegations of unproved abuses, Hassan said. "But you never threaten the regime with even a reduction in aid if such abuses do not stop. Egypt, after all, is America's ally, the first Arab state to make peace with Israel."

Egypt was locked in a classic vicious circle, he said. Arbitrary roundups, detention, and torture created more opposition to the government and pretexts for even more antigovernment violence, which, in turn, triggered more government assaults on freedom. Worse, the terrorism led citizens to tolerate abuses of human rights that were at the heart of civil society. Hence, the very notion of civil society was being undermined. The government's conviction that Islamic militancy was simply a security problem, its silence about the more subtle, semiofficial assaults on civil liberties, and its failure to defend its civil institutions were a boon to the militants.

Hassan's mood darkened. "Partly because of the government, we are losing the battle against fundamentalism. Each day, more and more women insist on wearing the *hijab*, and even the *niqaab*, which is not Egyptian dress at all. More and more men refuse to swim in integrated swimming pools. Islamic pressure to ban 'un-Islamic' books and movies is growing. Eighty percent of the material in my daughter's Arabic-language textbook in her private, secular school is from the Koran! It was less than twenty percent when I was a boy."

I knew that the problem was even worse in Egypt's twenty-five thousand public schools, especially in Upper Egypt, where Islamists had quietly infiltrated entire school districts. Whereas Islamic tradition required girls to cover their heads only after puberty, radical teachers now required girls as young as six to wear the *hijab*. Instead of teaching from government texts, they played cassettes of incendiary sermons by militant Islamic superstars — Sheikh Omar Abdel Rahman; Sheikh Kishk, Egypt's most popular militant preacher; and Sheikh Abdel Kafi, then the rage among the mystically inclined middle class. The government had confiscated more than 3 million illegal audiocassettes and videotapes containing propaganda mainly from the Gama'a.[29] Children were taught not to salute their flag or sing "*Biladi, Biladi*," or "My Country, My Country," a patriotic ballad dating back to the 1920s and Egypt's struggle for independence. They were taught not to identify themselves as Egyptians, but rather as Muslims, citizens of a worldwide *umma*, the Islamic community. Egypt's pharaohs were a corrupt race; their tombs, pyramids, and monuments were pre-Islamic pagan symbols and therefore idols to be smashed. Music classes and theater clubs had been disbanded by zealots. By the end of 1993 the minister of education had dismissed more than a thousand teachers — or, more accurately, transferred them to desk jobs, since it was virtually impossible to fire a low-grade civil servant in post-Nasserist Egypt. He had also banned the *niqaab* at schools and universities, which caused militant women to stage months of noisy demonstrations, some of which ended in violent clashes. But when the minister tried to restrict the *hijab*, the far less cumbersome Islamic covering, Egypt's supreme court had overruled him. So did the grand sheikh of al-Azhar. Now he was trying to purge the libraries of fundamentalist tracts and replace hundreds of suspect school principals. But these were awesome tasks: Egypt had more than 800,000 schoolteachers — twice as many teachers as soldiers.

" 'Secular' has become a dirty word in Egypt, thanks to the government's policies," Hassan told me. Sadat had used the ulema, the state-funded religious scholars, to legitimize his actions. For instance, he had called upon al-Azhar to denounce the food riots of 1977 and "bless" the controversial 1979 peace treaty with Israel. In return, Sadat had made religion compulsory in schools and universities and had rewritten the country's constitution to make Islamic law — sharia — which was barely mentioned in Nasser's 1962 National Charter, a "main source" of Egyptian law. Now Islamists were insisting that sharia be *the* source of all Egyptian law.

Hassan sighed. "I'm afraid our president doesn't realize that it is impossible to have a nonfundamentalist government in an Islamicized society. And unless things change, that's exactly where we are headed."

WHEN I HAD ASKED President Mubarak in October 1993 whether using state-sponsored Islam to counter its militant rival was counterproductive, he told me to turn off my tape recorder. I readily obliged, knowing from previous experience that he spoke most candidly when he was not being quoted — at least not immediately.[30] He could not "stand against the stream," the Islamic tide that was then so strong in Egypt, he told me. He could not say publicly that he was going to reduce the amount of religious programming on television or take other steps to weaken the Islamic current and strengthen civic society in Egypt. The fundamentalists would accuse him of being anti-Islamic. He had the militants on the run now, he said. He would not jeopardize that momentum by making statements that could be twisted to mean that he was attacking Islam. But "gradually," on a "smooth basis," government policy would change, he said. This was one of the goals he wished to accomplish in his third, and last, term. He had agreed to seek a third term "with great reluctance," he told me, though knowing Egypt's pharaoh syndrome, I was not convinced. His family had opposed a third term; so had his wife, Susan, partly out of fear for his safety. But he finally relented because he feared that Islamic militants would seize upon an interregnum to create more "chaos" and "violence." In his third term he wanted to push Egypt's state-dominated economy irrevocably toward the free market and to crush the radical Islamists once and for all.

He was tired of the well-intentioned advice he received from American and other Western officials about how he should handle the Islamic radicals, he said, pointing his right index finger at me to ensure that he had my undivided attention. Democracy, promoted by the Clinton administration as the cure-all for his country's political plight, could not come instantaneously in a country like Egypt. "If you have a dam and keep the water in until it begins to overflow and then suddenly you open the gates," he said, using a metaphor that came naturally to rulers of the Nile, "you will drown many people."

Egypt, he said, had been under intense pressure for many years. "So when you open the gates of freedom, you will find many terrible things taking place." Liberalization and democracy had to come slowly, he insisted.

Mubarak was nothing if not consistent. When President Chadli Benjedid of Algeria had tried to salvage his corrupt, inefficient regime by staging elections in 1990, Mubarak had privately warned him not to and also urged him not to recognize the Islamic Salvation Front, known as the FIS, a coalition of Islamic groups, as a political party. Algerian law, like its Egyptian counterpart, banned religious-based parties — for good reasons, Mubarak told me. But Chadli had ignored the advice: The FIS had won, the government had refused to accept the results, and Algeria was now fighting a deadly civil war in which an estimated forty thousand people had died.

The Egyptian public needed to be prepared for democracy. Private, independent associations and institutions needed time to take root. People needed to be taught political tolerance, "ed-u-ca-ted," he said, tapping out each syllable with his finger on the wooden conference table. "So we're doing things quietly, without giving the fundamentalists ammunition."

I thought about how much Mubarak had changed since I first met him, just after he became president following Sadat's murder in 1981. I could never forget the photograph that Gamal, our office manager, had taken immediately after the assassination. In the grainy black-and-white picture, a blood-splattered Mubarak, who had been at Sadat's side when the reviewing stand was riddled with bullets, was hunched over in the back of a covered military jeep, a look of utter bewilderment and terror on his large, square face.

Egyptians had taken to calling Vice President Mubarak *La Vache Qui Rit*, for the laughing cow on the wrapper of the bland French cheese of that name, which was widely sold in Egypt. The man I had described in print then as "timid," "unsure," and "modest" still moved carefully, but he had become determined and supremely confident in his judgment, perhaps overly so. He dyed his hair with what looked like shoe polish. He had also added a few pounds despite his daily squash or tennis game and an austere diet that included little meat and virtually no alcohol. But he looked much the same and still far younger than his sixty-five years. I still liked him and considered him a patriot who wanted only the best for Egypt. And I still found his candor disarming. "I always speak the truth," Mubarak often insisted.

A journalist, Emad al-Din Adeeb, once wrote that as a former pilot and air force chief of staff, Mubarak had learned the value of caution and maneuver — of "precision, keenness, how to move under cover of protection and how to circle to make sure that his target would be totally destroyed" — and most important, how to bring his aircraft home safely. He had needed those skills as Egypt's president, particularly since he lacked his predecessors' boldness, their pharaonic grandeur and charisma. Until the militant Islamists began to challenge him, Mubarak was not disliked in Egypt. In his first term he had substantially liberalized the country and increased political participation, and during my years in Cairo, most analysts agreed that the Egyptian press had enjoyed greater freedom under him than at any time since the overthrow of King Farouk in 1952.

If Mubarak feared for his life — and how could he not under the circumstances? — he refused to show it. He joked about his own mortality but not about his determination to rid Egypt of the plague of terrorism, at whatever price. No one would tell him how to rule, he declared, as his three senior aides shifted nervously in their chairs. He knew what he had to do and was prepared to do it. Egyptians knew that the militancy peddled by extremists was not Islam, he told me. Ordinary Egyptians supported him and the government. I should visit Egypt's towns and tiny villages and see for myself.

GAMAL MOHIEDDIN, the *Times* office manager for more than thirty years, and I sped along the new superhighway through the desert linking Cairo and Alexandria, Egypt's second-largest city, on the Mediterranean. Our destination was Kafr el Battikh, which in English means "Watermelon Village."

Egyptians, whether or not they lived in Cairo or Egypt's other giant cities, retained close ties to their native villages. It was impossible to understand modern Egypt without knowing something of life in the hundreds of hamlets, villages, and towns spread out along the Nile.

Gamal had taken *Times* reporters to this particular village ever since 1960, when President Nasser had scolded the press for paying so much attention to the glitter of Cairo, the modestly self-designated *Umm al-dunya* (mother of the world). Egypt, he said, was not Cairo, or even Alexandria. Egypt was Kafr el Battikh, a speck on the map of the Nile Delta, Egypt's most fertile region, where the Nile opened out into countless canaled tributaries. Egyptian journalists had laughed at what they presumed was Nasser's attempt at humor. The saying goes that Egyptian bumpkins didn't even know their "watermelons." But the *Times* reporter must have missed Nasser's joke, for he dutifully packed up the car for what was then a seven-hour drive north to the village. A few days later, he described in microscopic detail the place that Nasser had called "the true face of Egypt."[31]

What he found was a desperate backwater, a village that epitomized Egypt's poverty, squalor, and illiteracy as well as its inhabitants' utter dependence on the land and the river, a dependence that Nasser and his generation of "new Arabs" were determined to eradicate. In 1960, 17,800 people lived in Watermelon Village, four times more than the average Egyptian village population. Its inhabitants grew not only watermelons but many other crops. The village's most valuable asset was the 250,000 date-palm trees that produced a million dollars a year. But very little of this money was earned by the hardworking fellaheen who plowed the land and picked the fruit with the same implements pictured on the walls of pharaonic tombs, men who still wore the same galabias — the traditional flowing robes — that had been worn long before biblical times. Most villagers lived along disease-ridden canals in fired or mud-brick homes, numbed by drudgery and disease.

Four miles from the provincial capital of Damietta, only 116 miles northeast of Cairo, the village had no paved roads, public transport, or movie house, no electricity or running water, no veterinarian, no doctor, and only one barber, who also performed small operations in emergencies. The village had one mosque, one kindergarten, and two primary schools. Only a handful of adults could read and write. The average family had seven children, at least 20 percent of whom would not live to become adults. Watermelon Village, of course, had police. But there had not been a major crime in more than a decade.

The men, after toiling in the fields all day, gathered at night in coffeehouses over glasses of hot tea or thick coffee. They smoked their *narguilas* (water pipes) and hummed the ballads on the radio sung by Um Kalthoum, Egypt's beloved patriotic songbird, whose hits included "We Built the High Dam" and "Glory to Nasser and Arab Socialism." They also listened with rapt attention to Nasser, whom Gamal had told me the villagers idolized, perhaps because he was the first Egyptian leader ever to speak to them in their colloquial dialect. Nasser, in fact, was the first Egyptian leader in centuries who spoke fluent Arabic — colloquial or classical.[32] While his regime had not yet improved their lives, Nasser's stirring battle cry, "Raise your head, brother!" had found resonance in Kafr el Battikh. "Without losing their simplicity and charm," the reporter concluded, "they have ceased to be servile."

By 1966, Nasser's revolution had taken hold. While the land and the river were still the dominant factors of life, their influence was dwindling.[33] The new Aswan High Dam was making water available to cultivate sandy land. The first modern "popular housing," an ugly, squat six-story building, had been finished. A corps of seventy teachers and social workers had arrived from Cairo to offer instruction in health care and technology. There were five new schools — still barely enough for a population growing at an annual rate of over 3 percent — but water was now available through communal taps. Several new groceries had opened, along with a new police station. A new class of civil servants, merchants, and middle-class farmers was emerging. The three most venturesome coffeeshop owners had purchased television sets so that their customers could watch Nasser's speeches. But there were still problems: infant mortality, for example. The new medical clinic was mobbed — some two hundred patients came each day. More than 70 percent of patients had ancylostomiasis, or worms, and 65 percent, bilharzia, the parasitic disease endemic to the Nile and its irrigation canals. Though piped-in water was available, some villagers ignored the doctors' warnings and preferred drinking from the Nile.

By 1966 it was also clear that Nasser's land reform had failed. The government had expropriated without compensation most of the land owned by the village's largest landholder — a Levantine Catholic family which had lived there since the village's creation hundreds of years ago — and given twelve hundred of the seventeen hundred village families plots of less than five acres, which proved too small to provide a decent living. The fellaheen had thus become tenant farmers of the state, dependent on government cooperatives for seed, fertilizers, equipment, and pricing. Agricultural production was falling.

By 1977, the population had more than doubled to forty-four thousand. Television antennas topped many homes, and electric power lines crossed the main square. Some houses had toilets and sinks, but there was still no sewage system. Electric pumps had mostly replaced the water buffalo. Trade and small industry, which President Sadat had encouraged, already accounted for a quarter of the village's economy. Some one thousand villagers traveled the four miles to Damietta by train to work in small factories. The richest villagers even had cars and lived in brick houses. Life, on balance, was good, villagers said.[34]

By the time Gamal first took me to Watermelon Village in 1985, almost everything had changed except its name.[35] Agriculture, including its famed watermelons, was no longer the town's major source of income, and Watermelon Village was no longer a village. Its major industry was now furniture factories financed by workers' remittances repatriated by the three thousand villagers working in the Persian Gulf and Iraq. The town had doubled in area and tripled in population since 1966. Its sixty thousand people were about to be declared a city.

Gulf remittances had created not only local demand for imported food and products but also financed more than two hundred carpentry shops. Damietta was the carpentry capital of Egypt, so subcontracting work to villagers nearby made economic sense. Typical of the "new merchant" class was Mohammed Sayyid el Moazi, thirty-two, whose father had been a farmer. He had opened his shop in 1983 with money he had saved working in Iraq. By 1985 he had two assistants to help carve, sand, hammer, and paint the Baroque wooden bed frames, headboards, and mantels — just like the ones I was to see years later in Madiha Farouq's bedroom in Cairo. This elaborate "Louis Farouk" style had become fashionable in Egypt and throughout the Gulf, and villagers now made comfortable livings selling the sets — a double bed with headboard cost the Egyptian equivalent of about $165. "Luxury bedroom suites" — elaborately etched beds, headboards, and matching armoires — were exported to the Gulf for ten times as much.

The money that Nasser had invested in infrastructure and education had finally paid off. A sewage system was being built, and most homes in town had electricity and running water. Only farm and side roads remained unpaved. A decade earlier, Kafr el Battikh had only five agricultural engineers; by 1985, there were seventy. About 60 percent of the population were literate. Whereas in 1966 only one out of a hundred children who started school made it to the university, some three hundred university graduates had now returned to the village. Unfortunately, most worked for the government, but the majority supplemented their meager salaries with part-time jobs in farming, carpentry, or commerce.

Under Sadat, much of the government spending on infrastructure had stopped. While the population had tripled since 1966, only two more schools were built. After Sadat's "open door" economic policy in 1974, consumer goods had poured into Egypt, and workers had flowed out to lucrative work in the Gulf. Nasser's era of state socialism was gone, and residents of Kafr el Battikh did not seem to miss it. They were doing well enough on their own.

Social attitudes had also shifted dramatically. If in 1966 the fellaheen had felt uneasy about their new, largely unfulfilled ambitions, their sons and daughters two decades later had high, perhaps excessive, expectations. The young men dressed in Egyptian city style — blue jeans, sandals, and partly open shirts — and displayed what they termed a "modern" attitude. What that meant, in practice, was that they didn't want to have more than two or three children, and they didn't want to be farmers. The population growth rate had dropped from 3.0 percent in 1966 to 2.7 percent by 1985, still alarmingly high.

In 1985, Egyptian agricultural production, relative to other sectors, was still dropping. Once a net food exporter, Egypt was now importing about 50 percent of its food, and the gap between consumption and production was growing. Despite a vast population growth and substantial increases in yield per acre, Kafr el Battikh still had only thirty-one thousand acres of cultivated land, a negligible expansion since 1966. Five thousand more acres were being reclaimed, but four thousand of those had been taken by the government. Although farmworkers were paid more than four dollars a day — double what civil servants earned — the exodus of farm laborers to the Gulf and the disdain young people felt for farming had produced a labor shortage on the village's farms. Watermelon Village and Egypt itself were becoming hopelessly dependent on the Gulf and the West.

I hadn't visited this town since 1985 and was eager to see whether radical Islam had reached Kafr el Battikh. None of my immediate predecessors had mentioned Islamic violence in their dispatches. Neither had I in 1985. But now, in the fall of 1993, I was apprehensive even about making the four-hour car trip in such dangerous times. But Gamal would be with me, so I felt I would be safe.

Gamal, one of the kindest, most dignified men I have ever known, disliked the Islamic militants. A tall, handsome Nubian, he was fiercely patriotic: He even made a point of smoking rancid Cleopatra cigarettes rather than the imported Marlboros, which, before my latest ill-fated attempt to quit smoking, I had shared with younger Egyptian journalists. Since part of his family came from Sudan, Gamal knew firsthand the terror that had gripped Khartoum since an Islamic regime had seized power there in 1989. He feared such a fate for his beloved Egypt.

Deeply religious in his own unorthodox way, Gamal supported five children as well as his parents and in-laws. The numerous obligations that kept him away from our office occasionally for days at a time — the death of a third cousin of a mother-in-law, the marriage of a favorite niece who had no immediate family in Cairo, the school problems of a nephew of his wife's half brother — competed with the demands of putting out a daily newspaper. But they kept him in touch with Egyptians less fortunate than himself. Gamal's priorities, mirrored thousands of times over in Egyptian society, also meant that no matter how oppressive, incompetent, or bizarre the ruler, Egyptians would somehow get by. However wanting its political system, Egypt's social fabric was strong.

But Islamic fervor had touched even Gamal's own solid family, he told me as we drove along. The problem, he said, offering me a Cleopatra, was Aboodi —now "Sheikh Aboodi," one of several nephews whom he had employed as tea servers and messengers in the *Times*'s Cairo office. Aboodi, who had graduated the previous year from al-Azhar, had recently visited Gamal's family, with whom he had lived while he was in college. Gamal was stunned when Aboodi refused to kiss Gamal's wife or shake hands with his daughters, all of whom wore Islamic head scarves. "My wife virtually raised him; my daughters were like his sisters," Gamal told me. "But he refused even to touch them. He told me such contact was *haram*, forbidden by God! My wife was deeply hurt."

So Gamal had thrown him out. Where in the Koran did it say that showing respect for his surrogate family was *haram*? Gamal yelled at him. Aboodi could return to their home when he had apologized. But the young sheikh had not done so. He now lived and worked in Saudi Arabia—teaching the Koran at a remote desert mosque.

Was he worried that Islamic militants would come to power in Egypt? I asked Gamal. Despite having known me for so many years, Gamal was cautious. If the government were "just and strong," he replied, the Islamists would not succeed. But young men like Aboodi needed real jobs, he said. There were too many Egyptians without hope in Cairo and Alexandria, he said with a sigh. Only in places like Watermelon Village and other relatively prosperous Nile Delta towns had radical Islamists been thwarted.

I found bustling Watermelon Village a relief after Cairo's chaos, pollution, and political tension. The capital had deteriorated since I had lived in Egypt in the mid-1980s, and I must have had less patience now. Kafr el Battikh looked good to me, and the residents I spoke to agreed.

Gamal and I were shown into the offices of the Cairo-appointed town manager, an efficient-looking middle-aged man in a safari suit, the preferred attire of rural officials in Egypt. The trend away from agriculture had continued, he told me. Land had been lost to the new port of Damietta, which had opened in 1986, and since then had expanded. More arable land had been lost to the population sprawl.

Kafr el Battikh had become a town, but the entire area had been redistricted. So the town's population now stood at forty-five thousand, fifteen thousand less than when it had been a village. The boom that I saw in the mid-1980s was continuing, shakily. Red-brick houses and six-story cement apartment buildings were going up everywhere. Tiny cars now filled the still-unpaved side streets. But the recession in the Gulf had hurt the town, the manager told us. While three thousand villagers still worked overseas, the Arabs were not as eager to buy the elaborately carved bed sets as they once were.

"We had a rather serious problem a few years ago," said the manager, Farouk Abdel Attar.

"Islamic militants?" I asked.

Attar and his assistants exchanged amused glances. "No," he replied. "Drugs."

The port of Damietta made contraband smuggling a village pastime. But the government had sent police reinforcements in early 1993, and the problem had been "solved."

There were now seventy mosques in and around the town, he said, but all were *hukumi*, or government controlled. Kafr el Battikh had no *ahli*, popular mosques in private, and often militant, hands.

What was most encouraging, he added, was the number of educated young people who had returned to the town. Twenty years ago, students who went to study in Cairo and Alexandria would have stayed there. Today they lived better here.

There were, in fact, plenty of young people on the village streets, including women, some dressed in the traditional *hijab*; others, in Western-style clothes. I passed a video store en route to a café; two young women were selling and renting tapes, the Western and Asian action films that Egyptians, like everyone else, adored. Both girls wore lipstick and skirts that fell just below the knee, daring attire these days in rural Egypt. Had Islamists ever given them any trouble for the way they dressed and the Western tapes they sold? They smiled shyly and giggled. Not at all, they said. The sheikh's nephews were big customers.

Down the road from Kafr el Battikh was another new addition to the town: a $20 million power plant financed by American foreign aid. The entire area now had reliable power.

The equivalent of the mayor was a pleasant man in a traditional galabia who was also appointed by Cairo. His aides snapped to attention when he entered the room, muttering a subservient *hadir* (at your service) to their superior, whom they treated as if he were a pharaoh.

Mohammed Sadiq Raslan Selim and his wife offered us tea in their apartment. I started to light one of Gamal's Cleopatras but noticed that the coffee table, oddly, had no ashtray. Mohammed ordered his wife, Fadiha, to bring one, explaining that he wanted to discourage friends from smoking. He used this spacious living area for ceremonial occasions, he said. Fadiha's much smaller, spartan quarters were in the dingy back of the apartment. The couple were doing well, it seemed. The living room's white-stucco walls were covered, as in so many middle-class homes, with thick, shiny hangings that portrayed pastoral scenes and the Great Mosque in Mecca. A brightly lit chandelier made of glass hung over us, and a vase of plastic flowers sat upon a giant color-television set that broadcast an interminable Egyptian soap opera. The room, not surprisingly, was filled with local furniture — gifts, no doubt, from constituents grateful for the numerous, essential favors dispensed by such local potentates.

Mohammed's wife headed an American-funded family-planning clinic, only it was called a women's "guidance" center. Young women did not want more than two children, she reported happily. Two, which was what she had, were "more than enough," she said, laughing.

Mohammed and Fadiha had recently returned from the haj, the pilgrimage to the Prophet Muhammad's birthplace of Mecca required of all pious Muslims who could afford it once in a lifetime — a trip that had earned him in Egypt's elaborately coded language the honorific title of "hajji."

To commemorate their voyage, the couple had transformed one of their anterooms into a private mosque — the first in Kafr el Battikh, they boasted. Mohammed had painted the walls powder blue, lined the floors and wallboards with expensive mosaic tiles, covered the rest of the cement floor with prayer carpets, and even built a fountain for washing before praying. Some of their neighbors came to pray there. The room was clearly a hit. It was also tax-deductible, since Egyptian law encouraged mosque construction by exempting Muslims who consecrate a room in their homes as mosques from certain property taxes.

After our chat, Mohammed introduced me to Ibrahim Muhammad Ghanim, the third key figure in town, the head of the town council, the city's only elected post. A jovial, apparently well liked man who stopped and chatted with residents as he escorted us to his own furniture shop, Ghanim said there was no violence or extremist organizing in this town, not even a Muslim Brotherhood office, unusual for a town this size. This was his first four-year term in office, he told us, and he intended to make sure that things stayed that way.

And it probably would, I thought. Just as Kafr el Battikh was once a reflection of Egypt's poverty and despair, it now reflected the prosperity and stability that parts of Egypt enjoyed, particularly in the Nile Delta, where private business and trade flourished, with help from Cairo. At least three men counted here — two representing the central government, who watched each other as well as their fellow citizens, and a third chosen by town residents who negotiated with the other two. Kafr el Battikh's Islam was official — as solid, traditional, and unthreatening as its furniture. Competent leadership and continued economic progress held the place together. Not all Delta villages were as peaceful as this one, of course.[36] But this was how Egypt was supposed to be — when it worked.

His was a tough job, the council chief explained, especially since he still had to run his own business. People had so many problems, and solving them took so much time. Would he run again, I asked him, if furniture orders picked up? For how long did he wish to remain mayor?

Ghanim grinned broadly at his friends. "Forever!" he replied in Arabic as they all laughed. "Like President Mubarak."

KAFR EL BATTIKH was a model of Egyptian stability; Assyut was its opposite. The differences between them made generalizations about Egypt, the Mideast's oldest and most unified and homogeneous nation-state, misleading.

This bleak industrial city of more than 600,000 — Egypt's third largest — some two hundred miles south of Cairo on the Nile, was as drab in late 1993 as it had been during my previous visit in 1987. Assyut's endless rows of apartment blocks were still caked in grimy brown sand. The air was now even dirtier, choked with dust and car-exhaust fumes heavy with lead. The place reeked of sewage. Unlike Kafr el Battikh or Cairo, there was hardly any green to relieve the region's harsh, hot landscape — few parks and fewer trees, even along the Nile. I had never seen so many flies. When I nearly swallowed one, I gave up trying to breathe through my mouth.

The faces of Assyut were as hard and lined as its sun-baked mud. Most women's heads were covered; the only women who dared go bareheaded these days were Copts — between 20 and 30 percent of the city's population. Police in black and khaki uniforms lined major boulevards by day and checkpoints at strategic spots throughout the night, targeting their strobe lights at shadows.

"The past three years have been hell," said a Coptic friend who feared being identified even by his first name as we sipped tea at our semi-air-conditioned, Christian-owned hotel. "We have your hero Sadat to thank for this," he complained.

The Gama'a and other militant Islamic groups owed their existence in part to Sadat's efforts in the early 1970s to confront the threat from left-wing Arab nationalists by encouraging the formation of Islamic groups and associations. Sadat had also freed from jail hundreds of Islamic radicals, many of whom had been imprisoned for two decades.

Assyut was the main testing ground for his strategy. Under government protection and patronage, student Islamist groups known collectively as the *gam'iyat* — formed ostensibly to encourage Islamic behavior — had become the dominant force at the University of Assyut by the end of the decade.[37] Some members of these *gam'iyat* went on to form the Gama'a and join al-Jihad, the violent, secretive Islamic groups that would ultimately kill Sadat and challenge Mubarak.

The Christians of Assyut and other towns in Upper Egypt were the initial targets of the Islamic groups. "And why not?" my Coptic friend said bitterly. "We were the weakest — the easiest way of destroying the secular fabric of Egypt's political order." Christians, in other words, were not so much the fundamentalists' ideological enemy as a target of convenience.

"Their goal," my Coptic friend told me, "is to turn us into the *dhimmis* of the Koran, a so-called protected minority with fewer rights — second-class citizens in our own land."

In some towns, long-standing family vendettas between Christians and militant Muslims had been transformed into miniwars.[38] Gangs of young Muslims roamed Upper Egyptian villages blackmailing Coptic shopkeepers and landowners into paying a *jizya*, a special Koranic tax that Jews and Christians in a Muslim society were to pay for their "protection." Those who refused had their shops burned or their right arm and both legs broken as punishment and warning.

I recalled Sheikh Omar Abdel Rahman's despicable role in promoting such terror in 1981. In the trial of Sadat's murderers, Mohammed Abdelsalam Farag, a young electrical engineer who had boasted of his role in the assassination, described the counsel regarding Copts that Sheikh Abdel Rahman, the secret group's *alim* (religious guide), had given them. Rahman had ruled that it was "legitimate" to rob Christians to get money and weapons for their jihad. In his own interrogation statement, Sheikh Abdel Rahman said that he divided Copts into three groups: Copts who could be killed or, in his parlance, whose "blood was permissible" because they had fought or killed Muslims; those whose treasure and wealth could be seized for having aided the church; and those entitled to the same "rights as the rest of us."[39] When the police arrested the sheikh, they found some $20,000 as well as considerable quantities of stolen gold. Abdel Rahman's home, prosecutors concluded, had served as a laundry for loot. The cleric, in effect, was a fence. But Egyptian prosecutors somehow failed to prove either that Abdel Rahman had incited the group to murder or had provided religious sanction for the killing of Copts and the "pharaoh Sadat."[40] And he was never indicted, or even criticized, by the government for declaring in 1989 that Egyptian Nobel laureate Naguib Mahfouz, whom Islamic militants nearly stabbed to death five years later, was, like Salman Rushdie, an apostate for what he had written and that unless he repented, he, too, should be killed.[41]

Egyptian analysts told me that President Mubarak had not killed Abdel Rahman or thrown him in jail for fear of making him a martyr — a pattern of accommodation that Mubarak only reluctantly abandoned in 1994, when the sheikh was retried in absentia for one of his crimes, convicted, and sentenced to seven years in prison. But by then he was about to stand trial in New York on a twenty-count indictment for his role in the plot to blow up the United Nations and New York monuments in keeping with his perverse Islamic vision.

Throughout the 1980s the Egyptian police had failed to respond to the mounting attacks on Copts and their property, but the fearful Copts were conspicuously silent. They did not complain about the police raids on their homes and churches, or the insults and ostracism their children endured in public schools run by radical Muslim teachers. They lived with a constitution that proclaimed Islam the state religion and with laws that prohibited Muslims from converting to another faith and barred marriages between Muslim women and Christian men. They carried identity cards that stated their religion. They resisted using their political influence in the West to dissuade the government from using archaic Ottoman laws to ban the construction of new churches and repairs of old ones while private, fundamentalist-controlled mosques were doubling in number with official encouragement.[42]

For nearly thirty years Copts had been forced to petition the president — and wait years, often without result — for a presidential decree authorizing even modest church repairs.[43] No repair was too minor to require the pharaoh's consent. In 1991, for example, Mubarak issued a decree authorizing the Church of Mayiet Bara in Minūfiya Province to fix its toilet.[44]

Though Copts were still prominent within Egypt's elite and among Egypt's largest landowners, they were largely invisible in Mubarak's entourage. Christians represented no less than 10 percent of Egyptians in 1993—the government's estimate was 7 percent—but not one of the twenty-six provincial governors was Christian; nor were there many Copts among senior army or police officers of consequence.[45] Of Mubarak's 480 political appointments in 1991, only 5, or just over 1 percent, went to Christians. No major ambassador, city mayor, or state college dean was Christian.[46] Yet Mubarak repeatedly denied that there were dangerous sectarian divisions in Egypt or that his government discriminated against Christians. The Copts and Muslims were "very good friends," he told reporters in 1993 at a news conference in Washington. Not just some but "all" of his "best friends" were Copts.

Muslim-Christian vendettas in Upper Egypt grew increasingly ferocious in the early 1990s.[47] But only after Islamic groups began targeting non-Christian police and opinion leaders in Upper Egypt and senior officials in Cairo—as well as foreign tourists in October 1992—did the government launch an intensive antiterrorist campaign. Now there were thousands of soldiers and police in riot gear in this region, along with armored personnel carriers, helicopters, and missile launchers. Gamal and I had finished our interviews near Assyut escorted by the police in a heavily armed convoy. The police chief would not let us wander around alone—too dangerous, he said. The gentle countryside seemed menacing from the backseat of a bulletproof Toyota van where I was seated beside four nervous, khaki-clad policemen wielding double-clipped, ready-to-fire rifles—something I had not seen since the civil war in Lebanon. In the fall of 1993 the Assyut region was a war zone.

THE HARSH POVERTY of Upper Egypt made me reevaluate Egypt's long-term prospects. On the one hand, Egypt had made remarkable progress during Mubarak's years in office. The middle class was expanding; the economy was slowly opening up to a vibrant private sector; and numerous institutions cushioned change, such as a still-spirited press and Parliament. Income disparities that generated so much public outrage were still relatively small compared to many of Egypt's neighbors. The $35 billion in American aid since 1975 had not been wasted, though half of it had gone to the military.

In the past thirty years, average life expectancy had climbed from sixty-seven to eighty-one years; childhood deaths had fallen from thirty-four to eleven per thousand. Per capita gross national product had doubled from the mid-1970s to the mid-1980s, and adult literacy had risen from 35 to 49 percent; some 86 percent of Egyptians had access to safe drinking water, as opposed to 75 percent two decades earlier.

At the same time, the middle class was under enormous pressure. Nouveau-riche shop owners and real estate millionaires were making ten times as much as army colonels, the respected but increasingly impoverished pillar of Egyptian society. And the urban poor, once confined to a few of Cairo's slums and suburbs, were suddenly omnipresent and growing as a percentage of the population. Except for the military, the government had built almost no new public housing for the poor—housing of less than sixty square meters per unit—since

Nasser, a housing expert told me. The shortage of housing units stood at 3 million.[48] Now the government was building housing, clinics, and schools in blighted areas, but demand constantly overwhelmed supply.

These were the stubborn demographic facts: Mohammed Ali's Egypt of the nineteenth century had 2.5 million people; when I first visited Cairo in 1971, soon after Nasser's death, there were 35 million Egyptians; by the end of 1993 some 57 million Egyptians inhabited that same slim strip of fertile land along the banks of the Nile, about 3.5 percent of the land. By the year 2025 there would be nearly 100 million Egyptians, 50 percent of them under twenty.

Each year, deteriorating fertility due to overirrigation costs Egypt nearly 10 percent of its agricultural production. In 1840, 5 million Egyptians had lived on 5 million acres of cultivated land. Today, despite almost half a century of land reclamation and ambitious irrigation schemes, 60 million Egyptians still lived on just over 5 million acres of cultivated land.

Cairo, the monster of a capital, had trebled in size, and Egyptian cities were still growing on average by 3.7 percent a year. Two million people had lived in Cairo during Nasser's coup; there were 13 million now. By the early 1990s some 46 percent of Egyptians lived in cities, where population was grow-ing at an annual rate of 3.3 percent, almost twice the rural rate.

Since Mubarak became president in 1981, Egypt's population had increased by 16 million people — more than twice the population of New York and more than the combined population of Israel, Lebanon, Jordan, and the occupied territories of Palestine.

At the peak of Egypt's population boom in 1983, a new Egyptian baby was born every twelve seconds, more than a million each year. By the end of Mubarak's second term a decade later, the birthrate had slowed from 2.76 to 2.3 per family, but that still required the government to build a new school every day to keep pace with growth. Even with the now slower rate of growth, the government would have to create 400,000 new jobs a year for the foreseeable future — almost 4.5 million new jobs in the 1990s — just to employ new entrants into the labor force. That, in turn, required the economy to grow at a minimum of 5 percent a year. But Egypt's economy had been expanding in the early 1990s at an average annual rate of less than 2 percent, and by 1994 it had risen to only 3.9 percent. Between 1976 and 1986, Egypt added only 2.2 million jobs to its labor force of 15 million — less than half the jobs required. No wonder more than 75 percent of those unemployed (officially 9 percent in 1994 but more than 25 percent and some said even higher in the cities) were new entrants into the labor market — mostly young people under twenty-five, or roughly 60 percent of the population.[49]

Moreover, more than 90 percent of those who could not find work were men; of these, more than 90 percent held college degrees or had other advanced training. It was these young men, with their diplomas and high expectations, who often turned to militant Islam when their hopes of marriage, a decent home, and fulfilling work were dashed.[50]

While violent fringe groups like the Gama'a and New Jihad had lost ground by late 1994, the mainstream Muslim Brotherhood, the umbrella organization for Islamic political and social activities, with thousands of members across the world, including in Europe and the United States, was still growing richer and stronger. I had paid little attention to the group when I was in Cairo in the mid-1980s. At the insistence of our office manager, my friend Gamal, I would occasionally stroll over to the Brotherhood's dingy downtown office above a vegetable market to interview Ma'moun Hodeiby, the Ikhwan spokesman. And I had paid several courtesy visits to Zenab al-Ghazali, the leader of the Muslim Sisterhood, a woman of some physical and intellectual heft who had influenced previous generations of young Muslim radicals and never tired of trying to convert me to Islam. But during the mid-1980s the Brotherhood was a marginal factor in Egyptian political life. Mubarak had encouraged political debate and authorized several opposition parties and a freer press. The Brotherhood was no longer the only opposition in town.

Cairo in those days — with its teeming streets, Coca-Cola billboards, belly dancers, glitzy nightclubs, its passion for the recordings of Um Kalthoum and other nightingales of Arab nationalism — seemed an unlikely place for Islamic revolution. Young men were busy buying airline tickets to the Gulf for jobs that would earn them the apartment "key money" they needed to marry. The government-paid sheikhs of al-Azhar were also buying tickets for their annual pilgrimages to Mecca. The official ulema, or sheikhs of al-Azhar, would return with funds for new mosques, educational programs, charities, and Islamic invest- ment companies.

By the early 1990s, Cairo's mood had soured. There were fewer jobs to be had now that oil prices had fallen and brought recession to the Gulf. A million Egyptians had returned from Iraq or had moved to neighboring Libya, where jobs paid less well than in the Gulf or Baghdad. Egypt's grateful Gulf war allies had written off about $20 billion of what was a $51 billion debt. But America's Gulf war victory and Iraq's humiliation had produced an upsurge in anti-Western Islamic sentiment in much of the region. The Egyptian economy seemed stalled, and Mubarak's political liberalization had fizzled. Pharaonic caution had set in.

Meanwhile, the Muslim Brotherhood, with its partly Saudi financed net-work of low-cost clinics, social-welfare centers, clubs, and classes, had developed an impressive base of support within the economically squeezed middle class, and it provided essential services to neighborhoods that the government had effectively abandoned. A sociologist, Sa'ad Eddin Ibrahim, estimated that as many as 6 million Egyptians — a tenth of the population — now benefited regularly from such mosque-based services. Hisham Mubarak, the human-rights activist, said that the Brotherhood was now the largest, richest political organization in Egypt, though it was technically banned. The head of the Brotherhood acknowledged that the group received considerable funding and support from its offices in Germany, London, and the United States.[51] The elected heads of the most prominent professional associations — medicine, engineering, lawyers, and students—were almost all Muslim Brethren. The octogenarians who had long dominated the Brotherhood had even begun to recruit younger stars— men in their mid-forties. Dr. Essam Al-Erian, for example, a physician and gifted Islamist ideologue who in his student days had led a violent group at Cairo University, had told me that although the students had called their groups *gam'iyat* (Islamic associations)—as distinguished from the Gama'a Islamiya, Sheikh Omar Abdel Rahman's radical Islamic Group—the student associations in Cairo and Alexandria had long been part of the Brotherhood.

Erian's clipped beard and mustache, beige corduroy jacket, and wire-rimmed eyeglasses suggested an Islamic Trotsky—the Brotherhood's new face. Educated in the West, articulate in several languages, and smooth, he spoke in clipped and precise Arabic, dotted with classical Koranic phrases—"Islamic speech," Egyptians called it. Erian denied that he had ever encouraged strong-arm tactics; he had always favored making Egypt an Islamic state through democracy and reform.[52] The violence was the government's fault, he told me. After the 1987 elections, Islamists had lost hope of being able to secure power through the ballot box.[53]

The Brotherhood headquarters had changed little since my last visit in 1986. It still needed a coat of lime-green paint. Even its posters were the same. One depicted an octopus draped in an American flag, its tentacles encircling the earth. Another was of the Dome of the Rock mosque in Jerusalem, among Islam's holiest shrines. The mosque was locked with a chain that bore a Star of David.

In the spring of 1994 I was greeted by Ma'moun Hodeiby, a well-preserved seventy-three, wearing a gray Egyptian-style leisure suit like the one I had seen him in a decade earlier. Hodeiby's father had been a judge and the Brotherhood's second leader. Ma'moun Hodeiby was still the group's chief spokesman. Like the Brotherhood itself, he was a survivor.

Founded in 1928 in the Suez Canal city of Ismailia by Hassan al-Banna, a charismatic schoolteacher, the Brotherhood had rapidly become one of Egypt's largest political movements. Starting with four branches and fewer than a hundred adherents in 1929, the Brotherhood by 1949 had two thousand offices and more than 500,000 active members, and probably double that number of supporters. Like the Wafd, Egypt's oldest and largest political party, Banna's Brotherhood was determined to end Britain's colonial presence and restore Egypt's "dignity."[54] But unlike the Wafd, Banna did not seek an independent Egypt based on a Western democratic model. His dream was to build an Islamic society with neither Western democracy nor a constitution but with sharia, the Koran-given law of God. Nothing more was needed, Banna argued, as the group's slogan proclaimed: The Koran Is Our Constitution. Banna's movement was shaped by Islam's intellectual pioneers: by Jamal al-Din "al-Afghani," the nineteenth-century Islamic reformer who championed Muslim resurgence— the "Father of Muslim Nationalism," one scholar had called him—and also by Afghani's disciple, Muhammad Abdu, an Egyptian reformer who became

Egypt's mufti, the chief judge of its religious court and one of the leading ulema at al-Azhar University.[55] Banna's father, in fact, had studied with Abdu, who founded the influential Salafiya movement, which believed, as did Afghani, that the West had triumphed only because the Muslim world and its ulema were technologically backward. While rejecting Western science and technology, Muslim scholars and leaders had adopted Western political systems and cultural values, departing from the authentic spiritual and political principles of the *salaf* (literally, the "pious ancestors") — the Prophet Muhammad and the first four "rightly guided" caliphs.

Banna, like most contemporary Islamists, was vague about the nature of the state he wished to create, but one point was clear: Sovereignty, or *hakimiyya* in Arabic, rested not in the people nor in their rulers but in God. Not until Muslims acknowledged this dependence and created political systems that reflected it would they succeed in the present life or the next. Without sharia, Muslims were simply, in Banna's words, "a society of cultural mongrels and spiritual half-castes."[56]

While the Brothers initially focused on combating Christian missionary activity in Egypt, the fighting in Palestine gave the group its first significant international role. What began as fund-raising and propagandizing for Palestine in 1935 escalated into preparation for jihad through its secret military wing — its "special apparatus" — in late 1947 and, finally, participation in the ineffectual Arab effort in 1948 to prevent the Zionists from founding their state. The Brotherhood's enmity toward Israel would become an enduring theme.

Banna commanded fierce loyalty and was soon venerated by his followers in language like that Christians used to describe Christ. As late as 1985, one disciple referred to Banna not only as the "Restorer of the Cause of Islamic Principles," "builder of the nation," but also "innocent," "all-embracing," and "incapable of committing errors."[57] Given the respect of Arab culture for eloquence, Banna's fiery speeches and personal magnetism were largely responsible for the Brotherhood's early successes, an American historian argued. But Banna was an autocrat. "If Banna sneezed in Cairo, the Brothers in Aswan would say 'God Bless You,' " one critic complained.[58] His authoritarian instincts were also the source of the group's autocratic tendencies, its intolerance of dissent, and the political violence that ultimately gave governments the pretext to crush it — three times, in 1948, 1952, and 1954.

Banna was in some ways a prototype of today's modern militant Muslim — sly, ambitious, action oriented, and willing to embrace violence if it served his ends. In early 1949, Banna was gunned down on a Cairo street by the king's secret police.

The Brotherhood that reemerged from Nasser's horrific repression in 1954 was so different from Banna's — so cautious, so fearful of antagonizing the regime — that one scholar called them the "neo-Muslim Brethren" to distinguish them from the group that first the king and then Nasser had crushed.[59] Now it was guided by men fully aware of the horrific consequences of challenging the omnipotent pharaoh and his hard state. This time, the Brethren reasoned, they would fully prepare the ground for their Islamic state before they acted. They would renounce violence and work to become not only legal but indispensable. Never again would they move precipitously or openly challenge the regime if they could avoid it.

Not all the Brethren were chastened, however. Ever since Banna's death, a Brotherhood faction had resisted the group's more patient, accommodating strategy. In a prison infirmary, a sickly Brother — a schoolteacher and fiery essayist — had written a book that would shape the current Islamic revival: *Signposts on the Road*, an Islamist version of Lenin's *What Is to Be Done?*[60]

The true ideological father of modern Islamic militancy, more than Banna, is Sayyid Qutb, a Brotherhood leader and ideologue who spent more than ten years in Nasser's prisons and was himself atrociously tortured. His Islamic call to arms, a devastating Islamist criticism of Nasser's regime that was smuggled out of prison in the early 1960s and published in 1964, immediately became modern radical Islam's unofficial handbook.

In *Signposts*, Qutb set forth what was then a shocking thesis: Many Arab leaders, like Nasser, who called themselves Muslims were, in fact, nonbelievers; hence, their governments, too, were un-Islamic. True Muslims could never subject fellow Muslims to the torture and persecution that he and his brothers endured in prison. Indeed, such leaders and their societies were *jahili* — that is, spiritually akin to those Arabs who lived in "ignorance" and "barbarism" before the Prophet Muhammad founded his seventh-century state in Arabia. So, he wrote, real Muslims had a religious duty not only to reject such pseudo-Muslim creations but also to overthrow their leaders by force. From then on, jihad could be fought against ostensibly Muslim regimes.

Gilles Kepel, a French scholar, stressed that Qutb's manifesto was a radical departure not only from traditional Islamic doctrine, which maintained that even unjust Muslim rulers had to be obeyed for the unity and sake of the Islamic *umma* (community), but also from Muslim Brotherhood dogma. "Banna would never have dreamed of accusing the Egyptian society of his day of being non-Islamic!" Gilles told me. "But from Qutb's vantage point in a concentration camp, Nasser's United Arab Republic was even less Islamic than Egypt under the monarchy and the British."

Fouad Ajami, an American scholar of Lebanese origin, agreed: Qutb's deadly distinction "let the cat out of the bag." Before Qutb, and even for most traditional Muslims today, anyone who called himself a Muslim and prayed was a Muslim. No one had the right to challenge him. Qutb claimed the right to decide who was, and was not, a believer.

I had long been intrigued by Qutb, whose works I had seen on the shelf of every Islamist I visited in the Middle East. Like Banna, Qutb had secured a hallowed place among modern Islamic militancy's heroes by being "martyred" — sent to the gallows in 1966.

Unlike Banna, Qutb came to Islamic activism late in life. He was forty-five when he was inducted into the Brotherhood. Born in 1906 near Assyut to a family of poor rural notables, he was an inspector in the Ministry of Education until the end of World War II and wrote obsessively—not just essays but also literary criticism and fiction, even an autobiographical novel in which Qutb describes his disillusionment with love, which several analysts say explains why he never married. In 1948 the Education Ministry exiled him to the United States for study. As it did for so many other militant Arabs, Qutb's voyage to the New World served not to open his heart and mind to the West and so-called modern solutions to social problems but to drive him into Islam. Political scientists would later observe that many militant middle-class Islamists, in fact, were educated or trained in the West, particularly in the sciences.[61]

Qutb apparently rediscovered his faith as he stood on the deck of the ocean liner bound for New York. From that day on, says Kepel, he began praying five times a day and meeting with and preaching to fellow Muslims. In America, he exchanged his obsession with literature for Islam.[62]

While most scholars have focused on Qutb's political philosophy, I was more intrigued by the man himself and, in particular, his pathological vision of the West and my country.

Qutb detested America. The little-read account of his travels in the United States[63] is filled with disgust at American support of Zionism and the country's "synthetic civilization," materialism, and sexual depravity. But some of the America Qutb depicts in the 1950s is virtually unrecognizable to anyone who grew up in the United States in those years. While adherents of militant religious orders, and not just Muslims, often condemn practices and traditions that differ from their own, Qutb's writings, however fluent and occasionally humorous, reflect an absolute intolerance of the "other" so typical of his political writing in general and of his movement's brand of Islam.

Like most Islamic fundamentalists, Qutb was obsessed not only with sex but with the moral significance of women, and like many Muslim militants, he believed that their place was in the home. In a just society, a woman was not a "plaything created for man's pleasure" or a cog in the wheel of "material production" but the hub of the family, the guardian of humanity's most precious commodity: its children.[64]

I recalled his description of a church social in Greeley, Colorado, in 1950. When religious services ended,

> we made our way through a side door into the dance hall adjacent to the auditorium devoted to prayer. Every young man took the hand of a young woman. Among the young people were those who had just sung their hymns. Red and blue lights, with only a few white lamps, illuminated the dance floor. Songs from the record player whipped the dancing into a fury. The room became a confusion of feet and legs:

arms twisted around hips; lips met lips; chests pressed together. The air was thick with passion. And then, the minister came down from his office to scrutinize the place and everyone in it. He began to urge the hesitant young men and women who remained seated to join the dancing. When he noticed that the white lights were too bright — spoiling that dreamy, romantic atmosphere — he moved deftly around the room with subtle American efficiency, turning them off one by one. The minister feared that they were inhibiting the dancing and preventing couples from getting out onto the floor. In fact, the place did become more romantic. Then he proceeded to the turntable to choose a dance record that would be appropriate for the mood and that would encourage the participation of those still stuck to their chairs.

Qutb reports that the minister made "quite a selection," a "famous" tune called "Baby, It's Cold Outside." "The minister waited to see the steps of his 'sons and daughters' gliding to the music of that stirring song: then he was contented. He slipped out of the dance hall and went home, leaving the young men and women alone to complete this delightful, wholesome evening. The last to leave were responsible for depositing the keys to the church at the minister's house. The couples left one by one as they pleased!"

Qutb was not persuaded by the minister's explanation that churches used youth clubs and such innocent socials to recruit new members and attract the young to prayer services. To Qutb, the minister was a pimp. The churches saw nothing wrong with "using the prettiest and most elegant girls in the city" to lure Americans to prayer "in the same manner in which girls wearing tights and loud, colorful clothes are employed to stand in the entrances and corridors of cinemas." As it was for any "store manager," success was key, the "first priority; the nature of the means to success is no cause for concern." The more people joined his church, "the more his revenue increases, and therefore, the more his prestige and influence grow in his city." Americans, by nature, he wrote not inaccurately, were "truly enthralled by bigness — both physical size and number."

He had chosen such anecdotes from among "hundreds of similar scenes" that he supposedly witnessed as evidence of America's "total licentiousness." As a result, he wrote, "natural, licit, heterosexual relations no longer satisfy sexual urges," and "deviance has spread among young men and women alike." Qutb cites as proof the "precise and startling statistics" in what he called *The Kinsey Reports on Sexual Behavior in the Human Male and Sexual Behavior in the Human Female.*

Like most anti-American writers, he often quoted Western critics of Western culture to support his prejudices. Among those books he likes to cite is *Man, the Unknown* by Alexis Carrel, whom Qutb describes as a famous French scientist who lived and worked in the United States for thirty-five years and won the Nobel Prize for science in 1912. Carrel, in fact, was an American who was born in France and returned to his native land shortly before World War II. Having grown increasingly authoritarian and hostile to Western democracy, Carrel enthusiastically championed the pro-Nazi Vichy government in Paris. He died shortly before the end of the war and hence was never tried for collaboration.[65] But who among Qutb's modern readers would know that Carrel, so generously cited in Qutb's book, was a Nazi sympathizer?

As a result of his travels, Qutb decided that America and Europe — indeed, the entire West — was irretrievably decadent and in a "civilizational decline similar to the fall of ancient Rome." The decline that began with the Renaissance intensified, "especially during the Enlightenment," when society broke away "from the reins of the church, and simultaneously, strayed from God and from the course that He sets for human life." The moral crisis deepened in the nineteenth century with the advent of Darwin, Freud, and Marx, each of whom had "denigrated" humanity in his own way: Darwin stressed "the absolute animal nature of man"; Freud, the "totality of the sexual morass enveloping him"; and Marx, the "insignificance of human action in contrast to the power of economic forces and the material world."

Shattering the "fundamental principles of morality," such villains had "set the sexes loose like two animals pursuing desire and sensual pleasure for their own sake." As a result, Western society itself was adrift, and the church suffered from "neglect and alienation born of its irrelevance." Thus, the church "began to scramble frantically after society, grabbing at its coattails, no longer taking the lead in community affairs and directing the people toward religion, but, rather, chasing after society and pandering to base appetites."[66]

Jews, of course, played an important role in the creation of such barbarous *jahili* societies. Some appeared in the form of "Orientalists," besotted Western souls who attempted to understand Arab and Muslim society. Others, such as "Marx, Freud, Durkheim, and the Jew [sic] Jean-Paul Sartre," had all made inimitable contributions to the debasement of moral order.[67] Qutb cited the "Protocols of the Elders of Zion," a notorious czarist anti-Semitic tract, as evidence that Jews were behind "materialism, animal sensuality, the destruction of the family and the dissolution of society." But, Qutb added, it was wrong to blame Jews exclusively for Western materialism and imperialism, for "Western blood carries the spirit of the Crusades within itself."

Qutb's verdict on America, Europe, and the West was damnation. When he returned to Egypt in the summer of 1951, he denounced America so vehemently, according to Gilles Kepel, that he was forced to resign as a government teacher. And years later, in *Islam and the Problems of Civilization*, the same book in which he discusses his stay in America, he condemns Western civilization, explicitly pronouncing a death penalty. "What should be our verdict on this synthetic civilization?" he asks. What was to be done about America and the West given their "overwhelming danger to humanity . . . ? Should we not issue a sentence of death? Is this not the verdict most appropriate to the nature of the crime?"

Although the Muslim Brotherhood leadership officially rejected Qutb's most radical views, I would read many books and articles and hear endless mosque sermons in the next decade that echoed Qutb, though few as eloquent or original. Generations of disciples would "refine" his thinking. For example, the manifestos of both Jihad—*The Philosophy of Confrontation*—and the Gama'a—*The Program for Islamic Action*—borrowed heavily from Qutb. Those documents, both published in 1984, were partly written by militants in prison, as Qutb's *Signposts* had been.

Hisham Mubarak, who analyzed the manifestos in detail, noted that both groups paid homage, as had Qutb, to the spiritual ancestor of all modern Islamic revivalists, Ibn Taymiyya (1268–1328), the puritanical medieval scholar who spent his life protecting Islam from heretics and deviationists. Ibn Taymiyya, too, had done much of his work in prison and had died a martyr in a Damascus jail. He, like his militant successors, promoted a purist, literalist Islam, one stripped of what one scholar called "the dross accumulated during centuries of decline."[68] Ibn Taymiyya knew that his Mamluk sultanate of Egypt and Syria faced real enemies—the Mongols—men who called themselves Muslims but in Ibn Taymiyya's view were not. The Mongols, who had forced Ibn Taymiyya's family to flee their town when he was a boy, had abandoned most of the holy law, the sharia, he argued, and they had attacked other Muslims. In blessing those who fought the invaders and resisted such "illegitimate" power, Ibn Taymiyya, in effect, provided Jihad and the Gama'a with the theological underpinning they were seeking to fight contemporary Egyptian Mongols—Hosni Mubarak's godless state.[69]

But the conceptual framework of radical Islam's view of the West and of America—its rejection of the imitation by Arab regimes of Western systems and values and its devastating conclusion that every pious Muslim was religiously obliged to wage a jihad against such *jahili* societies—became accepted militant dogma by the time the Jihad and Gama'a theoreticians began writing in the 1980s. Those concepts are Sayyid Qutb's legacy to modern Islamic militancy, or "literalism," as a thoughtful Palestinian scholar prefers to call it.[70] The words and phrases that Qutb used are as old as Islam. Qutb's inimitable contribution was to make them mean something supposedly authentic and traditional but actually novel and radical. Qutb still matters, especially today, because his views penetrate "the mainstream of Muslim thought," as one scholar observed, and eventually helped change "age-old habits of passivity."[71] I did not fully understand this when I first read Qutb, but as I continued to encounter his words, I was also seeing how contemporary young Muslim literalists saw themselves and their world as well as me and mine.

THE NEO-MUSLIM BRETHREN were cautious. Ma'moun Hodeiby, for instance, had been among the fifteen hundred opposition figures jailed by Sadat in

September 1981, only a month before his murder. His message, and that of most Islamists I interviewed, was that the Brotherhood was now "mainstream" and "moderate" — no threat to Mubarak's regime and certainly not a group to be repressed.

"It is very frustrating." Hodeiby sighed, flashing a sincere smile through his scruffy gray beard. "What more can we do to demonstrate our peaceful intentions? We can publish our journal, but we cannot organize as a political party? What kind of democracy is this?"

A very "Egyptian" version, I thought, a "pharaonic democracy," as Egyptians jokingly called it, the other side of the president's "official" Islam, and equally disingenuous. But Mubarak, I knew, was adamant. "We have a law," he had told me in 1994. "It says no religious parties." As a youngster, Mubarak had been in the Brotherhood, he said. He knew what the Brethren were after: power, not Islam. He would let them run candidates through coalitions with legal parties, but not run as a party. Not as long as he was president.

Hodeiby insisted on his devotion to democracy, but I was as skeptical of him as I was of Mubarak's "Egyptian" democracy and "official" Islam. He assured me in the spring of 1994, for example, that in an Islamic Egypt all parties, "EVEN atheists," would be able to participate in politics. But a few months later, he told another reporter that while he might favor tolerating secular parties in an Islamic state, "the people would not accept it, and we cannot make people accept something they do not want."[72]

This was, of course, Islamic double-talk: There was nothing moderate or democratic about his credo. His Islamic state would ban many things as Egyptian as the Nile: belly dancing, for instance, and alcohol, a mainstay of the country's vital tourist industry, among its largest sources of foreign currency.

I asked him how Egypt would attract Western tourists without liquor. "Do you think they come here just to drink?" Hodeiby replied. "There is much to see in Egypt — the Pyramids, the tombs of Luxor. Tourists will still come."[73]

I was not so sure, recalling my own tours of the monuments in the furnace of Upper Egypt throughout the 1980s. A beer — even an Egyptian Stella, which critics said contained formaldehyde as a preservative — had never been as welcome.

Sharia, of course, with its death penalty for apostasy, its amputation of limbs for theft, and other medieval punishments, would be the law, Hodeiby continued, but women, a bulwark of the economy, would still be permitted to work. "Not as prostitutes, of course," he added quickly. "Or as judges or president. That's forbidden by the Koran."

Egypt's Coptic Christians, he said, would enjoy "full Koranic rights" as *dhimmis*, a protected minority. So why were they worried? he asked rhetorically.

In his Egypt there would be no place for relations with Israel, a sine qua non of militant Islam's doctrine. "They are killing our people," he said of the Israelis. And if they weren't? I asked him. If Israel satisfied the Palestinians and made peace with all its neighbors, as it had with Egypt in 1979, with the PLO in 1993, and with Jordan in 1994?

Hodeiby would not be pinned down. I knew that the Brotherhood had strongly condemned every peace agreement with the Jewish state, from Egypt's "Stable of David" agreements, as Brotherhood leader Muhammed Hamid Abu al-Nasr had called them, to the 1994 peace between Israel and Jordan.[74] The "only" way for Palestinians to achieve liberation, according to a Brethren communiqué after the 1993 Israeli-PLO accord, was through jihad. The Palestinians were weak; the "Zionist enemy" was strong. Thus, the PLO had not gotten the right to rule even 2 percent of historic Palestine. This "shameful" solution "imposed" on the Palestinians would not succeed. It would be "burned under the feet of the Mujahadeen."[75] But no matter how hard I pressed him, Hodeiby would not be specific about whether, or under what conditions, the Brotherhood would accept a Jewish state in *Dar al-Islam* (the realm of Islam).

Hodeiby and other senior Brethren were also determinedly vague about the size and operations of their group. Egyptian officials said that the Brethren had about 100,000 active members and more than a million supporters. But because the Brotherhood was both officially illegal and secretive, estimating its strength with confidence was impossible. Hisham Mubarak, the lawyer and Islamic expert, believed, however, that if the Brotherhood ever ran in a free election, it would win overwhelmingly.

Hodeiby was even more evasive when I asked about the Islamic violence plaguing Egypt and the Brotherhood's alleged role in aiding or inspiring it. "We operate through peaceful means," he insisted, thumping the Formica table separating us for emphasis. Only "Communists and other secular enemies of Islam" tried to link the Brethren to the extremist groups.

But did the Brotherhood condemn the violence? I asked.

He dodged my question by asking another: "Is there a more blatant terrorism than that exemplified by the state itself?" he replied.

Did the Brotherhood still maintain a secret apparatus, a secret military wing that aided or inspired the more radical Islamists like Gama'a and New Jihad?

"Nonsense!" he told me. "The government is living in a fantasy world."

My friend Said al-Ashmawi, a jovial, rotund, retired chief judge on Egypt's State Security Court, insisted that the Brotherhood and the fanatics were "two sides of one coin" when I visited him in the spring of 1994 in his shuttered apartment where four men with machine guns guarded him. Ashmawi, an outspoken critic of the radicals, had received numerous death threats, but he continued to denounce them. Of course, the Brethren had secret links to the violent groups, he told me. But they also had an effective division of labor. The radicals weakened the system through violence and terror; the Brotherhood stood by as the "peaceful" Islamic alternative to the government. The government was right about the ties. Hodeiby was lying, Ashmawi told me.

Only later did I learn why Ashmawi and others close to the police believed this. A high-level defector in the underground armed movement in Cairo had told the police in 1993 that Muslim Brotherhood supporters made secret payments to several violent groups, including his own, a senior official later told me. The official added that what the defector said was consistent with information the police had uncovered almost two years earlier at the offices of a computer software firm called the International Company for Development and Advanced Systems, known as Salsabil. In a raid in the Cairo suburb of Heliopolis in February 1992, the police said they had found computer disks and other documents that linked the Brotherhood to radical Islamic groups. The computer company was owned by two Egyptians, one of whom was the son of a Brotherhood leader in the 1950s. The material reportedly showed that despite the Brotherhood's denials, the Brethren still maintained a "secret apparatus," as they had in the 1930s and 1950s, and that this unit's goal was still to overthrow the government. While the Brotherhood was petitioning the courts to legalize the group, its secret branch was ready to take advantage of the government's "benign" attitude toward it, the official said, summarizing the material for me. Brothers with contacts in the security services were instructed to explore "the extent to which it is possible to realize the objectives of the party" through those good offices. The coded Salsabil disks also supposedly contained lists of Brotherhood banks and investment companies abroad, including in Switzerland and the Bahamas, as well as "reliable" Islamic contacts outside Egypt. While the government had immediately arrested fifteen people, including the two young store owners, and fifty others a few months after the raid and charged them with belonging to an "illegal" organization, the security services still had to verify the information and keep people on the list under surveillance. When in the summer of 1994 I read what was presented as an extensive description of the Salsabil documents in a pro-government magazine that was virtually identical to what the official had told me a year earlier, I realized that the government was probably planning to move against the Brotherhood itself.[76] Within days, the government, in fact, proposed legislation that would limit Brotherhood influence in the major professional syndicates, or unions. And some six months after the Salsabil documents were described in the press, the government arrested almost thirty senior Brotherhood leaders of the professional unions, including the suave Dr. Erian, charging them with membership in an "illegal" group.

I was never permitted to see the actual documents or to meet the elusive defector whom the official had described. But I was willing to believe that government supporters believed in their authenticity. Diplomats and human-rights workers, however, remained skeptical. Hisham Mubarak, for example, who had interviewed dozens of militants and read what they wrote, said that after Sadat, the Brotherhood was committed to coming to power by peaceful means. Perhaps some militants had ties to some Brethren, but that did not constitute formal cooperation between the Brotherhood and the violent groups, he argued. Moreover, he insisted, the Gama'a and Jihad detested the "co-opted" Brotherhood almost as much as they did the government. In August 1995, for example, both groups had denounced the Brotherhood for having condemned a Jihad-sponsored attempt on Mubarak's life in Ethiopia. The Brotherhood's expression of "joy at Mubarak's salvation" had not stopped the government from arresting Brotherhood leaders and jailing them at what a Jihad leader mockingly called the "Tura Prison tourist resort."[77]

As for the Salsabil documents, no case had ever been brought against a single defendant based on them, he argued. Eight of the fifteen people arrested at the company in 1992 had been released. While most of the fifty men arrested several months later were still in jail, none had been tried in court. Hisham had attended almost every hearing in connection with the Salsabil defendants and looked at the prosecutor's file, he told me. "I read the interrogation reports. There was not a single reference to those documents. No one I know has seen them, and no case has ever been brought to court based on them. What am I supposed to think?"

BY THE TIME I returned to Egypt in late 1994, the violence was still continuing; more than 460 people had been killed, including nine tourists, but police sweeps, coupled with government aid, had forced the armed militants to retreat to the villages of Upper Egypt. In February, a founder of Jihad acknowledged that his movement was "weaker now than it was in 1981."[78] Some fifteen people had been convicted in military court — only one was acquitted — of the assassination attempt on Minister Alfi. Four were sentenced to death; all were executed.

By the summer of 1994 the government's campaign to repress the Muslim Brotherhood was well under way. The Parliament approved legislation that denied university professors the right to elect their faculty deans, since many departments were dominated by Ikhwan activists. Then the Ministry of Awqaf, which oversees the nation's mosques, announced that the government would bring all of Egypt's 120,000 mosques and prayer rooms under its supervision — an ambitious goal, since officials had acknowledged the previous year that the state controlled less than half of them. But the statement served notice that the government could close any mosque at any time. Mubarak himself began denouncing the Muslim Brotherhood as a "terrorist" organization. Senior leaders, including the ailing supreme guide Abu al-Nasr, then eighty-one, and the aging leadership of the Labor Party, which was in a shaky alliance with the Brotherhood, were hauled in for questioning. The government also launched a public-relations offensive against the "terrorists," creating mawkishly patriotic soap operas and broadcasting "confessions" of repentant militant leaders.[79] It was hard to turn on your television or pass a café without seeing a now cleanly shaved Islamist in his ankle-length galabia sobbing over how he had been led astray from Islam's "straight path," a phrase from the opening chapter of the Koran that is repeated five times a day by devout Muslims. Some friends found the confessions unpersuasive. "I might say a lot of things after a few weeks of Interior Ministry hospitality at the receiving end of electrodes," said Mohammed Sid Ahmed, an engaging aristocrat and leftist intellectual who had spent time in Nasser's prisons.

Mubarak's policy also offered some incentives. In Cairo's Imbaba district, for example, where a million people were crammed into tottering mud-walled tenements along narrow, dark alleys and where an average of eight people shared each room,[80] the government was investing more than $10 million in a new medical and dental clinic—where the entrance fee was an affordable fifteen cents—paved roads, a sewage system, better garbage collection, new bus lines, more power and water lines, a vegetable market, and a youth center.[81] Two years earlier, the government had launched a brutal offensive against the Islamic groups in this same quarter, where the Gama'a had run a state within a state. Imbaba had been virtually sealed off for five weeks in late 1992 while fifteen thousand troops raided shops and homes, closed mosques, rounded up students, shot up militants' hangouts, and searched for members of the Gama'a. Now Mubarak was making amends. He also planned to spend more than $200 million on similar projects in other poor quarters and villages throughout Egypt beginning in 1994—$1.5 billion over the next five years. The militants' institutions still flourished in Imbaba, however. There, as everywhere, demand for government services and expectations still outstripped supply. Per capita income, after rising through much of the 1970s and 1980s, was falling, from $670 in 1980 to $610 in 1994, less than New Guinea, El Salvador, or the Congo. So were Egyptian living standards. While 42 percent of Egyptians lived below the poverty line in 1984, more than 54 percent of the country did so a decade later.

Perhaps that was why corruption—the "baksheesh" endemic at all levels of Egyptian society—was now so highly visible and more deeply resented than ever before. My friend Gamal had quietly waited fifteen years for a home telephone because he could not afford the $1,000 in baksheesh to expedite the process. But Essam, his university-trained son, was furious at having to pay what amounted to baksheesh to be admitted to a computer school, acceptance to which was supposedly based on merit. Like many in his generation, Essam lacked the *sabr*, the legendary patience that Gamal had tried, but failed, to instill in him or me. As income plunged, Cairene shopkeepers who made an average of $150 a month grew ever more bitter about the $30 a month they paid local policemen to avoid having their stores closed for obscure violations. And everyone was furious at the government—at President Mubarak, in particular.

In his first speech as president in 1981, Mubarak had vowed to end the corruption and nepotism that flourished under Sadat. Throughout the mid-1980s he was perceived as honest, if dull. Yet by the early 1990s the "gang of sons," as the young commercially minded offspring of government ministers were now known, were prospering. According to the opposition press, the son of Safwat Sherif, the information minister, had made a fortune selling government television programs to the Saudis. The son of Fouad Sultan, the former tourism minister, had been given the lucrative concession to sell furniture from Egypt's three hundred state-owned companies to state-owned hotels. The son of Prime Minister Sidki made millions, people said, as a trader for, among others, a Bahraini bank that engaged in foreign-currency exchanges. If you wanted a government job, the man to pay, one taxi driver and a diplomat told me, was a senior official in Mubarak's ruling party. One commentator, emboldened, no doubt, by his residency in America, said that everyone knew that the "government is controlled by Mubarak's in-laws."[82] Nor was it a secret that Libyan leader Muammar Qaddafi had attended the 1991 wedding of Mubarak's son Alaa, a Cairo business consultant whom American journalists and the opposition Egyptian press described as a partner in several Libyan investments in Egypt, particularly in the beleaguered hotel and tourism sector.[83] The government denied all this, but Alaa, according to American sources, was allegedly a partner in several Libyan-backed ventures, including sales of steel bars in which steel was bought in Libya and resold in Egypt at a high profit. American officials were particularly annoyed at Alaa Mubarak, since some of these alleged deals, not to mention his father's efforts to help his oil-rich neighbor, where more than 500,000 Egyptians now worked, were said to have helped Libya circumvent UN sanctions imposed on Qaddafi for his sponsorship of terrorism. *Al-Shaab*, among other opposition papers, had also accused Mubarak's attractive son Gihad, who then worked at the Bank of America in London, of having earned a $60,000 bonus for, among other deals, helping Egypt finance a multi-million-dollar trade deal with China.

Ordinarily, I would not have been shocked by such arrangements, nor would I have written about them. Corruption flourishes in every country, including my own. Everyone wanted power that ensured access and wealth. But in my twenty years of reporting from Egypt, I had never felt such resentment over what, in different times, would have been dismissed with a sigh and a *ma'alesh* (it doesn't matter). By 1994, corruption was perceived, by everyone except the president, as a major political problem.

Mubarak was enraged when I asked him about published reports concerning the "gang of sons," including his own. He was clean, he told me in 1994, and so was his family. "I have never taken any illegal money from anyplace all of my life," he said emphatically. Gihad's bonus was based on merit, on his overall performance, not on any single deal. Work for Egypt was a small part of his portfolio.

"If you give me ten million pounds or fifty million pounds, what would I do with it?" Mubarak said, his fist hitting the table once again. "Cars? I have lots of cars — all presents.

"A house?" Mubarak said. "I live in a good house. Food? I am eating less than any man in the street, less than anybody. What did you have for breakfast, Judy?" he asked, leaning toward me. I never eat breakfast, I told him. He seemed disappointed. "For my breakfast I had a piece of bread like this," he said, holding up two fingers to suggest a slice of bread no thicker than melba toast, "and a cup of tea." He didn't eat lunch unless he had guests. For dinner, he ate a salad, "boiled potatoes and a piece of fish or a very small piece of meat. I don't like meat."

Mubarak seemed sincere, but the furor persisted. If he attempted to ensure that his family and cabinet appeared above suspicion, he was not successful.

But he sent a very senior official to Washington to complain to senior editors of at least two publications about articles they had published on Egyptian corruption and proposed a tough press censorship law to bar reporters from attacking his family and government officials.

MY PERCEPTIVE FRIEND Tahseen Bashir, the scholar-diplomat, did not fear that Egypt would collapse or that the government would be overthrown by the militants. But he was afraid that the government's schizophrenic policy of fighting Islam with Islam and its inability to present an appealing alternative to Islamic rule would end badly.

On the surface, Egypt's civic institutions appeared vibrant and strong. Egyptians, who were to bureaucracy what Bach was to the Baroque, adored forming private associations. Egypt now had fourteen thousand of them, more than in all other Arab states combined.[84] Some had lofty names, such as the Ibn Khaldoun Center for Development Studies, named after the celebrated Arab historian, and the New Civic Forum, dedicated to political and economic liberalization in Egypt, a veritable "thunderbolt of common sense," a Western diplomat had called it. But such groups, alas, represented relatively few Egyptians, and this being Egypt, almost all were creatures of, or dependent on, the government. The associations that mattered were sponsored by Coptic or Islamic groups, many of them openly hostile to the secular state.

Many professional women, who had much to lose if Islamic literalists and their sharia replaced Egypt's secular government, however wanting, shunned politics for fear of the militants. The Arab Women's Solidarity Association, a group led by Nawal el-Saadawi, well-known physician and feminist author, had challenged the Islamists but also such politically sacrosanct government positions as Egypt's support of the American-led campaign against Iraq. As a result, the government had shut it down and awarded its license to an Islamic women's organization. Human-rights groups were also in trouble: The EOHR split up in 1994 after fistfights erupted at a board meeting over the group's political direction and spending priorities, leaving it in tatters.

Many Egyptian intellectuals, too, avoided confronting Islamic literalists and preferred not to explore the problems plaguing Egypt and other Arab societies. Egyptians who had forced Arab society to confront its weakness in 1948, after the Arabs were routed by the new Jewish state, and in 1967, after the Six-Day War,[85] were now mostly silent. There were exceptions, to be sure. Youssef Chaheen continued making provocative films; Adel Imam, the brave and talented actor/producer, mocked militants and leaders alike in his plays and movies. A new group of young writers was coming into its own. But many of the intellectuals who should have been leading the opposition to the avowed Islamic opponents of free thought and skeptical inquiry were now invisible in the struggle between the government and its fundamentalist foes by 1994.

While most young Egyptian intellectuals did not remember those terrifying days for freethinkers under Nasser, I did. Soon after Nasser died, I had spent half a night in 1971 driving through the capital in a dilapidated Fiat with its radio at full blast because it was the only place that the writer I was interviewing felt safe speaking candidly. But now the silence of intellectuals was not officially enforced; it was voluntary.

Some intellectuals had been terrified into passivity by Farag Foda's murder and the assassination attempt in the fall of 1994 against Naguib Mahfouz, Egypt's eighty-two-year-old Nobel Prize–winning author. Even before Mahfouz was attacked, he had softened his own defense of fellow writer Salman Rushdie to avoid antagonizing the militants. In early 1994, when I visited him at *Al Ahram*, the newspaper where he held court once a week, Mahfouz had told me that Rushdie's work, which he said he had not read, was "very disturbing." Rushdie had "insulted Islam," and insults had "consequences." The "right course," he said, would have been to put Rushdie on trial and let him repent before punishing him. "I would prefer to debate a book in court than kill its author."

I was saddened by Mahfouz's retreat on such a critical principle of free expression. His revised position was not all that different from that of the Muslim Brotherhood or, for that matter, from that of Sheikh Abdel Rahman in jail in New York.

Poverty had also humiliated and weakened Egypt's once luminous intelligentsia. The oil boom of the 1970s had a pernicious effect. Because of their fabulous wealth and Egypt's relative economic decline, Saudi Arabia and the Gulf had claimed the right to set the Arabs' cultural and political agenda, a "catastrophe" for Arab thought, said Hassan Hanafi, an Egyptian intellectual who was now also sympathetic to Islamism. Many an Egyptian intellectual, offered a choice between what Hanafi called "truth and a loaf of bread," had chosen the latter. In the Gulf the choice was between "a loaf of bread and a grilled steak in a fancy restaurant, luxury living, flats for one's children back in Cairo, junkets and sinecures." Thus, truth had been "banished," intellect had become "merchandise," and words had been turned into "whores at retail prices," Hanafi said. The glittering "petrodollar culture" of Saudi Arabia and the Gulf sheikhdoms had proved almost as inhibiting to intellectual discourse as Iran's Islamic *fatwas* and Saddam Hussein's Arab nationalism, a "straight path" of his own secular, authoritarian invention. "In the Arab world today," said Fouad Ajami, who, like so many of the most gifted Arab intellectuals, had chosen to live in the West, where he could express himself freely, "intellectuals have been either beaten down by the stick or seduced by the carrot." In his view, more thinkers had been bought off than bludgeoned into silence.

Economically dependent on Saudi Arabia, a culturally fundamentalist state that did not welcome provocative introspection in general and criticism of Islam in particular, Egyptian intellectuals teaching in Gulf schools or writing for wealthy London-based, Saudi-owned journals chose "safe" topics, such as Israel's wicked influence on Arab growth and development and Western hostility to Arab-Islamic culture.

In their unrelenting attacks on Israel and, in effect, on Egypt's pioneering peace with the Jewish state, Egypt's secular leftist intellectuals were accommodating Islamists, their ostensible foes. Leftists claimed that their objections to peace differed from those of the Islamists. For leftists, said Mohammed Sid Ahmed, opposition to Israel was the result of Israel's "expansionist" policies, its denial of "Palestinian national rights," and its "illegal confiscation and occupation of Palestinian land." But policies could change, he said, and the Israelis could theoretically redeem themselves. For militant Islamists, by contrast, and even for the supposedly "moderate" Brotherhood, the creation of Israel itself was an act of theft that could never be legitimized. Peace treaties with Israel, the Brotherhood and the Gama'a agreed, were disguised plots to enable Israel, the West's surrogate, to dominate the Middle East. "Crusader colonization by peaceful means," an Islamist thinker had called it.[86]

In practice, however, the hostility of leftists and Islamists to peace with Israel, Egypt's greatest foreign policy achievement in many Western eyes, was indistinguishable. Even after Israel made peace with the PLO and Jordan, Egyptian leftists continued to denounce Israel and boycott Israelis. Parroting the militant Islamist line, the leftist opposition said that the new peace agreements failed to guarantee the restoration of Palestinian land, rights, and Arab dignity.

Egypt's intelligentsia, ever eager to please the pharaoh, might reluctantly have endorsed peace with Israel had Mubarak embraced the treaties he inherited.[87] But Mubarak himself, lacking his predecessor's supreme confidence, seemed ambivalent about Camp David. Wanting to win the intellectuals back and fearing the combined assaults of the secular Left and the religious Right, Mubarak distanced his government from, and often apologized for, Sadat's peace. The result was yet another schizophrenic policy: The government, on the one hand, expressed pride that Egypt was the first Arab nation to have accepted political (and military) reality and to have recovered all its occupied land by making peace with Israel; on the other, it tried to calm its political elite and limit its own vulnerability by encouraging criticism of Israel and the peace and also by raising innumerable bureaucratic obstacles to normalization. The "cold peace" turned ever icier in the 1980s in response to Likud government policy: Israel's raid on Iraq's nuclear reactor, its continuing war in Lebanon, its repression of the Palestinian Intifada, and its unwillingness to withdraw from Palestinian land or acknowledge Palestinian rights.

Moreover, the peace had not produced the wealth that Egypt's leaders had promised. The Egyptian semiofficial press was now filled with warnings that Israel would use its new peace treaties with the PLO and Jordan to seek "hegemony." Disenchanted with its begrudging peace with Cairo and a paltry $20 million in Israeli-Egyptian trade a year, a young Egyptian diplomat told me, Israel would now join forces with its new Arab partners to "penetrate and dominate" Egypt's economy and destroy its "pivotal role" in the region. Israel, a small island in an Arab sea, was racist, greedy, and nuclear armed, the press said again and again. Egypt, whose per capita income was less than one-tenth that of Israel, risked being bypassed by the more ambitious, pragmatic men of the Levant—left out, ignored, debased yet again.[88]

Mubarak, politically weaker in 1993 than he had been ten years earlier, was in no position to champion the new peace treaties. During my years in Egypt, the elite had opposed Camp David, but the average Egyptians — the fellaheen as well as impoverished civil servants, and shopkeepers whose sons had died in a succession of Egyptian wars for Palestine — had either favored peace or were apathetic. But the decade-long anti-Israeli campaign in the mass media and universities, coupled with the growing influence of militant Islamic ideas throughout Egyptian society, had made peace with Israel less popular with more Egyptians at all levels of society than ever before.[89]

So the Egyptian government continued to discourage fellow Arabs from embracing peace. Reflecting government policy, Egyptian bureaucrats found ways of blocking the Israeli investment and expertise that Egypt so desperately needed. Every Egyptian artistic and professional union — of journalists, teachers, writers, artists, doctors — extended its ban on contact with Israel. Even Fifi Abdou, Egypt's celebrated belly dancer, refused to perform in Israel. Those who defied political convention were expelled and ostracized. Eli Salem, for example, the novelist and playwright who visited Israel in 1994 and wrote a sympathetic account of his travels, was expelled from the writers' union and denounced in the press. Israel, as usual, was not invited to Egypt's annual international book fair or its glitzy film festival. The film selected to open the 1994 festival was so anti-Jewish that Egyptian television had declined to broadcast it for three years. Saad Eddin Wahba, the festival's director, boasted about having banned from Egyptian screens *Schindler's List*, Steven Spielberg's movie about the "alleged holocaust massacre," as the English-language *Egyptian Gazette* called it, because the film contained "scenes of violence and seduction" and showed "naked women." In a sublime example of Egyptian compromise, the festival featured a special tribute to Naguib Mahfouz, the writer nearly murdered by Islamic militants, and Sha'adia, the popular actress who announced that she would not attend the festival because she had taken the veil.

During my visits to Cairo in 1994 and 1995, Egyptian newspapers were filled once more with crude caricatures of Jews — knife-wielding sadists with giant hook noses, pockets bulging with American dollars and tongues dripping with blood — who laughed as they stabbed Egypt in the back. Journalists quoted parliamentarians who accused Israel of exporting poisoned farm products to Egypt. One government newspaper asserted in 1995 that Satan had written the Talmud, the ancient code of Jewish law.[90]

"Israel is not Egypt's or the Arabs' main problem," Mona Makram-Ebeid, a sociologist and parliamentarian appointed by Mubarak, told me over tea one summer day in 1994 in her grand apartment with its Art Deco lobby, ancient wood-paneled elevator, and view of the Nile. "But you would never know that from the Arab press." Few ostensible intellectuals, she said — except, paradoxically, the Islamists — relished tackling real questions, such as what accounted for the Arabs' deadening authoritarianism, their stagnant economies, their lack of economic, scientific, and cultural creativity. Arabs preferred to pander to Egypt's exalted self-image, which alternated with intense self-pity.[91]

Nasir Hamid Abu Zeid, a professor of Arabic at Cairo University, told me that the roots of Egypt's economic and social crisis were too daunting for most intellectuals to confront. "At the dawn of our independence," he said, "Egypt had a small but educated middle class, a thriving intellectual life with two hundred Arabic newspapers and journals, plus sixty-five in foreign languages, superb theater, film, and music. We had real political parties and a thriving Parliament and political life. Thousands of books a year—as opposed to the 395 books we published last year—were written and imported in Arabic, French, and English. We had all the ingredients for takeoff," he said. "What happened to us?"

Abu Zeid's question was all the more troublesome when one compared Egypt with certain Asian countries that were now the envy of the Arabs and most developing nations and had achieved their post–World War II growth under conditions even less promising than those of Egypt.

The government, of course, could hardly blame Egypt's plight on the military bureaucracy that still ruled the country. But the Islamists had a ready explanation for Egypt's woes: The Arabs had failed because they had adopted alien Western systems and deviated from Islam. While some secular Egyptians asserted that lack of democracy was to blame for their country's ills, Islamists, who saw democracy as just another flawed Western import, observed, accurately to some extent, that authoritarianism had not prevented Singapore from prospering, to say nothing of China and the other autocratic Asian states.

Egypt's men of ideas were *ta'aban* (worn out), to use an Egyptian term. Secularists like Naguib Mahfouz, Tawfik al-Hakim, Lewis Awad, Ahmed Baha el-Din, Youssef Idris, Magdi Wahba, and many others—the generation trained by the British under the monarchy, the last survivors of an Egyptian era of truly free and independent thought—were dying or dead. There was a palpable nostalgia now among some Egyptian intellectuals for the British-backed monarchy that had ruled between 1922 and the 1952 coup, a period that only in retrospect became known as Egypt's "enlightenment." The Nasserite intellectuals who succeeded such men had been largely discredited, their ideology dismissed as a failure. Those raised under Sadat and Mubarak were too busy arranging their careers to face such difficult questions, much less train the next generation of thinkers.[92]

Still others, ever attuned to the prevailing political wind, had become Islamists themselves. I thought of Adel Hussein. Now in his early sixties, Adel had espoused many credos—a family trait. In the early 1930s his older brother Ahmed had helped found the Young Egypt Party, a parody of Europe's far deadlier Fascist movement, and then embraced a series of militant pharaonic, pan-Arabist, and socialist doctrines, all "draped in Islamic colors."[93] But Adel rivaled his brother in the role described by one scholar as Egypt's "quintessential chameleon." Adel began as a Communist and was imprisoned twice for membership in the party. Then, he told me during a visit in 1994, he gradually embraced Nasserism after becoming convinced, as he put it rather oddly, that "the Nasserist approach was correct, even after Nasser's experiment collapsed." Nasserism was the "interim stage" of Adel's transition from Marx to Muhammad. The shift occurred, he said, when he concluded that Marx did not sufficiently emphasize the cultural side of political identity.

"I couldn't find any serious explanation in Marxist doctrine, for instance, of why we Arabs felt we were one nation," he said, recounting this "defining" moment in his political evolution. "No set of 'objective conditions' explained why we felt this way — no tangible economic relationships or meaningful political structures. But I realized that just because Marxist theory couldn't explain these feelings did not mean that they did not exist. It meant that Marxism was deficient." And so Adel Hussein became an Islamist.

The more he studied, the more he decided that Islam was the solution, that it represented an "authentic, original model for Egypt." Even better, he said, Islamic militants needed intellectuals: He could play a key role in interpreting and defining the Egyptian Islamic model. As a formerly secular intellectual, he could "persuade a new generation of Muslim Brethren that civil society, rather than theocracy, was the key to development," he said, suggesting a new *mission civilisatrice* for leftist born-again Muslims. It was not, after all, such a great intellectual leap from Nasser's secular authoritarianism to Islam's "straight path." The sacred symbols of both faiths were interchangeable. *Al-Shaab*, the Socialist Party paper then allied with the Brethren, under its chief editor Adel Hussein, had no trouble defending the Islamist antagonism toward Israel. He had even less trouble defending the Islamic regime in Sudan, which, he said, was not a vicious violator of human rights, as the United Nations and other human-rights monitors insisted, but "an important experiment in destroying tribal-based political affiliations of African politics" and a "true miracle in economic self-reliance." The Arabs would be strong again, he told me, only when they united. But this time, the Islamic unity of the *umma* would prevail where secular pan-Arabism had failed.

Adel had more difficulty justifying the Koranic role afforded to women, since his wife — an independent woman and professional who would probably have thrown him out if he ever tried to exercise his Islamic right to a second wife — scoffed at wearing the *hijab* and at many of his new sacred ideas. Instead, Adel argued that Westerners did not understand Islam's view of women. In Islam, he said, women were "equal to men in the eyes of God" but, of course, "different from men" and therefore entitled to different roles and duties. The martyred Sayyid Qutb himself could not have put it more succinctly, I thought.

While certain Koranic verses could not, of course, be canceled — such as that instructing a man to admonish and then "beat" a wife "on whose part ye fear disloyalty and ill conduct" — they could be "reinterpreted," which was why Islam needed "enlightened" ulema, or sheikhs, and real intellectuals. In any event, such restrictions would not apply to the society's elite, he said with a smile.

A very few of Egypt's intellectuals continued to resist such Islamic cant.

One was Nasir Hamid Abu Zeid, the Arabic-language professor at Cairo University whose life was now threatened because of a perfectly respectable academic paper he had written on early Islamic thought. The trouble began in 1993 when a professor on his review panel blocked his promotion to full professor on the grounds that his paper was religiously unacceptable, filled with "perverse ideas" that bordered on "atheism." After the university denied him a promotion, several mosque preachers denounced Abu Zeid, accusing him of teaching "heresy." Soon he began to receive anonymous death threats — ominous in light of Farag Foda's murder. Then a group of zealous Islamist lawyers sued in court to have Abu Zeid's marriage dissolved on the grounds that a Muslim woman could not be married to an "apostate," a Muslim who had forsaken Islam. The case was initially thrown out, but the Islamists had appealed.

I had gone to see Abu Zeid in the summer of 1994 at his small apartment in the 6th of October City, one of those dreadful "new cities," constellations of drab apartment buildings thrown up in the desert to accommodate Cairo's sprawling population. The trip took an hour by car each way, but Abu Zeid said he was lucky to have the flat: The price of decent housing even this far from Cairo had soared. Only professionals and people with foreign connections could afford them now. Fortunately, Abu Zeid had saved some money when he taught Arabic in the 1980s at Japan's Osaka University. Though the Japanese had wanted him to stay, he missed Egypt. So he came home, and in 1992, at age forty-nine, he married Ibtehal Younes, a diplomat's elegant daughter who taught French at Cairo University and spoke four other languages. Together they now shared his tiny, book-filled flat. On his refrigerator door, Abu Zeid had pinned a drawing of one of his heroes: Don Quixote.

Abu Zeid's work, he explained, was to examine how Muslims had understood their sacred texts historically. He had noted in a scholarly paper that the Prophet Muhammad's companions had written the Koran after it was transmitted to them orally and that there had been terrific fights under each of the first four Muslim caliphs over its interpretation — what to include and in which Arabic dialect it should be written. Such simple statements of fact, however, had infuriated some Islamists, who maintained that the Koran was not only God's very words but as "eternal" as God, effectively precluding debate or speculation about when it was written or how the book was used in Islam's early political struggles.

"It has become dangerous even to explore Muhammad's human side," he complained to me, "despite the fact that the Prophet was, after all, a man, a passionate man who loved, hated, and made mistakes." But even to say this is to risk being accused of apostasy, he added. "I thought I was living in a civil society, in a secular country, with a civil code of law. To be sued in a court of law as an apostate has been traumatic for me and my wife. We are Muslims, good Muslims. But we no longer have objective social norms of legal and illegal, right and wrong, in Egypt. They have been replaced by religious norms — of *haram* (forbidden) and *halal* (permissible)."

In such a climate it was futile to argue that according to classical Islamic doctrine, no one had the right to challenge another Muslim's belief, that practices such as *takfir* (being declared an apostate) were akin to living in the Dark Ages, when people were judged by the church, he said. Under Islam, there was no coercion in religion theoretically. But the new intimidation in Egypt had nothing to do with religion; it was political.

Throughout its thirteen-hundred-year history Islam had always been politically manipulated. Rulers had always tried to hide their failure behind Islam — a "hallowed tradition in Arab society," he said. But now Egyptian officials professed to be "shocked" by the opposition's use of Islam — their very own cover — to delegitimize and challenge them. "When you call yourself the 'believing president,'" he said, referring to Sadat, "when you begin official speeches, as this regime does, with *Bismillah* (in the name of God), when you flood the papers and airwaves with the government's religious discourse, al-Azhar's religious discourse, and television's religious discourse, why are you surprised by the Muslim Brotherhood's success or the formation of a group like the Gama'a?"

The biggest problem, he said, was the government's growing reliance on al-Azhar for religious sanction in its informal competition with the militant Islamists to speak in the name of Islam. That strategy left the government vulnerable, he argued, because the opposition could always argue, no matter how Egypt diluted its secular framework, that the country was failing because it was not sufficiently Islamic. "If your terms of reference are Islamic rather than civil and secular, if your playing field is Islam, then the radicals will win every time," Abu Zeid warned. As long as the government could not, or would not, disenfranchise its Copts, alienate its Western donors by adopting Islamic law, or sharia, and break with Israel, the radicals would always be purer, more "Islamic," than the regime. "Just look at the recent *fatwas* from al-Azhar — supposedly the government's seat of Islamic wisdom. They are indistinguishable from those of the militants. Just look at those decrees and tell me which way the wind is blowing!"

MUHAMMAD SAYYID TANTAWI, Egypt's mufti, its state-appointed chief sheikh, and the senior religious experts at al-Azhar were silent in June 1995 when a civil appellate court ruled that Nasir Hamid Abu Zeid, based on his writings, was, in fact, an apostate — an unprecedented verdict in Egypt that annulled his marriage and put his life at risk. Because "believers" were now duty bound to kill him for having abandoned his faith, the couple had been forced into hiding. When I spoke to them by phone, Abu Zeid and Ibtehal vowed to continue living as man and wife. "I won't leave him," she insisted. "I will die with him if I must."

In the fall of 1995, the couple fled Egypt to Europe. Abu Zeid and Ibtehal were heartbroken over the ruling, and so was I. Egypt's judicial system was no longer a barrier to religious extremism. An Egypt without an independent judiciary and vibrant intellectuals like Abu Zeid was a land without an encouraging future.

More likely, Egypt's future was to be found on the sprawling campus of al-Azhar, where many students agreed that Abu Zeid should die for having insulted Islam. Founded in 972 by the Fatimid dynasty as a mosque to propagate its faith, al-Azhar had long ago outgrown its headquarters in the old Islamic part of Cairo. Its thousands of sheikhs and professors, many in their traditional gray robes and white turbans with red centers, its 125,000 students, and more than a dozen faculties occupied buildings throughout the modern city.

Al-Azhar's growth had always been dependent on the state. So its emergence in the past decade as the government's most problematic center of criticism was difficult to understand. My friend Malika Zeghal, a young French scholar then at Princeton who had just finished a fine book on al-Azhar, enlightened me.

Ever since its creation, but especially since the reign of Mohammed Ali in the nineteenth century, she explained, the ulema of al-Azhar had uneasily served the state. Al-Azhar and the ruler were mutually dependent: Al-Azhar granted the ruler religious legitimacy, and he, in turn, made the ulema his advisers, religious counselors, and partners in his own prosperity and the state's wealth. Determined to modernize Egypt by centralizing power in his own hands, Mohammed Ali had used internal al-Azhar feuds to break the ulema's personal power and seize much of their property. He built modern schools and ignored their advice on matters of state. If they opposed him, he went around them. When, for example, the ulema refused to issue a *fatwa* sanctioning dissection of human bodies, Mohammed Ali ordered medical students to conduct them in secret.[94] As long as the ulema did not interfere with his modernization schemes, he left them alone. But throughout the nineteenth century the grand sheikhs could not forgive the insult of being shunted aside. They indignantly issued *fatwas* condemning all forms of modernization — wearing hats and European clothes, studying arithmetic, imposing quarantine against plagues. Yet al-Azhar, the state-appointed guardian of Muslim tradition, also continued to preach that revolt against the state was the greatest of sins since it produced *fitna* (division) within the Muslim community. Even a murderous, incompetent, or corrupt ruler was preferable to no ruler at all, that is, to anarchy or the civil war that Islam had experienced in its first century. Rulers, however flawed, had to be obeyed, provided they were Muslim.

But destabilizing change, too, had to be resisted, and al-Azhar developed obstructionism to a fine art. Though foreign languages, for example, were included in its curriculum in 1901 and though King Farouk ordered again that they be taught in 1936, such instruction was just beginning in 1972.[95] The ulema resisted even their own enlightened reformers — Muhammad Abdu, who had taught the father of Muslim Brotherhood founder Hassan al-Banna, and Rashid Rida, who had impressed Banna himself.

Following an established pattern, Nasser initially courted the neglected al-Azhar ulema: The Free Officers needed them in their struggle against the rival Muslim Brotherhood. But once the Brotherhood was broken, Nasser nationalized al-Azhar and in 1961 made the grand sheikhs and ulema paid civil servants. The sharia courts were closed, and their judicial powers were integrated into the national system. While al-Azhar's ulema had sought only to advise and not to rule, this was too much. So the ulema resisted in their usual way, and some went further. A blind young sheikh named Omar Abdel Rahman, an unimpressive al-Azhar graduate, issued a *fatwa* condemning Nasser as a heretic and forbidding prayer at government mosques.

But even the secular socialist Nasser needed religious legitimation among his conservative and devout people, so he wound up justifying his devastating land confiscations and economic schemes on Islamic grounds: Socialism was Islamically "just." Continuing Mohammed Ali's campaign, Nasser tried to modernize the ulema by adding "modern" faculties — medicine, agriculture, and engineering — to al-Azhar's religious departments. "He thought that forcing al-Azhar to mix modern knowledge with religious knowledge would integrate Islam into the civil society," Malika Zeghal told me. "But it had the opposite effect." Combining modern knowledge with religious education helped produce the Islamism that plagued Egypt today.

Nasser also inadvertently emboldened and strengthened the ulema, she argued in her book, by letting them open the primary and secondary schools that now educated about a million students — between 7 and 10 percent of Egyptian children.[96]

Sadat compounded al-Azhar's influence in his war against Communist and other leftist foes by increasing its budget and also permitted the al-Azhar sheikhs to raise extra funds abroad. While precise figures are hard to come by, Malika Zeghal told me that the grand sheikh of al-Azhar alone had collected $3 million — including a $1 million contribution from Kuwait and $900,000 from Saudi Arabia — in a single written appeal to Arab leaders in 1976. Almost two decades of such Saudi funding had made the state's largest Islamic institution even more conservative. Many ulema had worked in Saudi Arabia, among them Mufti Tantawi, Egypt's chief sheikh, who had spent four years at the Islamic University of Medina.[97] Still others became proponents of Saudi, or "Wahhabi," Islam, a more austere, intolerant faith than Egypt's Sufi-influenced, or mystically oriented, religion, though that brand of Islam, too, was becoming increasingly rigid and insistent on the need to adopt sharia as the law of the land. While al-Azhar attracted less talented students and offered education and facilities that were distinctly second-rate, the al-Azhar system nonetheless enabled poor students to become doctors and professionals, to climb the ladder of social mobility in Egypt's class-ridden society. Many of these graduates were now Muslim Brotherhood stalwarts.

Nor was al-Azhar monolithic. Among its ranks were what Zeghal called "peripheral sheikhs," men deeply sympathetic to the militants' vision and program, if not their tactics, whose *fatwas* were virtually indistinguishable from those issued by the religious guides of the Gama'a and al-Jihad.

Usually, the ruler got the *fatwa* he wanted on key policy issues. Under

Sadat, for example, the sheikh of al-Azhar ruled that interest-bearing treasury bonds were consistent with divine law and that Sadat's trip to Jerusalem and subsequent peace treaty with Israel were in keeping with the faith. Another Azhari had even ruled that beer was *halal* because it did not technically fall under the ban on alcohol — which is why he was called Sheikh Stella, in honor of Egypt's leading beer.[98] While Mubarak granted al-Azhar great independence, he showed little forbearance on critical issues of state, such as the Gulf war. The ulema ruled, as they did in neighboring Saudi Arabia, that Islam permitted foreign troops on sacred Muslim soil in light of Iraq's aggression. But the relative freedom under Mubarak also increased debate, and eventually greater boldness, among the sheikhs, a trend that clearly displeased the president but about which he dared do little. "It is too late now to undo the militancy that took root under Nasser and Sadat," Malika told me.

Since 1989, al-Azhar's leading ulema had become ever bolder in challenging government policy. Gad al-Haqq Ali Gad al-Haq, the grand sheikh of al-Azhar, the seventy-seven-year-old scholar appointed by Mubarak in 1982, defended female circumcision — officially discouraged but still widely practiced in Egypt — saying that the Prophet had recommended it for both men and women. Girls whose genitals were not cut when they were young had a "sharp temperament and bad habits," he insisted in a recent *fatwa*, and would more easily be led into "immorality and corruption." Gad al-Haq also opposed the mufti, the state's chief sheikh, by arguing that bank interest was non-Islamic, and demanded changes in a UN draft document on population just weeks before it was taken up at a Cairo conference, declaring that it condoned extra-marital sex and unrestricted access to abortion.[99] Nor was the presidential palace pleased by his *fatwa* that the education minister could not dissuade girls from wearing the *hijab* to school by requiring parental permission or by his decision to grant the exalted title of *shahid* (martyr) to an Egyptian member of the Gama'a who had joined the Palestinian militants, Hamas, in a deadly attack in Jerusalem that left sixteen Israelis wounded and ten dead in 1994. When Israeli president Ezer Weizman made a state visit to Cairo later that year, Sheikh Gad al-Haq refused to receive him.

Other al-Azhar figures consistently tried to undermine Arab peace with Israel and other government policies. For example, Sheikh Ghazali, the defender of Farag Foda's murderers, strongly supported the Palestinian Intifada, sending a message through an Israeli Arab newspaper urging Palestinians to turn Palestine into a "land of jihad where the flame would burn continually."[100] In December 1994, when the Saudi mufti blessed the Arabs' peace with Israel (having denounced Sadat's historic trip to Jerusalem in 1977), Egyptian sheikh Youssef al-Qardawi, another al-Azhar-influenced thinker, attacked him with such fervor that the octogenarian Saudi chief scholar softened his endorsement. Sheikh Abdel Kafi, an agronomist who did graduate work at al-Azhar and who prided himself both on his al-Azhar connection and his talent for persuading Egyptian actresses to take the veil, openly advised his followers not to shake hands with Copts, attend their weddings and festivals, or wish them a Merry Christmas.

Malika Zeghal argued that President Mubarak himself was ultimately responsible for al-Azhar's increasing demands that Egyptian society be Islamicized. Because the state had sought the scholars' support to legitimize its crackdown on Islamic extremists and strengthen the government's Muslim credentials at the militants' expense, Mubarak, in exchange, allowed the sheikhs to regain a central position in Egyptian political life, thus ending their effective subordination to the state. In return for granting the government religious cover, the emboldened sheikhs felt free to demand a more Islamic society. So in defiance of Egyptian law they received informal permission to ban writing they considered inimical to Islamic values: essays by Farag Foda, movies by legendary Egyptian filmmakers, Nobel Prize–winning novels by Naguib Mahfouz, and even the Arab classic *A Thousand and One Nights.*[101]

Many secular intellectuals now saw the incendiary *fatwas* and al-Azhar's growing influence as evidence of a dangerous convergence between Egypt's radical and "establishment" Islamic trends. "The Islamic radicals have made common cause with the Muslim Brotherhood and now with al-Azhar, the official Islamic establishment. How can men of religion, in good faith, aid and abet such violence?" Tahseen Bashir asked. "And how can the government let them do so?"

The truth was: Mubarak felt he had little choice. He could not endanger this crucial bastion of legitimacy. With scant economic progress and political liberalization too risky, who but the al-Azhar sheikhs would bless his right to rule?

The longer he was in office and the more his regime failed, the more Mubarak relied not only on the sheikhs but also on the traditional sources of legitimacy in Egypt—the army and the fact that as *rais* (the president, or, literally, the head), he was not to be challenged.[102]

AT THE END of a trip to Cairo in 1995, I decided to cross the Nile on a felucca, one of the graceful sailboats of ancient design. As I sailed along to dinner with a senior Egyptian official, I thought about the strengths that kept Egypt so vibrant. An Egyptian intellectual once observed that Egypt's feet may be stuck in a swamp, but her brow touched heaven. Amidst Egypt's squalor were thriving pockets of intellectual brilliance that were key to its salvation, as well as a reflection of the genius of the land that had produced such towering intellectuals as Taha Hussein, Naguib Mahfouz, and so many others. A sturdy tradition of letters, of daring creativity, and of love of country remained evident in the fiction of such impressive young novelists as Yusuf al-Qaid and Son'allah Ibrahim, as well as in the trenchant, feisty journalism of magazines like *Rose el Youssef*, the essays of political economist Galal Amin, and the courageous prose of Rifaat Said, whose attacks on Islamic militancy grew ever more ferocious after Farag Foda's murder and who proudly defended Egypt's tradition of secularism and modernity. Among such intellectuals, there was little sense that Egypt's culture was dying.

Modern monuments like the Aswan Dam and the steady progress of places like Watermelon Village proved that Egyptians were capable of wondrous achievements. Many a vanquished foe had underestimated Egyptian determination. The temperament of its people, the civility of its society, and the legacy of its former splendor let me hope that Egypt would not only endure, but overcome the militancy and degradation that were the product of disappointments of the recent past.

But as I sailed along the Nile, I also thought about the great changes that had occurred in Egypt just in my lifetime. Eternal Egypt — the Egypt that Flaubert described only a century ago — was gone. The conditions that had made Egypt and Egyptians what they had always been had clearly changed. So it was senseless to project the future simply by extrapolating from the past. For most of Egypt's seven thousand years of existence, its population had lived in small villages and towns along the Nile. For the first time in its history, more than 50 percent of its people now lived in cities, more than 20 percent of them in greater Cairo alone. Also for the first time, most Egyptians no longer depended on the Nile and its agriculture. While Egypt's economy was once centered on food and textiles, modern Egypt was built on oil and gas revenues, workers' remittances from abroad, tourism, and Suez Canal tolls. The country now produces only 22 percent of its food, making it one of the world's most food-dependent countries.[103] Egyptians who once clung to the land, reluctant to move, were now forced to work abroad, exposed to ideas and cultures that differed sharply from their own. The coffeehouses that for five hundred years had dominated Egypt's social and political life were closing. Few had time to sit and listen to Um Kalthoum, play dominoes, or debate politics. The coffeehouses were becoming a relic, like my lovely felucca crossing the Nile. Egypt was in the midst of historic change; its ancient balances, its timeless traditions were under siege.

The objective conditions that had shaped Egyptian political character, having changed forever, could no longer exclude the possibility of a revolution simply because Egypt had never experienced one. But few Egyptians or non-Egyptian analysts thought revolution likely. Demographic and economic changes came swiftly, but character evolved slowly. It was hard to imagine an Islamic revolution in a country whose most popular soap opera was *The Bold and the Beautiful*, a cheap American series that made *Dallas* seem Sophoclean.

In the Sudan, however, militant Islamists had come to power not through the ballot box or revolution but by military coup. Could my Egyptian friends be missing the point? Could Egypt's next military ruler embrace Islam even more than Mubarak had to shore up his legitimacy? What would be so foreign to Egypt about an "Islamic pharaoh," a militant Muslim Mamluk? In this way, militant Islam could come to power without a revolution or even a coup.

For now Egypt had won its war against militant Islamic terrorism, but

Islamization of its culture was continuing. And Cairo was still not tranquil. I realized that with sinking finality as my felucca deposited me ashore in time for my dinner at the Paradise, an open-air patio at the Sheraton Gezira Hotel. My companion was a key adviser on whom both Sadat and Mubarak depended. It was a splendid night in late September. A crescent moon and scattered stars decorated the velvet sky. The air was heavy with jasmine. A damp breeze came in from the Nile as feluccas, lit only by gas lamps, glided silently by. An oud player on the patio plucked the lyrical quarter notes of an old Egyptian ballad. The official was discussing Arab life and Egyptian society — not always the same. Suddenly sharp voices shattered the calm. A customer at a table near us, an apparently middle-class man dressed in a blazer and tie, was yelling at the waiter. He and his wife were being overcharged for their beer, he complained. The waiter and the restaurant were thieves. Normally, the waiter would have demurred quietly to his "better" and called the manager to end the quarrel. Instead, the waiter screamed back. The prices were printed clearly on the menu. Could the customer not read! How dare he accuse him of stealing! He would pay his bill or answer to the police. In ordinary times, such angry outbursts were unheard of in "civilized" settings like the Paradise. But these were not normal times. I recalled nostalgically the donkey that had died on Kasr el Nil more than a decade ago — and in another Egypt.

Saudi Arabia

Money is the Great Lubricant.

SAUDI SAYING

Money isn't everything.

POPULAR SAYING

FARIDA WAS UPSET. We were having breakfast at a coffee shop on Madison Avenue in the fall of 1994. She had asked me to meet her there. She was subdued and smoked one cigarette after another. She barely touched her toast. I asked what was wrong.

"It's my cousin Hisham," she finally told me. "The Saudis arrested him eight months ago and won't let him go. My family has tried everything. My aunt is sick with worry; my uncle is a wreck. And I feel so goddamn helpless sitting here."

I had met Farida ten years earlier in Saudi Arabia. She was a spirited young college graduate then from a middle-class family who was determined to teach psychology, of all things. Since Saudi Arabia was so confining, this meant coming to the United States for graduate school, where she had met and married an American, a fellow psychologist from an Arab-American family. Like most of her family-oriented countrymen, she was terribly homesick and missed the daily meals and visits with her many relatives. But for her to have stayed in Saudi Arabia would have been intellectual suicide. We had become friends when she was trying to decide whether to stay or leave. She had not regretted her choice — until now.

"I know Hisham is a fool," she said bitterly. "He was a terrible student. He couldn't even get into KSU," she said, referring to one of the kingdom's better universities and a traditional choice of Saudi Arabia's more liberal, Western-oriented "technocrats." "So he went to Muhammad bin Saud Islamic University and studied the Koran all day. He calls himself a 'history' teacher, but he thinks history began with the Prophet Muhammad. God knows what he teaches his students! He was always a religious nut. In college, he went around Riyadh in a short, unpressed *thobe* and sandals and an unkempt beard, driving us all crazy. He wasn't really political, but his friends at the Islamic university were. He wanted them to like him. So he lent them his tape deck to help them record one of those cassettes that insulted the royal family — the ones that told about their corruption and 'un-Islamic' ways. They came for him at 2:00 A.M. Yanked him out of bed and hauled him off. They're holding him at al-Hayir, a prison twenty kilometers south of Riyadh. They won't let us visit him. Some prisoners have bathrooms and even televisions, but not him. He confessed, of course. But he was tortured. I can't tell you the things they did," she told me.

She didn't have to. In 1983 I had written an article about the torture of American citizens in Saudi jails that had embarrassed the normally solicitous American embassy into launching a formal diplomatic protest but had also gotten me banned from Arabia for several years.

Even so, the Saudis had never been nearly as ruthless as their "progressive" Arab neighbors. Iraq, Syria, and Egypt held thousands, not hundreds, of political prisoners. If Hisham had been arrested in Iraq or in the authoritarian Islamic Republic of Iran, he probably would have been tortured to death by now. And if he had joined Islamic radicals in Algeria, not only would he probably have been murdered by the government; he would have taken a dozen innocent lives himself. Yet here was Farida, her toast still untouched, lamenting her foolish cousin. For all its relative forbearance, Saudi Arabia was getting tough. The police were once more torturing Saudi dissidents, even men from "good" families, like Hisham.

The U.S. State Department annual report on human rights, uncommonly frank about the kingdom's human-rights record, given the strategic importance to Washington of the world's largest oil producer, concluded that the Saudi government engaged in torture, which included, among other methods, depriving prisoners of sleep, and *fallaqa*, beating the soles of the feet, which hurts terribly but leaves few bruises.[1] In 1994, Human Rights Watch, the private, New York–based monitoring group, concluded that respect for human rights in the kingdom had reached "a new low." "Saudi citizens today," an earlier report said, "have fewer civil and political rights than they had sixty years ago."

"It's all so horrible," Farida said bitterly. "We're impotent and humiliated. Prince Nayef, the minister of interior, has brushed my family off. If my uncle pushes too hard or threatens to protest publicly, they might take his passport away, which would ruin his business and all of us. So we're stuck. We hate them for it. I know the government has a serious problem with radical Islamists.

But Hisham is no threat to them. King Fahd once silenced enemies by buying them off, not torturing them. This is not the Saudi way."

I had never seen Farida in such a state. This was not my fierce, fearless friend. Nor, for that matter, was this the Saudi Arabia I had come to know and in some ways admire during the Gulf war in 1991. In 1990, the Saudi ruling family had permitted some 600,000 foreign soldiers, most of them American, to be based in the kingdom, ostensibly to liberate Kuwait from its occupation by Saddam Hussein but actually to protect Saudi Arabia from possible Iraqi aggression. I had spent more than two months in the kingdom before, during, and after the hundred-hour ground war in which Saddam's forces were humiliated.

My Saudi friends, most of them Western educated, thought that the war would make their country more open and progressive at home and bolder abroad. Saudis who had supported Saddam in his war against Iran a decade earlier could no longer deny the failure of their traditional policy of buying off whatever country, movement, group, or individual threatened the kingdom. Never again, said a Saudi friend, a brilliant young diplomat, would Riyadh finance regimes that had betrayed it. Never again would it fund so-called Islamic groups that had sided with the "Arab street," the Arab John Doe whose heart was with Saddam. "Those who stood with us will be rewarded," he told me resolutely as we sipped cappuccino in a lounge of the Hyatt-Regency, the marble-walled hotel where most Riyadh-based journalists lived during the war. "Those who betrayed us will finally be cut off — forever."

Saudi Arabia was now strong and "confident." The ruling family's decision to seek American protection had been vindicated. "*Al Shayukh Abkhas*," as the Saudis said — the royal family knows best, a saying that my Saudi friends had once used sarcastically in reference to the House of Saud's monopoly of power. Saudi Arabia's Islamic extremists and radical Arab nationalists who had argued that the war was an American "plot" to grab the kingdom's oil were proved wrong. The Americans had fought, won, and left. Thanks to the war, Saudi Arabia — the "magic kingdom," as we half-jokingly called it — was becoming a "normal" country, or so we all hoped.

The Gulf war undoubtedly changed Saudi Arabia, but not as my friends had predicted. While the confrontation with Saddam Hussein had stiffened Saudi foreign policy, it had also made the ruling House of Saud less legitimate in the eyes of some of its citizens. The reasons were largely economic; its consequences, political. The cost of the war had led first to a boom but later to a recession and soaring national debt. Years of massive spending on national infrastructure and extravagant industrial projects as well as widespread corruption had finally caught up with the Saudis, whose population had risen since the 1970s from an estimated 6 million to 12 million.[2] After a decade of stable oil prices and a 100 percent increase in population, Saudi per capita income had dropped to half what it was in the 1970s. The per capita income of Israel — with half the population and no oil — was now higher than Saudi Arabia's. Unable to continue borrowing, the government had reluctantly cut the budget and reduced the generous subsidies it gave all Saudis, "entitlements" that its citizens now took for granted.

Since the oil billions began flowing into the Saudi treasury in the mid-1970s, Saudis had received free medical care; subsidized mortgages, energy, and food; and inflated salaries for make-work jobs. Not only were college tuition and housing free, students were paid $270 a month in pocket money for attending. In exchange, Saudis were happy to leave the stewardship of their country—and monopolistic control of the kingdom's vast oil resources as well—to the House of Saud, or in Arabic, the Al Saud.[3] But now the royal family was unilaterally rewriting this unwritten social contract, which Saudi citizens deeply resented. Moreover, Saudis were being asked to make financial sacrifices without any significant increase in political participation. Some thought the government might even try to impose a sales or national income tax! At the same time, the royal family did not seem to be making much of a sacrifice. Abdulaziz bin Fahd, age twenty-five, the king's favorite son and a devoted Nintendo player— Azouz, as he was unaffectionately known—had recently completed a $300 million palace in Riyadh and was lobbying his father for yet another in Jidda, the old Red Sea port. The spoiled young prince, who in 1995 was named his father's "adviser," was also said to have gotten almost a billion-dollar commission on the kingdom's $4.5 billion contract with America's AT&T to modernize the country's telephone system.

Despite, or perhaps because of, the kingdom's financial squeeze, many princes were greedier than ever. Increasingly, the estimated four thousand male members of the ruling family, no longer content with a slice of the country's oil-generated income, were demanding a share in all private Saudi ventures. Princes and their retainers and front men were still taking 30 percent commissions—*sai*, in Arabic, meaning "effort"—disguised as "subcontracts" on major public projects. As a result, disdain for the ruling Sauds was growing, particularly within the middle class, and the country's traditional faith in its rulers was eroding.

After the Gulf war, the ruling family began a cautious crackdown on dissent from within the Islamic Right, the only group it felt threatened by. The police confiscated thousands of cassettes of sermons in which Saudi populist preachers denounced this most observant of Islamic countries as un-Islamic and its rulers as "traitors" to Islam.[4] The ruling Al Saud, the militant preachers said, was deviating from Islam's "straight path" by sanctioning "un-Islamic" laws, institutions, and practices and by embezzling and wasting the country's oil wealth rather than spending it on "sacred causes, such as the fight against Zionism and supporting the Islamic cause in Palestine."

The political mother of "fundamentalism," the land in which both the Prophet Muhammad and Islam were born, the state created by the Middle East's first modern militant Islamic movement—Wahhabiism—was now confronting a home-grown Islamic challenge to its legitimacy. The Al Saud, the family that had conquered and unified this vast kingdom in the name of Islam not once but three times in less than three hundred years, was now accused of being insufficiently "Islamic." Few of us who had witnessed the Gulf war in Saudi Arabia imagined that the victory would have such an outcome. But Saudi Arabia had always been a puzzle.

THE FOUNDER of the religion that is sacred to almost one-fifth of the world's people was not a Bedouin tribesman from the desert but a noble merchant from Mecca. Islam, in fact, was a religion of the city, of the *hadar*, the sedentary farmers, merchants, and traders — who were its first and most enduring followers — people who loathed and feared the nomadic Bedouin.[5] In the seventh century, Mecca was western Arabia's most prosperous town and a pagan sanctuary, but it was still backward and inconsequential compared to the cities of Byzantium and Sassanid Persia, the two empires that dominated and fought over the region's lucrative trade routes. In less than fifty years Muhammad would end Mecca's and Arabia's marginality.

Little is known about Muhammad's early years despite the many legends and hagiographies that have provided countless tales, most of questionable origin. After all, what is widely regarded as the most authoritative biography, that of the eighth-century believer Ibn Ishaq, was not written until 125 years after Muhammad's death.[6] Muslim historians and jurists admitted that many of the stories circulated about Muhammad — the so-called *hadith*, literally the "narratives" or the Prophet's recorded deeds and sayings — were fabricated to support a particular political faction or opinion. Less than two hundred years after Muhammad's death, one celebrated Muslim scholar is said to have discounted 596,725 *hadith* then in circulation.[7]

But whether or not one accepted Muhammad's divine mission — and I as a skeptic of all prophets did not — the man portrayed in Arabic sources was surely a remarkable figure and a political genius, or what historian Maxime Rodinson called a combination of "Jesus Christ and Charlemagne."[8] It was impossible to understand Saudi Arabia, contemporary Arabs, or modern Islamic militancy without knowing something about this extraordinary man. For the principles by which he lived and the state that he created are the models for today's Islamic radicals. Despite the many uncertainties about the Prophet's life and although his words and deeds can be interpreted in many ways, the militants, like all political men, select those parts of his life and example that support their own views on how Muslims should live and think.

Muhammad Ibn Abdullah was born sometime around the year 570 C.E. to a noble but not very prosperous branch of the Banu (sons of) Hashim clan of the Quraysh tribe, Mecca's leading traders. Orphaned in childhood and left virtually destitute, he was raised by his uncle, Abu Talib, who taught him the caravan trade. When he was still in his twenties, he became the commercial agent of a rich widow fifteen years his senior — a strong member of his own tribe — Khadija bint Khuwaylid. When he was twenty-five, she asked him to marry her. He agreed, and she bore him four daughters but no surviving sons, a source of shame in all Semitic societies. But as long as he was with this wealthy, determined woman, Muhammad took no other wives.

Muhammad did not begin receiving prophetic revelations until he was forty. At first these visions distressed him almost to the point of suicide. But his wife, Khadija—his first convert and closest companion—persuaded him that his supernatural visitor was an angel and not a delusion or the devil.[9]

While Christians have endowed their leader with divine status as mankind's Redeemer, a notion that might have dismayed the historical Jesus, Muhammad has remained to his followers God's Messenger, a prophet—albeit the last and most nearly perfect of them—but like Moses, entirely human.

Muslims believe that the angel Gabriel's first words to Muhammad, in Arabic, were: "Recite! You are the Messenger of God." The words he was given became the Qur'an, or as it is often written, Koran, literally "recitation." Muslims believe that what Allah told his messenger to repeat, indeed, every word in the Koran, was spoken by God through his inspired Prophet. Said to have been recorded during his lifetime on leather scraps, flat camel bones, and any other handy material, the verses constitute the first and some say the finest examples of Arabic rhymed prose, as opposed to the poetry that was Arabia's traditional art form. To believers, these words are divine and eternal, not to be challenged or even questioned.[10]

The religion Allah revealed to Muhammad acknowledged the legitimacy of his faith's monotheistic predecessors, the Jews and Christians—the so-called Peoples of the Book—as well as their prophets. His new religion's theological respect for the adherents of the two great monotheist faiths was politically shrewd, since seventh-century Arabia was populated by both Jewish and Christian tribes (at least two pre-Islamic Arab kings were Jews) as well as by Arabian monotheists called *hanifs*. Muhammad sought converts and allies among all of them.

Muhammad's religion, Islam—or "submission to God,"[11] a Muslim being one who has so submitted—was doctrinally uncomplicated. According to the Koran as elaborated by tradition and commentaries, those who wished to avoid eternal damnation and enjoy paradise after death must believe in and pray to the One God and share their wealth with the poor. Practically, what this meant was embodied in five key duties, or pillars, of the faith: the *shahada*, or professing that "there is but One God, Muhammad is his Messenger"; the *salat*, or praying five times a day; fasting from dawn to sunset for one month of the year—Ramadan; paying alms, or taxes, *zakat*, as the donation for charity was called; and, if a believer is able to do so, making at least one pilgrimage to Mecca. In addition, there was an unofficial pillar—the duty of holy war, or jihad. Dying to spread the faith canceled out all sins and led straight to paradise.

The vast majority of Meccans initially scoffed at the self-acclaimed Prophet, a tall, supposedly striking man with a gap between his two front teeth. They tolerated him only as long as he did not interfere with their worship of Mecca's many gods—of which Allah was the major deity—and more to the point, as long as he enjoyed the tribal protection of Abu Talib, his powerful and well-respected uncle. Initially, the community and Muhammad tried to compromise their theological differences. Meccans, after all, greatly prospered from pilgrimages to the Kaba, a cubic building the size of a small house in whose exterior wall a black stone — probably a meteorite — is embedded; both the Kaba and the stone are revered. When Meccans asked Muhammad whether their gods could be worshiped along with Allah, his One God, the Messenger received a timely ecumenical revelation that sanctioned recognition of Mecca's traditional gods — the "exalted birds," as Muhammad called them.[12] The answer must have delighted and relieved his fellow Meccans, who were also probably eager to avoid a communal split. But the archangel soon informed Muhammad that the verse he had received came not from God but from the devil. Horrified, Muhammad repudiated the revelation, calling it the "Satanic verses," the words used some thirteen centuries later by Salman Rushdie as the title of his controversial novel. Ultimately, Muhammad must have decided, whether through divine revelation or political acumen, that permitting Meccans to continue worshiping their more than three hundred gods would infringe on the "oneness" of his own true God and dilute his authority as Allah's Messenger.

As a result, Meccans increased their harassment of the more vulnerable members of Muhammad's new faith and mocked Muhammad himself by throwing sand, garbage, and even the wombs of sheep at him. An ancestral tribesman of a Saudi professor I know is said to have stolen the Prophet's sandals while he prayed. After Abu Talib's death in 619 — and his wife, Khadija's, that same year — a despondent Muhammad decided that his followers, who probably numbered less than a hundred, should abandon Mecca. The warring tribes of the town now called Medina, 280 miles north of Mecca, accepted this honest and charming dissident from the rival Qurayshis of Mecca, their arrogant neighbor, and made him the arbiter of their interminable local quarrels.

Muslims date their calendar from this acknowledgment of failure — the *hijra*, or emigration from Mecca to Medina in 622 C.E., an echo perhaps of Moses' flight into the desert.[13] But the *hijra* also marks the beginning of Muhammad's success as "political leader, spiritual guide, supreme lawmaker, and commander-in-chief."[14]

Militants tend to emphasize the Prophet's life in Medina, for it was there that Muhammad's community took root. And it was also in Medina that tensions mounted with the Jews, another fact of great importance to anti-Israeli Islamists. Muhammad's first agreement governing relations within his *umma* (community), the city's various tribes, included Medina's numerous Jews. This accord, a unilateral proclamation by Muhammad rather than a bilateral agreement, provided that as long as Jews and even pagans fought alongside Muslims against the Quraysh of Mecca or any other external enemy, refrained from "wronging" Muslims or aiding their foes, and helped finance the *umma*'s self-defense, there would be "sincere friendship, exchange of good counsel, fair conduct, and no treachery between them," and, of course, freedom of religion.[15]

Muhammad had expected to find natural allies in the Jews, this ancient People of the Book. Initially he made several concessions to them, such as instructing his followers to pray as they did toward Jerusalem and adopting some Jewish fast days. But the Jews disappointed him. They mocked what they regarded as his misappropriation of their own sacred texts.

Nevertheless, Muhammad's new faith grew in numbers and prestige. After Muhammad gained confidence, recruits, and wealth through raids on Meccan caravans, the Messenger decided to take on his rivals in Medina, particularly the Jews. To distinguish his followers from the Israelites, he banned Muslims from praying toward Jerusalem, ordering them instead to pray toward Mecca's Kaba. Then he expelled the Jewish tribe of Banu Nadir, one of whose members, tradition says, tried to assassinate Muhammad. This was followed by the flight of another Jewish tribe to the great oasis of Khaibar, north of Medina, which Muhammad would also later conquer.

In 627, after Medina, under Muhammad's leadership, survived a protracted siege by some ten thousand well-armed Meccans, Muhammad decided to eliminate his last potential internal enemy, the Banu Qurayza, Medina's last Jewish tribe. Muhammad accused them of having supported Mecca during the siege, a charge they ardently denied.[16] Muhammad refused to let the Banu Qurayza emigrate, unlike the other Jewish tribes. Disloyalty had to be punished. To decide their fate, Muhammad appointed a man who was dying of wounds received during the siege. The bitter arbiter condemned all adult Jewish males to death, a verdict that Muhammad was said to have praised as "the very sentence of Allah above the seven skies."[17] At least six hundred Jewish men, and even a woman, were beheaded in Medina the next day, their wives and children made slaves, and their property seized. However troubling its moral implications, the massacre was a political success. Never in Muhammad's lifetime[18] — and indeed, not until the twentieth century — would a Jewish tribe rise against the Arabs. To the militants, this saga of Jewish betrayal has a modern moral: Jews are not to be trusted; pacts with them are not to be made, and if they are made when Muslims are weak, they can be broken.

Even before this event, however, Muhammad had established many of the authoritarian principles that would govern his community long after his death and which modern militants would later stress to justify their own rigid political outlook. All executive, judicial, legislative, and religious authority rested in Allah and his Messenger. His state did not separate spiritual and temporal authority. Muhammad's theocracy[19] had no formal police force (though there was no shortage then, as now, of young zealots eager to implement the Messenger's word), no standing army, no bureaucracy; in fact, few institutions of any kind. Though the Koran sanctioned slavery and an inferior status for women, it softened existing inequalities and improved conditions for both. Muhammad's new faith revealed a decidedly egalitarian spirit, an intense conviction that tribe, wealth, and origin were less important in the eyes of God than the strength of one's faith and personal merit.

While legend has it that the Prophet was a charismatic man of almost infinite patience who valued those who questioned his orders, militants stress that intellectuals and other skeptics were not among his favorites. Muhammad, after all, was leading a revolution, not a debating society. While he often forgave those who had resisted or plotted against him — eager to avoid the vendettas and blood feuds at the core of the Bedouin code of honor and life itself — Muhammad abhorred being mocked in verse or song,[20] an intolerance that has endured in Arab culture. Soon after a successful raid at a place called Badr, Muhammad authorized the murder of an especially irksome critic — Islam's first politically sanctioned murder of an intellectual opponent — a woman poet. In her stinging verses, Asama bint Marwan had ridiculed her fellow Medinese's slavish acceptance of this foreigner from the loathsome Qurayshi tribe of Mecca. "Fucked men of Malik and of Nabit and of Awf, fucked men of Khazraj," she wrote of Medina's great clans and tribes in a verse that early Muslim scholars were honest enough to record. "You obey a stranger who does not belong among you."[21]

Enraged, Muhammad was said to have asked a question not uncommon among rulers: "Will no one rid me of this daughter of Marwan?" A volunteer went to the writer's house that very night and stabbed her to death as she slept surrounded by her children, a murder Muhammad was said to have praised as "a service to Allah and his Messenger."[22] A few months later, Muhammad ordered the death of a second critic, a male poet whose mother was Jewish. In this case Muhammad accompanied the assailants halfway to the scene of the crime and gave them a blessing, an early precedent for the modern *fatwas* sanctioning the murder of a *kafir* (nonbeliever) as well as intellectual "apostates," those who turn away from Islam. After he conquered Mecca, Muhammad reportedly killed only ten people for their affronts to him and Islam. But among them were an author of satirical (if not Satanic) verses about Muhammad and a young woman whose only apparent crime was to have sung them at a party.[23] Today, militants stress these examples as a warning to intellectuals — mock us at your peril.

A sensible politician, Muhammad accepted most of Arabia's tribal rules and customs, including male circumcision. Few other religions sanction a man's beating a disobedient wife, as does the Koran.[24] But other rules, such as his ban on a woman's being "inherited" as chattel by her late husband's eldest son, were decidedly progressive for the era and remained so relative to the West until the twentieth century. While Allah in his revelations to Muhammad limited to four the number of wives a man could take — excluding God's Messenger, of course, who was permitted to marry for reasons of state and had at least nine wives (at least one of them a converted Jew) and a Christian concubine when he died — he did not restrict the number of a man's concubines or slaves. (Slavery in Saudi Arabia was abolished de jure only in 1962.) But Allah required that men treat their wives equally, that women retain their own wealth, and that they be permitted under certain conditions to ask a judge to order their husbands to divorce them (men could end marriages at will) — all progressive measures compared to the practices of pre-Islamic society, the *jahiliyya*. Women themselves were entitled to a share of inheritance, although their portion was half that of men, as was the worth of some of their testimony in court. Islam outlawed the slaughter of infant girls, a common practice in desperately poor and perpetually hungry seventh-century Arabia.

Fatima Mernissi, a Moroccan writer, blames much of Islam's misogyny not on the divinely inspired Koran but on its all-too-human interpretation, the Sunna, that is, the *hadith* that Muhammad's companions and even later witnesses and scholars claim Muhammad uttered.[25] For example, the Koranic verse requiring Muslim women to wear the *hijab* (veil) outside their homes—the most obvious symbol of male supremacy—was imposed in Medina by the Prophet, she writes, to protect his wives and all free women against rape and harassment in the insecure streets of the city. But even Mernissi is hard-pressed to justify the Koran's determination that men are superior to women, that they alone can decide what kind of sexual positions a woman must submit to, and that husbands can use violence against their wives.[26]

It may be no accident that the Koran has two distinct voices. In Mecca, Muhammad was a rebel; in Medina he was head of state. The early Meccan verses—those recited while his new religion was being formed—concern mainly religious dogma. In the Medina verses, by contrast, Allah took what to a nonbeliever was a surprisingly detailed interest in the day-to-day problems of Muhammad's community, even in his Messenger's troubled love affairs. (To a believer, of course, God's concern for the welfare of his Prophet is not at all surprising.)[27] One of the most celebrated instances concerned Aisha, his favorite wife, who, as the daughter of Abu Bakr, the Prophet's companion and future first caliph, understood how to wield power. Muhammad had married Aisha when she was only six (a union said to be consummated when she was nine, child marriage being a not uncommon practice in Arabia and sanctioned by Allah).[28] Tradition has it that when a Medinese rival of Muhammad's accused Aisha of adultery, Allah himself exonerated her through a revelation—just in time, it seems, given Muhammad's doubts about her innocence. Muhammad's trance produced two other timely opinions aimed at discouraging such slander: first, the requirement that four male witnesses attest to an allegation of adultery and fornication, and second, that bearing false witness is to be punished by eighty lashes.

Since the dominant branch of Islam believes that Muhammad left no instructions about succession, Islam's first crisis, and an enduring problem in the Muslim Middle East, was not over religious dogma but over who should lead the state after his death. The Medinese wanted Muhammad's successor to come from among them. But the men of Mecca installed Abu Bakr as *Kalifa* (caliph in English), meaning "successor" and "deputy." To avoid future uncertainty over succession, Abu Bakr designated Umar the next caliph. But Umar was murdered in 644 by a disgruntled non-Muslim. The third caliph, Uthman, who won an apparent power struggle among six men whom Umar had named

worthy of succession, came from a great aristocratic clan of Mecca, the Umayyads. So many Muslims resented the choice, preferring the more humble Ali,
the Prophet's cousin and the husband of his daughter Fatima. Opposition to
Uthman grew, aggravated by his nepotism, his show of favoritism toward the
leading Meccan clans, and his determination to standardize religious dogma by
tolerating only his authorized version of the Koran. Uthman's murder in 656 by
Muslim dissidents, the first assassination of a Muslim caliph by Muslims, was a
"turning point" in Islamic history, which not only created what one scholar
called "an ominous precedent" but also "gravely weakened the religious and
moral prestige of the office as a bond of unity in Islam."[29]

The new caliph, Ali, was soon challenged by, among others, the Prophet's
widow Aisha. In 656, Aisha herself led a battle against Ali, the beginning of the
split of the Muslim realm into rival camps. At the Battle of the Camel, Ali
defeated her.[30] But in 657, Muawiyah, the late caliph Uthman's cousin, a fellow
Umayyad and then governor of Syria, challenged Ali's forces at Siffen, Islam's
first *fitna* (full-fledged civil war). The battle was inconclusive, and Ali agreed to
arbitration. Muawiyah ultimately prevailed, and in 661, Ali was murdered.

The war, the compromise over arbitration, and Ali's subsequent assassination were the events associated with the great division of Islam into rival camps
and the beginning of the political fragmentation that Muhammad had always
feared. For although Muawiyah and his Umayyad successors proved able rulers,
expanding the empire from their new capital, Damascus, into Europe and to the
borders of India and China, Ali's followers denounced the Umayyad caliphate as
illegitimate. Henceforth, these partisans of Ali became known as Shia, or Shiites.[31] In 680, Ali's son Hussein, the Prophet's grandson, led Shiite forces against
the Umayyads in a second round of the civil war, this time at Karbala in Iraq,
where he and almost his entire family were slaughtered. To this day, Shiites
mourn the "martyrdom" of the Prophet's descendant Hussein ibn (son of) Ali
in a day of atonement called Ashura. And to this day, Shiites, who make up less
than 10 percent of Middle Eastern Muslims, are a persecuted minority in several
Arab states, including Saudi Arabia. This historic division in Islam into Sunnis
—those who stood with Muawiyah and followed the Sunna, Muhammad's
teachings—and Shiites—the partisans of Ali—would never be healed.[32]

Another group of dissidents were the Kharijites, or secessionists—literally,
"those who go out." Originally, Kharijites were Shiites, partisans of Ali. But they
rejected him, too, when Ali submitted to arbitration: Men, they argued, had no
right to decide what Allah had already resolved in Ali's favor and what could be
determined on earth only through battle. In their fanatical idealism, they became anarchists, opposing both Muawiyah and Ali, Sunni and Shia, alike.
Though the Kharijites shared the Shia's sense of historical injustice at Ali's loss
in Islam's historic power struggle, the sect was ultimately rejected by all Muslims, including the Shia. For it was a Kharijite who murdered Ali.

Though less numerous and far more fanatically idealistic than other dissidents, the Kharijites had a profound effect on Islamic revivalist movements.

One writer called them a "prototype" for all modern Muslim militant groups — their spiritual forefathers.[33] While this was perhaps an overstatement, the Kharijites' doctrine, like that of modern-day militants, rejected compromise and branded those who disputed their interpretation of the Prophet's teachings "infidels" or "apostates." All such nonbelievers had to be killed — another disastrous precedent. For Kharijites, jihad, or spreading Islam by the sword, was their faith's "sixth pillar."

Islam became decidedly pragmatic in the mid–seventh century under Umayyad rule, reverting more or less to a secular kingship. Muawiyah, the gifted fifth caliph who ruled not from Arabia but from Damascus, introduced a dynastic element to Islamic rule and institutionalized practices that most modern Islamic militants reject as "secularism," the effective separation of religion and state. But when the Umayyads weakened, another branch of Muhammad's family, the Abbasids, launched Islam's third civil war against the Umayyads. Named for Muhammad's uncle Abbas, the Abbasids triumphantly relocated Islam's capital from Syria to Iraq in 750, thus intensifying a regional struggle between Damascus and Baghdad that has endured until today. While historians often describe the Abbasid caliphate (750–1258) as Islam's "golden era," it was even more autocratic than its predecessors. It was also less stable. A fourth civil war occurred in 809.

Modern Islamists argue that by the eleventh century Islam was in decline. "From then on," wrote my Islamist friend Abdelwahab El-Affendi, a thoughtful Sudanese scholar, "Muslims suffered calamity after calamity: the Crusades, the Mongol invasions, Mamluk tyrannies, and so forth," until the sixteenth century, when the "pax Ottomanica," the last and the greatest Islamic Empire and caliphate in Istanbul, restored "calm and order to the troubled Muslim realm."[34]

Given this history, it was easy to understand why, despite, or perhaps because of, their endless power struggles, most Muslims feared civil strife and unwarranted challenges to a ruler's authority. By the eleventh century, in fact, Sunni Islamic jurists had pronounced it sinful for Muslims to rebel against their leader — however cruel, corrupt, or unjust — as long as he was a Muslim who imposed sharia, the holy law.[35]

It was harder to understand, however, the militants' reverence for the "Rightly Guided Caliphs," that is, the first four successors to Muhammad — what they viewed as Islam's true "golden" age. For women, surely, the Rightly Guided Caliphs were a disaster. The limited freedom that women had enjoyed in Medina was quickly denied them by the Prophet's "righteous" successors.[36] Moreover, the repeated power struggles after Muhammad's death exposed major weaknesses of Islamic government that have endured to this day: the lack of a system of succession; the vagueness of what was meant by *shura*, or consultation with the community; the lack of guidance as to how the community is supposed to determine *ijma*, or what constitutes consensus; and how it should depose a leader who fails to live up to the Prophet's high standards. The Prophet himself seemed untroubled by such key questions of governance. "My community," he is reported to have said when asked how future Muslims would divine the "straight path" they were supposed to follow, "will not agree on an error."

Yet in this bloody epoch now glorified by today's Islamists, three of the first four Rightly Guided Caliphs had died violent deaths, two of them at the hands of fellow Muslims. Under them the Islamic world had split in two. Less than two hundred years after the Prophet's death, the Islamic community had suffered four civil wars, and rival factions and tribes were feuding over power, giving rise to, and justified by, disagreements over religious dogma.

From then on Muslims fought bitterly about the laws that governed them. Interpretation of the law was key in Islam, since for Muslims, God made law; man was left simply to interpret and enforce it. Modern Islamists insist that no society can be "Islamic" unless it is ruled by sharia, the holy law based on the divinely granted Koran and Sunna, the Prophet's traditions, or the secondhand accounts of what the Prophet supposedly said. But the holy law was systematized only after Muhammad's death. The *fuqaha* (legal scholars) and ulema (the guardians of doctrine) used reasoning by analogy and personal judgment to interpret law until the ninth century, when they decided that all the major questions had been answered and that the gate of *ijtihad*, as the process was known, should be closed. Shia, the minority branch of Islam, rejected this, although both Shia and Sunni jurists in practice were conservative, relying increasingly on precedent and shunning innovation and interpretation, a development that would have devastating intellectual consequences for Islamic thought.

The Rightly Guided Caliphs did not produce paradise on earth, but rather a powerful state with even more powerful rulers. This, it seemed to me, was at the heart of their attraction to modern Islamic militants: For all the chaos, bloodshed, murder, improvisation, and absolutism, the Rightly Guided Caliphs were a precedent for the type of Islamic regime — the autocratically "virtuous" state — that contemporary Islamists have sought to create. They seem impervious to the apparently inverse correlation between power and Muslim virtue: The more powerful the state (and its caliph) became, the further the polity moved from the ideals that Muhammad preached. But the longing for this ostensibly blissful past and a community ruled by the oxymoronic "just despot," an ideal that could be reestablished only by returning to the precepts established by the Messenger and his original companions, has proved remarkably durable. Eleven centuries later, this impulse would create the first Islamic militant reform movement in modern times to forge a state in — where else? — Arabia.

MODERN SAUDI ARABIA is actually the third Saudi kingdom. The first emerged in the late eighteenth century, drawing its enduring legitimacy from an extraordinary alliance between a local village chief and a fundamentalist sheikh who preached religious reform. Muhammad Ibn Saud, the village chief, and Muhammad Ibn Abd al-Wahhab, the strict and literal-minded teacher of Islam, banded together to spread Islam and Saudi political power.

Like many modern Islamists, Ibn Abd al-Wahhab railed against the superstitions and un-Islamic practices—worshiping saints, smoking, drinking, music, and wearing gold and silk garments—that had become prevalent in the Prophet's own peninsula.[37] But though he advocated a return to the original precepts and practices of Muhammad, as every modern Islamist does today, Ibn Abd al-Wahhab was, in fact, in many ways a very radical and modern thinker. His inspiration, not surprisingly, was the medieval revivalist Ibn Taymiyya, Islam's Luther,[38] the same theologian who would impress Egypt's Sayyid Qutb in the 1960s and today's Egyptian extremists—the Islamic Group and the Islamic Jihad.[39]

Ibn Taymiyya, like Ibn Abd al-Wahhab himself, followed the Hanbali school of jurisprudence, one of the four great schools of *fiqh*, or Islamic law, that had emerged by the tenth century.[40] Echoing his theological ancestor, Ibn Abd al-Wahhab argued that true believers had to fight rulers who called themselves Muslims but failed to implement sharia, the holy law. To challenge the established and, in his view, corrupt religious authorities, he stressed the need to reopen the gates of *ijtihad*, the process of independent thinking and learned interpretation of the Koran and the Sunna.

The marriage of convenience was a huge success initially. Spurred on by tribal and religious zeal, between 1773 and 1819 the Sauds and the Wahhabis united, often through bloody conquest, most of the land that Muhammad had ruled and which would become a century later the modern Saudi kingdom.[41]

But in 1818 the first state and its capital, Diriyya, were destroyed by Egypt at the urging of the jealous and powerful Ottomans—a humiliation for which Egypt has never quite been forgiven. The Sauds had overreached and lost, a mistake they would not repeat. The second Saudi kingdom (1824–91), also the result of an alliance between the Al Saud and the Wahhabis, ended in civil war and the temporary exile of the House of Saud in neighboring Kuwait.[42] The Sauds learned a second lesson: Family intrigues could be as deadly as political overreaching.

The third Saudi kingdom, the modern state of Saudi Arabia, had so far avoided its predecessors' failings. Much of the credit went to the modern kingdom's founder, King Abdulaziz, known as Ibn Saud, who, in 1902, at about age twenty, recaptured Riyadh from local rulers in a daring raid—the beginning of his campaign to reclaim the land of his ancestors.[43] To reconquer the rest of Arabia, Ibn Saud undertook what one scholar called a "unique experiment."[44] Relying on Wahhabi preachers, he mobilized the errant Bedouin, whose loyalty to Islam was "occasional and opportunistic," by persuading them to abandon the faithlessness inherent in their nomadic way of life and to move to a *hijra*, a settlement named after Muhammad's flight from Mecca to Medina. Each settler was called *akh* (brother). The movement itself came to be known as the Ikhwan, or brotherhood, from which Egypt's first Islamists, the Muslim Brotherhood, may have derived their name a generation later.

The Wahhabi Ikhwan were, in effect, reservists in Ibn Saud's army, well-trained warriors ever willing to fight, plunder, and die in jihad for Ibn Saud and their faith. One by one, they conquered Ibn Saud's Arabian rivals—the Rashids in the Najd, Sherif Hussein (the great-grandfather of Jordan's Hashemite King Hussein) in the Hijaz — until, by 1932, most of Arabia was theirs once more. Six years later, oil was discovered in the kingdom.

With the empire reconquered and their usefulness ended, Ibn Saud had to suppress the fanatical Ikhwan if he was to build a modern state, for they opposed the constitution he wrote and the courts he empowered because they were not based on the Hanbali school of jurisprudence that the Wahhabis followed; in addition, they denounced his approval of "un-Islamic" inventions: automobiles, radio, telephones, and, of course, taxes, particularly on tobacco, since smoking was technically illegal and severely punished. As so many later Saudi rulers would do, Ibn Saud patiently waited until public revulsion against the Ikhwan's extremism enabled him to persuade the ulema, the religious scholars, to sanction a military campaign against them. By 1930, Ibn Saud had crushed the rebellious zealots who had helped him unify Arabia.[45]

The Ikhwan's defeat meant that from then on Wahhabi Islam, the militant reform movement, would be confined, as it was in the second Saudi realm, to "Wahhabiism in one state."[46] Moreover, the ulema themselves, by approving Ibn Saud's destruction of the Ikhwan, had implicitly accepted the need at times to subordinate the spiritual to the temporal, by then a familiar pattern in Islamic (and non-Islamic) government. But tension between Wahhabi religious zeal and the Sauds' political requirements persisted. It was there, just below the surface, throughout the Gulf war. Only when I returned to Saudi Arabia after the war did I realize how intense these strains had become. Anyone seeking to understand the inherent tension in an ostensibly Islamic state between the "rule of God," on the one hand, and the realpolitik of the state, on the other, had only to look at modern Saudi Arabia.

I RETURNED to the kingdom in late 1991. The "welcome" sign at the Ministry of Information's desk was as frayed as the false hospitality it implied. The Saudis had been relieved by the departure of more than ten thousand journalists who had covered the war. I couldn't blame them.

My friend Nabil was still on duty, as he had been during the war, and after our de rigueur Arabic coffee and exchange of Marlboros, he handed me a letter in Arabic. "What's this?" I asked.

"Oh, nothing much," he replied nonchalantly. "Just show it to the hotel clerk at the Al Khozama when you check in and remember to keep it with you when you go out."

Later that night over drinks — rumless punch — in the evening shade of the Al Khozama's peaceful courtyard, an American-educated Saudi friend whom I shall call Abdullah deciphered the mysterious letter. "Basically, it says that you're not a prostitute," he said. The "I am not a whore" letter permitted me to register at hotels, rent a car and, of course, a driver, and venture out on my own — all unescorted by a male relative. Heaven help the woman who arrived without it.[47] The letter was also protection against being arrested in a morals sweep by the Mutawwaeen (volunteers), the zealous young bearded enforcers of prayer time, the segregation of the sexes in public places, and other Islamically correct conduct. Officially known as the Committee for the Promotion of Virtue and the Prevention of Vice, these religious thugs had become far more powerful after the war. Lately they had taken to scaling compound walls, even those inhabited by diplomats, to break up parties with alcohol and dancing, and to arresting unmarried couples in Akariya and Riyadh's other depressing shopping malls where young Saudis went to flirt and relieve their boredom.

Abdullah grimaced at the thought of our prospective visit to his hometown of Burayda, in the heart of the Najd, Saudi Arabia's Koran belt. "You'd better cover up tomorrow," he said anxiously. "The Mutawwaeen are everywhere."

Unlike Iran, where even foreign visiting women were forced to wear chadors or trenchcoats and head scarves, Saudi Arabia did not require women visitors to wear an *abayya* (a long black cloak with large sleeves that hangs over the head). But I had discovered that the *abayya* enabled me to move anonymously around the kingdom, particularly in the rural heartland of the Najd, which was even more xenophobic than the oppressive capital. Thanks to my *abayya*, I had once walked into a Saudi prison hospital a decade earlier to talk to Americans who had been tortured. The guards had assumed that this shrouded, veiled woman was a Saudi relative of a prisoner and had waved me through.

Abdullah reminded me that it was illegal for him to be driving off into the countryside alone with me. But I begged him to take me back to the conservative town that we had visited during the Gulf war. I loved the Saudi desert. Burayda was located near a range of red-tinted sand dunes that towered above us like small mountains. We had raced across the dunes in four-wheel-drive Land Cruisers and at night settled down to a lamb roast and traditional storytelling around a campfire near the crest of a large, silky dune. Abdullah's friend Muhammad had recited Nabati poetry, the popular vernacular verse that Arabians had performed for centuries on solemn or formal occasions to impel men to perform manly and chivalrous acts—an art that was disappearing as rapidly as the raiding and warrior life it glorified.

> My heart is set ablaze by anxieties; it simmers as if on glowing
>   embers.
> Oh, treacherous fate, how quickly it turns! My happy days
>   suddenly changed to adversity.
> When enemy horsemen attacked, I was the first to meet them
>   and cover the retreat of my kinsmen.
> But today, I have no mount on which to carry my baggage.
>   Oh, how shameful! I have been humbled and subdued.[48]

In Arabic it rhymed. The crackling of the fire and Muhammad's hypnotic chanting were the only sounds we heard. The bluish light of a full moon gave us a spectacular view of what seemed an endless sea of dunes. Our Land Cruiser was parked at the bottom of the dune and I had called my home in New York on the car phone. But the Bedouin campfire, the poetry, and the stories evoked pre-Islamic, simpler times. This was the Saudi Arabia that few outsiders knew.

Abdullah looked uneasy when he fetched me early the following morning. "The dunes are out," Abdullah told me as I climbed into his sleek Mercedes. "My cousin says the police are patrolling there at night."

As we drove through the sprawling, still-sleeping desert capital, I could only marvel at Riyadh despite my disappointment about the dunes. When I first saw it in 1976, the capital resembled an American frontier town. Now it was Phoenix without mountains. Out of this harsh desert, architects and planners had built a modern city for more than 2.5 million people. Giant black asphalt highways were sunken below street level to reduce car noise and protect the privacy of people who lived near them. Freeways and flyovers were immaculate and lined with flowering shrubs and more than a million date-palm trees. Hundreds of schools and playgrounds, thousands of housing units for less prosperous Saudis, spectacular public architecture, and dozens of fancy shopping malls, a Saudi favorite, had been built. Armies of Asian workers in bright orange uniforms collected Saudi garbage and litter. The wealthy hid their good fortune in Southern California–like suburbs behind high beige-toned cement walls — compounds that included acres of homes, all marble and coolness, with indoor and outdoor swimming pools, clay tennis courts, and family mosques for the many members of extended Saudi families. Within those walls we could swim, drink tea or scotch with friends, play tennis, and watch videos, theoretically banned in the kingdom. Saudis, like Californians, disliked infringements on their personal space. Behind these walls Saudis lived more or less as they wished; beyond them, Islamic virtue reigned.

Saudi Arabia had come a long way since I saw my first "camel crossing" sign twenty years ago.[49] The first road linking Jidda with the capital, Riyadh, was not finished until 1967. Today more than forty-five thousand miles of paved modern highways connect all parts of the kingdom. Investing more than $800 billion on development projects between 1974 and 1990, the government had built more than three hundred hospitals, seventeen hundred state-run clinics, seven universities, ninety-nine colleges, eighteen thousand schools, and twenty-nine airports.[50] Physically at least, Arabia had been transformed.

I recalled having visited Athuwayr, the hometown of another Saudi friend, Abdulaziz H. Fahad, an American-educated lawyer. The oasis village where he was born in 1954 was little more than a collection of baked-mud hovels, with neither electricity nor running water. Like many Saudis, he recalled with no nostalgia 120-degree days without air conditioning, the numbing desert winter cold, and huddling by a fire in a winter rainstorm on the dirt floor under the only section of palm-leaf-thatched roof that did not leak. Some even remembered hunger — catching locusts to eat for protein. To this day, King Fahd's sister ate locusts; old habits died hard.

"I grew up with ants the size of fingernails crawling around in my ears,"

Fahad had told me as we toured what remained of his former home, now slowly collapsing in the winter rains and blasting desert windstorms. "A decade later, I was attending Yale at government expense. So, yes, Saudis are grateful to the Al Saud; the ruling family educated us and made us rich."

The collapse of oil prices in the 1980s and the recession that followed, however, meant that after 1983 there were fewer large contracts with which to finance such projects and to buy the loyalty of Saudi merchants and citizens. The kingdom's current troubles may have been expressed in Islamic rhetoric, but their roots were economic. As Prince Bandar Bin Sultan, the kingdom's energetic ambassador to Washington, put it, parroting a favored American political axiom: "It's the economy, stupid."

Then came the enormous expense of the war and the inevitable questions about why the kingdom could not defend itself despite some $25 billion in annual defense spending—on a per capita basis, twice that of Israel and three times that of America. When the war came, Saudi Arabia had a 65,000-man army, 550 tanks, and 179 combat aircraft. Iraq, by contrast, had a million-man army, 5,500 tanks, and 513 combat planes.

As we drove along, I asked my friends about the war, which seemed to have receded as quickly in memory and import as a desert mirage. Had it made Saudis question the Al Saud's stewardship of the kingdom?

"Gratitude towards the Saudis still lingers," Abdullah told me. "The family developed the kingdom in record time without unhinging our traditionally xenophobic culture. But any idiot could have developed the country with almost a trillion dollars to spend! So after the war people began asking some questions: Where did all the money go? Why should the Al Saud have a monopoly on economic and political power? Why should idiot princes from the royal family be favored over talented commoners? Why was our patronage system now bankrupt?"

Saudis in business, he added, knew some unpleasant truths: that the kingdom had bought itself modern conveniences without real modernization; that many graduates of the state's universities, which devoted 30 percent of the curriculum to Islamic instruction, were too poorly educated to perform effectively in the private sector; that the government, which still provided about 90 percent of all jobs, would be unable to create sufficient employment for the sixty-five thousand graduates each year; and that for the first time unemployment among Saudi graduates stood at between 25 and 30 percent.

Abdullah was part of the kingdom's politically enlightened business class, the "technocrats," who were not "typical" Saudi citizens. With his luxurious compound in a Riyadh suburb, his winter home in London, and his summer house in Marbella, Spain, Abdullah traveled often and knew the world. He wanted what most technocrats wanted: political parties and real participation, the rule of law, a clearly defined penal code, CNN and a free press, a meritocracy rather than royal favoritism, and an end to the harassment by the Mutawwaeen and the Mabahith al-Ammah, or Mabahith for short, the Ministry of

Interior's dreaded security service. But this agenda was not, of course, what most adult Saudis wanted, only 65 percent of whom, despite the government's enormous education expenditures, were literate.[51] (While 78 percent of Saudi men can read and write, only 48 percent of women can do so.)[52]

Most of the country remained deeply religious, conservative, and xenophobic, suspicious even of the 4 million foreigners who made up two-thirds of the labor force and took jobs that few Saudis traditionally wanted. They were also opposed to democracy, women's and minority rights, and other "Western," "seditious" innovations.

"About a quarter of the country thinks the way I do," Abdullah told me. "About half wants nothing to change or is indifferent to the ruling family. And another quarter thinks that our recent failures result from our departure from Islam's 'straight path.' They want to return to the good old days and become even more Islamic — more closed to the West and, therefore, to modernization. Less than half of them — or about ten to fifteen percent — are religious fanatics who favor getting rid of the Al Saud, by violence if necessary." That was about the equivalent of the extreme Right in France or in America, he said.

Traditionally, the ruling family had balanced the liberal technocrats against its more conservative religious opponents to modernize the country. In the late 1940s, for example, Ibn Saud introduced radio despite opposition from some of the religious establishment. In 1959 his son King Faisal authorized education for girls. In 1963 he sent troops to the fanatical town of Burayda to protect the first girls' school when men rioted and more troops to Riyadh in 1965 to defend the television station when extremists attacked it as "an instrument of the devil." The king's own nephew had been killed after that fight. A decade later, the nephew's brother would assassinate King Faisal.

"The government was often more liberal than the majority of its people," Abdullah explained. "The country is littered with religious *fatwas* that the Al Saud ignored when the kingdom's interests were at stake." But now Fahd, the seventy-three-year-old monarch, had grown fat and lazy, and this worried Abdullah. The man who as minister and crown prince had surrounded himself with intellectuals, technocrats, and even foreigners now hated confrontation and resented any hint of criticism. His brothers held the occasional majlis, the informal sessions where people could see the family to complain and seek redress, especially financial help, but King Fahd almost never did. He spent his days sleeping and his nights with obsequious pals. A fortune-teller — very un-Islamic — had once told him he would die in Riyadh, so he hated the capital. He preferred looking at fish through an underwater glass wall in his $3 billion Al Salem palace in Jidda, whose white beach sand was said to have been imported from Greece. His brothers and the ministers were left to run the country but hesitated to act without him. So nothing got done. "It's total paralysis," Abdullah lamented, "and the system grows more sclerotic each day."

It was nearly dusk when we got to the Burayda farm where we were spending the night. I decided on a quick trip to the market, but Abdullah insisted on accompanying me. I could not go alone. Too dangerous, he said.

Engrossed in conversation, Abdullah and I failed to see the two young Mutawwaeen approaching us. Though I was wearing my *abayya* and a white head scarf that covered every strand of my hair, the religious police stopped us. Scowling, they ordered Abdullah to cover my face.

One of them, a young man who appeared to be in his early twenties, with an unkempt beard and a dirty, untied head scarf that flopped loosely on his head, reached for my head scarf to pull it down over my face. I'll never forget the hatred in his eyes. I was furious. I yelled at him in English: "Don't touch me! I am not Saudi. I am not Muslim. I am an American. American women do not wear veils."

Abdullah looked as startled as the Mutawwa, who, though he understood not a word of English, had felt my anger and backed off, unaccustomed to being challenged, especially by a woman. Instead, he turned on Abdullah. Who was this crazy woman, they demanded in Arabic, and what was I doing in Burayda? Abdullah told them I was an American reporter, a guest of the government, a woman who had helped defend their kingdom against Saddam.

The fiery-eyed Mutawwa grew even angrier. "We didn't need Americans to protect us, and we certainly don't need her," he shouted. "Allah defends us."

After Abdullah muttered a few suitably pious expressions about Saudi hospitality, Islam, and the Prophet — "peace be unto him," the phrase that invariably followed the mention of Muhammad's name — the young men softened. Wasn't Abdullah ashamed, they scolded him. How could he let me walk around half-naked?

The scene was almost comical, but I felt terrible. The Mutawwaeen would do little to me, but my outburst might have caused trouble for Abdullah, who could easily have been hauled off to jail despite the fact that the government now insisted that Mutawwaeen be accompanied by policemen when they arrested sinners. Far too polite to chide me, Abdullah was silent as we continued our stroll through the vast, dusty market's deserted stalls. The Mutawwaeen were out in force, tapping on windows of tardy shop closers with their metal-tipped bamboo switches. "Prayer! Come to prayer! Remember God!" they boomed, ordering merchants to close for the required thirty-minute break as the muezzins' throaty calls to prayer echoed through the market. These were human voices. Wahhabi Islam did not permit the tape-recorded calls to prayer that were now standard in Arab countries. In a fabric shop near the edge of the market, a merchant had lingered to chat with a woman customer, apparently a regular. *Thwack!* Down came the switch on the flustered Yemeni merchant's wrist. "Stop that!" the zealot shrieked at him. "Are you flirting with her? Close your shop now! And you," he said, his eyes narrowing as he inspected the woman's translucent veil, a middle-class hallmark. "Go home to your husband." I caught a glimpse of her face as she readjusted her veil before leaving the shop: humiliation, fury, and indignation. Glancing at my uncovered face, she shrugged under her veil. The Mutawwa was young enough to be her son. What had happened to the kingdom's traditional deference to one's elders?

Depressed, I asked Abdullah to take me home. "I told you that things had changed since you were last here," he said, sighing. "Everything now is *haram*, forbidden. Burayda and the entire Najd were always puritanical. But since the war they have become *haramstan*. The wartime economic boom is over. The family is under attack, so they let the zealots run loose. The new head of the Mutawwaeen was just given $18 million to train these three thousand idiots, most of them lower-class rejects from our good schools who can't get real jobs anywhere else. Now they ride around in brand-new red-and-white GM Suburbans with loudspeakers — big shots!" Abdullah said bitterly. "They love the power."

BACK IN RIYADH, I visited an old friend in the diplomatic quarter, the northeastern suburb twenty minutes from downtown Riyadh that houses most of the kingdom's diplomats and their families, along with some Westernized Saudis who paid high prices to secure the freedom the compound assures. How typically Saudi, I thought as my driver steered me through the heavily guarded, manicured community, with its high walls, lavish one-story villas, and sprawling ranch-style houses. Such compounds were the kingdom's quarantine, an ingenious system of separating Saudis from the estimated 4 million foreigners working here — "expats," as expatriate workers are known. The government knew that it could not yet do without the foreigners who each year sent some $18 billion in wages back home, so this was how it protected its citizens from exposure to the contagious ideas that some of us carried: our belief in human and civil rights, gender equality, democracy, the rule of law, freedom of speech, political expression, and religion.[53]

To the Al Saud, foreign journalists like me were the worst scourge, the intellectual equivalent of AIDS. Securing a Saudi visa, except during the Gulf war, was therefore an ordeal except for those whom the kingdom felt it had bought and could trust. Clearly I was neither. After the war I had written an article about Saudi life for *The New York Times Magazine*, which, among other things, described corruption among members of the royal family.[54] While all Saudis gossiped about such scandals, I had done so in print, and worse, I had named those allegedly responsible, an utterly unpardonable sin. King Fahd, Saudi Arabia's chief censor, was outraged. But it took the Saudi bureaucracy a while to connect me with the offending article. So I had gotten this visa, one last time. The diplomat friend predicted I would not get another. He was right.

"This is a land of silence, a culture of silences," the diplomat told me. "As the Saudis say, 'Not everything known is said.' Sins like corruption or sources of shame — suicide, mental illness, or AIDS — are all hidden away, discussed openly among themselves but rarely with strangers."

As my diplomat friend saw it, the Gulf war had fostered even greater xenophobia and discontent within most of Saudi society. The middle class, the technocratic elite, of course, was deeply disappointed that the kingdom had not opened up, that the family seemed determined to continue running everything and countenancing princely corruption and high-handedness. The government, for example, was still buying at inflated prices princes' land that it had previously given or sold them at bargain-basement rates. For their part, religious conservatives were furious that the kingdom had been unable to defend itself, that "infidels" had polluted the sanctity of the land of Mecca and Medina, and that un-Islamic products and ideas were still penetrating Saudi society. The king had responded as usual: He had tried buying off unhappy constituencies. To appease the liberal technocrats, King Fahd was planning to establish the long-promised *majlis al-shura* (consultative council), portrayed as a nascent Parliament that would enhance government accountability. To calm the religious establishment, he had unleashed the Mutawwaeen and was emphasizing the kingdom's and his family's Islamic credentials. To enhance the family's control of the religious establishment, he was creating the Ministry of Religious Affairs, another religious forum to complement, and some said compete with, the power base of Sheikh Abdulaziz Bin Baz, the Saudi mufti and head of the government-appointed Council of Senior Ulema, the kingdom's highest religious authority. The new ministry was to be headed by Sheikh, or Dr., as he preferred to be addressed, Abdullah Bin Abdul Mohsen al-Turki, the rector of Imam Muhammad bin Saud Islamic University.

I knew this pragmatic gentleman. In an interview at his spacious home shortly before the Gulf war, he had defended the country's strict Wahhabi interpretation of Islamic law and tradition, arguing that it was compatible with both modernization and social justice. Saudis who attacked the government and called for a "return" to Islamic traditions were "extremists," a distinct minority, he assured me. Saudi Arabia could not "return" to Islam because it had never left.[55] When I asked about his personal reaction to complaints about the growing Mutawwa raids on private homes and foreign compounds, the rector called such assaults "rare." Besides, he added cautiously, "those who are not violating God's law have nothing to fear." No good Muslim, he insisted, opposed the stationing of foreign military forces in the kingdom. The issue had been resolved by Islamic law. Recalling his words, I concluded that King Fahd had chosen the right man. In addition to having recruited an excellent manager to handle the kingdom's enormous religious assets, the family would be able to count on Sheikh Abdullah.

The Saudi government was to some extent a victim of its own success, my friend the diplomat told me — an exquisite irony. Whereas Islamic militancy in Egypt and other poor Arab countries was usually attributed to government failure to meet the needs of their citizens, religious opposition in Arabia was the result of a government that had done so all too well. For the past twenty-five years the Al Saud had made its citizens unimaginably prosperous. But now the government had less money with which to meet still-soaring expectations. Given the population explosion, the economy would have to grow at over 3 percent a year simply to maintain the same per capita income, a rate it had not achieved in the last decade. If the kingdom's population kept exploding, its political and economic system would be severely strained. Saudi Arabia was becoming too heavily populated to manage through its traditional informal majlis system, even in its enhanced form. A Saudi professor had told him that he had first cousins he had never even met. The kingdom's population boom, the diplomat said, was its largest single threat. "Dr. Muhammad Malthus is alive and all too well in Arabia."

In 1992 about 48 percent of Saudis were under fifteen; 58 percent were under twenty; and 68 percent were less than twenty-five years old.[56] Fewer and fewer Saudis remembered the poverty of time immemorial from which the Al Saud — and Arabia's oil — had delivered them. The "oil generation," as it was called, felt no gratitude for the past. You had to be over forty to remember anything but wealth. Telling the young about eating locusts was like telling Americans who came of age in the 1960s about the Great Depression. The kingdom's pampered youth, though still rich by Arab standards, judged the kingdom by its previous record and their own inflated expectations. To them, their country was suddenly and inexplicably broke.

THE CATALYST of the current fundamentalist revival was the women's driving demonstration, just before the Gulf war.

I visited a friend, Aza, I shall call her, one of the forty-seven women who had dumped their chauffeurs outside the Riyadh Safeway in November 1990 and savored ten minutes of freedom by driving their Lincoln, BMW, and Mercedes cars in convoy down a major boulevard before the Mutawwaeen stopped them and threw them into jail. It was a miserable reunion.

Aza was depressed, understandably. The king had suspended her for a year from the university teaching job she loved. She and her husband, and even some other relatives, were forbidden to leave the kingdom, a harsh, if temporary, measure in mobile Saudi Arabia, where professional people were accustomed to fleeing the heat and oppressive cultural restrictions for vacations abroad. They were ordered not to talk to Western reporters, but Aza risked a secret meeting with me.

She was "disappointed" by the king's action, she told me over mint tea at a friend's home, because the women had been on what she considered strong Islamic ground. "The Prophet's widow Aisha rode a camel into battle!" she told me. "What's the difference between a camel and a car? Islam does not require women to cover their faces; the Saudi ulema do. Our problem is not religion; it is politics. The government used us to deflect political protest during the war."

Aza was even more afraid of the fundamentalist sheikhs who had denounced the women — calling them "whores and prostitutes," "advocates of vice," and "filthy secularists" — from the kingdom's most powerful pulpit, the mosques. Militants had circulated leaflets containing the women's occupations, phone numbers, and addresses, some accusing them of having renounced Islam, an offense punishable by death.

The religious establishment, in effect, had encouraged the extremists. Shortly before the war, Sheikh Bin Baz, the blind octogenarian Islamic scholar who commanded enormous reverence among Saudis, issued a *fatwa* concluding that the women's protest "degraded and harmed the sanctity" of women. While many senior scholars believed that the informal ban on women drivers was not justified by the Koran, Bin Baz's ruling was no surprise. An unveiled woman, the sheikh had previously ruled, was "one of the great evils and patent sins" and a leading cause of "general depravity."[57] But even Bin Baz may have felt ambivalent about the driving *fatwa*, for uncharacteristically, he cited Saudi social custom rather than the Koran and Sunna to support its conclusion.

Aza was even more disappointed in the allegedly liberal friends who had shunned her, fearing that they, too, might be punished. Few technocrats wanted to jeopardize their privileged lives to make Saudi Arabia more modern and just.

"This society lives in terror of disapproval, of shame," she complained. "My colleagues rationalized their cowardice by saying that we had done immeasurable harm to our cause by choosing the 'wrong' time and way to make our point. But there never would have been a 'right' time to drive," she said bitterly. "The issue was not driving. It was whether or not I exist as a person in Saudi Arabia except from the belly button to the knees."

THE ROLE OF WOMEN in Saudi Arabia's reactionary culture — as well as a woman's place in most Arab societies — was at the heart of Arab obsession with *ird* (honor).[58] Almost no other single issue was as politically sensitive. The women's driving protest had polarized Saudi society, but not along gender lines: Most Saudi women and men were equally outraged by the protest. More than two thousand female students at King Saud University had signed a petition declaring that they did not want to drive. Aza's own students had confronted her after class: How could she have challenged the kingdom during a national emergency? How could she have embarrassed her country in front of foreigners?

Such hostility should have been predictable. Aza, who had studied in the West, was of a minority. In the early 1970s and 1980s, wealthy, educated Saudis had sent their sons and even daughters abroad to be educated. But after the kingdom opened its own universities (and ended foreign-study scholarships for women in 1980), most Saudis chose to educate their children in the kingdom. As a result, young Saudis were no longer exposed on a sustained basis at an impressionable age to Western culture or education. In the 1980s, there were more than 10,000 Saudis in American colleges and universities; by 1995, the number stood at about 3,300. As a result, the now-middle-age products of Western education — men and women in their forties — tended to be far more open and liberal than the young Saudis they were teaching or employing. "The liberal, Western-educated Saudi — we're a dying breed," Aza said.

One of Aza's colleagues told me that if the issue of women driving had been put to a vote, Aza would have lost overwhelmingly. "The king ignores *fatwas* when a change is supported by most people but opposed mainly by religious conservatives, who are a minority," her colleague said. "He cannot do so when both the religious authorities and most citizens are opposed."

Though tribal and blood loyalties crossed class lines and remained by far the society's strongest bonds, class antagonism had also hurt the women's cause. The list of drivers was a who's who in the kingdom, targets of envy. The "uppity rich bitches" had finally gotten what they deserved.

Moreover, Aza and my Americanized friend Farida were unlike other Saudi women I knew, many of whom seemed to enjoy life in the kingdom. They resented being considered oppressed or having their traditions denigrated as primitive. Saudi women were not abandoned and left to fend for themselves, as were women and even children in the United States, they reminded me. Nor were they robbed and killed on city streets. A Saudi sociologist trained at Indiana University said that while she missed the freedom of America, her society would have been torn apart long ago if the ruling family had pushed harder against the kingdom's cultural and religious norms. Maintaining the country's unique Islamic culture had held the kingdom together despite its enormously compressed economic transformation. If women had paid the heaviest price for maintaining social cohesion, so be it. "I'm proud of what we've accomplished," she told me. "I am a Saudi first, a woman second."

Many women had found satisfying work, even if segregated from men. Female Saudi journalists wrote their stories from dingy "women only" offices near their papers, calling officials on the phone without ever meeting them. Many others taught in universities. The economic slump was weakening some barriers, they told me. Because of the shortage of Saudi doctors, for example, women physicians were now treating both male and female patients.[59] Women were even beginning to live outside their families in distant cities to teach in girls' schools.[60] Change was coming, but slowly, they said — Saudi style.

Many of my friends who did not work said they did not want to. They preferred being home with their children and traveling abroad with their husbands. Many were married to first or second cousins in matches that had been arranged, or semiarranged, by their mothers or aunts. Many of these relationships seemed happier and more satisfying than those of my American counterparts.

None of my male friends had taken a second wife — not yet, anyway. Most told me they wouldn't dare; their wives would leave them. Among the middle class, taking a second wife except in case of illness or childlessness was neither fashionable nor affordable.

While Saudi Arabia is often portrayed as a land of total female subservience to men, its reality was more complex. Yes, Saudi women were barred from becoming engineers, architects, judges, ministers, and, of course, political leaders. Freedom of movement was highly restricted: Unmarried women could not live alone or travel without a male guardian or his authorization. Women were also deeply disadvantaged in case of divorce, legally unable to prevent it and forced to relinquish custody of their female children at age nine to their former husbands. But some Saudi women were veritable tyrants in their own homes. They decided where their children would go to school, when and whom they would marry, whether their husbands would accept new jobs, with whom the family socialized, and where the family would live and spend vacations. They promoted their friends' husbands, sons, and relatives to key jobs. "Saudi Arabians," concluded David Long, a former American diplomat who had taught school in the kingdom, "are the world's most henpecked men."[61]

Thanks to Islamic inheritance laws, Saudi women were also often wealthy in their own right. A Saudi female scholar concluded that in 1995 women controlled about 40 percent of the kingdom's private wealth.[62] Mai Yamani, the daughter of the former oil minister and a scholar in London, estimated that women now owned a fourth of all property in Riyadh and half of that in Jidda. Unable to work in most government offices, more than two thousand women had registered in retail trade with the Riyadh Chamber of Commerce, a threefold increase over the number before the Gulf war. Such economic clout would eventually have political repercussions, but slowly, given the extreme sensitivity of Islamic conservatives to any change in the status of women. Even this prospect, however, must have terrified Saudi men, for in 1995 the government stopped issuing trade licenses to women.

For poorer Saudi women who could not afford the chauffeurs, swimming pools, European vacations, and other luxuries that made life in the kingdom tolerable, the society's restrictions were far more onerous. I would never forget my own brief experience of living without money and on my own in the kingdom and my attempt one night to ride a public bus in Riyadh. I had been told that women had their own section in the back of the bus, like blacks in the American South when I was growing up. But I did not know that in Riyadh we had our own entrance as well. When I had tried to board the bus through the front door, men roared in indignation and threw Kleenex and an empty soda can at me. Rattled and humiliated, I descended and retreated to the proper door. There was only one other passenger in the unlit, stifling compartment, which was sealed off from the front of the bus by a thick wooden door. She must have heard the commotion, for she lifted her veil and smiled at me sympathetically. In excellent English she said: "You know, we are lucky to have this bus. The ulema wanted to keep us off them entirely." That would have been catastrophic for her: Her father and husband were dead; she hated her brothers-in-law, so this was her only affordable means of getting to and from her teaching job in a girls' school. "You get used to it," she said.

I knew I never could. Nor would I ever agree that she or Aza, however tiny a minority they represented, should be forced to accept such degrading abuse. My Egyptian women friends considered themselves good Muslims, but they did not cover their faces, nor were they secluded from men.

Saudi society, moreover, paid a price for its Islamic rigidities. An American defense analyst told me that the Saudi navy usually went to sea only during the day because its sailors, recruited from the kingdom's poorer classes, had to return home each night to take their wives shopping and help them perform other tasks that were difficult for unaccompanied women.[63]

Here was yet another irony. Whereas poverty and national ambition had induced countries like Egypt to accept some Western customs and values along with its development schemes, Saudi Arabia had long been rich enough to afford its fanatical ways. Because of its affluence, the government could keep women — half the able-bodied workforce — unemployed, or at least underemployed. Because of its oil, it could ignore protests from human-rights groups about the kingdom's failure to provide equal rights to its citizens regardless of race, gender, or religion. Because it could buy friends and influence, it did not need to defer to Western sensibilities. By buying off its opposition and playing dissidents — the liberal technocrats and the conservative religious critics — off against each other, it had quelled potentially deadly opposition that might have destroyed poorer, less cohesive regimes.

The government's relatively harsh reaction to the women's protest also reflected an ugly pragmatism that had prevailed since the early days of Islam. Just as the early Muslim caliphs had sacrificed women's rights to appease the men for the sake of the *umma*, the Islamic community, contemporary Arabians had sacrificed women to placate Islamic hard-liners whose support was vital to the Al Saud. During the Gulf war, for example, the religious opposition had opposed both the foreign troops and the women's driving demonstration. The government had made an implicit deal: King Fahd had cracked down on the women but in return had demanded acquiescence of the troops. For a time he got it. But some militants mistook the king's concessions for weakness, and after the war they decided to push ever harder. They were unprepared for the ruling family's decision to shove back.

DISCONTENT after the war was reflected in two separate petitions to the king: one from liberal technocrats; the other, and far more significant, from religious conservatives. Even the decision to put their concerns in writing and to have them published in Egyptian newspapers shocked traditionalists. Although ostensibly the petitions sought radically different things, both of them, stripped of ideological and theological cover, were really demands to share power.

The liberals had moved first. In early 1991 more than forty technocrats signed a petition calling for a consultative assembly and a legal code that would grant legal equality to all citizens "regardless of race, tribe, social status, or gender." While raising children was the "noblest vocation" of Muslim women, the document said, women should have a "public voice" and enjoy the "basic legal and social rights" as long as they were "within an Islamic context."

The second petition, signed by more than four hundred clerics and intellectuals, ostensibly "under the direction of Sheikh Abdulaziz Bin Baz," worried the government more. It, too, called for a consultative council and human rights but demanded an end to what it called official corruption, "harassment" of Saudi religious critics, "widespread favoritism and nepotism," government monopolies, and misappropriation of oil revenue for "frivolous luxuries while Saudis lack money for daily bread," themes that had broad resonance in Saudi society.[64] The signatories also protested government regulations written by "secular laymen," many of whom were "attorneys influenced by the temporal laws" who "lacked the minimal understanding of Islamic law needed to arrive at optimum Islamic rulings." They condemned commercial statutes that contained "blatant violations of Islamic law" that were "unbefitting" the kingdom, the "birthplace of the call to Islam, a guiding star for Muslims, and a standard for the Islamic world." They demanded lifting the ban on Islamic banks (which do not charge interest) and "justice" in distributing Saudi wealth. In veiled criticism of the king's decision to invite half a million American forces into the kingdom, the petition called for the creation of a powerful, well-equipped army to defend the country. Most telling of all was the call for what one naive Western analyst described as "freedom of the press and expression."[65] What the conservatives wanted, in fact, was a purge of "all that would undermine" Islam in the Saudi media: television serials, for example, "overflowing with adorned women, unveiled faces, suggestive remarks, and sexual innuendo"; songs that speak of "flirtation and love"; and video stores that sell "tens of thousands of provocative films that show women in overt sexual situations that sanction sin and even promote damaging ideas and deviant behavior." Finally, they demanded a ban on the "many articles, especially on literary pages, by writers known for intellectual perversion and even for hostility to the kingdom."

The ruling family correctly saw both petitions, but particularly that of the conservatives, as a challenge to its authority. The conservatives were demanding an even more Islamic state — a plea that put the ruling family on weaker religious and, hence, political ground.

While the kingdom's crusading puritanism often led Western analysts to portray the Saudi rulers as "strict constructionists," this was not quite the case. The Al Saud, one prominent scholar argued, had made Islam compatible with modern society through its skillful reliance on the Hanbali school of law.[66] Though the Hanbalis insisted on strict adherence to the Koran and the Sunna and were therefore in many respects more rigid than the juridical schools of other Arab Muslim states, Hanbali tradition had always emphasized *ijtihad* (independent reasoning) in areas where the Koran and Sunna offered no specific guidance. So for Hanbali ulema, the "gate of *ijtihad*" had theoretically never closed. If the Koran did not specifically prohibit something, it was permitted, provided it was consistent with the sacred law's basic principles.[67] Thus, although Muslims believed that only God made law and that all holy law was enshrined in the Koran and the Sunna, Hanbali jurists and Saudi bureaucrats enacted what amounted to laws, calling them instead "regulations." Since the early 1950s, the government had issued thousands of such regulations governing commercial and social activity. The conservatives' petition, in effect, challenged its right to do so.

Initially, the government did not respond to either petition. But in January 1992 young radicals, calling themselves the "Islamic Awakening," threatened to stage a public protest — anathema in conservative Arabia. The following autumn, 107 religious militants, representatives of leading religious institutes and universities, circulated an even tougher "Memorandum of Advice," which insisted not only that the government rigorously apply Islamic laws to every aspect of Saudi life, but that it also repudiate relations with non-Islamic governments and the West in general.

Sheikh Bin Baz, no stranger to youthful rebellion, was initially perceived as sympathetic to the dissidents' demand for greater justice and religious purity. The family feared that if Bin Baz and his deputy sided with the petitioners — however unlikely that might be — its situation would become untenable. The militants, for their part, had tried to curry the ulema's favor, sensing that the ulema were their ultimate protectors.[68]

The family, as it always had, turned to the Council of Senior Ulema to back its repression. The age-old alliance between Muslim rulers and their spiritual guides was about to be tested yet again.

FROM THE BEGINNING of modern Saudi history the House of Saud had relied on the ulema to justify and defend the family's rule. But the Al Saud had also sought to ensure that the balance of power between the temporal and spiritual was always in its favor.

Before the kingdom grew rich, Saudi Arabia's most influential religious voice was that of the mufti, its chief Islamic scholar, Muhammad bin Ibrahim Al al-Sheikh, a descendant of the great Ibn Abd al-Wahhab and a man widely revered for his piety and theological expertise. While the family often disregarded his individual rulings, they would never have dared to dismiss or permanently alienate him. After Sheikh Muhammad's death in 1969, however, the Al Saud decided not to appoint a new mufti, obviously reluctant to permit a single individual to gain such influence. Instead, the family tried to rein in the religious establishment by institutionalizing the issuing of *fatwas*: In 1971, it created the Council of Senior Ulema as the kingdom's supreme religious authority, a panel of some seventeen to twenty-two scholars, to rule on the Islamic correctness of political questions. Though individual scholars on the panel could continue issuing their own *fatwas* on theological issues, the council, as a group, was to state its view only on issues specifically raised by the Al Saud. In addition, the recently established Ministry of Justice was given power that the mufti had previously exercised.[69] Ministers, unlike muftis, could be hired and fired.

For a while, this new structure, coupled with the oil billions pouring into the kingdom, shifted the balance of power strongly in favor of the Al Saud. But in 1979 the family's authority was shaken by two traumatic events: Ayatollah Ruholla Khomeini's militant Shiite Islamic revolution in Iran and the seizure of the Great Mosque at Mecca.

From its inception Iran's revolutionary government had excoriated the Al Saud, whose oil it, too, coveted. "There Is No King in Islam," the Iranian slogans declared, challenging the Saudi monarchy's Islamic legitimacy. Equally if not more jolting was the seizure in November of the holy sites of Mecca by several hundred Sunni Islamic militants—Ikhwan, they called themselves, after the kingdom's original religious warriors. Suddenly, the kingdom was under attack not only by its historical foes—Iran's Shiites—but also by its own Sunni radicals from the Wahhabi heartland. It took the Saudis, assisted by French (infidel) paratroopers and poison nerve gas, two weeks and the death of 127 security officials to evict the rebels from the mosque and the basements and safe houses to which they retreated. The holy places had been profaned by bloodshed, undermining the Al Saud's role as Mecca's protector.[70]

At about the same time, Saudi Shiite Muslims, aroused by Iran's revolution, rioted to protest systematic discrimination against them. The kingdom was home to roughly 700,000 Shia, the vast majority of them in the oil-rich Eastern Province. More than twenty people died, dozens were injured, and hundreds more were detained in the campaign to repress them.

Given this dual challenge, the kingdom's nervous rulers had little choice but to stress their religious credentials and make concessions, most of them superficial, to Islamic hard-liners. After the mosque rebellion, for instance, the government removed women broadcasters from the Arabic television channel (though they remained on the English channel) and ordered that photos of women not appear in Saudi newspapers.[71] Yet another reflection of royal anxiety was King Fahd's decision in 1986 to be addressed from then on not as "Your Majesty," but as the "Custodian of the Two Holy Mosques, King of Saudi Arabia," a reference to the Al Saud's stewardship of the holy sites of Mecca and Medina, on whose maintenance he was spending more than $100 million a month. But although the pendulum had swung back slightly toward the religious establishment, the shift was ultimately blunted by the kingdom's huge prosperity and the Al Saud's even more enormous generosity. On key issues, the family could still afford to have its way.

As tensions abated, the family returned to centralizing authority. Increasingly the government tried to use the ulema for what many Saudis considered political rather than religious ends. In 1980, for example, after Libya's erratic Muammar Qaddafi challenged the kingdom's right to control Mecca and Medina, the government not only severed diplomatic relations with Tripoli; it secured from the ulema, in an ominous echo of early Islamic days, a *fatwa* calling Qaddafi an apostate.[72]

The ulema, for their part, chafed over their marginalization but understood that no honorable Sunni Muslim jurist would criticize the ruler publicly. Their role was to persuade the Al Saud privately that its actions were misguided. Not until the Gulf war was the balance of power between the sultan and the "sultan's jurists," as Khomeini called the Saudi ulema, at issue again.

BY THE TIME of the Iraqi invasion of Kuwait in the summer of 1990, most of the malleable Senior Ulema Council members were no longer taken seriously by the public. Most Saudis saw them as creatures of the state, beholden to the royal family for their posts and salaries. But Saudis still had a high regard for the council's aged, blind chief, Sheikh Bin Baz. Despite his espousal of some obscurantist views, the sheikh was widely admired for his humility, religious wisdom, and piety. Unlike so many in Arabia, he did not crave worldly goods or power. Something of a rebel himself in his younger years, Bin Baz had been assigned to a faraway post in Medina for his theological differences with other senior ulema.

Given Bin Baz's moral authority as well as his usually staunch defense of government policies, the ruling family had overlooked many of the sheikh's controversial and, in some cases, downright discomforting rulings. When in 1966, for example, he had condemned what he termed the Copernican "heresy," insisting, as the Koran said, that the sun moved, Egyptian journalists, much to President Nasser's delight, had mercilessly mocked the leading cleric as a reflection of Saudi primitiveness.[73]

The family was usually able to ignore Bin Baz when his rulings clashed with the kingdom's modernization plans or when the issue at hand was not likely to arouse public passion. The government, for instance, had disregarded his *fatwa* that photography was *haram* and that the makers of such graven images, or even those who refused to tear them up, would suffer "the severest punishment on the Day of Resurrection."[74]

During the Great Mosque seizure, a crucial test of ulema loyalty, Bin Baz had proved supportive of the family, but only to a point. King Khaled secured a *fatwa* from the Senior Ulema Council sanctioning the use of force to evict the young militants. But when the government asked the ulema to declare them "apostates," as they had Qaddafi, they refused. Instead, the scholars called them "outlaws"—*muharbin* in Arabic, or those who rebel against authority, a serious crime in Islamic law but not as grave a spiritual matter as renouncing one's faith.[75]

On the eve of the allied land invasion in the Gulf war, however, Bin Baz not only sanctioned the presence of foreign forces in the kingdom, he also blessed the war as a jihad, thus implying that soldiers killed during this holy conflict would go straight to paradise.[76]

To reward such loyalty, King Fahd in 1992 named Bin Baz to the long-vacant post of mufti, the kingdom's chief religious guide, having previously taken the precaution of shifting many of the post's functions to the government. But when the militants circulated their first petition demanding a purer, more Islamic government, Bin Baz was ominously silent. Only after the second petition became public did he criticize the petitioners, and only then at the government's request. Such protests, he ruled, were "totally against the teaching of Allah and His Prophet."

In 1993 the Al Saud, increasingly confident that Bin Baz and the other senior ulema would not oppose the family publicly, cracked down harder on religious dissidents. It dismissed many militant preachers and scholars, most notably Sheikh Safar al-Hawali, the dean of Islamic studies at Mecca's Umm al-Qura University, and Sheikh Salman al-Audah, a charismatic thirty-eight-year-old preacher from conservative Burayda, known as "Arabia's Khomeini."

At the same time, the government also closed down the kingdom's first "human rights" committee, the Committee for the Defense of Legitimate Rights (CDLR). Founded by Muhammad Massari, a burly American-educated physicist who had been tortured in jail,[77] the committee had a rather unconventional approach to human rights, even by Saudi standards. One of the CDLR's founders, Sheikh Abdallah bin Jibrin, had asserted that the 700,000 Shiite Muslims in Arabia were apostates — a crime punishable by death. Another CDLR stalwart, Abdella Hamoud al-Taweijri, had demanded that the women drivers be jailed as "prostitutes." Other members had supported a total ban on women working, the creation of religious committees in each government ministry to review the compliance of all laws and regulations with the sharia, and further restrictions on the already stultifyingly insipid state radio and television.

After Massari sought political asylum in London, his relaunched CDLR began flooding Saudi offices, even royal mailboxes, with unsolicited faxes detailing the defection of two Saudi diplomats in London and New York, stories of corruption within the House of Saud, its repressive practices at home, and its manipulation abroad by Israel, the United States, and the degenerate, atheist West. From their safe haven in Britain, government critics had finally found a public forum other than the mosque from which to publicize their grievances.

At first the CDLR bulletins were enthusiastically received by Saudis, but as CDLR bulletins became increasingly strident, the group became less credible.[78]

In late 1994, Bin Baz attacked the London-based dissidents. "My advice to all is not to read their bulletins," he said, since they were aimed at "dividing the ranks of Muslims" and were hence "absolutely evil."[79]

In the fall of 1994, the government arrested more than four hundred dissidents, including Sheikhs Hawali and Audah. Initially the government denied having arrested anyone. The next day, it said it had only detained 110 "fanatics." But a subsequent announcement stated that it had released 130 people and was still holding 20 more.[80] While the government maintained that the religious establishment had supported the arrests, the state-controlled press published only a year-old letter from Sheikh Bin Baz stating that the radicals should be "questioned" about their views by a committee of religious scholars. Apparently the dissident sheikhs were questioned and given an opportunity to recant but had refused to do so. Bin Baz was suddenly and inexplicably unavailable for further comment.

The government chafed. Bin Baz seemed reluctant to be as supportive of royal policy as expected. Only a month before the arrests, for example, he had denounced the 1994 UN population conference as "an insult to Islam." The ruling not only forced Saudi Arabia to skip the meeting, an insult to its Gulf war ally Egypt; it also complicated government efforts to tackle a real threat to the regime's stability: the kingdom's burgeoning population. In late 1994, Sheikh Bin Baz, without being asked to do so, also guardedly blessed Israel's peace agreements with the PLO and Jordan. The sheikh, who had condemned Egypt's peace with Israel a decade earlier, now ruled that Islam permitted peace with Israel, the Arabs' implacable foe, at least until Muslims gained the strength to evict the Jews from Palestine or make them pay tribute. Each Middle Eastern state, he said, had to pursue "its own interests." If Muslim interests were served by making peace with Jews, exchanging ambassadors, and bilateral trade, "fine." [81] Bin Baz's personal initiative mortified the Al Saud, which was resisting Washington's prodding to play a more publicly prominent role in the peace process. The *fatwa* was soon denounced on theological grounds by Muslim Brotherhood–aligned sheikhs in Egypt. The criticism was so intense that Bin Baz soon "clarified" his *fatwa*, stressing that he had blessed Arab-Israeli peace as only a temporary measure.

The Saudi government decided it needed yet another vehicle to contain what officials called "extremist" threats and to control religious activity. In October 1994, King Fahd set up a Supreme Council of Islamic Affairs, headed by his brother Prince Sultan, the defense minister and a man not known for his religious sensibilities. The council was to consider aid requests from Islamic groups and act as what one official called an ombudsman on Islamic affairs.

With the Ministry of Islamic Affairs now in charge of mosques, religious property, and *da'wa*, or Muslim education and proselytizing, and the Supreme Council of Islamic Affairs monitoring religious donations to, and cooperation with, foreign Islamic groups, the Al Saud had effectively shifted even more of Bin Baz's power to state functionaries. Because it could neither dismiss nor publicly berate the mufti, it had tried instead to drown him in religious bureaucracy. This trustworthy but aging scholar, Saudi officials quietly told me, could not be relied upon to keep militants out of the mosques and prevent charitable contributions from reaching the kingdom's Islamic enemies.

Although the family and friends of those still under detention continued to grieve bitterly, most Saudis were talking less about the CDLR and the jailed dissidents by mid-1995 than they had the year before. Bin Baz still refused to sanction the government's arrests on religious grounds, but he refrained from criticizing the royal family publicly. I recalled a notice I had seen in the *Saudi Gazette* in the spring of 1995. Mufti Bin Baz had issued a *fatwa* concluding that marking sale items "nonreturnable and nonrefundable" was contrary to Islamic practice — an important commercial matter but hardly of pressing political import.

Had the Al Saud finally managed to bring the potentially troublesome ulema under firm control? Unable to get another Saudi visa, I met my friend Abdullah in a Paris café and asked him to interpret the sensitive interaction between the family and its religious scholars. Had the family finally prevailed?

"Yes and no," Abdullah patiently told me, puffing on his Marlboros and sipping espresso, a poor substitute, we both agreed, for Arabic coffee around a campfire in the dunes near Burayda. Yes, the Al Saud had temporarily tamed, contained, and marginalized the role of the Senior Ulema Council and even that of Sheikh Bin Baz. But the ruling family was still vulnerable, Abdullah asserted.

The militants who challenged the government on Islamic grounds emerged precisely because there was a religious vacuum in the kingdom, because the senior ulema's authority and integrity had been compromised. "In a Wahhabi Islamic state like ours," he said, "people and the state feel a need for such legitimation. So the people looked elsewhere."

What they found were Dr. Massari's CDLR and other militant Islamic opponents. These dissidents were unlike those who had seized the Great Mosque in Mecca and challenged the state's adherence to Islam seventeen years ago. The modern rebels were not only college educated and often familiar with the West, their movement was truly national — no longer sectarian or regionally or tribally based — and hence potentially a genuine threat, Abdullah told me.

The Islamists, he said, were able to mobilize and exploit essentially middle-class aspirations and economic frustrations "in the name of Islam" because the family had banned all alternative forms of political expression.

But why did the Al Saud care? As long as the senior ulema were unwilling to side openly with the militants — no matter how sympathetic they might be to the radicals' goals, if not their methods — as long as the ulema stood publicly with the family, was the balance of power not comfortably with the Al Saud?

"Power has shifted, yes. But not legitimacy," he replied. By using the scholars as a shield against demands that had national resonance, the family had undermined them and hence its own Islamic credentials. In an avowedly "Islamic" state, that was a problem.

HAVING DONE what they could to contain their own internal Islamic challenge, the Saudis moved to counter Saudi-based radical threats to the kingdom's Arab allies. In 1995, Prince Nayef, the Saudi interior minister, met openly with his counterparts from Egypt, Tunisia, Algeria, and other quasi-secular Arab regimes to enhance cooperation against Islamic "extremism." In what was by Saudi standards remarkable candor, Prince Nayef conceded that wealthy Saudis were still funding militant groups abroad, but without the "knowledge or consent of the government or the bulk of the people." He also blamed the kingdom's internal unrest partly on "some Arab brethren who used to work in the kingdom." Such men, he said, a reference, Saudis inferred, to the most extremist Muslim Brethren and members of its spin-off groups, were no longer welcome. "Any hand that is extended to tamper with the security of the Saudi citizen or the country, to whomever it may be," he said, would be "cut off." [82]

Nayef meant it. In response to the kingdom's soaring crime rate after the Gulf war, the government had sharply increased its beheadings of murderers, rapists, and drug traffickers, executing a record eighty-five men in 1993 and fifty-nine in 1994, most of them foreigners. Public executions, amputations, floggings, and other sharia-mandated punishments suspended during the Gulf war were reinstituted in what foreigners called Riyadh's "Chop Square," in the heart of the old downtown. In May 1995 the government executed by "crucifixion", six foreigners in Jidda for armed robbery, murder, and drug trafficking. [83] An Interior Ministry statement warned that anyone who disturbed the kingdom's

or tranquility would "meet the same fate." Such penalties, of course, were
itory under sharia, but they were imposed only by the Islamic states of
Saudi Arabia, Iran, and Sudan — so far.

To contain dissidents like Dr. Massari more effectively, the government
had quietly authorized the Ministry of Interior to assemble a seventeen-man
team to study the backgrounds of some twenty-eight hundred militants. Not
surprisingly, the study found that many radicals were veterans of the Saudi- and
American-financed jihad in Afghanistan. They had returned to the kingdom
expecting to be welcomed as heroes, but society had ignored them. According
to scholars familiar with the study, the psychological profiles of the militants
were similar to those of drug abusers and other dysfunctional Saudis: Many
came from poorer backgrounds and were victims of abusive fathers; a higher
than usual percentage came from homes in which fathers had taken second
wives; many of their own mothers had been forced to leave their homes. A
second, older group from which the militant leaders emerged had been sent
abroad for advanced studies, but had failed as students. The study concluded,
ominously, that their militancy was not a passing phase, that firm action was
needed to control them.

After the war the government severed aid to Islamic groups that had stood
with Saddam.[84] Responding to pressure from Egypt and other Gulf war allies
facing militant Islamic challenges, the government in 1993 banned the collection of money within the kingdom for "charitable" Muslim causes without
Interior Ministry permit. The regulation, officials explained, was aimed at di-
minishing the annual subsidy to ostensible Islamic causes of at least $1 billion,
some of which was funneled to militant groups throughout the Middle East.

In a rare action the government revoked the Saudi citizenship of Usama
Bin Laden, a wealthy young financier known for his passionate support of the
Afghan rebels and other Islamic causes. One radical Jordanian splinter group
he had financed, "Muhammad's Army," had attempted in 1993 to assassinate
Prince Abdullah, the son of Jordan's King Hussein, according to senior Arab
officials. During the war, a Saudi prince told me, Bin Laden had marched into
several princes' offices with maps and flowcharts to demonstrate how the kingdom could defend itself without foreign forces. Expelled from Riyadh, Bin
Laden now shuttled between London and Khartoum with a new passport provided by Sudan's radical Islamic regime.

For years Arab leaders had complained that Saudi Arabia's phenomenal
but undiscriminating generosity toward any vaguely Islamic group or cause had
made the kingdom the region's most important, if unwitting, purveyor of Islamic
fanaticism.

Saudi ties to Islamic radicals dated back to the 1950s and 1960s, when
the kingdom took in hundreds of militant Muslim Brethren fleeing Nasser's
murderous anti-Brotherhood campaign. While the Wahhabi religious establishment had sharp political and dogmatic disagreements with its fellow Islamists
from Egypt,[85] the ruling family initially considered the Egyptian radicals useful.

Not only did their presence help reinforce the kingdom's legitimacy against challenges inspired by the godless, Communist-inspired Arab nationalists of Nasser's Egypt; the Brethren were also needed in the kingdom's new schools and colleges as teachers in a society that was then 85 percent illiterate. In 1960, for example, most professors at the kingdom's new Medina University were Egyptian Muslim Brethren, except in the all-important theology department, from which non-Wahhabis were excluded. By the time the ruling Sauds had trained their own teachers and could send the Egyptians home, the kingdom was facing the Islamic challenge of Iran's revolution. After the 1979 attack on Mecca's Great Mosque, the Saudi government and the Egyptian Muslim Brethren made a pact to insulate the Sunni kingdom from further mayhem: The Egyptian Ikhwan was granted permission to remain in the kingdom, provided it did not operate independently within it; in return, the Brethren agreed to help the Saudi government, through organizations like the government-sponsored World Muslim League, maintain contact with foreign Sunni Islamic groups. Thus, the Egyptian Brotherhood, according to one scholar, was instrumental in determining which groups received Saudi support.[86] Only after the Egyptian Brotherhood supported Iraq in the Gulf war did this cozy relationship end.[87]

The Gulf war, more than anything else, persuaded Riyadh to abandon, at least temporarily, its policy of trying to co-opt militant Islamic groups by buying them off. The radicals did not accept being cut off gracefully. In 1994, for example, Hassan al-Turabi, the de facto ruler of militantly Islamic Sudan, denounced his early and generous patron almost as harshly as he did communism. The Saudis, he told me, "with their monarchy and their secular laws and secular elites," had propagated a "very conservative Islam throughout the Middle East." But now they, too, were facing a "full-fledged Islamic movement" that would no longer be "bought off." The House of Saud, he gloated through his thin, pursed lips, was "in quite a mess."

Only after the Gulf war did the government finally understand the extent to which many of its own citizens had been "contaminated" by the anti-Saudi propaganda spread by the very groups it had supported, a Saudi prince told me. The Saudis were not alone in this error, however. Before the collapse of the Soviet Union, the American CIA, Egypt's Anwar Sadat, and even Israel had tried to combat radical nationalist movements by "playing the Islamic card" as a counterweight to leftist revolutionary groups.

Meanwhile, Riyadh was strengthening its ties to America as further insurance against a militant upheaval in the kingdom. Contrary to many published accounts, Riyadh-Washington ties were strained after the war. For one thing, King Fahd had been stunned by America's decision to end the war before Saddam Hussein was destroyed. According to knowledgeable Saudi and American officials, Riyadh had done its best to keep the conflict going. First, senior Saudi officials had urged the Americans to continue the aerial bombing of Iraq's retreating army for two or three more days. When that failed, they recommended that the allies bomb Republican Guard divisions on the outskirts of

Baghdad. When this request, too, was denied, the Saudis deliberately slowed down the translation of Iraq's acceptance of the terms of surrender, which President Bush insisted that King Fahd approve before it was signed. When the translation was done, an administration official told me, Saudi officials ordered their linguists to translate it again.

Fahd was still determined to topple the ungrateful Saddam, to whom Riyadh had given more than $25 billion in aid during Iraq's war with Iran. For Fahd, the fight had become personal: After the war Saddam sent an assassination squad to the kingdom to try to kill him.[88] But Saudi Arabia, also keen to retain U.S. favor, maintained diplomatic silence when American officials blamed the war's sudden end on Riyadh's concern about the possible disintegration of Iraq in the wake of Saddam Hussein's death or sudden departure.

I recalled what seemed the king's genuine anguish over the impending war when he delivered a ninety-minute monologue to a small group of reporters, including me, in the Saudi desert in January 1991, just before the war. The king, who rarely gives interviews to foreign reporters, was an imposing figure, well over six feet tall. Dressed in his crisp white *thobe*, a gold-embroidered, camel-colored cloak, and the traditional red-and-white-checked head scarf, he greeted us in a makeshift tent at King Khaled Military City, one of the world's largest military installations. His was the face of a hawk: His shrewd, piercing brown eyes inspected our little group, the majority of whom were women. In his younger years, Fahd had a well-documented reputation as a gambler and rake. But as king, a new, more sober (if not thinner) Fahd had emerged — protection in part against enemies who sought to disparage his piety and religious credentials. He seemed to me deeply distraught over the crisis. A man's word was everything in Arab culture, and Saddam had betrayed him. His eyes also told me that the Gulf war was, as I feared, inevitable. But Fahd said that he expected — and hoped — that Saddam would withdraw to "spare everyone bloodshed and catastrophe."

After the war, the Saudis demonstrated their gratitude for America's backing by, among other things, supporting the Bush administration's effort to convene an Arab-Israeli peace conference in Madrid and quietly agreeing to pay for much of it. Riyadh even ordered its notoriously anti-Jewish media to begin referring to "Israel" rather than "the Zionist enemy" and took other steps, most unpublicized, to advance the cause of peace.[89]

But the mounting Islamic criticism of the Sauds' pro-peace, pro-Western stance complicated the kingdom's bold partnership with America. Gradually, the kingdom retreated to its prewar public posture; at least publicly, the Al Saud began distancing itself from Washington. While the Saudis, America's largest arms purchasers, continued ordering American weapons and goods, Riyadh became distinctly unhelpful on other matters. The Saudis repeatedly rebuffed American requests to base a brigade's worth of equipment on Saudi territory, even after Saddam moved his forces toward the Kuwaiti border in a feint in October 1993.[90] American diplomats protested, unofficially, of course, Mutawwa harassment of Bee Bentsen, wife of the then U.S. treasury secretary, during an official visit in 1993, according to Washington officials. Finally, the kingdom spurned American pleas to bolster Jordan's King Hussein—whom King Fahd despised for having "betrayed" him during the Gulf war—by selling oil to Jordan at concessionary prices in order to end Amman's dependence on Iraqi oil imports.[91] Such diplomatic "favors" for Washington, a Saudi diplomat explained, would expose the ruling family to charges that it was an American pawn, and hence strengthen militant forces in the kingdom. Aid to some Islamists was quietly resumed.

In Washington, I had lunch with the visiting Saudi diplomat who had so confidently predicted the emergence of a bolder Saudi foreign policy after the Gulf war. He dismissed the diplomatic tensions as marginal. The Saudis knew they needed American support to defend the kingdom. Though twice as large as they had been before the Gulf war, the Saudi armed forces could not fend off potential threats unilaterally, nor even in alliance with the Gulf Cooperation Council. ("Big shell, little snail," an American diplomat had once denigrated the group.) Despite appearances, the U.S.-Saudi relationship was growing stronger. Saudi foreign policy was far more pragmatic than it had been before the Gulf war, he insisted. "It's still 'No More Mr. Nice Guy'—sort of."

By MID-1995 the House of Saud had buttressed its stewardship of the kingdom's holy mosques—in Mecca and Medina—and, of course, the Saudi treasury. To assuage its liberal technocrats, King Fahd had finally created in 1992 a *majlis al-shura* (Shura Council), the consultative council that every Saudi king since Abdulaziz had vowed to establish. Saudi liberals were stunned and delighted to see that none of the council's sixty members, appointed for four-year terms, was a prince and that most were fellow technocrats—lawyers, engineers, journalists, professors, and civil servants. At least thirty-two held doctorates, twenty-two of them from American universities. There were no radical Islamic members.[92] The council's chairman, Muhammad bin Jubeir, was a commoner, a former justice minister, and a highly regarded judge on the Senior Ulema Council, which had upheld the death sentences of Juhaiman al-Utaibi, the leader of the 1979 uprising at the Great Mosque, and sixty-two of his followers.

Before long, though, Saudis were joking about the council, which was theoretically responsible for preparing new legislation for royal approval, but was soon derided as impotent. Offered the gift of a parrot while traveling abroad, one joke went, the Shura Council speaker was said to have replied: "No, thank you. I have sixty of them already." By the end of 1995, however, Saudis were laughing less. Slowly, quietly, the council was having an impact. During the summer of 1994, Prince Saud bin Faisal, the foreign minister, had spent six hours testifying on the kingdom's foreign policy. Then the finance minister had asked the majlis to support budget reductions that King Fahd was resisting. That same year, Fahd also sought the council's advice on whether the kingdom should scale back its massive entitlements, and if so, how. To the majlis's credit, it politely refused to endorse the government's preferred plan to impose excise taxes. The king imposed the increases anyway. But he felt the need to claim that he had secured the majlis's indirect endorsement.[93] By the summer of 1995 every cabinet minister had appeared before the council at least once.

Nathaniel Kern, an American oil analyst and one of the few Americans to have attended a Saudi university, took the Shura Council seriously. While it was hard to gauge the council's impact, since its proceedings weren't published, he told me, even skeptics now acknowledged that the kingdom would probably not have ended its costly subsidies without it. Kern thought that within five years the council's proceedings would be broadcast on television and that the group might soon be called on to confirm the appointment of ministers. Most liberal Saudis, he said, hoped that the council would evolve into a quasi-Parliament.

Unlike many American analysts, Kern was not concerned about what Washington called the Saudi "succession" problem, although King Fahd was ailing and now seventy-three and the kingdom's designated successor, Prince Abdullah, who in early 1986 temporarily assumed power for the ailing king, was about the same age. The third kingdom had always enjoyed smooth power transitions no matter how its kings had ended their rule: through natural death, deposition, or assassination. The order of succession among the sons of King Abdulaziz was fairly clear.[94] If there was to be a succession struggle, it would occur when the grandsons' time to rule had come.

Few seasoned analysts thought the family would destroy itself, as it had during the second Saudi kingdom, by feuding over succession. The family went to extraordinary lengths to prevent outbreaks of ill will among them. After King Faisal was killed in 1975 by his twenty-six-year-old nephew, for example, the Al Saud ensured that the assassin's branch of the family would not be punished by, among other things, blessing the marriage of the nephew's daughter to one of King Abdulaziz's more promising grandsons, now the deputy oil minister. Knowing that blood feuds in Arab culture were endless and highly divisive, the Al Saud did not kill unless it felt it had to. This was the Saudi way.

The government's economic retrenchment — its elimination of inefficient subsidies and scaling back of entitlements — also reflected a serious attempt to solve a problem that, if unaddressed, might eventually weaken the throne.[95] While Saudi officials initially called expressions of concern about the kingdom's reckless spending evidence of a "Zionist plot" to undermine international financial confidence in their country, the family had moved within a year to control the budget. Unlike the United States, which, by 1995, was struggling simply to reduce the rate of growth in government spending, Saudi Arabia had cut actual spending by 20 percent in 1994 and by 6.2 percent the following year. Saudis wound up paying more for water, electricity, oil, and domestic airfares. Defense spending remained constant — which it had as a percentage of GNP since the birth of the kingdom — but education and several other ministries were cut by 20 percent. Saudis grumbled but seemed to adjust.

The government also realized that it had to reduce the 4 million foreigners working in the kingdom to create jobs for young Saudi graduates and correct its balance-of-payments deficit. So, among other steps, the government dramatically increased foreign-residence fees to induce employers to hire Saudis rather than foreigners for jobs that young Saudis would once have spurned but now wanted. A company that had advertised for ice-cream vendors—a job that most Saudis would have been ashamed to take five years ago—received three times the usual number of applicants for each opening.

In addition, the government was cautiously addressing the problem of corruption. In 1993, two years after the scandal first surfaced in *The New York Times*, the king finally shut down Chemvest, a controversial joint venture between Mobil Oil and the son of oil minister Hisham Nazer, which critics complained gave Nazer's son preferential treatment. In August 1995 the long-serving Nazer was replaced. Also dismissed was Alawi Darwish Kayal, the telecommunications minister. Several months earlier, the minister had rushed to the bedside of a business associate, Muwaffaq Al-Maydani, as he lay dying at Minnesota's Mayo Clinic. Maydani, according to Saudi businessmen, owed the minister a share of a commission for a contract his ministry had awarded. From his deathbed, Maydani made Minister Kayal the executor of his estate. But Maydani's sons challenged their father's decision. A well-connected lawyer wrote a letter demanding restitution to Maydani's heirs, copies of which were faxed throughout the kingdom. The scandal led some Saudis to believe that King Fahd must have approved the letter's dissemination and that Minister Kayal's days in office were numbered.

But cracking down on corruption among commoners was easier than controlling the princes. That would occur, Saudi analysts agreed, only when the ruling family felt truly threatened. At the moment, it did not, despite a bombing attack in November 1995 at the National Guard office that left seven dead, most of them American trainers.

"They said the kingdom would fall apart in 1973 because we had too much money," my friend the Saudi diplomat complained one day. "In 1993 they predicted we would collapse because we didn't have enough money. What kind of an economic crisis is it when you are sitting on between twenty-five and thirty percent of the world's oil reserves—another hundred years of production at current rates—with an estimated value of more than four trillion dollars?"

The Sauds were realists, for as Prince Bandar Bin Sultan, Riyadh's ambassador to Washington, had noted, Saudis lived in the desert. "You have to distinguish between a mirage and the real thing. Your survival depends on it."[96]

Even before the Gulf war Saudis knew they could not rely on their neighbors, that their region, in Bandar's words, was "filled with poisonous snakes." Iran, for one, saw the kingdom as its main rival as the uncompromising bearer of the flag of Islam and no doubt coveted Saudi oil as well. Egypt was Saudi Arabia's historical competitor, having destroyed the first Saudi kingdom's capital, Diriyya, in 1818, massacred vast numbers of civilians, and sold Arabian men, women, and children into slavery in Cairo. I had visited the forlorn former capital. To this day it remained a ruin. Iraq, for its part, had never forgiven the Wahhabis for the nineteenth-century massacre of Shiites at Karbala.

The Saudis had even fewer illusions after the Gulf war. They knew that most Arabs resented the fact that God had played a perverse trick on the more numerous, more cultured Arabs of Damascus and Cairo — the "city Arabs," as Mohammed Heikal, Nasser's chief publicist, had called them: Allah had placed enormous financial power in the barren land of the few, primitive Saudis, the marginal and backward "Desert Arabs" who had once barely survived on earnings from the annual Muslim pilgrimages to Mecca. Suddenly the Saudis had become rich — and astonishingly generous. Throughout the 1980s the kingdom spent between 4 and 7 percent of its GNP on foreign aid, or roughly $4 billion a year, the world's highest rate. But their charity had won them few Arab friends. "God had favored the hillbillies," my Saudi diplomat friend said. "Other Arabs couldn't hate God for being our friend, so they hated us instead."

Saudis sensed the contempt their "brotherly" Arabs felt for them — "tribes with flags" was how an Egyptian diplomat had dismissed them. "Oil wells with flags," a Jordanian writer during the Gulf war had agreed. They knew that the city Arabs' flattery, their sycophancy, barely masked their scorn as well as their conviction that Saudi oil was somehow rightly theirs, a conclusion expressed most vehemently by the Arab "masses" during the Gulf war. Poorer Arabs still flocked to the desert to seek their fortunes in "secular pilgrimages" of the oil age. But under their breath and their hypocritical smiles, the city Arabs muttered a traditional Arab curse: "Kiss the hand you cannot bite and ask God to break it for you."[97]

The Sauds were not fooled. They resisted reckless foreign adventures and the political "reforms" being promoted by well-meaning Western and Arab allies. The family had no intention of embracing American-style democracy, a Western form of government that was alien to its Islamic tradition of centralized, autocratic rule. "There is no democracy in Islam," Nazer, the former oil minister, once told me candidly, admitting what militant Islamists usually denied. "Ours is a society of deference, of respect for one's elders and superiors. These are our limits, but they are also our strength." King Fahd was equally blunt. In a postwar speech whose realism utterly depressed the kingdom's liberal technocrats, Fahd vowed that Saudi Arabia would never be a Western democracy.

"This state," wrote Adel al-Jubeir, a Saudi diplomat, "has overcome three challenges that would have destroyed weaker states: Nasser's radical pan-Arabism, Khomeini's militant Islamic revolution, and Saddam Hussein. Years from now, the kingdom and its brand of Islam will still be here."

He was probably right, I thought, barring some unforeseen foreign challenge — to which the United States did not respond — or a cataclysm of some kind within the kingdom.

Some of my liberal Saudi friends disagreed. Since the war, the royals had become so convinced of their virtue that they interpreted any criticism of them as an attack on Islam, my friend Abdullah complained as we drove one afternoon through Riyadh, the sun pounding against the glistening skyscrapers, stark against the sharp-angled city. "There is no dialogue with them, only deference. If you hesitate to kiss a prince's shoulder as a sign of respect at his weekly majlis, you are suspect. If you contradict him, you are subversive. Enemies abound. There has been a centralization of authority and a tightening of control. For Islamists and liberals alike, there is less freedom today than there was before the Gulf war, despite the new majlis."

A private poll conducted by Interior Minister Nayef in November 1994 confirmed the lack of public enthusiasm for the ruling family. According to an academic who was permitted to study the survey data, 10 percent of those polled expressed support for the Al Saud, 10 percent were hostile, 40 percent seemed indifferent, and another 40 percent said they were unsure how they felt.

King Fahd's remoteness and failing health, as well as his growing insensitivity to Saudi resentment of his enormous personal wealth and power, had also enhanced public disdain. A telling example was the king's meeting after the Gulf war with a delegation of American former diplomats and prominent businessmen. Fahd had expressed indignation about reports in the Western media that estimated his personal wealth at $18 billion. "Eighteen billion!" he exclaimed. "If anyone can prove I'm worth more than nine billion, I'll share it with them." His guests were stunned by what one called Fahd's declaration of a new royal "poverty line."

I understood, of course, the anger and unhappiness of my Westernized Saudi friends. Though the militant Islamists endlessly denounced the kingdom's un-Islamic ways, it was hard to imagine a more naysaying "fundamentalist" country. With most of its law based on sharia, its punishments mandated by the Koran, its strict separation and veiling of women, and its religious establishment at its ruler's right hand, Saudi Arabia seemed in many ways the quintessential militant Islamic state.

Given its brand of Islamic autocracy, Saudi Arabia was dead—for thinking men and women alike. While the kingdom was entrepreneurial, it was not truly dynamic. Public discourse and academic freedom were highly restricted. The authorities still prohibited the study of evolution, Freud, Marx, music, and Western philosophy. Professors told me that government and conservative religious informers monitored their classroom comments and that masters and doctoral dissertations were screened to ensure consistency with the "kingdom's public image." The government controlled all forms of public artistic expression. Cinemas and public theaters were banned.

Its zero tolerance of written dissent meant that there were few Saudi scientists of international standing or scholars outside religious circles with world-class reputations. There were no internationally known Saudi playwrights or film directors. There were, in fact, virtually no Saudi writers of international stature, no Saudi Naguib Mahfouz. The kingdom's one well-known novelist, Abdelrahman Munif, had hardly lived in the kingdom. After the first of a multi-part novel about life in the kingdom was published, the Saudi government revoked his passport. He had lived ever since in Damascus, of all places.

Petrodollars may have physically transformed the kingdom but not its soul.

Riyadh in the 1990s could still be described, as it was by a visitor in the 1920s, as a place where "all that redounds to the glory of man is banned."

Of course, Abdullah and his middle-class friends were unhappy. Saudi Arabia was terminally dull, and its deadness had awful consequences for Arab culture. Over the past decade the kingdom had invested hundreds of millions of dollars to acquire a friendly and influential press in Arab print, radio, and television.[98] "There is nothing now which may be called a dialogue in the Arab world," lamented Egyptian journalist Mohammed Heikal, Nasser's former champion, blaming the desperate state of affairs on Saudi Arabia.[99]

"Our intellectual landscape is as arid as our deserts," Abdullah agreed. "Young Saudis have nothing to do except visit their families and hang out in shopping malls. Intellectual life means debating whether women should be permitted to drive and the appropriate length of one's *thobe*. That is our Islam."

But I doubted that either Abdullah in Riyadh or Farida in New York was sufficiently embittered to risk a direct challenge to the family's power. They were both too frightened and had already prospered too well in the kingdom. Nor were they likely to join the CDLR of Dr. Massari, whom Britain, under Saudi and American pressure, in early 1996 announced it would deport. Why would they risk all to replace what Abdullah called the "Al Saud's authoritarianism" with "Islamic totalitarianism"?

But without the support of middle-class people like Farida and Abdullah, the radical Islamic opposition was unlikely to acquire sufficient strength to spark a coup or riots that would topple the regime.

Most of my friends seemed resigned: If the kingdom's economy prospered, stability would most likely prevail. "If the average Saudi is given a choice between revolution and a bonus, he'll take the bonus," Abdullah conceded when we last met for drinks in London. And so would he, I thought to myself. "Even if the choice is between political participation and a bonus, he'll take the bonus." While the kingdom's wealth and ardent Islam had clearly not immunized it against an "Islamic" challenge, its particular mixture of money and faith would most likely prevent such a challenge from succeeding, especially because the militants lacked a charismatic leader who could mobilize modern Saudis, as King Abdulaziz had done almost a century ago. After all, what did the militants really want? Surely not democracy. Though the Islamists invariably included it in their demands, nothing in their political program suggested that their commitment was sincere. A truly Islamic government, they said, would institute meaningful *shura* (consultation) and distribute oil revenues more equitably. But based on what they wrote and said to one another, I suspected that what they really wanted was what their Islamic counterparts in Egypt wanted — power.

With so much at stake, the family was not likely to cede it or self-destruct. If the Al Saud could no longer afford to buy off its opponents, it would continue repressing them. And if one day Sheikh Bin Baz and the Saudi religious establishment ever turned on the ruling family — a highly unlikely event, since it would mean defying its traditional Islamic role and the historical alliance between faith and power that had created the kingdom of Saudi Arabia and sustained it for so long — the ruling family would probably do what Arab leaders, Islamic or not, had always done: It would crush the ulema. Abdullah insisted that the ruling family could not do that and survive, that the Saudi people would not tolerate it. But no one knew what the family would do, or be able to get away with, to preserve its rule; perhaps not even the Al Saud.

SUDAN

IN SUDAN in the summer of 1994, a life was worth between 80,000 and 100,000 Sudanese pounds, or 372–465 U.S. dollars at the official exchange rate, half that sum on the black market, the real rate of exchange. That is what it cost to buy back a Christian or pagan child from one of the Islamic schools in which thousands of Sudanese children were being held against their will.

The self-proclaimed Islamic government of Sudan denied, of course, that it was running de facto prisons where black, non-Muslim children from southern Sudan were forced to become Muslims. It denied routinely rounding up children from marketplaces and displacement camps in the south, and even in the capital, Khartoum, and sending them to schools that gave them new Islamic names and a Muslim identity. It denied feeding them just enough beans, bread, and water to keep them alive and subjecting them to hours of daily Koranic indoctrination. The children, Sudanese officials maintained, were "orphans" of the devastating civil war between the Arab Muslim north and the Christian and animist south—"delinquents," the government spokesman insisted when I asked about the charges by human-rights and church groups. "Conversion by force is not Islamic," declared Hassan al-Turabi, the mastermind who created Sudan's Islamic regime. Turabi, a suave, radical Sunni Muslim with London University and Sorbonne degrees, was militant Sunni Islam's reigning philosopher-king, an inspiration to millions of young Arab Islamists throughout the world. "Islam," he continued, flashing me an easy, handsome smile and adjusting his white turban, "relies totally on persuasion."

Had Majok Kwai Jok been "persuaded" to change his faith? For nearly two years this twelve-year-old Christian from the south had been imprisoned in one of five government "orphanages" in Khartoum. In May 1993 he was finally "retrieved." This was the euphemism relief groups and church workers used for the process by which expensive lawyers challenged the state's custody of abducted children. When judicial remedies failed, the money went to local imams and to school officials who were quietly bribed to release children in their care.

Majok, a frail boy with short, crinkly hair, night-black skin, and bright white teeth, had been picked up along with his older cousin, Alier, near the southern town of Bor and brought to Khartoum by a Captain "Mohammed." In school, Majok and his cousin were separated and given Islamic names. He spent his day studying the Koran, parading in military drills, and learning about jihad, the holy war that the Arab, Muslim north was waging against the mostly black, non-Muslim secessionist south. In 1993 his frantic parents had come to the capital searching for him and miraculously, in a country with 2–3 million people displaced by the civil war, managed to trace Majok to the school that was holding him. With financial aid from church groups, the family petitioned the courts to rescue their son. The attorney general dismissed their petition, saying that Majok and his cousin "wanted to remain with Captain 'Mohammed,'" the Sudanese officer who had brought them there, according to a church group's memorandum on the case.

"Majok's parents learned only later that school officials had warned the boys that they would be killed if they asked to leave the school," said a woman whom I shall call Mariam, a relief worker who intervened in Majok's case.

Turned down by the courts, Mariam's friends approached the school directly. Quiet negotiations began; money was handed over. Captain "Mohammed" agreed to relinquish his ward.

"We are still looking for Alier, Majok's cousin," Mariam told me as we sipped Arabic coffee in the church's sweltering office on an airless Sunday morning in June. "We know that he is now named after the captain, but he is no longer in the school. We can't locate him."

Mariam was especially concerned because of Alier's age. "We've seen lots of children between the ages of seven and twelve. There are almost four hundred of them in the school where we found Majok. But we see almost no one older than that," she said.

I asked her what happened to all the teenage boys.

"We don't know for sure," she told me, gazing out the cracked, sand-covered glass window. There are reports that some were sold to Libya and even Saudi Arabia as slaves. "But the boys tell us that the fifteen- to seventeen-year-olds are sent to the south to the front to fight," she replied. "After they are Islamized, they become mujahideen, soldiers in the holy war against the southern Christians and animists. In other words, they are sent south to kill 'infidels' — their parents."

The forced Islamization of non-Muslim children was one of many heart-breaking facts of life in Hassan Turabi's putative Islamic regime, which, during my last visit in June 1994, was about to mark its fifth year in power.[1] The children were being enslaved by the descendants of Sudanese Arabs who less than a hundred years ago had run some of the world's richest slave markets.

The legacy of the slave trade and the triumph a century ago of revolutionary Islam under the thirteen-year rule of the man who called himself the Mahdi, the Muslim Messiah, continued to haunt modern Sudan. In fact, Turabi's Islamic state was in many ways a throwback to the harsh and uncompromising rule of the Mahdi, the messianic revolutionary and Islamic leader who, in 1885, had killed Britain's eccentric general Charles George "Chinese" Gordon, expelled his Egyptian-Ottoman forces from Sudan, flattened Khartoum, and established one of the region's first modern, militant Islamic states.

Except for the revenues derived from its market in human beings, Sudan had — and still has — few economic resources; it had always been poor. Now it was bankrupt. Inflation, which exceeded 100 percent for the fourth consecutive year, was still rising when I visited Hassan Turabi; foreign debt, estimated at more than 280 percent of its gross domestic product, was unprecedented in Sudan.

The civil war between the Muslim Arab north and the Christian pagan south, home to more than a quarter of the population, raged on. More than 1.3 million of the 25 million Sudanese had been killed in the war, most of them southerners, but no end to the slaughter seemed near. Though most Sudanese were understandably desperate about the future, the Islamic government was ever more deeply entrenched.

This Sudan was strikingly different from the land I had first visited almost twenty years before — the first of many visits. While the Sudan had always been poor and disorganized, what a gentler, more hopeful place it had been only two decades ago. My affection for this land, however, was not shared by most journalists or by many earlier visitors.

The ancient Egyptian pharaohs who periodically ruled Sudan rarely mentioned Cush, as they called it, without adding the epithet "wretched."[2] In 23 B.C., a Roman army had moved south from Egypt into the Sudan and razed Napata, the capital of the kingdom then called Meroe. But the Roman commander soon withdrew, concluding that Meroe was "too poor to warrant its conquest."[3] Four centuries later, the kings of Meroe and two adjoining states formed a kingdom called Nubia and converted to the ancient form of Christianity practiced by Egypt's Copts. Two hundred years later, the Arabs carried Muhammad's Islam to Nubia, laying siege to the city of Dunqulah and destroying its grand cathedral. But once again, the price of conquest was too high: The Nubians, brilliantly effective archers — "eye smiters," they were called — repelled the Arabs. Their efforts to conquer the Nubians having failed, the Arabs signed the first of a series of treaties with them that would determine the relationship between the Arabs and Nubian Africans for some six hundred years. These accords, among other things, required the Nubian kings to provide the Arabs with an annual tribute of hundreds of male and female slaves — and, later, with elephants, giraffes, and other wild beasts.[4]

Over the centuries the area was gradually Islamized, not by the sword but through trade and wandering holy men (*fugara*), who performed miracles and attracted popular followings. This so-called Sufism, a highly personalized, mystical interpretation of Islam, was different from the dry, rigid Islam that had emerged in nearby Arabia. By the fifteenth and sixteenth centuries Muslims had become a majority in the old Nubian areas, which, in the nineteenth century, would be unified for the first time and called the Sudan. In Arabic, *bilad al-Sudan* meant "country of the blacks"; it was not a compliment.

In 1820 the Egyptians, under the Ottoman khedive Mohammed Ali, conquered the Sudan and placed their garrison at Khartoum, the windswept plain where the White Nile and the Blue Nile merged. Like Shendy and Zanzibar before it, the city soon distinguished itself as Africa's greatest slave market.

By the mid–nineteenth century Khartoum's reputation had not improved. "A more miserable, filthy, and unhealthy place can hardly be imagined," said Samuel Baker, the English explorer of the Nile who visited Khartoum in the early 1860s and was later chosen as its governor-general by the Egyptian-Ottoman rulers. Alan Moorehead, the historian of the Nile, described the Khartoum that Baker and his wife inhabited. "Dead animals lay rotting in the undrained streets and the only supply of water was a muddy fluid brought up from the river. . . . Nothing in the town [of thirty thousand people] could be done except by bribery; torture and flogging took place as a matter of course in the prisons. Throughout most of the year the heat was overwhelming."[5] Baker, like so many nineteenth-century travelers, was even less impressed with southern Sudan, or the region known as the Upper Nile. "All is wild and brutal, hard and unfeeling," he wrote; and, unlike the north, there were no "no ancient histories to charm the present with memories of the past."[6]

Sudan's history was forever changed — and its despotic Islamic destiny foreshadowed — when Muhammad Ahmed (1845–1885), a remote descendant of the Prophet and the son of a poor boat builder, declared in 1881 that he was the "expected one," the "Mahdi of Islam." Though there is no mention of a Mahdi in the Koran, a *hadith* foretold the coming of such a savior one day. So the miserably poor Sudanese, prone to Sufi mysticism and superstition, flocked to join him. Did not their Muhammad, like the Prophet himself, have the same V-shaped gap between his two front teeth? The Mahdi's supporters became known as the Ansar, a Koranic word meaning "helpers," the name that the Prophet had given his first converts in Medina after fleeing Mecca. As the Wahhabis had done in Arabia, Muhammad Ahmed mobilized the Sudanese to conquer for their faith. And like the Wahhabis, what the Mahdi's men lacked in arms, they made up for in organization, discipline, and willingness to die.

In 1885 the Mahdi's forces enraged Britain by storming Charles Gordon's palace, killing Britain's odd hero, and planting his head, with its neatly clipped white hair and matching mustache and once piercing blue eyes, on a stake near the Mahdi's tent.

Gordon had also been a man of stubborn religious fervor, a Christian version of the Mahdi. Disobeying orders to evacuate the city, he had stayed to defend Khartoum and the reforms he had imposed as governor-general — a ban on slavery and some of the harshest traditional punishments, and also on bribery to secure an audience with the governor and his aides—an enduring custom in the Middle East. But it was Gordon's efforts to end the slave trade, a mainstay of the Sudanese economy, that had helped unify the powerful slave-trading Muslim tribes and Islamic sheikhs under the Mahdi's leadership. For all their faults, the Mahdi and Caliph Abdullahi gave the Sudanese their first taste of independence and an Islamic state.

Their reign was harsh indeed. Like religious fanatics before and since, the Mahdi and Abdullahi insisted on absolute obedience. Any believer who challenged them was an "infidel," worse than the nonbelievers and a handful of Western captives who were slaves. Blasphemy meant death. The smallest infractions resulted in punishments mandated by sharia—floggings, stonings, and amputations.[7]

The "Mahdiya" imposed a return to the basics of their faith: Singing, dancing, swearing, alcohol, and jewelry were banned. So was the wearing of fancy clothes, the fez, and even shoes (the garb of the heretical Egyptians). According to Father Joseph Ohrwalder, an Austrian Catholic priest who was held hostage for ten years, all women, even girls over five, had to be veiled.

As it would his successors, power soon corrupted the once fierce young puritan. The Mahdi soon grew so fat from date wine that he had to be carried to Friday prayers by several strong adherents. None of this, however, affected his public standing. Ohrwalder and the other European hostages who hated him conceded that Sudanese of all tribes and classes adored the Mahdi. Beggars praised him as they rattled their cups; poets composed verses in his honor. Women, it was said, were mad for him. "The Mahdi is the light of our eyes," a popular song began.

Even his critics were impressed with his success at unifying Sudan's fractious tribes and sects. "There is no doubt that, until he was ruined by unbridled sensuality," wrote Francis Reginald Wingate, the head of British intelligence in Egypt's army who had studied his enemy with care and dispassion, "this man had the strongest head and the clearest mental vision of any man in the two million square miles of which he more or less made himself master before he died."[8]

The cruel and quick-tempered Caliph Abdullahi, the Mahdi's successor, managed to expand the Mahdian empire to include territory half the size of Europe and to maintain a primitive but effective postal service, which was more than Sudan's current Islamic government could do.

There were other similarities between the Mahdiya and Sudan's modern Islamic despots. In 1888 and 1889, when famine hit the Sudan, the *kalifa* and his entourage ate well while thousands starved and died, resorting even to cannibalism. Under Abdullahi's reign some 75 percent of Sudan's then 9 million people died or were killed.[9] "It seemed as if the entire Sudan lay under a curse," Father Ohrwalder wrote.

In 1898, Britain avenged Gordon's murder, and by 1899 it had reconquered most of Sudan. A young correspondent under Herbert Kitchener's command, Winston Churchill, described the breathtakingly futile last assault by the caliph's fifty thousand men upon the British: "The whole face of the slope beneath became black with swarming savages," Churchill wrote. "Above them waved hundreds of banners, and the sun, glinting on many thousand hostile spearpoints, spread a sparkling cloud." Apart from some obsolete Remington rifles the Sudanese had captured in battle, however, those "hostile spearpoints" were the *kalifa*'s only weapons; Kitchener's forces had machine guns and heavy artillery. Undaunted, the Sudanese charged straight into what one correspondent called a fiery "wall of lead." Churchill said that the battle was "the most signal triumph ever gained by the arms of science over barbarians." G. W. Stevens, a British war correspondent, was more objective: "No white troops would have faced that torrent of death for five minutes," he wrote. "It was not a battle, but an execution." More than ten thousand of the *kalifa*'s men were killed; British casualties stood at four hundred.

Kitchener then rebuilt Khartoum. So as to leave Gordon's killers in no doubt about who was in charge, he laid out new Khartoum in the pattern of a Union Jack.

IN 1976, when I first visited Khartoum — meaning "elephant's trunk" in Arabic, an allusion to the city's shape — the capital was a flat, sand-colored strip of 2 million people sprawled chaotically along the banks of the Blue and White Niles. Sudan's hodgepodge of humanity was like nothing I had ever seen before. Neither Arab nor African, Sudan was a mixture of both. Unlike busy, cosmopolitan Cairo, Khartoum had people of many colors who never seemed to have much to do. I was repeatedly struck by their great gentleness, their generosity and kindness toward one another and strangers. The men were forever smiling and greeting one another happily in their flowing snow-white robes — djellabas — and half-foot-high turbans wound from four yards of white cotton. "In the Sudan people are not content with a single handshake," a nineteenth-century English journalist had observed. The interchange of courtesies and caresses was "interminable."[10]

Sudanese women were equally striking — tall, slender, and alluring in their *thobes* — translucent or brightly colored wraps that they draped casually over their chocolate bodies and around their sleek black hair. No wonder they were once so sought after as slaves and concubines in neighboring Egypt and Turkey and in modern times as mistresses and second wives in the wealthy Gulf states.

Khartoum's sun-baked skyline, without tall buildings, was full of light. Its most elegant streets and buildings were those the British had built in stolid, neoclassical brick. Wealthy Sudanese traditionally shunned the ostentation of their Arab counterparts in the Levant and the Gulf. The rich hid their money behind crude mud walls that enclosed fairly simple houses with lush, beautifully kept gardens — fruit, palm, and olive trees, acacias, jasmines, and the dramatic jacarandas, whose reddish orange flowers bloomed in spring and early summer, decorating wealthy and poor neighborhoods alike. The homes of the rich were maintained by black servants from the south; their children sought prosperity abroad — as accountants, lawyers, doctors, and other professionals, well-paid and prestigious retainers of Gulf princes and wealthy *effendi* of Egypt.

In Khartoum it was hard to escape the old-fashioned hum of electric fans; only the Hilton, diplomats' homes, and those of the very wealthy were reliably air-conditioned. But every Sudanese home and office offered visitors something to drink: Pepsi, or "Bepsi," as the Sudanese call it, pronouncing, as most Arabic speakers do, the sounds "p" and "b" as if they were the same, Arabic coffee with cardamom, iced tea, freshly squeezed lemonade, iced carcaday — the bitter beet-colored herb that makes a refreshing tea — or in the very poorest houses, plain water. It was in the Sudan that I understood what accounted for the Arab hospitality I so missed in America. The unrelenting heat and haboobs, the choking dust storms that gusted in from the desert, demanded such hospitality: If you didn't keep drinking in this forbidding, dehydrating climate, you would die.

The Sudanese were much poorer than the Egyptians I had lived among in Cairo, but prouder and even more patient. Like the Egyptians, they had a quick sense of humor, and they detested public displays of violence or humiliation. Unlike the Egyptians, they scorned begging and the age-old custom of baksheesh for services actually or theoretically rendered.

Fate had not been kind to Sudan. Since independence from Britain and Egypt in 1956, the Sudanese had gone through eight governments in a depressingly repetitive rotation: A brief period of inept sectarian democracy gave rise to military rule, which, in turn, would collapse or be overthrown; the new rulers would then return the government to the same incompetent tribal, sectarian leaders who had wrecked the country in the first place. So it had gone for nearly forty years. Under military or civilian rule, the Sudanese had tried everything: socialism, Marxism, democracy, military dictatorship, and now Hassan Turabi's uncompromising Islamic militancy. The experiments in democracy were predictably brief: Military rule had prevailed for twenty-seven of the thirty-eight years since independence, and many Sudanese had preferred the military to the anarchy of Sudan's stupefyingly ineffectual civilian democratic coalitions.

IN 1976 many Sudanese still expected their country to become, as its then ruler Gen. Gaafar al-Nimeiri promised, the "breadbasket of the Arab world." His vision did not seem as preposterous then as it does today. Nearly $800 million a year — more than half of the Sudan's national budget — was pouring in from the Gulf, Japan, Europe, and the United States. Sudan had 200 million barrels of proven, recoverable oil reserves, much of it in the south and, because of the war, yet to be exploited. Nimeiri was building an ambitious irrigation system along the Nile, known as the Jonglei Canal Project, intended to carry life-giving Nile waters to the potentially fertile desert. The British-inspired Gezira Scheme — more than 2 million acres farmed by almost 100,000 tenant farmers — produced three-quarters of the country's lucrative cotton crop, which accounted for more than half of Sudan's export earnings. A UN study estimated that by 1990 as many as 40 million acres of land could be under cultivation.[11]

President Nimeiri had made peace with the rebellious south in 1972, ending a seventeen-year-long civil war in which at least 500,000 Sudanese had died. The Addis Ababa accords granted southerners considerable autonomy, the right to continue using English along with Arabic, a more equitable share in resources, and most critically, religious freedom, exactly what the southern rebels, who later were known as the Sudan People's Liberation Army (SPLA), had demanded as the price of peace. Sudan, the largest country in Africa, one-third the size of the continental United States, was too large and too diverse to be governed centrally. Southerners were almost one-third of the population. Only about half of the Sudanese were Arab Muslims; Sudan was divided among more than five hundred tribes who spoke more than a hundred languages. Christians and pagans in the south would never choose to be ruled by northern Muslims in the name of Islam.

When I first met him in 1973, I was impressed with Nimeiri, a Muslim Arab who came from a family that was devoted to the Mahdi and his descendants. Though mercurial and corrupt, Nimeiri was a shrewd conciliator, a patriot, and flexible enough to shift alliances and political course if circumstances warranted it, as they often did in Sudan. Coming to power in a 1969 military coup as an admirer of Egypt's Gamal Abdel Nasser and radical Arab nationalism, Nimeiri eventually tried to crush all his major opponents: the Ansar, the strongest neo-Mahdist Islamic movement in the Sudan, headed then, as now, by Sadiq al-Mahdi, the Mahdi's great-grandson; the Khatmiya, the second-largest Muslim tribal grouping; Hassan Turabi's then insignificant Muslim Brotherhood; and the more influential Sudanese Communist Party. After the Communists nearly ousted Nimeiri in 1971, Nimeiri concluded he had more to fear from his once-leftist allies than from the Islamic parties. So in what would become a recurring theme in Sudanese politics, he embraced Islam, purged his government of leftists, and offered senior posts to men with Sufi and traditional Islamic backgrounds. Courting Sufi leaders by giving them money to build more mosques and religious centers, Nimeiri himself began conducting Friday prayers at mosques in different towns and villages.[12]

Nimeiri, alas, lacked charisma. Flabby, black-skinned, and tainted in the eyes of many of his racist northern countrymen by his facial scars — inflicted by tribal healers to protect children against the Nile's innumerable eye diseases — he was a poor orator. Unable to attract Sudanese support away from traditional rival political and religious groups, particularly Sadiq al-Mahdi's Ansar, Nimeiri switched tactics in 1977 and did what President Sadat of Egypt was unwilling or unable to do: In addition to his own embrace of Islam, he made a deal with other Islamists — with the Ansar and Turabi's Muslim Brotherhood — to stay in power. Sadiq al-Mahdi ended his overt opposition to Nimeiri's regime. His brother-in-law Turabi not only broke with the opposition but joined Nimeiri's government. In 1979 his loyalty was rewarded: Turabi was named attorney general. Nimeiri increasingly emphasized his own "Islamic" orientation and, more significantly, let Turabi open an Islamic bank, a decision that would have far-reaching consequences for Sudan in less than a decade.

Turabi and Sadiq al-Mahdi continually pressed Nimeiri to make Sudanese law conform with sharia, the Islamic holy law. But Nimeiri resisted, imposing Islam on his heterogeneous country, for southern leaders had repeatedly warned him that doing so would mean relegating Christian Sudanese to *dhimmi*, a "protected" minority community, and denying Sudanese pagans, who are not even "Peoples of the Book," any rights at all. The south would have little choice but to resume the ruinous civil war.

But the longer Nimeiri ruled, the more eccentric and autocratic—and apparently devout—he became. Soon he was speaking more and more openly about the need for an "Islamic" lifestyle in his country. In 1980, a year after the Islamic revolution in Iran, he published a book, *Al-Nahj al-Islami Limadha?* (Why the Islamic Path?), in which he praised Islam as the best way to achieve Sudanese unity. While the ghostwritten book stopped short of endorsing the imposition of Islamic law, Nimeiri's apparent effort to capitalize on growing Islamic fervor in Sudan and bolster his popularity in the Arab Muslim north worried southerners. At about that time, Nimeiri issued a directive to government ministries—"Sober Leadership," it was called—that warned officials against drinking in public or engaging in un-Islamic conduct. In the early 1980s he ordered senior army officers to take Islamic indoctrination classes three times a week at a center where Turabi, his former nemesis and now senior foreign affairs adviser, lectured. Among Turabi's students were several young officers who would later oust Nimeiri, including President Omar Hassan al-Bashir, Sudan's current Islamic ruler.[13]

Even supposedly well-connected diplomats had difficulty explaining Nimeiri's stunning decision in 1983 to impose sharia, the so-called September laws. Nimeiri's Islamic legal code surprised even Turabi, who was then heading a committee charged with revising Sudan's laws to ensure their consistency with sharia.[14] Sadiq al-Mahdi and other Muslim leaders denounced Nimeiri's new penal code as too harsh. But Turabi embraced it, and until Nimeiri imprisoned him less than three months before his overthrow in 1985, Turabi, who had admitted to having fainted when he saw his first Islamic amputation, defended the new laws and their severe corporal punishments.[15] Such punishments, he told me at the time, did not "shock" the Sudanese. "In Zaire and elsewhere in Africa," he said coolly, "thieves are often crucified or beaten to death. So Africans are used to amputations and flogging."

The civil war that Nimeiri had ended resumed.[16] And the war, in turn, led to economic stagnation that further weakened Nimeiri's hold on power.

Former advisers and aides have long speculated about why Nimeiri imposed an Islamic code, with its gruesome penalties, such as amputating the hands of thieves, in a country where hunger was so prevalent. Nimeiri told me that a "revelation" had come to him in a dream.[17] Some former advisers argued that faced with a deteriorating economy, Nimeiri was trying to bolster his plummeting popularity through an alliance with a political faction that he thought needed him more than he needed them — Turabi's Muslim Brotherhood. Turabi, for his part, always insisted that his inclusion in Nimeiri's government was mere "window dressing," a ploy by the sly Nimeiri that never translated into real power for him or the Brotherhood. Still others thought that Nimeiri, sensing that Islam was on the rise after the Arabs' humiliating 1967 defeat by Israel, Iran's 1979 revolution, and the assassination of Egypt's Sadat by radical Islamists in 1981, was trying to position himself in the forefront of what he considered a winning trend. Besides, becoming more Islamic would mean even more aid from wealthy Saudi Arabia and the conservative Gulf. But desolate, isolated Sudan was hardly a likely leader of the region's Islamic revival. And virtually all of Nimeiri's opponents had better Islamic credentials than his. Some wise analysts argued that Nimeiri had simply lost touch with political reality after ruling for so long.

Years later, Selim Issa, a Lebanese wheeler-dealer who had served for almost a decade as a senior Nimeiri adviser, provided an even more intriguing explanation. "When I first joined him, Nimeiri was as pragmatic, as shrewd a leader as I had ever met," Issa told me over Arabic coffee in the shade of his cabana by the Nile Hilton's pool in the early 1990s. "The Sudan was potentially rich. We were signing contracts left and right. But Nimeiri was becoming a desperate man."

Nimeiri had four daughters but no sons. "He used to say to me," Selim recalled, inhaling his Marlboro, " 'What is a ruler in this part of the world without an heir?' He tried everything — doctors in Sudan, in Cairo, in Europe, even in the United States. He saw priests, mystics, fortune-tellers; he took herbal medicine. Nothing worked."

Finally, Nimeiri sought advice from a Sufi Muslim sheikh, a man known, as Sufis often are, for his magical powers. "The son of a bitch told him that if he imposed sharia and returned to the true path of Islam, he would have a son! And Nimeiri, who also turned out to be a stupid son of a bitch, believed him!"

The Saudis, who loved to promote the concept of Islam, were nevertheless appalled by Nimeiri's imposition of sharia; so was Egypt, which shared the waters of the Nile. "Once sharia was imposed, we all knew there was no way to prevent a resumption of the civil war," Selim confided. "I tried to dissuade him from this lunacy, but Nimeiri ignored everyone. And he never did have a son!"

WHEN I RETURNED to Khartoum in January 1985, even northern Arab Muslims were fed up with Nimeiri's unpredictable, autocratic, ostensibly Islamic regime. The civil war was bleeding the country dry. Much of the Western and Saudi "development" aid had been wasted or, according to Selim and former Sudanese advisers, sent to Nimeiri's Swiss bank accounts. The economy was staggering.[18] Despite Nimeiri's promises to develop Sudan's infrastructure, there were still only twelve hundred miles of asphalt roads and another twelve hundred miles of dirt or gravel ones in a modern country nearly four times the size of Texas. Worse still, Nimeiri's regime was battling a severe drought that had devastated the harvests and sent more than 500,000 starving refugees from neighboring Ethiopia, Chad, and Uganda into the Sudan. Much to his credit, Nimeiri had accepted all of them, though Sudan itself was short of food. "The breadbasket has become a basket case," said my friend Ali Abdullah Ali, a Sudanese economist who was then editing a newspaper that covered what was laughingly called the Sudanese economy.

Nimeiri's government was also accused of being savage and heartless — "un-Sudanese," critics said. Since Nimeiri had imposed his version of Islamic law in the fall of 1983, eight men had been hanged for adultery and other capital crimes, and fifty-four convicted thieves, including Christians and pagans, had had their hands amputated. Men like Nouredin Ahmed Aissa, a twenty-seven-year-old former thief, displayed their stumps in dirty cafés and told their stories to sometimes titillated, more often horrified foreign journalists. Aissa, a repeat offender, had lost both his right hand and left foot under Nimeiri's Islamic penal code. These "cross-amputations" were performed as Islamic law required, in public, in Aissa's case in Kobar Prison's courtyard. Kobar had seen so many political prisoners come and go under Nimeiri that the elite half-jokingly referred to it as "the National Hotel."

Aissa had recounted in nauseating detail what happened the day of his punishment: the tingling of the anesthetic, the unsheathing of the thick, heavy knife that had been imported for the occasion from Saudi Arabia, the black mask that was placed over his eyes, the roar of the crowd at the prison. He remembered lifting the mask and seeing a prison guard holding his severed hand and foot aloft before a cheering crowd. The guard was smiling. Then Aissa had fainted.[19]

The hanging of Mahmoud Muhammad Taha, the founder and moderate opposition leader of the Republican Brothers, a nonviolent Islamic group, outraged both Sudanese and Western critics. Taha's public execution for alleged apostasy in January 1985 led Washington to conclude that its pro-Western, anti-Communist ally was becoming unhinged. European, American, and Egyptian diplomats had all pleaded for clemency for the seventy-six-year-old Islamist, but Nimeiri would not hear of it.

The day after the hanging, my friend David Blundy, of the London *Sunday Times*, and I visited Mohammed Omar Beshir (no relation to the ruling Islamist general Bashir), a popular intellectual who taught political science at Khartoum University and crusader for human rights. As we sat in one of those cool, shaded gardens in which northern Sudanese intellectuals muse about life and their country's prospects, M.O.B., as he was known to correspondents, was glum. Our discussion was interrupted by his servant, who leaned over to whisper something in his ear.

Suddenly, Beshir leaped up and ushered us into a large, dark, cool study whose battered wooden shutters were closed tight against the intense winter sun. He flipped on the fan and an ancient black-and-white television set.

The television camera was fixed on a small room in what appeared to be a prison. The place resembled a disorderly café. Half-empty tea glasses were strewn across the table, which was covered by a plastic tablecloth. Flies buzzed overhead.

One by one, four men in tattered djellabas were led into the strobe-lit room. Each was carrying the iron chains that bound his feet. I thought of Sudan's nineteenth-century Messiah, the Mahdi: He and his successor, the *ka-lifa*, had kept their prisoners in such chains. Beshir gasped at the sight of men he clearly knew. Blundy and I exchanged bewildered glances.

Around the table sat six Muslim "judges," two of whom wore mirrored sunglasses. They had been sent to encourage the four convicted heretics — followers of Taha and fellow Republican Brothers — to repent. The men had chosen repentance rather than death a day before their own scheduled executions. Their "crime" was having distributed a leaflet opposing Nimeiri's interpretation of Islamic law. On camera, the judges asked each of them to sign a confession stating that he had deviated from the "straight path" of Islam. After each had signed, the judges ordered them to denounce their former leader on television as a heretic.

One of the four hesitated. He had worked with Taha for thirty years, he said, tears welling in his eyes. He would admit the error of his ways and vow to remain a good Muslim, but he could not denounce his friend.

The judges stared at him silently. Finally, one in a bright white turban and sunglasses shook his finger at him. Unless he denounced Taha unequivocally, "RIGHT NOW," the judge warned, he would be taken straight to the gallows. Moments later, the convict succumbed. Sobbing openly, he was led out of the room. The judge who had bullied him leaned back in his chair and smiled at the camera. His name was Haj Nour; he was notorious, Beshir told us, for his cruelty and he was the subject of rumors about his sexual preferences. It was this "pillar of the community," Beshir said bitterly, who had sentenced Taha to death and staged the recantations we had just seen on television. Less than a decade later, Haj Nour would emerge under Turabi's ruling National Islamic Front as the imam of the Khartoum University mosque, the place where Turabi, Bashir, and other senior "Niffers" — as members of the N.I.F. were known — prayed on Fridays and where Islamic-minded students received the latest Islamic line.

Our host shut the set off. While Taha's execution had been open to the public, no pictures were permitted. The crudely taped recantations, by contrast, had been broadcast repeatedly. "If Fellini had wanted to film a modern Spanish Inquisition, he could hardly have found a more suitable event," Beshir said.

"What you have just seen has nothing to do with Islam!" Beshir thundered. "Nimeiri can impose lashings and flogging and hangings and crucifixions from now until Judgment Day and he still won't have an Islamic regime." Beshir, who had briefly been a roving ambassador for Nimeiri, now hated the man. "Nimeiri may have intended this to show that he is still in charge, that he must be feared and obeyed. But such humiliating displays are morally repugnant to Sudanese. This is the beginning of the end for him."

I, too, sensed that Nimeiri would not endure when I interviewed him shortly after Taha's hanging in January 1985. Nimeiri, who usually relished hearing the latest political jokes from Egypt or news from Kansas, where he had been a military cadet, was on edge. Meticulously attired in his olive-green uniform, laden with medals, he insisted on speaking in his quite good English. But he shifted mood and subjects quickly during our three hours together and would countenance few follow-up questions. The Americans, Egyptians, and Europeans were full of "idiotic" advice about how he should run his country and end the civil war, he told me agitatedly. "They have all the answers! All I have to do is guarantee the southerners a greater share of economic resources and a larger role in Khartoum!"

But wasn't that an appropriate solution? I asked him, risking an interruption.

Nimeiri glared at me coldly. "Those diplomats don't know what the hell is going on in this country," he snapped. It wasn't true, he declared, that imposing Islamic law had inflamed the largely Christian and pagan south. All Sudanese understood that Islamic law was a deterrent. "There haven't been any serious thefts since the amputations started," he maintained. "Khartoum is the safest city in Africa. Your cities would be safer if you amputated a few hands now and then."

Wasn't the death penalty for minors in some American states enough of a barbaric "deterrent"? I wondered. Yet it hadn't curbed a soaring murder rate in America.

"Why did you kill Mahmoud Taha?" I asked him, shifting to even more uncomfortable ground.

"You called him a moderate. But he was no moderate," Nimeiri replied, refusing to elaborate. "The Koran prescribes death as punishment for heresy. Even presidents, kings, and sultans cannot change that."

Nimeiri sank into his chair and fell silent. He reached for a handkerchief and wiped his brow. Seeming to forget my presence entirely, he ran his hand absentmindedly through his curly black hair. His face, so animated only moments before, suddenly collapsed, his jowls expanding as he sighed and dismissed me with a wave of his hand. This would be my last interview with President Nimeiri.

FOUR MONTHS LATER, Gaafar Nimeiri was gone. In the first week of April 1985 thousands of Sudanese, led by trade unionists and students, who had a long and proud tradition of political activism, rioted to protest food shortages and rising prices. Nimeiri was visiting President Reagan at the White House at the time. On April 6, 1985, the defense minister, Gen. Abdel Rahman Mohammed Hassan Siwar el-Dahab, considered Nimeiri's close friend, seized power in a bloodless coup, citing "the worsening situation in the country." Thousands of people thronged the streets singing in celebration of Nimeiri's ouster.

Liz Colton, of *Newsweek* magazine, and I were the first American correspondents to arrive after the coup. As our taxi made its way to the Khartoum Hilton, Sudanese were still rejoicing in the streets, tearing down portraits of Nimeiri. Although traffic was light because of gasoline shortages, people were everywhere. There was little visible military presence.

Later that day, Liz and I simply walked into the presidential palace, and much to our astonishment, Gen. Siwar el-Dahab, Sudan's new ruler, gave us an interview. Escorted into the room where I had last seen Nimeiri, I saw at once that the president's picture had been removed, leaving a large rectangular shadow on the wall. Siwar el-Dahab, in his first interview, told us that he had no intention of staying in power, that military rule would be a transition to civilian rule and would last "less than a year." During that time, a painful economic austerity program instituted by Nimeiri would be maintained so that Sudan would not be blacklisted by the International Monetary Fund. But sharia would have to be "amended" and "modified" to eliminate "incorrect and excessive" punishments inflicted by Nimeiri. I made a mental note that even the new secular military government hesitated to repeal "God's law" in Sudan.

What about Nimeiri? I asked him. Would Nimeiri be put on trial, as was rumored, for "crimes against the Sudanese people"?[20] "We have more important issues to deal with," he replied.

While there had been sporadic calls for retribution against Nimeiri and those who had worked for him, most Sudanese did not seek the vengeance that was so common in other Arab countries. "Nimeiri is gone — *khalas!*" said Ali Abdullah Ali, the economist, when I embraced him at his office after the coup. "It is over — let's forget it," unusual forbearance in the Middle East, where every injustice or perceived slight is rarely forgotten and almost never forgiven.

Even the coup itself had mirrored Sudanese society's restraint. Hume Horan, then the American ambassador and a well-respected Arabist, had summed it up as we had tea together at the American embassy. It was "small potatoes as a coup or revolution by Arab standards," he said, his air conditioner on full blast. "There was a week of strikes and demonstrations; only a few people were badly beaten by the security police; fewer still were killed. When the military finally took over, reluctantly, to prevent further bloodshed, some students had gone to Kobar Prison and shouted, 'No more amputations!' That was about as wild as it got. It was more like a stock takeover than a revolution."

Horan was astonished that it had happened at all. There was something "oxygenless" about Khartoum that made conflagrations hard to ignite. Maybe it was the heat, I thought, or the Sudanese people's nearly infinite patience that bred such inertia, such passivity, and such willingness to forgive.

"Good riddance!" Beshir proclaimed when David Blundy and I visited him a few days later. We had joined Beshir and some other friends for a picnic celebration commemorating the first day of spring. Our little group was surrounded by thousands of Sudanese families ignoring the searing heat of the white desert sun and picnicking along the banks of the Blue and White Nile. For many young Sudanese, this was the first spring ever without Nimeiri as president, and they were joyous.

The bloodless coup of 1985 had released an intense, long-suppressed yearning for political freedom that I shall never forget. While Nimeiri tolerated no political parties except his own, some thirty-five parties had emerged since his ouster the week before. Hardly an evening passed without a political rally. The previous evening, Blundy and I had joined some ten thousand people — many trucked in from villages and towns hours away from Khartoum — at an N.I.F. rally where Hassan Turabi, the Brotherhood leader just released from jail, had urged the faithful to "fight for a real Islamic revolution," a government "that will not beg," a regime that was "neither East nor West." "Islam is the solution!" the mob chanted as Turabi spoke. But there were many other voices and points of view. The euphoria contrasted sharply with M.O.B.'s somber mood at our picnic.

The Sudan was in economic misery. Four million Sudanese and a million refugees had been affected by drought and famine. Government debt was soaring; Sudan's pathetic infrastructure continued to collapse, particularly the links between the north and south that had been attacked by the rebels. Much of the middle class had emigrated. Would they return? Were development and democracy conceivable without them?

But there were even deeper reasons for concern, Beshir said. Modern Arab and African history were strewn with examples of military officers who had seized power and then refused to relinquish it. Even if the new military junta turned power over to civilians, would they govern more wisely and justly than the previous regime? Why would modern Sudanese history make one optimistic?[21]

"All the political systems we have tried since independence have failed. The system that the British left us, by definition, would not work." The British, he said, had not only insisted on military-based rule in Khartoum; they had kept the south poor and underdeveloped, an "arcadia of primitives," a "human zoo."

Neither David Blundy nor I wanted Beshir's gloom to lessen the infectious euphoria that gripped Sudan that day — a rare enough event in this land of sorrow. As Beshir's guests retired for their afternoon naps — a hallowed tradition in the stifling heat of Sudan — Blundy and I took a walk along the Nile. Removing our shoes, we ignored the parasitic snails and walked barefoot through the sand.

The rough beauty of the land overwhelmed us. Earlier in the day, the heat had shimmered above the yellow sand, and the sun had made the desert rocks too hot to walk on. But now the red-orange sun was setting harmlessly over the Nile. Storks gazed at us as they stood, one-legged, against the setting sun in the shallow water. Birds of extraordinary color flew overhead. As we neared our hotel, a felucca, with its distinctive slanted sail, pulled up to the shore and dropped anchor. Its weary crewmen disembarked and were beginning to haul the day's catch up from the hold when a man on shore summoned them. Suddenly, they dropped their nets and scrambled up the riverbank. Facing northeast toward Mecca, they fell on their knees and began chanting their evening prayers. Oblivious to all else, they pressed their foreheads into the still-warm sand in submission to God. David and I watched them, transfixed, as the sun set behind them. The Muslims of Sudan, we were reminded yet again, were not fanatical, but they were pious. While they had not been fooled by Nimeiri's attempt to use Islam to prolong his rule, the sailors' reverence was yet another reminder that any government that flouted Islam in northern Sudan was risking everything.

Whereas most Sudanese Muslims probably thought that sharia should be the law of the land, Christians and pagans in the south opposed Islamic law, and who could blame them? M.O.B. was right: Establishing peace and equality between the Arab north and the non-Muslim south would be dreadfully difficult. Personal rivalries and ethnic and sectarian tensions were deep and historic. The two leading parties were both religiously based and had roughly equal support in the country. Thus, the fringe parties — the Communists and the Muslim Brotherhood — were decisive in any coalition government, an inherently unstable situation. The north was deeply racist toward the "infidels," the nonpeople of the south whom, less than a century ago, Muslim Arab slave traders had bought and sold. Many northerners still considered this the natural order of things, though it was unfashionable to say so. "We were the slavers; they were the slaves," Beshir had reminded us — a bitter legacy, as the protracted civil war had shown.

Given the Sudan's dilapidated infrastructure, rampant corruption, and devastated economy, a new democratic government composed of the same petty old men with their endless quarrels would probably not succeed. Beshir's mood had not improved a week later when we went to the sprawling, dusty university to say good-bye. "The traditional civilian leaders won't dare abolish sharia, and there can be no peace with the south without that," M.O.B. predicted. "I'm sorry to say this, but there will be another coup, probably in about three years." That was in 1985.

He was wrong by less than a year.

HEAT STRUCK ME like a fist as I poked my head out of the plane in June 1994. Pulling my hat down even lower over my sunglasses, I made a dash for the airport's reception hall. Perhaps it would be air-conditioned. It wasn't. Summer was not a good time to visit Sudan.

I had vowed never to return to "Islamic Sudan" after spending time in Khartoum in 1992, three years after Turabi's National Islamic Front had seized power. What I had seen during that trip had shocked and depressed me. But I had agreed to return once more to interview Turabi, now militant Sunni Islam's chief theorist, for *Foreign Affairs*, the foreign policy journal read by American and foreign members of the policy elite. I had really come back to see whether this Islamic paradise was on the brink of being overthrown, as my dissident Sudanese friends had told me.

I looked around for my old driver, Muhammad Tawfik, whom I had tried to telex from Cairo. There was no sign of his battered old yellow taxi. Instead, a businessman I met on the plane gave me a ride to the Hilton, which was clean and cool inside. It was also empty. "You can have your choice of rooms, Mrs. Miller," the reception manager whispered, welcoming me back. "We're less than a third full."

I asked the bellman whether Muhammad was still in Khartoum and driving a taxi. Yes, Muhammad was still here, the doorman beamed. The hotel would send for him. I told the doorman to ask Muhammad to meet me at the home of a diplomat I had long known and trusted. Since the hotel security men would know where I was going and whom I was meeting, I wasn't betraying a source, just simplifying everyone's life logistically. Gasoline was rationed, and additional fuel on the black market was exorbitant. I would never find another taxi at the diplomat's home.

Things in Sudan were worse than ever, my friend the diplomat told me. Turabi's modern, self-styled Islamic government had seized power in June 1989 in what seemed a standard military coup d'état. The democratic but ineffective government of Sadiq al-Mahdi, the Mahdi's great-grandson, was ensured legitimacy, respect, and political influence by his illustrious name alone. But Sadiq had been a disastrous prime minister. His indecisiveness, particularly his unwillingness to do what was needed to end the protracted civil war, had further impoverished Sudan and exasperated even his staunchest supporters.

Initially, few had known what to make of Lieutenant General Bashir and the junior officers who had arrested their commanders and seized power. After seven years of democratic chaos, the relieved Sudanese hoped that the new military junta would, as it had promised, end the debilitating civil war and save their country.

Within months, however, it became clear that Sudan was not ruled by the traditional Egyptian-tutored military alone but also by a clique of militant Islamists who had infiltrated the government, only a few of whom had risen through the armed forces. These quiet men behind the coup — Sudan's real rulers, as it would turn out — were activists in the National Islamic Front, the Muslim Brotherhood group long dominated by Turabi, who was, I recalled, also the deposed prime minister Sadiq al-Mahdi's brother-in-law.

Turabi, fluent — and persuasive — in at least four languages, had served in almost every one of Sudan's democratic governments and military regimes when he wasn't imprisoned by one of those same governments. Though he was jailed briefly after the 1989 coup, he soon emerged as the leading behind-the-scenes counselor to the young and inexperienced "Niffers."

In 1992 the regime had administered capitalist shock therapy to the economy. It had isolated the money-losing parts of the country—almost all of Darfur in the west, and Kordofan, southwest of Khartoum, as well as parts of the central and eastern regions, leaving its impoverished inhabitants to fend for themselves under the harshest of conditions. It invested only in enterprises that might show a profit. It had drastically devalued the Sudanese pound, lifted price controls, and ended subsidies that constituted half the budget.

In 1992, Abdul Rahim Hamdi, then the economics minister, had told me that within a year Sudan's traditionally statist economy would be functioning according to free-market rules, "because this is how an Islamic economy should function." Hamdi, a disciple of Milton Friedman, was determined to implement his harsh reforms no matter how they might hurt the average Sudanese, whose real income was less than $100 a month and plunging. Hamdi himself, of course, would not suffer. A former Islamic banker in London, he still had a bank there. "The population accepts these hardships," he asserted with a confident little smile, "because it supports Islam and us."

Hamdi knew as well as I did that the population had little choice. The N.I.F. had banned strikes and protests; a curfew had been in effect since the coup. And by now many Sudanese were simply too discouraged by their experience with democracy to rise up and oust dictators, as they had done in 1964 and 1985. We both also knew that this economic shock therapy, which had increased the price of bread 500 percent, could never be implemented in a democratic state.

Nor, it turned out, could it be imposed on Sudan. By 1994 the regime had backed away from the most extreme free-market reforms so beloved by the IMF and international financiers. Hamdi had resigned, though he remained important in the N.I.F. Sudan was virtually bankrupt: National debt stood at $15 billion, the highest ever. Imports were more than four times exports.

The government was now relying on what my diplomat friend called "slogan economics" for survival. The regime's stated commitment to economic self-reliance—"we eat what we grow; we wear what we sew"—had prompted savage caricatures in the Sudanese exile press. One cartoon in London portrayed a naked General Bashir hunting for watermelon seeds. Sudanese friends were fond of telling the story of a thief sentenced to forty lashes for stealing an apple. When the court tried to defer the punishment, the thief objected. Why? the judges asked. "Because today I'll receive forty lashes; if inflation continues, it will be eighty lashes tomorrow."

The civil war, of course, was partly responsible for the economic ruin; the war that had cost an average of $300,000 a day under Nimeiri was now costing more than $1 million a day. The human cost was far worse: Between two hundred and three hundred wounded men a week were trucked in to Khartoum hospitals. There was no medicine, of course. The N.I.F. had "privatized" medical care, which meant that patients, even the wounded, had to pay for every service or pill, when they were available. A doctor had recently warned a Sudanese friend scheduled for surgery to bring his own catheter; the hospital didn't have any. Hospital directors and department heads still had their titles and offices, but hospitals were run by so-called salvation committees, whose main task was not to heal but to spy on doctors and patients. Only eight hundred of Sudan's ten thousand doctors were still in the country; the others had fled. The government denied the high number of war casualties. So the dead and wounded were slipped in after midnight so that the public would not see how many there were. But everyone knew.

On paper the government's proposals to southern leaders for ending the war seemed more forthcoming and flexible than any previous regime's since the Addis Ababa accords of 1972: decentralization, federalism, and the abolition of sharia in the south. But the government had refused to clarify these proposals, the diplomat explained. So negotiators had gotten nowhere. And Khartoum had continued spending money on weapons, hoping to secure a military victory in the conflict it ostensibly wanted to resolve peacefully. As a result, John Garang and the other southern leaders — and there were now several, as the SPLA had split into several warring factions in 1992 — were now utterly disaffected and even calling for secession, something most of them had not done before. In addition, the government was secretly arming the SPLA's rival factions and actively promoted ethnic divisions among the southern rebels. A political solution seemed unlikely.

Did this mean that the Turabi regime would weaken and fall? I asked my friend. "No," he said, shaking his head sadly. "The government has persuaded many Arab Muslims that the war is winnable militarily. And the emigration of talented opponents has continued. Finally, the security apparatus has taken an ever firmer hold. Young Sudanese now know that to get ahead, and sometimes just to survive, you must join a security force. If you inform, you may get a job, a house, a car, the oh-so-precious requirements to marry. If you remain aloof, you'll starve, or be sent to the south to fight in the war — and probably die." [22]

What the Islamic regime in Khartoum had added to the savage civil war was religious sanction. The war was no longer merely a fight over natural resources and deep-seated racial hatred and ethnic rivalries; it was a jihad, a struggle mandated by God to crush infidels who opposed the spread of Islam.

Though Turabi himself had apparently never declared the war a jihad, a holy war against a non-Muslim enemy of Islam, as the Koran required a leader to do, President Bashir and the state-run media routinely used that term. So did preachers in the state mosques. And in 1994 the Sudanese government defended its designation, arguing that the term "jihad" was "part of the cultural and linguistic heritage of the Sudanese people." Khartoum would make "no apologies for using the term in the context of the just war that the majority of the Sudanese are waging to safeguard the common interest of society," Ali Mohamed Osman Yassin, Sudan's permanent representative to the United Nations, had stated in an extraordinary response to an even more unusual denunciation of his country's human-rights record. [23]

Since General Bashir had come to power, all political parties and trade unions had been suppressed; the country's constitution had been suspended; private publications not licensed by the new regime were banned; and the civil service, judiciary, and army were purged of nonbelievers. Roughly 80 percent of the civil service had been replaced. The government had demolished the makeshift homes of more than a million people, most of them non-Muslims from the south, and moved them into camps on the outskirts of the city that lacked even basic amenities. Students, once the vanguard of political activism, had been tortured and frightened into passivity. I recalled the university student whom I had visited in a Khartoum hospital in 1992. The boy had lain on a dirty cot in a dingy room swarming with mosquitoes and flies, his head covered in bandages. His hands and back were scorched by burns, some still oozing. Islamic militants had hit him on the head during a demonstration with a bottle of flammable liquid that set him afire. No Islamist had been punished for the assault.

The level of violence seemed to be one of the few rising indicators in Sudan. In 1990, after less than a year in power, Bashir and Turabi's Islamic government had already been branded by Human Rights Watch/Africa, a private human-rights group, the most "brutal" to govern Sudan since independence. Bashir's regime, stated the report, was guilty of human-rights abuses "never before seen" in the country. The fierce, systematic repression of political opposition already surpassed "even the worst excesses perpetrated by Nimeiri."

By 1990 several of the regime's most articulate critics had been hanged, allegedly for violating harsh new laws governing foreign-currency transactions. The government justified its executions by comparing their war against currency speculators to America's campaign against drug dealers. "Drugs are a very sinister force that must be dealt with by your government in a harsh manner," a government spokesman had said. "Foreign currency dealers are the equivalent of drug dealers in the Bronx. They are sapping the will of our people."[24]

In March 1991 the regime had introduced its own version of sharia that broadened the code to cover more offenses than were included by either Nimeiri or Sadiq al-Mahdi. This time, the penal code, the centerpiece of the new ostensibly Islamic order, reflected Turabi's literal interpretation of Islam's injunctions. Apostasy, defined as "every Muslim who propagates the renunciation of the creed of Islam, or publicly declares his renouncement thereof, by an expressed statement or conclusive act," meant death if the apostate did not "repent." An armed robber could be killed and then crucified if the robbery involved murder or rape; a thief could lose a right hand and a left foot. A married female adulterer was to be stoned to death; a Muslim who drank alcohol received up to forty lashes; a suicide attempt was punishable by a year in prison and/or a fine; an abortion that was not required to save the mother's life or was not the result of rape could result in up to three years in jail and/or a fine; a homosexual was subject to a hundred lashes and imprisonment of up to five years. "Gross indecency," which was defined as "any act contrary to another person's modesty," brought forty lashes, the same as the penalty for someone who wore an "indecent or immoral uniform which caused annoyance to public feelings."

Prison was not what it had been before. Sadiq al-Mahdi had once told me that he had found prison under Nimeiri "relaxing." He had written a couple of books; on weekends, his family had visited; amnesties and early releases were common. Turabi, too, had described the experience as "very pleasant." "We had air conditioning, TV, access to our families and food from home."[25] But under the so-called Islamic regime, imprisonment meant torture, disease, disappearance, and death.

The United States, however, had not rushed to judgment about the Islamic regime. Fearful of offending Islamic sensibilities, the Bush administration initially downplayed reports of atrocities by its former ally.[26]

Turabi, whom the Reagan administration and Saudi Arabia had warmly supported for his staunch anticommunism, particularly in Afghanistan, was given a visa to the United States in 1992 even after Khartoum supported Iraq in the Gulf war and over the strong protests of human-rights and Sudanese exile groups. Sudan was not added to the State Department's list of countries that sponsor or aid terrorism until the summer of 1993, and only after five Sudanese nationals were indicted in New York in connection with the latter phase of the World Trade Center bombing plots—the scheme to blow up the United Nations and New York bridges and public buildings.[27]

"The worst thing of all," my friend the diplomat concluded, "is that there is little likelihood of getting rid of this regime." At least five coup attempts, three of them sponsored by Egypt, had been quashed; at least thirty-five officers had been executed, and no fewer than fifteen hundred officers had been cashiered. "Detention centers—those 'ghost houses' we talked about before—are still operating. And the opposition is in an even greater mess than usual—disorganized, plagued by traditional rivalries, and utterly lacking in astute leadership."

I was thoroughly depressed by the time I left the diplomat's house. In 1986, when Sudan held its last free election, Turabi's N.I.F. had won less than 20 percent of the national vote. Now Turabi and his friends were well entrenched. As the guard escorted me to the huge padlocked gate like those that now protect most diplomatic missions, I saw a familiar face pressed against the tall iron bars. It was Muhammad, my driver. It took me a few seconds to recognize him because he was dressed not in his Western-style chinos and plaid shirt that he had worn when we worked together but in a flowing white djellaba and turban. After a brief puzzlement, I recognized his unforgettable smile.

We had no time to lose, I told him, since the government had given me a visa for only five days. Because most telephones no longer worked, we had to go to people's homes and offices to fix appointments. Khartoum was a vast city with at least 5 million inhabitants; only the main roads were paved; in traffic, it could take more than an hour to cross the forty-mile stretch from one end of Khartoum to the refugee camps on the outskirts of Omdurman, its sister city across the river.

"Okay," I said, taking out the list of names and useless telephone numbers that I had brought with me, "let's start with Mohammed Beshir, and then let's see Abdalla Nageeb."

Muhammad stared at me blankly, his round black eyes widening. "You don't know?" he said tentatively. "Beshir is dead. M.O.B. died almost two years ago — of cancer. Didn't anyone tell you?"

I had not heard. The Sudan was a distant planet for someone in New York, even for people in the rest of the Middle East. Poor, dear, prescient Beshir. How much David Blundy and I had loved and admired him. But Blundy, too, was now dead, killed by a sniper in Salvador. "What about Abdalla?" I pressed him.

"You won't find him, either," Muhammad said, shaking his head as he steered his rattling car around the potholes that punctuated the bumpy sand road. "He took his family and emigrated to Australia. Sold his home, his land, everything."

Most of the country's political opposition had fled to Egypt, Britain, Canada, the United States — wherever they could get entry visas and work. But Abdalla was a Coptic Christian from Sudan's second-largest political party who had told me he was determined to stay and fight for his people's rights. Now he, too, had given up.

Maybe Professor Abdelrahman Abu Zayd was still here. He had been the head of Omdurman Aliya University when I had seen him last and was fiercely critical of the Islamic regime. I vividly recalled what he had told me: The pan-Arab nationalist soldiers who had seized power were no different from the Islamist officers now in charge. "It's all a racket," he said. He had also belittled the notion that Islamic militancy could ever be "moderate," as many Western analysts hoped and predicted. To attract the young, Islam had to be fierce and militant. It had to oppose the existing order. So to speak of a moderate political Islam was "a contradiction in terms."

Muhammad grimaced when I mentioned Abu Zayd. "Your friend has become a spokesman for the government!"

Suddenly, I was frightened and confused. Everything Abu Zayd and I had discussed — and everyone we had talked about — would now be known to the regime.

"What about Nogoad?" I continued. "He must be here!"

"Yes," said Muhammad. "But who knows where. He's underground. The government has been hunting for him everywhere! They're embarrassed and furious that they can't find him."

So Muhammad Nogoad, at least, had been true to his word. He had vowed never to leave his homeland. When we last met in 1992, Nogoad had just returned from twenty-two months in prison and was still under house arrest. Even then he was pessimistic about the prospects of ousting Turabi's regime.

The opposition, the so-called National Democratic Alliance, was neither national nor democratic, and it was certainly not effective. Southern leaders of the rebellion, moreover, had little rapport with their northern Arab counterparts in exile.

Nogoad, now in his early sixties, had been an early member of Sudan's now-banned Communist Party, once the largest in all Africa. He had spent almost fifteen years of Nimeiri's twenty-six-year rule underground. When he was arrested by Turabi's regime soon after the coup, he had been placed in the same section of Kobar Prison where he had been kept thirty years earlier.

Nogoad had warned me not to take Sudan's political parties seriously. They were not parties as Westerners thought of them. Parties in Sudan were superimposed on the country's religious sects to give ethnic politics legitimacy. Scratch any member of Sadiq's Umma Party and one would find an Ansar, descendants of the original followers of the Mahdi. The Umma (the Prophet Muhammad's "community of believers") was traditionally Sudan's strongest party because the Mahdi's Ansar sect included many of the numerous and powerful cattle-owning northern Arab tribes and thus had the largest following in Sudan.

The second strongest was the Khatmiya, another religious *tarika* (sect), founded by Osman al-Mirghani, an Islamic missionary from Arabia who proselytized in Sudan in the early 1800s. Mirghani's descendants, too, still led their party, the Union Party, now the Democratic Union Party. Though the Khatmiya were just as uncompromisingly pious as the Mahdi's followers, they had not believed that the mystical son of a carpenter was the Messiah — the Mahdi, who would cleanse and restore Islam and crush its enemies. When the Mahdi had declared that he was, in fact, the expected redeemer, in a telegram to the government, the Khatmiya had scoffed. They had refused to join the Ansar in their fight against either General Gordon or Kitchener.[28] Grateful to the British and Egyptians for having overthrown the Ansar's tyrannical caliph who had persecuted them, the Khatmiya had served as clerks and administrators in the colonial administration. While they did not oppose independence, they had long favored merger with Egypt, or at the very least, a close, continuing relationship.

The rivalry between Ansar and Khatmiya had been transposed onto the Umma and Union Parties. They hated each other, which not only paralyzed efforts to govern effectively during Sudan's brief attempts at parliamentary democracy but doomed many of the early attempts to oust Nimeiri and now Bashir's military rule.

Nogoad, my Communist friend, knew his historical enemy, the Muslim Brotherhood's N.I.F., all too well. He had been Turabi's classmate. "A punctual and disciplined schoolboy," Nogoad had called Sudan's Islamic guru.

The Islamists and Communists had been the fiercest of rivals since independence, particularly at the University of Khartoum, then Gordon College, perhaps because both groups lacked an overt tribal base and as a result rejected traditional forms of political identification. But unlike the Communists, Turabi's N.I.F. had benefited from Nimeiri's rule. After a Communist-sponsored coup against him failed in 1971, Nimeiri had outlawed the party and banned leftists from the armed forces. The jubilant Islamists had then joined the military academy and his government in droves.

Saudi Arabia had also used Turabi and his N.I.F. to promote its own Islamic agenda, and Turabi had used Riyadh. Having spent several of his years in exile in Arabia cultivating wealthy Saudis and encouraging them to finance his movement, Turabi and his Saudi patrons had persuaded Nimeiri in 1978 to license the Middle East's first Islamic bank in the Sudan. Though Islamic banks were banned in Saudi Arabia, Faisal Islamic Bank was funded by Saudi Prince Mohammed bin Faisal bin Abdulaziz. Exempted from taxes, government scrutiny, and most banking regulations, Faisal Islamic rapidly became Sudan's second-largest bank, financing Islamic trading companies, insurance agencies, and other Islamist-owned companies, which employed only Islamically inclined graduates of Sudanese universities. Wealthy, disciplined, well organized, and convinced of the righteousness of its cause, the N.I.F. spread rapidly. According to Nogoad, Turabi virtually controlled the bank; his party had operated from a penthouse in the bank's headquarters. Through the bank and its Geneva-based holding company, the Islamic Financial Holding Company, registered in the Bahamas, Turabi had slowly but steadily built a formidable economic and political network in Sudan. Today dozens of these Islamic banks help the N.I.F. control business and trading in Sudan.

Until the creation of the Faisal Islamic Bank, agriculture had been dominated by the Ansar; commerce and trading, by the Khatmiya. But Turabi slowly filled economic and political niches, never turning down an opportunity to buy a building or fill a slot in a ministry that would strengthen the Islamists' *da'wa*, their social welfare network. In other words, Turabi's N.I.F. had built the network that the Communists had tried but failed to build.

Now that the Soviet Union had crumbled and the notion of a single mass party led by the vanguard of the proletariat had been discredited, Communists like Nogoad favored creating a democratic, secular state. But this being the Sudan, the secular state would still have to lean on Islam. Sudan's two major parties, after all, were both Islamic, and the Communists needed allies if the N.I.F. were to be overthrown. Islam was part of Sudan's tradition, its psychological makeup. So Nogoad was determined to "borrow from Islam." Just what kind of communism was this? I wondered.

I recalled that Nogoad had chuckled. In this country, he had told me, those who wanted to succeed in politics could never forget the importance of tribe, sect, and religion. In Sudan, Islam ran so deep even the Communists were Islamists.

Since Sudan's independence, in fact, Islam had played a major role in Sudan's ostensibly secular politics. As early as 1957 leaders of the Umma and Union Parties had demanded — with Muslim Brotherhood endorsement — that

Sudan be declared an "Islamic parliamentary republic," with sharia established as the "main source of legislation." Only the Communists had opposed this. But Islamic fundamentalism and communism were, after all, expressions of the same human desire for perfection on earth — militant Islamists inspired by an idealized past, Communists, by an equally idealized vision of the future. And both were committed to imposing their own utopian vision by force, if necessary. I had noticed the same impulse in Egypt, Syria, Lebanon, and even my own country. The dream of transforming human nature to create paradise on earth was universal, a characteristic of the species, and it usually ended badly.

"WE SAY that when Allah made the Sudan, he laughed," Muhammad told me as we bumped along what passed for a road. "But I think when Allah made the Sudan, he cried."

I held a handkerchief over my mouth, vainly trying to block the dust that permeated the car as a fuel truck overtook our tiny yellow taxi on the right. It was 9:00 A.M. and already 110 degrees. I did not say what I was thinking: When Allah made the Sudan, he probably could not decide whether to laugh or cry, but I was sure he spent the month of June elsewhere.

Muhammad and I had been working since six-thirty that morning. We were exhausted and perspiring. It is hard to describe such heat if one has not experienced it. I couldn't imagine how anyone survived it in a prison or a ghost house. We were on our way to see Sid Ahmed al-Hussein, who had, in fact, survived such an ordeal — six times since Turabi's men had seized power in 1989. He had been released again from prison only days before. Hussein was acting head of the Union Party and had once been minister of the interior, responsible for the same security services that had imprisoned him. Though he had lost his right hand in a childhood accident, his infirmity had not kept the government from torturing him.

Tall and in his early sixties, Hussein, a lawyer by training, had the aplomb of a diplomat. Apologizing to friends who were sitting with him on cushions on the floor, he led me quickly into his Western-style study, where we sat on comfortable sofas and were served ice-cold carcaday by a black servant from the south. Hussein removed his turban, revealing short-cropped white hair that matched his neat little mustache.

Hussein had been an early inhabitant of what the Sudanese called ghost houses, since people taken there were rarely seen again. In 1989 he had been interrogated for more than a month in the "Citibank" ghost house, so named for its former occupants. The N.I.F. located its interrogation and detention centers in some of the best houses in Khartoum, the former villas of British colonialists.

Thrown into a space the size of a kitchen cupboard — three feet long by six feet wide, without lights or windows — Hussein was literally "swimming" in his sweat, he told us. "The stench and the insects were disgusting.

"At night they strung me up, hanged me from a ceiling hook by my arms.

I mean, by my arm," he added with a smile. "Loudspeakers broadcast readings from the Koran all night long. During the day I was chained from my elbow to my foot. I spent a month like that."

What had his interrogators wanted to know? I asked him. What crime had he been accused of?

"It was never clear," he said. "They asked me which ambassadors and foreigners had come to see me. But they already knew that! They had been watching my house for weeks."

Once, he had been accused of treason and taken off to a prison in Kordofan to be shot. For some reason — he was never told why — the execution was canceled.

The Citibank ghost house was better prepared for guests by his next visit. The government had built nineteen cells around what had been a garden. "There were nearly two hundred prisoners, most of them young, from the university. They treated me all right, but it was impossible to sleep at night because of their screams."

Once uncommon in the Sudan, torture was now widespread, especially in the south.[29] Non-Muslim women were raped, their children taken from them; paper bags filled with chili powder were placed over men's heads, and some were tied to anthills; testicles were crushed and burned by cigarettes and electrical current, according to a 1994 report by Human Rights Watch/Africa. Gaspar Biro, a Hungarian law professor and the United Nations' special envoy to Sudan in 1993, had accused the Sudanese government of "widespread and systematic torture" of political detainees and "degrading treatment" in front of their family members.[30] While Biro's report also accused the SPLA of similar atrocities, it focused on Khartoum's abuses, especially on the Islamic government's policy of "depopulating" the Nuba Mountains, a thirty-thousand-square-mile area in the heart of the Sudan, where almost a million Nubas, a tall, black cattle-herding people, had lived for centuries.

In response, the Sudanese government had formally accused Biro of "dishonesty," "lack of professionalism," and disseminating "lies about Muslims."[31] He was unqualified "in view of his age" — Biro was thirty-six years old — careless in his reporting, guilty of "malicious elaborations," and "a confirmed anti-Muslim fanatic." There were no summary executions in the Sudan, the government said, no reprisals against non-Muslim civilian populations, and no "ghost houses." Even the use of such a "pejorative expression" in a UN document, Ambassador Ali Yassin complained, demonstrated a "lack of objectivity." As for Biro's call for the repeal of Islamic sharia, whose amputations, lashings, stoning, and other corporal punishments mocked decent and widely accepted standards of human rights, Yassin called the recommendation "blasphemous." Abolishing sharia would be "against what was ordained by God" and therefore constituted a "flagrant attack on Islam." As for torture, there wasn't any.

The regime was still "brainwashing" the young, Hussein told me. The "Holy Koran societies," cells of militant volunteers who spied on teachers and students, were now everywhere. So were neighborhood "popular committees" and the Popular Defense Forces, paramilitary police groups composed of students and civil servants who were given two months of basic military training and religious indoctrination and sent to the front. Except for these security mechanisms, Hussein said, the state was collapsing. "Everybody knows by now that this is not an Islamic state."

MUHAMMAD HAD ARRANGED for me a meeting at 10:00 A.M. with Sadiq al-Mahdi, leader of the Ansar and the now-banned Umma Party. Mahdi was exceedingly punctual. Muhammad and I were always late, and at ten we were still racing along the Nile in his taxi, honking the horn to move slower cars to the right and persuade Sudanese ambling across the roads either to stop or move more quickly. But Muhammad's horn, a demure sheep's bleat, was hardly authoritative, and the pedestrians were unimpressed. They looked up at us speeding toward them, glanced down again, and kept inching across the road. It was just another miserable day here in Islamic paradise. Why hurry?

"You can't criticize, you can't question anymore," Muhammad told me as he leaned on his horn. "We live in a country where words no longer have meaning. There is a Ministry of Peace but no peace. There is a House of Parliament but no parties or democracy."

There were no nightclubs any longer, no mixed dancing in public, only third-rate action films at the few remaining cinemas. I pointed to a crowd of more than 250 young men outside the Friendship Palace, the giant conference center the Chinese government had built for Nimeiri. They were waiting for an afternoon film to begin. "It's a lousy Indian film," Muhammad said. But it was one of the few air-conditioned public places in Khartoum. Sudan did not need prisons, he complained; the whole country had become one giant, stifling prison.

Not for everyone. An intelligent and charming Sudanese friend had invited me the previous evening to a relative's wedding. My friend, educated in the United States, now worked for a government financial institution. Her family was well connected. She herself ardently believed in the new Islamic order and its goal of economic independence. Farmers were now more important in her country than civil servants, she told me approvingly. Sudan's dignity was being restored.

She and her relatives welcomed me at the wedding as if I were part of the family; I was delighted by the evening. More than 250 people — friends, relatives of the bride and groom, dignitaries — had come to the outdoor party. Men and women were theoretically segregated by being seated on folding chairs in separate areas, but once the music began, all pretense of Islamic puritanism vanished. The men in djellabas and women in *thobes* of pure silk and other exotic fabrics undulated together on the dirt-floor courtyard, the women's bodies moving provocatively in their understated traditional dances. They swayed back and forth to the rhythmic African drums and an electric keyboard. The groom was lifted into the air by his friends; his bride, in her white satin Victorian wedding dress and rhinestone tiara, danced with family and admirers. Pepsi flowed, and the guests were served a dinner that included meat. A video cameraman recorded the revelry late into the night. The party was still going strong when I left to get some sleep. This was the Sudan I had first known and would always love.

The wedding had been expensive, a display that only the elite could afford, and a diplomat later reproached me for having enjoyed it so uncritically. For ordinary people, the government arranged marriages en masse in soccer fields so they could avoid the expense of such ceremonies. Some two thousand people had recently been married like that a few days before my arrival; couples were paid to marry. A Sudanese friend told me that her cousin had recently gotten "married" just to collect the government's 2,000 pounds ($6.25 U.S. at the official exchange rate); she and her boyfriend had then split the dowry and resumed their single lives.

The lavish wedding I had seen was yet another example of the regime's hypocritical double standard, the diplomat said. Only a few weeks before, the Egyptian diplomatic club had been raided and closed after the security police found its members engaged in "mixed dancing." Everyone knew there was one set of rules for ordinary Sudanese and unwelcome foreigners—and Egyptians were particularly unwelcome—and quite another for the Sudanese elite.

As we bumped along toward our appointment—now twenty minutes late—I tried to lift Muhammad's spirits by pointing to some improvements in Khartoum since my last visit. Streets and neighborhoods were cleaner than before, I told him. Unlike Syria and Iraq, whose streets and buildings were festooned with photos of "the leader," there were hardly any photos of Bashir or Turabi, no banners plastered with empty politico-Islamic slogans. The 11:00 P.M. curfew, in effect since the coup, had finally been lifted, and there were far fewer policemen on the streets today than two years ago.

Muhammad was unimpressed. The regime's undercover intelligence apparatus assured more subtle control today, he replied; the government no longer required so visible a presence. As for the streets, yes, they were cleaner, he conceded, largely because of one of the more intriguing figures in the N.I.F., Youssef Abdelfattah, a young militant whom the Sudanese called "Rambo" for his daring, perhaps hopeless, assault on rubbish in the capital. He was known for careening around Khartoum in his Range Rover and safari suit, looking for litter. He was something of a folk hero, mocked by many government critics but genuinely popular among young Sudanese who desperately wanted to believe in something, perhaps that they could improve their society. But Abdelfattah was deemed too independent by the jealous, faction-ridden N.I.F. So this Islamic warrior on waste had been transferred to another ministry. He would no longer be giving interviews.

There was little for young people like Muhammad to do or to hope for in Sudan. Sudanese called their television station the "public bus" because their screens were constantly filled with throngs of people chanting the Koran, singing Islamic songs, and citing *hadiths*, which was why satellite dishes providing access to foreign programs had become the latest status symbol in Khartoum for the few who could afford them.

Sadiq al-Mahdi's house had one. His compound was in Omdurman, the "Arab" part of the city from which the Mahdi, his great-grandfather, had ruled.

Unlike Khartoum, Omdurman, across the river, had little definition. It sprawled in all directions from the Mahdi's magnificent tomb along the Nile — a sand-colored honeycomb of flat-roofed mud huts and multicolored inhabitants. There were no grand forts and palaces, no English gardens along the Nile, no broad streets. All roads seemed to lead to the central meeting place by the Mahdi's tomb and to the adjacent outdoor mosque where the *kalifa*, his successor, had insisted that important followers pray. It is said that the *kalifa* had never left Omdurman. He did not need to. His vast spy network informed him of all threats to his authority. Even today in Omdurman, one felt the presence of the enigmatic Mahdi and his ruthless caliph.

A servant led me to the cone-shaped straw gazebo where Sadiq al-Mahdi received visitors. Dark in the Nubian way, tall and thin, Sadiq wore elegant sandals, a flowing white djellaba, and an embroidered skullcap. He looked the part of the Mahdi's heir.

The morning was hot, but Sadiq's gazebo was surprisingly cool. I noticed that it had been purged of insects. As we chatted, another servant brought tea in delicate imported porcelain cups from England.

"I am the only major Sudanese leader left who has not been driven into exile or underground," Sadiq declared. "But this regime, which illegally toppled my government, is failing."

I had always found Sadiq brilliant, and in June 1994 he was as biting as ever. As he spoke, his graceful hands accompanied his words as if he were conducting himself in a one-man performance. I had almost forgotten those hands, those mesmerizing, long, thin, delicate brown fingers, their translucent eggshell nails so well filed and buffed. When we first met in 1985, Sadiq had just been released from prison after Nimeiri's ouster and was about to run for office. I had stared at those elegant hands for hours as he fingered his carved walking stick and debated politics late into the night on his airy terrace.

Sadiq and his brother-in-law Turabi both thought of themselves as the natural leaders of a country that was inherently Islamic. Both had sympathized with Iran's Islamic revolution and were critical of the "outdated" Gulf monarchies; both saw renascent Islam as the most powerful ideological force in the post–cold war era, and both believed that the West neither understood nor appreciated the force of the Islamic revival. "But there are two kinds of Islam — enlightened Islam," Sadiq said, turning up his left palm, "and reactionary or absolutist Islam," as his right palm took its place beside the left. Unlike Turabi's N.I.F., the Umma Party had championed the former, Sadiq said, the "tolerant," "inclusive" Islam in which Islamic law was administered with extensive guarantees of due process and minority rights.

I had watched those same expressive hands punctuate his speeches at rallies after he was elected prime minister in 1986. I had seen those hands gently slice the air to dismiss criticisms of his government—that he was moving too slowly in abrogating sharia and ending the civil war, that his cooperation with Libya was alienating the West, that his coalition with Turabi's Muslim Brotherhood was dangerous for democracy. Finally, I had seen those same hands pressed emphatically to his chest after General Bashir seized power in the 1989 coup, catapulting Hassan Turabi, his brother-in-law and Islamic rival, to power. "Sudan was already an Islamic society," he told me. "Why did the N.I.F. impose its reactionary brand of Islam here?"

He was not, Sadiq asserted, "the great ditherer," as critics charged, a man who aspired to be both a modern, secular leader and a traditional, Islamic one, a man whose intellectual couch was crammed with contradictions. Democracy had slowed down what he was trying to do, he said. But finally all parties, except the N.I.F., had agreed to suspend sharia so that talks with the south could begin. "And that's when the N.I.F. struck!" he said. "They knew we would succeed, that this was their last moment."

Now the N.I.F. was taking "Lenin's route," using force to achieve what persuasion could not. But the regime was still failing, he repeated defiantly. "Officials must accept bribes to live. Prostitution and other immoral practices have increased dramatically. Their Islam is only rhetoric. They haven't dared cut off a single hand for theft!"

The regime tried to appear unified, he continued, but its unity was as fictitious as its Islam. Several power centers were competing for dominance, some even more radical than the ruling trend. "The N.I.F.," he said smugly, "is divided on almost every issue except staying in power."

As we said good-bye, I pressed once more that elegant hand, so soft, its pressure so gentle. I was reminded of what his friend in the Umma Party had once told me: "Sadiq is a jolly fellow, a good man to discuss philosophy or play tennis with. But he was no ruler. His indecision was catastrophic for our party and our country."

As we parted, he motioned me back for a second. "Don't be too hard on my brother-in-law," Sadiq said quietly of Turabi. "He's not a bad fellow, and others in the N.I.F. are far more radical and dangerous. We may both live to see a harsher man in charge than Turabi."

What I was hearing, of course, was the endlessly forgiving spirit of Sudan.

SADIQ'S DELICATE WORLD was a planet removed from that of his ancestor, the Mahdi. The Mahdi and his *kalifa* were in possession of conviction that intellectuals like Sadiq lacked. That was probably why he had found it so hard to govern. Men with so many doubts, such noble goals often in conflict, and such gentility were rarely effective leaders in the Middle East or anywhere else for that matter. This harsh land demanded even harsher men. Men with self-doubt or compassion were usually swept aside by more determined men like his brother-in-law, Turabi, whom I was now on my way to interview and who would no doubt already have heard of my meeting with Sadiq. A diplomat had told me the night before that even flies didn't move in Sudan without Turabi's knowledge, and perhaps his permission as well.

There was nothing to suggest such power at Turabi's nondescript offices in the building occupied by his Popular Islamic and Arab Conference, a barebones but air-conditioned office. On the enclosed veranda, young Sudanese, many of them Western educated, I assumed, and speaking foreign languages with visitors from many continents, were waiting their turn to see Sudan's modern Islamic guide.

The Egyptians argued—and had persuaded at least some American officials—that Turabi was using the Popular Islamic and Arab Conference he created after the Gulf war as an Islamic "Comintern," or a "Khomeinitern," as an Egyptian intelligence officer had called this alleged center of the militant Islamic conspiracy against moderate Arab governments. Every extremist Muslim group in Africa, the Middle East, and Asia was represented in the conference, which seemed better funded than most Sudanese ministries. At least the phones and faxes worked—some of the time.

Egypt estimated that there were "thousands" of Iranian Revolutionary Guards in Sudan. American intelligence officers put the number at no more than two hundred. But even this relatively small number of Iranian advisers was not insignificant in a country like Sudan. And intelligence analysts said that several key Niffers, such as Sudan's interior minister, had received training in Teheran. Khartoum, moreover, had given diplomatic passports to several Islamic militants being sought by other Arab countries, men like Rashid Ghannouchi, the head of Tunisia's Islamic movement, who had won political asylum in Britain, and Usama Bin Laden, the young Saudi financier of so many violent Islamic groups and causes, now a part-time resident of Khartoum.

While America had put Sudan on its terrorist list, what poor, remote Sudan mainly offered terrorists, several U.S. officials said, was a refuge in which to refresh themselves between operations—"a shower and a shave." But Egypt in 1995 accused Sudan of trying to assassinate President Mubarak in Addis Ababa; Cairo feared its Islamic neighbors.[32] Most of Sudan's neighbors, in fact, complained openly about Sudanese support for Islamic and other rebel groups in their own countries.[33] When I had asked Hassan Turabi on a previous visit in 1992 about reports of Sudan's growing ties to Iran and its support for terrorist groups, he had dismissed the allegations as "rubbish."

Turabi himself now welcomed me into his private room, an unadorned office whose plastic venetian blinds were shut tight to protect the simple couches and Formica furniture against the noonday sun. The fluorescent light was cool and harsh and made Turabi's snow-white turban, salt-and-pepper mustache, and closely clipped beard seem whiter against his dark skin. He had changed little since our last meeting in New York in 1992: the same boyish face, the same tense energy. Here, in his Khartoum office, there was no physical sign of the murderous assault on him during his 1992 North America trip by a Sudanese dissident and martial-arts champion in Canada, though the attack left him partly paralyzed and unable to speak for weeks.

Turabi seemed his old self, excitedly pacing around the office in his djellaba, beaming at me. His smile was still irresistible! Like the Mahdi's, I thought. Everyone who had written about the Mahdi, and of Hassan Turabi as well, had mentioned that ineffable smile. The Mahdi had smiled even as he ordered executions or hideous tortures of some poor Sudanese who had offended God, and hence him, by chewing tobacco or sneaking a sip of wine. "A smiler with a knife," one historian had called him.

"He gave me four blows, that black belt in karate!" Turabi exclaimed, recalling the assault at Ottawa airport. "And yet I survived! And now I'm even more famous," he said with his disarming giggle. "I've become a symbol of Islam."

The supreme guide's regard for himself had apparently been undiminished by the attack. Both he and Islam were destined not only to survive but to triumph, he told me. "Islam can no longer be denied! It is the only force that motivates young people in the developing world. You in the West must understand that; you must not fear it. You had better get used to it. Because we are not your enemy, and Islam is the future. You won't be able to stop it, anyway. Objectively, the future is ours."

As he saw it, most of the world's civilizations were in decline. The Arab nationalist states were "going downhill." Africa was plunging headlong into tribalism. Even his patron Iran, where Shiite Islam had triumphed, was too "negative," too focused on "tearing the West and its enemies down" rather than inspiring hope and a new vision. Turabi did not really approve of clerics who governed, as they did in Iran. He, after all, was no cleric. Only Asia, with its "cultural solidarity," and "disciplined, hardworking people," had a bright future, he told me.

The United States was "leaderless." President Clinton, though "young and energetic," was "aimless." And his secretary of state, Warren Christopher, he added, his smile broadening, "he hasn't a clue."

Turabi had met most recent American presidents. When he had been Nimeiri's foreign affairs adviser, he met President Ronald Reagan in Washington. "Reagan thought Sudan was in Latin America — literally," Turabi told me. "At least George Bush had expertise — in the CIA, as vice president," Turabi said. "I met him several times; he impressed me." Turabi, however, had not impressed Bush. In 1992, when Boutros Boutros-Ghali, the UN secretary-general, had met with President Bush to ask him why Hassan al-Turabi and a then obscure Egyptian sheikh named Omar Abdel Rahman — later convicted of plotting to bomb New York's tunnels, bridges, and monuments — had been given visas to the United States, Bush looked puzzled. Taking out a small pocket notebook and pen, he had asked Boutros-Ghali to repeat the two names. "T-A-R . . . how do you spell that Sudanese guy's name?" Bush asked. Recalling the incident, I smiled. Turabi would have been crushed to know that Bush did not even remember him.

Turabi said that he knew my country well. When he was studying at the Sorbonne in Paris, he had spent the summer of 1961 touring America as a "student leader" and government guest. Turabi had traveled widely. He had even visited Alcatraz with his American girlfriend. Though he liked America, he told me, he had found the country racist.

One group that had impressed the young Turabi unfavorably was the Nation of Islam, the radical black Muslims now led by Louis Farrakhan, the virulent antiwhite, anti-Semitic black separatist. "They reacted differently to an Egyptian or an Arab who was lighter skinned," Turabi recalled. "Most of them were more antiwhite than they were Islamic." But Turabi must since have overcome his antipathy to the group, for Farrakhan had recently visited Khartoum as a guest of his government.

But what about racism within the Sudan? I asked him. Wasn't northern Arab racism toward black southerners partly responsible for the unending civil war?

Turabi's smile dissolved; the supreme guide scowled at me. There was no racism in Sudan, he said. And slavery itself? I pressed him. That northern Arabs had enslaved southerners throughout history, that slavery had been among his country's most profitable endeavors — this had no legacy?

"All Sudanese were victims of colonial oppression," Turabi replied. Slavery, he said, was never a "substantial institution" in Sudan until "Mohammed Ali and his European friends came here in the nineteenth century." In Islam, all men are equal, he said, growing irritated. So racism is un-Islamic. Therefore, I wrote in my notebook, it did not exist.

But Arab society, like most societies, was deeply racist. I recalled the seventh-century treaty between the Arabs and the black king of Nubia, part of modern Sudan, which had provided the Arabs with an annual levy of Nubian slaves. I also thought about the brilliant Arab historian and geographer Ibn Khaldun, who, in the fourteenth century, had written that "Negro nations are, as a rule, submissive to slavery, because [Negroes] have little [that is essentially] human and have attributes that are quite similar to those of dumb animals."[34] Northern Sudanese had long considered the south part of those "Negro nations" not really part of their country. The kalifa, for example, had ultimately forgotten about conquering the southernmost Sudanese province of Equatoria, which was now the SPLA's stronghold. Sudan's most important slaver was not Egypt's Muhammad Ali but Zobeir Pasha, a Sudanese tribesman and a hereditary religious authority among northern Arab Muslims. Finally, I thought of the subliminal hostility reflected in the Sudanese Muslim Brotherhood's perception of the south, in the words of an important Islamic political theorist, as a "distant, vaguely symbolic place," an "alienated, lost brother, who had to be retrieved through the spread of Islam, the Arabic language, and better communication."[35]

Turabi surely knew his country's tormented history. So why was he saying this?

In addition to being racist, Turabi continued lecturing, America was anti-Islamic. Turabi didn't believe Washington's declaration that America was critical not of Islam but of Islamic extremists who threatened America's Arab friends and allies. America was anti-Islamic "because of certain lobbies," he said, like the "Zionists," a very "powerful lobby in the media and public life in general." But Islam had other American enemies as well — "fundamentalist Christians," for one, private charities and relief groups, for another.

Turabi had long despised the groups that had helped sustain many of his starving people, particularly Christians and pagans in the south. It was the relief groups that had accused the N.I.F. of tying food and aid to conversion to Islam, an un-Islamic practice by any devout Muslim's definition, since the Koran stated that there was no "compulsion in religion." Most relief groups just wanted contributions, Turabi complained. "They show skeletons and bones of children so that people pay. But most of the money goes for administration. If these groups were really humanitarian, they would help people grow their own food and become independent."

Although Washington's designation of Sudan in 1993 as a country that sponsored terrorism had severely limited international aid and loans, the United States still gave Sudan more than $80 million a year in relief. I knew that the Islamic government wanted the aid without strings or donor interference.

Sudan would not expel most relief groups, he said cautiously, but having been deprived of much of its aid, Sudan had become more "self-reliant," he asserted.

But the country's standard of living was plunging! I interrupted him. "People are desperate and hungry; many in the south are starving."

"We are living well," he insisted. "Go out in the streets! People are not hungry or begging; you will find more beggars in Egypt than in Sudan. America has done everything it can with the United Nations, with Europe, with the Arabs to stop aid to the Sudan. But we're surviving."

Turabi was denying the obvious, just as he had denied charges of human-rights abuses leveled by the United Nations, the Catholic Bishops Conference, Amnesty International, Human Rights Watch/Africa, and many other humanitarian and religious groups. There was no forced conversion to Islam in Sudan. There was no torture. The Sudanese were simply overly sensitive to "bright lights being shined in their face," Turabi had said. There was no official corruption. Women were not fired or flogged for refusing to wear Islamic dress. There were only some twenty to thirty political detainees in the entire country. Egypt's human-rights record was much worse, "a thousand times worse" than Sudan's. And he knew "damn well" that Sudan was "not worse than America." It was "more peaceful than Chicago or Philadelphia. Or Washington. Or New York," he insisted. Yet Sudan received more pressure on human rights than any other country.

"Is Saudi Arabia, which does not let women drive or work with men, which has no parliament, no democracy, no accountability to its people, worse than the Sudan?" he said heatedly. But Washington never criticized Saudi Arabia or any other allied Arab regime that arrested people, which was true, of course. As for the condemnation by the United Nations special envoy, "nobody" believed Gaspar Biro, said the still-smiling Turabi, though obviously furious by now. "He is the worst lawyer I've ever seen. He is stupid. The southerners got hold of him. He thinks he'll please the Americans. He'll keep working to get his dollars. He's East European, you know," Turabi said, staring at me coldly. "He needs those dollars badly."

So anyone who criticized the Sudan, in Turabi's view, was either stupid or venal. This, indeed, was a new Turabi, a man I had not seen when I had first interviewed him in 1983, when he was Nimeiri's adviser on foreign affairs. And this was certainly not the man I had met when he was in the opposition, writing his provocative, quasi-liberal tracts that few Western liberals could fault.

In the early 1970s, Turabi had favored Islamic emancipation of women and respect for individual dignity. Islam, he wrote, did not believe in coercion. It prohibited torture and required democracy. In Turabi's Islamic paradise, the ordinary Muslim citizen would be obliged to practice *ijtihad*, to interpret Islamic principles himself; authority did not reside solely with the ulema but also with the people.[36] Turabi had been praised as a "liberal" and "modernizer" in a bitter ideological and personality struggle within the Ikhwan in the late 1960s. Turabi's "political school" had favored creating an Islamic state by building a broad coalition of forces sympathetic to an Islamic revolution and by participating in government to gain experience and contacts whenever the Brotherhood could; the hard-line "educationalist school" had argued in line with orthodox Muslim Brotherhood doctrine that such a state could be brought about only by an uncompromising militant elite who shunned those who resisted the Brotherhood's discipline and credo and who operated in relative isolation from mainstream society. In 1969, Turabi's faction had prevailed and had begun implementing his high-risk strategy. Soon the Brothers had infiltrated the army, the bureaucracy, the security services, and any other government sector that would have them.

In 1983, Turabi had taken another dramatic step: Citing the need for local autonomy, he officially broke with the authority of the Cairo-based Brotherhood. Since many Sudanese still resented their historic subjugation to Egypt, the move, though controversial among the disciplined, internationalist Muslim Brotherhood, had strengthened the group's appeal within Sudan.[37]

In 1986, after Nimeiri was ousted, Turabi had joined Sadiq al-Mahdi's coalition government, vowing to respect the rules of parliamentary democracy and abide by the will of the majority. But by 1989, Turabi's Niffers were well enough placed throughout the army and government to make their own bid for power.

Once in power, Turabi discarded the liberal sentiments expressed in his early writings.[38] By 1994, he no longer even bothered to rationalize or justify or explain. He simply denied things that he knew I had seen and heard firsthand and knew to be true, abuses that could never be defended by Islamic principles or any other moral standard.

Turabi's transformation should not have been surprising. In Islamic politics, as in all politics, timing was pivotal. Turabi had been tolerant in opposition when a democratic outlook was useful. Out of office, Turabi had spoken the language of reform and pluralism; ruling, however, was something else.

Martin Kramer, the Israeli analyst of militant Islam, argued that as a rule, an Islamic militant's "moderation" was inversely correlated to his proximity to power; the farther away from power Turabi had been, the greater his so-called moderation. Bernard Lewis, another fierce critic of Islamic absolutism, had put it this way: "Moderation," or "pragmatism," in a radical fundamentalist movement usually reflected a lack of alternatives. An Islamic "moderate," he quoted Arab friends as saying, was one who had "run out of ammunition."

Turabi was now the de facto leader of a well-entrenched regime; he no longer had to justify his government's actions. He could simply lie. He had, in other words, assumed a defense common to all dictators: denying obvious truths, as if to say, of course we both know I'm lying, but what are you going to do about it?

Though Turabi still insisted that he had no official role in government, he now admitted having what he called "considerable influence" in society, the "primary institution in Islam, rather than the state." [39] His was the "only portrait" in the State Department's 1993 report on terrorism, he boasted.

I asked Turabi about articles in an Islamic newspaper that accused his son Essam, a rifle-toting young militant with a weakness for fast cars and American jeans, of speculating in foreign currency on the black market. [40] According to a journalist I knew, Essam had gone to the newspaper office after the article appeared and attacked the reporter who had written it. Soon after, the regime closed Sudan al-Dawliya (Sudan International), arrested its editor, and charged him with subverting the Islamic state. "The gossip doesn't bother me," Turabi insisted. "Even the Holy Prophets were subjected to it!"

"Why, then," I pressed him, "was the newspaper closed and its editor arrested?"

Turabi was aggrieved. It was terribly sad, he said, with only a hint of his habitual smile. The editor — a friend and a leading member of the N.I.F. — had become a paid Saudi agent. "It was a shock to all his friends. I myself was shocked." [41] Journalists wrote all kinds of lies about him and Sudan, he told me. For example, the "Zionist" New York Times had written that Sudan supported terrorism, which was untrue. Sudan did not provide a safe haven to the Palestinian Hamas and to the Islamic Jihad, to Lebanon's Hezbollah, to countless organizations that killed civilians and opposed the Arab-Israeli peace process. "There is not a single Hezbollah Sudanese here. Not one!" he thundered. "And Hamas!" he said, referring to the radical Palestinian branch of the Muslim Brotherhood that opposed peace with Israel. "History is going the way of Hamas. But do you know how many Palestinians are here? Maybe, with families, two thousand in all. How many are there in the United States? Hundreds of thousands! I meet Islamic Jihad and Hamas members — in America!"

The day before I saw Turabi, Muhammad and I had driven past Hezbollah's busy office in Khartoum on our way to interview a Hamas leader at home. At least twenty Palestinians worked full-time in the Hamas office. Turabi was lying about the presence of such groups in Khartoum, but he was accurate in saying that Hamas had a strong presence in the United States. Until the World Trade Center bombings in 1993, both Hamas and the Islamic Jihad had increasingly used America as a logistical, and even an operational, base.[42]

Turabi denied any connection with the plots to bomb the World Trade Center and other public buildings and landmarks in New York, though there was substantial evidence of Sudanese complicity with the Islamic radicals involved in the conspiracy. Sheikh Omar Abdel Rahman, the Egyptian cleric who had inspired and blessed some of the operations, had spent several weeks in Sudan at Turabi's invitation shortly before his arrival in New York. Five of the eleven people convicted for their involvement in the planned attacks, moreover, were Sudanese nationals. Two members of Sudan's mission to the United Nations had developed extensive contacts with these compatriots, American investigators had told me. And Sudan's entire mission to the United Nations had been named as "unindicted coconspirators" in the plot to blow up New York bridges and monuments.

"I never met Omar Abdel Rahman here," Turabi asserted. "He never met one important person in this country. He wanted to go to Yemen, and there was no direct flight. So he came and stayed here for seven whole days!"

Turabi had seen him only once in Pakistan, he said. The sheikh, he told me, was "not much of a scholar" or an intellectual. "He's blind. He's not capable of what you've charged him with. And those charges are illegal. Silly. That's why most people think your government is anti-Islamic."

As for the Sudanese involved in the planned New York attacks, he said, they were innocents duped by Egypt's double agent Emad Salem, a key prosecution witness. The young men thought they were building bombs "to protect Muslims in Bosnia against the Muslim-killing Serbs," Turabi explained.

I smiled, knowing from American investigators what Turabi did not then know: Sidiq Ali, one of the Sudanese defendants in the World Trade Center trials, was cooperating with prosecutors in the case and had already implicated his fellow Sudanese defendants. But what Turabi must have known was that Sidiq Ali not only had worked briefly for the Sudanese government but also had long-standing ties to Turabi's N.I.F. When I interviewed the Ali family in a Khartoum suburb just before my meeting with Turabi, their house was being guarded by plainclothes Sudanese security men.

The United States had not acted properly toward him, Turabi insisted, speaking ever more quickly but still without a break in his frozen smile. Washington, he declared, had sent the CIA to assassinate him in Canada! The agency was behind the 1992 attack on him by the Sudanese karate champion. "But even if they kill me, if they silence me, does that mean that Islam will disappear simply because I'm not there? What happened to communism after Lenin died?

"Your government has behaved very badly," he declared. "Five months ago, your ambassador came here, to this office, to read me a piece of paper," he said. I made a quick calculation. That would have been soon after Sudan was placed on the terrorist list in 1993. "He said to me: 'If you do anything to prejudice American interests anywhere in the world, anything, we'll take military measures against you that will destroy your economy entirely.' The paper had no heading, no signature. He read it without hearing anything from me. It was tantamount to war, an awful thing!" Turabi exploded.[43] "I told him this was stupid of your government. Because if you threaten the Sudanese, they won't be frightened. They will be provoked, and they will react!

"And if you bring Americans here, they will love you as in Vietnam. We would enjoy it! This is what I told your ambassador," he recounted. "So I know the American government is anti-Islamic." By now the smile was gone.

WHEN I LEFT his office, I thought about the debate among Arabists over Turabi's character. Some argued that there were really "two Turabis": a pre-coup Turabi, a tolerant, democratic, and liberal Islamic intellectual, and a post-coup Turabi, brutal, heartless, and single-minded. But really there was only one: the same focused, determined, and militant Islamist, now obviously somewhat paranoid, who had always done whatever he had to do to acquire and maintain power. Turabi had won by never losing sight of his goal of securing enough power to transform his country into an Islamic model — under his guidance, of course. Turabi once told me that Sadiq al-Mahdi, his brother-in-law, had made "too many compromises with too many people" but that he himself was "a resolute man."

Perhaps the United States, as he asserted, was looking for a new enemy now that the Soviet Union was gone, but Turabi had always needed enemies. Today they abounded: not only Communists, leftists, and secularists but Zionists, relief groups, UN envoys, Islamists who disagreed with him, the SPLA, Sadiq's Ansar movement, the Khatmiya, and finally the United States. His enemy — and Islam's enemy — was anyone who stood in his way.

Many Sudanese now believed that their government had degraded Islam, Gassan Bedri, the dean and son of the founder of Afad University, a private college in Omdurman, told me. "Islam, to them, has become merely a slogan," he said. Restaurants, roads, and buses have been given Islamic names, but only their names had changed. The economy was still ailing; roads were still unpaved; buses were still overcrowded. "They must brainwash the young," he said, "because their Islam is increasingly at odds with the people's Islam."

I recalled the frustration of Turabi's true spiritual and political predecessors — the Mahdi and Kalifa Abdullahi — over their inability to change Sudanese character. Charles Neufeld, a German merchant who had been enslaved in the Mahdiya for a decade, noted, for example, that Sudanese had never approved of the stonings of confessed women adulterers, though such punishment was mandated by the Koran. The government, he wrote, was unable to persuade those in attendance to throw stones with the sufficient force to stun or kill a sinner.[44]

Increasingly, the modern-day Islamic regime was confronting that same

Sudanese culture. Sudanese women might be forced to wear a head scarf under their *thobes*, but the N.I.F. would probably not "persuade" them to abandon *thobes* altogether. Public life may have become as arid as the desert surrounding Khartoum, but in private Sudanese tried to live normal lives, to celebrate the festivals they had always cherished. The Mahdiya had not changed Sudanese character, much less human nature. But many more Sudanese would suffer while Turabi's regime tried.

It was fashionable now to say that Turabi's government was dramatically different from those that had preceded it since independence. But was it really? Nimeiri, when he grew desperate enough, had imposed a crude Islamic penal code and vowed to build an Islamic state in Sudan. His ostensibly democratic successor, Sadiq al-Mahdi, had resisted abrogating sharia and had never tired of telling anyone who would listen that Sudan was an Islamic society. Like Turabi, he had dismissed Salman Rushdie as a "silly man" who had written a book "offensive" to Islam. The main difference between them was that the fastidious Sadiq, with his English porcelain, had believed in Islamic "democracy" and did not feel that people should be killed for apostasy that "undermined" an Islamic state.

Most Sudanese governments, to a greater or less degree, had reflected the spirit of Sudan's first Islamic regime: the nineteenth-century Mahdiya. Unlike Egypt, whose independence was secured by secular Arab nationalists, national liberation in Sudan was still connected in the country's consciousness with the Mahdi and hence with Islam. It would be difficult for Sudan to escape its twin legacy of slavery and militant Islam no matter who governed. This, in turn, had grave implications for Sudanese efforts to build a "secular," democratic state and to end the civil strife between the Arabized north and Africanized south.

These sad thoughts depressed me as Muhammad took me to the airport the morning my visa expired. I knew that we might not meet again, at least not in Sudan. "Don't forget us," he pleaded. I urged him to be careful. As I boarded the plane, I felt guilty, knowing there was little I could do to help the many wonderful people I was leaving behind. I could only hope that one day the Sudanese would rise up, that they would pour into the streets, as they had in 1964 and 1985, to rid their country of these vile rulers. But the regime was prepared to kill thousands, and even if the Sudanese somehow managed to oust this "Islamic" police state, then what? Would the country not succumb to the same pathology that had debilitated it for so long? I could not help thinking about what Father Ohrwalder wrote after he had escaped from captivity in the Mahdiya almost a century ago. "The old days of rejoicing have vanished, all is anguish and fear, no man's life and property are secure; everyone has perforce to break the laws, which are most of them quite impractical, and at the same time, are in constant fear of spies, who are everywhere. There is no security, justice, or liberty; and happiness and content are unknown," the priest lamented. "The Sudan lies open in its desolation and nakedness. In the name of the Sudan people, whose misery I have seen, and in the name of all civilized nations," he wrote, how long would the civilized world "watch unmoved the outrages of the *kalifa* and the destruction of the Sudan people?"

This time, however, neither Britain nor anyone else would come save Sudan. Only the Sudanese could do so, and the price might be terrible — the outcome dubious.

ALGERIA

Tomorrow Algeria will be a land of ruins and of corpses that no force, no power in the world, will be able to restore in our century.

ALBERT CAMUS, 1955

. . . those barbarians will some day devastate the earth and drink all the water of the lakes and rivers. Your lands will revert to their primordial dryness. I know that you have had to forget History, the tragedy of subjugation, the pangs of misery, the doubts of the night. And yet, your unhappiness is only just beginning.

RACHID MIMOUNI, *The Honor of the Tribe*, 1992

IT HAPPENED SUDDENLY. In the chilly thrall of an early spring in 1993, a young lawyer, whom I shall call Ali, was escorting me through the alleys of the Casbah. We were on our way to interview the family of one of Ali's clients, a teenage boy whom the Algerian security police had tortured nearly to death and then sent to a detention camp in the Sahara. It was early, but the dank, narrow streets were already filled with shoppers and young men going to the mosque for Friday prayers. Ali was on my right. I felt a tug at my left arm. Instinctively, I clutched my shoulder bag to my chest. Then I felt a sharp jab at the back of my neck. The small gold pen that I always wore attached to my necklace crashed to the ground. I lunged to retrieve it and swerved around just in time to see a young man in a black leather jacket disappearing with the necklace through the crowd.

Ali screamed, "Thief!" in Arabic. "Help us!" But the unsmiling pedestrians just stared at us. No one chased the culprits as they would have in other Arab capitals; no one came to our aid.

I did not realize at the time how lucky I had been. Only a few months later, the jab in my neck would probably have been a knife. For after warning all foreigners to leave the country in October 1993, Islamic militants began targeting foreigners, and by the end of 1994 they had killed at least ninety of them, mostly Europeans. Also targeted were Algerians who looked, sounded, or were presumed to think like Europeans: politicians, teachers, tax collectors, hairdressers and beauticians, dressmakers, priests, entertainers, sports figures, lawyers and judges, businessmen, women who ventured out in public with their heads uncovered, intellectuals, and any civilian whose lifestyle was seen as inconsistent with the militants' Islamic values. Journalists were particularly vulnerable. The Armed Islamic Group, or the GIA as it was known—Algeria's own Khmer Rouge—flaunted its list of journalists to be killed. Eighteen of my colleagues had been murdered in 1994 alone, forty by early 1995. Two of them were forced at gunpoint from their homes, shot, and then decapitated. Another was shot as he stood over his mother's grave. More than two hundred journalists had fled abroad.[1] Others were living in a heavily guarded compound in Sidi Efredj, a suburb of Algiers, by the sea. "We see other friends only at funerals," said Abdelwahab Hébatt, a photographer in the compound.

I knew that one day the fighting would end, whether by negotiation, a military victory, or sheer exhaustion. But what would be left of Algeria when it did? I had already lost so many friends to the savage civil strife. Among them was Azzedine Medjoubi, director of the national theater. Medjoubi, a popular film actor with a comical drooping mustache, was gunned down by two young men as he left his theater after having organized a children's play. His other crime, as the militants saw it, was his adaptation of Tennessee Williams's drama *A Streetcar Named Desire*, a favorite on Algerian television. Theater was *haram*, the militants warned—forbidden by God. So was music. Cheb Hasni, twenty-six years old, the most popular singer of *rai*, Algeria's unofficial national music, an alluring blend of Arabic, Berber, and Western tones, was murdered in Oran in the fall of 1994. His haunting songs offended God, claimed the Islamic militants who boasted of their "eradication" of this "evil on earth." Only after the Berbers, Muslims who represent more than 20 percent of the population and cling to their own culture and language, threatened to "declare war on Islam" was a Berber singer, Lounes Matoub, released after being held captive for two weeks. Aziz Smati, a television producer who had been so helpful during my first trips to Algeria, was still alive after being attacked by Islamic militants, but he was now a paraplegic. My Algerian friends were still discussing the death of my friend Rachid Mimouni, Algeria's finest novelist, because, unlike so many other writers whom he had defended, Rachid had died of natural causes at age forty-nine in a Paris hospital.

There were others—so many others I did not know. Human-rights groups estimated that about ten thousand Algerians had been killed since the army declared a state of emergency and took effective control in January 1992, after the opposition Islamic Salvation Front, known by the French abbreviation FIS, was on the verge of winning electoral control of the legislature. Unofficial estimates put the death toll by 1995 at forty thousand, four times the official estimate.

The violence, of course, was not one-sided. The government's security forces, or vigilante squads backed by them, had killed thousands of civilians, human-rights groups said. Torture, which had been eradicated after 1989, was common again. The security forces' favored methods included the *chiffon*, in which a detainee was tied to a bench and a cloth stuffed into his mouth along with huge quantities of dirty water mixed with detergent or other chemicals; the *chalumeau*, using a blowtorch to burn off a man's skin; and *gegène*, electroshock to the genitals and other sensitive body parts—French terms for the methods used by the French during their struggle to hold the land they had colonized in 1830 and ruled for 130 years. Detainees also reported having been subjected to mock executions, beatings, and sexual abuse. Some said the security police had used hand drills to bore holes in their back, feet, and legs.[2]

Aicha Lemsine, the feminist writer who visited me in New York in early 1995, could barely suppress tears of fury as she described her country's descent into barbarity, its transformation into a land of death squads and warlords, of "armed state groups" and "armed Islamic groups" terrorizing the nation. Aicha, who, as a young girl, had fought along with some ten thousand Algerian women in the war of independence, blamed both sides for the growing savagery. But she could not ignore the fact that the militant Islamists, deprived of their election victory in 1992, now seemed determined to destroy whatever remained of Algeria's once-vibrant cultural life. Even children were not exempt. A fourteen-year-old boy from Medea who had befriended several policeman in his neighborhood had recently been killed, she told me. His body was found hanging from a street sign, his head in a nearby town. A tally maintained by *Le Matin*, the French-language paper whose editor was murdered in December, reported that in 1994 alone, eighty-two schoolteachers had been killed, many in front of their horrified students. The militants, who had declared war on state schools in which girls were unveiled and classes unsegregated, had also burned down and vandalized schools throughout the country, officials said.[3]

Aicha was shaken by the militants' campaign against women. Just before she left Algeria, fifteen Islamic gunmen had forced two young girls and their mother from their home in a village near the capital. The thugs dragged the women into the forest, "practically right under their neighbors' noses," Aicha said, and gang-raped them so that their sexual defilement would forever bar their entry to paradise. Then the militants slit their throats—the "Kabyle smile," as the silent slayings were called forty years ago when the mujahideen, the holy warriors who had fought for Algeria's independence, used this tactic against the French and Algerian collaborators. Not since the war for independence, in fact, had Algerians killed one another with such intimate brutality. What made this particular incident so appalling, Aicha said, was that the targeted family was religious. An illiterate farmer, the father had fought the French and was proud of the fact that his daughters could read and write. In the 1960s, 85 percent of Algerian women could do neither. Their mother was a *haja*, a woman who had made the pilgrimage to Mecca that is required of all believing Muslim men once in a lifetime. The girls wore the *hijab* and never socialized with boys at school. The fanatics did not touch the father, his young son, or the daughter who did not attend school. They took only the mother and her daughters, Zoulikha, nineteen, and Saida, fifteen, believers whose only crime was wanting to be educated. This primitive paganism and ignorant fanaticism were what passed for Islam in Algeria today, Aicha said. The state was no better, she said with an even-handedness that in such polarized times made her distrusted by both sides. The self-proclaimed "democratic" intellectuals and "civil society" were promoters of what she called "the culture of the lie." They were created and manipulated by the state in the name of national security. Algerians were caught between state repression and Islamic terrorism. "We are now Bosnia and Rwanda all in one. The death knell has become our national anthem. The country is everywhere in mourning."

Algeria was disintegrating. Outrage followed outrage. In January 1995, the GIA claimed credit for a car bombing outside Algiers's main police station that killed 42 people and wounded 286. Less than a month later, the security forces took revenge by killing 99 Islamic prisoners and wounding 10 more in an alleged "uprising" at Serkadji Prison in the capital—the single bloodiest incident to date since the current cycle of violence began. The Middle East had not witnessed such shocking state revenge against prisoners since 1982, when the Syrian regime had murdered some five hundred defenseless Islamist inmates in jail in Palmyra.[4]

Could this be the same country I first visited during its brief, intoxicating "democratic" moment between 1989 and 1991? Had I known Algeria better at the time, I might have sensed that even President Chadli Benjedid's "great political opening" was not what it seemed and that, as Aicha had warned me, what was visible in her country was only camouflage. Algeria taught me as much about political cynicism and self-delusion as it did about the alleged struggle between "democracy" and "political Islam" taking place in this tortured land. For almost nothing in Algeria was what it seemed or purported to be.

MOST VISITORS to Africa's third-largest country, one-fifth the size of the United States, have been impressed by Algeria's beauty. While much of the country is uninhabited desert, the seven-hundred-mile-long coastal strip along the Mediterranean, where most of the 28 million Algerians live, offers a temperate climate and magnificent scenery. Algiers, the capital, niched in hills overlooking a bay of the Mediterranean, is particularly stunning—a North African Marseilles. Alexis de Tocqueville, who visited Algiers in 1841, a decade after the French had conquered it, wrote that he had never seen anything quite like its "astounding mixture of races and native dress—Arabs, Berbers, Moors, Blacks, French," all of whom went about their business feverishly amid the din of perpetual construction. In Algiers, as in America, which he had also described so perceptively, "one hears only the sound of the hammer." Algiers, he said, was "Cincinnati on African soil"; Algeria was "Sicily with French industry."

The French were reconstructing the capital, replacing its narrow, twisting streets with their "grand boulevards" and victory arches, its splendid Moorish houses with modern French villas. The Moorish homes, built around open courtyards and hidden behind tall, white walls, were well suited to the Muslim population's lifestyle — its polygamy, seclusion of women, and absence of public life. Behind those walls, Algerians "could hide much about their lives" from Algeria's "sly, tyrannical government."[5]

Tocqueville quickly sensed Algeria's malaise as well as the problems France would encounter in its *mission civilisatrice.* France's attorney general in Algiers warned him that "nothing would come of Algeria" and that it would be best if the French left "as soon as possible." Algeria, said the chief doctor at Algiers hospital, was "a study in evil" even within France's "detestable colonial system." Algerians were bitter about being overtaxed by and governed from Paris, without local advice, much less consent. Tocqueville was also impressed by the Arabs' devotion, despite their war weariness, to Sheikh Abdelkader, a young tribal chief who managed to unite some but not all of the country's quarrelsome tribes and clans against French rule and who, to this day, is one of the few heroes in Algeria's past revered by all groups in this contentious society. And he was appalled by the French commander of Philippeville who boasted of having decapitated a murder suspect and spiked his head on the city gate of Constantine. "Nothing succeeds with these people," the French colonel had told Tocqueville coolly, "except terror and force."

Tocqueville wondered whether the "cascade of violence and injustice" in Algeria would not necessarily end in "an indigenous revolt and the ruin of the Europeans."

That it did. But five generations of crushingly brutal French rule, coupled with the barbaric eight-year-long struggle between 1954 and 1962 to end it— what historian Alistair Horne called Algeria's "Savage War of Peace"—deeply scarred Algerians, helped mold the country's modern politics, and at least partly explains the country's current misery.

The French were not Algeria's first invaders or the cruelest. Once known as Numidia, Algeria was ruled for seven centuries by the Carthaginians and in the second century B.C. by Rome. After Rome came Vandals, Byzantines, Arabs —who brought with them the Islam that would forever change this land— Spaniards, and finally Ottoman Turks. The Turks succeeded where others had failed, according to one historian, because they refused to mingle with, or take an interest in, the local population. Instead, they insisted only on the steady payment of hefty local taxes.[6] They also maintained order through their superbly trained Janissaries, equipped with modern cannons that no Arab or Berber opponent possessed, and by appointing the most powerful Arab tribes as their tax collectors. Finally, the Turks made concessions to the country's religious nobility: Algeria's marabouts, its holy men and charismatic leaders of mystical Sufi orders, were exempt from taxes and given special privileges. Independent-minded marabouts were killed, as was anyone who threatened Ottoman order. But rather than fight the local religious and tribal system, as the French would later do, the Turks profited from it. Pirates and slavers flourished during much of the three centuries of Turkish rule. In fact, piracy, a bloody and violent enterprise, was Algiers's principal occupation.[7]

The pretext for France's invasion was pique — an "insult" by the Turkish-appointed dey of Algiers, the local ruler. In 1827, the dey was said to have lost his temper during trade talks with the French consul, struck him with a fly whisk, and called him "a wicked, faithless, idol-worshipping rascal."[8] France waited three years before demanding satisfaction. The invasion itself was a relaxed affair. Pleasure boats carrying elegant "grandes dames" were invited to witness the naval bombardment of Algiers at "a respectful distance," as one newspaper advertised.

After seventeen years of often brutal "pacification" and the surrender and exile of the rebel marabout and tribal chief Emir Abdelkader in 1847, the French felt secure in Algeria. Despite continued fighting in the interior, much of it led by other local marabouts whom the French eventually killed or co-opted,[9] relative security prevailed by the century's end. But France eventually recognized its error in having eliminated the Muslims' natural leaders. By destroying the most powerful tribes and grand families, Algeria's governor-general complained in 1894, France was without any "authoritative intermediaries between ourselves and the indigenous population." What remained in Algeria, he said, was "human dust."[10]

France's occupation left Algeria with the trappings of modern European civilization: good roads through often challenging terrain, railways and airfields, ports and great cities, electricity and gas, a medical service, agricultural development, and North Africa's most productive vineyards. But last, and surely most critical, was its legacy of the French language and French educational institutions, which, paradoxically, produced many of Algeria's revolutionaries. For as historian Horne noted, not only were allusions in French history books to "Our ancestors, the Gauls, painfully incongruous" to Arab and Berber students, the educational emphasis on the "Great French Revolution" could not help but impress young Algerians with the virtue of rebellion. Demands for change came not from those who had suffered most under French rule but from this relatively small group of partially integrated, French-educated Muslims who were denied full acceptance in French life and politics.[11]

Another source of national resistance was Algeria's Islamic community, which was even then as divided and faction-ridden as its modern-day counterpart and the rest of Algerian society. The early Islamic movement had at least two major competing strands, each with its own leader and counterpart in contemporary society and both copies of the Islam of the Mashreq, the Arab East. The reformist Islamic movement in the 1920s — when the Muslim Brotherhood was being formed in Egypt — was led by Sheikh Abdulhamid Ben Badis, a Berber from Constantine whose family had been religious and local clan leaders for generations.

The conservative Ben Badis was a "Salafi," a believer in Islam *pur et dur*, as the French put it, the Islam ostensibly practiced by the Prophet Muhammad and his first four caliphs. Algerian Muslims had to return to Islam's founding principles — the Koran and the Sunna — and to the example of the "ancestors," he argued.[12] Like the Arabian Wahhabis and other Salafis, Ben Badis asserted that sports, alcohol, tobacco, music, and dancing were forbidden, and he also opposed Algeria's traditional religious establishment. The beloved marabouts, he scoffed, had corrupted the faith with their superstitions, saints, and miracles and had helped divide the *umma*, or Muslim community, by becoming tools of the French, as they were of the Ottomans. But unlike many Salafis who rejected territorial-based nationalism as a "Western" invention, Ben Badis was fiercely nationalist.[13] The association he formed,[14] which gave Algerian nationalists their initial momentum, coined what became a rallying cry of the independence war: "Islam is my religion; Arabic is my language; Algeria is my fatherland."[15]

Ben Badis, however, was no radical or revolutionary. He insisted that his movement was primarily cultural, and he repudiated violence as well as the notion that Algeria's national identity could not be expressed within a French-ruled state. He was willing, in effect, to accept the de facto separation of religious and political authority that had prevailed throughout most of Sunni Arab history.[16] Despite his relentless promotion of the Arabic language and an Islamic identity, Ben Badis was basically a reformer.[17]

The revolutionary within the Islamic camp was the son of a shoemaker named Messali Hadj, Algeria's first modern Islamic populist. A former Communist who had married a French Communist, Messali had turned from communism to Islam — but a modern brand. He endorsed violence against colonialism and was repeatedly jailed by the French. A passionate orator and charismatic rabble-rouser, Messali led a Paris-based group[18] whose program the ruling secular National Liberation Front, known by its French abbreviation, the FLN, would later endorse: universal suffrage, socialism, and land distribution among the fellaheen. On the eve of the revolution, the fellaheen, 85 percent of the population, still lived in the countryside; 90 percent of them were illiterate.

Neither of these rival Islamic groups, however, wound up leading the fight for independence. That honor went to the FLN, led by nine "historical chiefs" whose average age was thirty-two. Not only did most of these men have only a vague religious commitment — despite the FLN's incorporation of Islamic nationalists within their ranks; their Islam was cultural, an essential element of their national identity, but used mainly to mobilize Algerians.[19] The FLN, as its name suggests, was not a political party but a loosely structured coalition of clans, factions, and cliques that sought the overthrow of French colonialism. Miraculously, it held together during the eight-year war for independence despite staggering levels of mistrust and intrigue, personal and political feuds, and substantive and petty rivalries.

One scholar concluded that Algeria's instability and stagnation were the result of the debilitating conflicts within the revolutionary political elite after independence in 1954, which, in turn, were the product of the colonial system and the political dynamics that had led to revolution.[20] Each new Algerian group entered the political system in reaction to the failure of an earlier group. Before independence, for example, Algerian reformers had sought integration into French life. But when Paris rejected their demand for citizenship and other inclusionary reforms, the reformers were supplanted by "radicals," who favored violence to end colonial rule. The radicals, in turn, were replaced by even more militant "revolutionaries" when Paris spurned the radicals' demands for more autonomy and made it impossible for Algerian Muslims to become French citizens without effectively renouncing Islam. Because new politicians were not recruited into a system with well-defined "rules of the game," Algerian groups developed narrow ideas about how best to rule, and "intransigence" prevailed over "bargaining and compromise."[21] This psychosis soon infected all segments of Algerian political life.

Algerians, collectively and individually, remained "complex and full of complexes," or as one Algerian radical observed, "an absolutist people" whose mentality was "characterized by the right angle."[22] The FLN, and Algerians in general, had been united only by their hatred of French rule. In keeping with French political tradition, they were *contre* (against). What they were collectively *pour* (for) was elusive. So it was hardly surprising that the FLN, like many anticolonialist movements, did not remain cohesive after the French left and the object of their rage disappeared. Algerian identity had never been resolved, said my friend Rachid Mimouni, the writer. Was Algeria French or Arab, Berber or Arab, Middle Eastern or North African? Mashreq (the East), or Mashreb (the West)? Was it Mediterranean Algiers and the coastal cities or the country's "authentic" interior? Was it open and modern or backward and closed? Revolutionary or reactionary? Duality marked virtually every aspect of Algerian life. "In politics, religion, and culture," he told me, "there are at least two Algerias. And each Algerian is at least two people. Algeria's dualism is individual and collective."

While the FLN leadership was commonly thought of as secular, it manipulated Islamic symbols. The war for independence was a jihad; FLN rebels were mujahideen.[23] After the war, the ulema pressed for, and to a limited extent secured, government support for the development of a nominally Arabo-Islamic society to which the revolution, at least rhetorically, was committed and through which it had mobilized the illiterate, more religious, and traditional interior of the country. In 1964, Algeria's first president began "Arabizing" the school system and made religious instruction compulsory in state schools. The government also tolerated the creation of the Al-Qiyam (Values Association), responsible for the cultural renewal of Algerian Islam. But while the ulema were given a role in education and religious affairs, they were discouraged and often prohibited from becoming involved in broader policymaking. Lip service was paid to Islam; concessions were made, but mostly to co-opt the ulema, as the French, the Turks, and Arab leaders throughout the Middle East had always done. In 1966, when Al-Qiyam, for example, protested Egypt's execution of Sayyid Qutb, the Egyptian Muslim Brotherhood radical who had so loathed America, the government promptly dissolved it.

Not all religious Algerians accepted the state's "official" Islam or religious co-optation. While some pressed for radical change, but within the system, others became convinced that the FLN state itself was the problem. The only way to build an Islamic society, a minority concluded, was through force.[24] The military leader of this faction was Mustafa Bouyali, a young Islamic radical who founded one of the first Islamist maquis.[25] Between 1982 and 1987, the year Bouyali was killed by government security forces, his tiny group — about twenty-five men and fewer than two hundred to three hundred sympathizers — led an increasingly violent struggle against the "impious" government. Despite their tenacity, however, such radicals were marginal in Algeria's Islamic politics until the 1990s.

The government controlled Islamic forces through its secret police and its vast oil and gas wealth. During the 1970s, when state power reached its zenith, most Algerians, and even state-blessed religious leaders, acquiesced to the government's "Islamic secularism." Few seemed to notice, much less protest, the antithetical planks in the 1976 national charter, which stated, on the one hand, that Algeria was "socialist," that is, secular and revolutionary, and on the other, that "Islam is the state religion."[26] The revolution, after all, owed its legitimacy not to Islam but to its triumph over the French.

At the peak of its power, Algeria's ruling FLN adopted a policy that unwittingly undermined its leadership and the state. In an effort to silence critics, President Houari Boumédienne, the general who had overthrown Algeria's first president in 1965, began emphasizing the country's "Arab" and "Islamic" character. A graduate of Egypt's al-Azhar, Boumédienne imported thousands of Egyptian schoolteachers — many of them Muslim Brethren — to teach Arabic in Algerian schools and help make Arabic, rather than French, the educational system's primary teaching language.[27] But along with their language the Egyptian instructors brought the radical new ideas of Muslim Brother Sayyid Qutb and other militant Islamic thinkers. A decade later, Muslim preachers who had once preached the state's quietest Islam were encouraging now-radicalized Muslim students to fight secular leftists first on campus and later in the streets.

President Chadli, Boumédienne's successor, intensified efforts to co-opt the religious trend. In the early 1980s, Chadli inaugurated a new Islamic university in Constantine and lifted the ban on the publication of religious books. Hundreds of young Islamists flocked to hear university lectures by the great

Islamic stars of the Arab East—among them, Sheikh Muhammad al-Ghazali, the former Muslim Brother and Islamic expert at al-Azhar University who a decade later would defend the murderers of the writer Farag Foda, the Egyptian "apostate." Sheikh Ghazali, who taught in Constantine for seven years in the 1980s, attracted thousands to the Islamic cause through his mesmerizing sermons. An Egyptian diplomat in Algiers recalled having heard one of Ghazali's more incendiary sermons on television in which the sheikh attacked Egypt's Copts as "infidels" who had sided with foreigners against their own Muslim *umma*. When Sheikh Ghazali left Algeria in 1989, his farewell party was hosted by President Chadli, the sheikh's good friend, whom he had informally advised.[28] Young Algerian Islamists, too, were devoted to the Egyptian preacher. A young FIS activist who later became the group's spokesman in exile called Sheikh Ghazali his "reference," a source of inspiration who had urged the movement's warring factions to "put aside ideological and personal quarrels and work together for Islam."[29]

At first, Chadli implemented the FLN program he had inherited: the half-cocked socialism of Arab postcolonial societies, centralization of state power, and the destruction of independent labor unions, professional associations, political parties (except the sacrosanct FLN), the souk, or bazaar, and other intermediary institutions on which vibrant civil society depends. Algeria's command economy continued to place priority on glamorous heavy industry at the expense of the productive farm sector; it had nationalized land, collectivized agriculture, and steered loans and credit from the country's food sector to exploiting Algeria's vast natural gas reserves, which accounted for more than 95 percent of hard currency earnings. Incompetence and corruption were rampant. But Minister of Energy and Heavy Industry Belaid Abdesselam still boasted in the mid-1970s that Algeria would become by the century's end "Africa's first and the world's second Japan."

Such illusions crumbled with a population explosion and the collapse of oil and gas prices in the mid-1980s. The smug government had actively encouraged a more than doubling of the population after independence, shunning, despite demographers' warnings, population planning until 1983. Young Algerians flocked to the cities, tripling their size in less than twenty years. These semieducated youngsters inhabited the hovels of the Casbah and the shantytowns ringing Algiers—seven to a room, many of them sleeping in shifts. They lacked sewage or water. But they were *parabolisé*, as the French said, linked by television *parabols* (satellites) to Parisian and Western culture. They knew enough to want, but not enough to be able to secure the marvels they saw on television: the spacious apartments, refrigerators filled with Evian bottled water, cars, motorbikes, *le jeans*, and other trappings of French consumer culture.

By the time I arrived in Algeria in 1990, the consequences of Algeria's demographic explosion and misguided development strategy were apparent: The population soared from 8 million in 1962 to 28 million by 1992. Forty percent of Algerians were under fifteen; 75 percent were less than twenty-five years old. Since the early 1970s, 200,000 new job seekers had entered the labor market each year, while the number of available jobs had peaked at 150,000 in 1984.[30] Nearly 50 percent of new workers were unemployed. The government would have to create 4 million jobs by the year 2000 simply to maintain current employment levels. Algeria's national debt was soaring; more than two-thirds of its annual earnings went to servicing its debt. The country, which in 1962 was self-sufficient in food, was now importing 75 percent of its needs. Its nationalized industries were running at 25–30 percent capacity.[31] The ultimate welfare state could no longer fulfill its commitments, and the young citizens of what should have been a wealthy paradise were understandably furious. To save the country from insurrection and economic ruin, the Chadli government had radically shifted policies in 1989 and embraced capitalism, though, loath to utter the reactionary word, ministers called it "liberalization" and economic "reform." Algeria's troubles had just begun.

THE ARGUMENT began at the airport. While I was waiting for my baggage in the arrival hall in the fall of 1990, I asked a baggage handler standing near the carousel whether the tiny beard he was growing signaled his support for the Islamic Salvation Front, the FIS. The previous June, the FIS had stunned Algerian and foreign political analysts alike by sweeping the municipal elections, winning 55 percent of the municipal and gubernatorial votes and gaining control of more than 850 of Algeria's 1,500 municipalities. Many Algerians were jubilant about the message they had sent their stuffy, autocratic rulers, but others were terrified that Algeria would become a "second Iran," or "Qum on the Mediterranean."

The wiry, dour young porter—descriptions of Algerians in newspaper articles were invariably preceded by the adjective "unsmiling"—suddenly beamed and nodded vigorously. "Ah, *oui!*" he declared as he lifted my bag into a trolley. "Islam is the solution." Overhearing our conversation, another porter joined in. "Ali," he said, poking his colleague gently in the ribs, "you are an idiot. *Tout à fait Majnoun!*" he giggled, blending French and Arabic—100 percent crazy. "Will Islam build you an apartment so you can get married? Will it get us better pay or decent jobs?"

Before long, eight young porters, all wearing the blue uniforms of porters in France, were ardently debating their country's future. Almost all were pro-FIS, or more accurately, antigovernment—Algerian versions of disgruntled American voters keen on "throwing the bums out." I had difficulty following their debate, however. They spoke a curious mixture of Arabic and French, with a smattering of Berber words and expressions. The Arabic was so different from the soft, melodic Egyptian tones I was accustomed to; the French was mostly slang; and the Berber was utterly incomprehensible to me. But they were clearly enjoying themselves. They were still arguing heatedly as I left to clear customs.

Only two years earlier such a scene would have been unthinkable. But Algeria was then exploding with what Algerians called democracy. There were fifty-eight political parties (and eventually sixty-four), some thirty independent newspapers — a real press, unlike Egypt's ritualized official, semiofficial, and opposition newspapers — and a flourishing debate about Algeria's future. It was exhilarating. For the first time, Algerians had enough freedom to engage in real politics.

I should have suspected, however, that Algeria was more complicated than it initially seemed when I checked into the Hotel El-Djazair, the Arabic name for Algeria, and spent twenty minutes searching for my room. The hotel was a stunning white structure with high ceilings and vaulted arches, intricate mosaic floors and inlaid tiles, Arabic lanterns, spacious rooms and vistas. Under the French, it was the Hôtel Saint-Georges, opened in 1889, though part of the building was built on the ruins of an Ottoman villa, I was told: Its exact origins, like most things Algerian before the arrival of the French, were somewhat vague. The hotel's interior was a maze, a defiance of logic and common sense. Rooms 1101–1124 were on the first floor (the French first floor; the second floor to Americans), but so were rooms 2101–2124 as well as 3101–3133. Rooms 1204–1224 were on the second floor (i.e., on the third level), as were rooms 1210–1233 and 3201–3233. Eventually, I reasoned that the second digit of the number must indicate the room's floor, but no one actually told me that. Algerians detested what they called the "service" mentality of Egyptians and other Arabs, which meant that getting anything done in Algeria was an ordeal. No one, of course, had even considered posting a sign or a floor map in the hotel to aid the befuddled, baggage-laden traveler.

Algerian politics resembled the hotel's layout. Nothing was quite what one expected or what it pretended to be. While the government had billed Algeria's new political liberalization as a bold foray into democracy, a cause for hope and optimism, diplomats and cynical Algerians called it a ploy by President Chadli and his ruling elite to retain power, to continue "talking left, and living right," as one scholar put it.[32]

Change had been forced on the government by the bloody riots of October 1988. To protest rising unemployment, soaring prices, and the FLN's monopoly on power and privilege, thousands of young people had spontaneously taken to the streets, smashing government buildings and state-owned property. The army had responded brutally: Several hundred young protesters were killed; hundreds were tortured. Calm was restored only after Chadli met with Abbassi Madani, the former FLN activist turned Islamist and professor of education, and a delegation of leading Algerian Islamists.[33] In return for helping calm public passions through the mosques and the vast social support networks that Islamists ran in semiclandestinity, the government promised the Islamists greater political freedom and, specifically, the right to organize and compete in elections for their Islamic cause. With order restored, Chadli announced that Algeria would embark on a democratic path: free elections, pluralism, decentralization, economic liberalization, and market reform. Suddenly, this colorless former army officer, whom the army and the FLN elite had selected as president in 1979 precisely because his blandness offended no one, was being compared to Mikhail Gorbachev, minus the charisma or charm.

British historian Hugh Roberts argues that Chadli, in effect, colluded with the FIS to authorize and encourage the then fledgling Islamic political party. Chadli viewed the FIS as less a threat than the "Boumédiennists," the radical socialists and other opponents within his own ruling FLN. Evidence of a tacit alliance is impressive: For instance, Chadli legalized the FIS in 1989—against the advice of most ministers, not to mention Egyptian president Hosni Mubarak and even Libyan leader Muammar Qaddafi[34]—despite the fact that the new Algerian constitution and implementing laws banned religious-based parties and any political association that advocated abrogating the people's sovereignty. In October that same year, he permitted the FIS to overshadow the government in taking charge of large-scale relief operations after an earthquake in Tipasa, a seaside resort forty miles west of Algiers.[35] Moreover, the government did not station police at voting stations during the 1990 municipal elections to stop the well-deployed FIS from intimidating secular voters and lobbying the undecided to vote for "God and the Koran." Even after the FIS swept the local elections, Chadli continued telling diplomats that Islamists did not threaten his regime and that several key Arab leaders had praised his experiment in democracy.[36] He also persisted in overlooking the FIS's illegal use of the country's ten thousand mosques for political organizing and proselytizing.[37]

Several experts on Algeria dismissed the notion that Chadli and the FIS had actively "conspired" against rival militants in the ruling FLN as "too conspiratorial," even for Algeria. But most conceded that the FIS would probably not have scored its impressive electoral gains without at least the tacit support of Chadli's FLN faction.[38]

Just as the ruling FLN was first and foremost a "front," that is, a coalition, so, too, was the FIS. If the FLN was a politically opportunistic assembly of bickering clans and ideologically divergent factions, its Islamic mirror image was the FIS. The FIS's cantankerous groups and individuals, with their disparate ideologies and backgrounds, were united only by a vague Islamic program aimed at creating popular support for an equally vague Islamic state. The splits within the FIS—never mind those between the FIS and its non-"front" Islamic rivals—were just as bitter as those within the FLN. The abbreviation FIS, after all, sounds like "fils," or "son" in French. The Islamist son proved disturbingly similar—in ideological diversity as well as in its talent for cynical manipulation and political opportunism—to the FLN, its secular nationalist "father."

Only after I met several key FIS leaders did I understand how truly diverse the FIS was. The organization's genius was its appeal not only to Algeria's petite bourgeoisie—the small merchants, craftsmen, and shopkeepers who had been pushed aside by socialism—but also to the jobless underclass—the *hittistes*, the young men whose sole function in life was leaning against the *heet*, the Arabic word for "wall." The FIS's fifteen-point platform contained something for everyone, but curiously, barely a mention of the country's debilitating economic woes.[39] The Islamic coalition's very use of the word "front" was intended to elicit nostalgia for the original national front's victory over France (the West) and to enable the FIS to posture, according to Hugh Roberts, as the FLN's "lineal successor and rightful heir." It was no accident that Abbassi Madani, an FIS founder and leader, was a former FLN patriot who had spent much of the war for independence in jail. And it was also no accident that the group's name was chosen by Abbassi.[40] The FIS deliberately sought to assume the FLN's mantle of leading the struggle against Western exploitation and the fight for justice, equality, and true Islam. Just as the FLN leaders had sensed the need to incorporate Islamic symbols in their fight for independence from France, the FLN veteran Abbassi shrewdly grasped the utility of appropriating Algerian nationalism's central themes and symbols in his campaign for Islam.[41]

I first met the then sixty-year-old leader of the FIS at his modest home in Algiers that fall of 1990, soon after Iraq's invasion of Kuwait. There was no sign of the English wife he had married while completing his doctorate in education in London in the mid-1970s or of Ali Benhadj, the Islamist hothead and FIS coleader whose speech was as violent as Abbassi's was measured.

Offering me coffee and tea in his simple living room, Abbassi was the model Islamic host. Dressed in a flowing white djellaba and a crocheted white skullcap, he looked more like a sheikh than the seasoned FLN politician that he was. His discourse was moderate and filled with common sense. He exuded a confident serenity despite the fact that the Gulf crisis had put him in the uncomfortable position of having to choose between his key financial patron, Saudi Arabia, and the intensely pro-Saddam sentiment of the Algerian public. (After a short-lived effort as a self-appointed "intermediary" between Baghdad and Riyadh, Abbassi, ever the politician, chose the street.) Despite the Saudis' ire, Abbassi sensed that his political moment had come.

He was a short, portly man and very soft-spoken. Islam, he told me, was just and tolerant. It was also supportive of free-market principles, he added quickly, remembering that I was an American. The political cartoons and caustic newspaper articles about the FIS's shoddy and sometimes fanatical administration of municipalities since 1990 were part of a government-inspired "smear campaign" to discredit Islam and his party.

I had been told that the FIS's performance in local government since the June elections was mixed. Reports from Tipasa were mostly positive despite the city government's unpopular and largely unenforced ban on women in shorts within city limits and bathing suits at the beach. Militants had tried to segregate beaches by gender, but they were overruled by more pragmatic colleagues. Tipasa City Hall had gained a reputation for being a more efficient, "polite" place where ordinary Algerians and their concerns were taken seriously. In Kouba, the teeming, hilly suburb of Algiers into which more than eighty-six thousand Algerians were crowded, the new Islamic government had introduced literacy classes in mosques, delivered food and services to the poor, and prodded an unresponsive welfare bureaucracy. It had also replaced the old FLN revolutionary slogan "For the People, By the People" on city hall with a new plastic sign designating Kouba as "An Islamic Community of the Region." During Ramadan, the Muslim holy month of dawn-to-dusk prayer and fasting, city officials served a free meal to religious and nonobservant men alike at the municipal auditorium to celebrate *iftar*, the breaking of the daily fast—an unprecedented act of charity and Islamist grassroots politicking.

In some cities, however, disputes raged between secularists and Islamists. In one such town, officials had infuriated Algerian feminists by segregating public transportation: men in the front of buses and women in the back, behind a curtain, Saudi style. Women's groups across the country had also protested the mayor of Annaba's dismissal of an office secretary of thirteen years because she refused to wear a veil. In religiously inclined Constantine, local officials had banned coeducation. Several cities had closed liquor stores and tried to prohibit the sale of wine to nontourists in restaurants. In Oran, a port city of 700,000, officials outraged music lovers by banning a popular annual festival of traditional *rai* during Ramadan. Some disputes had turned violent. In Algiers, for example, fourteen people were injured when militants attacked a crowd at a popular Ramadan concert, throwing stones and Molotov cocktails after their effort to block the concert hall's entrances failed.

Abbassi told me that he "deplored" the violence and that such attacks had been staged mainly by "government agents provocateurs" to discredit the FIS. He had always denounced similar disruptions, he told me, despite the fact that such concerts were "inappropriate" during the holy month of Ramadan, supposedly reserved for meditation and prayer. People had called the FIS to complain about the music and noise, he told me. "Algerians have a right to listen to music, but their countrymen also have a right to pray at home in tranquility and to get some sleep. If your neighbor took a hammer and started pounding at your walls, what would you do?"

There should be limits to such insensitivity; compromises had to be made, he said. This was the "middle way" favored by the FIS and Islam. This was true democracy, a "balancing of freedoms."

Abbassi's gentle, trilling voice was hypnotic. I found myself nodding in agreement and struggling to marshal skeptical questions. "Freedom is the basis of democracy, as it is in America," he continued. "It is the expression of the popular will, the collective will. What is important is that we have ended one-party rule in Algeria. Our democracy may be weak, but it exists."

I knew that Ali Benhadj, the then thirty-four-year-old coleader of the FIS, did not share Abbassi's ostensible enthusiasm for America or democracy. In his Friday sermons at Kouba Mosque, which had become best-selling cassettes, this brash orator maintained that whenever democracy and Islam collided, Islam had to prevail. The FIS itself, he said, was only a "means to an end," the creation of an Islamic state in Algeria and, ultimately, the restoration of the Muslim caliphate to guide all the world's Muslims.[42]

For Benhadj and other FIS militants, democracy was automatically suspect because it was an "imported" idea of "impious" Western origin and American sponsorship.[43] Democracy was based on the people's sovereignty, whereas believers knew that sharia, or sacred Islamic law, derived its legitimacy from God. Individual interpretation, executive authority, and judicial maneuvering had to be subordinated to, and constrained by, the sacred law. Even "majority rule" could not thwart its implementation by a virtuous caliph: If he governed by sharia, his rule, as interpreted by the virtuous few (i.e., Benhadj and his followers), had to be obeyed. Look at what democracy had reaped in America and the West: AIDS, homosexuality, sexual promiscuity, hedonism, greed, egotism, and rampant individualism! Man was weak and easily tempted; self-mastery of lust and passion was impossible, Benhadj said, echoing the view of an earlier, more celebrated Algerian fundamentalist: Christianity's St. Augustine.

The message had been elaborated upon by the medieval jurist Ibn Taymiyya and by more modern militants like Egypt's Sayyid Qutb, both of whom, Benhadj said, had inspired his own beliefs.[44] Because they were not governed by sharia, Westerners lacked moral proportion. "The Europeans do not respect human rights alone but go further and defend animal rights in the manner of that tart Brigitte Bardot," he declared. "They even defend vegetation rights like those of public parks!" he added. Westerners, moreover, confused freedom with sexual permissiveness. "This is what they call 'syphilization,'" he scoffed in a rare attempt at humor.[45]

For Benhadj, democracy, like the FIS itself, was useful only in securing power. In his future Islamic state no "anti-Muslim ideas" would be "aired in public," he candidly told the faithful. A virtuous order, not democracy or human rights, was his goal. And revenge was his motive. The FLN would pay for its shallow emulation of France, he warned. "Just wait!" Benhadj told more than thirty thousand people who had crouched on prayer rugs in Kouba Mosque and on the streets surrounding it after the FIS municipal victory in June. "The day will come when we will settle the account for the blood of our martyrs that you have shed. The day of accounting has come!"

This was the "democrat" praised by so many Western scholars. This was the "yin" to Abbassi Madani's "yang," the ugly face of Algerian Islamism that had made so many Westernized Algerians fear for their future.

Abbassi seemed unperturbed by my questions about Benhadj's rantings. Such intemperate statements were only further proof of the FIS's pluralism, he said calmly. Yes, some excesses had occurred in municipalities under Islamic local rule, but they were "exceptions." The FIS was still learning. Benhadj was young, he reminded me—young enough to be his "son." Several Algerians, in fact, had told me that Benhadj, whose father had died when he was an infant, deferred to Abbassi as the father he never had. And Abbassi was clearly protective of this young Rasputin. The preachy righteousness that had alienated so many Algerians would diminish once FIS officials were given the task of reviving the country's moribund economy, Abbassi assured me.

The FIS knew that Algeria's problems could not be solved overnight. Moreover, the FLN had undermined the FIS's municipal rule by reversing its local edicts and cutting city budgets. In response, FIS supporters had organized voluntary patrols to pick up garbage, clean streets, and perform other essential services that the government would no longer finance. But local officials lacked the resources and authority to build housing, provide more power or drinking water, and pave decrepit roads. To do that, the FIS needed to rule. "Restoring civic pride and a sense of identity takes time," Abbassi said. "But we will succeed — there is no doubt," he said, his voice rising in conviction for the first time in our interview. "The whole world is watching Algeria. We have an appointment with history. Under Islam we will do what the FLN set out to do and failed. Our deserts will be more fertile than California. We will rebuild our cities and make our barren land fertile once more. We will revive our nation!"

WHEN I RETURNED to Algiers in February 1992, Abbassi Madani's boast was as hollow as Belaid Abdesselam's two decades earlier. Algeria was neither California nor Japan. It was an armed camp.

Abbassi and Benhadj were in prison, arrested the previous June after the end of an FIS-led strike that had turned violent. In December 1991 the long-delayed parliamentary elections were finally held, and the FIS, despite the imprisonment of its two leaders, had won 188 of the 430 seats in the assembly in the first voting round; the FLN won 15. Most analysts predicted that the second round would give the FIS not only a majority but the two-thirds majority needed to change Algeria's constitution to create an Islamic state. After intense, secret negotiations, senior army officers, led by Gen. Khaled Nezzar, the defense minister, had forced the resignation of a devastated President Chadli, who, according to diplomats, had suffered several near-nervous breakdowns since the riots of 1988. The second voting round was canceled, the initial results annulled, and a state of siege declared.

In February 1992 the army established the High State Council to rule for the next two years. In March the FIS was banned. While many denounced the coup, Tunisia, Jordan, Libya, and Egypt — all plagued by militant Islamic movements — gasped with relief. So did France, whose southern port Marseilles is only five hundred miles from Algiers. The last thing Paris wanted was an influx of Westernized Muslims fleeing an Islamic Algeria. Relief, too, was shared by many of Algeria's Westernized, secular middle class, especially women. But much of Algeria, and the world, were outraged.

The head of the High State Council was Mohammed Boudiaf, one of the few surviving historical "chiefs" of the 1954 revolution, who was widely regarded as an incorrupt patriot and pluralist. Boudiaf had spent twenty-eight years in exile in Morocco rather than live under what he had denounced as Algeria's military dictatorship. But a senior member of the High State Council had finally persuaded the obstinate revolutionary hero to take the job,[46] and now Boudiaf was attempting to explain his decision at his first — and last — international news conference.

Standing before me was a bit of history. Wearing a no-nonsense navy-blue business suit, starched white shirt buttoned tight at the neck, and a crimson tie, Boudiaf came across as a tough-minded fighter with few illusions about his country's jagged-edge politics or its smoldering resentments. He was small but strongly built. His hands were uncommonly large and powerful. His long, hawkish nose, sharp eyes, and large ears were accentuated by his baldness. He resembled a bird of prey. He did not look his seventy-one years.

He had returned, he told the assembled journalists in French, because Algeria needed him. It was that simple. "You in the foreign press expected civil war!" he said, sizing up his audience. "Thank God we have avoided that curse."

Algeria, he said, had stopped the election process temporarily in order to save it — an argument that seemed all too reminiscent of America's assertion during the Vietnam War that it had destroyed Vietnamese villages in order to save them. "You have to respect the rules of the game in order to play," Boudiaf said. "The FIS did not respect those rules. The Koran would have destroyed democracy."

The state had receded from public life; anarchy, not democracy, had prevailed. He had fought for democracy for thirty years, he said. He was not about to see it usurped by "fascists," like those who threatened Europe in 1939. I would hear this argument often in the fearful months that followed, and not just from officials. Some of the country's best writers and intellectuals, among them Rachid Mimouni, cited Nazi history to justify what they called Algeria's "suspension" of democracy. "Judith, put yourself in our place," Rachid had told me one night over a dinner and a good bottle of Algerian red wine at Le Bardo, a restaurant that served French cuisine to Algeria's Francophone elite. "If, in 1933, in Weimar, Germany, you could have found a nondemocratic way to stop Hitler after an election in which he, too, won roughly the same proportion of votes as the FIS, shouldn't you have done so? Make no mistake. These Islamists are fascists — green fascists."

An "Islamic Republic" could not be democratic, Boudiaf continued. "Is Iran democratic?" There was nothing Islamic or patriotic about sending young Algerians to kill other Algerians in the name of God, an apparent allusion to an FIS list of "heretics" slated for murder that the government had reportedly found in the city of Mascara. I had dismissed the existence of such lists as government propaganda. Only later, when journalists and other "heretics" began to be killed, did I realize that my judgment was probably rash.

"At the same time," Boudiaf added, pausing for effect, "we've heard those who voted for the FIS. We've known your sorrow, your pain. We advise young believers to be patient. We are ready to talk. We are ready to listen."

The High State Council was running Algeria, he asserted, not the army. "It's good to have an army that does not want to seize power," he told us. The army had stepped in, he concluded, only to "prevent civil war and save the country."

This being Algeria, I suspected that the army's role was not quite so selfless.

The 120,000-man armed forces had been Algeria's driving force since independence in 1962—a privileged group indeed. Since the beginning of Chadli's liberalization in late 1988, senior officers had warned the government that it would not permit the country to descend into anarchy. General Nezzar hated the FIS, and Ali Benhadj in particular. For in February 1991, Benhadj had mocked the military in a noisy demonstration of 400,000 in front of the Defense Ministry to protest Algeria's neutrality in the Gulf war. "We will defend Iraq and fight the United States if our pathetic military, the 'protector of the revolution,' refuses!" Benhadj had declared. Nezzar, a sixty-four-year-old graduate of the War College of Paris and Soviet Military Academy and a ferocious opponent of Islamic radicals, seethed, awaiting the moment for revenge.

I finally heard a credible version of why the generals had ousted Chadli when I visited a senior government official late one night at La Résidence Mithaq, the elegant, heavily guarded government guest palace turned fortress where the army chiefs, the High State Council, and senior officials met to make policy. La Résidence, whose grand, if understated, reception room was filled with soft leather sofas and mahogany coffee tables, was about as far from the squalor of the Casbah as one could get. The luxury surprised me, for although there was a large gap in living standards between the rich and poor in Algeria, wealthy Algerians tended not to flaunt their good fortune as ostentatiously as their counterparts did in other Arab countries. I recalled visiting my friend Mohammed Yazid, an FLN founder, at his modest villa. He had picked me up in his five-year-old Mercedes. His chauffeur addressed his boss by his first name, and Mohammed rode at his side, not in the backseat. "This is Algerian egalitarianism," Mohammed joked.

As I waited in the lobby of La Résidence, a silently attentive staff served me endless cups of French coffee and tea in imported French porcelain demitasse cups. The silver boxes on the tables were filled with imported cigarettes—none Algerian. The exhausted official finally received me close to midnight. His jacket and tie were off; his collar was undone. His eyes were ringed by shadows, raccoonlike. He insisted, as so many Algerians did, that he not be identified.

After the FIS swept the municipal elections in June 1990, he told me, Chadli's clique concluded that its effort to build up the FIS in order to balance hard-liners within the FLN had been all too successful. "The FIS's wings had to be clipped," he told me. The army was losing confidence in Chadli's ability to control the situation. So Chadli fired the prime minister, who had engineered the reforms, and replaced him with Sid Ahmed Ghozali, a bright, French-educated engineer and former minister addicted to Marlboros and bow ties. The government passed a new election law designed to contain the FIS's future gains and amplify what Chadli's out-of-touch advisers assumed would be a slight plurality for the FLN in the next elections. Districts were then gerrymandered.[47] Outraged by such steps, Abbassi and Benhadj called for a strike despite warnings from the prime minister that the government (i.e., the army) would not tolerate such a hostile action. Ghozali told his aides that, curiously, Abbassi did not seem alarmed by the government's threats. Only later did he learn that Abbassi had been meeting secretly with President Chadli to set ground rules for the strike.[48] When Ghozali finally confronted Chadli about his secret contacts, the president denied having made any "deal" with the FIS. As a result, Ghozali grew increasingly suspicious of Chadli, the official said.

The strike fizzled, probably because so many FIS supporters had no jobs to stay away from, but the street protests surrounding it, as Prime Minister Ghozali had feared, turned violent. The army came out of its barracks, not unhappily. After a month of unrest and a state of emergency, Abbassi called for an end to the strike, but too late. By then General Nezzar had arrested his nemesis Benhadj, hundreds of activists, and even Abbassi Madani himself.

Tension within the ruling elite mounted. Senior army officials urged President Chadli to ban the FIS, but Chadli refused. The army also wanted the election deferred, a demand Chadli had also ignored. Ghozali and other aides supported Chadli, insisting that the FIS could not possibly win given the new election system and with its leaders in jail. The referendum, Chadli and his aides insisted, would be held. Neither the FIS nor the FLN would win a clear majority, Chadli reassured the army's leaders. That's what the polls showed.[49] So Parliament would be divided, and Chadli would be able to stay on as arbiter between the FLN elite and the FIS.

The FIS landslide in the first round of voting in December 1991 was followed by an eerie silence from the presidential palace. The election results were ironic. The FIS had won 3.2 million of the approximately 6 million votes cast (about half of the 13 million people eligible to vote had not done so) — about a million fewer votes than the Islamists had won in the 1990 municipal elections. But since the FLN vote had collapsed (from 17.5 percent of the electorate in 1990 to 12.17 percent in 1991), the government's owned rigged "winner take all" system ensured that the FIS would win almost a majority of seats on the first ballot and probably get the two-thirds majority it needed in the runoffs to make Algeria an Islamic state.[50]

As speculation soared about whether the army would prevent the second voting round, Chadli remained at home, unwilling to receive some of his closest advisers, who waited ever more anxiously for him at the presidential offices. Meanwhile, Chadli was meeting — secretly, he assumed — with Abdelkader Hachani, the then thirty-five-year-old engineer who had become the acting FIS leader following the arrests of Abbassi and Benhadj. According to a senior official's account of the meeting, Hachani, intent on pursuing Abbassi's strategy of using elections to come to power, offered Chadli a deal: The FIS would permit Chadli to remain president after the second ballot provided he agreed to fire the defense and interior ministers as well as the minister of foreign affairs and replace all three with FIS appointees. What the FIS was seeking, the official told me, was control of the security apparatus of the state.[51] Chadli had accepted the offer, the still-astonished official recounted. "Chadli was prepared to remain in his post as a 'flowerpot' — a powerless figurehead — rather than step down," he said bitterly.

Chadli's meetings with the FIS, it turned out, were no secret to Defense

Minister Nezzar, whose office was monitoring the president's every move. Nezzar and other senior army officers did not see themselves as dispensable in a power-sharing agreement between Chadli's faction of the FLN and the FIS. Nor were they prepared to turn over the country's armed forces to the Islamists. Ghozali, informed by General Nezzar of Chadli's discussions, confronted Chadli, who denied, as he had the previous May, that any secret deals had been made. General Nezzar gave Ghozali a choice: He could back the army or Chadli. Ghozali sided with the system—the army. On January 11, 1992, the army moved. Chadli was out.

RADWAN, I shall call him, one of the 25 percent of Algerians who had voted for the FIS, was devastated by the coup. Unlike those who had cast their ballots against the government rather than for the FIS, Radwan was a true believer. For the past year he had written for *El-Mounqid* (the Savior), the FIS's weekly newspaper. As prearranged in a guarded telephone call, he picked me up at dusk in his battered car on a deserted street near the cemetery in Kouba, an FIS stronghold. Graffiti that warned *"Attention aux traîtres"* (Beware of traitors) was painted on the cemetery's entry gates. Unlike others in the FIS, Radwan had not shaved his beard. "I would rather die than shave it off," he said as I quickly got into his car.

Not many young Algerians had Radwan's conviction—or his recklessness, some would say. Diplomats passed along cruel jokes about how the coup had prompted a razor shortage in Algiers as young militants scrambled to shed the telltale sign of Islamic affiliation. A beard alone was enough to get a young man picked up in one of the nightly police sweeps of popular quarters. By mid-February 1992 more than ten thousand FIS activists were being held in camps in the desert, though the government claimed that no more than six thousand men were under arrest and that none were being tortured.

Radwan and I had met when I toured his newspaper in the fall of 1990. He had the emaciated look of all revolutionaries, but like so many of the Islamist brand, he was soft-spoken and seemed utterly sincere. We had argued in French about the role of women in an Islamic state and about the impending Gulf war. Radwan was pro-Saddam despite the secular Iraqi leader's instant conversion to Islam on the eve of the war and his ruthless repression of Islamists and all other opponents. Radwan had also defended the FIS's economic program, which, he said, favored "economic liberalism," but opposed "savage capitalism" and "the dictatorship of the dollar." The FIS, he said, was also against monopolies, the country's "trabandist" economy—the informal contraband markets that kept most Algerians afloat—and, of course, the sale of drugs, wine, and other alcohol. Algeria was rich, he said; but Algerians, 99 percent of whom were Muslims, were poor. The FIS would end the rampant corruption, the informal Paris-based "mafias" that took a cut of every foreign project in the country. It would build housing and create jobs; how he could not say. It would pay women to stay home, "protected," to take care of their children—their "proper role." "If you don't have enough jobs," he continued, "wouldn't you give the job to a man, the head of a household who must support a family, rather than a woman?" Women would be persuaded—"Islam does not believe in coercion," he added quickly—that this was best for Algeria, he said. I laughed out loud. "Not the Algerian women I've met, Radwan!"

We disagreed, but I had admired his spirit. Now the intense young man hunched down over his steering wheel looked terrified. He hadn't been home for more than a week, he told me. His newspaper was closed, and several of his colleagues and FIS leaders had been arrested. The FIS was still issuing communiqués calling upon the army to release activists from jail, restore the democratic process, and avoid shedding the "blood of their brothers." The FIS was still determined to "work within the system," he told me.

It was hopeless, I thought, as we drove aimlessly through the ugly suburb, with its endless clusters of gray cement and cinder-block tenements—unmarked, unfinished, uncared for—graffiti in several languages defacing the crumbling walls. Radwan was naive if he thought the army would voluntarily relinquish power. All he had to do was look around. Tanks guarded the entrances to bridges and tunnels. Machine gun–toting soldiers in the blue uniforms worn by their French counterparts, and riot police, their faces hidden by male "veils," black-visored helmets, patrolled the city's broad boulevards and the Casbah's labyrinthine alleys. After the 10:30 P.M. curfew the normally bustling city was deserted. Only the cats would be out, scrounging for food through the pyramids of uncollected garbage that littered the streets.

"There's one basic fact they cannot change." He sighed as we slowed down. "We chose democracy; the government did not."

Radwan dropped me off near the Martyrs' Monument, an imposing concrete memorial to the victims of the war of liberation that was built atop the ruins of a poor quarter that the government, with its typical sensitivity to the "masses," had flattened.

"The West fears us because it suspects that Islam is fairer than your system. And it fears it in Algeria because Islam may succeed in a rich country. So Jews and Zionists have tried to distort our religion and give our movement a bad name."

I made a mental note of the unusual reference to the radical Islamists' "Little Satan"—Israel. Algerians tended less than other Islamists to blame Israel for their woes. There were so many other convenient villains at home and in nearby France.

"We will win in the end," Radwan vowed as we parted. I waved good-bye, knowing he would not shake my hand. "And when we do, we will remember who stood with us—and who was against us."

I shuddered as he drove off into the chilly night toward Kouba. My young friend had grown so bitter. He was now a part of his country's historical cycle of repression and revenge. I feared for his enemies, and I feared for him. I asked about him on my subsequent trips, but I never saw Radwan again.

•

YASMINE BELKACEM was just as committed to her position as Radwan was to his. "They will never win," she declared in perfect French over mint tea in her small villa in fashionable Hydra. "The half of me that remains will fight them to the death."

Her declaration was not hyperbole. Yasmine had no legs. They were blown off at the hips when she was fifteen years old fighting the French, an early recruit to the "maquis." The bomb she was carrying went off in her handbag in front of the police station instead of inside it, as its makers had intended. Her partner in the daring raid was killed instantly. She was tortured in the hospital. The French had then tortured her mother when Yasmine refused to talk. An Algerian doctor, a secret FLN sympathizer, had kept her alive, even though, in pain, she had pleaded to die.

Yasmine wheeled herself around the apartment with ease born of decades of practice as she fixed our tea. Her housekeeper was off that day, she apologized. The smell of burning incense mingled with the soft, damp air of spring. The house was immaculate, serene, and filled with plants—a welcome relief from the din and chaos outside. I looked at a photograph on the white wall of her simple villa. A beaming, much younger Yasmine stared out at me. Seated next to her was an equally radiant President Ahmed Ben Bella.

"That was taken the day Algeria was admitted to the United Nations," she said proudly. "I accompanied our official delegation to New York. I cried as the Algerian flag was raised alongside all the others. After so much suffering and sacrifice, we were a free nation at last! An independent state. A progressive, secular country. It was," she said more softly, "the finest day of my life."

Her large brown eyes stared out at me as she poured the tea, searching, it seemed, for a sense of my own political sympathies. Algeria was grateful to America, she told me. "Your President Kennedy said that Algeria should be free. We never forgot that. Now the Islamists denounce 'the West.' But America supported our fight for liberation—in spirit at least. France would have killed every one of us if it could have. So what exactly is 'the West'? There is no West. It's another example of the extremists' ignorance and demagoguery."

It was hard not to admire this woman, to respect her spirit and determination. She was the embodiment of the "revolution," as Algerians called their war for independence, a struggle that was now ancient history to the more than three-quarters of Algerians born after 1962. For many Americans my age, Algeria evoked memories of romantic rebellion. Throughout my own youth in the 1960s, Algeria had epitomized the gallant struggle of so many "Third World" nations to evict colonialists, as America had done, to chart an independent course. Algeria was a "vanguard state," as the Arabs had called it, a symbol of stubborn independence in an artificially divided world. To me and other youthful opponents of America's own protracted "imperialistic" war in Vietnam, Algeria was a testament to the power of "oppressed" people to defeat authoritarian or imperialistic regimes. Algeria was Egypt with oil. It had everything—

natural gas, proximity to Europe, talented and politicized citizens, and an iron determination to pursue neutrality — all of which granted it a special place not only in the Arab imagination but throughout the developing world.

Few of us in faraway, democratic America understood what deep scars the war had left. The war, Algerians said, had uprooted 1.8 million Muslims and claimed a million Muslim lives (the French estimate was 300,000) — more than one out of every ten Algerians. All sides had tortured. All had engaged in mutilations and unspeakable reprisals, for the "revolution" was a civil conflict as well as a war for liberation. The French withdrawal was followed by some of the worst slaughter, of political "cleansings." The worst was reserved for the *harkis*, Muslims who had fought for France. Of the more than a quarter million who had sided with the French, fewer than fifteen thousand escaped from Algeria.[52]

"The FIS is killing the very people who liberated this country. And Chadli helped them do it," Yasmine said. "Chadli is the father of this epidemic. After Algeria was muzzled for thirty years, he decided on instant, full-blown democracy. He knew what that would do to Algeria. He didn't care. Not as long as he and his rotten clique survived."

Listening to her, I understood how divided the *nomenklatura* really was. Yasmine had voted against the FIS, but also against the FLN, she told me. And she was not just relieved that the army had taken over to "protect democracy" in Algeria; she was thrilled. Tolerance was not a word that came easily to her lips. "Why should it?" she glared at me. "Chadli, that bastard, nearly wrecked our country. He destroyed everything we fought for. If I had the chance, I would cut him to little pieces."

KHALIDA MESSAOUDI, a younger-generation Algerian feminist, was gentler in tone but no less militant than Yasmine. A small woman in her mid-thirties, with short auburn hair and wearing a well-tailored gray business suit, Khalida picked delicately at the shrimp on her plate. While I was ravenously hungry — the result of yet another attempt to quit smoking — her mind was clearly on politics, not food. We gazed through the scratched picture window at the Mediterranean below and the hills around us. The restaurant at the Aurassi Hotel, a Stalinesque structure built during the heyday of Algerian gas wealth and nonalignment, was as stolid and unimaginative as its food. But the view was spectacular. So was Khalida.

Like Yasmine, she was determined not to flee her country. She agreed that what had begun as a power struggle within the ruling clique had become what she called a battle between a military dictatorship and religious zealots. "As a democrat, as a feminist," she told me in excellent French, "I have no good choices. I'm being offered the plague or cholera. But I'll pick the military over an Islamic state like Iran any day. Because two blueprints for society are at stake: one that appeals to the Enlightenment and human rights and another that is rooted in obscurantism and religious fanaticism."

While most analysts focused on Chadli's deals with the FIS in 1989 and 1990, the government's first major concession to the Islamists was made in 1984, soon after Chadli came to power. His government proposed a regulation that would have required Algerian women to have their husband's or guardian's permission to leave the country. But Algerian women had fought back, Khalida told me, and the order was rescinded. The first major defeat for women also came in 1984, when Algeria adopted a new "family code" that denied women equal rights. "Women, as usual, were the government's first sacrificial lambs," she said, biting her lip as she smiled. "The FIS did not invent misogyny. It merely blessed Algeria's patriarchal structure and its antifemale bias with religious sanction." Many women complained bitterly about earlier drafts of the family code, which took key provisions directly from Islamic sharia. But the final document was even more disappointing. It sanctioned polygamy, enabled a man to "repudiate" his wife, forbade Muslim women from marrying non-Muslim men, and effectively required women to have their husbands' consent to work. For a country that prided itself on its "progressive" credentials, the code was shocking, she said.[53]

Yet it was also another indication of the extent to which the country's self-image conflicted with its reality. The writer Frantz Fanon, the 1960s theorist of the Third World and the rage of young leftists of my generation, had argued that thanks to women's participation in the war for independence, sociosexual relations in Algeria would forever be changed.[54] What Fanon failed to appreciate, or chose to ignore, given his apparent disdain for letting facts inhibit his boosterism of any manifestation of anticolonialism, was not only the depth of Algerian traditionalism and patriarchy but also the inevitable backlash that would occur against French culture, particularly the quintessentially French concept of *égalité* for all citizens, even women. It was the French, not Algerians, who had insisted on educating Algerian women, who had propagandized against the veil, and who had given Algerian women the right to vote for the first time in 1958.[55] And it was men like Sheikh Ben Badis, those revered patriots, who had led the campaign against such un-Algerian measures.

In 1958 the FLN picked up the theme of promoting "authentic" Arabo-Islamic civilization by opposing the women's vote. While Algerian women "freedom fighters" were touring Arab and Third World capitals as propaganda for the new regime, the head of the FLN was telling a leading feminist and former freedom fighter that, now that the war was over, women like her could return to their "couscous." While most societies told women to return to "hearth and home" once a national crisis had passed, Algerians, as usual, went to extremes. The Islamic Values Association in 1964 demanded from its inception that the government restrict certain jobs to Muslim men; its leader openly argued that women were inferior on grounds that "no women prophets have been known." President Boumédienne maintained in 1969 that the role of Algerian girls was "as mothers and upholders of Islamic Arab morality," while boys were expected to "assume political responsibility for the state." But because Boumédienne's

economic goal of industrializing Algeria required a minimal level of literacy for
the society, his government continued emphasizing education, even for girls, at
least until the university level. By the time Chadli became president in 1979, a
new generation of educated women were demanding change. This was about
the time that Khalida, a mathematics professor, became politically active.

"Algerian women had been fighting for a decade for equal rights. We had
organized protests and petitions to our leaders. Imagine our despair when we
learned that Chadli had drafted a code—secretly, behind our backs, without a
single woman adviser—that diminished our legal status! Law is like oxygen.
You can't change culture and mentality without it. Thanks to Chadli's code,
the law was on their side."

Only 6 percent of Algerian women worked, she told me, a dismal rate
when compared with that of conservative Morocco and neighboring Tunisia,
where women represented between 15 and 20 percent of their respective labor
forces.

However appalling the government's record, however, the FIS would be
worse for Algeria and for women, she asserted. "Listen to Ali Benhadj," she said,
referring to the jailed FIS coleader. "His words make your blood run cold. He
would stone adulterers, burn homosexuals, ban women from working. Why not
believe that he means what he says?"

I recalled one of the young sheikh's more spirited commentaries on the
subject. Woman, he said, was a "producer of men." A woman's function was to
"consecrate herself to the education of men." Women produced "no material
goods, but this essential thing which is the Muslim."[56] For men like Benhadj,
even Algeria's retrogressive family code was too permissive.

"His words smack of Ayatollah Montazeri of Iran," she said. "I keep won-
dering, who are these Islamic 'moderates' that Western academics keep talking
about? There are none when it comes to women."

Islam concentrated on the virtue of women, she said, because women
were "the ultimate" mechanism of control. "If you terrorize a man, you don't
automatically terrorize his wife. But if you terrorize a woman, you get her, her
children, and her husband, because by terrorizing her, you've emasculated him,
the patriarch, the head of the household.

"What the Islamists have done is simply take St. Augustine a step further,"
she said. "Augustine, an Algerian, of course, knew that if you controlled sexual
impulse, you controlled the man. The FIS understands that if you control sexual
impulses by controlling women, you've secured ultimate societal control—
supersubmission. Under the FIS, the *umma*, that amorphous 'community,' will
decide whether I work, what I wear, how I make love. It's ultimate power the
Islamists are seeking."

The FIS had intimidated women before they won the National Assembly
elections. Students had accosted a professor friend of hers dressed in jeans,
warning her that "when we take over, you won't be able to 'dress Texan.' " They
had thrown acid at the legs of young unveiled women—"femmes easy," they

called them—prostitutes. The children of working women were referred to as "abandoned." The vice president of a communal assembly had refused to shake her hand. The teenage son of a businesswoman friend had told his mother that he could no longer kiss her good night. His teacher had told him that kissing women, even his mother or sisters, was *haram.*

What was worse, she told me, was that "the attire the Islamists are pushing isn't even Algerian." Algerian women wore the *haiq,* a white cotton or silk scarf, with a smaller piece of white cloth that covered the mouth and chin, that some of her male colleagues found coquettish. The *hijab* worn in Egypt or Iran did not exist in Algeria before the FIS. It was as foreign as the miniskirt. "They not only want to impose Islam on us," she said. "They want to impose a foreign Islam, an Oriental, or eastern, Islam."

Khalida vowed she would never submit to them. "I'll pick up arms if I have to. But I won't leave."

By the end of 1994, Khalida was virtually in hiding. She had not resorted to arms, but she had been forced to abandon her apartment and her teaching post and to spend more time in Paris. Friends told me she had stopped counting the death threats.

THERE WAS no shortage of Algerians who, unlike Khalida, had picked up the Kalashnikov after the 1992 coup. Those who had hoped that President Boudiaf, the last of the FLN historic leaders, would reunify the country and end the violence were devastated when he, too, was assassinated in late June 1992. The man charged with the crime—who by early 1995 had still not been tried in court—was a member of the security forces who was accused of working with Islamic militants. But few Algerians believed that and, typically, were soon spinning conspiracy theories to explain the murder of what many viewed as Algeria's last good hope.[57] The FIS, for its part, denied any role in the killing.[58]

Given the deep rifts that plagued the FIS, however, it was probably inevitable that the group would split first into military and political factions and then be taken over by the most violent elements in the Islamic movement—a typically Algerian pattern. But the FIS, like most Islamist movements, shunned public discussion of its structure, ideology, and tactics. Experience had taught the Islamists that a clever, ruthless state would use such information to exploit the movement's internal tensions. Because of this mafialike vow of silence, much of the FIS's inner workings remained secret.

Unable to interview Benhadj or Abbassi in prison, I began hunting for key FIS founders who had been pushed aside in early power struggles. I tracked down several of them, including Said Gueshi, widely acknowledged as an FIS "father." I found this frail man, who looked older than his forty-seven years, at a quiet hotel on the outskirts of Algiers. Gueshi seemed still very upset over the derailment of his Islamic project.

Nationalism, not Islamism, was his original passion, he told me in French. "I was literally born on a banned Algerian flag." Gueshi was first arrested when he was only ten for having written *"Vive le FLN"* on a school wall. In 1960 the French sentenced him to eight years in prison, but he was freed with independence in 1962. Like many young Algerians, he quickly soured on the FLN but continued working in his native town of Sétif in a government post. Gueshi, who was not religious, told me he had "discovered" Islam's potential utility in attacking the government in 1977 when he and his new wife made the haj to Mecca. He began reading the work of early Islamists, especially Afghani, the nineteenth-century Islamic reformer. The following year, he met Ali Benhadj, and another Islamist who deeply impressed him: Mustafa Bouyali, who would soon lead a jihad against the state and who was also close to Benhadj. In 1982, Gueshi, Benhadj, and other Bouyalists were arrested. Benhadj was sentenced to five years in jail; Gueshi was given three years, "for writing a pamphlet," he says. But Bouyali was not caught, and in 1985 he began conducting fierce hit-and-run guerrilla attacks against the state. In 1987 he was cornered and killed "like a dog," Gueshi told me.

After the traumatic riots of 1988, Gueshi moved to Algiers and met again with Benhadj and other Islamic opponents of the regime. "I understood the implications of Chadli's opening: This was a unique opportunity for us to participate in the political process. The Kabyles were forming a party to fight for their Berber language. If they could do that, I thought, why couldn't we create a party to fight for Islam? As long as it wasn't exclusively a religious party, as long as we had a political program, it would be hard for the government to stop us."

On January 3, 1989, he and ten key figures in the Islamic movement met at the late Bouyali's home to plan what became the FIS. "I proposed forming an Islamic party, a group that advocated not just the Koran and the Sunna but a complete economic, social, and political program — a modern program reflecting modern times."

After more discussions in late January and early February 1989, Abbassi Madani, Ali Benhadj, and the core group announced the creation of the FIS before tumultuous worshipers at the Sunna Mosque in Bab el-Oued, a popular quarter. "It was," Gueshi recalled with tears in his eyes, "the most exciting day of my life."

But Gueshi knew all too well that the brave words and seemingly solid front were illusory. Several key figures in the Islamic movement had rejected the new Islamic front[59] or were rejected by it. The most important was Mohammed Said, the leader of Djaz'ara, the "Algerianists," an informal group of French-speaking Islamic academics and intellectuals who had lobbied for Islam on college campuses in the 1970s and 1980s in the tradition of Ben Badis in the 1930s and the ill-fated Al-Qiyam (Values Association) in the 1960s.[60]

Secretive and elitist, Mohammed Said and his friends had only disdain for lower-class rabble-rousers like Sheikh Ali Benhadj. Said, in particular, detested the young rival. But Abbassi knew that the intellectuals of Djaz'ara could be useful, so he had encouraged Said to join the FIS leadership. Said refused, unwilling to be subordinate to an upstart like Benhadj. Instead, Said denounced the FIS, calling its leaders "ignoramuses." Only after the FIS swept the municipal elections in 1990 did Said realize his error and decide to make a serious bid for FIS leadership.

Even those who joined the new Islamic Salvation Front had severe ideological disagreements. Many were Salafi, who preached a return to the "original" Islamic values and traditions of Islam's "ancestors." But the Salafi house had many rooms, and almost as many tendencies as it had followers. Some, like firebrand Ali Benhadj, shared the radical outlook of the violent Mustafa Bouyali; others favored long-term reform and nonviolent action, even cooperation with the government, to secure an Islamic state. Abbassi Madani was widely considered a bridge between these two main factions within the Salafis as well as between the Salafis and the Djaz'ara.

The FIS executive council, its *majlis al-shura*, quickly fell out over many issues: membership, the structure of its leadership, the Gulf war,[61] and most critically, the strike of June 1990. For Gueshi and several other FIS founders, Abbassi's insistence on the strike to protest the government's election reforms was a fatal turning point. It also proved to him that the FIS was not "democratic." The majlis members were appointed, not elected, Gueshi told me. "We could not agree on what to have for lunch, much less a coherent concept of an Islamic state. We spoke a double language — one for the mosques and another among ourselves. And Abbassi disregarded us whenever he liked." A majority of the majlis, for instance, including Ali Benhadj at first, opposed the strike, he said, but Abbassi had insisted.

Abbassi had also argued that unless the electoral gerrymandering and ostensible reforms were annulled, the FIS could not hope to come to power through the ballot box. Unless it jettisoned its entire political strategy, a strike was essential. Gueshi and others argued — accurately, it turned out — that the army would use the strike as a pretext to crush the movement and that a strike was unnecessary because the FIS would win at least 40 percent of the vote despite the government's machinations. A strike was "suicidal," Gueshi maintained. But Abbassi prevailed. A three-day strike was approved. Once it began, Abbassi refused to end it despite the opposition of a majority of the majlis.

In protest, three leading majlis members denounced the strike and Abbassi's "authoritarian" leadership on state-controlled television, one of the first public indications of the deep rifts within the FIS.[62] Gueshi resigned.[63]

After Abbassi and Benhadj were arrested, Mohammed Said's Djaz'ara took advantage of the splits and confusion within the FIS to seize control of the movement. "Imagine my shock," Gueshi said, echoing others, "when I turned on the television and saw Mohammed Said, a man who was not even a member of the FIS, much less of its majlis, speaking in the name of the FIS!"

At a hastily convened "loyalty" congress in July 1991 in Batna, southeast of Algiers, the Djaz'arists completed what amounted to an internal coup d'état within the FIS.[64] A new majlis, or executive council, was named, though the FIS was still theoretically beholden to the imprisoned leaders Abbassi and Benhadj.

Several of the more militant members were expelled. Abdelkader Hachani, the cautious antimilitant who had secretly met with President Chadli before the coup to work out a deal, became the FIS spokesman. Djaz'ara, which also wanted to marginalize the Islamic radicals, became the effective leaders of the movement.

The intrigue and jockeying within the FIS proved that Islamic politics were, like all politics when much is at stake, fierce. But the constant shuffling of posts and leaders — because of arrests, leaders fleeing or going underground, personal quarrels, and ideological rivalries — had made me increasingly wary about predicting what the FIS would do when, or if, it ever came to power. It was increasingly hard for anyone to know who and what the FIS was.

I WAS IN ALGIERS when a mysterious armed Islamic group launched its initial attacks on *le pouvoir*, an almost untranslatable French term that means literally "power" but in French conveys not only the government but all its authority and force. It was February 1992, only a month after the coup. Some FIS leaders were still issuing conciliatory communiqués begging the army to "uphold" the constitution and restore the democratic process. But some militants within and outside the FIS had already concluded that such appeals were futile.

A journalist who specialized in Islamism, Omar, I shall call him, and I were to head out to Bab el-Oued, a former FIS stronghold. The FIS had called on Friday for a "march for democracy" in downtown Algiers. The day was chilly but sunny. The streets were deserted. The army's awesome display of force had deterred prospective protesters. The boulevards were lined with riot police and army troops equipped with automatic rifles, shotguns, and tear-gas launchers. Water cannons were installed near the FIS mosques; their loudspeakers had been unplugged. "No sane person will march through these guys," said Omar.

We retired to a café near the Casbah to contemplate the latest rumors. Suddenly, we heard what sounded like machine-gun fire. It was coming from the direction of the Place des Martyrs, less than a quarter of a mile away. We got up from the table and trotted forward toward the site, but it was impossible to get through. The once-empty streets were now filled with panicked and confused Algerians tearing about in all directions, asking what had happened. We retreated to our café and soon heard the news: Armed militants had opened fire with machine guns on soldiers in the square. Several were killed, along with a child who was caught in the crossfire. The army was now chasing the militants through the Casbah. All afternoon the sound of sporadic gunfire echoed through the celebrated quarter. In the evening we heard an explosion. But the curfew was just a few hours off. We could never find the site of the explosion in time.

Omar called me from his newspaper that night. No one had claimed credit for the attack in the square. But the paper had received another communiqué calling for a jihad against the government. It was signed by *Fidèles au Serment* (Those Loyal to the Oath). It was odd, he said, that no one had claimed responsibility for the attack or for an even more daring assault a few days earlier

—also in broad daylight—on the Admiralty building near the port of Algiers in which seven sailors and two policemen had been killed. "But the killing has begun. Those radicals who disagreed with FIS's conciliatory stance have surfaced."

By 1993, the *Fidèles* would have different names. More than half a dozen tiny bands of armed extremists were attacking the government whenever and wherever they could.[65] The most deadly among them would eventually be known as the Armed Islamic Group, the GIA in the French abbreviation. The GIA was headed by a former member of Mustafa Bouyali's gang who had never joined the FIS.[66] Its members also included so-called Afghans from among the more than twenty-eight hundred Algerians who had participated in the jihad in Afghanistan[67] as well as young members of splinter extremist groups who saw violence as their first and only resort. By 1994 its membership included at least two FIS leaders—for one, Mohammed Said, who, having despaired of coming to power through elections, had finally picked up the gun. The government's repression of the FIS had a predictable effect: At least some of the Islamists who had wanted to achieve power nonviolently by playing on divisions within the ruling elite—to contest the system within the system—had been forced into violence.

Early the next morning Omar and I made our way through the Casbah past the Crémerie du Bonheur (the "Milk Store of Happiness") to the smoky remains of a house at the bottom of an alley. We entered the wreckage. Suspecting that Islamic militants who had attacked the policemen had taken refuge here, the army had blown it to bits. The house still smelled of burning metal.

At least eighteen people had shared the tiny house. Four men were asleep on cots in the room that received the direct shell hit; three of them were killed instantly. Leading us by flashlight, Khaled, a survivor, guided us up the shattered staircase to what had been the bedroom, warning us to avoid the sharp and twisted metal shards that dangled from the crumbling ceiling. The room was smoldering and smelled of acid. Except for pieces of twisted metal bed frames and a blood-soaked mattress that had been pulled from the burning room, most of its contents had melted. Six children had occupied an even tinier adjoining room. They were alive, Khaled's wife told us, but the police had beaten her and thrown her onto a cot in another room. Khaled and his wife swore that no one had fired at the police from this house, that no militants had taken refuge here. But who would ever know?

As we were leaving, an anguished young man made his way toward the ruin that had been his friend's home. "What kind of animals can do this?" he cried in Arabic, weeping openly. "We want an end to this violence. We want an Islamic state. God will give us food and housing and money when we are guided by Muslims. God will provide."

Omar, no friend of the fundamentalists, was moved. "Such misery," he said as we left the quarter. "If they want Allah or anyone to save them, who can blame them?"

•

EVEN A YEAR after the coup, Selima Ghezali, a thirty-four-year-old divorcée and mother of two young girls, was still determined to put out her woman's magazine, *Nyssa* (Women). I had met so many strong, talented Algerian women, but Selima's quiet resolve had touched me most deeply. She and her children lived not in one of those comfortable bourgeois neighborhoods favored by intellectuals but in the village of Khemis el Khechna, near Boumerdès, a poor suburb of Algiers. Each day she spent two hours in a public bus commuting to Algiers, where she edited her magazine and described the desperation of women she knew firsthand in her "village" of forty thousand people.

"We were only thirty-five miles from Algiers, but it seemed like a foreign country when I first arrived to teach school," Selima told me in French as we drove to her suburb. "Algerians there had become 'urban,' but they were still 'rural' at heart. We had all the strains of an uprooted community—a perpetual tug-of-war between archaic and modern reflexes."

The mosque preachers were strong in places like Boumerdès; their word was law. This was the district from which the militant Bouyali had led his holy war in the mid-1980s against the "impious state." He had been ambushed and killed there in 1987, his followers arrested and imprisoned. But President Chadli had pardoned them in November 1989—a gesture of national reconciliation. Others who had escaped in 1987 had never stopped dreaming of overthrowing the illegitimate secular government. The struggle between those who favored the creation of Islamic rule on earth and supporters of secular government was always more intense here than in cosmopolitan Algiers. If the FLN and the FIS were now deeply divided, her village had always been so.

Selima recounted the commune's protracted fight over whether to license *parabols*, the satellite dishes omnipresent in Algiers. The "modernists" had won, but imams in the local mosques never stopped attacking the promoters of "degenerate Western culture" and satellite dishes, "diaboliques," in FIS lingo.

"All the Islamists ever wanted was space for more mosques, not a garden or even a soccer field for the kids," Selima told me. After three years, she had won a fight to open a sports club for girls. "But after 1990, when the FIS won the municipality elections, the local Islamists shut it down."

We were on our way to visit the Bouzeraa family, her next-door neighbors in the Cité de 56 Logements, a drab gray-and-white four-story stucco complex that had defaced a hill overlooking the old village. The *cité*'s name came, unimaginatively, from the unit's fifty-six apartments into which more than three hundred people were crammed.

The Bouzeraas were Berbers, the country's original inhabitants who remained wedded to their own language and culture. Berbers, who make up at least a fifth of the population, were usually considered hostile to Islamism, but this, like most generalizations, Selima explained, was untrue. First of all, there were four major Berber-speaking groups, the largest of whom were the Kabyles—like the Bouzeraas—who came from Kabylia, the mountainous region east of

Algiers.[68] Many Kabyles who opposed the government's "Arabization" program and the suppression of their own language and culture had opposed the pro-Arab FIS, but some of the FIS's key figures were Berber. Many Berbers, who were also Muslim, had voted for Hocine Ait Ahmed, the Berber leader of yet another "front," the Socialist Forces Front (FFS), one of two main Berber-based parties. But while the smaller Berber party had supported the military coup, the FFS had not. Ait Ahmed's FFS was against the FIS, but even more opposed to the government's coup and its savage repression.[69] "You see why generalizations about anything in Algeria are so often wrong," she said.

Selima had befriended the Bouzeraa family when they moved to the village from Algiers, unable to afford the capital's high rents. The family of fourteen was deeply troubled. Selima had taught several of them in high school, including Khaled, the eldest son, "a beautiful boy but not a gifted student," she remarked. Khaled, who became an early FIS activist, wrote her a letter in 1989 criticizing her for having encouraged village women to protest for women's rights. In his letter, Khaled asked Selima whether what the imams said about her was true: Was she against the *hijab?* Was she against the Koran (and Algeria's ostensibly secular family code), which permitted a man to have four wives? Was she against the Prophet and Islam?

"His questions were menacing," Selima said. "Khaled ended by saying that if the imams had spoken the truth, I should 'repent and return to God.' But if it was slander, then I should prove to him that I was a believer."

Selima had written to Khaled. Thanking him for his letter, she told him that her religious convictions were a private matter. His former professor did not have to justify her actions or beliefs to her former student. "I closed by saying that if he wanted to discuss such matters, I would be glad to receive him at home. Khaled never replied."

Khaled's parents were not religious, but he had "mobilized" them for the FIS, she said. After he was elected to the town council, his parents became even more openly devout, since this once-unpromising young man, a teacher, like his father, was suddenly a "big man in the *cité*," Selima said.

Selima became concerned about Khaled's sister Rashida, who could not adjust to village life and had refused to wear the *hijab*. To punish her, the family would not let her leave the apartment. "She had no radio or television, no right to socialize, no work. Two months after Khaled was elected, she got a mysterious fever and died. Just like that. The family told me that Rashida had gone crazy. But I think she died of despair, of isolation. She was only twenty-four, but she no longer wanted to live. She had been close to Khaled before he turned religious, but after his re-Islamization, he shunned her—an 'unbeliever,' he called his own sister. She became even more distraught. Rashida's sister Soued, another 'believer,' had screamed at her less than a year before her illness. I heard Soued say: 'I hope you die. You are not fit to live.' This can be a very tough society," Selima said quietly.

After the coup, Khaled was arrested. Later that year, after thousands in the camps were released, Selima encountered him in the market. "He had grown fat in prison, but he still had his beard. He no longer lived at home but with other FIS activists. We talked a little, but it was awkward: Because I was a woman he no longer wanted to look me in the eye."

Khaled joined the maquis, as the armed Islamic groups called themselves after the FLN original. He disappeared. But the military came looking for him. "He was one of three men who had killed a village policeman we all knew and liked. Friends in the village had recognized him.

"His family was crushed," Selima said. "They had disavowed the FIS and withdrawn in shame. But Soued was still a 'believer.' 'Her FIS' was not violent, she told me. But after the car bombs against civilians and the assassination of President Boudiaf, she is no longer sure."

After tea at Selima's small, neat apartment, we went downstairs to the entrance of the Bouzeraa flat. As we rang the doorbell, a tall, plain girl dressed in an olive-green trenchcoat and black head scarf—typical attire for young Iranian women—came up behind us. She had been buying milk at the store. It was Soued. "Come in," she beckoned as she opened the lock of the flimsy front door with what looked like a paper clip.

The airless apartment was poorly furnished. The kitchen was its main room, a plasticized table and rickety wooden chairs its furniture. The "living room" was a bedroom filled with cots masquerading as sofas, a few ragged pillows thrown on top of them. The lime-green paint was half-peeled from the walls. Though the day was sunny and bright, the apartment was dark and cold. We huddled by the gas stove as Soued prepared the tea. As we talked, I heard the muffled sound of neighbors' conversations through the paper-thin walls.

Soued, twenty-four, had studied architecture in college but had been unable to find work since graduating. "There's almost no construction, so no one needs architects," she told me in her poor French. "I look every day, though. Selima is helping me. If the FIS had come to power, I wouldn't have to work," she said provocatively. "The FIS would have paid me to stay at home!"

"But wouldn't you want to work, Soued?" Selima asked.

"Not really," she said, laughing. "Only because I need money."

"The FIS took over in this *cité* and in many municipalities, Soued," Selima continued, accepting the bait. "Did your life improve?"

"No," Soued conceded. "But it was a start!"

"What did they accomplish? They closed sports clubs for girls and segregated school buses!"

"That's not important," Soued replied.

"They stopped concerts."

"They had to. Music is *haram*. That is Islam."

"But Soued"—Selima pressed her young friend's hand—"don't you like music?"

"Yes, but I have enough discipline not to listen to it!"

"And going out with men?"

"That's not only a sin," said Soued, pulling her long chestnut hair back into a ponytail. "It's a waste of time."

I hadn't been able to see her hair until she had removed the *hijab*. The long, wavy hair was Soued's best feature. What a pity she covered it up in public. "I want a prince charming. A man who is going to take me out of here," she said, gesturing around the dingy, fluorescent-lit apartment.

"Do you want the life your mother had?"

"No," Soued said softly.

"Do you want as many children?"

"God will decide that. Limiting births is thwarting God's will."

"But do you want twelve children?"

"No," she said, suddenly depressed. "You don't understand, Selima. For me Islam is everything. It is all I have. Especially now. I want a real life, not just living. Our country should have been rich, but they squandered and stole it all. And we live in dumps like this. We will be able to solve all our problems through Islam."

I slowly realized that I was understanding only part of what Soued said. Unable to speak either French or Arabic well enough to express herself, she resorted to a mixture of both. Such linguistic confusion was part of Algeria's duality. I recalled the graffiti I had seen scrawled on a battered cement wall in the Casbah the previous day: "*Vive le FIS!*" it declared. Perhaps the young proponent of Islamic rule was unable to write his slogan in Arabic. Or perhaps he had concluded that too many Algerians would fail to understood his appeal if it was not expressed in French. Algeria's official Arabization campaign had only intensified the nation's cultural confusion and the alienation of its youth. Poorly done, it meant that most Algerians spoke neither language well. Moreover, the graduates of Arabic-speaking university programs found themselves unable to compete for prized jobs in the private or public sector, which required French as well as Arabic. These new unemployables, like Soued, were understandably bitter about their exclusion.

"Soued, were the FIS delegates elected to our city hall the best men in the neighborhood?"

Soued stared silently at Selima for a minute before replying. "My brother Khaled was good," she asserted defensively. "The others, no. They were not the best. But the FIS was not given a chance to solve our problems."

"Wouldn't they have forced women like me to quit work, to wear the *hijab*, to shut my mouth?"

"They would not have forced you. You would have been persuaded. Islam does not believe in coercion."

"In fact, wouldn't they have killed people like me?"

"No."

"Oh, yes they would have," Selima replied. "Just as they killed our policeman," she added, deliberately leaving the perpetrators unidentified. "If they were ordered to, you know they would kill me — in the name of God."

Soued's pale face flushed with rage. "They didn't start the violence, Selima. You know that. The FIS warned that if they were denied the right to rule democratically, there would be violence. They didn't start it. The military started it. Islam permits us, instructs us, to fight for our faith! I'm comfortable with the choice I made. I would do the same thing again."

And so it went: two friends, the former teacher and former student, locked in a debate that neither could "win." Selima, realizing the pointlessness of the discussion, rose to leave. At the door, she paused, remembering that she had not inquired about Soued's family. Were they fine? Had she news of Khaled?

Soued froze. No, she replied curtly in Arabic, her eyes fixed on the floor. There was no news of her brother.[70] The silence that followed seemed to last an eternity. She did not say good-bye.

JUST AS the FLN had split and the FIS had exploded, just as Algerian neighbors like Selima and Soued were now divided into warring camps, pressure was mounting within le pouvoir. General Nezzar became ill in the summer of 1994 and was commuting between Algiers and Paris for medical treatment. The military was now led by Gen. Liamine Zeroual, but within its ranks were, of course, two camps: éradicateurs and réconciliateurs.[71] The conciliators were said to favor a negotiated solution to the conflict. The eradicators, as their Star Wars name suggested, believed that annihilating the Islamist challenge was the only solution. The army had toyed with negotiations in the summer of 1994, but in retrospect, it appeared that the effort was aimed mainly at buying time to crush the armed groups and to obtain emergency debt relief from the International Monetary Fund.

In January, remnants of the FIS—Anouar Haddam, in Washington, and Rabah Kebir, chief of the executive committee in Germany—joined seven other Islamist and secular opposition parties in Rome in a proposal to end the country's civil strife. The Rome platform called for an end to the militants' campaign against the army and Algerian secularists in return for the release of ten thousand jailed militants and the legalization of the FIS. This was to be followed by talks to form a national unity government and hold new elections.

Though the proposal was greeted warmly by Washington and even Paris, which had staunchly backed the military government, General Zeroual angrily rejected it, reiterating the army's insistence on keeping the FIS out of politics. Soon after that, two armed groups also opposed the platform: the GIA and the Islamic Salvation Army, the armed group more closely associated with the FIS that had competed for turf with the GIA since 1993. The chaotic response to its own ostensible plan proved that Algeria's Islamic movement had become too factionalized to speak with one voice.

Supporters of the Rome platform noted that the FIS, for the first time, had endorsed democratic pluralism. But did the FIS as an organization even exist any longer? And at this stage why would anyone think that the army would take the Islamists at their word? Or vice versa?

I recalled the words of Miloud Brahimi, the former head of Algeria's League of Human Rights, when he unhappily supported the military coup. It was "fine for others to talk about conducting a grand political experiment with Islamic rule in Algeria," he had told me. "But what do we look like—white rats?"

I understood his fear. While I found Algeria an often harsh and heartless place, I hoped it would not become another Iran or Sudan. Journalists used to joke that the FIS actually stood for "Front: Iran and Sudan." There was no way of knowing, of course, what the FIS would have done had it been permitted to come to power. But there was little reason to believe that it would have remained a coalition attempting to strike a balance among its competing points of view. The FIS itself, after all, had never been governed democratically. The most likely outcome was that one faction—probably the strongest and, given Algerian politics, the most ruthless—would have emerged and tried to impose its will on dissident Islamists and opposition secularists alike. In all likelihood, the military, at one point or another, would have balked and challenged them. The result would probably have been civil strife not dissimilar from that which now prevailed.

Meanwhile, Washington scrambled for a coherent policy toward Algeria that would, on the one hand, encourage "democracy" and human rights and, on the other, not offend its ally France or alarm Egypt, Tunisia, Morocco, and other Arab states that also faced militant Islamist challenges. The administration had divided the Islamists into "moderates," whom it would support, and "extremists" who endorsed violence and intolerance, whom it would shun.

Scholars, too, were fond of placing the Islamists in ideological or professional boxes. But Islamists, like most political men, defied the convenient labels we gave them. Algeria taught me that such categories obscured more than they revealed. Sheikh Mahfoud Nahnah, the Muslim Brother, for example, who sided with the government and said he insisted on a pluralist, democratic Islamic state, was often described as "moderate" by Algerian experts. Yet this moderate—among the sanest, most reasonable Algerians I had met—had been sentenced to fifteen years in prison in 1976 for blowing up power lines and conducting other terrorist acts rather than accept a national charter that marginalized Islam in Algerian political life. Abbassi Madani, the "moderate" leader of the FIS, espoused the pragmatic line of the small business class he represented. In secret meetings, the pragmatic Abbassi had assured the Spanish government and other large purchasers of Algerian natural gas that all contracts would be honored when the FIS ruled, and that no gas installations or personnel would be attacked. But there was nothing moderate about his views on human rights, if women were considered human. A woman, Abbassi said in 1989, citing a well-known *hadith*, should leave her home only three times: "when she is born, when she is married, and when she goes to the cemetery."[72] Moreover, the moderate Abbassi persisted with a strike that he must have known would turn violent rather than abandon his movement's strategy of coming to power through elections, an Islamic version of the ends justifying the means. It was Ali Benhadj, the infamous FIS "radical," who initially opposed that strike. After his own arrest, Benhadj wrote a letter from prison in September 1991, three months before the national elections, informing believers that a state that did not impose Islamic law was not a Muslim state. Since Algeria's law of the land was not sharia, the implication was clear: Believers were obliged to wage a jihad against it. While his letter was shared with senior Islamic activists and known to senior government officials, it was not distributed to the general public, which might have questioned the FIS's commitment to a system it was willing to destroy before the people's voice could even be heard. In January 1993 and on several occasions after that, Benhadj, still in prison, reaffirmed clearly and unequivocally his call for jihad despite the growing violence and deliberate slaughter of intellectuals, of women who refused to marry Islamic militants, and of other innocent civilians.

Another presumed "moderate" was Anouar Haddam, the FIS representative to whom the United States had given shelter and political legitimacy.[73] Haddam, whom I had met soon after he arrived in America, had mastered a few tributes to pluralism, equal rights, and democracy in his newly acquired English. But Haddam told me at a conference in April 1993, after Islamic militants had begun killing Algerian intellectuals, that such violence was "justified." The targets were not "innocent," he said. Haddam told me that one murdered man about whom I had inquired was the "brains of the regime." In fact, the victim had been in charge of his university's statistics department. Later that year, Haddam broadcast his view about "justifiable" murders more openly, though his European counterpart, Rabah Kebir, was usually more cautious.[74] An American human-rights group concluded that the moderate Haddam, America's guest, was the source of "the clearest support among FIS leaders in exile for the killing of civilians."[75]

If Algeria taught me anything, it was that the terms "moderate" and "extreme" meant little as descriptions of the various players in the Islamic movement. Moderate at what point? On which issues? Men evolved. Circumstances changed. Mohammed Said, who had once been part of the moderate Djaz'ara, had become the political director of the GIA, the deadliest of Islamic groups. Another former FIS moderate was its information director. Gueshi, a man with a violent nationalist past, had found Abbassi's FIS too extreme and quit the movement.

After the coup, such terms meant even less. Few knew who was directing the FIS, if such an organization existed at all, or who was committing the terror in Algeria. The atmosphere had become so charged that most Algerians believed that hard-liners in each camp were deliberately murdering and terrorizing their own people to incite even greater indignation and intransigence.

The Islamists spoke with many voices because there were many voices. But while the Islamists had once been divided over elections and the use of other moderate means to secure their ends, I doubted that there would be anything moderate about the Islamic state they were seeking to impose on secular Algerians. The closer the FIS had gotten to achieving national power, in fact, the less moderate its statements had become.[76] The issue was not how the FIS secured power but what it would do with it once acquired. The fashionable American notion that supporting elections automatically made people moderates or democrats was historically naive. It was wrong to assume that parties that came to power democratically would necessarily be democratic: There were too many examples to the contrary, the most notable, Nazi Germany.

The French, who continued to meddle in Algeria for reasons of history and geography, had no such illusions. For France, the issue was not dealing with moderates rather than extremists but supporting men and factions that were "pro-French," whether within the army, the FLN, or even the FIS, secular democratic France's ostensible ideological foe. Paris sought the triumph of men with whom it could maintain its "special relationship," not the nationalists, Algerians who wanted such ties, economic favoritism, and financial deals to end and for Algeria to go its own way. Paris, its rhetoric notwithstanding, had ardently supported the military government's bloody repression until members of the GIA nearly succeeded in late 1994 in hijacking a commercial airliner in order to explode it over Paris. After the Islamists proved capable of carrying their war to French soil, Paris began pressing for a "political" resolution of the conflict that incorporated Islamist demands. Specifically, it began supporting a political "compromise" with men such as Taleb Ibrahimi, an FLN member who, though known to be sympathetic and acceptable to the FIS, was also considered reliably "pro-French." But Paris continued supporting the military government, providing more than $1 billion in grants and loans in 1995 and importing more than $1 billion in Algerian natural gas. Outraged, the Islamists launched a campaign of terror against the French inside France. Between July and October 1995, militants planted eight bombs in the Paris subway and commuter trains, killing seven and wounding more than two hundred.

Meanwhile, the Algerian army maintained that it had seized power to spare the country a civil war. Perhaps what Algeria was experiencing was not technically such a conflict, but the violence had no contemporary equal in the Arab Middle East. Algeria was enduring precisely what the army had ostensibly seized power to prevent. Moreover, for those Islamists who believed in compromise, or said they did, the army's brutal repression could only increase mistrust and make them less willing than ever to lay down the arms they had picked up as a last resort. For just as France's refusal to accept a loss of control had driven colonial Algerians into ever more militancy — a radicalization that had ended in military rule — the Algerian government's repression of the FIS half a century later had shattered the original group and driven Islamists to ever greater extremes. Perhaps the radical elements of the FIS would eventually have prevailed even if the army had not intervened early on, but given the mistrust and divisions so endemic in Algerian society and the political elite's determination to continue ruling, a harmonious outcome to the power struggle had always been unlikely.

Algeria was riven by two irreconcilable national visions. As far as I could see, neither side enjoyed a clear majority, though both sides claimed they did. And while Islamists were fond of comparing their struggle to Algeria's war for independence, the differences between the conflicts were more striking than the similarities. Yes, France had defeated the FLN militarily and had still lost Algeria, but the French had their own country to retreat to. The Algerian army and its 2 million family members, with their subsidized housing, imported, duty-free cars, and other privileges, had no other place to go. And while most Algerian Muslims by the 1950s had wanted independence, at least a substantial portion of the country in the 1990s rejected the notion of an Islamic state. Negotiations to end the brutal conflict would be productive only when one side felt its goals could no longer be secured through violence. In Algeria, the only "moderation" would be in response to weakness.

Both the army and the FIS appeared to represent only minorities. Most Algerians had played no role either in the elections—a majority had not even voted—or in the violence. They were trapped, anxiously waiting to see who would prove stronger in the savage scramble for power. If history was any indication, it was unlikely that armed militants would be able to destroy *le pouvoir,* unless the army itself crumbled internally or lost its resolve. That was not likely, especially after General Zeroual won a strong majority in elections in late 1995 from which the FIS and its candidates were excluded. I thought again of Rachid Mimouni's novel *The Honor of the Tribe.* "Remember," he had written shortly before he died, "victory often belongs to the more resolute and not the more powerful."

Until it became clear which side was more resolute, Algerians would continue to suffer and die.

LIBYA

If you stay at the Mahari Hotel in Tripoli, don't lose your room key.

In April 1993, twenty-five of the three hundred rooms at the Mahari, the Libyan capital's largest, most elegant hotel, could no longer be rented because guests had lost the keys to these rooms and the Libyans couldn't import new ones.

"It is a big problem," said Mottah Elyounsi, the front-office manager who looked after Libya's most important guests. "The sanctions make very big problems."

Limited economic sanctions were imposed by the UN Security Council in 1992 to induce Libya to stop supporting terrorism and to "provide a full and effective response" to American and British demands for the surrender of two Libyans accused of having placed a bomb aboard Pan American Flight 103, which exploded over Lockerbie, Scotland, in 1988, killing 270 people, most of them Americans. The American-led sanctions were responsible for the Mahari's "key crisis."

The hotel was gaudy and expensive. Its floors were marble and granite; the lobby's thirty-foot ceiling was decorated with imported, hand-carved wood, trimmed with polished brass. Elaborate chandeliers adorned the lobby and other reception areas, with their thick leather sofas, where guests could sip coffee and chat, under the eyes of Libyan intelligence officers. But unlike the Kebir, once the capital's best hotel, the surveillance at the Mahari was not obvious. And there was no trace of the revolutionary propaganda that adorned the Kebir, no brass plaques above the reception area featuring the regime's often mystifying slogans — "In Need Freedom Is Latent" and the slightly more intelligible "Partners, Not Wage Workers."

There were plenty of wage workers at the Mahari, almost all of whom, except the Libyan intelligence agents who manned the reception desk, telephone, and telex rooms, were Moroccan. These foreigners kept the hotel running despite the sanctions: cooked the imported food, emptied the ashtrays, and cleaned the spacious rooms whose balconies overlooked Tripoli's graceful port. And they despised Libyans. "They don't speak any language but Arabic. They don't know how to do anything, and they don't like to work," my Moroccan waiter told me in perfect French. "I came here to make money. And I have made a lot of it, since there is nothing to spend it on here—no nightclubs, concerts, cinemas. There aren't even decent coffeehouses."

Before the UN sanctions, the hotel had bought the latest equipment from France, including clunky metal keys, custom-made by a French company, that could now no longer be replaced.

"Official delegates are very busy people," Elyounsi, a Libyan, explained in his awkward French. "So many lost their keys while they were staying with us. We had to let them into their rooms each time with the master key. It was very inconvenient." It apparently never occurred to Elyounsi that the imported locks could have been replaced with local ones.

The key crisis, however, was among the few immediately obvious effects of the sanctions. Libyans were furious that international flights had been suspended, and economists estimated that the sanctions had cost Libya between $2.4 and $4.6 billion. But Tripoli looked smarter and appeared to function better in the spring of 1993 than it had in years. When I had visited a decade earlier, it had been hard to find a decent loaf of bread in the dilapidated capital despite Libya's vast wealth. Now Tripoli, though still not beautiful by Mediterranean standards, was a little cheerier and a lot cleaner, and good bread was easier to find. Many buildings had been painted white and then trimmed with green, the country's national color, the color of Islam; buildings that were literally falling down had finally been demolished.

Before the sanctions, Muammar Qaddafi, Libya's aging enfant terrible, had embarked on a tepid "privatization" of Libya's 140 bankrupt or money-losing state enterprises. Though the private stores that lined Omar al-Mukhtar Street and 18th of September Avenue were still technically illegal, business was flourishing in the spring of 1993. Prices were exorbitant—which the government hypocritically blamed on the sanctions—but at least there were goods to buy. The black market, where the Libyan dinar was traded daily for dollars and other real currencies at six times the official rate, was booming. Because of the sanctions, Qaddafi had not been able to buy arms or spare parts. But because the sanctions still permitted Libya to sell oil, the government was cash-rich. Libyans were buying up shares in previously state-owned farms and ranches. One Libyan had recently bought a public hospital.

The sanctions were not aimed at destroying the regime, as in the case of Iraq, but at isolating Libya and forcing its quixotic ruler to behave by internationally accepted standards of rational conduct, which meant, first and foremost, surrendering the two intelligence agents accused of the Lockerbie bombing. So far, Qaddafi had refused to do that. Economic sanctions rarely forced leaders of oil-rich countries like Libya or Iraq — or even impoverished ones like Haiti and Cuba — to mend their ways.

Although Tripoli looked better, depressingly little had changed in terms of political and human rights since my earlier visits. Libyans, a kind, gentle, and passive people, were still terrified to talk to foreigners. Interviews were still difficult to arrange without official blessing. And in a country almost as large as Alaska and twice the size of neighboring Egypt, a nation of less than 5 million people that contained the world's third-largest oil reserves and earned more than $10 billion yearly, services and infrastructure were still primitive. There were no public buses; Alexander Graham Bell would have recognized the phone system. But Libyans still talked bravely about self-reliance and mouthed other revolutionary slogans from the *Green Book,* in which Qaddafi had outlined his weird ideology, the "Third Way," his own quixotic path to an "Islamic" utopia. Schoolchildren still memorized passages of Qaddafi's *Green Book,* his very own Koran, an often incomprehensible blend of mystical Islam, socialism, and Libyan folk wisdom. And, most important, Qaddafi was still the supreme ruler, the *khaid* (leader). Only four of the eleven junior officers who had helped him topple King Idris in 1969 had survived. Some of the others, as well as numerous other "stray dogs," as Qaddafi called critics who sought sanctuary abroad, had been gunned down, poisoned, or kidnapped and killed in Arab or European capitals, even in the United States.

Qaddafi watchers had long predicted this mercurial dictator's demise. But in 1996, at age fifty-four, or so he claims, he was still among the Arab Middle East's most enduring, if bizarre, leaders. Analysts have always had difficulty capturing his essence, perhaps because they initially took him and his lunatic theories seriously. They wrote respectfully of his "personal piety," his dramatic reassertion of Libya's "Arab-Islamic heritage," and his use of Islam "to buttress its national ideology and Arab nationalism/socialism."[1] They wrote volumes on the meaning of the *Green Book,* the three slim volumes, published from 1975 to 1979, that contain his crudely crafted blueprint of how the world should work, filled with such insights as "woman is a female and man is a male" and "it is an undisputed fact that both man and woman are human beings" and, finally, most aptly in Qaddafi's case: "The natural person has freedom to express himself even if, when he is mad, he behaves irrationally to express his madness."

Some Arab leaders had initially embraced Qaddafi, at least officially. Devastated by the Arabs' humiliation by Israel in the 1967 war, pan-Arabists had called Qaddafi *el amin,* the "trustee" of Arab nationalism. After Nasser's death in 1970, they said, the mantle of Arab leadership had fallen on his shoulders. He was lionized by the young, restless gangs of Beirut. Even Mohammed Heikal, Nasser's hagiographer, gave a roundabout blessing to the man he had privately denounced to Nasser as "shockingly innocent" and possibly deranged.[2] Qaddafi, for his part, adored the attention and public acclaim. And after Nasser's death he saw himself as Nasser's successor and blamed fate for having made him a leader without a real country while Egypt remained a country without a real leader. But gradually Libya's Arab and African neighbors tired of Qaddafi's antics and his efforts to subvert their regimes. They increasingly resented the young maniac who kept dropping in on them, usually unannounced, and proposing immediate union with Libya and the merger of all Arab states. Less than five years after Qaddafi came to power in 1969, President Gaafar al-Nimeiri of the Sudan denounced the Libyan as a "split personality — both evil." And Egyptian president Anwar Sadat spoke of Qaddafi as *al walid majnoon* (that crazy boy) and later as a "vicious criminal" who was "100 percent sick." Sadat had also scoffed at Qaddafi's *Green Book*, which claimed to contain the world's political wisdom in a volume "no bigger than a toaster manual."

But long after Sadat and other Arab leaders had disappeared, often violently, Qaddafi remained. He was still Libya's sole omnipotent ruler, its unchallenged, if deranged, guide. He was still, as hip young Libyans called him, "the man."

QADDAFI WAS NOT the first egomaniac to rule here. Most of Libya's history was sad and brutal. Its land had been repeatedly overrun by foreigners — Phoenicians, Greeks, Romans, Arabs, Sicilian Normans, Knights of St. John, Turks — and later by France, Italy, Germany, and Britain, to say nothing of the United States during World War II's North African campaign. The country we know today did not exist until 1951, when the United Nations patched together the former Italian provinces of Cyrenaica, Tripolitania, and Fezzan to form Libya. Its name came from the ancient Greeks, who had called all of North Africa west of Egypt "Libye."

Among its earliest historical mentions was by Herodotus, writing twenty-five hundred years ago, who recounted a story he had heard about the "wild young fellows" of Cyrene, "sons of chieftains in their country," who had "on coming to manhood planned amongst themselves all sorts of extravagant adventures," among them to "explore the Libyan desert and try to penetrate further than any one had ever done before."

In the Middle Ages, the independent state of Fezzan, now part of Libya, controlled stops on the great Saharan trade route that crisscrossed the desert with goods, news, and during Ottoman times, slaves, the most valuable trans-Saharan cargo. Situated on the Mediterranean, providing the closest access to the Sahara, Tripoli was "the gateway to the interior of Africa."[3] From the mid–sixteenth century, the Ottoman Empire ruled Libya, at least nominally. Unlike other invaders, the Turks were content to control the province's cities and leave the Berber and Arab tribes of the interior largely to themselves.[4] As long as they paid their taxes, the inhabitants were left in peace.

Libya's first native-born strongman was Ahmed Karamanli, the son of a Turkish officer and an Arab woman, an Ottoman cavalry officer whose dynasty ruled between 1711 and 1835, when the Turks finally deposed the last of the Karamanlis and reoccupied Tripoli. The brutal Ottoman campaign to control not only the cities, where 98 percent of the people lived and still do, but also the solitary, obstinate people of the desert gave rise to a second local liberator— Abd-al-Jalil Saif-al-Nassir, chief of the powerful Awlad Slaiman tribe. It took the Turks twenty-four years to defeat him.[5]

Libya's third great figure, a man responsible for the brand of Islam still practiced by many Libyans, was Sayyid Muhammad Ibn Ali al-Sanusi, or the "Grand Sanusi," as he would become known. Born in the late 1780s in Algeria, a descendant of the Prophet Muhammad on his mother's side, Sanusi was a Sufi—one of the mystically inclined sheikhs who emphasized meditation and personal piety in ascertaining God's "straight path."[6] After extensive study in Morocco, he traveled to Cairo's al-Azhar, Sunni Islam's great center of learning. But Sanusi found the Egyptian ulema intellectually timid and in thrall to Pasha Mohammed Ali and the Ottomans who ruled Egypt. He deplored their lack of spiritual zeal. In response, the al-Azhar scholars and the mufti, the state-appointed chief sheikh, denounced what they considered Sanusi's heretical views in a lengthy *fatwa*. Among other things, they challenged Sanusi's belief that learned Muslims had the right, in fact, the duty, to disregard the four classical Muslim schools of law and Koranic interpretation and engage in *ijtihad*, or individual interpretation of the sacred texts and traditions.

Undeterred, Sanusi left Egypt and found more sympathetic religious ground in Mecca, where he eventually founded his own *zawiya* (monastery), whose disciples were heavily influenced by the Arabian Wahhabis.[7] Forced out of Mecca in 1840 by the city's religious elite—jealous of the Grand Sanusi's growing appeal—he traveled throughout North Africa gathering disciples and preaching a return to Islamic "purity," resistance to the infidels (European Christians), and greater Arab Islamic unity—themes later embraced by modern Islamic militants.

In 1843 the Grand Sanusi settled in Cyrenaica—which was then free of European influence and of the conservative Islamic establishment that dominated Cairo and Istanbul—and founded a series of *zawiyas* aimed at "reminding the negligent, teaching the ignorant, and guiding him who has gone astray."[8] North Africans were increasingly receptive to his message, for more of their land was coming under European rule and their region was growing poorer. Europeans by 1840 had suppressed most of the trans-Saharan slave trade, North Africa's most lucrative venture, and Europe relied increasingly on sea routes rather than the desert to the markets of the East.

As his popularity spread, the Grand Sanusi's disciples, the Ikhwan—as their militant Wahhabi brethren in Arabia and Islamic reformers in Egypt would later be called—were sent throughout North Africa to open lodges to educate the tribes and promote through example, not force, a return to a pure Islam. The Ottomans, wary of another twenty-five years of war with the province's unruly inhabitants, gradually ceded tax collecting and other authority to the Grand Sanusi, who, in turn, accepted nominal Ottoman sovereignty. But the Sanusis became Libya's de facto rulers. The Grand Sanusi was the absolute master of his missionary brotherhood, consulting his advisory council only as he saw fit, an arrangement that apparently satisfied both locals and Ottomans. British visitors disparaged Ottoman rule, but the Sanusi-backed Turks held Cyrenaica with only a thousand men; fifty years later, the Italians would need twenty thousand men to do so.[9]

Under the Grand Sanusi's son in the 1880s, the Sanusi order reached the peak of its influence. Some fifty lodges dotted Cyrenaica, the Sahara, and even sub-Saharan Africa, as far south as modern-day Chad. But for all its local power, the Sanusiya, the Turkish-Sanusi condominium, was surrounded by enemies: To the west were the French, who had conquered Algeria and coveted Chad; to the east were Anglo-Egyptian forces that had retaken Khartoum from Sudan's Islamic messianic leader, the militant Mahdi, or "expected one," who had previously tried but failed to recruit Sanusi's son as his own disciple.[10] In 1902, when the French captured the Sanusi lodge in Chad and killed Sanusi's son, a French army captain and Arabist warned prophetically that France's victory would be fleeting. Because of the Sanusi order's "influence" and "pan-Islamic dreams," he wrote, "never will a Muslim accept, without serious reservation, Christian domination."[11]

Just as the Mahdi had linked in Sudan's national consciousness the concepts of independence, unity, and national dignity with his Islamic revival, the Sanusi's Islamic campaign, with its appeals to resist the encroaching infidels and its hostility toward all Western occupiers, infused what became modern Libya and the descendants of the tribes that had flocked to the order's defense, among them the al-Qaddafa, Muammar Qaddafi's tribe.

As the Ottoman Empire weakened and Europeans scrambled for North African possessions, Italy saw a chance to reclaim the land that its ancestral Romans had ruled. In 1922, Benito Mussolini launched his infamous *Riconquista* of "Libya," a name that had not been used since Roman rule two thousand years earlier. For ten years, Omar al-Mukhtar, a leading Sanusi sheikh who became the young Qaddafi's favorite national hero, battled the Italians led by Commander Rodolfo Graziani, the "butcher," as he was known to Libyans. Qaddafi claimed in a speech I heard in 1979 that some 750,000 Libyans — more than half his countrymen — had died fighting the Italians, an exaggerated figure, according to most historians. But scholars agree that the campaign was one of the century's most brutal colonial wars and that between 250,000 and 300,000 Libyans died from 1912 to 1943 in their struggle for freedom.[12] The Italians closed Sanusi lodges, arrested sheikhs, confiscated mosque land, and according to some accounts, dropped captured Libyans alive from airplanes.[13] In Cyrenaica, where most of the Sanusi-inspired resistance was based, at least half the province's population was driven out or died from starvation and disease, Fascist aerial bombardments, and "the use of mustard gas and napalm."[14]

In 1932, when the rebellion ended and Omar Mukhtar was hanged before twenty thousand of his followers, Fascist Italy launched an ambitious resettlement program on former Sanusi-owned lands to transform Libya into Italy's "fourth shore." To counter enduring Libyan, Arab, and Islamic enmity toward Italy, Mussolini declared himself in 1937 the "Protector of Islam." He also encouraged non-Sanusi education and promoted conservative Sunni Muslim sheikhs, hoping to destroy Libyan devotion to the rebellious Sanusi order.[15] By 1940 more than 110,000 Italians lived in Libya — almost 12 percent of the population — proportionately more Europeans than in Algeria during the peak of French occupation in 1954.[16]

The British drove Italy out of Libya in 1943. The North Africa campaign devastated Libya's coastal cities, and the desert countryside was ravaged. To this day, an estimated 11 million unexploded land mines remain buried in Libyan soil.[17] When World War II was over, Libya, with a per capita income of twenty-five U.S. dollars, was among the world's poorest countries. In 1951, when the United Nations created the Royal Kingdom of Libya as an independent monarchy, the man who returned from exile in Egypt with British blessing to become Libya's first king was Idris al-Sanusi, the Grand Sanusi's grandson.

Under King Idris I, Sanusi dominance in political and religious life was restored. The non-Sanusi Islamic establishment that the Italians had cultivated was pushed aside. The monarchy incorporated the sharia courts into the royal-run judicial system and made the mufti and other senior religious figures part of the state bureaucracy. The ulema became salaried employees, as they were in Nasser's Egypt, while the king retained family control of the Sanusi institutions, including the rebuilt zawiyas, the fraternal Islamic lodges.[18] The government made clear that the non-Sanusi religious elite would be punished for its collaboration with Libya's colonial oppressors and its alleged betrayal of Islam.

During the first decade of Sanusi rule, Libya's largest source of income was from the sale of scrap metal from war debris; later, it came from American and British rents for military bases. Then Libya discovered oil. In the early 1960s the monarchy plunged into development, building schools, irrigation canals, and roads. By 1971, a decade after the first barrels of oil were shipped to Europe, Libya was the Middle East's third-largest producer, pumping more than 3 million barrels per day. Some scholars argue that King Idris and his advisers adopted many of the nationalist measures for which Qaddafi later claimed credit and for which he has been inaccurately credited by too many writers.[19] To defuse criticism that he was the West's lackey, Idris required that Arabic be used in public life, launched negotiations to end British and American presence on Libyan military bases, and redrafted Libya's commercial code to increase Libyan earnings from oil. But these steps still lagged behind soaring Libyan expectations, and an increasingly overwhelmed, unresponsive, and corrupt political patronage system made matters worse. Opposition mounted — from the non-Sanusi ulema, the growing middle class, and the young, restless new generation to whom Egypt's Nasser was God. Libyans, whose average age was fifteen, had no memory of colonialism or the war and felt little gratitude to, or affection for, the eighty-year-old king. They yearned to imitate Nasser's Egypt: to unify the Arabs, expel the West, and eradicate Israel. They did not have long to wait.

•

ON SEPTEMBER 1, 1969, Qaddafi and a small group of junior officers seized control of the country while King Idris, dispirited and preparing to abdicate, was on vacation in Turkey. The coup itself was farcically inept. It was postponed at least once after Qaddafi learned that Um Kalthoum, the legendary Egyptian singer known for her long, lyrical odes to Nasser, Palestine, and the Arab cause, had scheduled a concert that same night in Benghazi. To fervent young Nasserites like Qaddafi, even the idea of disrupting an Um Kalthoum concert was counterrevolutionary.

When the young officers finally moved, there were further glitches. One conspirator left his rifle and ammunition in a taxi. Another got lost and could not find the officers he was supposed to arrest. Two plotters had a car accident en route to their mission.

Yet Captain Qaddafi (he soon promoted himself to colonel) and his eleven coconspirators prevailed, partly because the monarchy was so vulnerable and because several other groups were also plotting coups. Egypt, for one, was helping a rival group of Libyan officers intent on seizing power, and Nasser was stunned when his journalist-envoy, Mohammed Heikal, told him that an unknown group of dangerously "naive" plotters had succeeded instead.

Western diplomats and intelligence agencies were also initially surprised and confused by the coup, or the "revolution," as Qaddafi called it. "I was in the CIA station chief's office the morning of the coup, and I guarantee that nobody had ever heard of, much less cultivated a relationship with, Muammar Qaddafi," said Henry M. Schuler, a former U.S. official and head of W. R. Grace & Co. in Libya at the time. "The names of the Revolutionary Command Council [RCC] members were not even announced until more than a week after the takeover."

Whatever reservations Western governments may have had, they rushed to seek favor with the new regime once its new military leaders assured diplomats that they would honor Libya's oil agreements and protect the resident foreign community.

At first, Qaddafi's takeover seemed to be typical of other Middle Eastern nationalist coups whose hallmark was Nasser's dictum that the army must "permanently patrol society." As in Egypt, Syria, and Iraq, the army established a single nationalist party and "popular" organizations, but as empty shells to mask and legitimate military rule.[20]

Once in power, the young officers, predictably, decided to keep it. The Libyan army doubled in size; untrustworthy senior officers were arrested, pensioned off, or sent abroad. The government closed ten newspapers, banned party politics, and destroyed vestiges of Libya's colonial past by closing churches and cathedrals. Foreign banks were converted into Libyan companies; Americans were required to live up to their prior agreement to withdraw from Wheelus air force base, as were the British from their air base at Al Adem (events celebrated henceforth as "Evacuation Day").[21] Some thirty thousand Italian settlers — crafts-

men, farmers, and middle-class tradesmen whose skills Libya badly needed —
were deported (and subsequently commemorated in "Revenge Day"); several
hundred Libyan Jews, whose dwindling community had already suffered in riots
after the 1956 Suez crisis and 1967 Arab-Israeli war, were also expelled — an
uncommemorated event.

Qaddafi initially saw Islam as a means of legitimizing his rule. While
Nasser proved a determinedly secular leader who wanted no competition, even
from God, Qaddafi preceded Iran's Ayatollah Khomeini by a decade in invoking
Allah to serve his political agenda. He also lost no time in dismantling the
Sanusi-dominated religious structure and replacing Libya's leading Islamic figures with pliable, non-Sanusi scholars he thought he could trust, just as the
Italians had done half a century earlier. As mufti, or chief religious guide,
Qaddafi chose Tahir al-Zawi, an orthodox sheikh with no strong Sanusi links
who was also a fine historian. The mystical Sanusis, Qaddafi told fellow Libyans,
had betrayed Islam by ordering them to obey a corrupt, unjust, and hence
un-Islamic royal dynasty that had insulted Islam by tolerating such sins as drinking and dancing in nightclubs. Sanusi *zawiyas* were placed under government
supervision, and permits to build new ones were revoked. Within a month of
the coup, the RCC required Arabic and the Muslim calendar to be used in all
public announcements. Alcohol was banned, and Islamic punishments were
reinstated, in theory but not in practice.[22]

The Sanusiya, however, was not the only independent religious power base
and, hence, potential competition that Qaddafi feared. Libya's new leader was
equally suspicious of the Muslim Brotherhood, the enemy of his idol Nasser.
The Ikhwan, he told a Beirut newspaper in the early 1970s, worked "against Arab
unity, against Socialism, and against Arab nationalism, because they consider all
these to be inconsistent with religion." In opposing these ennobling goals, the
Muslim Brethren had "cooperated" with the British and other colonialists.[23]

In Qaddafi's view, most of the Islamic elites had collaborated with reactionary, imperialist Western forces — the orthodox ulema with the Italians, the Sanusis with the British, and the Muslim Brotherhood with the British-backed
Egyptian monarchy. Obsessed with Arab unity, Qaddafi also despised the Islamic scholars' endless disputes over interpretation of the Koran and the Sunna,
the Prophet Muhammad's practices according to his companions and early
followers. Such theological quarrels led only to debilitating divisions among
Muslims that confused and weakened the Arab masses, he said.

In 1970, soon after the coup, Qaddafi told a correspondent from the French
newspaper *Le Monde* that the Koran was the "only source of truth," implicitly
rejecting, as his Sanusi forefathers had done, orthodox Islam's insistence that
believers confine themselves to previously accepted interpretations of the
Sunna. "Here," he told the correspondent, "read the Koran and reread it." The
book contained the answers to "all your questions," he said — from "Arab unity"
to "the inevitable fall of the Roman empire" to "the destruction of our planet
following the intervention [sic] of the atom bomb. It's all there for anyone
willing to read it."[24]

Like the Grand Sanusi before him, Qaddafi insisted, in effect, that the established ulema should not have the final say on religious interpretation. Individuals—or as it turned out, one individual with virtually no religious train-ing—had the right to interpret the Sunna. "We must not restrict ourselves to one *ijtihad*," Qaddafi said. Whether or not he realized it, Qaddafi was advancing a view of Islam not all that different from what Libya's Sanusi founders had preached.[25] But also like the Grand Sanusi, Qaddafi would become, in practice, the final arbiter of all religious as well as political disputes. Those who disagreed with the supreme guide faced imprisonment, exile, and murder—a sharp depar-ture from the Sanusis' relatively tolerant tradition.

Qaddafi's campaign to reinstitute Islamic law and abrogate laws that con-flicted with Islamic principles was primarily a way of ridding Libya of the "corrupting influence" of Western culture and securing his rule.[26] His Islamiza-tion campaign, the first launched by a modern Middle Eastern government, linked the revolutionary regime with what one scholar called "traditional Libyan values and Islamic symbols." But while Qaddafi praised sharia, Islamic holy law, in speeches, his changes in Libya's legal code were "superficial and designed to be so," this scholar concluded.[27] In other words, Islam was useful, in its place, as long as it consolidated his rule.

In 1975 the first volume of Qaddafi's personal *ijtihad* was published: volume 1 of the *Green Book*, which outlined the Third Universal Theory, or "Third Way," his proposed "alternative" to both Soviet-style communism and Western capitalism. There was no mention of Islam in volume 1, which focused on politics, or in volume 2, in which Qaddafi offered his own version of socialism, the "Solution" to man's "Economic Problem." Volume 3, published a year after volume 2 in 1979, clearly subordinated Islam and all other religions to national-ism: From then on, the Third Universal Theory would take precedence over both Islamic law and Libyan traditions. Qaddafi later explained his *Green Book*'s omission of Islam. If his Third Universal Theory had presented Islam as its religion, a message intended to be universal would exclude non-Muslims, "something which we [meaning himself] evidently do not want." Thus, the "Third Theory," he said, presented applications of Islam "from which all man-kind may benefit."[28]

Since Qaddafi wanted to remold his society, any law or tradition inconsis-tent with his goals had to be abolished. Women, for example, who, in Arab Muslim societies, were traditionally segregated from men and often excluded from public life, were not only to be integrated in society but educated, and even armed! Qaddafi later underscored his commitment to women's rights and further enraged his traditional, male-dominated country by surrounding himself with female bodyguards—the "Amazons," journalists called them.

The regime had turned ugly long before Qaddafi outlined his Third Uni-versal Theory. The revolution was in trouble, Qaddafi told a youth conference in 1973, because "perverts" at the university and elsewhere were subverting it. All such "feeble minds" and "poisonous ideas"—that is, those that diverged from his thinking—had to be "weeded out"; the bourgeoisie and the bureaucracy had to be destroyed; laws had to be repealed and replaced by the popular committees and congresses by "revolutionary enactments." Within days of the speech, at least a thousand leading academicians, lawyers, writers, officials, businessmen—Marxists, leftists, and Muslim Brotherhood members—were arrested. In a population of then only 2 million, the arrests gave Libya proportionately the world's largest prison population.[29]

Qaddafi's RCC supervised "popular committees" that were mobilized to implement his cultural revolution, a "green" version of Mao's ruinous popular upheaval. By year's end, some, though not all, of the political prisoners who agreed to "confess" their crimes on national television were released. By then, however, Libya's nascent middle class had understood the drift of things and fled. Some thirty thousand Libyans eventually left the country, including many of its most talented people. The exodus was further encouraged in 1977 by Qaddafi's military interventions in uranium-rich northern Chad, a decade-long conflict in which more than three thousand Libyan soldiers were killed and wounded.

By 1977, Qaddafi was preparing to take on the ulema, whom he increasingly saw as a source of resistance to his political program. In an article in the official daily newspaper under what was probably a pseudonym for Qaddafi himself, a certain Ibn al-Tayyib argued that religious scholars and functionaries could not represent the Libyan people and that even the powers of the mufti were incompatible with popular authority.[30] Enraged by the article but afraid of ignoring such an obvious hint, Mufti Tahir al-Zawi, then in his nineties, resigned. Qaddafi, who wanted no competition as Libya's supreme religious guide, did not name a successor.

The official ulema interpreted the socialist measures endorsed by the *Green Book*, particularly the Third Way's insistence that "land belongs to no one"—not even *waqf* (land donated to mosques for religious purposes)—as a declaration of war by the regime against Islam and their own prerogatives. By this time, however, Qaddafi welcomed a confrontation with the ulema, even the usually quiescent men he himself had appointed. In a series of speeches in 1978, Qaddafi accused them of having "remembered Islam" only after their own land was confiscated. The religious establishment, he said, had "propagated heretical stories elaborated over the course of centuries of decadence" and conducted "a reactionary campaign against the progressive, egalitarian, and socialist concepts of the regime." He urged the masses to "seize the mosques," which they did.[31] He also tried to downgrade the role of the Prophet Muhammad, who was, after all, a member of the despised merchant class,[32] and he also asserted explicitly for the first time that the Sunna, the Prophet's traditions, had been so corrupted and misinterpreted by self-serving Muslim scholars that they could no longer be regarded by the devout as binding. The Koran, he argued, could not be interpreted by such suspect sources, and, in fact, it should not be interpreted at all.

What Islam needed was a "revolution" that would "purify" the faith of its reactionary impulses and present Islam "correctly," that is, consistent with his own views. To make his point, Qaddafi revised the Muslim calendar. No longer would time be dated from the *hijra,* the Prophet Muhammad's emigration in 622 from Mecca to Medina. From then on, time would begin with the Prophet's death, the end of his prophecy and the revelation of the Koran. In 1979, Libya officially revised the country's calendar, setting official time back ten years behind that of other Muslim countries.[33]

I FIRST VISITED Libya in 1978 during this destructive post-Islamic, revolutionary phase. Qaddafi had just banned private property, told Libyans they could occupy only one home or apartment, encouraged workers to seize their factories, and outlawed retail trade. Barbers and cobblers, he said, were "decadent capitalists." In those days journalists were assigned to the Beach Hotel, whose damp, dingy corridors smelled of urine and whose toilets dripped water day and night. My diary contains only a few references to the Beach — all unprintable. Libya was then still the darling of radical anti-Westernism, though Libya and the United States were doing roughly $4 billion in trade a year. Tripoli was then what Beirut, Damascus, Teheran, and Khartoum would later become — a haven for every anti-Western, anti-Zionist group in the region.

When I next visited Libya in 1984, Qaddafi was strengthening his "Revolutionary Committees," composed of young guardians of the revolution whose loyalty was unquestioned and whose mission was to promote the Third Way by arresting state enemies and implementing their leader's order to eliminate — by whatever means necessary — "antirevolutionary" thoughts and even colors.

Libya still seemed obsessed with the color green. The beige cement buildings of the drab, sprawling capital were decorated with green shades and shutters. Libya's new flag was green. So were car license plates. A plastic toothbrush I bought in the market was green; so was the toothpaste. At a session of the People's Assembly I covered, an earnest young man in olive-green military fatigues gave a speech saying that while America could "threaten and terrorize" Libya, "nothing, but nothing," would stop "the green mind." Diplomats told us that Qaddafi had intended to call the cavernous People's Congress the Green House until an American-educated aide told him that the phrase, in English, meant a place where vegetables were grown.

Not only was green the color of Islam; it was also for most Arabs who dwell on the edges of deserts a sign of water — of life itself. Westerners took the emerald-green and chocolate-brown landscape of Europe for granted. But after I had spent several years in the region, a wave of relief would sweep over me as I gazed down from my airplane seat during my rare vacations at the lush, fertile European tapestry.

Equally as ubiquitous as artificial green, and as dulling to the senses, were the revolutionary slogans that Libyan youth chanted at the People's Congress meetings; their rantings filled the airwaves and were piped into the lobby and even the elevators of the Grand Hotel. A Libyan friend whom I shall call Ahmed once complained about his sore arm — "Qaddafi arm," diplomats called it, an affliction that came from being obliged to spend hours at People's Congress meetings waving one's arm in the air and clenching one's fist.

Also omnipresent in 1984 were pictures of the leader. Qaddafi would later complain in interviews about the growing personality cult around him. To defuse it, he told me, he had ordered newspapers not to print his picture or feature his activities. "But they won't listen!" he said, throwing his hands helplessly in the air but flashing a self-satisfied smile. "Look at them," he said, pointing to the television, which was showing a rally where Libyans were shouting his name. "They're all wearing vests. You know why? Because yesterday I wore a vest! I can't help it! They *insist* on imitating me."

Invariably, the government did nothing to discourage the idolatry of the man who considered himself Islam's latest political prophet. New official portraits of the colonel kept appearing at my local newsstand, featuring sayings from the *Green Book*. The manager had just received new green-colored felt-tipped pens. The newsstand, which always had stacks of unsold issues of *The Green Path*, regularly received fresh batches of Qaddafi postcards quoting his favorite homilies. I sent a postcard to my sister that showed Qaddafi on horseback in the desert, instructing: "Teach your sons marksmanship, swimming, and horsemanship." My father liked the card showing Qaddafi playing soccer. Good legs, he said. My mother had two favorites: the colonel with his parents in their tent (which he perversely insisted they continue to live in years after he seized power) and another entitled "Qaddafi meets militant women." The newsstand operator told me that the most popular card was a mosaic of photos of Qaddafi engaged in different activities, entitled, in English, "Human Images from the Life of Muammar al-Qaddafi."

The leader, to be sure, was charismatic. And it was difficult not to write about him, for he was, and remains, a splendid performer, a demonic impresario who appreciates the value of political extravaganzas.

I witnessed my first such performance in August 1984. The occasion was the inauguration of what Qaddafi called "the eighth wonder of the world," the $30 billion "Great Man-Made River Project," or as it came to be known, the Great "Madman" River Project. The venue was the Libyan desert. Thousands attended, of whom hundreds, including journalists and diplomats, had been flown 650 miles from Tripoli into the desert town of Sarir in central Libya to witness the opening of the first stage of Libya's most ambitious, and the world's most expensive, development project: a system of 270 desert wells, reservoirs, and pipes that would bring 1 million cubic meters of water a day through more than twelve hundred miles of pipeline from the heart of the Libyan desert to Libya's northern coastal towns and cities. For Qaddafi, the Great Man-Made River was to be the principal monument to his revolution, which was then marking its fifteenth anniversary.

The project had infuriated neighboring Sudan and Egypt, which feared that tapping vast aquifers some 170 feet below the Libyan desert would diminish their own water supplies. Other foreign experts had questioned not only its technical feasibility but its financial wisdom. Water experts had estimated that the aquifer feeding the gigantic pipeline would last no more than fifty years. For the $5 billion cost of the project's first phase, they added, Libya could build as many as five desalination plants, each of which would produce nearly 4 million liters of water a day.[34] But Nasser, his hero, had built the Aswan Dam, so Qaddafi, too, wanted a grand project. He also wanted to make the desert bloom, as the despised Israelis had done. In Tripoli the previous evening he had scolded Cairo and Khartoum for rejecting his invitation to help exploit the underground reservoirs so that their joint deserts could be transformed into a "garden of Eden." Egyptians had to "liberate" themselves from Israeli domination and the rule of Sadat, whom he had denounced as a "coward," a "traitor," and most ominously, possibly "of Jewish origin."[35] The Sudanese, too, had to get rid of their "sick, lying leader," alluding to President Nimeiri, who was, in fact, overthrown the next year.

Despite his poor relations with Washington, the water project was being managed by Americans. Standing near me at the ceremony were representatives of the British office of Brown & Root Inc., the Houston-based engineering company that had won the $100 million contract to oversee the project's preliminary engineering. Price Brothers Company, an American concern based in Dayton, Ohio, was the technical consultant. The construction workers were mostly South Korean. Libya's national project, in fact, was mainly the work of foreigners, as in the oil-rich Gulf states.

Though it condemned Libyan terrorism, the Reagan administration, in fact, initially did little to discourage Brown & Root or the five American oil companies operating in Libya, whose exports to the U.S. accounted for roughly 40 percent of its oil revenues. As I later learned from Henry Schuler, a former U.S. official now at a Washington think tank, who loathed the colonel's murderous regime, this was part of a pattern. Schuler told me — and Libyan exiles confirmed — that Washington had repeatedly protected Qaddafi in the regime's early years by warning him of at least three coup plots against him. At first, he said, the CIA had foolishly hoped that Qaddafi could be won over and used to extricate Soviet forces from Egypt and that Libya's wealth could substitute for the Russian aid that Egypt so badly needed. America's cold war obsession with reducing Soviet influence in the Middle East had blinded U.S. policymakers to the ugliness of Qaddafi's tactics and his dangerous megalomania until 1973, he said, when Libya financed a terrorist attack on an oil ministers' meeting in Khartoum in which an American ambassador was killed.[36]

Several of the American businessmen sitting with me on the podium in the middle of the desert that day seemed nervous, though not about terrorism. Qaddafi was in financial trouble. Because of the world oil surplus and concomitant drop in prices, Libya's revenues, based almost entirely on the production of 1.1 million barrels of oil a day, had plunged from some $22 billion in 1980 to less than $10 billion by 1983.

It was evening by the time Qaddafi's show began and the burning desert

had turned pleasantly cool. A carefully screened crowd of Qaddafi's faithful had
been imported for the occasion; more than five hundred stage Bedouin supporters, many still dressed in city clothes, cheered loudly and waved green banners
as the presidential jeep pulled up and the leader mounted a portable staircase
to a podium opposite us. Across the desert, hundreds of horses began racing
toward us, their real Bedouin riders hoisting torches in the air and screaming
"*Allahu Akbar!*" Qaddafi, clad in a *zirt* (a traditional winter woolen cape), his
curly brown hair protruding coquettishly from under his sand-colored turban,
acknowledged the adulation with a smile, a wave, and a defiant clenched fist.
As an amber sun slipped slowly into the Great Sand Sea, Qaddafi pushed a
button painted iridescent green — a nice touch, I thought. A giant geyser of fresh
water rose a hundred feet into the air.

The crowd went wild, clasping each other, singing, and dancing on the
sand. A hundred bulbs flashed as cameramen captured Qaddafi, in profile
against the setting desert sun, gazing stoically at the water shooting toward a
newborn crescent moon, the symbol of Islam. Now this was a photo opportunity,
I thought, a show worthy of Ronald Reagan himself!

BY MY NEXT TRIP to Libya in 1986, the colonel's act was wearing thin. But those
who even thought about removing him were eliminated, or as Qaddafi said,
"crushed like rats and cockroaches," which he later insisted America was breed-
ing to export to Libya to destroy its "agriculture and industry and get into
everything." [37]

Nevertheless, these were exciting days for Qaddafi. Though still unwilling
to discourage American companies from doing business in Libya, the Reagan
administration had been obsessed with Qaddafi since its inauguration. Citing
Qaddafi's support for international terrorism, Washington had expelled Libyan
diplomats in 1981. In 1985, the administration charged that Libya had funded
and assisted several major Palestinian terrorist attacks, among them the bombing
of a West Berlin discotheque in which two people, one of them an American
serviceman, were killed and 230 others injured; and, in December, twin attacks
on Rome and Vienna airports in which nineteen people were killed and more
than a hundred others wounded. Reagan, using Qaddafian rhetoric, had called
Libya's leader a "mad dog," the "most dangerous man in the world," and had
warned that America would retaliate. So Qaddafi had decided to import a little
insurance — in the form of Western reporters.

Thanks to Qaddafi's concern about what Washington might do next, I had
my first extended interview with the philosopher-king in January of 1986. I had
just checked into the Kebir Hotel and was still dressed in a heavy winter raincoat, a long skirt, and heels when an agitated Ministry of Information official
raced into the lobby. "Come quickly," he yelled, waving his arms in the air. I
followed the official out the door and boarded an empty green-and-white bus
that was then supposed to pick up other journalists at the Foreign Ministry.
Neither the journalists nor the foreign minister could be found, however, so the

two of us headed into the desert. An hour later, we arrived at El Azizir, a new three-thousand-hectare state farm.

As I stepped off the bus in my high heels, I sank into a freshly plowed barley field. At the far end of the field I could dimly make out a tent, and as I squinted against the noonday sun, I saw a tractor speeding toward me. When it pulled up, the driver commanded, "Hop in." It was Qaddafi.

"Are you alone?" he said, grinning at me.

"I suppose so, Colonel," I replied idiotically, gesturing limply at the empty field and returning the grin.

"Good. Then we shall talk and try out the tractor."

Qaddafi laughed as he noticed my mud-covered shoes, one of which had lost its heel. His shoes, of course, had no mud on them. In dry, drab Libya, Qaddafi's wardrobe was more colorful than anything else in sight. Dapper as ever, he was wearing a jumpsuit, a salmon-colored turban, black knee-high riding boots, matching black gloves, and his omnipresent sunglasses. But he did not know much about driving a tractor. The vehicle lurched violently as the leader ground the gears and cut an erratic path across the field, mangling the young plants. Qaddafi's mind was on weightier things.

"This farm is one of many projects that will help Libya become self-sufficient in food. We need to be independent in all things," he lectured. "The people are lazy; they don't want to work. It is a problem of all petroleum societies."

Qaddafi had pretended to try to solve the problem by expelling some eighty thousand foreign Arab workers—the Egyptians, Moroccans, and Tunisians who kept Libya running. The expulsions, I knew, were not, as he maintained, the result of his quest for self-reliance but of a shortage of foreign currency now that oil prices had fallen. On a trip the previous year, I had visited the main state supermarket in Tripoli and found neither fresh vegetables nor meat, no toilet paper, matches, detergent, or soap. The only commodities in ample supply were 110-pound bags of Cuban sugar, boxes of tea from China, canned tomatoes from Cyprus, salt, and dented cans of insect spray. I had bought the repellent and, to cheer up my hotel room, one of the dozens of potbellied teddy bears on display —a big hit with the country's four thousand Russian military "advisers" and their families. The only other well-stocked item was hundreds of pairs of men's huge tennis shoes, all size 45, stamped "Jamahiriya." The word, which was Qaddafi's neologism for Libya and translates roughly as "gathering of the masses," was stamped on each pair of soles. The shoes, I later learned, had been made in Asia.

This was a difficult period for the Jamahiriya, Qaddafi declared, theatrically sweeping back his turban's tail with one hand and steering the tractor with the other. But he was not intimidated by Washington. Reagan was "a monster, a bully."

Americans love Ronald Reagan, I told him. Qaddafi seemed astonished. "They love him?" he asked in disbelief. But Reagan had created so many crises, and did Americans not know that Reagan was under Zionist control? Did Americans not understand the suffering of the Palestinians, "the pain of a people whose land has been stolen from them"?

Despite Reagan, the Jamahiriya, or the Socialist People's Libyan Arab Jamahiriya — the SPLAJ, as journalists called it — would never abandon social- ism, Arabism, or the search for Arab unity. The SPLAJ would not be intimidated by the "Reagan Black House," nor would it ever recognize "the Stable of David agreements," another Qaddafiism for the peace treaty between Israel and Egypt, a phrase later picked up by militant Islamists. And it would never abandon the Palestinian cause. But, he added, finally coming to his point, there were no Palestinian training camps in Libya, as Washington had charged. Had the Pales- tinians asked for such assistance, he would have granted it; but they had not asked. Nor had his country sponsored or assisted the twin airport attacks in Rome and Vienna in late 1985. Qaddafi did not explain, nor did I ask him as we zigzagged messily through the field, why, if Libya had not been involved, Libyan passports were found on the Palestinians killed in the raids.

Yes, he acknowledged, he knew Abu Nidal, the Palestinian terrorist for hire who had killed as many mainstream PLO officials as he had Israelis and Westerners. But he had not seen him in Libya "for a long time." That was a lie. An American intelligence official I trusted had traced the offices of Abu Nidal to a nondescript building not far from the Kebir Hotel where I was staying and where two rogue ex-CIA officials, Ed Wilson and Frank E. Terpil, who sold explosives and arms to Libya, had also stayed.[38] Qaddafi and Abu Nidal had met for lunch only two weeks earlier, the analyst had told me. And the U.S. National Security Agency, which operates America's spy satellites, had aerial photos of the training camps whose existence Qaddafi denied. Israel estimated that some seven thousand Palestinians and other "revolutionaries" were training that year in no fewer than a dozen Libyan camps.[39]

He would not be cowed, Qaddafi declared. American retaliation against Libya would lead to "World War III." "Suicide missions" would be launched against America and Israel. "Our aircraft bombers are fedayeen [freedom fight- ers] who can reach anyplace. We will act inside American streets if we are attacked."

But I should not feel threatened, Qaddafi said, placing his gloved hand on mine. Americans in Libya — and in 1986 there were between fifteen hundred (the State Department's estimate) and three thousand of them (according to a diplomat in Tripoli) — were "welcome." "You will never be harmed," he purred.

As the colonel spoke, I noticed that a busload of correspondents had arrived and were now racing across the field toward our tractor. Alarmed by the throng of camera-wielding reporters charging Qaddafi's vehicle, dozens of khaki-clad bodyguards and soldiers had leaped onto their own tractors and were trying to cut them off, heading straight toward us at top speed from the right. To our left was a huge irrigation ditch that Qaddafi's tractor was veering toward. We were close to a collision.

"Which way shall I go?" Qaddafi asked playfully.

"A *la tule!*" I yelled, Egyptian slang meaning "straight ahead." "Straight!" I said again as Qaddafi, probably to scare me, made a sharp right turn toward the oncoming tractor fleet whose drivers seemed no more adept than their leader. "For God's sake, Colonel, go straight! Qaddafi always goes straight!"

Qaddafi roared with laughter and corrected his course. "Tell Reagan that!" he shouted as the tractor screeched to a halt. "Tell America I always go straight!"

WHILE LIBYA clearly financed and supported terrorism, so did Syria and Iran.[40] But neither was singled out by the Reagan administration, as Libya had been. Damascus and Teheran were serious regional players militarily capable of defending themselves and inflicting American losses in the event of an attack. Jimmy Carter had been humiliated when he used military force and failed to rescue American hostages in Teheran in 1980, and Syrian intervention in Lebanon was seen by Israeli and American officials alike as that war-ravaged country's only hope for stability. America's desire to show its strength was intensified by President Reagan's ignominious withdrawal of American forces from Lebanon in the wake of the 1983 Iranian-and-Syrian-backed car-bomb attack on the U.S. Marine compound. The administration desperately needed a place in the Middle East where America, one Reaganaut had told me, could "stand tall" without seriously risking American lives. So why not pick on the runt? What better place to make a stand against international terrorism than absurdly well armed but pathetically weak Libya?

While a wiser man might have sensed America's growing agitation, Qaddafi grew increasingly reckless. He relished taunting the administration by virtually daring Reagan to attack him. Qaddafi popped a threat a day. My favorite will always be his foray into the choppy waters of the Gulf of Sidra to defy Reagan by "confronting" America's Sixth Fleet.

He looked splendid that gray morning in February 1986 in his royal blue jumpsuit trimmed in emerald green, wearing his navy captain's hat at a jaunty tilt. About twenty journalists had been flown to Misurata harbor, 120 miles east of Tripoli, to witness Qaddafi's defiance of U.S. air and naval maneuvers off the Libyan coast. At a shipside news conference, the leader had vowed to sail along parallel 32.5 to underscore his legally absurd claim to the entire 150,000-square-mile Gulf of Sidra as Libyan territorial waters. Pointing his green swagger stick out to sea from the deck of his patrol boat, Qaddafi declared parallel 32.5 his "line of death." "Here [in the water presumably] we shall stand and fight with our backs to the wall," Qaddafi vowed.

Then, to a seven-gun salute, his 350-ton patrol boat, the *Wamid*, which means "lightning," headed out to sea. The press quickly climbed aboard his British-made luxury yacht and followed him out into the gulf. I looked back at the shore and at Misurata airport. This did not look like a country ready for war. The tarmac was lined with eighteen Soviet-made MiG fighter jets, but many of them were under tarpaulins. Other than a few camouflaged oil trucks and helicopters parked under date palms along the road, there was no sign of the "full military alert" that Qaddafi had declared the previous day.

The yacht began pitching in the choppy bay as we sailed ever deeper into the gulf. Several of the Moroccan waiters on board—and nearly all of the Libyan crew—were beginning to look seasick. One of them, I noticed, was gripping the rails, his knuckles white and teeth clenched. Ten minutes later, the sailors were vomiting over the ship's sides. Suddenly, the yacht pitched violently, and we heard a crash. A table of porcelain plates, crystal goblets, and sterling silverware—hardly seaworthy utensils—that had been set for lunch had crashed onto the deck. The sailors and Ministry of Information officials, now pea green, scrambled to pick up shards of the presidential china and cutlery. By the time we turned back, Qaddafi's patrol boat was nowhere in sight. We never learned whether he had reached his line of death or what happened if he did.

While such flamboyant spectacles made splendid stories in the Western press, Qaddafi's revolutionary theatrics no longer fooled Libyans. Many were fed up with his reckless taunting of America, where at least four thousand Libyan students were still studying, and increasingly furious about food and other shortages in what should have been a land of plenty. But they were powerless to get rid of him. Qaddafi had carefully sprinkled his inner circle with representatives of Libya's influential tribes. And he had crushed any group that threatened him—the army, the merchants, civil servants, and, of course, the Muslim ulema, who, inside Libya and abroad, were furious about Qaddafi's religious interpretations and his claim that they were now superfluous, since Muslims needed no intermediaries between themselves and God.

The Revolutionary Committees had grown by 1986 to a vanguard of between one thousand and two thousand zealots, many now from his own tribe to assure absolute loyalty. Based at the Azziziya barracks, this ugly force spied on and intimidated everyone. Created in 1978, the guards had grown in both numbers and influence after May 1984, when twelve soldiers had attacked the barracks in one of more than ten documented attempts to kill Qaddafi. Ordinary Libyans may have had to scrounge for decent bread, but Revolutionary Committee members lacked nothing.

In early 1986, I had dinner one night at the home of Ibrahim and Fatiya Zakkah, Qaddafi's committee leaders who were then in their early thirties. Ibrahim, who, like his wife, came from Qaddafi's home village, supervised the Ministry of Information, which made him far more powerful—and dangerous to journalists—than the minister. Fatiya, who had three children, was an unpaid worker on Qaddafi's personal staff. The Zakkahs had benefited from their propaganda and intelligence work: Their spacious villa, richly furnished in the finest Arabic style and located in what before the coup was Tripoli's American compound, had been expropriated from American "exploiters," as Fatiya called them. The low-slung crimson-velvet sectional sofa was new, as were the velvet-and-brass dining-room chairs and the Oriental carpet on the living-room floor. Fatiya was especially proud of a crystal vase and glasses decorated with revolutionary slogans from the *Green Book* and four cherished items on her mantel-piece: an Arabic lantern, a brass statue of a camel, a gold-leaf Koran, and a framed photograph of Qaddafi.

"I was fifteen when the revolution came," she said as she served us hearty portions of meat, vegetables, and fruit—all unavailable then to the average Libyan. "He was the most handsome man I ever saw. So tall and thin! (Qaddafi is six feet tall, a giant—in green—by Libyan standards.) I was inspired by his vision for our country. I joined his Arab Socialist Union at school. One day he noticed me at a rally and asked if I would come work for him. I've been there ever since."

Their passion for the colonel seemed heartfelt. Libya, they said, had spent twenty times as much on development under Qaddafi as it had under the monarchy, five times as much on agriculture, seven times as much for industry —all of which was true.[41] The regime had built hundreds of new schools and hospitals and hundreds of thousands of miles of roads. There had been a 321 percent growth in individual income, a 600 percent rise in national income. Although there was little to buy, Libyan per capita income was among the world's highest. My hosts did not mention that defense spending had risen faster than any other sector or that Qaddafi had spent at least $20 billion on Soviet arms,[42] to say nothing of what he had wasted on the Great Man-Made River Project, which was still not finished and might never be.

Fatiya was proudest of the progress women had made under Qaddafi's rule. Although male university students still outnumbered females three to one, girls and boys now attended primary and secondary schools in roughly equal numbers; there had been a fivefold increase in the number of women in college. Child brides were banned, and the minimum legal age for marriage was now eighteen. Women and men had roughly comparable rights in demanding a divorce, a very un-Islamic concept. And young Libyan women were no longer shrouded in *farshiyahs,* the traditional white cover that left only one eye exposed. The conservative ulema had fought these measures, Fatiya said. But Qaddafi had persevered, insisting that women, like men, receive military training and be able to serve in the armed forces. Libya's military academy, she boasted, had trained some seven thousand women since it opened in 1978.

I had interviewed one of the recruits earlier that week: Fawzia Abdullah, a twenty-one-year-old first lieutenant, was trying to become the first female captain in Libya's army. Like most of her male counterparts, she had been trained to fire Russian-made surface-to-air missiles, to dismantle and reassemble Kalashnikov rifles in less than a minute, and to handle recoilless antiaircraft guns. She also played bagpipes in the marching band. But her makeup was impeccable. Her short fingernails were painted crimson, and she wore fishnet stockings under her medium-high-heeled miniboots. Solid gold-drop earrings offset her jet black hair and jangled alluringly as she spoke of her dream of earning that extra star. But, she added with a giggle, "I would also like to get married." Some things in revolutionary Libya had not changed.

Women had made great strides, Fatiya lectured, snapping me out of my reverie. She blamed Libya's continuing inequality between men and women not on Qaddafi's muddled views on the status of women but on her tribal patriarchal society. Many Libyan fathers refused to send their daughters to high school because of the compulsory military training, she complained. Others insisted that their daughters cover their heads with scarves in Islamic virtue. And there was still no abortion or serious birth control in Libya, partly because the ulema objected and partly because, as Qaddafi explained, Libya needed more people to defend the vast, empty country. The People's Congress had also rejected Qaddafi's recommendation that polygamy be abolished. (Every now and then, a diplomat told me, the congress was allowed to veto an "inconsequential" proposal to give the rubber-stamp Parliament a patina of respectability.) Women had a long way to go, Fatiya conceded. Most remained housewives and mothers; few held prominent jobs in politics or finance. Even Safiya, the colonel's second wife, who had met Qaddafi when she was a fifteen-year-old nurse tending to the leader after his appendicitis,[43] was bored by politics, Fatiya said, sighing.

I decided not to ask Fatiya how the colonel squared his alleged feminism with his *Green Book* declarations that although women should be educated and even armed, men and women could not be truly equal because of "innate" characteristics. According to a "gynaecologist [sic]," Dr. Qaddafi had explained, a woman "menstruates or suffers feebleness every month, while man, being a male, does not menstruate." After a woman gave birth, she was "feeble for about a year"; if she miscarried, she suffered puerperium. As the man "does not get pregnant," the author of the *Green Book* observed, "he is not liable to the feebleness which woman, being a female, suffers." If a woman is forced to abandon her "natural role" of wife and mother, "she falls victim to coercion and dictatorship."[44]

If such insights — consistent, of course, with orthodox Islam's subjugation of women — troubled Fatiya, she did not let on as we sipped thick Arabic coffee after our sumptuous meal. "There is no contradiction between Islam and the revolution," she asserted, the "reactionary" ulema's muted protests notwithstanding. "I do not cover my head, but many women do, even at the military academy. Last year, Ibrahim and I made the haj," she added proudly, referring to the pilgrimage to Mecca pious Muslims must make at least once if possible. "I dress modestly for Islam," she said. "But I would willingly take off all my clothes and run naked into battle for Qaddafi and the defense of my country."

FOR ME, the sincerity of Qaddafi's commitment to women's dignity, as well as his sanity, was called into question by a truly bizarre incident in early 1986. Qaddafi had summoned five female correspondents, all representing major Western media, to spend some relaxed and private moments with him, his wife, Safiya, and their seven children. His ostensible aim was to convince the West that he was not a terrorist, as Ronald Reagan charged, but a devoted husband, loving father, and champion of women's liberation.

Qaddafi was ebullient that night. Flamboyantly attired in his best Bedouin layered look—a collarless shirt of cranberry cotton under a blue-denim vest that was covered by a camel-colored, gold-embroidered cape and topped by a salmon-colored turban—he had performed brilliantly, stressing with great warmth and apparent sincerity his desire for peace and his respect for the American people. In what I later learned was a well-rehearsed speech for Western journalists, he quoted Gloria Steinem and Betty Friedan and said that he had decided to grant interviews only to female journalists because "women in Libya and all over the world are oppressed and I want to liberate them." He was sorry that he had only one daughter, Aisha, he told us, lifting his then eight-year-old daughter onto his knee. But Aisha was his favorite because she was "political —just like me!"

He wanted Aisha and all other Libyan girls to grow up not in a backward country dominated by powerful tribes and autocratic sheikhs but in a true Islamic paradise, a progressive democracy without race, class, or sex distinctions, a land in which girls could become whatever they wanted to be.

The colonel might have fooled some of us with his devoted family-man performance if not for a second invitation when we left the tent. We were led to a nearby office building to join him for tea. Once inside, Qaddafi invited us to ask him questions individually and then disappeared into an adjacent room. One after another, we were invited into the room for our "exclusive" interviews. But something told me to decline. All but one of my colleagues accepted, however. One by one, each emerged from the room, clearly upset. Later on, I learned what had happened.

The room, as narrow as a nun's cell, smelled of Givenchy, Qaddafi's favorite cologne at the time, and contained only a single bed and a television that featured nonstop scenes from the leader's speeches. Behind the closed door, a waiting Qaddafi, having slipped out of his Bedouin garb and into a baby-blue jumpsuit, had made a crude pass at each of the three women, each time without success. One of my colleagues described the leader's technique: Qaddafi had simply gotten up from the bed where he was watching pictures of himself—the ultimate aphrodisiac—and put one hand around the back of her neck and the other around her waist. Then he had pressed himself against her. Stunned for a second, she pushed him away and ran out of the room.

My colleagues were furious when I told them I intended to write about Qaddafi's stunt. Was I mad! they shouted when we got back to the hotel. Qaddafi would have us expelled from Libya and would then ban our newspapers, too. We would all miss the American military retaliation that we sensed was imminent. Our editors would be furious, and not at Qaddafi. The colonel would have us barred from every country on our beat. Or worse. "Judy," one colleague reminded me, "this guy kills people!"

Finally, after hours of negotiation and an entire pack of Marlboros, despite yet another resolution to give them up, we reached a compromise: I would write about the incident (and I did), but only after we had all left Libya. After all, the colonel's behavior was news: How many rulers in the Middle East, or anywhere else, were crazy enough to make a succession of passes at correspondents from leading newspapers and television networks? Nothing even remotely like this had ever happened to any of us before. The incident was important because it proved, at least to me, that the "Leader" — whom reporters politely referred to in print as "quixotic," "erratic," and "mercurial" — was, in fact, insane.

I STAYED SO LONG in Libya in early 1986 because I was sure that the United States intended to respond to Qaddafi's taunts and terrorism. But in March 1986, the *Times* ordered me to leave. My foreign editor felt that almost three months in Tripoli had been more than enough. I would have protested more vigorously were it not for my own ambivalence about staying. Two events were particularly unsettling.

The first was an interview I had conducted in great secrecy — and never published — with a young British woman who had become ensnared in Qaddafi's terrorist network. Gail, I shall call her, was a working-class nineteen-year-old nurse from Britain who had met and married a young Libyan in London, moved to Tripoli, and rented an apartment beneath his parents' flat. When I met her, Gail's two small children were tearing around her small, dingy downtown apartment that smelled of rotting couscous. Her husband had told her that he worked for the Foreign Ministry as a courier; he often traveled abroad. Then, as she listened to the BBC one morning, she learned that her husband, ostensibly a courier, had been arrested in London and charged with attempted murder. He had given a Libyan dissident a package of peanuts that contained a highly lethal poison. The dissident had survived, but his two children, who had shared the peanuts, had become suddenly and violently ill. They were saved only by a prompt and correct diagnosis at the emergency hospital to which they were rushed. The family dog had licked some peanut remnants off the floor and had died instantly. Gail, a blondish waif who still spoke almost no Arabic, was distraught. The man she loved had lied to her. He was a murderer, part of Qaddafi's international hit squad, thugs who had killed Libyan dissidents throughout the world, who had tried to kill King Hussein of Jordan and several other Arab leaders, and who had targeted at least two American ambassadors: Herman Eilts, a former U.S. ambassador to Cairo, and Frances Cook, America's ambassador to Burundi, who had bravely refused to give Qaddafi the satisfaction of abandoning her post. Gail's husband was being tried for attempted murder, a crime for which he was eventually sentenced to life imprisonment. No one in the Libyan government would explain anything or help her. Her husband's parents held her passport and refused to let her leave. They had also threatened to take her children away if she said anything critical of Libya or their son. Could I help her? she pleaded. There was nothing I could do but listen sympathetically, share my American cigarettes with her, and lend her my handkerchief as she dabbed her eyes and described the nightmare her life had become.

The second episode involved Qaddafi himself. It was well after midnight when I was summoned to the barracks by a telephone call from Ibrahim, the Revolutionary Guard. The colonel wanted to see me — now. I did not particularly want to see more of the colonel, and certainly not at this hour, given his overtures toward my colleagues. But I dressed quickly and rushed to Al-Azziziya barracks, where I was escorted to a tawdry reception room dimly lit by a flickering fluorescent bulb. There, watching television, was a radically different Qaddafi. His jaw sagged; his face had swollen to almost twice its normal size. His shoulders drooped, and dark rings circled his eyes. It looked as if he had not slept for days. Diplomats had told me about Qaddafi's depressions. A doctor at Tripoli's Hadra Hospital told a diplomat he trusted that he gave the leader a potent daily cocktail of antidepressants, barbiturates, and amphetamines to combat his frequent and extreme mood fluctuations. Another doctor told me that Qaddafi had manic-depressive symptoms. The facial swelling, an intelligence analyst had told me, was caused by cortisone, a drug he took to relieve acute back pains from a slipped disc; it tended to make the eyes puffy and the face swell. While I had heard many rumors about Qaddafi's precarious psychological state and his drug treatments, I had never before seen physical evidence of it.

"Sit down," he mumbled. "Write down what I say, word for word," he said, his usually strong voice trailing off into a whisper. I had been summoned, it turned out, because the leader wanted to send "condolences" to the families of the Americans who had been killed earlier that day aboard the space shuttle *Challenger*. Only after I entered the room did I notice that the television was broadcasting pictures of the *Challenger* exploding in air, again and again. "It is a very sad day not only for all Americans but for all humanity," he said, his glazed stare shifting between the television set and me. He had sent for me, he continued, so that his message could be delivered "by an American to the American people." The *Challenger*'s crew were "victims of imperialist impatience." The space program itself was part of Reagan's effort to militarize the skies. "Those innocent Americans were sacrificed for nothing!" Qaddafi declared, his voice growing louder. "There are thirty thousand Americans in New York without homes!" he shouted. "They are sleeping in the streets of your city! The dollars should build housing for them, not be wasted on military maneuvers in space." Every now and then, despite his dementia, I thought, Qaddafi spoke plain, if unpalatable, truths.

Qaddafi dismissed me. As I started to leave, he called me back: "Write exactly what I said!"

It was close to deadline in New York by the time I got a call through to the paper. My editor was unimpressed with the colonel's condolences. But I pleaded for space — just two hundred words. "Print something. Anything," I pleaded. "Or you may be sending condolences to my mother."

The *Times* printed a small box featuring Qaddafi's message, but it was time to leave Libya.

•

IN THE EARLY-MORNING hours of April 15, 1986, the United States bombed Tripoli and Benghazi in a ten-minute-long raid in which at least fifteen people were killed and scores more injured. The air attack threw Tripoli into utter chaos. Qaddafi, who normally dominated Libyan television, appeared only a few times after the strike in which American planes had flattened his compound and other strategic targets. Libya had won a great victory against America, he had told his people. Henceforth, the name of the Socialist People's Libyan Arab Jamahiriya would be preceded by the adjective "Great," or as we called it from then on, the "Great SPLAJ." Two of Qaddafi's sons had been injured, and among the dead was Hanna Qaddafi, his fifteen-month-old "adopted" daughter. Hanna, however, was not among his acknowledged children when I had met the Qaddafi family in January. And I vividly recalled his complaint about having only one daughter: eight-year-old Aisha. A small child had obviously been killed in the raid, but her relationship to Qaddafi, if any, was obscure.

In June 1986, Qaddafi gave his first interview after the raid to an American reporter: Marie Colvin, a friend and fellow journalist with whom he instantly became infatuated. Qaddafi was virtually incoherent, she later told me. Reagan had once been a Nazi, he told her. Then he had joined Israel's Mossad, its CIA, to cover up his Gestapo past. "Reagan has caused the death of thousands of Jews," he ranted. "We have a file on this."

Colvin was to see more of the colonel. At one session, Qaddafi was waiting for her on a couch, dressed in a gold cape, red silk Nehru shirt, white silk pajama pants, and gray lizard-skin slippers. Arrayed neatly on a nearby couch was Marie's intended attire: a white Libyan wedding dress and a pair of tiny green slippers. She had feigned a headache and backed quickly out of the room. On a subsequent trip to Libya, she was awakened by pounding on her hotel room door, which she blearily opened. An aide to Qaddafi and a nurse entered the room. The nurse, a Bulgarian, Marie subsequently learned, pulled a giant syringe from her black medical bag. Qaddafi wanted to see Marie, the nurse explained, but not before he was sure that she was not one of the AIDS-bearing agents that the CIA had sent to Libya to destroy the people. Would she mind giving Qaddafi a blood sample?

When it finally dawned on Qaddafi years later that his affections for Colvin would not be reciprocated, he confessed to her his secret passion for yet another American woman, Margaret Tutweiler, the Bush administration's influential State Department spokesman. He watched her every night on CNN, he confessed. Did Marie know her fax number? Could he get a message to her? he pleaded. "Tell her that I love her. And that if she loves me, she should wear something green at her next press conference. I shall be watching and hoping."

WHILE LEGAL SCHOLARS argued that the American raid was a clear violation of international and possibly of American law,[45] Qaddafi was chastened,[46] if only for a while. Then, in 1988, the lull in Libyan-sponsored terrorism ended when

Pan Am 103 was blown up, and in 1989 a French civilian airliner exploded en route from Brazzaville to Paris, killing all 171 people on board. In 1991 a French court issued arrest warrants for four senior Libyan officials, including Abdullah Sennousi, Qaddafi's brother-in-law and the deputy head of intelligence, charging them with having destroyed the plane. By early 1992, American officials had concluded that the Abu Nidal group was still in Libya and that Qaddafi was still operating at least five training camps and making only "cosmetic" concessions to Western demands that he end support for terrorism.[47] Moreover, Washington accused Libya of having produced as much as thirty tons of deadly mustard gas, enough for 150 chemical bombs, at a pharmaceutical plant at Rabta, and of attempting to build a second production facility in the southern desert outside Sabhah, some four hundred miles south of Tripoli.[48]

In April 1992 the United Nations for the first time accused a nation of sponsoring terrorism and imposed limited economic sanctions aimed at forcing Libya to turn over the suspects in the two airline bombings. Qaddafi was desperate to get the sanctions lifted. The collapse of the Soviet Union and departure of the remaining seventeen hundred Russian advisers and technicians had devastated whatever military infrastructure the American raid had not destroyed, leaving Qaddafi isolated and without a superpower ally. But he could not surrender the two Libyans to America. One was a relative of his deputy, Abdel-Salaam Jalloud, a member of the Megraha, one of Libya's strongest tribes. Turning him over to the West for trial could risk not only offending a tribal pillar of the regime but also exposing other terrorist actions conducted by Libya's security establishment, without whose support Qaddafi could not rule.

To ingratiate himself to the West, however, Qaddafi had closed several training camps and finally expelled Abu Nidal and other terrorists long sought by the West. He had also turned over to Britain information about the Irish Republican Army, which Libya had once sheltered, armed, and trained.

But nothing worked. The Americans would not relent. He had to find some other way of persuading the Americans to lift the sanctions — another charm offensive. That was how I found myself in April 1993 back in Libya at the Mahari Hotel.

I HEARD the glass break as soon as Raffaello Fellah dropped his suitcase on the cold tile floor of Tunis airport. "It's the Passover wine!" he cried as the crimson liquid oozed across the arrival hall floor. "Such a shame," he sighed. "There's none in Libya."

That was not surprising, I thought, as I helped my distraught traveling companion dump glass shards into a waste bin. There were only six Jews left in Libya, all of them very old. Before Israel's war of independence in 1948, Libya was home to 35,000 Jews, part of the 870,000 Jews then living in the Arab Middle East.

Raffaello's family had been in Libya for centuries. The first Jews had arrived in Cyrenaica from Egypt in about 300 B.C. Raffaello's father, who sold "Oriental" clothes to the Italians, had been wealthy. He had nine children, a "soccer team," said Raffaello. They were all born in the city's old quarter and at home spoke Judeo-Arabic, the Yiddish of the Middle East. In 1945, Raffaello's father was killed in a pogrom in which some 158 Jews were murdered and two thousand injured in forty-eight hours as the British occupiers looked on indifferently, he said. A second pogrom followed in 1948. Some Jews fought back; others emigrated. Not Raffaello, who continued to believe in "Jewish-Arab reconciliation and in Libya," he told me as our limousine sped toward the Tunisian border. We were driving from Tunis to Tripoli because ever since the sanctions, international flights to and from Libya had been suspended.

After the 1967 Arab-Israeli war, Raffaello was finally forced to flee his beloved Libya along with some forty-five hundred fellow Jews who left at night on special Alitalia flights. "We were permitted to take one suitcase each—and no gold," he said. He had immediately formed an emergency committee to help Libyan Jews. His own property in Libya was safeguarded by his Palestinian partner in the family's oil business. Then, in 1968, Fellah, sensing political turmoil, had returned to Tripoli and sold off everything. In 1969, when Qaddafi nationalized property and industry after his coup, Raffaello created the Libyan-Jewish Society to preserve the Jewish community's rights and heritage in Libya. Fellah, who now lived in Rome, had finally met Qaddafi in early 1993. He was convinced that the leader wanted to reconcile with Jews and the West and was even prepared to recognize Israel. Qaddafi had already fulfilled his earlier pledge to renovate and restore synagogues and ancient Jewish homes in Tripoli's Islamic quarter; more gestures were planned.

When Raffaello first introduced himself on the phone and tried to talk me into returning to Libya to interview Qaddafi, I thought he was as mad as the leader himself. I had been banned from Libya ever since my article on Qaddafi's crude sexual advances was published in the *Times* in 1986. But this portly, excitable man with piercing hazel eyes and infinite determination seemed to know many of my friends—Arab and Israeli. So I checked him out with my Israeli colleague, Smadar Perry, a journalist in Tel Aviv. Fellah was definitely "kosher," she reported a few days later. "A dreamer; a bit of a schemer. A businessman like everyone in our happy region. But on the level," she said. "And some people here are very interested in what Qaddafi might tell you." I decided to take a chance.

The young man assigned to "assist" us in Tripoli—and undoubtedly to spy on us as well—was waiting at the Mahari when we arrived. He was tall, thin, and elegant: His double-breasted suit was Armani, I thought. Very expensive. He wore a diamond-studded Rolex watch, a Hermès tie, and smart Italian sunglasses. His longish hair was slicked back and plastered down with hair spray. "Yo. I'm Fawzi Shalgam," he introduced himself, extending his hand and an MTV smile. "Welcome back." His English was as smooth as his Gucci loafers. "Sorry I can't offer you a real drink," he said, pouring us some nonalcoholic beer from the minibar of his hotel suite. "But when you visit my farm, I'll make it up to you. I don't drink, myself. But I love a Jack Daniel's atmosphere."

Fawzi, which is not his real name, worked in Germany for LAFICO, the Libyan foreign investment company, Qaddafi's bankers. Through LAFICO, Libya had spread its oil wealth, buying into Fiat and more than twenty-two hundred gas stations in Italy, some $700 million worth of stations and outlets in Germany, Switzerland, and France and some $3 billion worth of assets in Europe and Canada.[49] "Even in the United States!" Fawzi laughed. "We own lots in your country — indirectly, of course. There are no borders for businessmen."

Fawzi was the new Libyan, the unlikely product of Qaddafi's "revolution," his demented Islamo-socialist regime. There was little that this well-traveled young man with a bachelor's degree from an American business school had not done or tried. Only thirty-four years old, he seemed far older. His twenty-three-year-old Italian wife lived in Munich, and because he traveled so much, he saw far too little of his two-year-old daughter. Only when he spoke of his child did a softness spread across his angular face, with its practiced smile.

Fawzi was amazingly efficient at getting things done and warning me about what I would not be able to do. I tried, for example, to find Fatiya and Ibrahim Zakkah, the Revolutionary Committee leaders who had been so hospitable during my last visit. But Fawzi urged me to abandon the search; such people were now in disfavor. I would not find them, and I did not. Nor could I find Gail, the stranded British woman who had poured out her heart to me seven years earlier. I could never learn what had happened to any of them.

Raffaello had insisted that we tour the old city, which Qaddafi had finally decided to preserve. I had never visited the quarter before: The Islamic villas and medieval walkways were exquisite despite years of neglect. And the restoration was impressive. "The sanctions are hurting us," I was told by Fawzia Shalabi, a feminist who had helped persuade Qaddafi to save the deteriorating quarter where thirty-five hundred people still lived and some sixty-five thousand worked. Her team had money; what it lacked were enough skilled restorers and technicians. "Old Tripoli should be like Venice! The whole world should be helping us," she said. Fawzi looked bored.

"Hey, man," he complained as we left a newly restored synagogue. "It's 1993. What's the point of saving this old stuff?" Raffaello stared at him blankly. "The streets are too narrow for cars. Putting in sewage, water, and phone lines is very expensive. And only old people live here. Why bother?"

Ms. Shalabi stared at him warily. Knowing that Fawzi probably worked for intelligence, she was cautious. "This is part of Libya's heritage," she said, trying not to patronize him. "We must connect people like you with your past. One day, tourists may come to admire what we built and saved."

Fawzi brightened at the mention of tourists. Tourism, he said, was a growth sector for Libya. LAFICO owned many hotels around the world, including the giant Abu Nawas chain that operated throughout the region, except, of course, in Israel and Libya. But even before the sanctions, Libya had attracted only fifteen hundred visitors a year. Now almost no one came despite a 1991 law that authorized the issuance of tourist visas in twenty-four hours.

Libya had as much potential for tourism as terrorism. Tripoli and Benghazi were lovely Mediterranean cities with constant sun and good climate. Their Italianate squares and villas and tree-lined promenades overlooking the sea were perfect for outdoor restaurants and clubs, if only the government would permit them. I could still find occasional remnants of Tripoli's former lives: the Roman ruins of the City of Oea, on which it was built, and monuments built by Mussolini's colonists. The site, now filled by the cement-covered catastrophe known improbably as Green Square, was once a manicured garden with a fine fountain. A merchant in the formerly thriving gold souk had shown me old photographs of Tripoli under Italian occupation. The Italians were horrible, he said. But the city, "ah, it was splendid."

Beyond Tripoli lay thousands of miles of open, unspoiled dunes and flat lands and, along the coast, the breathtaking ruins of the Roman cities of Leptis Magna and Sabratha. Under a different government, Leptis Magna, the world's largest ancient Roman city on the sea, would attract thousands; in Sabratha, only forty-five minutes from Tripoli, was the exquisite mosaic known as the Tree of Life. Once a temple floor, it depicted a giant tree in which the birds known to the ancient Romans were perched.

All along Libya's undeveloped coastline, surf crashed against golden, sandy beaches lined with high, stalky date palms and luxuriant patches of green. If only the government would pick up the garbage on the beach and clear away the fetid piles of trash that marred city streets and back alleys.

Instead, Qaddafi had chosen "revolution" and isolation. A flood of tourists would undoubtedly threaten a regime based so totally, if subtly, on control. Rather than permit real commerce, Qaddafi had used Libya's oil revenues to finance handouts in a dysfunctional welfare state. Some 750,000 Libyans in a country of just under 5 million worked in theory for the government, representing roughly three quarters of Libya's million households. But more than a million foreigners, most of them Egyptian farmers, did the real work. Despite their contribution, Libya still imported $500 million worth of food in 1992. Oil now accounted for 98 percent of all foreign-currency earnings. While the leader still talked bravely of self-reliance, his country had become the classic *rentier* state, a Bedouin version of Kuwait.

In the late 1980s, Qaddafi had attempted to defuse growing opposition through tepid economic liberalization and a massive release of political prisoners. By 1993 he had begun distributing part of Libya's annual oil income directly to Libyan families.[50] I suppose these reforms were better than buying more weapons to rust in the sand or building more vast industrial complexes and grandiose projects that would continue losing money, such as the massive steel works at Misurata and, of course, the Great Man-Made River. The country had imported ten transistor radios for each citizen, and the average Libyan household owned three videotape machines, but Libyan hospitals lacked modern equipment and qualified staff. Schools had ample supplies of *Green Books*, but no chalk or desks. Qaddafi had often proposed abolishing schools, anyway—along with money. Children would be better off, he said, if they were taught by their parents at home, and bartering was more democratic than trade.

Chaos was all that Qaddafi had institutionalized. In 1992 he ordered property records burned after tribal chiefs had quarreled over land. Only Libya's four major intelligence agencies and LAFICO had computers. Fawzi and I spent several hours one day hunting in government ministries for a typewriter I could borrow after my laptop was defeated by Libya's electrical system.

Piped water, despite the Great Man-Made River Project, had become so brackish—ten times the internationally accepted level—that most Libyans had to make their coffee and wash clothes with bottled water. Qaddafi was deeply troubled when experts told him there would be 14 million Libyans by the year 2025 but only enough water for fifty years. Perhaps he should expel millions of Libyans, he asked his technical experts, but failed even to discuss the possibility of introducing serious birth-control policies in his country.[51]

Indoor plumbing, postal services, and garbage collection operated sporadically. So did international telephones. "Paris is out of order," a sweet young operator told me after she had been unable to get through to France all day. Libya as I found it in 1993 was a mess despite its oil wealth—testimony to an economic paradox: Money alone did not make a nation rich, efficient, or satisfied. Half Hitchcock, half Marx Brothers, Libya had become a prop for the ego of one particularly foolish and dangerous man.

FAWZI, RAFFAELLO, and I made a requisite pilgrimage to Qaddafi's house at the Azziziya barracks, which the Americans had bombed. The house was now a museum. Children were taken on class trips to see how America had defiled their leader's home.

Qaddafi had made the most of this defining moment in Libyan history. The post office had issued commemorative stamps of the 1986 raid. And Tripoli's planetarium featured a sound-and-light show entitled *How the Stars Stood When America Attacked the Jamahiriya*, complete with flashing strobe lights to simulate lightning and the earsplitting noise of low-flying jets and exploding bombs. Dirk Vandewalle, a scholar who had also seen the show, credited the convincing sound-and-light effects to a team of East German technicians.

A bomb had landed outside the front door of Qaddafi's former house, blowing out the kitchen's glass doors and windows and collapsing part of the living-room ceiling. Wreckage from the raid and rotting orange peels left by a guard were on display inside the salon, along with gruesome pictures of the raid's victims, including children, and what appeared to be several charred bodies. Bomb casings were propped up like shadeless lamps next to a Goodrich airplane tire and a section of a wing of the single F-111 jet that had crashed in combat. Bits of fuselage, along with pieces of the ceiling, were suspended from a makeshift roof by steel wire like modern sculpture. The room itself was covered with dust and debris, as if it had been bombed only yesterday rather than seven years ago.

The house was modest by Arab-ruler standards. On the second floor were two identical "his" and "her" master bedrooms, each containing a large oval bed under a matching seascape, like those found in American honeymoon motels. Several pieces of gypsum from the collapsed ceiling that had nearly killed Qaddafi's wife were displayed on her bed. The children's bombed-out rooms contained poignant artifacts: a green school bag, some partially burned schoolbooks, a framed photo of Hanna — Qaddafi's "adopted" daughter said to have been killed in the raid — her plastic high chair and tambourine. It was a simple house for such a powerful man. But Libyan visitors, accustomed to a low standard of living, considered it luxurious.

The centerpiece of the museum was a floor-to-ceiling mural of *Tripoli Under Siege*, depicting — who else? — a smiling and confident Qaddafi confronting the fleet of American planes that rained bombs on his capital.

Raffaello inscribed a lengthy tribute to Libya's suffering in the international guest book, which I also dutifully signed, as Fawzi looked on, bemused.

The next day, I returned to the Azziziya barracks for the interview with Qaddafi and was quickly escorted into his Bedouin-style tent, as I had been so many times before. The leader was seated in a large stuffed armchair; he did not get up. How he had deteriorated! Once proud of his slim figure and chiseled features, Qaddafi was now bloated and visibly tired. Though he claimed to have been born in 1942, he looked far older. His once-wavy brown locks were now shoe-polish black, like President Mubarak's. The dye emphasized the raccoon rings around his eyes.

The tent was different, too — sleeker, better furnished, and now reinforced with concrete. With cushions covering the floor for Arab guests, its brightly colored patchwork quilt into which Qaddafi's sayings were embroidered, its modern bathroom, color-television set, video recorder, stereo system, and green telephone, the tent blended Bedouin chic with high tech — vintage Qaddafi.

I asked Qaddafi whether he now believed that he had erred in adopting socialism and ruining his economy. Wasn't his recent decision to privatize the economy an acknowledgment of failure?

"I have no power," he declared in passable English, which he had learned at a military training course in Britain in the mid-1960s. "I've been in revolution, not in power. Power is in the hands of the people. The masses have power — through the People's Congress." Ownership of companies and land, too, he said, was also in the hands of the people. "Popular socialism," he called it, unwilling, even now, to utter the detested word "capitalism."

"My goals and principles haven't changed," he told me. "We have simply taken world developments into account in devising new paths to achieve them. As you told me the day we met," he said, suddenly brightening, "Qaddafi always goes straight."

"What was that, Colonel?" I asked him.

"Straight . . . you said: 'Qaddafi always goes straight,' that day on the tractor!"

I had almost forgotten our first interview in 1986. Qaddafi may have been crazy, I thought, but there was nothing wrong with his memory.

Qaddafi soon steered the interview to his purpose. President Bill Clinton was the "savior of the world," he told me: Libya prayed for his success. A seemingly chastened Qaddafi poured out his desire for improved relations with America, the West, and the "Jews of the world," and even indirectly with Israel. (He left the distasteful task of acknowledging that Libya was prepared to recognize Israel to Omar Montasser, his able foreign minister.)

Tripoli would soon extend an invitation to Jewish leaders, including Israelis, to a conference of the three major monotheistic faiths; he would permit a group of Libyan Muslims to visit holy shrines in Jerusalem; he would compensate Italians and Jews who had left property in Libya when they had fled. While he could not surrender the Libyans who were wanted by London and Washington for the Pan Am bombing, Libya had closed the camps that the West had alleged were terrorist-training facilities, he assured me, and had invited UN inspectors to visit any site they chose. Libya, he vowed, would never develop or seek to purchase nuclear weapons, though he had attempted to do both, in one case, a senior official told me, offering India and China as much as $15 billion for a single atomic bomb. "I'm afraid of nuclear proliferation," Qaddafi said solemnly. "All this atomic material and people with nuclear skills are for sale. A black market is developing. Against whom would such weapons be used? It would mean the destruction of all our region, of the world!"

Finally, he denounced the Muslim Brotherhood and other "Islamic militants" as "mad dogs and terrorists" and called for close cooperation between Arab and Western countries to fight them. The Gulf war would only strengthen them in the long run, Qaddafi said. "It has bred a new generation of hatred that may one day produce an Arab and Islamic earthquake." If they took over, he said, a "minority in the name of God" would impose its will — the veiling of women and segregation of schools — on the "majority."

The bombing of the World Trade Center in New York, he said, was a bad omen for America. The Islamists' militancy "is coming home to destroy the country that adopted them." If America was not careful, it could become like Egypt or Algeria. "But what did you expect? You funded Islamic militants in Afghanistan and all over the world and then were surprised when they turned on you," he said, shaking his head sadly. "You brought it upon yourselves." There were those unpalatable truths again.

I knew that Qaddafi still hated his Islamic challengers. In 1989, Amnesty International reported, hundreds of religious activists had been arrested after they had fought with Qaddafi's Revolutionary Committees and security forces. Calling Islamic militants "worse than cancer and AIDS" and demanding that they be crushed, Qaddafi had arrested some three thousand of them after Islamic fundamentalists tried to assassinate him.[52] In September 1995, the regime was forced to suppress a riot in Benghazi that, according to Arab officials, was instigated by the underground Muslim Brotherhood and other Islamic activists. Most Libya watchers continued to see militant Islamists as the best organized threat to his rule.

Qaddafi had responded with predictable ruthlessness at home. He had also popped in on Algerian president Chadli Benjedid in 1990, according to an Algerian official, to warn him against proceeding with national elections and his democratization program. "What you are doing is sheer madness!" Qaddafi had lectured Chadli. "They are merely using elections to take over."

Weeks after my interview was published in April 1993, it became clear that it was a small part of a far broader Libyan campaign to persuade the United States to lift sanctions without surrendering the Libyan agents. Qaddafi felt isolated. No one was paying attention to him. His fellow Libyans were complaining about not being able to fly in and out of the country. Fatalities on the Tripoli-Tunis road, always high given the way Libyans drive, had quintupled. Qaddafi had watched President Hafiz al-Assad of Syria successfully court Washington through Israel's heart; he, too, could use the Israeli card to win forgiveness and the favor of the sole remaining superpower. But Libya was not Syria, and Qaddafi was neither as shrewd nor as patient as Syria's Assad. And Assad, moreover, was depressingly sane.

A few days after I had published my interview and what I had called in print Qaddafi's "astonishing" series of "about-faces,"[53] Henry Schuler, the American Qaddafi watcher, faxed me a copy of a speech to Libyan university students that the leader had given shortly after I had seen him. The Islamic fundamentalists conducting terrorism in Egypt and Algeria, Qaddafi told the students as he reverted to true form, were part of a "Western plot to weaken and divide the Arab world and guarantee Israel's absolute superiority."

Israel soon soured on Qaddafi's overtures. Initially breaking ranks with the West on contacts with Libya, Israel had publicly promised Qaddafi in June 1993 that a delegation of two hundred Libyan pilgrims to Jerusalem would be welcomed. Even Qaddafi himself would be welcome, a wary Prime Minister Yitzhak Rabin told journalists. But the welcome cooled when a spokesman for the Libyan pilgrims visiting Jerusalem called for the liberation of Islam's third-holiest city at a packed press conference attended by, among others, a mortified Raffaello Fellah, who had accompanied the delegation on its eighteen-hundred-mile overland trip to Israel.[54]

"I have no illusions," said Israeli foreign minister Shimon Peres, who never saw a diplomatic opening he did not want to test. "The Libyans came to us to make a good impression on America." Soon after the Libyan press conference, the Israeli Foreign Ministry, while reaffirming the "principle of religious freedom and the safeguarding of free access to religious shrines for all faiths," attacked Libya for its sponsorship of "brutal terrorism against innocents." Israel, the statement declared, fully endorsed "all international sanctions and measures taken against Libya for its terrorist activities." Libya's experiment in glasnost was over.

•

MONTHS AFTER I left Libya, Fawzi turned up in New York and offered to buy me a real drink. He ordered Coca-Cola; I drank scotch. He was still smoking; I had stopped — yet again. He asked me whether I had been disappointed by my trip. I told him that I wondered whether I had captured the strangeness and sadness of Libya, the joylessness and helplessness of the people, the sinister confusion of everyday life, or Qaddafi's utter corruption of Islamic and political norms.

How did I really feel about the bombing? Fawzi pressed me.

I was still of two minds about the raid, I told him, speaking more honestly than I would have in Libya and hoping, somehow, that he might reciprocate. Qaddafi had grown increasingly provocative in the mid-1980s. His support for terrorism, efforts to buy or make weapons of mass destruction, and growing repression and idiosyncratic rule at home had provoked a Western response. The rules of Middle Eastern politics were not subtle. The raid had gotten Qaddafi's attention, and it had put others in the region on notice that weak nations would be wise not to target Americans no matter how great their antipathy toward the West. At the same time, I agreed with those who argued that the raid had inadvertently helped Qaddafi. Not only had it reinforced the regime's pathological distrust of the West; it had also seemed to many Arabs opportunistic as well as out of proportion to the damage Libya had inflicted on American interests.[55] Finally, it had enabled Qaddafi to continue portraying Libya as a victim of history, of Italy, of its corrupt and inefficient monarchy, and now of the United States rather than his own idiotic regime.

There was yet another compelling reason to be critical of the raid: It had not achieved its stated goal of containing Qaddafi's terrorism, as the families of the victims of Pan Am 103 knew all too well. Nor had it killed Qaddafi — its unacknowledged objective. Sanctions had not yet worked and probably would not work unless they were strengthened. But only an embargo on Libyan oil was likely to inflict true economic pain on Libya, and European allies would not support this, given their dependence on Libyan crude.

Finally, Fawzi spoke. Why was I obsessed with Qaddafi? he said. "The Arabs are like children," he told me. "They need a dictator." Qaddafi was no worse than the others. "Democracy," he said, draining his Coke, "is a system in which you're taken to the cleaners unwittingly. In dictatorship, you're being had and you know it."

Qaddafi's revolution was "over, long gone," he said. Maybe it had never existed. Islam, too, was irrelevant, he laughed. The Sanusi patronage network had been smashed, and the Muslim Brothers were hypocrites who wanted to take the colonel's place as the country's supreme guide, if they could. "Money is all that matters," Fawzi told me. "It is all that has ever mattered."

And power. In one sense Qaddafi had always "gone straight": He had done whatever he had to do and taken whatever ideological coloration he needed to survive. Qaddafi's Islam, though ostensibly grounded in the Sanusiya's drive for moral purity and intellectual independence, was as peculiar and self-serving as his socialist "revolution." Survival was all that mattered.

Fawzi, too, was obviously a product of his leader's cynicism, a young man for whom racing cars, his "dream" farm with billiards room, heated swimming pool, thoroughbred horses, and giant movie screening room were as important as Qaddafi's revolutionary slogans had been to his father's generation.

"Don't spend too much time worrying about 'the man,' " Fawzi advised as we parted. "Money makes the world go round today, not religion or politics. Islam and politics are only cover."

I liked Fawzi, but as he threw his Burberry raincoat over his shoulder and left the bar, I felt a moment's pang for Qaddafi's tent and the bit of the desert that the Libyan leader had so poignantly tried to preserve in his bitter world of power and intrigue. Qaddafi still belonged to his desert tradition, aspiring, if clumsily, even madly, for authenticity. But Fawzi believed in nothing; he belonged to nothing; and he was attracted merely to the ephemera of Western culture. Fawzi was a man of his age, yet another of the modern Middle East's cynical schemers, like so many Islamists themselves, beside whom Muammar Qaddafi seemed almost innocent.

LEBANON

IN DECEMBER 1993 I was dining along the Mediterranean coast in Burj al Hammam, a fluorescent-lit restaurant in the Christian enclave of Jounieh, a recently built Levantine Riviera a few miles north of Beirut. The Burj was filled with pre-Christmas revelers. Waiters in crisp uniforms navigated through rows of wooden chairs and linen-draped tables, starched white napkins over their forearms.

The giant room resonated with laughter, French, Arabic, and the tinkling of wineglasses. The heavily made up women wore Dior suits and low-cut dresses; their Chanel handbags were draped carelessly over the backs of their chairs. Their heavy gold bracelets clanked against the tables as they flirted with the plump men whose suede jackets bulged with the American dollars and Lebanese pounds required to pay the hefty checks. Dinner for two usually ran over $150, and few Beirut restaurants had accepted credit cards since the civil war that began in 1975.

Amid this gaiety, a fierce and unlikely argument was about to ensue. Rima Tarabai, the Lebanese prime minister's press secretary, had invited me to dinner with Maroun Bagdadi, a Lebanese filmmaker whose work I had greatly admired but whom I had never met.

Rima worked for Rafic Hariri, the Sunni Muslim who became prime minister in October 1992, three years after the war had ended—officially. A fifty-year-old billionaire who had made his fortune in construction in Saudi Arabia, Hariri was initially hailed as Lebanon's "master builder" and putative savior, a symbol of the country's resurrection after seventeen years of civil war. Hariri had spent more than a billion dollars of his own money to rebuild his shattered land and restore investor confidence. But many Lebanese now accused him of having "bought" the job that most sane men would have shunned and denounced him as a Syrian pawn. Damascus, which, at the request of Lebanon's Christians, had intervened in the early days of the civil war, had remained to pursue its own interests, ruthlessly, and now unofficially controlled cantankerous Lebanon.

Maroun Bagdadi blamed Hariri for Lebanon's postwar supermaterialism and cynical pragmatism. A slim forty-three-year-old man with gentle brown eyes and a ring of curly hair the same color, he was as sensitive and engaging as his films. "Look at my countrymen!" he said, gesturing around the room. "Can you believe this? There is not an empty seat in the place. Look at the food! The wine! The jewels! The bonhomie! They hate one another, the Lebanese. A few years ago, they were all killing one another. But today they sit and joke as if nothing had ever happened."

It was true. No one would ever guess that we were dining in a wreck of a city that was slowly emerging from a civil war of intermittent savagery. I had not visited Lebanon since 1983, when Americans were the main targets of Shiite Muslim extremists determined to expel the "Great Satan" from their country and Western visitors were valued primarily as hostages. The Islamic extremists' ultimate goal was the ejection of Israeli forces that also still occupied part of southern Lebanon and the establishment of an Islamic state in what had been the Middle East's most freewheeling capital. Maroun had also avoided Beirut since the mid-1980s, when the growing power of Islamic militants had finally driven him out. He had been making films about his beleaguered land from Paris.

"Does no one remember anything in Lebanon?" he said. "Does this country have no collective memory of the war? Is there not a rather curious lack of introspection about what happened?"

"Maroun," said Rima, running her fingers through her chestnut hair, "there is nothing special about the Lebanese. People always want to forget war once it's over. After so much suffering, people need to forget."

Maroun looked at his beautiful friend quizzically. "No, Rima," he said finally. "People have not repressed the memories of the war. They never even stopped to think about it."

Rima ignored him. "We Lebanese love life, Maroun," she continued. "There's nothing wrong with that. Arab countries do not have our zest, our *joie de vivre*. It is the secret of our resilience. It is what makes us—well, different from other countries in the region, like Egypt. They're constantly talking about their glorious past. And just look at the place! It's a wreck—filthy and disorganized. Egyptians have given up. They're not only poor; they're beggars, broken people. Everywhere you go everyone has his hand out. It's uncivilized."

"Uncivilized!" Maroun exploded with laughter. "Egypt is one of the most civilized countries on earth. How can you talk about civilization in a country that has indulged in our sort of slaughter for seventeen years! Egyptians never did that to one another. You don't like Egypt, Rima, because it is 'Arab.' But what did your 'Phoenician' civilization ever bring us? It brought us Bashir Gemayel!"

Rima reddened at the reference to her alleged ancestors, the seafaring Phoenicians who in ancient times, long before the Arabs came, had ruled what is now Lebanon and their self-styled modern successors, the Maronite Christians, some of whom now called themselves Phalangists. Bashir Gemayel had been one of them, a tough, young, charismatic Christian who had led the Lebanese Forces, the private militia of the Phalange Party, Lebanon's largest and oldest Christian political organization. The Phalange, founding in 1936 by Bashir's father, who was deeply impressed with European fascism, embodied Christian fantasies of establishing a purely Christian ministate in Lebanon or at the very least a state in which Christians would dominate Lebanon's Muslim majority indefinitely. Bashir was elected president by Lebanon's Parliament in 1982, having promised to establish a cantonized, federal country like Switzerland in which each of Lebanon's denominations would be able to live in accordance with its culture and heritage. "If I want my children to learn physics in French and not Arabic . . . that is my right," Bashir was fond of saying. He also promised an end to the oligarchy of feudal patriarchs — men like his father — who had dominated Lebanon since its creation. Threatened by the prospect of a truly sovereign Lebanon, one that Syria could not control, Syrian agents had killed Bashir before he could assume power in 1982 and with him Christian dreams of political hegemony. While there were many who saw Bashir as an impulsive, ruthless thug, a man who had murdered his way to the top, many Christians, including Rima, still worshiped him.[2] She swallowed hard but did not respond.

"Face it, Rima," Maroun persisted with good-natured firmness. "You lost! The Christians lost the civil war and the right to dominate Lebanon. So now you've switched sides, typically Lebanese. You're working for a man from the winning side — a Sunni Muslim billionaire! You're promoting Rafic Hariri, a man who offers Lebanon dollars instead of dreams, who promotes materialism as an ideology, who is turning our country into his personal limited holding company. Maroun chuckled at her obvious discomfort. "Hariri thinks he can buy anyone and anything — even peace and stability in Lebanon!"

Maroun was not optimistic about Lebanon. "I hate what's happening here," he said as Rima grew angrier. "I loathe the greed and superindividualism that Hariri has made respectable, the rapaciousness he has unleashed in the name of saving Lebanon. And you, my dear, are helping him. You are a naive sellout."

Rima blanched. "And you, Maroun, are an antiquated leftist who still wants to create a Lebanon that never existed and never will. Rafic Hariri may not be perfect, but he's pragmatic. He sees beyond our silly ideologies. And he sincerely wants to rebuild Lebanon, which is more than our pathetic traditional leaders have done. There will be real peace soon. That means markets and tourism and economic competition. Hariri is trying to position Lebanon to compete in that environment.

"Besides, Maroun, you are in no position to judge us," she said sharply. "You were sitting in Paris while I fought to save Lebanon."

"And how were you doing that, Rima?" he said, raising his voice for the first time. "You were part of the stubbornness and blindness that kept the war going, the intolerance that ruined this country."

All three of us knew what he meant. Before joining Hariri's office, Rima had been a spokeswoman for the Christian Lebanese Forces, whose leadership was now being hunted down by the Syrian-dominated Lebanese government. When the militia was finally disbanded in 1990, after the Lebanese war officially ended, Rima had traded in her fatigues and AK-47 for a designer pantsuit and the lucrative job with Hariri. Rima had told me that she honestly believed that Lebanon needed a rich patron to restore peace and prosperity. But many Christian colleagues, some jealous of her beauty and success, whispered that she, like so many others, had been bought by the fabulously wealthy Hariri.

Rima was startled by Maroun's oblique allusion to what he considered her unsavory past. He had violated an unspoken agreement among Lebanese not to discuss what they had done during the war. Maroun, too, was now angry.

"Yes, Rima," he replied, lowering his voice. "I was in Paris while you were here. But I was never far from Lebanon. I made films about Lebanon; I yearned for Lebanon. And I suffered in exile."

"You suffered?" Rima scoffed.

"You can suffer in exile, Rima. You can die of nostalgia."

I FELT AS IF I had barged in on a family quarrel. It was such differences as these that had haunted Lebanon since its creation as a state under French mandate in 1920 and had subsequently wrecked the country. To Maroun and other unreconstructed Arab nationalists, Lebanon was an "Arab" country, inseparable from Arab culture, politics, and history. For Rima, Lebanon was an exception, a Western-oriented sanctuary founded not by Arabs but by the Phoenicians; Lebanon was a cedar — its national symbol — a mountain tree towering proudly over an Arab desert. She detested Hamra, the main shopping street of West (or Muslim) Beirut, with its cafés frequented, she complained, by every imaginable brand of Arab revolutionary and political weirdo. Her Lebanon was Ashrafiyeh, a clean, orderly, staunchly Christian neighborhood in East Beirut whose very existence proved to her that the country's values would remain Western, entrepreneurial, secular, and modern — in other words, the opposite, so she assumed, of Arabism.

Had Maroun been a Muslim and Rima a Christian, I would have anticipated their differences. But they were both Christians. He was Greek Catholic, a Christian sect that had lived for centuries among the Sunni Muslim majorities of the cities of the Levant and from whose ranks, like those of the Greek Orthodox, came many of Arab nationalism's most prominent exponents; she was Maronite, the tough, proud, isolated people of Mount Lebanon who had inhabited this land since the tenth century and for whom France had created a modern nation-state.

Even in a society as religiously stratified as this had become, Christians and Muslims were often as divided within their own sects as they were from one another despite their sectarian leaders' preposterous claims of ethnic solidarity. Though their friendship was strong, Rima and Maroun would always disagree.

Yet as much as they disagreed with each other, they loathed and feared another political solution being promoted for Lebanon: the Islamic state that Hezbollah, the Iranian-dominated, militantly Islamic "Party of God," sought to create.

Maroun was flying to Paris the next day, he told me as Rima and I dropped him off at his apartment. His wife was about to have another baby; he was anxious to get home. Would I come see them on my way back to New York? *Inshallah*, I replied. God willing.

Maroun Bagdadi died later that very night in a strange accident. He had arrived back at his apartment in East Beirut to find his building dark. The electricity had gone off again, and not being a seasoned veteran of the war, he had neglected to bring a flashlight. Attempting to navigate the spiral staircase, he had stumbled into the elevator shaft.

Rima called the next day to tell me what had happened, her voice choked with anguish and disbelief. Given the anti-Hezbollah films he made and the left-wing positions he had taken, Maroun's death might not have been accidental, as friends would suggest days, even months, later. In Beirut, one could never be sure. A familiar despair shot through me. Later that day, in my dingy room at the once-elegant Bristol Hotel, I remembered friends and others who had died in Lebanon and all the acts of wanton destruction I had witnessed here. Lebanon specialized in them.

MOST OF MY COLLEAGUES adored antebellum Lebanon. It wasn't that they believed in the Lebanon touted by tourist brochures. Nor were they taken in by the Lebanon of its own imagination: the mythical East-West crossroads, the cosmopolitan trading center where 3 million Muslims and Christians of some seventeen officially recognized sects had fashioned a political compromise that had produced the Arabs' only lively, liberal, tolerant democracy. Resident journalists like Tom Friedman, my *Times* colleague, had eloquently described the encrusted sectarian hatreds just beneath Lebanon's glitzy façade.[3] No. Journalists were infatuated with Beirut because it was, as my colleague Jonathan Randal described it, "the perfect base." Journalists were suckers for information, especially for news provided in sexy settings.

Lebanon, a state the size of Connecticut, had made the most of its national myth as the "Paris of the Orient." It pretended to have overcome the small-minded quarrels, sectarian backwardness, and dictatorships of the Arab states in pursuit of a greater goal — making money. For its sophisticated bankers, traders, intellectuals, and foreign visitors, Lebanon was synonymous in the Arab psyche with openness, modernity, and all that accompanied political pluralism and fast money — a freewheeling, if shallow, press, a dynamic, if notoriously corrupt, Parliament, real politics, provocative theater, designer boutiques, fast cars and women, and bars, restaurants, and discos where Arabs and Westerners could mix anonymously. And it was beautiful. The red-tile roofs of its mountain villages really did "glisten" in the sun and the snow, just as the brochures promised. Amid the French landscaping there was only the occasional dose of Middle Eastern sloppiness. Lebanon's ancient ruins at Byblos and Baalbek, the famed Greco-Roman-Phoenician "City of the Sun," attracted thousands of visitors. Baalbek's annual summer culture festival had featured top entertainers; in 1964, Rudolf Nureyev and Margot Fonteyn opened the dance program with *Swan Lake.* No other country in the region had such theater or cuisine.

But Lebanon had always frightened me. Ever since my first trip in 1971 I sensed that Lebanon was not what it seemed, that its Western sophistication was thin. Though I admired Lebanon's exuberance and vitality, its culture of selfishness and lack of discipline — the almost total absence of a collective sense of civic culture so obvious in a country like Egypt — made me wary.

Lebanon was historically a refuge for persecuted minorities and regional oddballs, but its sects had never lived easily together. According to Kamal Salibi, Lebanon's preeminent historian,[4] there had always been tension between the two main groups on Mount Lebanon: the Maronite Christians, the thirteen-hundred-year-old sect loyal since the twelfth century to the Roman Catholic church that came to the mountain to flee persecution, and the Druze, an eleventh-century Muslim sect that was a schism of a schism of Islam and that also sought shelter there. While the Druze had originally welcomed the Christians, the Maronites had not returned the favor. Far more dynamic, the Maronites increasingly challenged Druze stewardship of Mount Lebanon, which fell under Ottoman rule, as did Syria and much of the Middle East, in the sixteenth century.

After open conflict between Christians and the Druze erupted in 1840, the Ottomans divided Mount Lebanon into two administrative units, one for the Maronites, the other for the Druze. But in 1860, the Druze, attempting for the last time, as Salibi saw it, "to reassert a vanishing Druze ascendancy," attacked Maronites throughout the mountain in Lebanon's first civil war. More than 11,000 Christians were killed, 4,000 more died of hunger or exposure, and 100,000 were displaced. Encouraged by the Druze example, Sunni Muslims in Ottoman-ruled Syria slaughtered some 5,500 Christians in Damascus in a single day.[5]

The massacres sparked indignation throughout the West. "It is a crime which cries to Europe for punishment," exclaimed Thomas G. Appleton, a

Christian American who described his encounters with Christian survivors.[6] France, which had cast itself as the protector of fellow Roman Catholics since the Crusades, demanded that Istanbul create a special autonomous province in Mount Lebanon for the Christians; the Ottomans, weakened by war and internal strife, yielded and created a *mutesarrifate*, a semiautonomous region, guaranteed by the major European powers, that was ruled from 1861 until 1915 by a non-Lebanese Ottoman Christian. It was at this time that the area was first officially designated "Lebanon," named for the mountain that the two sects shared. The creation of this special entity undoubtedly reinforced Maronite belief that Christians were entitled to rule or at least to a special status.

During World War I, the German-allied Turks abolished the Christians' autonomous status and tried to starve the French-allied Maronites out of Mount Lebanon. At least 100,000 Maronites — one-quarter of the mountain's population — died of hunger or famine-related disease. Once again passionate appeals were heard on behalf of the Levant's endangered Christians.[7]

After the war the French yielded to Maronite insistence that the port cities of Beirut, Sidon, and Tripoli as well as the fertile territory of the Bekaa Valley and the south be added to the modern state of Lebanon. Never again, vowed the Christians, would Mount Lebanon be subject to foreign embargo or vulnerable to the political whim of Muslim occupiers. But with the ports and the land came a huge Muslim population — what Chaim Weizmann, one of Israel's founders, later called a "biting gift" — the political consequences of which were frighteningly obvious to at least some perceptive Maronites.[8]

The decision to trade its strong Christian majority for Muslim-inhabited land may well have been a fateful error for the Maronites (as well as a warning to Israel later on about the risks of a multinational state). Some scholars argue that this decision doomed Lebanon's ethnic balance and was ultimately responsible for the civil wars that erupted years later. The trade-off should have been clear: If Christians got the land they wanted, they would have to incorporate the Muslims who lived on it.[9] And for Muslims, Lebanon was not the Holy Land, but *Dar al-Islam* (the Abode or House of Islam), where Muslims, not Christians, were supposed to rule.

By the time Lebanon gained its independence from France in 1943, the Druze were no longer the Maronites' primary preoccupation. Sunni Muslims had become numerically and politically stronger. Thus, observed Fouad Ajami, the Lebanese-born American scholar, just as a Maronite-Druze entente had resulted in the creation of modern Lebanon in 1920, a Maronite-Sunni accord, a philosophical and numerical compromise between the two largest sects, was essential for Lebanon to achieve independence.[10]

Though it was not an easy compromise, each religious group, then under enlightened leadership, agreed to relinquish part of its identity to create what became independent Lebanon in 1943: The Christians renounced French protection and the notion of an exclusively Christian homeland and accepted a vague Arab component of its identity; the Muslims relinquished their goal of becoming part of a pan-Arab nation and accepted Lebanese sovereignty and statehood.

The so-called National Pact was in effect a three-way power split: The presidency and other key posts were to be held by Maronites, then 30 percent of the population (Christians overall were probably a slight majority); the prime minister would be a Sunni Muslim, representing what was then 22 percent of the people, and the Speaker of Parliament, last and definitely least in the power structure, would be a Shiite Muslim, then about 19 percent of Lebanese.[11] This "confessionalism," or power sharing according to religious sect, was based loosely on the Ottoman "millet" system. But in Lebanon's rendition, Christians, rather than Muslims, were dominant, which made it unique in the Arab Middle East.

The framers of the pact had pledged themselves with typically Lebanese vagueness to "Lebanize the Muslims" and "Arabize the Christians," that is, to postpone agreeing on a common identity. Lebanon's national identity, in fact, was fudged: Lebanon, according to the pact, would be "neither East nor West" but a state with an "Arab face," whatever that meant.

As it became clear that Muslims were outstripping the Christian population, demands mounted for greater Muslim power. But the political elite, particularly Christians, ignored the growing tension, certain that the country's prosperity would paper over the deepening ideological rifts and demographic imbalances.[12]

Some scholars say that Lebanon's modern civil war began not in 1975 but in 1958; it was contained, they argued, only by the United States, which, fearful of expanding Soviet influence in the Middle East, landed fourteen thousand troops in Lebanon—a force the size of Lebanon's national army. The American intervention worked, if only temporarily. But it did not resolve the dispute over Lebanese identity or which sect would rule. After the 1958 conflict, both Christian and Muslim camps, led by men who saw personal or communal advantage in altering the founding political system, became more and more rejectionist. Now the Muslims had numbers on their side. By the mid-1950s, Shiite Muslims had already become the country's largest sect; Sunni Muslims were second, and the Maronites ranked a distant third.

By the mid-1970s what the historian Kamal Salibi called the "polite fiction" of Lebanese unity and the alleged numerical equality of Christians and Muslims that justified Christian domination could no longer be sustained. The balance had been further upset by the influx of some 300,000 Palestinians, most of them Sunni Muslim refugees from Arab-Israeli wars and from Jordan.[13] The PLO joined forces with leftist Lebanese Muslims who also wanted more power; together they shattered the country's fragile cohesion and prepared the ground for civil war.

I was visiting Beirut in April 1975 when the civil war finally erupted. My Lebanese friends, particularly Christians and Shiite Muslims, were fed up with the state within a state that the PLO had created inside their country. Palestinians, guests in Lebanon, were acting as if they owned the place; Jordan's King Hussein had done the right thing, they argued. Unwilling to let the PLO take over his country, Hussein had killed thousands of them in the civil war of 1970. But Lebanon was not Jordan. The Lebanese state was too weak and far too divided to respond to the PLO's challenge, as Jordan had.

As Palestinians and Lebanese Muslims grew in number and influence, the Christians trained their own militias, with Israeli help. So did the Palestinians, with aid from Syria and Saudi Arabia, as well as the Druze, ever on guard against real and imagined enemies. By 1975, each group was staggeringly well armed. Even before the civil war began, Beirut's murder rate rivaled that of Washington, D.C. Rather than try to work out their differences, each sect had reached out, as it always had, to a foreign champion—another Lebanese tradition that hastened the country's disintegration.

I was having lunch in Beirut on the terrace of the glorious St. Georges Hotel when word came that Christian militiamen had ambushed a busload of Palestinians, killing twenty-six of them. The ambush was in retaliation for an attack earlier that day on a church in East Beirut that was to be visited by Pierre Gemayel, the Maronite father of the Christian Phalange, in which four Christians had died. The militias began fighting the next day. The war that would forever change Lebanon was on.

NOTHING PREPARED ME for the Lebanon that I returned to in 1983. In less than a decade, the Lebanon that I knew had been obliterated. Beirut was a wreck.

Some of the destruction was the result of Israel's invasion the previous year. In response to repeated Christian pleas for intervention, Israel had entered the Lebanese civil war vowing to eradicate the PLO and end its Lebanese-based attacks that had emptied northern Israeli kibbutzim and villages. Israel's secondary goal was to help the Christians create a Christian-dominated Lebanon that would be friendly to Israel. In the summer of 1982, Israel besieged Beirut, mercilessly pounding Muslim sections of West Beirut from the air, land, and sea. For two and a half months Beirut had held out. Finally, Lebanese leaders of all sects demanded that the leader of the PLO, Yasir Arafat, end Beirut's suffering by leaving Lebanon, and the PLO had reluctantly agreed. The Israelis, too, soon began withdrawing from Beirut; a multinational "peacekeeping" force of American, French, Italian, and British soldiers entered the capital in their stead. Bashir Gemayel, Lebanon's president, was killed by Syrian agents in September 1982, and his brother Amin, whom Israel considered weak but friendly, became president. In May 1983, Israel signed an agreement with the Christian-led government that provided for the normalization of Lebanese-Israeli relations and the subsequent withdrawal of all foreign forces from Lebanon. In the summer of 1983, Israel began a slow, staged withdrawal from Lebanon. But Syria strenuously objected to the accord, since it had no intention of withdrawing its own forces. With Syria determined to control land it had once ruled and senior Syrians dependent on Lebanon's lucrative black market,

Syrian president Hafiz Assad demanded that Lebanon abrogate the May agreement.

Such was the state of affairs when I returned to Beirut in 1983. The *Times* had sent me to help cover the infamous suicide truck bombing of the U.S. Marine Corps headquarters on October 23.

I first saw the outlines of what had been the four-story Marine headquarters the day after the attack at dawn after having traveled most of the night by taxi from Israel. Giant strobe lights illuminated what was left of the compound, giving the ruins a surreal glow. As we got closer, it was obvious that few of the three hundred Marines in the building could have survived the blast. Seabees, aided by rescue workers from several countries, were using picks, shovels, and finally their hands to remove debris from the bodies of 241 Marines who had been killed.

Over the next few days, Ihsan Hijazi, the *Times*'s veteran local reporter in Lebanon, helped me understand which of the lunatic factions or their foreign sponsors might have been responsible for blowing up not only the marine base but, two minutes after that, some fifty-eight French soldiers in their barracks across town. Hijazi, a Palestinian Sunni Muslim and Lebanese citizen since 1958, loved his adopted homeland, but he had few illusions about Lebanon or the region's violent politics. The Americans would abandon Lebanon, he predicted. The Lebanese had a long history of occupation but also a talent for getting rid of conquerors, mostly by ruining their nerves. Occupiers had all left, even if it had taken time — more than four centuries in the case of the Ottomans. The Israelis, too, would retreat. (They had already started doing so.)

Syria insisted that Lebanon remain firmly in its orbit, as history and geography dictated, which explained why Syria was insisting that the May accord, supported by Washington, be abrogated. Syria would withdraw its troops only after ensuring that Damascus could impose an agreement to its liking, what Syria's President Assad diplomatically called an "Arab solution." Iran, too, wanted the Great Satan humiliated, driven out of Lebanon; the Shiite Islamic republic in Teheran was Syria's ally and, at the time, its major source of oil and of support and inspiration for Lebanon's million Shiite Muslims, or the Shia, as they were also known, the country's largest single sect. For more than four hundred years, Shia from Iran and what was now Lebanon had mingled as they traveled back and forth.

This analysis led Hijazi to conclude, accurately, that we would eventually find Syrian and/or Iranian fingerprints on the truck and its suicidal driver, a twenty-four-year-old Shiite.

American intelligence officials eventually determined that Syrian agents, in fact, had helped build the truck bombs that had killed the American and French soldiers and that the Lebanese Shiite sheikhs who would later create Hezbollah, the Party of God, had recruited and inspired the young suicide bombers, or "martyrs," as the movement called them. And the Americans would be told by their Phalangist allies that Sayyid Muhammad Hussein Fadlallah, the Shiite sheikh who was the most articulate and influential advocate of the Islamic cause in Lebanon, the spiritual guide of Lebanon's Islamic movement, a man whom many American academics and the more credulous students of radical Islam would eventually call "moderate," had personally blessed the bomber before he headed out to martyrdom, a charge Fadlallah would repeatedly deny.

HIJAZI OFFERED what was to be our last cup of tea together in Lebanon a few weeks after the bombing of the peacekeepers. Before we parted, he urged me to do some reporting outside Beirut. Reporters often confused Beirut, the city-state, with Lebanon itself, he complained. The real story of Lebanon was being written beyond Beirut's mutilated borders. In Beirut reporters were obsessed with the Palestinians and the fate of the PLO. But Palestinians were a brief interlude in Lebanon's history. In towns and villages throughout southern Lebanon the country's Shiite Muslim majority was being mobilized. "Their day is coming," Hijazi told me.

The day had already come in Jibsheit, a town of fourteen thousand in southern Lebanon. Though less than forty miles southwest of Beirut, Jibsheit might well have been a world away. This was the home of Sheikh Raghib Harb, a charismatic young Shiite mullah who was known for his fierce opposition to the Israeli occupation of southern Lebanon and his determination to turn Lebanon into an Islamic state.

I had heard about these young militants in the Bekaa Valley east of Beirut and throughout southern Lebanon who were determined to see Islam rule the earth, starting with their tiny part of it. From the vantage of Hamra Street, Beirut's integrated, sophisticated commercial area in West Beirut, I had always dismissed them and their objective as ludicrous. How could a country as spiritually secular, unfailingly materialistic, and religiously diverse as Lebanon ever become a religious state of any kind, much less an Islamic republic like Iran?

But the idea seemed less preposterous as Ali, my Shiite driver, and I drove ever deeper into the south. This, indeed, was the "other" Lebanon. There were none of West Beirut's cosmopolitan young Muslim women, immaculately coiffed, sauntering down the streets in their low-cut silk shirts, tight-fitting blue jeans, and red high heels. The women of Jibsheit seemed to have no limbs or hair at all. Virtually all of them, even little girls, were covered in Islamic garb: arms and legs hidden, hair and half their foreheads covered by thick scarves.

Jibsheit had been for much of its history a clerical crossroads between Iraq and Iran, a place known for its heavy concentration of sayyids, descendants of the Prophet Muhammad.

As Ali and I drove into Jibsheit, the visage of the imam Musa al-Sadr, the Shiite spiritual leader who had disappeared in 1978 while visiting Libya, peered down at us in posters hanging from telephone poles, apartments, buildings, and offices. To the Shia, Musa Sadr was an almost mythical figure. Born in Iran and sent to Lebanon to awaken the quiescent Lebanese Shia when he was thirty-one years old, Sadr had helped transform the Lebanese Shia spirit from one of complacency to militant wrath. "Tall with striking looks and great ambitions for himself and his flock," as Fouad Ajami would later write of the strange and seductive mullah who so fascinated him, "Musa al-Sadr had set out to reinterpret Shia history, to strip it of its quiescence, to stand the Shia rituals of grief and mourning on their head, to read into the old Shia tales of dispossession a new politics of commitment and daring." [14]

Throughout the 1960s and 1970s, Musa al-Sadr had railed against the Shia's plight, against the shocking inequalities of Lebanon. The rulers of Lebanon, he told his people, had cheated them of what was rightly theirs. "Oh, men in power," he had cried in a speech from Baalbek in 1974, a year before the civil war began, "do you not feel ashamed that a few kilometers away from your homes are houses that are not fit for human habitation?" [15] It was Musa al-Sadr who had established, reluctantly, Ajami maintained, the first Shia militia in the summer of 1975: the group called Amal, an acronym which in Arabic means "hope." But despite his decision to join Lebanon's sordid new order of militias, Musa al-Sadr was no radical. He continued to believe in power sharing with Christians and in Lebanon's special identity; he instinctively knew that Lebanon could not be an Islamic republic, as so many of his fellow Iranians desired.

But five years had passed since Musa al-Sadr had vanished in Libya. The stage was now filled with cruder men bred by the culture of violence in Lebanon, men like Sheikh Harb.

While many Shiites had initially welcomed Israel's invasion in 1982 as a way of ridding their land of the despised Palestinians, their enthusiasm for Israel did not last long. In fact, many Shia, whose economic misery was inflamed by the harangues of such uncompromising clerics as Sheikh Harb, had already concluded that Israeli soldiers were even more heinous than their Palestinian predecessors. Israel would be driven from the land, Ali, my Shiite driver declared, quoting Sheikh Harb in Jibsheit, his own hometown. Sheikh Harb, the mullah I had come to see, was a "good man," as was Sheikh Fadlallah, whose Beirut mosque Ali also frequented.

"And what about him, Ali?" I said, pointing to the giant metal cutout portrait of Iran's Ayatollah Ruholla Khomeini, whose glum countenance graced Jibsheit's main square and stared down at us from roadside signs — a holy Marlboro Man in a turban. "*Zaim!*" Ali said, a "leader," smiling broadly and poking his thumb into the air. "But not Lebanese."

The bearded, unkempt young men in Sheikh Harb's outer office did not look Lebanese, either; in fact, they weren't. Ali told me that they had recently come from Iran to protect Sheikh Harb, a frequent visitor to Teheran. The young men shoved a head scarf into my hand and insisted that I wear it during the interview rather than my white Egyptian sun hat, which covered my offending locks as effectively.

Unlike Musa al-Sadr, whose height, elegance, and gift for oratory had contributed to his aura in Lebanon, Sheikh Harb was a short, uncharismatic man with a scraggly beard and bulldog face. A former Marxist, Harb had embraced Islam as a more effective way of mobilizing the downtrodden Shia masses. Clad in a long gray cloak and a black turban, the sign of his membership in the family of the Prophet, he received me in a small, bare office with a cold, gray cement floor. His voice was thin and raspy. Seated beneath a calendar marking the victory of the Islamic revolution in Iran, Sheikh Harb called Israel a "cancer" that would eventually be cut out of Lebanon and the Middle East. He denied responsibility for the growing attacks on the Israeli forces that were still occupying southern Lebanon but applauded them. "We are fighting through civil resistance," said the sheikh as I nervously stirred another lump of sugar into my already sweetened tea. "Others are fighting with guns. It is entirely appropriate that they do this."

And what about the bombing of the U.S. Marine compound and the French barracks? Was that "appropriate"?

"Your country supports Israel and its occupation of Lebanon," he said. "The Muslims must defend themselves. So such acts should not surprise you."

Years later, such talk would be standard among Islamic militants. But as a young foreign correspondent in 1983, I was shocked by his words. Harb's contempt for my secular country, and for me, an infidel woman in trousers with a borrowed head scarf, America's sole representative in his hometown, frightened me. I glanced out the window to make sure Ali's battered taxi was still there.

Neither Israel nor the United States frightened him, the sheikh continued. The previous spring, Israeli security forces had detained him for seventeen days after he refused to pledge not to speak against them. His detention had done them no good, he said, permitting himself a tight little smile; he had continued his tirades against them in his mosque sermons. Though I did not know it at the time, Israel would soon decide that Sheikh Harb was more than merely an irritant.

Israel had tortured Shiite boys whom it had picked up on its raids throughout south Lebanon, Harb asserted. "The fury of the Muslims of Nabatiye is only the start of Islam's revenge," he warned.

I had heard about the incident in Nabatiye when I visited this large southern Shiite city the day before. Israeli analysts would later regard that event as a turning point in their country's relationship with Lebanon's Shia. Ashura, the Shiite's holiest day, which commemorates the death of Hussein, the grandson of Prophet Muhammad and the Shiites' most sacred patron saint, had fallen on October sixteenth that year. To mourn the seventh-century death in battle of the man who Shiites believe was the rightful leader of all Muslims, men took to the streets with whips and olive branches, beating themselves and one another until their shirts and kafiyehs were shredded and wet with blood. Israeli soldiers had been ordered to avoid the city on this day. But as some ten thousand Shiites were leaving the main square after prayers, an Israeli convoy had entered the town and encountered the frenzied crowd. The nervous Israelis had opened fire, killing one civilian and wounding ten more. In the riot that ensued, eight

Israeli soldiers were wounded, and two jeeps were burned. A curfew was declared.

Shiites throughout Lebanon were indignant. In Beirut, Sheikh Fadlallah railed against Israel, the "cancer" in the region that Shiites had a religious duty to destroy. But more ominous was a *fatwa* from Sheikh Mohammed Mahdi Shamseddine, then the deputy president of the Supreme Shiite Council, usually known for its centrist views. Shamseddine denounced Israel and urged fellow Shiites to engage in active civil resistance against the occupation. Cooperation with Israel, he said in a widely publicized *fatwa*, was tantamount to "high treason" and "betrayal of Islam." Other Shiite leaders followed suit and called for an end to political, economic, and social contacts with Israelis. At least six shops in Nabatiye that openly stocked Israeli fruits and vegetables were bombed. The Shia's jihad against Israel had begun, to Sheikh Harb's evident delight.

"Mark my words carefully," he told me in Arabic. "As long as Israel stays here as occupier, it will have no peace. And as long as your country helps them, neither will you."

I WAS GREATLY relieved to leave Sheikh Harb's office. I wanted to get away from him, from his Iranian "minders," from Jibsheit, and from southern Lebanon as quickly as possible. Though unaware of it at the time, I had just interviewed a local leader of the group that had become Hezbollah, the radical militants who were staging the suicide raids on Israeli and Western forces in Lebanon and who would soon be kidnapping Americans and Europeans in Beirut.

As the taxi climbed the hills of a neighboring village, I began to relax. I saw a group of children apparently at play. But as we got closer to the village school, I realized that the children were not playing; they were marching up and down a small hill like soldiers, wielding wooden sticks like rifles. They couldn't have been more than five or six years old.

I asked Ali to stop the car and find out what was going on. Shrieking with delight, the children immediately abandoned their military drill and surrounded the "enemy" as Ali and I emerged from the taxi. Suddenly, I heard an angry voice admonishing them to stay away from me, the *ferenge* (foreigner). The voice belonged to a thin young man in a crisply ironed white shirt and plain black jeans. His triangular face was pimply and gaunt; his features were sharp and hawklike. He had a tiny black beard that ended in a point, accentuating his geometrically shaped head. Ali told me that this young man was the village's new kindergarten teacher. He, too, had just returned from Iran.

I smiled and asked him what the children were doing. He did not return the smile. His black eyes stared out disapprovingly at my uncovered head and baggy but still offensive trousers. "They are playing martyr," he said in Arabic. "When they are older, they may have the honor of dying for Islam."

How many such "teachers" had come from Iran to villages and towns like this one? What else, I wondered, was this young man teaching the children? What was going on here under Israel's very nose? Iranian Revolutionary Guards protecting Sheikh Harb? Kindergarten teachers sent from Iran to teach Lebanese toddlers to be martyrs? And all this on Lebanese land from which Israel had not yet withdrawn?

By the time we got to Tyre, I realized that what I had seen in Jibsheit was not unusual. In village after village local Shiite clerics were railing against Israel and its occupation, urging Muslims throughout the world to rise up and exterminate Israel, the alien body in the Abode of Islam. Ever since their arrival in force in Lebanon in early 1980, Iranian Revolutionary Guards had been openly training young Lebanese men for combat, villagers told us. In almost every southern village, schools and pharmacies were run by young, bearded men with the same intense look as the teacher Ali and I had encountered. Most of them, too, had recently returned from school in Iran's Qum or from the Iraqi Shiite clerical center of Najaf.

Did the Israelis understand the implications of what was happening on the ground in southern Lebanon? I stopped at the Israeli military headquarters in Tyre to see what I could learn. Ali, who had been genial and accommodating until then, was suddenly angry. How could I possibly meet with *them?* he yelled indignantly. My brief lecture on the duty of journalists to speak with people on all sides of a conflict made no impression. He refused to drive into the command post, and after an extended argument over politics and payment, especially the latter, Ali dumped me and my luggage at the compound entrance.

To an outsider, the two-story, L-shaped compound, once a Palestinian school, seemed impregnable. Ali had said it was a security center for policing the Tyre region as well as a place where Lebanese and Palestinian suspects were detained, interrogated, and tortured. The thirty yards of unpaved road leading to a high steel gate was set within a steel fence and with the same rock-filled barrels and cement barricades that I had seen at the U.S. Marine and French army compounds in Beirut. But here there were many soldiers and Arabic-speaking, paramilitary border police on guard.

I finally found the deputy base commander. Yes, he said, there had recently been a surge of resentment against Israel among Shiite Muslims in southern Lebanon. He gave me a paper prepared by Clinton Bailey, an American-born Israeli political scientist and a liaison officer in southern Lebanon, who was among the few Israelis to warn that growing Shiite militancy in southern Lebanon jeopardized not only Israel's forces in Lebanon but also Israel's broader goal of peaceful coexistence with the Shiites, Lebanon's single largest religious community. The paper showed a sharp increase in recent attacks against Israeli forces in southern Lebanon,[16] all after the Israelis had opened fire on Shiites in Nabatiye.

Israel's "mistake" in Nabatiye had also strengthened Iranian-backed fundamentalist forces at the expense of Amal, the more pragmatic, centrist Shia group that Musa al-Sadr had established. Even within Amal, whose leadership Israel had once cultivated, pragmatic and militant factions were struggling for control. The incident in Nabatiye had strengthened the most uncompromising elements within Amal.

A few hours after leaving the Israeli post at Tyre, I reached East Jerusalem and the American Colony Hotel, the favorite of journalists who covered the Arab world. Exhausted from my trip, I passed up a drink with other itinerant journalists who invariably congregated at night at the bar and went straight to my room. When I awoke the next morning, the Voice of Israel was broadcasting the latest news from Lebanon. "In the wake of the suicide bombing attack at dawn today on the military headquarters in Tyre," stricter security measures were being implemented throughout southern Lebanon, the announcer said. "An estimated thirty-nine people were killed and thirty-two wounded in the worst terrorist attack to date on an Israeli military target."

I immediately thought of Sheikh Harb — of his self-satisfied smirk at the mention of the dead American Marines, his disheveled Iranian guards, and his warning to Israel and America. What pride he must have felt at this attack.

Three months after I had returned to the relative safety of my home base in Cairo, three bells signaling important news rang out over the wire machine late one evening in February 1984: Sheikh Raghib Harb had been assassinated as he left a neighbor's house in the village of Jibsheit by men whom Lebanese sources described as Israeli operatives. Israel had also closed down the crossing on the Awali River, the south's economic lifeline to Beirut. But cutting the supply lines to the south, according to Israeli and Lebanese scholars alike, had crushed what remained of southern Lebanon's economy and further antagonized the Shia.[17] And militant Islamists had won something dear to their cause: Lebanon's radical Shia, whose religious history was steeped in usurpation and dispossession, had secured, thanks to Israel, their first home-grown clerical martyr.

IN THE YEARS between Sheikh Harb's assassination and my next visit to Lebanon in December 1993, Lebanon continued to unravel. The American Marines abandoned Beirut, ingloriously, in February 1984, and Lebanon's Christian government, defenseless, abrogated the May agreement with Israel, as Syria had insisted. By 1985, Israel had withdrawn from Lebanon except for a six-mile-wide buffer — its so-called security zone — to prevent the radicalized, pro-Iranian Hezbollah militants who ran southern Lebanon from shelling Jewish towns and settlements. As Israel had withdrawn, Druze and Muslim militias pummeled the Israeli-allied Christian Lebanese Forces. A few years later, the Druze and Muslims battled each other. What wasn't destroyed in those battles was demolished in subsequent intra-Muslim and intra-Christian battles that raged throughout the country in the mid- and late 1980s. So it had gone, on and on, till Lebanon was out of victims, almost out of buildings to destroy, and out of tears for the dead, the wounded, and the missing.

In 1989 the Saudi-sponsored Taif accords, negotiated, appropriately, in Damascus, had reshuffled the political deck to reflect the war's winners and losers.[18] Although Lebanon's president was still a Christian, the Sunni prime minister would from then on be the dominant figure. Christians were required to admit that Lebanon was an "Arab" country; in return, Muslims agreed to perpetuate the fiction of numerical equality between Christians and Muslims so that power could be shared — temporarily. For Taif also called for the eventual elimination of Lebanon's sectarian political system and its replacement with a majoritarian, American-style democracy. But a "one man, one vote" government meant that Shiite Muslims would rule Lebanon, a prospect that Sunni Muslims feared almost as much as Christians.

The Taif agreements, moreover, did not stop the fighting. Although Syria had helped Hariri's government disband most religious militias and slowly curtail the car bombs, assassinations, and other terrorist acts that had punctuated daily life during the war, random violence persisted — so much so that even by late 1995 the U.S. government continued to ban travel to Lebanon for American passport holders.

The cost of the Lebanese war, or wars, because there were really several, was immeasurable: They had devastated a country of nearly 4 million people that only two decades ago had led the Arabs in national levels of income, longevity, literacy, and quality of life. According to official estimates, 150,000 Lebanese had been killed, twice that number wounded, and a million (at least 600,000 of them Christians) had fled the country along with some $30–$40 billion in capital. Lebanon itself had become a metaphor for barbarity and chaos. Most of my close friends had either died or left. In 1992, Ihsan Hijazi, after thirty-one years as the *Times* representative in Beirut, had finally retired, leaving his adopted home for the safety and tranquility of San Diego. Most of his children had fled years before.

But in December 1993, after almost twenty years of civil strife, Lebanon was being rebuilt, or so Hariri's government said. *The New York Times* and the *Washington Post* had run glowing articles about the resurgence of little Lebanon. "Beirut's revenge," Nora Boustany, a Lebanese reporter at the *Washington Post*, had called it, an all-too-familiar word in Lebanon's political lexicon.

Prime Minister Hariri was about to announce that his government had raised, through a stock offering, more than $650 million for the first phase of a controversial $2 billion scheme to rebuild Beirut's financial center and an even grander ten-year, $14 billion plan to reconstruct the entire country.

Since becoming prime minister, Hariri had attracted investment and loans from the Gulf, though not as much as the Lebanese had expected. Most of Beirut now had eighteen hours of power a day. Water and telephone service were slowly being restored. So were the traffic lights that had been out of commission for a decade. Contracts for a million cellular telephones had been signed. Some eleven thousand buildings were being rebuilt in Beirut; seventeen universities were operating in the country. Thanks to Hariri, long-paralyzed government agencies were now functioning, an almost miraculous achievement. Lebanese were trickling back to the country; despite the State Department's travel ban, more than 100,000 Lebanese Americans had visited in 1992.

Based on what Maroun Bagdadi and others had told me, however, Hariri, despite his enormous generosity, was increasingly seen by many political notables, of all sects, as a rapacious profiteer, a Saudi and Syrian pawn, or more charitably, a dangerous political amateur.

The Lebanese were now saying that Hariri did not even look Lebanese, whatever that meant. In fact, with his pronounced hawk nose, bushy mustache, and sharp brown eyes, he did strongly resemble King Fahd of Saudi Arabia, under whose rule Hariri had made much of his fortune. The resemblance reinforced the charge that Hariri, who was born and raised in Lebanon's Sidon, was a Saudi at heart. Riyadh had given him a Saudi diplomatic passport—a prized possession in the Arab world—as well as a job as special envoy to negotiations to end Lebanon's civil war, including the Saudi-sponsored 1989 Taif conference at which the unhappy compromise supposedly ending the war was hammered out. Most well-connected Lebanese had dual nationality, but Hariri's twin citizenship was often cited, unfairly, I thought, as evidence of his loyalty to another state.

Rafic Hariri was trying to "save" Lebanon by offering his country not just money but a new ideology—"tycoonism." [19] Hariri's supporters argued that tycoonism would succeed precisely because it was, in some sense, the antithesis of ideology—a polite metaphor for the wheeling and dealing, the materialism, and the goalless pragmatism of Lebanon and other Arab societies in the wake of their numerous military and economic failures. It was also a symbol of the prosperity that pragmatism promised and which the average Arab craved. In Lebanon, where money could traditionally buy almost anything, tycoonism, rather than Islam, had to be the "solution." The Lebanese, after all, had always been more attached to themselves, their immediate families, and their clans than to their little country; selfishness and greed were never regarded by Lebanese as pejorative. A Lebanese, one French consul general lamented almost eighty years ago, had always been willing "to set his country on fire in order to light his cigarette." If tycoonism could not work in such a country, where would it work?

Tycoonism, however, was not without its competitors, and many wondered whether it would be able to swamp the other "isms" that had fueled the civil war—Pan-Arabism, "Maronism," communism, and now the latest bidder in Lebanon for temporal power, Islamism.

To assess the competition between Islamism and tycoonism, I visited southern Lebanon, a traditionally poor Shiite Muslim stronghold that was closest to the Israeli-occupied buffer zone. My first stop was Sidon, Hariri's hometown and Lebanon's third-largest city, only twenty miles south of Beirut. A Sunni Muslim enclave in a Shiite Muslim sea, Sidon, like Beirut, was a port surrounded by gently rolling mountains; and like Beirut, its population had exploded during the war. About 250,000 people now lived in Sidon and its suburbs, in the surrounding mountain villages, and the squalid Palestinian refugee camp of Ein Helway, which had no fewer than 100,000 inhabitants.

The Hariris were Sidon's third-largest family, but Rafic Hariri's fortune had made them preeminent. The Hariri family compound dominated the highest hill overlooking the city. The well-guarded, marble-heavy fortress reminded me of the hotels and royal palaces I had seen in Saudi Arabia, many of which Hariri's firm had also built. Rafic's father, mother, and sister graciously received me for lunch. Bahiya, Hariri's younger sister, had given away many of Rafic's millions through his Hariri Foundation and as a result had been elected in 1992 to Parliament, one of three women in the 128-member body. She and her parents had filled our table with enough food to have fed half of Sidon — typically Lebanese culinary ostentation that was often confused with hospitality in the Middle East.

Rafic's younger brother Walid, or Shafiq as he was known, had also made a fortune in construction, first in Arabia with Rafic and later on in Lebanon. Unlike his siblings, Shafiq detested politics. "Those politicians are making my brother miserable," he complained as we sipped tea in one of his immense marble villas, this one in downtown Sidon. The business of Lebanon was business, he declared. The discredited political class should let his brother get on with his mission: restoring an attractive investment climate in the country. Lebanon's traditional rulers were "pathetic" — petty, jealous, greedy, and unwilling to relinquish, or even share, power with younger, more pragmatic men. The traditional Sunni Muslim leaders disliked his brother Rafic because they envied him. Shiite Muslims, now Lebanon's single largest sect, thought that they, not a Sunni Muslim, should run the country. The Christians could not accept the fact that they were no longer running Lebanon. And the Druze, who were supposedly supporting Rafic, were always playing the angles, cheering him when he succeeded, positioning themselves to capitalize on his defeat should he fail. But no group hated his brother as much as the Islamic militants did, especially the Shiite Hezbollah.

The Party of God knew that only Hariri was rich and generous enough to threaten its own hold on the population by restoring government services that Hezbollah now rendered to build support for "Islamic" government. While Shiite Hezbollah tried to discredit Hariri as a Saudi, Sunni "import," the Party of God itself was financially dependent on Iran, Shafiq charged.[20]

Hariri's wealth had certainly transformed his Sunni Muslim hometown. Perhaps Hariri's tycoonism could not solve all of Lebanon's problems, but it had clearly worked miracles in Sidon. The Hariri textile plant, the town's largest factory, employed more than a hundred workers. Donations from Hariri had paved roads and created parks and landscaped streets with palm trees and shrubs. Suddenly, there were new schools, clinics, social centers, renovated mosques, and infirmaries — all gifts from Hariri. His personal fortune had even helped pay the local police. In gratitude, Hariri's picture adorned most squares and office buildings; a dozen facilities had been named for him.

But even in Sidon militant Islamism had made inroads. Two flags were flying side by side in the city's main square during my visit: Lebanon's national flag, the distinctive red-and-white-striped banner with a green cedar in the center; and a black flag emblazoned with Koranic script, the symbol of Sidon's militantly Sunni group, the Gama'a Islamiya, the Islamic Group. Because Sidon was a Sunni enclave, the Shiite Hezbollah had little appeal within the city, but the Islamic Group, led by Haj Ali Amar, had considerable support despite

. Hariri's popularity. The Gama'a was clearly trying to copy Hezbollah's formula for success: Its militant young supporters from the city and the wretched Palestinian camp nearby were kept busy training to fight Israel; within Sidon, the Gama'a offered social services and payments to the poor. But Hariri's pockets were deeper than the Gama'a's: Hariri supporters gloated that Haj Ali Amar's own children attended one of Hariri's schools.

Beyond Sidon, Hezbollah still reigned. The Party of God had used Israel's continued occupation and bombing raids to sink roots in the south, although most of the senior Hezbollah activists came from the Bekaa Valley, a far rougher and even poorer region in eastern Lebanon.

Most Shia villages and towns, in fact, were still aligned with Hezbollah's Shiite rival, Amal, the more mainstream Shiite movement headed by Nabih Berri, the parliamentary speaker who was an ally of both Hariri and Syria. Some of the fiercest clashes in the Lebanon war were those between the Shiite militias of Amal and Hezbollah. Many Shiites in the south still resented Hezbollah, whose rocket attacks on Israeli settlements had made their towns and villages targets of Israeli retaliation. Who were these young upstarts, these uneducated Shiite interlopers from the backward Bekaa Valley, to tell them what to do? Who were these "Iranian agents" who paid fellow villagers to spy on them, to report on Muslims who drank, danced, or listened to music, to identify those whose daughters refused to veil? The Shia's fury was compounded by their powerlessness: They could evict neither Israel from its buffer zone nor Hezbollah from their communities, since the Party of God had both financial backing from Teheran and Syrian blessing.

After a particularly destructive Israeli reprisal assault in July 1993 — "Operation Accountability," Israel's own dreadful term — Rafic Hariri sensed an opportunity to strike at his militant Shiite rival.[21] Using the Israeli bombing raids as a pretext, he had deployed the Lebanese army in the south. But the move, applauded by Lebanese, particularly in the south, infuriated Syria, which publicly reprimanded Hariri for having interfered in a "security" issue. The prime minister should stick to economics, he was told in Damascus. Forbidden by Syria from using Lebanon's army to challenge Hezbollah's unpopular hegemony in the south, Hariri decided to fight the Party of God on his own turf with his own militia — money. In the weeks after Israel's raids, Hariri and Hezbollah had vied for preeminence in rebuilding the south. Jihad al-Benaa, or Holy War Construction, as the Party of God's "Islamic development" division is known,[22] moved first, removing bodies from under bombed-out buildings, burying the dead, opening rubble-strewn streets, and demolishing unsafe structures.[23] But soon Hariri's government mobilized, landing eleven relief planes in the south before Iran, Hezbollah's patron, had even announced its own relief plans. In addition, the government gave each family whose home had been demolished $11,500 to build new accommodations and distributed tens of thousands of food packages. Even this aid was insufficient, and Hezbollah remained long after government relief workers had returned to Beirut, but the central government had made its presence felt in the south for the first time in more than a decade.

The incident, Hariri's supporters said, was a potential harbinger: If Syria made peace with Israel and permitted the Lebanese government to disarm Hezbollah and send its militants back to the Bekaa Valley, if relief and prosperity came to be associated not with Hezbollah and the money it doled out for Islamic good behavior and the services it rendered, but with the Lebanese government, Hezbollah would be reduced to the marginal force it had once been in the south.

HEZBOLLAH DETESTED Hariri, but it was not alone. Christians, Maronites, in particular, also resented him. Many of them considered Hariri a traitor whose lust for power had led him to accept Syria's domination of their country and the continued presence of some forty thousand Syrian troops throughout Lebanon.

In late 1993 signs of Syrian influence abounded. Throughout the south and even in Beirut, President Assad's chilling smile peered down at Lebanese drivers from posters pinned above the numerous sentry posts. Gen. Ghazi Kanaan, the head of Syrian intelligence in Lebanon, was a fixture on the Lebanese social scene. His plainclothes agents staged midnight raids, especially in Christian villages, where resistance to Damascus was strong.

Maronites had been closely watched by Damascus ever since Gen. Michel Aoun had staged his futile war against Syrian domination of his country. In 1988, Lebanon's outgoing Christian president had named Aoun, the Christian former commander of the Lebanese army, interim prime minister — a post normally reserved for a Sunni Muslim — until Parliament could choose a successor. Aoun soon became wildly popular among Christians and even some Sunni Muslims by pledging to restore Lebanese independence and to disarm all domestic militias. First, Aoun took on militiamen loyal to the Lebanese Forces, the old Christian Phalangist militia. But while battling fanatical Christian forces in 1989, he simultaneously declared a suicidal "war of liberation" on Syria's occupation of Lebanon. In October 1990, a year after the Taif agreements and more than a year of fierce fighting, Syrian forces finally routed Aoun's army, bombing his positions, invading the presidential palace, and forcing him into exile in Paris. Since then, the embittered Maronites, like other Lebanese, had acquiesced to Syrian hegemony. Some now openly vied for Syrian favor.[24]

Obsequious Lebanese politicians were accustomed to prostrating themselves before representatives of stronger powers — Syria, Israel, Saudi Arabia, and Iran — seeking money or blessing for their particular causes.[25] Such solicitations, in fact, were not purely Lebanese but a veritable Arab tradition; the Lebanese were simply better at it than other Arabs. Moreover, they rarely conceded that there might be a contradiction between their eloquent pleas for the restoration of Lebanon's independence and their willingness to traipse to Damascus or another foreign capital for special pleading.

My Christian friend Habib Malik, a professor at a private Christian college in Beirut and the son of a staunchly pro-American Greek Orthodox politician of the 1950s and 1960s,[26] feared that Hariri's government would make Lebanon Syria's pawn, but also that it would strengthen the "Islamization" of his homeland.

Through Habib I obtained an interview with Nasrallah Sfair, the Maronite patriarch, the spiritual leader of Lebanon's shrinking Maronite community and, in the absence of any dominant Christian political leader, increasingly its spokesman. As we drove out of Muslim West Beirut into the hills of Lebanon toward Bkirke, the Maronite patriarch's seat, Habib complained that most Westerners did not appreciate the imbalance in communal fears. While Muslims feared being underrepresented, "we fear that in twenty-five years Christians may not exist as a community in Lebanon. Our fears, unlike theirs, are existential." Hariri, he added, had not allayed them. "Having a few Christians on your payroll is not confessional balancing, and it's not national reconciliation."

Christians were fighting Islamization by begging friends not to sell their land, and the Maronite church had weighed in: "Selling land," its statement declared, would harm the "demographic structure of Lebanon and consequently the situation in Lebanon as a whole." But the appeal had failed: Land prices were now twice as high in West Beirut as in the Christian enclaves, a sign of excess supply.

The Muslim birthrate was now almost double that of Christians, and many more Christians than Muslims had emigrated during the war — especially the wealthy and middle class, the highly educated, and those with close ties to the West. In the past seventeen years — three out of every five emigrants were Christian.

The Christian plight was exacerbated by a lack of serious leadership, Habib argued. Some militia leaders were dead; others, like Aoun, were in exile; a few were under arrest; still others had been "co-opted" by Syria and had joined Hariri's government. For example, Elie Hobeika, the Phalangist intelligence chief who helped maim and massacre more than four hundred Palestinians at the infamous Sabra and Shatila camps in 1982, sparing not even their cats, dogs, or horses, was now a minister in charge of — what could only happen in Lebanon — the handicapped.

The sun was setting when we arrived at Bkirke, the monumental 250-year-old stone fortress dominating the highest hill overlooking the capital. The stolid, unadorned church, whose architecture seemed to be a metaphor for the Christians' determination to endure in Lebanon, had been shelled several times during the war but escaped major damage.

Inside, the church was quiet and cool and smelled of incense. Ushered into a vast, rectangular room the length of a basketball court, which was lined on four sides with wooden chairs, I glanced at the picture of Pope John Paul II hanging on the wall over the patriarch's large chair. Patriarch Nasrallah Sfair, who had served since 1985, turned out to be a tall man who seemed even taller in his floor-length black cloak and huge black hat. His face was younger than his long white beard suggested; he had shrewd black eyes.

Yes, he told us, the Christians had lost more than the Muslims during the war. Yes, he had initially endorsed the Taif accords as the only way to end the fighting. But Taif had given too much power to the Muslims. The Christians had been disarmed, but Hezbollah and some Palestinians in the south had not been. The Syrians had pledged to leave Lebanon, but after seventeen years they were still here.

Christians were underrepresented in Parliament because 87 percent of the Lebanese had boycotted the 1992 elections. But he had endorsed the boycott, prompting an almost total Maronite abstention, because, he said defensively, as long as "foreign" troops were on Lebanese soil, no election could be fair.

Washington was responsible for this sorry state of affairs, according to the patriarch. "We were expecting more support from America," he said, attempting a smile while narrowing his eyes. "We may be small, but we have a role to play. And we share your values, your ideals. We may be an imperfect democracy, but a democracy nonetheless. And yet an Arab-Israeli peace may be at our expense. If Israel keeps a piece of us and Syria has a piece, Lebanon will be lost. Your president goes to Geneva to meet the Syrian president. But your secretary of state can't spare a few minutes to come to Lebanon. We deserved a few minutes of his time."

A sense of abandonment hung in the room.

"Lebanese Christians have a clear identity," he continued. "We are in the midst of an Arab world. We are Christians who speak Arabic. But if being Arab continues to become increasingly synonymous with being Muslim, then we cannot be Arabs."

Lebanon's future depended on Christians and Muslims being equal under the law. "That is not the case in other Arab countries where Muslims are a majority," he said. "We in Lebanon should provide a model of equality for the others; Muslims and Christians must have the same rights, the same duties. Pope John Paul II said that Lebanon was more than a nation; it was an example, a message of liberty and pluralism."

Was the patriarch serious? Could the Lebanon of the past seventeen years be an example of anything to be imitated?

"We must find a formula for living together," he declared. A state in which Christians and Muslims lived together with equal rights, the patriarch said, was possible only through a "democracy of communities," not one based on numbers. Smart Muslims, he said, would give minority Christians equal rights because they would understand that a Lebanon without Christians would not be an independent or democratic Lebanon but part of Syria. Lebanon needed decentralization — local confessional autonomy — the right of each community to teach its history, its values, its ideals. A federation of autonomous confessions made sense now that most of the country's sects were effectively divided into cantons. Seventeen years of war had ensured that there were very few "mixed" neighborhoods left in Lebanon. The Taif formula, which called for the replacement of sectarian power sharing with an American "one-man, one-vote" system, would never work in his country.

As we drove away from Bkirke, Habib stressed that Christians would never accept second-class status in a conglomerate state no matter how small their community became.

"We will not become like the Copts of Egypt!" Habib said as he careened down the treacherous road in the shadowy light of dusk in his ancient Pontiac. "We will not be Lebanon's *dhimmis*, its Christian minority, 'protected' by Islam. We will not watch our pharmacies be burned, our churches go unrepaired, our spirits crushed as they have been in Egypt," he said, picking up speed as his anger grew and the mountain road became ever more twisting and unpredictable.

The Maronites, stranded by geography and history, had good reason to worry. It was unlikely that Christians who had left Lebanon would return. Several Lebanese friends in New York had gone home for a visit, but few were willing, or financially able, to return for good. Though many exiles were rich, most were middle class — the mainstay of any thriving democracy. They had been Lebanon's bankers and builders, its restaurateurs, wine makers, and jewelers. They had opened its first newspapers and made Lebanon the Middle East's publishing center. Now they were gone, and not just from Lebanon.

What Maronites wanted but now knew they would never have in modern Lebanon was a state of their own; in effect, a Christian Israel. Maronites, in fact, had long been impressed by the European Jews who had created their own modern Jewish state. Zionism had insisted on a Jewish majority as the primary means of ensuring Jewish rights in a democratic state. Militant Maronites, in fact, had more in common with Israel's Jews than they did with Egypt's Copts or other non-Muslim minorities in Arab states. For "Maronism" and Zionism were both doctrinal responses of embattled peoples who saw themselves as beleaguered outposts in a hostile Islamic "Orient." Both believed they had a covenant with the land and with their kinsman. Both had sacred geography — the Qadisha (holy) Valley of Mount Lebanon for Maronites, "Eretz Israel" for the Jews. And both were determined to infuse whatever land they held with their own traditions and Western values.[27]

But Maronites knew after the civil war that they could not count on Israel. Although Maronite-Zionist contacts had long predated the state of Israel and though the Maronite church, unlike the Vatican, had openly supported Israel's creation,[28] Israel's relations with the Maronites were always ambivalent. While some Israeli officials had supported dismembering Lebanon and helping the Maronites install a "Christian" government that would support Israel, those who opposed such intervention had usually triumphed. And while the Zionists and, later, the Israelis maintained cordial relations with the Maronites, the Jews understood how divided the Christians were and that open Israeli support for a Christian state in Lebanon might mean war with Syria, which Israel was eager to avoid.

During Lebanon's civil war in 1958, Israel had sent Lebanon's embattled Christian president arms and supplies, but intense contacts between Israel and

Lebanon's Christians had not begun until the 1970s. Though Lebanese often blamed Israel for helping to provoke their civil war, even as sharp a critic of Israel as Jonathan Randal concluded that Israel was not at fault, that Israel, in fact, had done little more at the beginning of the conflict than "watch Lebanon fall apart."[29] By the time Israel invaded Lebanon in 1982, the civil war had been raging for seven years.

Nevertheless, Israel's war in Lebanon was ultimately expensive — for Israel and the Maronites. While Israel had succeeded in ridding Lebanon of the PLO as a fighting force, its intervention helped expose Maronite weakness and undermined the Christian hold over Lebanon. Israel, moreover, had turned out to be the inadvertent midwife of Shiite militancy in Lebanon.

Maronite hegemony was over.

IF THE MARONITES had flourished under Lebanon's original power-sharing system, another sect, Arab and non-Muslim, had also benefited disproportionately: the Druze, a small but fierce 180,000-member sect whose followers, along with the Maronites, had been Mount Lebanon's early inhabitants. In late 1993 I drove for two hours up the perilously narrow roads that led into the Shuf, the southern part of Mount Lebanon, to see Walid Jumblatt, now the unchallenged feudal lord of the Druze, at Mukhtara, his fortress and ancestral home.

At least fifty men were milling around the stone palace's chilly waiting room, sipping coffee, chatting, and fiddling with worry beads. Dressed in their best three-piece suits, their hair slicked back for the occasion, they had been waiting, many of them for hours, to seek advice, a favor, or the support of Walid "bey," the "big man." I was ushered into his inner office quickly, bypassing the masses of grown men patiently waiting like children for their moment with the undisputed leader of their clan.

What was Lebanon's future? I asked him.

"There is no Lebanon," Walid declared. "The very idea is an absurdity; we're Arabs, not Lebanese!"

Walid had not changed much in ten years. He still loved to shock. The top of his head was bald, but what remained of his unruly black hair tumbled down over his shirt collar. He still favored casual clothes: a tie and sweater but no jacket. Tall and full of nervous energy, he seemed in perpetual motion. His knee bobbed up and down as we spoke; his thick mustache framed an excessively mobile mouth; his intelligent eyes darted around the room in pursuit of his words.

The view that Lebanon was an inseparable part of the "Arab nation" was a Jumblatt family position but hardly a constant one. Walid's remarkable father, the late Kamal Bey, one of Lebanon's most talented and influential politicians, had once espoused Lebanon's *mission civilisatrice*, as the French put it, his country's role as a model to other Arabs of the "humanistic, civilizational, and democratic paths." But Kamal had converted to Nasser's Arab nationalism in the 1960s and had dismissed Lebanon as an "artificial construct."[30]

The Jumblatt family's political flexibility and its shrewdness in maximizing the leverage of its small sect had made the Druze far more powerful than they would have been in other Arab states. They were among the primary beneficiaries of the system that Kamal Jumblatt denigrated after his belated, and some said opportunistic, conversion to the Arab cause.

The Druze were Arabs but were not considered Muslims by Sunnis or Shiites. Their origins and religious doctrines are somewhat obscure, but according to the historian Kamal Salibi, the sect had begun in Egypt in the eleventh century as followers of Caliph al-Hakim, an Ismaili (a schism of the Muslim Shiite Fatimids) who had declared himself divine.[31] Driven by religious persecution into Mount Lebanon, the Druze had fought battles for their allies the Turks, which had forged them into disciplined fighters. But unlike the Maronites with whom they shared the mountain, the Druze church and their political leaders were one and the same. The Druze, like Shiite Muslims, practiced taqiyya (religiously sanctioned dissimulation), that is, lying to protect their faith from hostile dominant groups. Beleaguered and persecuted, the Druze were secretive, recognizing one another among strangers through signals known only to the faithful.

Although the Druze's disciplined, feudal structure and a leader, or zaim, as gifted as Kamal Bey, Walid's father, assured them disproportionate influence within Lebanon's political system, Jumblatt's minority status nevertheless "strictly delimited the boundaries of his political ambition," as one scholar argued.[32] If the system stood in his way, Kamal Bey reasoned, the system would have to go. So when the PLO challenged Lebanon's confessional order in 1975, Jumblatt, the ideological friend of radical Arab causes, supported the PLO, thus helping to fuel Lebanon's civil war. But Kamal Jumblatt miscalculated: He did not believe that leftist, Arab nationalist Syria would intervene on behalf of the Maronites. When Syrian president Assad ordered Jumblatt to accept a Syrian-brokered compromise with the Christians, one that did not enhance his own power significantly, Jumblatt had refused. Less than a year later, he was assassinated in broad daylight near his feudal seat at Mukhtara, not far from a Syrian checkpoint.

Kamal's murder had impressed other putative Lebanese leaders, chief among them Kamal's son Walid. As a result, the Syrians would have nothing to fear from this Jumblatt. Walid Jumblatt's Syrian credentials were impeccable. I had asked him when we first met a decade ago in Damascus how he could work so closely with the men who had murdered his father. "Why assume it was Syria?" he had snapped. "Anyone could have done it! My father had many enemies, especially the Israelis! This is Lebanon!"

Perhaps he was engaging in his sect's time-honored tradition of taqiyya, but Walid had appeared genuinely indignant. However, this, as he reminded me, was Lebanon. And Walid and his clan were survivors, people who constituted some 6 percent of the population but who had managed to acquire roughly 24 percent of Lebanese government posts. The Druze knew how to maneuver. So it did not surprise me to discover a decade later that Walid was still close to Damascus or that he still officially hated both Israel and the Maronites and did brisk business with them both.

Walid was among those traditional communal lords who had flourished as a militia leader, thanks partly to his Syrian connections. Through looting, the imposition of impromptu "taxes," and the franchises acquired by his militia for distributing oil and other essentials during the war, Walid "bey" had become a very rich man.

Walid's devotion to Syria was evident in his warm support of Prime Minister Hariri, though he had not always been so admiring of the tycoon. Only a few years before, Walid had described Hariri as a "balloon filled with dollars." But Hariri's generosity toward Walid and Syria's support of Hariri had made Jumblatt an ally. In return, Hariri had put Jumblatt in charge of helping the 500,000 Lebanese "displaced" by the war to return home. The man whose own militia had killed and expelled tens of thousands of Christians was now officially responsible for their return and reintegration into Lebanon.

WHILE THE MARONITES and Druze had sought expression of their communal culture and protection of their rights by sticking solidly to their tribes, some Lebanese had always rejected their country's sectarian power sharing. Though Arab nationalism was born in Syria and found its most powerful exponent in Nasser's Egypt, it had lived longest in Lebanon, particularly in the hearts of some Arab followers of the Greek Orthodox church, Christians who disputed the Maronites' insistence on the primacy of tribal affiliation. How did the Greek Orthodox feel about Lebanon's prospects?

Najah Wakim, a Greek Orthodox parliamentarian, did not attempt to hide his rage about Rafic Hariri — a "liar," "gangster," and financial "thug" who, according to Wakim, was destroying Lebanon. "He is not educated. He is not cultured. He gave money to all the militias during the war, and now he bribes anyone who stands in his way. He bought his way into power and is turning Lebanon into a limited holding company. He's Lebanon's chairman of the board, not a statesman. He doesn't want Lebanon to be liberated. To be free you need *assabiyeh* (patriotism). He doesn't even understand the concept. He wants to privatize everything, our very souls. He thinks you can reduce everything to market forces — love, hate, ideology."

But Hariri, he continued, pausing only to catch his breath, was a mere "shill" for those pulling the strings — "the Saudis, and the United States, our greatest enemy, and behind them both, Jewish capital."

Hariri was not the sole cause of his rage. Najah Wakim was a shipwrecked man, an ideologue whose ideology, whose vision of a just order, whose dream of Arab greatness through unity, had foundered on the shoals of forty years of Arab history. He also typified many in Lebanon's Greek Orthodox community, Christians who had featured prominently in the Arab nationalist movement throughout the Levant, who had then rallied to the Palestinian cause, and who, before that, had pressed for Lebanon's absorption into Greater Syria and for Syrian unity with Egypt in 1958. To Wakim, Nasser was still a god.

Born in 1947, he was an Arab nationalist baby boomer, one of a generation raised on the secular pan-Arabist faith. He had hoped that the Lebanon war would not only end Maronite domination but replace the country's political system with a secular, majoritarian democracy. But the city-dwelling Greek Orthodox were few in number and had neither guns nor other Christian allies; so they, too, were now stranded by the war.

It was not only his country but Wakim's entire world that had collapsed during the two decades of war. The Soviet Union was gone; Israel had proved it could thwart any military challenge by any combination of Arab states; Iran had unleashed and legitimized religious politics that secular Arab nationalists had once ridiculed as childish and atavistic; Egypt had made a separate, heretical peace with Israel; Iraq, the strongest Arab nation after Egypt, had been humiliated by America; and the world now saw America as the strongest military power, inheritor of the right to create a new world order in its image. In 1993 even the PLO had sued for peace with Israel and the favors of Washington. In 1994 so had Jordan. In late 1995, Syria, too, was inching toward peace.

Wakim still affected the look of a radical Arab nationalist. Tieless, fond of French blouson suede jackets and expensive Italian loafers, he continued to command media and public attention because of his rabid attacks on Hariri's "soulless" capitalism. But he had ceased to be relevant to Lebanese or Arab politics. And he seemed to know that he and his movement were now marginal. Most of his own family, after all, had moved to the United States. And he was powerless to stop Hariri's programs or the deepening individualism and materialism he accused Hariri of promoting.

Wakim's bitter attacks vaguely annoyed the establishment, but they were also useful to those in control: Syria could present them as an example of Lebanon's freedom and pluralism. In fact, almost no one, not even Najah Wakim, took them seriously anymore.

IF LEBANON'S HISTORY was Maronite, its future was Shiite, as Fouad Ajami, the Shiite scholar born in southern Lebanon, never tired of predicting. Just as the first great demographic shift in Lebanon — when Maronites began to outnumber the Druze in the nineteenth century — had awesome political implications, so, too, did the second demographic change — the rise of the Shia underclass as Lebanon's largest sect a century later.

Historically, the minority Shiites, though Muslims, were disenfranchised outsiders in much of the Middle East. Only in Lebanon, Iran, Iraq, and Bahrain did they outnumber Sunnis. Almost everywhere else, the word "Muslim" was synonymous with Sunni.[33]

But after the war, the Shia community in Lebanon, traditionally ruled by its own feudal lords, was undergoing great change. Its traditional *zaim* and beys were being cast aside partly by secular newcomers like Nabih Berri, the Speaker of Parliament, who, in one scholar's view, epitomized "the drive of a new Shia middle class grasping for its own place," and partly by clerics trained in Iran and Iraq—upstarts like Sheikh Fadlallah and other proponents of an Islamic order in Lebanon.[34]

Since the war, the power struggle between the more mainstream and the radical Shia had intensified; its outcome was by no means clear when, in 1993, I visited Sheikh Mohammed Mahdi Shamseddine, leader of the Shiite clerical establishment. Though a distinguished cleric, Shamseddine was very much a product of confessional Lebanon and, as such, a rival to Sheikh Fadlallah and other Islamic militants of Hezbollah, who also claimed to speak for the dispossessed.

Sheikh Shamseddine looked the part of an Islamic leader. Tall, with an exquisite white beard and matching turban, he exuded authority as he entered the sparely furnished living room in his brown woolen floor-length coat. Trailing behind him respectfully was an even taller, thinner, younger replica of the sheikh: his son Ibrahim.

I had wanted to meet Shamseddine for years. For one thing, he was the first leader to assert that all Lebanese bore some responsibility for the catastrophe of the war, an unusual acknowledgment in Lebanon. Second, as deputy head of the Supreme Shiite Council, it was he who had issued the famous *fatwa* against Israel in 1983, after the Israelis had entered Nabatiye during the commemoration of Ashura. That decree, which called upon the Shiites to engage in civil disobedience and "to soar and sacrifice" to end Israeli occupation, had officially launched the Shiite war against Israel. Had Shamseddine acted out of religious conviction, or was he afraid of losing political ground to the radical Shia clerics of Hezbollah who were leading the resistance against Israeli occupation?

"In principle," the sheikh told me in a surprisingly thin voice, so different from Sheikh Fadlallah's resonant tones, he did not oppose an Islamic state in Lebanon. But since no religious sect had a clear majority (the Shia were now about 40 percent), the only solution was an "atheistic" state, a "state without religion."

Shamseddine had long taken this position. When Iran's Ayatollah Khomeini had expounded his theory of *walayat al-faqih* (state of the jurists), in which the enlightened clergy were required by God to rule, Shamseddine had dissented. He knew that Khomeini's theory was a total break with Shia practice, which had traditionally viewed temporal power with suspicion, as something to be shunned. Shamseddine, a conservative, had grasped the revolutionary implications of Khomeini's position and wanted no part of it. An Islamic government, he believed, would only cause more havoc in pluralistic, multireligious Lebanon. And Shamseddine, despite his robes and turban, was very much a man of the traditional order in Lebanon as well as a man of the world. As he spoke, his elegant Arabic cloak opened slightly, revealing its hand-embroidered label: "Made in England."

The sheikh's refusal to subscribe to Khomeini's line had infuriated Hezbollah and other Islamic militant groups. His life had been repeatedly threatened, but Shamseddine stood his ground. Though often so accommodating on other issues as to appear almost cowardly, Shamseddine could be a tough opponent, religiously unassailable. Trained at the Shiite seminaries in Iraq's Najaf, he had given the oration at the funeral of Sheikh Fadlallah's father in 1984. He knew these younger, ambitious clerics who sought to turn Shiism on its head and replace its patient and submissive faith with aggressive frenzy. He did not approve of them. His own son Ibrahim, who sat quietly at his father's side, taking notes, worked for Prime Minister Hariri on the committee overseeing Lebanon's reconstruction. Men like Ibrahim were Lebanon's future, he believed, not those noisy proponents of hatred and historical revenge.

The sheikh was committed to the political reconstruction of Lebanon in accordance with the original principles of confessional democracy embodied in the National Pact of 1943, the agreement that assured each sect a share in power. The Shia, of course, should have greater representation, since they now constituted the largest single sect. But their numbers did not justify either exclusive Shia rule or a religious state. "Most Lebanese, no matter what their religion, do not want a theocracy in Lebanon," he told me. "They want a civil state and a democratic government. The Lebanese are sick of violence and those who promote it. I am against violence, even in political dialogue."

Shamseddine did not have to criticize Hezbollah by name. His remarks were obviously aimed at the Party of God and its patron, Iran. While he had excellent ties with the Iranian clerics, Shamseddine had sided with Syria, and hence with Amal, the Shia militia and political organization favored by Damascus.

Now that the war was finally ebbing and Syria had emerged as dominant in Lebanon, Shamseddine's choice seemed shrewd. But in the passion and chaos of militant Iran's ascendancy in 1979 and Israel's invasion of Lebanon in 1982, mainstream Shia figures like Shamseddine and his ally, Nabih Berri, the head of Amal, seemed to be overtaken by the Islamic extremists. It was this challenge, an adviser told me, that had prompted Shamseddine to issue his famous *fatwa* against Israel. Not to have done so would have further eroded his credibility among the outraged Shia.

Hezbollah was still the Shia mainstream's fiercest rival. Shamseddine knew that Hezbollah had deeper roots in the impoverished Shia communities of Beirut's southern suburbs and the rough-and-tumble Bekaa Valley than Amal or the Supreme Shiite Council. Only in the more learned, tamed, and timid south could Amal hope to become dominant, and then only if the fighting stopped and Israel withdrew.

As Ibrahim walked me to my car, he said that both he and his father believed that Rafic Hariri was the "right man" for the postwar period. Lebanon needed a builder, he said, someone who would literally and figuratively sweep away the rubble. He had recently persuaded Hariri to spend a quarter of a billion dollars on infrastructure in Beirut's southern suburbs. He did not add what we both knew: Spending that much money would enable the government to challenge Hezbollah's political hold in the Shiite slums. The rivalry between mainstream Amal and radical Hezbollah had obviously been passed on to the next generation.

BEIRUT'S SOUTHERN SUBURBS, or "Little Teheran," as they are known, reminded me more of the poorer cities of Iran than of Lebanon. The muddy, unpaved streets were filled with barefoot children in tattered clothes and smudged faces and women hooded in black. The shop and street signs were in Arabic, not French or English. Makeshift telephone and power lines crisscrossed the narrow, sunless streets. Laundry hung from the balconies of the unpainted, four-story, cement-block buildings. Again and again the muezzin's call to prayer could be heard throughout the neighborhood. The Party of God's water trucks, schools, and medical clinics were everywhere, and badly needed. There was little government-supplied electricity for the 800,000 mostly poor Shiites who now lived here. The sound of small private generators hummed through the dank, unpaved side streets, where puddles of rainwater mixed with sewage.

In late 1993, I was on my way to see Hussein Musawi, a member of Hezbollah's ruling Politburo and the founder of a radical allied group. "Rafic Hariri," Musawi told me calmly, had been "implanted in Lebanon by the United States so that Lebanon would make peace with Israel." Hariri's "only concern" was "profits for the rich from his casinos, bars, and hotels. He does not care about the poor. He is a dangerous man," Musawi said.

Hussein Musawi knew about dangerous men. He was one of them. American and Israeli intelligence officers had long identified him as a key figure in Hezbollah, an early Lebanese disciple of the Iranian revolution that had initiated the hijackings, kidnappings, and murders of Westerners in Lebanon in the early 1980s. American intelligence officials put him at the center of the planning and execution of several successful terrorist operations — among them, the bombings of the American embassy in Beirut in April 1983, the U.S. Marine and French compounds six months later, and the kidnapping of William Buckley, the CIA station chief who was tortured to death. In the spirit of taqiyya, Musawi had long denied responsibility for these actions, though he had condoned them as acts of "self-defense" against Israeli and American aggression in Lebanon.

At the moment, he did not look very dangerous. With his soft almond eyes and engaging smile, his neatly clipped salt-and-pepper beard, his charcoal-gray sweater and matching woolen trousers, and, of course, his Iranian-style shirt with no tie, the fifty-year-old Musawi was the image of modesty and political probity.

The Hezbollah office, like most militant Islamic headquarters, was functional and spare. There were none of the expensive, hand-carved wooden chairs with stuffed leather seats and embroidered ottomans found in most rich private homes and government ministries. Tea was served in small, plain glasses, without the usual gold trim. There were no paintings or decorations on the wall other than pictures of Shiite Islam's heroes: Khomeini; the vanished imam Musa al-Sadr; and Hezbollah's latest martyr, Abbas Musawi, the late leader of Hezbollah and Hussein Musawi's cousin.

Israel had killed Abbas Musawi, his wife, their six-year-old son, and five bodyguards in February 1992 in a dramatic helicopter attack on his motorcade as it was leaving—where else?—the southern Lebanese town of Jibsheit.[35] Sheikh Abbas, who only the week before had asked God in his Friday mosque sermon to "bless and honor us with martyrdom," had imprudently traveled to Hezbollah's southernmost outpost to deliver an impassioned sermon marking the eighth anniversary of the murder of Sheikh Harb, the man I had interviewed in that same stony, dirt-poor town a decade ago.

Less than three miles from Israel's "security zone," Jibsheit had been the repeated target of Israel's efforts to crush Hezbollah by, in American spy parlance, "neutralizing" its local leadership. First, Israelis had killed Sheikh Harb. Then, in 1989, Israeli commandos had kidnapped Sheikh Abdul Karim Obeid, who had succeeded Harb as Jibsheit's imam, or chief sheikh, despite his lack of formal religious training.[36] As I sat in Musawi's office, I knew that only a few months earlier Israel had struck Jibsheit again. During Operation Accountability, much of the town, including Sheikh Harb's tomb, was flattened.

I also knew that Israel's most intricate and successful covert operation against Hezbollah had never been publicized. This was in 1985, when fifteen people were killed and more than fifty-five wounded in an explosion in the Shiite village of Marakah, near the southern port of Tyre. Lebanese officials accused Israel of having planted the bomb in the village's main mosque, which Israel denied. In fact, Israel had set the charge that had destroyed almost the entire regional leadership of the Party of God and a visiting Iranian dignitary.

Before it withdrew from the village, Israel had hidden explosives and monitoring equipment in the mosque, which was also a center of political activities, under a false ceiling that soldiers had constructed virtually overnight—an exact replica of the original but some eight inches lower. Israeli agents had then monitored activity in the mosque and detonated the explosives during an important Hezbollah strategy session in March 1985, according to Israeli officials.[37]

No wonder that Hussein Musawi was far more cautious about security than his cousin Abbas had been. My translator and I had walked through metal detectors before we were allowed to enter his office; the contents of our handbags were meticulously examined.

Only a few years ago, Musawi would probably not have received an American journalist, and an American journalist would have hesitated to meet him. But kidnapping Westerners was passé, at least for now, and Hezbollah, like so many other radical Islamic groups, was courting Americans.

"We have nothing against the American people," Musawi told me in Arabic. "But why does your government side with the Jews against the Muslims?"

he said, flashing a sincerely mystified smile. "Why does it side with five million Jews rather than three hundred million Arabs and more than a billion Muslims?" The Jews had a "black future." The future belonged to Muslims. So America should improve its relations with Muslims now, he argued. "If you recognize your own interests, we will forget all the past problems between us."

The allusion to unspecified "past problems" obviously meant Hezbollah's suicide attacks against American and Western facilities in the 1980s, its relentless car bombings, and the kidnappings and barbarous treatment of more than forty civilian foreigners whom it had held hostage in Lebanon, including journalists.

American policy had always been shortsighted in the Middle East, Musawi continued. During the Gulf war, for instance, Washington had "flattened Baghdad and killed half of the Iraqi people. Why didn't you just kill Saddam Hussein?"

Musawi was obviously not opposed to violence that furthered what he considered a worthy cause, in this case, the destruction of Iraq's leader. Hezbollah detested Saddam for his persecution of Iraqi Shiites. But while it was hardly surprising that Musawi detested secular Baathist Iraq, he had no trouble condoning Syria's murderous campaign against its own Islamic militants, the Sunni Muslim Brotherhood. President Assad, Musawi said of Hezbollah's ally and patron, was a "man of honor" despite his having massacred as many as thirty thousand Syrians in the Syrian city of Hama in 1982. "Everywhere in the world," Musawi had told one of my colleagues, "governments maintain law and order in the way they see fit"[38] — an omen of what Musawi might do in the name of "law and order" if Hezbollah ever ruled Lebanon.

Musawi was predictably vague when I asked about Hezbollah's strength, estimated by diplomats in 1993 at between two thousand and four thousand militia members. For almost a decade Hezbollah had received as much as $100 million in annual subsidies from Iran, enough to have fought and bought its way into the hearts of perhaps half of Lebanon's Shiites. "We have no membership cards," he said, batting away the tiresome question like an annoying fly. "Everyone opposed to Israel is with Hezbollah."

Musawi was a survivor in the cutthroat world of militant Islamic politics. An early member of Amal, he had broken away from the group in June 1982 after Israel's invasion of Lebanon and founded his own organization: Islamic Amal. What prompted this first of many splits, Musawi told me, was a ferocious dispute over how to fight Israel.[39] Islamic Amal had now merged with Hezbollah.[40]

Despite his radicalism, Musawi had supported Sheikh Fadlallah's controversial decision in the early 1990s that Hezbollah should participate in the 1992 Lebanese elections. The Party of God, in fact, had done exceedingly well, fielding well-funded candidates, sometimes on sectarian lists, in every Lebanese district, and mobilizing its mosques, media, and social-welfare network to get out the vote in a campaign that one scholar had called "more evocative of Tammany than Teheran."[41] Because of its shrewd campaign and the votes of the twenty-eight thousand Shiite families to which Hezbollah gave a monthly stipend, God's warriors had won eight assembly seats, a victory that made them — along with four closely allied deputies — the single largest bloc in the fragmented, 128-member Parliament.

What would Hezbollah do, I asked him, when the Parliament it had joined was called upon to ratify peace with Israel?

"At such a point" — he scowled — "we would have to reconsider our participation in the Parliament."

Only reconsider? It seemed a curiously cautious, conventionally "political" response from a man who hated Israel and the political status quo in Lebanon. But whether Musawi approved or not, Hezbollah was now deeply enmeshed in the politics of a state whose very legitimacy it had once denied.

Only a few years ago, both Musawi and Sheikh Fadlallah had rejected the notion of a Lebanese state almost as fervently as they had Israel's right to exist, for in militant Islamic theory, the twin struggles were sacred — mandated by God — and uncompromisable. In those days, it had been fashionable at Hezbollah rallies to burn not just Israeli, but also Lebanese, flags.[42]

But the civil war had demonstrated that Lebanon was probably here to stay in one configuration or another. Like Kuwait and all the other supposedly "artificial" entities created by Western imperialists after the collapse of the Ottoman Empire, Middle Eastern states had shown a surprising and — to fervent Arab nationalists and Islamists alike — a disturbing durability. If seventeen years of anarchy and mayhem could not destroy Lebanon, its existence would probably have to be accepted, even by those whose ultimate goal was to dismantle or transform it. Thus, the Party of God shifted tactics so as to remain credible, which meant becoming, or appearing to become, a conventional political player.

Hezbollah's decision to run for Parliament, in fact, was a turning point for the group — what one scholar called the beginning of the Party of God's reluctant transformation from a "coterie of disgruntled Shiite clerics and violent zealots" into "a true *hezb* (party) — a real political party of its followers.[43] "We need a political role," Musawi told me. "We're tired of carrying guns."

Some scholars argue that Sheikh Fadlallah began to abandon the goal of creating an Islamic state in Lebanon as early as 1987, that is, as soon as the extent of Syria's influence in Lebanon became clear. Syria sought order, predictability, and the advancement of its own interests in Lebanon. It was Syria that had ordered an end to kidnappings in the Bekaa Valley and in other Lebanese sectors it controlled; Hezbollah had no choice but to comply. Fadlallah also knew that unsentimental and tacitly brutal Syria wanted to ensure that Damascus, not Hezbollah or any other Lebanese faction, and certainly not Iran, controlled Lebanon.[44]

Sheikh Fadlallah, who understood Assad's calculus,[45] had persuaded his reluctant Iranian patrons to endorse Hezbollah's participation in the 1992 elections so that the Party of God could develop an independent political base in Lebanon. Revolutions, after all, were not the only way to change societies.[46]

Hezbollah's new style had evolved over the past decade. It had replaced its once mysterious "spokesmen" and shadowy *shura* (consultative council) with a publicly named secretary-general of what was now called its Politburo. Hezbollah now referred to Elias Hrawi as Lebanon's president, not the "president of the Maronite regime," as it once had.[47] Hezbollah's television channel, in search of higher ratings, now broadcast American movies that showed men and women touching and, yes, kissing. The Party of God had even established its own soccer teams; one of them, Al-Rissala, or "the Message," had done well in 1993.

Sheikh Fadlallah had also concluded that even Hezbollah's goal of destroying Israel had to be reformulated if Hezbollah was to remain relevant. While men like Musawi continued to argue that President Assad, that "man of honor," would never make peace with Israel, Fadlallah had implied to me that Syria, like the PLO and Jordan, would eventually make a deal.

Since Hezbollah depended heavily on Syrian protection — its Iranian arms, men, and money came through Syria — the Party of God had put itself at Damascus's mercy. If Israel insisted that Syria curtail Iranian support for Hezbollah as a price of peace, Hezbollah's militias would be disarmed and the organization reduced to a network of mosques, social-welfare institutions, and media outlets. A strong political base was therefore essential.

Sheikh Fadlallah had long been preoccupied with staking out a fallback position against the day that the Arabs and Israelis made peace. In speech after speech, he had attempted to set new ground rules for the Islamists' continuing war against Zion. If peace treaties between Israel and its neighboring Arab states could not be blocked, peace between the Israeli and Arab people could be. "Just because Arab states are forced to accept the existence of Israel, we do not have to succumb to such pressure," Fadlallah told me when I visited his home in Beirut in 1994, shortly before Israel and the PLO signed yet another peace accord in Cairo.[48] Fadlallah urged that *fatwas* that barred trading and any other contact between Muslims and Jews be strictly obeyed.

Did he have the authority to issue such *fatwas*, and did he intend to do so? "Many people" believed that he, "as an Ayatollah," an Iranian title that he told me he preferred, had the "necessary spiritual and legal standing to publish such edicts," he said in a display of Islamic modesty, placing his ascendancy in the mouths of unnamed others. But, he added, such rulings were "unnecessary" because Lebanese-Israeli contacts had been banned in *fatwas* ever since the bloody Israeli-Shiite confrontation in Nabatiye in 1983.

Had he ever issued a *fatwa* authorizing a suicide mission against Israel or a Western target in Lebanon? I asked. No, he had not, he said. Was the sheikh also engaging in *taqiyya*? Many Lebanese thought so. "He lies the way we breathe," Prime Minister Hariri had once said of his bitter rival. Western intelligence officials agreed with Hariri. Some asserted that Fadlallah had explicitly sanctioned early kidnappings and the bombing of the U.S. Marine compound in Lebanon. Others, however, likened Sheikh Fadlallah's role to that of Sheikh Omar Abdel Rahman, the Egyptian cleric who had obliquely blessed Sadat's assassination and the 1993 attack on New York's World Trade Center by branding the targets "anti-Islamic" or "traitors to Islam" and, hence, legitimate targets of attack.

Fadlallah appeared to have read my mind. That he had not issued such rulings, he said, did not necessarily mean that he disapproved of the attacks. While he had condemned the hijacking of airliners and kidnapping of foreigners in Lebanon since the mid-1980s, he added, "any means of self-defense is acceptable in war." Any means? I asked. "Yes," he declared. Self-martyrdom, Fadlallah said, was "certainly less abhorrent than the atomic bombs the United States dropped on Japan or what it did to Iraqi soldiers during the Gulf war. You buried them alive in their bunkers."

I was fascinated by the contrast between Fadlallah's words and his tone. Had I not been following his words, the sheikh could have passed for Santa Claus. A plump man with a bushy white beard, twinkling, bright eyes, and a broad smile, Fadlallah was usually referred to as "moderate" by Western students of Islam. He was said to be an impressive scholar — a poet, essayist, and stirring orator. He was the author of many books; few of them had been translated from Arabic, but they were hotly debated among Arabs.

His *Islam and the Logic of Force* had honed the theology of violence expounded twenty years earlier by Egypt's Sayyid Qutb and Iran's Ayatollah Khomeini. Written in 1976 during the early years of the savage Lebanese civil war, it had encouraged the Shia, in the tradition of Imam Musa Sadr, to shake off their quiescent submission to "illegitimate" authority, as one scholar put it, and to "exalt force and power." God preferred the "pious strong" to the "pious weak," the sheikh wrote.[49] But now in the 1990s, it was Fadlallah's pragmatism that prevailed as the Party of God entered the sordid game of Lebanese politics.

Unlike the Maronites, Shia leaders had numbers on their side, but they were also much shrewder. The divided, wretched Christian leaders had not grasped reality; they had not been flexible enough to bend or remain silent until their enemies flagged. While Hezbollah benefited from the 1992 parliamentary elections, the Maronites had boycotted them. While Hezbollah's leaders were being quoted by the press and courted by politicians, most Maronite leaders were dead, in exile, or being hunted. And while the Shia were growing in numbers and influence, the Christian community was shrinking.

Many analysts believed that Hezbollah's evolution into a political player, albeit an exotic one, meant that the group would eventually moderate its rhetoric, actions, and goals to protect conventional interests: parliamentary seats, constituents, government-assigned jobs and benefits. Hezbollah had tasted power and liked it. In the fall of 1993 a Hezbollah parliamentary delegation had gone to Brazil — the first such overseas visit — and been royally received.[50] Even Fadlallah admitted the advantages of political respectability. "When you are a parliamentary deputy, the newspapers and media report your words," Fadlallah had said. "Just try, if you don't have a seat in the political club, even if you're well known, and you won't even get a little corner in the newspaper or media. Parliament represents an advanced propaganda podium for the Islamists." Moreover, he noted, being in Parliament enabled the Party of God to persuade others "to support some of what you want. In this way, you can pass a law for Islam here and secure a position for Islam there."[51]

Thus, Lebanon would not be "Islamized"; Hezbollah would be "Lebanized." But both Martin Kramer, an Israeli analyst, and Marius Deeb, a leading Lebanese expert on Hezbollah, remained dubious. What Hezbollah had in mind was taking power — legitimately, if possible. But if it failed in the polls to achieve its ambitions, it might return to violence. Either way, Lebanon's future with a Shia majority was dicey. Running for office had not led Hezbollah to embrace pluralism, tolerance, or democracy; quite the opposite. The very idea of "popular sovereignty," Kramer said, quoting Fadlallah, was anathema to Islamic thought because "rule in Islam" was "a prerogative of God." It was God who appointed the Prophet, God who prescribed the general precepts for rule. Therefore, Islam could not be reconciled to any government that "accords the majority, however large, the right to legislate in opposition to Islamic law," Fadlallah had repeatedly stated. Nor was Hezbollah or other militant Shia Islamists likely to abandon their determination to destroy Israel. Given America's current military strength, its resounding defeat of Iraq in the Gulf war, the disunity among Arabs and Muslims, and Israel's military superiority and political cohesion, the goal would have to be deferred. But it could never be discarded, at least not rhetorically.

No one could predict, of course, how Hezbollah would evolve or what a Lebanon in which Hezbollah played a key role would be like. But even if the militants had no intention of abandoning their radical agenda, participation in government, especially in Lebanon's free-for-all politics, might transform them despite themselves. The Islamists, after all, were vulnerable to the same earthly temptations and vices as their secular counterparts.

Acquiring power, of course, had not "moderated" the repressive Islamic regime in Iran. While so-called moderates and radicals fought for power in Teheran, the government remained intolerant, oppressive, and antidemocratic. But Lebanon was not Iran. Lebanon's foremost characteristic was its ability to corrupt. As one scholar had argued as early as 1985, any radical Shiite movement in Lebanon would end in "isolation and frenzy." There was no "agricultural hinterland in Lebanon to sustain a zealous state of the faithful," and unlike Iran, Lebanon had no oil. Beirut, always a "tough and cynical city," had now been further hardened by "war and ruin." The Lebanese saw scoundrels everywhere, and they were usually right. This was not exactly an "ideal site for great movements of redemption."[52]

Moments of virtue are fleeting in the life of nations, and Lebanon had been bourgeois to its bone, even after the civil war. There was no place for radical Hezbollah in this bourgeois culture. Even if the middle class had fled or been impoverished by the war, many of those who remained still perceived themselves as middle class. And the bourgeois spirit of many middle-class Shia, especially the 600,000 who worked overseas to send money home, was an even tougher opponent of radical Islam than Hafiz al-Assad's repression.

To test this theory, I returned in April 1994 to the ancient city of Baalbek,

Hezbollah's unofficial capital in the Shiite Bekaa Valley, a mini-Islamic state in Lebanon.

BAALBEK IS only forty-five miles northeast of Beirut and thirty-five miles northwest of Damascus, but once you drive up into the mountains overlooking Beirut and the sea, you abandon the Levant in topography and spirit. While Beirut is balmy and mild, the snow-capped mountain pass that gradually descends into the Bekaa Valley is at least fifteen degrees colder.

Long before Hezbollah arrived, the Bekaa Valley was an unruly place that government troops had prudently avoided. A valley on a high plateau wedged between the Lebanon and the Anti-Lebanon Mountains, the fertile Bekaa was home to Lebanon's second-largest Shiite population. The Shia of the Bekaa were sharply different in tradition and temperament from those of south Lebanon or Beirut's southern suburbs. The southern Shia grew licensed tobacco; in the Bekaa, the Shia favored illegal hashish, which is how one scholarly friend summed up the difference.[53] The clannish Shia of the Bekaa were as assertive of their independence as the peasants of the south were patient and subdued. While Amal ruled in most of the south, it had less appeal in the wild, generally poorer Bekaa badlands.

The valley had always been a quarrelsome place, with its infamous blood feuds. Even Hezbollah's Hussein Musawi, for instance, had been forced to avoid his home village of Nabishit for several years because of a family vendetta.[54] Isolated and poor, anarchic and clannish, the Bekaa was just the place for the politics of holy revenge to take hold.

Baalbek, the largest city in the valley and an ancient place of worship, pilgrimage, trade, and conquest, had become legendary during the civil war for its brisk drug business. Since conventional tourism had died during the war, drugs now dominated what was left of the local economy. Hezbollah had not tried to hide its partial dependence on the billions of dollars in drug revenues and the counterfeiting of $100 bills that flowed from or through the Bekaa — Lebanon's biggest business — the proceeds of which were shared with Syrian generals and others who were "well connected." In fact, Sheikh Subhi al-Tufayli, a particularly militant Hezbollah leader, had repeatedly refused to condemn the Shia for growing poppies and processing heroin in Bekaa-based laboratories. Such a ban, he had explained, would further penalize the impoverished Shia of the Bekaa. Although the taking of drugs was condemned by Islam, Hezbollah did not object to a believer's financial salvation.

Only four months earlier, in December 1993, I had visited the Bekaa for the first time in a decade. To ensure that I was not picked up or harassed by Hezbollah, I was accompanied by a Shiite friend, Hassan Husseini, the son of Hussein Husseini, the former Speaker of Parliament and the first head of Amal, the rival Shiite group. One of Baalbek's most prominent traditional families, the Husseinis owned the dilapidated Palmyra, a venerable hotel built in 1874 that once attracted royalty and dignitaries during the summer festivals and offered a stunning view of the ruins.

Hassan and I had arrived at night, delayed by the many Syrian checkpoints along the road. A full moon cast an icy light over the temple ruins, which were deserted, even in daylight. We had sipped steaming tea and warmed up in front of the fireplace at the Palmyra bar, which had few guests.

I was shocked by the urban mess in what had once been an empty, agricultural valley. The Bekaa was now littered with ugly concrete buildings hugging the road, most built during the war by the thousands of Shia who had fled here to avoid fighting in Beirut or the south. Before the war about 200,000 people had lived in the Bekaa, 80 percent of them Shia; by 1994, the valley was home to more than half a million. Baalbek, too, had exploded in size, from 17,000 before the war to some 120,000 now.

In December 1993, Hezbollah had few rivals in Baalbek; the Lebanese government in Beirut was not among them. The Syrians, too, though they supposedly controlled the valley, had given Hezbollah wide latitude. Only weeks earlier militants had picked up a young Swedish tourist from Damascus who was visiting the ruins. Though they held him for less than a day, Hezbollah had reminded the Lebanese and Syrian military that the Bekaa was its turf. A month later, Hezbollah militiamen had arrested a young Shia from Baalbek whom neighbors accused of having robbed and killed a woman and her two sons in a neighboring village. Dragged before a committee of Hezbollah officials, Hussein Assem Awada, age sixteen, had confessed to his crime and was executed under Hezbollah's interpretation of sharia, Islamic law. "God's law now rules in Baalbek," one militiaman had boasted after Awada was shot in the head in the Khawwam Hotel, a Hezbollah center. Though Lebanese officials and confessional leaders in Beirut denounced this vigilantism, they had taken no action against Hezbollah.[55]

Hundreds of Christian families had left Baalbek after the Party of God began operating here in 1982. The first to be abducted in this city was Elias Zoghbi, the Roman Catholic bishop of Baalbek. The militants held the bishop for only two days, long enough to make their point: They were strong enough to kidnap a religious notable who would once have been untouchable. Christians got the message and fled. Baalbek's prewar Christian population of some ten thousand now stood at fewer than a thousand. In 1975, Baalbek had three large churches; now only one was open, which I had visited in December 1993, joining some fifty parishioners crammed into a small, icy prayer chapel on the side of St. Barbara's, once among the largest Greek Catholic churches in the Middle East. Most of the huddled Christians chanting their prayers in Arabic were old. The familiar smell of incense floated above the dank, narrow, vaulted room, badly in need of paint. Along with the incense, I smelled fear. The priest in his long white cassock, with a large gold cross, and his tall black hat, seemed not to notice his flock's sad faces. He was deep in incantation, his eyes almost shut, his arms outstretched as if pleading for help.

The rest of that visit to the Bekaa had been equally depressing. Portraits of the Ayatollah Khomeini were everywhere. Above the main square hung a giant banner: "Relations with Israel Are Forbidden." Sullen young militants patrolled the streets, ensuring that women and even little girls wore head scarves and stayed away from men.

Hezbollah had been quietly preparing for the day when subsidies from Iran might end. In Baalbek, the Party of God operated the city's electrical generators, a well-stocked food cooperative, several health clinics, a hospital, and pharmacies. It was also building a shopping center on the edge of town, one of many new businesses in the valley in which the Party of God had a financial stake.

In April 1994, four months after my winter visit with Husseini, I returned to Baalbek with Hikmat Shehabi, a journalist from the French news agency Agence France-Presse. As we approached the familiar mountain pass that led down to the valley, I shuddered with apprehension.

Shehabi, the only reporter based in the Hezbollah stronghold, was able to live there because he came from a large Shiite clan from the neighboring town of Yamoune, which protected him: Hezbollah did not want an enemy among the numerous, well-armed Shehabis.

Hezbollah's roots, Shehabi told me as we drove along the mountain range, could be traced to the arrival of the first contingent of Iranian Revolutionary Guards in Baalbek in 1980,[56] long before Israel's massive invasion but a few months after Khomeini's Shiite revolution and two years before Hezbollah itself emerged, unofficially. Not until 1985 would the Party of God publicly declare its existence.[57] Until they established their own base, the Iranian volunteers were given shelter at a school founded by Hussein Musawi's cousin, a graduate of a Shiite seminary in Najaf.[58]

Both Syria and Iran were instrumental in Hezbollah's founding, Shehabi told me. For several years after its creation, Hezbollah took orders directly from its spiritual and operational godfather, Ali Akbar Mohtashami, then Iran's ambassador to Syria.[59]

But the PLO, too, had played a key role, Hikmat said. The secular PLO had helped create Hezbollah by training a few hundred Iranians in the Bekaa ever since the early 1970s, long before the shah of Iran was overthrown, a vanguard of those who would arrive later. Many of these Iranian "trainees" returned to the Bekaa in 1980 as "trainers." One of their first camps was located near Yamoune, Hikmat's village. In all, about ten thousand Iranian militants were eventually trained by the PLO, he said.[60]

The PLO had also helped Imam Musa Sadr create Amal, the Shiite militia, in the mid-1970s, according to Shehabi. And the PLO had given Sheikh Tufayli, a radical Hezbollah founder, his first car, a personal gift from PLO chairman Arafat. When Hussein Musawi left Amal to found his own group, Islamic Amal, the PLO helped again. These groups had, of course, a common enemy in Israel; but the PLO also believed that the militant Islamists could help contain its Lebanese opponents, the Maronites. But in helping the Islamic opposition in Lebanon, the PLO did not anticipate that it was aiding the movement that would eventually support Hamas and other radical Islamic rivals to its own status as the "sole, legitimate representative" of the Palestinians. Thus, Arafat made a mistake similar to Israel's, which had also permitted Islamic groups in Gaza and the West Bank to organize as a way of dividing support for the PLO. What neither fully appreciated at the time was that the fury of such Islamic groups would not be directed solely at the intended enemy.

It was Israel's invasion of Lebanon in 1982 that gave Lebanon's militant Islamists their real momentum. In response to Israel's assault, Iran sent through Syria to the Bekaa some 150, and by the year's end an estimated thousand, Revolutionary Guards, including the "kindergarten teachers" I had encountered in Jibsheit in 1983, where they established their own bases at the Islamic seminary just east of the city and at the French-built Ecole Normale de Baalbek inside the town. At the same time, Hussein Musawi's Islamic Amal in Baalbek and the Iranian Revolutionary Guards had taught, in the words of Hussein's cousin Abbas, "the Muslim youths to love martyrdom," which led to the first grenade attacks on. multinational forces in March 1983 and the subsequent suicide bombings of the U.S. embassy in Beirut and the U.S. Marine and other "peacekeepers" compounds.[61] By 1983, Islamists in Baalbek had seized from the Lebanese army the Sheikh Abdullah barracks, the huge fortress atop the city's highest hill, which could hold up to five thousand soldiers. Later, Hezbollah would use the barracks as a makeshift prison for several Western hostages.[62] It was in 1985 in Jibsheit that the Party of God made its first official appearance. To commemorate the first anniversary of the assassination of Sheikh Raghib Harb, Hezbollah published a forty-eight-page manifesto, an "open letter" to "the Oppressed in Lebanon and the World," calling upon believers to "rise above the ostentation of this world's ornaments"—no small sacrifice in a country as materialistic as Lebanon—and to "yearn for paradise and martyrdom in the path of God."[63]

Hikmat and I drove straight to the main square of Baalbek where, during my previous visit in December, Iranians and their Lebanese supporters had pitched stalls for a giant food and crafts fair. But now the tents, along with the Iranians, were gone. So was a giant metal portrait of the Ayatollah Khomeini that had dominated the square. In fact, nearly all the huge posters of Iranian and Lebanese martyrs were gone. What was going on here?

We drove past the park where, four months earlier, Hezbollah had erected a speaker's podium surrounded by Islamic banners proclaiming Koranic slogans of jihad. Again, there was no trace of Hezbollah's podium and its banners. Instead, the park was tranquil. Women—more than half of them without head scarves—sat on the grass chatting or pushed baby strollers; children played soccer; old men sat on benches, gossiping in the morning sun. Could this be the same Baalbek that I had visited in December? What had happened to Hezbollah's Hyde Park? I asked Hikmat.

He laughed. "You notice some changes since your last visit?"

I could hardly believe what I saw. Tour buses filled with Lebanese children were lined up at the ruins, which had been all but deserted during my last trip. Gone were the sour-faced Islamic vigilantes who had patrolled the city with machine guns and rifles four months earlier. Gone were the slogans, banners, photos, and posters.

Hikmat explained. Shortly before our trip, some five hundred to six hundred young Hezbollah militants had paraded through the Bekaa to commemorate "Jerusalem Day," flouting Lebanese law by openly carrying weapons. Hariri had seized on this display to launch a long-planned crackdown. In cooperation with Syrian troops, the Lebanese army began rounding up militants during the night and reoccupied the Sheikh Abdullah barracks. A new government edict declared that anyone carrying a weapon had to go south and fight Israel; anyone else found with a gun in public would be arrested. Lebanese and Syrian soldiers then began removing Hezbollah's pictures, slogans, and other tangible signs of its presence.

"Some Islamists have taken their weapons and headed south. Others have hidden their arms. But everyone is now lying low," Hikmat told me. "Hezbollah is still here — everywhere — but they are playing along."

Hikmat and I tried to visit Sheikh Tufayli. When we arrived at his house on the outskirts of Baalbek, the windows were closed; the shutters drawn. A black Hezbollah flag still flew over the building, but the government guards who once patrolled the street to protect the sheikh were gone. Tufayli was now guarded only by family members, who told us that he had gone out unexpectedly; they did not know when he would return. The men who surrounded our car seemed fearful, now that they were isolated, afraid of the government they had once mocked and the Syrian allies they had taken for granted.

As we left Tufayli's neighborhood and headed back to the main road, we came across several of the giant metal posters of Islam's beloved martyrs that had once decorated Baalbek's roundabouts and squares, most of them facedown in the dirt. A few had been propped up against the side of an abandoned building. There was Khomeini's familiar wave and sour countenance, staring out at a garbage dump.

Along the main road Syrian soldiers were hoisting a freshly painted banner over the entrance to the town. "Yes, yes!" the red Arabic letters proclaimed. "Yes to Hafiz al-Assad."

BACK IN BEIRUT the following day, I stood on what had been the most dangerous ground in Beirut during the civil war: the "museum crossing." Lebanon's National Museum, a vast neoclassical structure built in the monumental, fascistic style of the 1930s, had the misfortune to be situated on a hilltop that straddled a major highway dividing East, or Christian, Beirut from West, or Muslim, Beirut. Before the war many neighborhoods had been integrated, but militiamen had deliberately pushed each sect into its own psychological and geographic ghetto. Those who resisted sectarian segregation were killed or bombed into submission. Because of its strategic location the museum had closed in 1975, just after the war erupted. But it had not been spared. The repository of Lebanon's cultural history had been fought over by most militias. In April of 1994 the museum, like

Beirut itself, was a wreck. Maurice Shehab, its dedicated curator, a Maronite descendant of the family that had run Mount Lebanon under Ottoman rule for 250 years, had sensed that the conflict would be long and bloody. So he had hidden many of the smaller, precious objects or sent them out of the country. And he had encased the statues, stelae, and sarcophagi that were too heavy to move in huge blocks of cement. He had died without seeing the restoration of his museum or his country.

In November 1993 the museum had opened for ten days for the first time in eighteen years to raise money for its reconstruction. Hariri himself had given a million dollars to the campaign. Camille Asmar, the new director, said that some Lebanese had wept when they saw the devastated building and its pathetic exhibition of photographs of Lebanon before, during, and after the war. Some twenty thousand Lebanese, many of them children who had never been to a museum before, were taken on tours of the place they had known only as a metaphor for fear.

Asmar, who had worked at the museum throughout the war, escorted me through the burned and leaking building. Almost every window was gone; so was much of the staircase leading to the second floor. A giant shell hole in the roof provided the only illumination. Shehab's concrete blocks still stood like massive tombs in the deserted halls; the museum itself felt like a funeral vault.

I froze as we entered the hall that had once featured the museum's breathtaking mosaics. There was little that the imaginative Maurice Shehab could have done to protect them. But I still was not prepared for what I saw. In the lower left-hand corner of a fifth-century mosaic of Christ as a shepherd tending a flock of exotic animals was a jagged sniper hole the size of a watermelon. One of the militiamen who had slept, eaten, urinated, and fought from here had desecrated the holiest site, I thought, in Beirut.

My eyes filled with tears — of rage. Asmar looked away. "The mosaic came from Jenah, a suburb of Beirut," he said quietly. "There was nothing quite like it in all the Middle East."

Had the militiaman not understood? Was he so ignorant, so frenzied, so filled with hate and fear, that he had failed to notice what he had destroyed? Couldn't he have knocked his goddamn hole a foot or two away from the mosaic?

And then I noticed the graffiti in Arabic just above the mosaic: *Bismillah al rahman al rahim* (In the Name of God the Merciful), the Islamic inscription began. So the young sniper had known what he was doing, after all. Jesus would mean nothing to him. A mosaic from the *jahiliyya*, the era before the Prophet Muhammad, the pre-seventh-century era of "ignorance," was probably worse than nothing: The mosaic depicted a man, and this was *haram*, forbidden by Islam. That the mosaic should be revered not for its subject but for its beauty, rarity, and age would never have occurred to him.

I asked Asmar about the graffiti. "There is scribbling like this all over the building, left by all the sects," he said with a sigh. "There are crosses and crescents, Islamic and Phalangist slogans. They even left us their names and addresses. They wanted to be remembered."

The fate of Lebanon's National Museum was like that of Lebanon, a country so divided and atomized by its competing religions and sects, so filled with rage, envy, petty resentments, and ancient grievances that successions of militiamen had thought nothing about using the shrine of their common heritage as a killing field.

Brave individuals had tried to stop the carnage. The Maurice Shehabs of Lebanon had done what they could to protect the country's cultural wealth. The historian Kamal Salibi and other patriots had tried to save their integrated, civilized neighborhoods. Those who believed in Lebanon had remained and rebuilt, again and again. But they were outnumbered by those who wanted only to destroy. They had been repeatedly deceived and disappointed by the *zu'ama*, their traditional leaders, patronage-hungry politicians whose selfishness and stupidity had fueled the conflict. And they had been betrayed as well by Lebanon's new men — the usurpers with guns — the thuggish militiamen who had ravaged the land and slaughtered its people because of their identity cards. What had happened to compromise that had created a free, democratic Lebanon?

Through most of its torment, Lebanon had been deserted by the "Arab world." Syria used Lebanon's weakness, greed, and disunity to secure influence, profit, and hegemony. Syrians had "helped" Lebanon by helping themselves. The more distant Arabs had watched the slaughter for years and done nothing. Many, in fact, had gloated over Lebanon's agony. This is what came of too much money, freedom, and lack of discipline, they sniffed in the stultifying safety of their own capitals. Despite the ritual tears shed for Lebanon and the hollow words of countless books, magazines, pamphlets, and newspapers about the sacred Arab "cause," the solidarity and ultimate triumph of the greater Arab nation, Lebanon had fought and bled and died alone. Fouad Ajami, a man of Lebanon despite his determined effort to disengage from his tragic land, could not hide his bitterness when he complained that the Lebanon war had been launched against a background of "Arab indifference and quiescence." Only Saudi Arabia, the conservative kingdom opposed to Arab nationalism, envied and despised by most non-Gulf Arabs for its unearned riches, had tried to end the slaughter — a decade after it started — by sponsoring talks that eventually culminated in the successful Taif accords of 1989. The Arab-Israeli war of 1967 had exposed the hollowness of Arab military claims; the war in Lebanon had revealed the absurdity of pan-Arabism's political myth. Lebanon had suffered in agony, and no one cared.

"Lebanon is a rotten piece of wood," a young architect told me soon after my return from Baalbek. "You can put fresh paint on it, but that will only disguise the fact that it has been eaten out by termites, that it is hollow and won't support real weight."

Another architect I knew, Assem Salam, a patrician intellectual, had argued, on the other hand, that Hariri's plan to demolish much of what remained in the downtown area and build two thousand new buildings — skyscrapers, a new port, giant parks, banks, and highways — was "overambitious, megalomania-cal, and self-destructive," like Lebanon itself. What Beirut needed, he said, was "invisible mending," a patient restitching of torn fabric, not the destruction of whole cloth and its replacement with a new, untested fabric.

Meanwhile, Hariri and his supporters were determined to do whatever it took to rebuild Lebanon. But could Hariri, for all his sound intentions, build something new and strong that would not be wrecked again by the next fanatic's bomb? Or was he, in fact, simply putting new paint on rotten wood?

Was this the flaw in Hariri's tycoonism? The idea that a billionaire Leba-nese Santa Claus could remake his tormented nation? Yes, Hariri could pay to clear the rubble away, rebuild the streets, fix the phones, and restore power. Yes, he could buy off critics and woo allies, domestic and foreign, with money and deals. But could all the money in the world reweave Lebanese society? Could money alone repair a generation's worth of damage? Could money buy the trust, peace, and stability that Lebanon needed if it was to restore itself? And even if all this could be done, would Lebanon, given its sectarian nature, not always be vulnerable to foreign meddling and malicious interference? Wasn't Hariri's tycoonism as perversely visionary as Sheikh Fadlallah's dream of trans-forming Lebanon into an Islamic state?

It was hard to be optimistic. Few of my Lebanese friends questioned whether Lebanon could recapture its former glory and status. But with computer bank transfers, faxes, Touch-Tone telephones, and jet travel, was there still a need for a financial service center in the Middle East? Could Lebanon ever again attract tourists? Israel's new peace with the PLO and Jordan made tourist investment in that part of the Levant more promising. Lebanon's beaches and rivers were filthy. It would take more than a decade to clean them up. Most of the country's cedar forests had been destroyed, the land stripped bare. Before the war, 27 percent of Lebanon had been forest; now 2 percent was. Where there had been lush greenery that enveloped the mountains there was now only cement.

An entire generation of middle-class Lebanese had grown up outside of Lebanon. Even Prime Minister Hariri's children were at school in Paris. Would a Shia bourgeoisie replace the deported Christians? Perhaps the materialistic Shia, those whom Ajami called "the faithful children of Lebanon," would prevail over those who sought meaning and purpose in God. Even Hezbollah was not immune to Lebanon's infectious commercialism. By 1995, the Party of God had begun advertising in Arab newspapers "package tours" through the ruins of Baalbek and the "historic Bekaa," where Western hostages had once been tortured and killed. At the American University of Beirut the young mili-tants who once patrolled the campus walkways and parks warning students not to smoke or drink and ordering women to don the veil were gone. I recalled a copy of the campus newspaper I had picked up at the university's canteen. It featured a half-page photo of a buxom junior under the headline "Babe of the Week."

The war had reshaped Lebanon's political system so as to cede some Christian power and privileges to the numerically dominant Muslims. The Lebanese Parliament was now half Christian, half Muslim. While the president remained a Christian, some of his powers had shifted to the Shiite Speaker of Parliament and to the Sunni prime minister, and given Hariri's enormous wealth and generosity, particularly to the latter. In addition, many of the most useless *zu'ama* and beys had been cast aside in favor of new, more talented men. Lebanon's three leaders—Hariri, Hrawi, and Berri—had all acquired power that had traditionally been denied descendants of the nonprominent. Hariri's rise, in particular, had also reversed another Lebanese, and Arab, tradition: Power usually yielded wealth in the Middle East, not the other way around. Yet Hariri had used his personal fortune—estimated at about half of Lebanon's $7.5 billion gross domestic product—to buy power; and unlike many other Arab politicians, he returned enormous sums to his people, thus breaking another Lebanese tradition.

The war, however, had still not resolved major questions of identity and power sharing that prompted it. In Lebanon, loyalty to the vague concept of nation had never transcended preexisting loyalties to family, tribe, sect, or clan, especially not in times of stress. Could majoritarian democracy now produce peace and stability? Were the Taif accords mainly a temporary fix, a bandage— fresh paint that could not conceal the rot inside?

Many in Lebanon chose not to raise such questions, much less dwell on the war itself. Lebanon was suffering from a highly selective amnesia, just as my friend the filmmaker Maroun Bagdadi had argued. Lebanon, of course, had never been an introspective society; it had always made up in energy what it lacked in depth. Because it contained so many different sects and ideologies, Lebanon had always encouraged superficiality. People with so many differences who sought harmony and democracy could not afford to look at themselves or their society deeply.

This "cultural amnesia" was a theme that Elias Khoury, a Lebanese writer, had repeatedly revisited in his essays and plays. Before leaving Lebanon, I went to see him. His new play about the disappearance of some twenty thousand Lebanese men during the war had become the talk of what was left of Beirut's intelligentsia.

Khoury clearly relished his role as intellectual agent provocateur. Slender, with heavy black glasses and thick black wavy hair, he looked like an intellectual. He would have been at home in Paris, where his play would soon be performed, or in New York, where he had taught for two years during the war. His office at *An-Nahar* was as cluttered as my own. Khoury had helped found *Mawakif* (Positions), a now-defunct journal created after the 1967 Arab-Israeli war that had attempted to explore with brutal candor the causes of the Arabs' massive defeats. The effort had been highly unusual in Arab intellectual life.

I asked Khoury why there was no equivalent of *Mawakif* today, when the Arabs needed such a journal. "Because there is no Beirut," Khoury replied. "We are living in a collapsed society. Where else in the Arab world would you have Arab intellectuals rich enough, independent enough, and free enough to dare to ask the questions we raised then?"

None of today's models of government suited either the Arabs or the Lebanese, Khoury said. Lebanon's traditional system did not work because "it gave Muslims the impression that Christians were governing Muslims with European backing." Besides, the system had failed even to protect Christians. "It proved that even if we Christians govern, we will not necessarily be protected." The Arab nationalist model, too, had failed: It had not liberated Palestine, nor had it liberated, enriched, or empowered Arab citizens. Most Arab states were "confessional," that is, comprised of several minorities and one dominant sect; but under Arab nationalism, ethnic diversity had been denied, deliberately suppressed. Turkey's secular model was now facing stiff internal opposition not only from Islamists but also from its Kurds, a despised, much-mistreated minority. "Some Arabs glorify the Turkish democratic, secular model now," he said, "forgetting that modern Turkey began with a massacre — of Christian Armenians."

Lebanese today were being offered a choice "between Hariri's money and Hezbollah's God." He, for one, wanted neither. The militant Islamists offered seemingly compelling solutions, he said; but like all simple solutions, they would create more problems than they solved. "I'm not sure the militant Shiites could ever win in Lebanon," he said. "Most Lebanese, including the Shia, simply want to be left alone and make money. We are very pragmatic — at times."

If there were peace in the region and Lebanon prospered, it would be harder still for Hezbollah to win, he added. "They have long fed on economic and political discontent and disenfranchisement."

I wondered. Most social revolutions — in France, Russia, and even Iran — had occurred not during times of economic despair but of growing prosperity.

Lebanon's culture was chaotic but strong, Khoury insisted, which was "bound to affect the fundamentalists." Hezbollah, in his view, would become "Lebanized" before Lebanon became "Islamized" because no minority had ever ruled tyrannically for long in Lebanon. There were too many competing, complaining zu'ama.

"But we have endured a monstrous ordeal. And monstrous ordeals tend to produce monstrous solutions," he said, picking up the other side of his argument. And no one could predict what would happen in the next decade in the region. "If militant fundamentalism were to triumph in Syria, or Egypt, or Iraq . . . ," he said, his voice trailing off.

For Khoury, a secular Christian, an Islamic future in Lebanon would force him into exile, something he disliked even contemplating. For him, Lebanon's past and its future were inseparable. That was why his country's aversion to pondering the causes and implications of the war had so troubled him, as it had Maroun Bagdadi.

"People disliked my play because it forced them to remember," he said, returning to psychologically more comfortable ground. "It forced them to admit that we were all responsible for the carnage in Lebanon, that this was not a war caused by foreign meddling, '*une guerre des autres*,' as too many still call it. How can we rebuild souls when there is no soul-searching? Our amnesia is dangerous because it is destroying our ability to leave the war behind. If you don't examine the past, you can't really leave it behind."

Suddenly, we heard what sounded like an explosion. Khoury and I exchanged worried glances. Two minutes later, we heard the ambulances and fire trucks as they sped toward East Beirut.

If the Lebanese thought about the past, Khoury said, trying to continue our discussion, they would realize that they must find a new formula for ensuring, that Lebanon remained democratic but a society in which "our confessional and ideological differences are tolerated."

But there was no consensus in Lebanon on a system that would satisfy all, or even most, of its seventeen sects; "salami" sects, one scholar had called them.[64] How could one speak of what the Christians wanted? Which Christians? Maronites, Greek Orthodox, Greek Catholics, Roman Catholics, Protestants? So far the Lebanese had only determined what my friend Habib Malik had called their "negative identity." The Lebanese now knew only what they were against: They were opposed to the 300,000 Palestinians remaining in their country, to Syrian hegemony, and to the rabble-rousing militias that had pillaged and plundered the land.

"The world is now beginning to ask itself very Lebanon-like questions," Khoury said. "Look at Bosnia, Somalia, Sudan, Russia, and even Belgium! Everyone is struggling with the issue of how minorities — peoples of different colors, religions, or races — can live together in freedom, harmony, and prosperity. The whole world is becoming Lebanized!" That was bad for Lebanon, he added lightheartedly. "It only increases our megalomania."

It was dark by the time we finished talking. The smell of smoke and the wailing of sirens had become more intense. Khoury turned on the news and learned that at least three people were dead and thirty more wounded at the site of the explosion: the headquarters of the Christian Lebanese Forces.

Who could have done such a thing?

Khoury looked out the window sadly and sighed. "Anyone."

SYRIA

Arabism is love.

MICHEL AFLAQ,
founder of Syria's ruling Baath Party

We want to establish a state in which there is no egoism,
despotism, or suppression. We want an *umma* that finds death
agreeable and that shakes mountains.

MUSTAFA AL-SIBAI,
Syrian Muslim Brotherhood founder[1]

ON A COLD, BRIGHT DAY in March 1994, more than a hundred thoroughbred
horses, shrouded in black, paraded silently through the deserted central square
of Damascus. The normally bustling souks were closed, their metal shutters
drawn. So were offices. The streets were empty. Radio stations broadcast only
classical Western music and readings from the Koran. Syrian television carried
a single program: a live broadcast from Qardaha, a remote mountain village in
northern Syria, more than two hundred miles from Damascus. There, in his
hometown, sat President Hafiz al-Assad, stiff and shriveled, in an overstuffed
armchair on a makeshift podium, listening to unctuous tributes to him from
Syrian and foreign notables in an audience of hundreds of diplomats, Middle
Eastern dignitaries, members of the large Assad clan, and almost as many
tense, mustachioed bodyguards. Hour after hour, the cameras panned
back to the familiar solitary figure in the giant chair, his large, peanut-shaped
head dwarfing his deceptively frail body. His usually penetrating brown eyes

stared out at the crowd blankly. During more than six hours of eulogy, he did not stir.

The occasion was the commemoration, forty days after his death, of President Assad's eldest son Basil, heir apparent to Syria's long-standing dictatorship. On January 21, Basil Assad, thirty-two, was killed in his Mercedes as he was speeding on the airport road and hit a curb at the turnoff. Assad's eldest son was racing to catch an early-morning flight to Frankfurt or speeding just for the thrill of it, since the plane undoubtedly would have been held for so influential a passenger. The car hit the curb at more than 125 miles an hour and, according to official accounts, spun like a top twenty feet through the air. Basil's cousin in the passenger seat and his bodyguard in the back were badly hurt. Basil Assad died instantly.

By the time I arrived in Damascus a month after the ceremony, Syria was still in deepest mourning. Despite the momentous developments in the Arab-Israeli peace process — the 1993 agreement on a framework for peace between Israel and the PLO and the imminent withdrawal of Israeli troops from Gaza and Jericho — Syria was subdued, convulsed by what a diplomat friend called "Basilmania." Posters of Basil and of father and son were emblazoned on mountainsides and were nailed to the entrances of every spice and rug shop in the capital. Syria's new martyr could be seen in a variety of poses: in military uniform; with his father in military or civilian attire; in parachute gear; as a rock star sporting heavy black Ray-Ban sunglasses; in black tie; or riding horseback — jumping, trotting, galloping — staring beatifically toward the heavens (my personal favorite); and in a photo never before revealed in determinedly secular Syria, on his knees in prayer in Mecca, clad in a traditional white prayer robe, making an *umrah*, the lesser pilgrimage to Islam's holiest city.

Politically astute merchants had paid for personalized posters of him, their names featured prominently at the bottom. For the truly well connected or those who fancied dictator kitsch, there were Basil key chains, pens, and even diamond-studded watches. A giant banner showed Basil waving at shoppers who entered the Souk al-Hamidiyeh, Damascus's ancient market, among the world's oldest: "Good-bye, my people," the banner proclaimed in what were presumably Basil's last thoughts. "I would have liked to serve you longer, but Allah did not will it."

"People were actually weeping in the streets when they heard the news," a diplomat's wife and old friend told me as we sipped gin and tonics at the Sheraton, one of Syria's few first-class hotels. "They stood below Assad's balcony, waiting for him to appear, which, of course, he never did.

"Some of the hysteria was managed, as things always are around here," she said, lowering her voice as she glanced nervously around the room for unintended listeners. "But some of it was genuine. People were truly sorry for his father. And they were frightened for themselves."

My friend was right. While Syrians had cause to be terrified of Assad, many were even more frightened of what might happen in Syria without him. Though universally feared, Assad was also respected, even by many of his most vehement critics. The tremendous outpouring of grief at Basil Assad's commemoration was, in effect, an advance wake for Hafiz Assad himself and his suffocatingly stagnant, reassuringly stable regime. Less than forty-eight hours after Basil died, the government was prominently featuring Bashar, twenty-eight, a soft-spoken physician who had practiced medicine in London and Assad's second-eldest son. Though he had never shown an interest in politics, Bashar was suddenly omnipresent on television and in the newspapers. But few Syrians found the instant production of a new heir apparent credible.[2]

Basil had said in 1988 that he doubted that either his death or that of any of his brothers would have a "political impact on our father."[3] But he was wrong. With Basil's death, assurances of political continuity in Syria had vanished. And Syrians, mindful of their country's chaotic history, found the prospect of a return to anarchy or yet another prolonged, bloody power struggle — and perhaps even the triumph of militant Islam in the most secular of all Arab states — alarming.

SINCE HIS ASCENSION to power in 1970 in a military coup — known not as a "revolution" but as the "Corrective Movement" — Hafiz Assad had become synonymous with Syria. In his authoritative but respectful biography of the leader, Patrick Seale had praised Assad for transforming Syria from an Arab plaything into a "substantial regional power."

Assad's regime had built schools, roads, dams, and hospitals, but also the third-largest — after Iraq and Egypt — and arguably the least successful, army in the Arab Middle East. Assad had struggled to combat, again without much success, the country's intense regionalism, the vast gap in living standards between peasants and city dwellers, and the ferocious sectarian rivalry in this land of 14 million people, half of them less than sixteen years old. He had built a heavily centralized, bureaucratized system that stifled individual incentive whenever and wherever it could. He had erected ludicrous statues of himself at the entry to every major Syrian city and town. But he had made Syria matter, for which Syrians, so desperate to be taken seriously, were deeply grateful. Most of all, Hafiz Assad had survived. He had been in power longer than most other Arab rulers except Libya's erratic Muammar Qaddafi, whom he despised, and two monarchs, Hussein of Jordan and Hassan II of Morocco, both of whom, as descendants of the Prophet Muhammad, had legitimacy that Assad could only envy.

Like many of his counterparts, Assad had endured because he was willing to kill. In 1982 he had ordered an infamous massacre in the ancient city of Hama, Syria's fourth largest, following a sustained uprising by Islamic militants. Some 10,000–30,000 of Hama's nearly 200,000 residents — the precise number is unknowable[4] — were killed by Syrian soldiers. The slaughter made Assad's name — and Syria's — synonymous with state terror. Apart from his neighbor and rival Saddam Hussein, no other current Arab ruler had shown such bloody determination to survive. In the modern Arab Middle East only Hafiz Assad was known primarily for a massacre.

According to a senior Syrian diplomat, Assad would tell guests that thanks to the "measures" he had taken in Hama, Muslim fundamentalists no longer troubled Syria as they did his neighbors. Human rights, Assad said in late 1994, was merely a phrase "now in fashion."[5] In a conversation that year with Dennis Ross, the Clinton administration's special envoy, Assad had berated Egyptian president Hosni Mubarak for being, on the one hand, "too insensitive" to the public demand for Islamic symbols in daily life and, at the same time, "too weak" toward Egypt's Islamic militants. Because they did not fear Mubarak, Assad said, the regime itself was threatened.

The justification for the Hama massacre was terrifyingly simple: It had solidified the regime and Assad's personal power and ensured the near absence of organized political violence in Syria ever since. And it successfully refuted Western liberals and other supporters of the militant Islamic agenda who maintained that brute repression alone would curb neither Islamically inspired violence nor demands for Islamic government. Just as terror had crushed violent resistance to Lenin's Soviet Union and concentration camps reinforced by massacres had suppressed the democracy movement in modern China, Hama had ended public dissent in Syria, not, as some analysts contended, because the Arabs were "tribal" or "authoritarian" or "submissive" by nature but because they were human. Assad had ordered the massacre not because, as some scholars maintained, Syria was torn by tension between the "city against countryside," "rich against poor," "secular versus religious," or "majority against minority sects," though all these cleavages have complicated his rule to this day. He slaughtered the citizens of Hama because Assad, too, wanted to survive.

I wondered what scars the Hama massacre had left on the soul of this nation. Murder on such a scale and governing by what Tom Friedman, my *Times* colleague, had called "Hama rules," had to have left a mark.[6] Armed with a notebook containing names and addresses of several Hama residents, I set off to visit the chastened city.

ONE OF THE OLDEST CITIES in the Middle East, about 120 miles northwest of the capital, Hama is nestled on the Orontes River — Nahr al-Assi, which in Arabic means, appropriately, "Rebel River." Hama's domed stone houses with gracefully arched windows, manicured walkways, and well-tended parks still line the riverbanks. But the city's famed *norias*, the giant wooden waterwheels thirty to sixty feet in diameter that have churned since Byzantine times, were no longer turning when I arrived by taxi on a warm spring day in April 1994. After two years of abundant rain and snow, a fierce drought gripped the region. There was no longer enough water to turn the wheels; the mighty Orontes had been reduced to a foul stream.

I visited a man whom I shall call Fares at his law office on the east side of the river. Since I had been sent by friends, he invited me home to lunch, an example of the famous Syrian hospitality I had so often enjoyed. Dining at home offered not only better food than most Syrian restaurants; it assured privacy, an even more precious commodity in a country where fifteen intelligence services spy on fellow Syrians and on one another.

Fares and his wife lived in a spacious two-story villa on a steep hillside overlooking the Orontes and Hama. The house, deserted by their grown children, seemed empty and forlorn, as empty nests do. The ceilings were high—a reminder of days without air conditioning—and the living room was furnished in the ornate Syrian style. I admired the carved wooden tables and chests, with their intricate inlay of ivory and mother-of-pearl, and a vitrine filled with antique porcelain from China and hand-painted Syrian goblets in colored glass. As we sat stiffly on the traditional embroidered silk–covered chairs, I noticed that several panes of glass in the front windows were cracked. "From the events," Fares said, using the Syrian euphemism for the three-week rampage that had forever changed his family's life only twelve years ago. "We left them broken so we would remember," he said, his voice dropping. The windows had been shattered by the sheer pressure of shell fire pounding the town below from the tanks that were stationed directly opposite his house.

While many of the campaign's details were still in dispute, its broad outlines were well known. On the night of February 2, 1982, Muslim Brotherhood militants had killed some ninety soldiers as they attempted to raid a house in the old section of Hama, where the Brotherhood had stored caches of Saudi- and Iraqi-financed arms. The next morning, insurgents who had occupied the city's mosques, roofs, and turrets announced through megaphones that Hama had been "liberated" and that the rest of Syria would soon be free. Ransacking government offices and the local armory, they had killed at least fifty officials and other "collaborators" on the first day of what Patrick Seale called a "full-scale urban insurrection such as had never occurred under Asad's rule." Assad's response, Fares told us, was five hundred tanks, along with helicopters, artillery, and almost 100,000 soldiers, far more than the 12,000 reported by Amnesty International or the 50,000 estimated by the Muslim Brotherhood in its own account of the massacre.[7] After the city was sealed off, the guerrillas retreated into the labyrinthine warren of the ancient town, taking refuge in mosques, shops, and houses connected by serpentine courtyards. In response, the army demolished entire neighborhoods, leaving "thousands of innocent people out in the cold, without food or shelter during one of our worst winters," Fares recalled.

On February 15, Syria's defense minister and deputy prime minister, Maj. Gen. Mustafa Tlas, Assad's friend since childhood, announced that the uprising had been crushed. But for two more weeks soldiers conducted house-to-house searches, arrested and tortured residents, and undertook what Amnesty International condemned as "collective killings of unarmed, innocent inhabitants." Many of the dead were buried in predug, unmarked mass graves. Amnesty received reports, which Syria denied, that cyanide gas containers had also been brought to Hama and piped into buildings believed to house insurgents.

"To this day, I cannot forget the smell—the stench of rotting corpses," Fares told me. After the slaughter, army bulldozers had crushed all buildings damaged beyond repair and flattened out the rubble "like parking lots," according to one account. On February 22 the Syrian media broadcast a letter to

President Assad from Hama's Baath Party, Syria's ruling party, praising the reprisals against the Muslim Brothers and their sympathizers that had "stopped them from breathing forever." Assad himself responded in late February: "What happened in Hama has happened and is now over."

Fares took me to see the major battlefields in this lopsided urban guerrilla war. The government had built new apartment buildings on one of the worst killing fields. Yes, he conceded as we strolled through what remained of Hama's ancient quarter, the Muslim rebels had started the war. But they were relatively few and badly armed. "Their revolt could not have succeeded. The army recaptured the town after the first day of fighting. Only then did the real killing begin," he said. Almost forty mosques were destroyed, along with Hama's most beautiful churches. (The city was 10 percent Christian.) Several ancient water-wheels had also been deliberately burned. The government had not even bothered to distinguish between insurgents and innocent bystanders, he said bitterly. Fares's cousin, a senior Baath Party official who lived in the ancient quarter in what was a Muslim Brotherhood stronghold, had been dragged out of his home during the second week of the siege with some twenty other residents of his building. The men were lined up against the wall and shot. "Abdellah, my cousin, screamed at them: 'Don't shoot, I am a senior member of the Baath!' But he was mowed down like the rest. He was lucky, though," Fares added. "He got three bullets, but only in his arms and legs. We were able to save him, but not his limbs."

No family in Hama was untouched by the massacre, Fares said. The official register showed payments to some ten thousand widows in Hama, "and that's not counting the men, women, and children who disappeared beneath the rubble."

Fares still took pride in his city despite these horrors. He led us to a fourteenth-century Turkish bath which had only recently been restored. "We managed to save this after the army left," he said to me. "Go in. It's lady's day."

The bath was steamy and warm inside. A dozen women sat cross-legged on the mosaic-tile floor, washing themselves and their children with large loofah sponges. They were gossiping and laughing as if nothing had happened here. A heavy woman with large breasts and a towel wrapped around her waist grabbed my hand and guided me through the gaggle of women, who shrieked with delight at the appearance of a foreign female in this most private of sanctuaries. She offered me *melisseh* (verbena tea) and a free hair wash. I thanked her but declined, for Fares was waiting outside. Taking the side of her towel, she rubbed clean my now misted sunglasses and held them up to the afternoon light that filtered through the newly replaced stained glass in the bath's ancient dome. "You are blind," she observed in Arabic after inspecting the lenses. I laughed in agreement. Would I like a cigarette? she offered, lighting her own half-wet Marlboro with difficulty. I declined, with difficulty. Her husband, too, did not permit her to smoke; she could only enjoy her cigarettes inside the bath, she confided as beads of water fell from her glossy black curls onto her round white shoulders. As she tried to blow smoke rings through the mist, I wondered which relatives of this friendly woman had been murdered near this bathhouse.

As Fares and I continued our walk down a narrow cobblestone street, I noticed some graffiti in Arabic on the wall of an ancient house near the bath: "In memory of Mahmoud," someone had written. "You see such inscriptions all over town," he said. "People just imagine where their friends or family might have been killed and write their names on the spot. There are many graves in Hama, but few gravestones."

The razing of the city was deliberate, he insisted. Many of the instigators had fled by the time the government arrived. But soldiers laid mines and blew up ancient buildings for weeks after the resistance had collapsed. This was not self-defense or even a civil war, he insisted. The government wanted to make an example of Hama. Aleppo, Syria's second-largest city in the north, had also been plagued by Islamic resistance. But Hama, with its smaller population, was easier to encircle and isolate — the perfect object lesson.

We walked past a construction site where Hama's Great Mosque, once its most celebrated structure, was being rebuilt. "It was a Byzantine church before it was a mosque, and probably a synagogue before that; centuries earlier, it had been a Hellenistic temple," Fares said. In 1982 it became rubble. As we walked through the site, more than a dozen men were lifting giant stones that had been numbered for eventual replacement in their original spots. A sign in Arabic announced that the Office of Islamic Reconstruction was managing the project. "The government destroyed it, so now the government is rebuilding it," Fares explained. "The logic is very Syrian, which is to say no logic at all. The government abolished logic in Hama."

THIS WAS NOT the first time that rulers of Syria had created a ruin only to rebuild it. I thought of the trip I had made a few days earlier to Palmyra, or Tadmor, as it is called in Arabic, the ancient oasis and site of Queen Zenobia's opulent third-century empire. Under the reign of Odenathus, Zenobia's husband, Palmyra had prospered, the result of its loose alliance with Rome. But after Odenathus was murdered — by whom is not clear — and Zenobia succeeded him, she challenged Emperor Aurelian. Zenobia was a student of history and philosophy and spoke several languages. She craved independence for Palmyra and calculated that Aurelian was too distracted by other wars to punish her insubordination, or if he did, that Parthia or Persia would support her revolt against Rome. This assumption was no less wrong than the Islamists' belief some eighteen hundred years later that Assad lacked the strength and determination to suppress a revolt and that Syria's Sunni Muslim majority would rise up — with help from Iraq — against Assad's minority sect, the Alawites, once a rebellion began.[8]

Aurelian "fell upon the citizens without mercy," according to an American writer who visited Palmyra a century ago and became fascinated by its tragic queen. Its palaces and temples were sacked and despoiled, and the city became, "as the word Tadmor signifies, a ruin."[9] At length, Aurelian then decided that the Palmyrans had been "sufficiently slaughtered and cut to pieces." So he had launched a grand rebuilding campaign and returned to Rome with his prisoner Zenobia stumbling under the weight of her gold chains in what Roman historians called "sumptuous bondage." Aurelian did not attack other Syrian cities; he did not need to. Palmyra had taught the ancient Syrians that he could be ruthless, and as the American visitor observed, "The Orientals did not need a second lesson."

But the city itself never revived. Even today, a visitor could somehow sense its ancient suffering. Though Palmyra was now, by Syrian standards, a major tourist site with a population of more than thirty-five thousand people, its glorious monuments remained unlit at night. There was only one more or less modern hotel and, for such an impressive ruin, relatively few tourists.

At the edge of Palmyra, behind an olive grove and a stone wall topped by barbed wire, is a government prison that once housed mostly Muslim militants. My driver seemed frightened at the very mention of its name and refused at first even to drive by it. And no wonder. Amnesty International had singled out Tadmor as a prison where detainees were routinely "whipped, kicked and punched," where cigarettes were "stubbed out on their bodies as they enter or leave their cells," where their faces were "slashed with razor blades and shaving knives." [10] Visitors to modern Palmyra are welcomed by a banner declaring in English: "Welcome to Syria — Country of Safety and Peace." But the tranquility, one soon sees, has to do with death.

BECAUSE OF THE HAMA MASSACRE, Assad, in Aurelian fashion, had secured peace with, or had at least assured himself the acquiescence of, Syria's Sunni Muslim majority. The despised son of a despised community — the Alawites — he had broken Syria. Assad did not ask Syrians to love him, only to fear him. And like his Roman predecessor, Assad spent lavishly to rebuild the city he had destroyed. Along with the Great Mosque, he had built a new 230-bed hospital in Hama, a central market in classical Arabic design, new government centers for Baathist unions and federations, a teachers college, and a girls' sports center. He had also built two ugly new mosques to compensate for some of those his forces had blown up and also a new church. "The Baath is a popular party that comes from the heart of the people," declared a banner in Arabic draped across the new town hall's façade in April 1994. The building was one of the few in Hama to feature one of his giant portraits that are ubiquitous in other Syrian cities. At the edge of Hama the government erected a bronze statue of the frowning leader that stands twenty-five feet high. Seale noted that Assad had wanted not merely to rebuild the shattered city but to change its reactionary attitudes. So he instituted mixed bathing in 1983 and inaugurated the first mixed dormitory for male and female college students. Despite conservative Muslims, who disdained the idea of sports for women, the girls' sports center was a success, Seale reported; by 1985, only three years after the massacre, Hama girls were the national Ping-Pong champions.

But like ancient Palmyra, Hama could not bury its awful past. Fares's hatred of the regime that his family had once championed — and that of other Hama residents whom I had interviewed over the years — suggested that the massacre would not be forgotten.

Late that afternoon, I had tea with Fares on the terrace of the Apamee Cham Palace, a new luxury hotel with inlaid mosaic fountains, its marble surfaces polished like glass. A recording of "Plaisir d'Amour" played softly on the hotel audio system. Visitors to the hotel had a spectacular view of the western side of the river where less than fifteen years before soldiers had pursued and tortured fellow Syrians and set the giant waterwheels on fire. Fares whispered that the hotel was built on the site of a grave; we were literally sitting on bones.

As we left, a young Syrian behind the reception desk who was not from Hama told us that the hotel was fully booked. I could not imagine why. Perhaps tourism was picking up, but then again, why? Despite the new apartment buildings, the neatly landscaped roads and shops, the parks and sports center, Hama made me uneasy. This stunted city in a stunted land was quiet but not at peace. The rage that Fares could barely contain seemed to me everywhere.

The markets had been rebuilt, but there was little from Hama to buy. Before the events in 1982, Hama was known for its cotton tablecloths, bedspreads, and curtains, with their distinctive black stenciled prints in unusual patterns — doves, roosters, flowers, and geometric forms. Now they were difficult to find, and not only in Hama. Charlie Glass, a friend and colleague, had told me why: Four of the five families that once made the cloth had been killed in the "events."[11]

APOLOGISTS FOR Assad's massacre, or those who wish to minimize the horror, usually try to put the crime in what they call historical context. What had happened in Hama was inevitable, they argue, given three factors: Syria's tortured past, the city's fanatical history, and Assad's nature.

There was some merit to the Syrian argument that history had been unfair to Syria. Philip Hitti, the historian, observed that until the end of World War I, the name Syria was primarily geographic; the ancient Greeks had used the word to cover the lands that became known in our time as Palestine, Israel, Jordan, Lebanon, and even part of Turkey. Until modern times, all of Syria had only twice been an independent sovereign state, the center of empire: during the later Seleucid kingdom at Antioch (301–141 B.C.) and the Islamic Umayyad caliphate at Damascus (661–750 C.E.). For the rest of its turbulent history, Syria was either part of a foreign empire or divided among native or foreign states.

Syria's strength as well as its misfortune had always been its geography. The British officer John Glubb, or Glubb Pasha, as he was known during his days as military adviser to King Hussein of Jordan, argued long ago that Syria could best be understood as a narrow strip of land between two seas, the Mediterranean and the desert, both of which were the constant target of foreign invasion.[12] On the west were Mediterranean pirates; on the east, Bedouin raiders, their desert counterparts. This narrow isthmus, only seventy-five miles wide, was the only land thoroughfare joining Europe and Asia to Africa, the only terrain between the Nile and the Euphrates, essential for trade but irresistible to plunderers. Hence, for most of its history Syria was, as one writer put it, an imperial doormat.

In Roman times Syria supplied the empire with vast numbers of lawyers, doctors, philosophers, and even imperial secretaries. The Syrians, Glubb wrote in an era that still believed in the now politically incorrect notion of national character, were known for their "cleverness, quick intellect, and fluency rather, perhaps, than for their profundity," traits, he dryly observed, that "still distinguish them today."

Syria owed its rise to an early civil war among Muslims. Umar, the second caliph, had declared that Arabian Muslims who ruled conquered lands should constitute what Hitti called a "religio-military aristocracy, keeping their blood pure and unmixed, living aloof and abstaining from holding or cultivating any landed property." In 644, Umar died and Uthman succeeded him as caliph. But the Shiites — or those who supported Ali, Muhammad's son-in-law and cousin — murdered Uthman, insisting that Ali should be caliph. Ali moved Islam's capital from Medina to what he hoped would be more hospitable ground for his caliphate: Al-Kufah (Karbala), in modern-day Iraq. But in the chaos and bitterness that ensued, Muawiyah, the ambitious governor of Damascus and the Prophet's cousin from the aristocratic Umayyad branch of their tribe, sensed opportunity. Portraying himself as the avenger of the martyred caliph, Muawiyah dramatically challenged Ali by unfurling in his Damascus mosque Uthman's blood-soaked shirt and displaying the severed fingers of the caliph's wife that had been chopped off as she defended her husband.

Ultimately, Hitti argued, the conflict was not one of personalities but "whether Iraq or Syria, Kufah or Damascus, should head the Islamic world."[13] The issue was settled, as were most early conflicts within Islam, in blood — and with Ali's murder — in favor of Muawiyah and Damascus, which in 661 became Islam's capital, a turning point in Muslim history.

Under Muawiyah, Islam's fifth caliph and the first head of the Umayyad empire, Islam flourished, expanding from Spain to India. Muawiyah departed from Umar's ruling creed by surrounding himself with Syrian Christian advisers and taking a Christian wife, ingratiating himself with the people he had conquered.[14]

The dynasty became associated, as did Syria itself, with another landmark in Islamic history. By including non-Muslims in key positions in court, by introducing tolerant "innovations" opposed by religious conservatives, and by appointing his frivolous son to succeed him as caliph, thus introducing the principle of hereditary rule that has been followed ever since by Muslim dynasties, Muawiyah "secularized Islam and transformed the theocratic caliphate into a temporal sovereignty," according to Hitti. While Islamic doctrine would continue to insist that there was no separation between politics and religion, between the temporal and the spiritual in general, the two realms had indeed been effectively separated and would remain so throughout the world of Islam.[15] Generations of future Islamic "fundamentalists" would never forgive Muawiyah or the Umayyads for this violation of political *tawhid*, the "oneness" of church and state, a cardinal principle of Islam.

When, in 750, the Abbasids, another branch of the Prophet's quarrelsome family, defeated the Umayyads, Damascus suffered a fatal blow. The second Abbasid caliph founded the city of Baghdad and proclaimed it Islam's capital, thus ensuring eternal rivalry between Damascus and Baghdad—yet another characteristic of modern Syrian politics.

With the rise of the Abbasids, Syria became a doormat again, caught between Islamic rivals in Baghdad and Cairo. Between 962 and 1000, Syria was invaded—even before the Crusades—at least eight times.[16] In the early fifteenth century the most terrifying of invaders, Tamerlane the Mongol, sacked Aleppo, then Hama, the city's first noteworthy massacre, and later Damascus. Ottoman rule in 1516 brought peace to Syria but also neglect. After the discovery of the Cape of Good Hope in 1497, trade routes shifted away from the desert caravans that had made North Africa and Mediterranean Syria a wealthy crossroads. Politically and economically irrelevant, Syria, at last, was stable.

As INTENSE AS its yearning to be respected but utterly at odds with this goal were the communal hatreds and rivalries of Syria's many sects. "The population of Syria is so inharmonious a gathering of widely differing races in blood, in creed, and in custom," wrote Mark Sykes, a British traveler and Arab enthusiast at the turn of the twentieth century, "that government is both difficult and dangerous."[17] After World War I, parliamentarian Sykes, who may have conveniently forgotten his earlier concerns about the inherent difficulty of ruling the volatile Middle East, redrew the region's map—and changed Syria's future—in the notorious, initially secret imperial power grab by Britain and France that bears his name.[18]

Among the most quarrelsome of Syrian cities was the ancient city of Hama, known for its religious and political conservatism—a xenophobic, zealous, and feudal place.[19] Under Ottoman rule the Hama region had been controlled by four of Syria's great families—all Sunni Muslims.[20] These feudal lords had only contempt for the sect to which Assad belongs, the Alawites, a minority offshoot of Islam that neither orthodox Sunni nor Shiite Muslims considered Muslim.

While the origins of the Alawites, or Nusayris, as they were once known, remain unclear, the low esteem in which they were held by Syria's Sunni Muslim Arab majority and even its Shiites, Islam's minority branch, was legendary. Ibn Taymiyya, the medieval Syrian theologian and one of Islam's early "fundamentalists," had denounced Alawites as more dangerous even than Christians and had urged fellow Sunni Muslims to declare a jihad against them.[21] Concentrated in the impoverished northwest of the country and making up less than 10 percent of the population, Alawites had served mainly as servants of the proud and privileged Sunni aristocrats who saw themselves as Syria's natural rulers.

The Sunnis despised France not only for its sometimes brutal occupation but also for the privileges and autonomous area that Paris gave the Alawis in 1920, and the state it created for them in 1922, to protect this beleaguered, constantly feuding minority from Sunni exploitation and persecution.

As Arab nationalism spread throughout Syria and other mandatory states in the Middle East, Alawites feared that their European protector would withdraw. In 1936 six Alawi notables begged the French occupiers not to do so. Given Sunni Arab Muslim hatred of "everything non-Muslim," the notables wrote, French withdrawal would expose Syrian minorities to "death and annihilation" and would "end freedom of thought and belief." A "dark fate" awaited Jews, Alawis, and other minorities if, as the Sunnis desired, Muslim Palestine were united with Muslim Syria, the notables warned. Among the letter's signers was Sulayman al-Assad, Hafiz Assad's father.[22]

Their anxiety proved justified. In 1946, France, confronted by rising Syrian national sentiment, withdrew from the Levant, granting Syria independence but also abandoning the Alawis and other minorities that had helped Paris govern for more than two decades.

Sunni Muslim aristocrats would also never forgive the French for having dismantled Syria: Under the Ottoman agreements ceding Syria to the French, much of Syria's coast was given to Christian-dominated Lebanon, and large sections of the Syrian province of Aleppo were ceded to Turkey. When the French finally withdrew, Syria was about half the size it had been under the Ottomans. Assad rarely omits to mention this historical injustice to visitors.

Syria's leading Sunni families had long and lavishly supported the Muslim Brotherhood, founded in Syria in 1946 as a paramilitary organization and branch of the Egyptian Brotherhood.[23] While the Brotherhood everywhere was rigid and doctrinaire, the Hama branch, according to Tammam al-Barazi, a journalist who was born there, was especially uncompromising.

The Syrian Brotherhood, or the Ikhwan, had hated the ruling Baath Party ever since its creation in the 1940s as a nationalist alternative to communism. The Baath, which in Arabic means "renewal" or "rebirth," favored everything the Brotherhood detested: socialism, secular government, and Western-style nationalism.

Despite religious and Sunni aristocratic opposition, the Baath's ideological commitment to equal standing for all who embraced pan-Arabism had tremendous appeal within a country as ethnically varied as Syria, especially to such persecuted minorities as the Alawites. Among those attracted by the party's policy of inclusion was a young student from Latakia whose family belonged to the least important of the Alawites' four main tribal confederations—Hafiz Assad.[24] While young Assad shared his father's disdain for the arrogant Sunni Muslims, he was part of a younger, more nationalist generation that, instead of embracing the French as his father had done, joined the Baath. In 1948, Muslim Brotherhood activists cornered the Baathist student leader and stabbed him repeatedly in the back. It took Assad several months to recover from the attack. The psychological wounds never healed.

When the Baath seized power in a military coup in 1963, Hama's Sunni religious and political elite was outraged. Rioting erupted against Baath rule throughout Syria in 1964, and predictably, Hama's Sultan Mosque became the rebellion's headquarters. The militants, as they would do in 1982, used the mosque to hide weapons and as a sanctuary. More than a hundred men were killed, and the mosque's minaret was toppled when Syrian soldiers shelled it to flush out insurgents. The attack on so holy a shrine inflamed Muslim passions: The then prime minister was forced to resign, yielding power to a Baath founder, Salah al-Din al-Bitar, a Sunni Muslim teacher of humble origins. Patrick Seale argued that the 1964 rebellion based in Hama had been yet another "formative experience" for Syrian Baathists, among them, a rising star: fighter pilot Hafiz Assad.

Failing to unseat the Baath from power in 1964, Islamic militants fled abroad, many of them to Aachen, West Germany, a Syrian Brotherhood base to this day, to Saudi Arabia and to Jordan, or underground to organize armed resistance to Syria's godless usurpers.

Assad's ascent in 1970 was doubly offensive to the Brethren: Syria's new leader was not only a Baathist but also an Alawite, a minority sect that, according to Islamic tradition, had no right to rule. In 1973, only three years after Assad seized power from his fellow Baathists in yet another coup, riots erupted again throughout the country, especially in Hama. The protesters were particularly enraged that Assad's new constitution omitted the traditional requirement that the head of state be a Muslim. Assad, then weak and unsure of power, relented. The requirement was reinserted into the new constitution. But Assad took the precaution of securing a *fatwa* from a prominent Shiite cleric in Lebanon—the pragmatic Musa Sadr—ruling that the Alawites were, in fact, Shiites and hence Muslims.

All the while, the Brotherhood organized—in schools, in mosques, and underground. By the late 1970s an estimated ten thousand Ikhwan supporters were ready to confront the state. In May 1979 the Brotherhood tried to assassinate Assad as his convoy drove through the capital. The assault failed, but the Ikhwan's next attempt, the Aleppo Artillery School, was a spectacular success as well as a declaration of war on the regime. More than eighty mainly Alawi cadets were killed and a hundred more wounded when militant Muslims, led by the school's own drill commander, a Sunni Muslim, stormed into the dining hall at dinnertime firing automatic weapons. Because a Muslim Brotherhood sympathizer had locked all the doors except the one through which the Ikhwan had entered, there was no escape.[25]

Between 1979 and 1981, the Muslim Brotherhood waged a deadly campaign against Assad's state, murdering Baath Party officials, two of Assad's physicians, the rector of Damascus University, and the director of police and blowing up cinemas, ministries, and airline offices. In those two years, Islamic militants killed more than three hundred people in Aleppo alone.[26] Outraged, Assad was now powerful enough to respond.

In April 1981, Syrian forces swept into Hama in what one newspaper described as the "bloodiest retribution so far" in Assad's crackdown on opponents.[27] There was no resistance as the soldiers dragged men and even boys from their homes for what most Hamaites assumed would be a routine interrogation. Instead, between 350 and 600 young men were shot, their bodies picked up later by city garbage trucks and buried in pits at the edge of the city.

Retaliation reached its peak in 1982. In addition to their campaign in Hama, Syrian soldiers under Rifaat Assad, the president's brother, stormed Tadmor Prison early one morning and massacred five hundred Muslim Brotherhood inmates in their cells the day after an assassination attempt on Hafiz Assad. No wonder my trembling driver, a decade after the slaughter, was reluctant to drive past it.

I VISITED DAMASCUS briefly in the summer of 1971, but my first extended stay as a reporter was not until December 1983, following my depressing assignment in Beirut covering the U.S. Marine compound bombing and the growing Shiite militancy in southern Lebanon. At first, I was relieved to be in Damascus, to stay at a first-class hotel where the thud of shell fire and the rattle of automatic weapons no longer kept me awake at night and Americans were not being blown up or assassinated. But I soon found myself as tense in Damascus as I had been in Lebanon. I could not help noticing, for example, the plainclothes *mukhabarat* security agents in the lobby of the Sheraton Damascus, which is owned by the government and has long been the city's unofficial information center.

My favorite spy is still an agent who seemed to live in a three-piece black suit with bold red pinstripes. Mustafa, as his friends called him, would sit for hours in the leather divans of the hotel lobby, sipping coffee and fiddling with a strand of gold worry beads, trying without success to look nonchalant. Mustafa had apparently been assigned to watch Walid Jumblatt, the Lebanese Druze political leader and frequent visitor to Damascus, for every time Jumblatt left the hotel, Mustafa would heave his paunch out of the sofa to chase after him. Because Jumblatt was always in motion, the overworked Mustafa was highly visible. Liz Colton, *Newsweek* magazine's spirited Cairo bureau chief, used to harass the beleagered Mustafa by yelling, "Hi, Walid!" whenever she passed Mustafa's sofa.

The Soviets were a force in Syria in those days. Some four to five thousand lived in Damascus alone, though they kept out of sight in their fortified compound at the city's edge, since they, too, were hunted by the Muslim Brotherhood. Secular Arab socialism reigned in Syria at that time, and Baath Party members still referred to one another in the now-quaint jargon of Soviet solidarity.

"Under Comrade Assad's inspired leadership," Mohammed Heidar, the director of foreign relations for the ruling Baath Party, told Liz Colton and me in a rare interview with Western reporters in December 1983, many attempts had been made to unify the Baath Parties of Syria and Iraq, where rival wings ruled. But reconciliation had failed, he said, because Saddam Hussein feared Arab unity. Iraq, he told us, had constantly "conspired" with such "reactionary elements" as the Muslim Brotherhood to topple Syria's Baathist regime and to "suppress the will of the masses." Unity and victory would continue to elude the Arabs, Heidar predicted, until "that man vanishes."

I expected such bitterness to be directed at Syria's "eternal" enemies: PLO chairman Yasir Arafat, whom Assad loathed, and Israel, which had humiliated Assad by capturing the strategic Golan Heights during the 1967 war when he was defense minister. But the hatred between Damascus and Baghdad was older and more intense than that between more predictable, contemporary foes. The two cities had been vying for the seat of Arab power ever since the Umayyads and Abbasids clashed in the early days of Islam. Prompted in part by its hatred of Saddam Hussein's Baathist Iraq, Syria and Muammar Qaddafi's Libya were the only Arab countries to oppose Iraq's invasion of Iran in 1979 in the wake of the Islamic revolution in Teheran. Militant Iran had rewarded its Syrian ally with weapons, free and subsidized oil, and tourists — some two thousand Iranians a week who came mainly to visit the crypt of the Prophet's daughter Zenab in a gaudy mosque on the outskirts of Damascus. "We befriend according to political stands, not ethnicity or religion," Heidar told us, defending the alliance that had made Syria a maverick among Arab states.

For several years Syria had permitted Iranians to pass through Damascus into Lebanon to help Amal and Hezbollah, the Lebanese Shiite militias, fight Israel, he told us. But Syria had no fear that Hezbollah or other Islamic militants being trained by Iran would encourage religious unrest within Syria. Lebanon was not Syria. Lebanon's "confessionalism" — its sectarian power sharing — bred civil strife and unrest. "Syria," he said with satisfaction, "is a secular society, undivided by religious or sectarian slogans. Religion is for God; the homeland is for everybody. We won't tolerate anything else."

Heidar did not mention the regime's slaughter at Hama the year before. He did not need to.

By my next trip, in February 1984, security had become God. Syrians grumbled about the invasions of their personal lives, but they tolerated them not only because they had no choice but also because Assad had produced the stability that had eluded their country. Syria, its officials told me again and again in the official mantra, was stable. That meant much to people who had endured twenty-one coups between independence in 1946 and Assad's takeover in 1970. Syria had become so synonymous with coups, countercoups, and political chaos in those years that an Egyptian newspaper concluded that Syria was not a state but an insane asylum. "It became something of a ritual," recalled Fouad Ajami, the American scholar who had grown up in neighboring Lebanon. "Syrians became accustomed to waking up to the crackle of military music on radio and then a somber voice announcing: 'Military communiqué number one.'"

I got a taste of the chaos and bloodshed that Assad's absence might mean during that visit in February 1984. James McManus, a British journalist then writing for the *Guardian* of London, Jonathan Randal of the *Washington Post*, and I had bumped into one another in Amman and shared a taxi to Damascus, a three-hour journey. Seasoned in the ways of the Levant, Randal immediately sensed that something was wrong when we were held at the border for more than an hour despite our valid visas. The Syrian border guards and the stocky intelligence agents who monitored all Syrian borders seemed edgy. "I don't like it," muttered Randal, who even in his most tranquil moments could hardly be called calm. "Something's wrong."

By the time we reached Damascus, we knew Randal was right. An unusual number of Syrian soldiers manned the main road to the capital; the roadsides were lined with tanks, their tarpaulin covers removed. At a road junction near the city limits were hundreds of soldiers from the "Defense Company" brigades, a reinforced division of some fifty thousand soldiers headed by Rifaat Assad, the leader's brother who had overseen the Tadmor prison massacre and whose soldiers were responsible for protecting the capital. Normally, I couldn't tell one soldier from another, but Rifaat's elite troops were unmistakable in their tight-fitting pink-gray-and-green camouflage uniforms and cinnamon berets.

The Sheraton Damascus was deserted. On the far side of the huge traffic circle that led to the hotel, the roof of the Defense Ministry was piled high with sandbags. We could see rifle barrels protruding from them, pointed down at Rifaat's troops across the square. Eventually, we learned that we had stumbled on the first open split among the ruling elite since Assad had seized power in 1970. It had begun the previous November, when Assad was hospitalized for what Syrian officials initially described as appendicitis but which the embassy suspected was a heart attack. Assad had long suffered from diabetes, which was aggravated by his fondness for sweets and his chain-smoking. But clearly a major power struggle was under way whose outcome was uncertain. Syria was suddenly leaderless and hence panic-stricken.

Rifaat was furious that Assad had excluded him from the six-man committee that was to rule during his convalescence. Apparently at the urging of fellow military officers, Rifaat had decided to reverse this injustice. The man who had helped save Syria from militant Islamic insurrection only two years earlier had a right to succeed his brother. To make his point, Rifaat had redeployed his Praetorian Guard throughout the capital and had even moved surface-to-air missile batteries onto Kassyoun Mountain, which overlooked Damascus.

Speaking softly, McManus, Randal, and I exchanged notes at the bar later that night. We knew that we were witnessing a major story, but how could we report it? The telephone lines were bugged. Even hinting over the phone about a power struggle, much less an incipient civil war, meant expulsion or worse.

We could leave Syria and file stories from our home bases, but then we would not know the outcome of Rifaat's power play firsthand. Randal decided to leave Damascus after a day or two and not to write about the struggle. He had been banned from Damascus before. This time it would be permanent. An account could be written just as well by the *Post*'s diplomatic correspondent from Washington, with help from him. McManus argued that we had to stay to see how the crisis was resolved. He and I made a deal: I would remain until the struggle was over; he would leave Damascus at week's end. We would both file our stories on the same day. When he got to Amman, he would dictate my story to New York. And he would urge the foreign editor not to question me about it over the phone. I told McManus to ask the desk to make sure that my byline was not on the story and that the dateline was Washington, not Damascus.[28]

I felt abandoned a few days later as I waved good-bye to James and watched his dilapidated yellow taxi speed off toward the Jordanian border. I was now the only American reporter in Damascus, and the atmosphere was tense. But I tried to pretend that things were normal and told the Information Ministry that I wanted to stay on to write some pieces about Syrian culture: a squabble over the planned restoration of a part of the Old City; a profile of Tamara, an American belly dancer from Glendale, California, whom Damascenes (particularly Rifaat Assad) adored; and an article on Syria's cuisine that I told the minister Americans would enjoy.

I arranged to meet a Syrian source — Farid, I shall call him — the following day at the Nour Eddin bathhouse in the Old City of Damascus. I loved the old market, the Souk al-Hamidiyeh. I could walk for hours through the stalls along Straight Street, where Saint Paul was said to have undergone his conversion some two thousand years ago, a market as timeless as the street itself. Although many of the female shoppers in this determinedly secular state now covered their glossy black hair with head scarves, their beauty was evident. No wonder that Syrian women were the first choice of wealthy Gulf Arabs as second or even first wives. Boys carrying goods on their bicycles maneuvered through the crowds of shoppers. The souk's stands were piled high with sacks of herbs and spices, walnuts, pistachios, olive-oil soap, candles to commemorate almost any occasion — even circumcisions — finely carved and polished wooden boxes, bolts of silk and hand-spun cotton, rugs, gold, silver, and "antiques" of wildly varying authenticity, all described as "priceless" by the merchants, who sipped tea and gossiped about politics while making a sale.

The Nour Eddin bathhouse, which dated from the twelfth century, was still crowded with men when I arrived. Once there had been more than a hundred such establishments in Damascus, but the government had preserved only this one, with its mosaic tiles and marble fountains. I noticed at least one official I had met earlier in the day. An orange Nour Eddin towel was wrapped around his head, and another was tied like a sarong across his ample stomach —a tribute to Damascus's irresistible sweets. He was puffing contentedly on a Cuban cigar, one of the many benefits of Syria's "revolutionary" friendship with

Fidel Castro. As I was about to ask for Farid at the reception desk, he appeared and grabbed my arm, steering me silently to a nearby restaurant. Seated as far away as possible from other guests, he ordered a good bottle of wine, hoping that the secret police would interpret our rendezvous as a fellow Syrian's romantic encounter with a Western journalist.

By the end of dinner I had dragged some genuine news out of my reticent friend. President Assad, though still frail, had recovered from his illness. "*Al-Hamd ul-Illah* [thanks be to God]," Farid added. Hikmat Shehabi, the armed forces chief of staff and one of the few Sunni Muslims in Assad's inner circle, together with Shefiq Fayadh, a fellow Alawite and the head of the Syrian army's powerful Third Division, and Ali Duba, another Alawite who headed military intelligence, were all bitterly opposed to Rifaat's challenge. President Assad, it turned out, was also displeased by his younger brother's power play, which, he was persuaded, was American-backed. Assad had decided to teach his brother a lesson.

Later that night, I was asleep in my hotel when the phone rang. It was the foreign desk. "We have a few questions about your Syrian soup story," said Anne Zusy, then a desk editor.

"About what?"

"About that excellent piece you filed on Syrian soup," she replied.

"What are you talking about?"

"Your article on Syrian cooking, Judy. Your description of the soup in which all ingredients are mixed together to enable the strongest flavor to emerge."

"Oh," I said warily, "*that* soup story."

"Abe likes it. He may even put it on the front page, but he had some questions," she said, referring to Abe Rosenthal, then the executive editor. "Is this a good time to discuss the recipe?"

Anne had been given the thankless task of devising a way to ask me questions she knew I could not answer on the phone. She had succeeded, in a way. For the next thirty minutes, Syrian phone monitors were treated to a discussion of Syrian spices and soup ingredients as Anne tried to get me to clarify questions about the power struggle that I had described and that McManus, as promised, had dictated to the paper. Could I tell her whether the pink-gray-and-green vegetables were more or less dominant in the broth than other, more standard ingredients?

What the censors made of this I do not know. But I was not expelled from Syria. And the story ran without a byline, datelined Washington — and on the front page. And it appeared more or less as I had written it except for one dictation error. Because of James's reluctance to spell out each and every Syrian name, Ali Duba, Syria's military intelligence chief, would henceforth be known to *New York Times* readers as Ali Buba.[29]

Less than a week later, the crisis was over. According to Patrick Seale, Hafiz Assad had confronted his brother in an angry meeting at Rifaat's house. Unwilling to risk armed conflict with his brother, Rifaat had ordered his troops to stand down. Assad shuffled his cabinet and named three new vice presidents, including Rifaat. But what looked like a promotion for Rifaat was, in fact, a defeat, for he was forced to relinquish control of the Defense Company Brigades. Rifaat's friends were punished, too. Mohammed Heidar, the senior Baath official I had interviewed, whose daughter was married to one of Rifaat's sons, had his party membership "frozen"—the Syrian equivalent of a Siberian vacation.

Two months after the cabinet reshuffle, Assad sent Rifaat and a planeload of some seventy officers to Moscow for a cooling-off period. All but Rifaat soon returned to their posts. Rifaat, who reportedly owned land in Damascus, Paris, and even at the time in Potomac, Maryland, near Washington, D.C., went into luxurious exile in Geneva. General Tlas, the defense minister and Assad's ally since childhood, declared in an interview later that year that Rifaat was now *persona non grata* in Damascus.

IN FEBRUARY 1985, less than a year after Rifaat Assad's challenge, Syrians expressed their gratitude to Hafiz Assad by giving him a third seven-year term as president with 99.9 percent of the vote. Assad clearly enjoyed winning by that margin. In December 1991, Syrians again endorsed an unprecedented fourth seven-year term for Assad—by 99.9 percent of the 6.5 million Syrians eligible to vote and only 50,000 abstentions. There was, as usual, no opposition.

During the 1991 election campaign, in which Assad had never once spoken at a rally, I met a Syrian writer for drinks at the Sheraton, which, in keeping with Syria's determined secularism, displayed a giant Christmas tree and crèche in the lobby while "Jingle Bells" played on the hotel's loudspeaker.

"Even if Allah had run, he wouldn't have done as well," my friend complained. He was indignant about the campaign frenzy, the *bayaa*, as the referendum was called, an Arabic term referring to the pledge of loyalty that Islam's elders gave the Prophet Muhammad's successor. "This eighty-million-dollar show of devotion was truly revolting," he sputtered. "How many rallies and tributes could they stage to 'our father,' 'our savior,' 'our beloved,' the 'darling of the people'?" Even Syria's then tiny Jewish community of 3,800, whose numbers had stood at 100,000 in 1900, before mass emigration began, had been called upon to demonstrate their "love" for Syria's modern messiah.

The election had belonged as much to the Marx Brothers as to George Orwell. Assad was repositioning his traditionally pro-Soviet state toward America, but this resort to the electoral tactics of the defunct Kremlin could hardly enhance his standing in the West. Another Arab friend, a senior Arab official close to Assad, explained that despite the Syrian president's mastery of Middle Eastern politics, he knew little about the outside world, about Israel and America, in particular. Assad used to ask him about internal American and Israeli politics, but only when they were alone. A leader who was viewed as wily and omniscient as Assad was supposed to be could hardly afford to let his subordinates discover that their president had no idea how real democracies functioned or, as he once asked my friend, whether there was any substantive difference between Israel's Labor and Likud Parties. "He probably did not even realize that people accustomed to holding real elections might be offended by such a display," he told me.

Dr. Jamal Atassi, a former cabinet minister and one of the few opposition politicians permitted to criticize the government openly because of his participation in Assad's 1970 coup, insisted when I visited him at his cold, poorly staffed medical clinic that Assad had intended the election to be an insult. "It is his way of saying: 'You want democracy? Here it is.' It was his way of portraying Syrians as backward, as a rabble who should appropriately be ruled by a strongman."

The minister of information had another explanation. "Ten years ago," said Mohammed Salman, who sat in a silk-embroidered armchair in front of a giant holograph portrait of the leader, "when Muslim Brothers were assassinating officials in our streets, we couldn't have risked turning a million people loose in Damascus for election rallies. But today we did that, and not a single stone was thrown."

IN EARLY 1992, Mustafa Tlas, Assad's long-serving defense minister and friend, told me that Assad had begun repositioning Syria long before the Soviet Union's collapse, in fact, even before 1989, when Moscow informed him that it would not — indeed, could no longer afford to — provide him with weapons that would supposedly guarantee Syria's "strategic parity" with Israel. Assad had been particularly shaken by the collapse of East Germany and of Romania's Nicolae Ceauşescu in the late 1980s, Tlas said. Syria's ambassador to Bucharest had described Ceauşescu's fall to Assad in horrific detail, reinforcing the urgent need for a strategic about-face. The ambassador, Walid al-Moualem, had deeply impressed his boss: He was now Syria's ambassador in Washington D.C., charged, among other things, with overseeing the sensitive Arab-Israeli peace talks.[30]

The Gulf war had been a godsend for Assad. Ignoring the sympathy so many Syrians harbored for Iraq, Syria had sent twenty thousand soldiers to Saudi Arabia. Assad had made his critical decision to join the coalition in less than five minutes — astonishing speed, given his usual caution.[31] Since Assad had long detested Saddam Hussein and had denounced him since the early 1980s to Egypt's President Mubarak as "aggressive" and "treacherous," the Syrian president sensed in the crisis an opportunity not only to win Washington's favor but also to eliminate his durable Baathist rival and foe.

Assad had another reason to support Riyadh: Despite his insistence on independence as a hallmark of national dignity, Assad was loath to offend the Gulf Arabs who had generously supported him for so long. According to Selim Issa, my late Lebanese friend who had worked for Sudan's President Nimeiri and for Saudi intelligence, Syria had been receiving money from the Saudi royal family ever since the mid-1970s. Issa, a courier who claimed to have personally delivered Saudi checks to Damascus, told me how surprised then King Faisal of Saudi Arabia had been to discover how "cheaply" the Assad regime could be bought. "It only cost the Saudis twenty-five million a year," Selim told me, plus such "extras" as Assad's presidential palace, the austere, glass-walled fortress atop the mountain dominating Damascus that was used mainly on ceremonial occasions. In exchange for the millions that flowed into Syria's treasury and private Swiss bank accounts, Assad could usually, but not always, be counted on to side with Riyadh, provided Syrian national interests would not be adversely affected, according to Issa.[32]

The Syrians, as usual, were well rewarded for supporting Riyadh during the Gulf war. Although Syrian soldiers never fought at the front, their presence earned Damascus more than $1 billion in Saudi gratitude — roughly $100,000 per soldier. In return, American officials said, Syria had urged its ally Iran to be neutral toward the American-led effort and had given Washington critical information about planned terrorist attacks on Western targets, including details of a plot to assassinate the U.S. ambassador to Greece by blowing up the Athens embassy.[33]

Assad's challenge, according to his senior aides, was to adjust his country's policies without fundamentally changing the country itself, to adapt to an American-dictated world without relinquishing political control, and to continue exploiting what he saw as Syria's natural role as a power broker in the region.

This would not be easy. In a world of crumbling dictatorships and decentralized communications, of faxes and mobile phones that intelligence services found frustrating to monitor, Syria's autocratic, repressive regime was an anachronism, as antique as its staged election rallies, its frayed telephone lines, and the 1950s-vintage De Sotos, Packards, and Studebakers that rattled through the city's ancient streets and broad modern boulevards.

To redress the heavy-handed statist policies that had crippled his country's Soviet-bloc counterparts and to rejuvenate the economy, Assad had reluctantly embarked on tepid economic liberalization and privatization in the late 1980s. But because the regime could not risk a free banking and insurance system, Syria had attracted little foreign investment. And because of his regime's economic bungling and the widespread corruption of its ruling elite, Syria's middle class, once the largest and most entrenched of all Arab states — the backbone of any flourishing economy — was being steadily pauperized, as in Egypt. More than 40 percent of Syrian workers worked for the government, most of them earning salaries of about seventy-five dollars a month, not enough to live on. Second jobs were a necessity. Roughly 60 percent of the national budget still went to the military and security services.[34]

Unlike neighboring Iraq, Syria was no longer ruled primarily through visible terror but by the mere threat of it. Most of the regime's most committed opponents had been killed, driven out, or jailed long ago. The government no longer needed to act with brutality to make its point. "The most deadening censorship is now self-censorship," Mamduh Udwan, a witty and popular Alawite playwright, remarked over dinner one night at one of the city's few plausible French restaurants.

The more time I spent in Syria, the more I agreed with a clever Syrian scholar who argued that the Syrian regime depended on what he called a "merchant-military complex."[35] The Alawite ruling clique, which controlled the military and most of its four hundred generals as well as the vying intelligence and paramilitary services, needed the country's merchants to survive. The merchants had risen largely at the expense of the country's "traditional elite, the Sunni landowning aristocracy," he told me. This new bourgeois class of merchants and deal makers — many of them Alawites — had grown ever richer, often by bribing corrupt public officials for lucrative government contracts and other preferential treatment. "To this day, there is no Alawite producer class," the scholar said. "They have all made their money as deal makers and fixers. As long as they avoid politics, merchants are given enormous latitude."

Assad sensed that his regime would be destabilized by change that was too rapid or radical. The Soviet Union's demise had brought more than enough change, much of it unwelcome. Assad had lost Moscow's $2 billion a year in arms and soft loans. Though he had been given roughly the same amount from the Gulf states for his astute decision to support the American-led coalition that evicted Baghdad, that sum was a onetime injection, and he had spent it almost immediately. Syria's military had also benefited from the smuggling of drugs and other items in Lebanon, the world's largest producer of hashish, an estimated $2 billion a year business in the early 1990s. But Washington had insisted that Syria crack down on the drug trade in Syrian-controlled areas, and Assad, who felt he had no choice but to court the Americans, had to some extent complied. His oil exports, thanks to expertise from Western oil companies, totaled 500,000 barrels a day by 1994, with reserves estimated at 1 billion barrels. Even this windfall, however, would soon be exhausted by a birthrate of 3.7 children per family, which ensured a doubling of the population every fifteen years.

Even riskier from Assad's standpoint, modest economic liberalization might incite demands for more political openness, which Assad saw as suicidal. Hence, a man who was innately cautious had reason to be even more so.

PARTICIPATION IN the American-sponsored peace process was one of the many concessions Assad made to win Washington's favor. While Assad sent his foreign minister to the Madrid peace conference in October 1991 because he felt he had no choice, the Syrian president had concluded that there was little chance of an agreement. At best, he told a senior Arab leader at the time, he stood an outside chance of getting all his territory back, securing Western blessing for his "indispensable role" in maintaining stability in Lebanon, and hence continuing de facto control of land that was historically part of "Greater Syria" and winning political rights for, and the gratitude of, the Palestinians, 300,000 of whom lived without passports or citizenship in his own country. Though he initially feared that Washington might try to pressure him into making unacceptable concessions, he was gradually persuaded that Israel, then under right-wing Likud Party leadership, would not yield land for peace and that there was little danger either of such pressure or an accord. Moreover, neither the Palestinians nor Jordan would dare make a "separate" peace with Israel, as Egypt had done, until Syria's demands were satisfied.

While his delegates engaged in fruitless talks in Washington, Assad lost nothing. Indeed, he had gained a great deal: trade with the West, Arab cash, and time to solidify his hold on Lebanon. Assad could still lecture foreign visitors about the benefits of peace while championing the eternal Arab cause at home. He did not even have to abandon his long-standing support of international terrorism.

I recalled my interview in early 1992 — an audience, actually — with Farouk Sharaa, Syria's handsome, smooth-talking foreign minister. Born in 1938 and having graduated from Damascus University in English literature, Sharaa had also studied law at London University. Between 1963 and 1976 he was an executive at Syrian Arab Airlines, hardly traditional training for the country's senior diplomat but useful in his previous life with the *mukhabarat*. Sharaa's English was fluent and his manner beguiling when he wanted it to be. Like so many diplomats, he had perfected the ability to say nothing in many words. That day, however, Sharaa had a message to send Washington: Damascus was outraged that Washington refused to remove Syria from its list of countries that sponsored terrorism.

If Syria wanted to be removed from the terrorist list, I asked him, why was it hosting so many Islamic terrorist groups, some of which were even informally allied with the Syrian Islamists who had repeatedly tried to overthrow Assad's regime?

I had been brainwashed by Israeli propaganda, Sharaa replied coolly. Syria did not support terrorism.

If Syria was not a terrorism sponsor, which nation was? Damascus had been on the American terrorist list ever since the list's creation — for good cause.[36] Assad's regime had been involved in some of the worst terrorist attacks of the past two decades. In 1983, Syria had helped Lebanon's Shiite Hezbollah blow up the U.S. Marine compound without having been punished for it. Throughout the 1980s, Syrian agents had killed numerous opposition figures abroad, just as Libya and Iran had done.

Some of those Damascus helped were non-Syrian militant Islamic groups that, like the Muslim Brotherhood it had crushed at Hama, were trying to destroy Israel and overthrow their own secular Arab rulers in favor of Islamic states. Damascus and the Syrian-controlled Bekaa Valley in neighboring Lebanon were home to at least five radical Palestinian "rejectionist" groups — two of them Islamic. The most deadly branch of the Palestinian Islamic Jihad was now based in Damascus. In August 1994, less than three months before President Clinton's meeting with Assad in Damascus, leaders of Hamas had announced in the Syrian capital that Hamas and Syria had reached "a firm, clear stand on ways to confront the Zionist occupier." In October 1994, an Israeli official told me, the orders for a suicide bomber to blow up a bus in the streets of Tel Aviv during the morning rush hour had been issued from Damascus.[37] At least two leaders of Hamas, the Palestinian Islamic militants who reject peace with Israel, had moved to Syria after being expelled from Amman in the wake of Jordan's peace with Israel.

But while terrorism had long been Syria's favored blood sport, I knew it was pointless to challenge Sharaa's assertion that Israel was terrorism's true sponsor in the region. This was how Syrians viewed the long-standing Arab-Israeli conflict: They believed that the creation of Israel was responsible for most tensions in the Middle East. They believed, as Sharaa and his boss repeatedly asserted, that Syria had not provoked its wars with Israel, that Israel was aggressive and expansionist, and that Damascus itself was threatened. For Assad, support of such terrorism was a form of self-defense — as in Hama.[38]

Unlike Libya's Qaddafi and Sudan's Turabi, Farouk Sharaa did not deny the existence of terrorist groups in his country. Nor did he or his boss fear them: Islamic Jihad, Hamas, and the Popular Front for the Liberation of Palestine, whose secular Christian leader was now openly courting militant Islamic financiers, would never dare abuse the hospitality of their secular Syrian hosts — again, thanks to Hama.

ASSAD WAS CAUGHT off balance — indeed, infuriated — by Yasir Arafat's peace accord with Israel in September 1993.[39] The two men had loathed each other since 1966, when Assad briefly imprisoned the PLO chief for unauthorized political activities in Damascus. The feeling was mutual: Arafat never forgave Assad for having driven his PLO out of its comfortable base in Lebanon in 1982 during the Lebanese civil war.

Assad abandoned all pretense at calm when Jordan made peace with Israel in October 1994. In July 1993, after King Hussein and Israel signed an accord ending the state of belligerency between them — on the White House lawn at the Clinton administration's insistence — the Jordanian monarch had traveled to Damascus to assure Assad that he would not sign a formal peace treaty until Syria had negotiated its own agreement, a senior Syrian official told me. But now Hussein had betrayed him. Assad was livid.

In a visit to Cairo in late 1994, Assad denounced Jordan's peace treaty as "apostasy," an ironic condemnation from the leader of a supposedly secular socialist state that had repeatedly massacred Islamic militants. In private meetings Assad was even more bitter. Sadat had been assassinated after having made a separate peace, Assad told a visitor in early 1995. "Arafat could be killed tomorrow. And King Hussein could well wind up like his grandfather Abdullah — with a bullet in his head," Assad had said, leaving his visitor with the impression that his comment might have been a threat as much as a prediction.

But Assad was now trapped. His "brotherly" Arabs had moved without him. Most analysts thought that Assad no longer had a choice. As his old friend and ally Iran's Ayatollah Khomeini had been forced to do in 1988, he would have to drink from the "poisoned chalice" of peace — eventually.

Assad cautioned visiting envoys that he could not "rush" into peace: His country had to be prepared for such a radical change. Even after Madrid, the state-controlled Syrian press had avoided printing the name Israel, referring instead to "the Zionist entity," or "the entity," "occupied Palestine," "the usurper," and simply "the enemy." Making peace with Israel meant reversing a half century of propaganda depicting Israelis as pure evil.

I recalled my visit in 1993 to the capital's Ibn Khaldoun High School for boys, where the state-mandated curriculum included books that taught children as young as twelve how to assemble and dismantle automatic weapons to defend their nation against "the enemy." Another textbook not only showed Syria's old borders with Palestine, Lebanon, and the land north of Aleppo as part of the historic Greater Syria; it also highlighted great moments in Middle Eastern history, among them the 1983 suicide car-bomb attack by pro-Iranian Shiite militants on the U.S. Marine compound in Beirut that killed 241 Americans. Even by 1994, a handbook for Syrian teachers instructed them to tell students that the "liberation of the land occupied in 1967" was only "an intermediate goal."[40]

How would Assad's Syria, the "beating heart of Arab nationalism," as Nasser had called it, explain that peace with the Arabs' "eternal" enemy was probably inevitable? How could the leader who, in 1966, declared that Syria would "never call for nor accept peace," that he would "drench this land with our blood to oust you, aggressors, and throw you into the sea for good," now cozy up to Washington and fly the Israeli flag in Damascus? Preparing Syrians for the reversal of what had been an ideological pillar of his Baathist regime would not be easy, Assad had told a fellow Arab leader.

At Egypt's suggestion, Assad had enlisted some of Syria's wealthiest businessmen in the pro-peace campaign. Men like Badreddin Challah, the eighty-eight-year-old patriarch of Syria's most venerable Sunni business clan, and Saeb Nahas, a wealthy Shiite trader who was proud to be the largest exporter of women's chadors to neighboring Iran—a Syrian version of coals to Newcastle—had both expressed their enthusiastic support for Assad's peace the moment he signaled his desire that they do so.

The country's intellectuals, however, were a greater challenge.

SOMETHING OF an intellectual life had managed to survive in Syria despite the regime. Although many of the country's best writers and artists had been driven into exile long ago, some had refused to budge, risking harassment or worse, but providing Syrian culture with refreshing pockets of vitality. In particular, poets and their protest poetry retained their traditional popularity. University students in Aleppo, a more freewheeling commercial city than the capital, packed halls to hear such favorites as Ali Kanaan. At a dinner party in Damascus in 1992, Kanaan repeated his rendition of "Shards" for a small group of friends. The beautiful poem in Arabic, which suffers greatly, as does most Arabic poetry, in translation, appeared to attack Assad: "The King is made of glass," the poem begins. "His castles are of clay. But in his henhouse, rights are luxuries."

I asked Ali whether "the King" was, in fact, the president and whether the starved poultry were fellow Syrians. The room fell silent. Ali smiled with evident relief when our hostess suggested that we listen to a new cassette by a beloved Syrian singer. But when we were alone, Ali told me that he had written "Shards" as a protest against his own "crime of silence" about the government's outrages. The regime had not tolerated the publication of "Shards" in Syria; it had been published in Tunisia.

I had dinner a few nights later with Duraid Lahham, Syria's Woody Allen, a slapstick comedian and director whose films and television serials present often savagely satirical portraits of Arab life and politics. He explained that he and his scriptwriter, Muhammad Maghut, avoided censorship by criticizing previous regimes — "our own regimes think they look good by comparison," he said — and by never mentioning venue. "All of my signs, streets, and names are fictitious," he told me at a private screening of one of his films. "You can never tell in my films what country you're in. I called the site of one of my films ArabCarlo; in *Borders*, a film about a young Arab who loses his passport and is trapped between two 'brotherly' Arab countries, the countries are called East-stan, Weststan, Norstan, etc.," he said. "I called the Arab League Allstan. Because there is so much corruption and tyranny in the Arab world, audiences in each Arab country invariably believe my film is about them!"

Lahham was permitted to work thanks to the influence of a powerful fan: President Assad. "I met him in 1969, before the Corrective Movement, when he was still defense minister," Lahham recalled, using the regime's stilted jargon for the coup. Assad had come to see a scathing play about politicians that Lahham had staged at the Damascus Theater Festival. Some officials had urged that the play be banned and that all the actors, including Lahham, be imprisoned. "But Assad told them that we were 'revolutionary' actors who should say whatever we wanted," the director said. "He invited me to his office to discuss my other ideas for plays. After he came to power, the president made a point of coming to most of my openings — just to make the actors feel safe."

Nevertheless, some of Lahham's work has not been shown in Syria, and much of it was banned in other Arab countries that dared not tolerate the criticism of Islamic radicals that was sanctioned by the state in Syria. In Bahrain — generally regarded as far more tolerant than neighboring Saudi Arabia, where all theater is banned as un-Islamic — local censors insisted that Lahham delete a line from his play *Wildflowers* before they would permit it to be staged. The offending passage concerned the relationship between God and man in Islam. A character in the play asks why religion makes man fear God, why God was inevitably portrayed as jealous and angry, smiting mankind with floods, volcanoes, and plagues whenever he was displeased. "I told the censor: 'I'm not afraid of God, and I'm certainly not afraid of censors and other self-appointed demigods.' As you might have guessed, my play was not performed in Bahrain."

Lahham blamed Syria's heavy-handed censorship not on Assad or on his long-serving minister of culture, Najah al-Attar, the only woman in the cabinet — whose brother is still a leading Muslim Brotherhood ideologue in Germany — but entirely on the "demigod bureaucrats."

"They outdo each other in poetic obsequiousness," Lahham complained. "One television producer shows five minutes of the president, so his successor shows seven minutes the next night; the third, fifteen minutes; and so on." I thought about the loony presidential election campaign I had recently witnessed. A few days before the voting, Assad had appeared on the balcony of his modest villa to greet his fans. That night, twenty-three minutes of Syria's thirty-minute evening news program was devoted to Assad, on his balcony, waving to the crowd but uttering not a word.

"Bureaucrats hate original ideas," Lahham said. "In fact, they hate ideas. They only feel comfortable with orders. If a mayor likes fountains, the city builds them everywhere; his successor does the same with trash bins. When a Baath Party official visited Vietnam in 1967, he noticed that streets were lined with concrete ditches where people hid during American air raids. So when he returned to Damascus, he built concrete-lined ditches and barriers along our streets. No one has ever hidden in them, of course, but we are still tripping over them."

Mamduh Udwan, the Alawite playwright who had complained to me about intellectual self-censorship in Syria, told me that the government itself had loosened up since the Hama massacre, sensing that it no longer faced a serious challenge to its rule. But, of course, there was still no play about the Hama massacre. Besides, people were now so preoccupied with the daily struggle to make ends meet that they had little time for protest. "Disappointed people are easier to govern," he said. Nevertheless, three of Udwan's plays were banned in Syria, and none had yet been published there. He had little hope that things would improve. "Anything but yes-men are considered opposition. If you stick to what's allowed, you have no problems. But then again, you have no theater."

Neighboring Lebanon, even under Syrian occupation, still had theater. It also had jokes, like the one about the two Lebanese dogs. One decided to go to Syria to flee the war in Beirut. A week later, he returned. "What's the matter?" his canine friend said. "Didn't you like Syria?" "I liked it a lot. There was no fighting; food was great," the second dog said. "But after a while I wanted to bark."

Sadallah Wannous, one of my favorite Syrian playwrights and social critics, told me that Syrian officials tolerated some of his more critical work because it enabled them to show the West that Syrians enjoy freedom of expression. "My very existence is propaganda," he said. I had first met Wannous, who is also an Alawite, in early 1992, after Syrian censors had banned his play *The Rape*. "Do you know that *Al-Thawra* and *Al-Baath* newspapers are barred from even publishing my name?" he told me. "Like Israel, I am an abstraction."

His play's political sin was that it contained a sympathetic and hopeful dialogue between the author and an anti-Zionist Israeli psychiatrist. I was struck by Wannous's boldness to include an Israeli in his play, but even he could not bring himself to create a sympathetic Jew who believed in Israel's right to exist.

This was the paradox: Syrian intellectuals, long in the vanguard of Arab nationalism and ever faithful to its empty slogans, could hardly contemplate the prospect of peace with the nation they had long denounced for having raped and occupied Palestine (stolen from Greater Syria), invaded neighboring Lebanon, humiliated Arab pride, and debunked the sacred dream of Arab socialism and renewal.

Not only was Arab nationalism one of the last pillars of Hafiz Assad's legitimacy; it was Syria's own home-grown religion. Arab nationalism was born in Damascus. Its founders and leaders had been Syrian intellectuals. Baathism's creators were two Syrian schoolteachers — Michel Aflaq, a Greek Orthodox Christian, and Salah al-Din al-Bitar, a Sunni Muslim — both of whom had attended the Sorbonne and were determined to bring to their native soil the Western nationalism they had learned there, along with Western development. For Aflaq, Arab nationalism was also a way of legitimizing Christians, about 8 percent of the Syrian population, as full-fledged, first-class Arabs rather than submitting to Muslim assertions that being Arab meant being Muslim. No, said Aflaq: Islam was the most sublime expression of Arabism, not the other way around. Islam flowed from the genius of Arab history and civilization. There was no contradiction between them. His was an ideology, as one analyst described it, that was "all things to all Arabs."[41] Above all, it was vague. Because Arab nationalism was "spiritual," it would not clash with religion, he wrote. It was racial in that "we hold sacred this Arab race." It was revolutionary in that it sparked "hope in the soul." Its imperatives were three-pronged and sounded good in Arabic slogans: "Unity, Freedom, Socialism."

Aflaq was equally opaque about the nature of the pan-Arab socialism he and Bitar peddled, in particular, about how it should be translated into concrete policy. "When I am asked to give a definition of socialism," he wrote, "I can say that it is not to be found in the works of Marx and Lenin." Socialism, he continued, was "the religion of life, and of its victory over death." By giving work to all and helping everyone develop his talents, "it keeps the patrimony of life for life, and leaves for death only dried-up flesh and scorched bones."[42] The words were fetching, particularly in Arabic, but what did they mean?

While Aflaq and Bitar were euphoric when Baathist military officers seized power in 1963, only three years later these thinkers — however wanting — had been pushed aside by soldiers. By 1972 the military had gained "complete control over the party, remoulded it, and fashioned it into an obedient instrument," according to Itamar Rabinovich, an Israeli expert on Syria who, as Israel's ambassador to Washington, now oversees Syrian-Israeli peace talks. "Their tragedy," he wrote of Aflaq, Bitar, and other political reformers and ideologists, "was that cooperation with the military was at one and the same time indispensable and self-defeating."[43]

After a rival wing of the Baath took power in Iraq in 1968, Aflaq was given a place of honor in Baghdad as the party's founding father, a trophy intellectual whom Iraqi Baathists could lord over their Syrian Baathist brothers who had forced him into exile. In my visits to Iraq in the mid-1980s, Aflaq was the only man whom Saddam Hussein would honor each year with a presidential visit.

But Aflaq died in this exalted exile and never saw his native Syria again. Bitar, Baathism's other founder, was assassinated in 1980 by Syrian agents in Paris as he campaigned against Assad's regime.

Though Syrian intellectuals were unable to criticize their own society, they had been encouraged to criticize foes. With glee, they had savaged militant Islam and Israel. And despite countless political disappointments, most still believed in the bankrupt ideology that the regime pretended to hold dear and the goals, however muddled or simplistic, that had shaped them. It was too painful for many of them to renounce their secular, socialist faith by endorsing peace with their historical enemy, an Israel that would continue occupying much of Palestine. To change their views was tantamount to rejecting whatever remained of their political identity, repudiating their very soul. It also meant failure of the Arab and Baathist cause, of the Christian dream that non-Muslims could claim equal status with Muslims in an Arab state, and of the movement whose motto was "One Arab Nation with an Eternal Message." Suddenly, the message had changed.

While I respected the courage of my Syrian intellectual friends, I had to acknowledge that many of the most ardent proponents of liberalization and democratization within Syria were also the harshest critics of Syria's participation in the Gulf war on Kuwait's side and the American-brokered peace with Israel. Udwan, the playwright, for instance, was among sixty intellectuals who had signed a petition protesting the American bombing of Baghdad during the war. Sadiq al-Azm, Syria's best political philosopher and a leading defender of Salman Rushdie, had denounced America's intervention as an imperialist plot while he was a visiting scholar in Washington. Duraid Lahham, the film-maker, complained that Israel was inherently aggressive. It was "shameful" that 150 million Arabs were no match for Zionism, that they had been forced to call upon the United States to balance and pressure Israel. "We are in an impossible situation," Lahham told me one night: "War is suicide, but peace is surrender."

Intellectuals, moreover, were not alone in their hostility to peace. Resentment was widespread in 1994, even among many younger businessmen. Thaer Lahham, Duraid's son, an ambitious entrepreneur, echoed Egyptian anxieties by arguing that Israel wanted to accomplish through peace what it had failed to win through war. If peace prevailed, Israel would launch an economic invasion: a cultural, political, and tourist offensive that would crush Syria's soul. Like his father, Thaer had been enraged as he had watched first the PLO's Yasir Arafat and then King Hussein of Jordan declare an end to war with Israel. "Arab dignity suffered by what they did," he said. "It was humiliating."

In theory, young entrepreneurs like Thaer had the most to gain from the economic liberalization and reduction in Islamic fervor that peace promised the region. Unlike most Syrians, these privileged sons of the establishment were educated; they had traveled; they knew the world; they had been as pampered as Hamaites had been pounded. They had "connections," what Syrians called *wasta,* or "vitamin W"—access to capital to start new businesses and buy imported cars, modern phones, fax machines, and satellite dishes that were still officially banned in Syria, but not for the rich and well connected. They could frequent discos that blared the latest MTV tunes on giant screens and watch American movies on private VCRs; they could cut through much of the state's red tape that drove so many businessmen to despair and their capital out of the country. Yet despite their apparent worldliness and commitment to secularism and free enterprise, many members of this young Damascene elite still viewed their region and Israel through the traditional lens of the Arab-Israeli conflict. Even they could not escape fifty years of propaganda. The slogans of Arab nationalism had been stamped on their hearts. Never, said Thaer, would he shake an Israeli's hand; never would he do business with an Israeli company.

Perhaps their fear of Israeli domination was not so surprising or unrealistic. More than most Syrians, these entrepreneurs understood their country's weakness. Israel's population was less than half that of Syria's, yet its gross national product was almost three times as large. In a country that had yet to build its first supermarket, much less a stock exchange or a computerized banking system, Syrian businessmen feared being devoured economically by their dynamic neighbor. They knew firsthand the suffocating consequences of the government's chronic extortions and its unwelcome interventions in the private sector. Although commerce had boomed since Assad embarked on his hesitant economic liberalization, most wealthy foreign and Syrian businessmen were still reluctant to invest in Syria.

Among ordinary citizens, quiet resentment of their own economic plight, of Syria's abandonment of them and its socialist tradition, and of peace talks with the Arabs' eternal enemy was reinforced by the aging regime's corruption and the special place afforded Alawites. While Assad prided himself on living simply, charges of smuggling and corruption in high places were rampant. His brother Jamil, as well as Jamil's sons, were said to be major smugglers in Latakia, the Alawite stronghold in northwest Syria. The scale of the problem had gotten so large, one Syrian friend told me, that Hafiz Assad had sent his eldest son, Basil, into Latakia in 1993 to clean house and restore order. Rifaat, Assad's brother, had been permitted to return to Syria from exile in 1992, although he was not truly politically rehabilitated. But he, too, had continued to profit handsomely under his brother's rule.

Before his fatal auto crash, even heir apparent Basil Assad was known to have had substantial business interests, among them, Syrian friends asserted, the resale of cars stolen from Kuwait during Iraq's occupation and the Gulf war.

In Malki and other posh Damascus suburbs, the villas of senior military men, and those of their sons, were readily identifiable not only by their bodyguards but by the brand-new Mercedes parked in front of them. There were now more Mercedes 500s in Damascus than in Germany, a Syrian friend complained. Anger over the car shortage, in particular, was widespread, as most Syrians relied on dirty, dilapidated taxis that picked up several passengers on a route rather than the city's ancient, even more cramped and decrepit public buses. In 1994 there was one car for every ninety-seven Syrians, among the lowest ratios in the Middle East.[44] So severe was the shortage that the thousands of candidates who ran for seats in Syria's People's Assembly, a rubber-stamp parliament with virtually no power, did so mainly because assemblymen were given a new car.[45]

Members of Assad's ruling clique insisted on making themselves partners in everyone's new business, whether an automobile assembly plant, pharmacy, or hotel. Only those already in league with the government—the sons, or in a few cases the grandsons, of Assad's cronies—were willing to risk capital on something new.

I thought about the city's disheartening restaurants. The government was theoretically promoting tourism. Any Syrian with sufficient cash or the connections needed to get a loan from the government-owned banks could open a restaurant. On paper it should have been a good investment, given the middle-class Syrian's passion for good food and revelry and the shortage of sophisticated restaurants catering to this class. Yet the number of passable restaurants had hardly increased since my early trips to the capital. A business friend explained why: "You always have a silent or not-so-silent partner here," he complained. "It's hard to make money if someone is taking between ten to thirty percent of your profits off the top. Why bother when I can invest in France?"

As a result, most new Damascus restaurants were run by the "sons of the revolution," as they were sarcastically known, or the "Abu and Sons Club," *abu* meaning "father of." The Sahara, for example, was reportedly owned by a son of Rifaat Assad; Le Villa, another popular restaurant, belonged to a son of Hikmat Shehabi, the military chief of staff. The son of Shefiq Fayadh, another senior army commander, was also in the restaurant business.[46]

Bitterness about payoffs to military officers was also widespread and building. I recalled my previous visit in early 1992 to Madaya, a picture-postcard mountain town near the Lebanese border where the shops had been piled high with boxloads of smuggled goods from Lebanon. But after a local wood smuggler had refused to make his routine payoff of some six hundred dollars a week to a local army commander, the military had cordoned off the town and rampaged through its shops to teach town residents a lesson.

No one seemed to have a reliable estimate of how much money the Syrian military took from smuggling in Lebanon, which it occupied. But one scholar valued black-market sales of imported cigarettes alone at $1 million a day.[47] In response to American complaints about Syrian drug smuggling and Syrian-supervised counterfeiting of hundred-dollar bills in Lebanon's Bekaa Valley, Assad began reining in those responsible for the most egregious abuses in early 1994. But the bulk of the smuggling and stealing continued: Assad would not alienate the military and security services, his only reliable and indispensable base.

The ruling clique was not bound by Syrian laws affecting mere mortals—

yet another source of anger. Syrians complained bitterly about "untouchables" like Ribal Assad, Rifaat's youngest, twenty-something-year-old son. Ribal had shocked Damascus by obsessively pursuing a young woman whose father wound up sending her to study in Geneva to avoid young Ribal's attentions. They also complained about the son of Ali Duba, the intelligence chief, who Syrian businessmen said was running with a wild gang that included some young car thieves. President Assad himself, a prominent Syrian confided, had finally ordered Ali Duba to do something. Duba sent his son abroad until the furor subsided.

THE PEACE PROCESS was stalled in mid-1994 as I headed off for a Friday lunch with well-to-do friends at their country home in Zabadani, a fashionable retreat in the Syrian foothills, near the Lebanese border, about thirty miles from Damascus.

The day was cold, the air fresh and clean after the smog of Damascus. Travelers throughout history had praised Damascus's beauty. But modern times had not been kind to the ancient city. A century ago, its population was 150,000; today it approaches 4 million. Syria's birthrate, among the highest in the world, meant that even with growing oil exports the government would be hard-pressed to provide jobs and housing for the thousands of new university graduates each year who looked to the state to meet their perhaps inflated expectations. Despite massive investment in education, nearly a third of the population was still illiterate.

Compounding the effects of population growth, Syrians, like people in most developing countries, had flocked to cities in search of jobs, education, and excitement — to Damascus, in particular. Whereas less than a third of Syria's population were city dwellers in 1970 when Assad seized power, more than half of all Syrians now lived in cities. Damascus's population was growing at 15 percent a year; the city could not build housing fast enough. During my first trips to Syria twenty years ago, the land between Damascus airport and the capital was mostly empty. Today gray cement apartment blocks sprawled across land where neat rows of crops once grew. Syrians now faced daily power shortages. Tap water, rarely reliable in these new instant slums, had become so brackish that those who could afford to do so drank bottled water and even cooked with it. Most of these new neighborhoods were surrounded by piles of rotting garbage: tin cans, discarded food, broken wire, dead animals, and the ubiquitous empty blue plastic water bottles.

Yarmouk refugee camp, home to thousands of Palestinian refugees from the 1948 and 1967 wars, was near these ugly new suburbs. Yarmouk had electricity, but the state made no pretense of providing a sewage system or other basic services. While the leaders of the Palestinian rejectionist groups lived in relative comfort, their foot soldiers inhabited these ramshackle stucco and cement boxes, struggling to survive. Syria, like most Arab states except Jordan, had never given its Palestinian "guests" citizenship. Most children in these camps lived pathetic lives, stateless, amid filth and squalor. The last time I visited Yarmouk, I had interviewed a traumatized family. Their twelve-year-old son had been arrested by the *mukhabarat*—the camp's only efficient service—as he was preparing to spray a graffiti slogan on the dreary cement walls. It would cost the Palestinian family the Syrian pound equivalent of thirty thousand dollars in bribes to get him freed and six hundred dollars just for the right to visit him in jail. Since the average Syrian earned about fifteen hundred dollars a year—and Palestinians made considerably less—the family was in despair. But for Syria's nearly 300,000 Palestinians, this cruelty was common.

Our hosts in Zabadani, whom I shall call Karim and Nadia, were a planet removed from such woes. Zabadani was an elite resort; freshly painted villas on well-paved roads dotted the hills. Nadia's major worry was whether the day was warm enough to serve her fine Oriental spread outdoors on the terrace: her hummus, or chick-pea puree in local olive oil; baba ghanouch, the ubiquitous eggplant with oil and sesame paste; muhammara, a savory red dip made of walnuts, garlic, peppers, and paprika; and kishke, dried, fermented yogurt with green onions and garlic. Syria was no place to diet.

Friday luncheons were a hallowed Syrian tradition, relaxed and unharried. More than a dozen well-to-do Damascenes, many of them owners of similar well-appointed villas in this expensive enclave, had come on this glorious spring day to chat, gossip, and enjoy Nadia's excellent cuisine.

The talk on the terrace was of commerce and peace. I asked our hostess and a small group of women seated near her about religious militancy at Damascus University: More than a third of the young women I had seen on campus the previous day were wearing head scarves. Did such Islamic dress suggest sympathy for the Muslim Brotherhood or antipathy toward the regime?

The women fell silent. Nadia frowned. "It's only fashion," she said, a little too quickly, I thought. When I got up to get more juice, she leaned over and squeezed her sister's hand. Over lunch I asked her sister Nadine why my question had troubled her. Nadine, an elegant woman in a Pucci-style silk blouse and expensive Italian trousers, had been educated in Europe. Fluent in English and French, she ran a major travel agency in town. She and her husband were prominent, part of the elite. But suddenly this affable, witty woman seemed hesitant.

"I'm sure the head scarf is, well, as my sister told you, just a fashion statement," she said, pushing an errant strand of her well-coiffed, streaked blond hair behind her ear. "But maybe it's more than that. Perhaps these young people are searching for meaning, for identity, for a way to live an honorable life. I'm sure it's not a threat to the government. Not at all."

How did she know that? I asked her.

Nadine's mouth tightened. All at once she looked a decade older, beaten down with worry. "Because my daughter—my only daughter—is one of them."

Suddenly, the words flowed in torrents as the saga of her daughter's conversion poured out. It had started at the university, she told me: Her daughter came home one day and simply announced that she wanted to wear Islamic dress, that she wanted to live a "Muslim life."

"She said to me: 'Mama, we *are* Muslims! I want to live as Muslims.' So she threw away her blue jeans and T-shirts, all her cosmetics, her American music and videos. She stopped seeing her old friends. She avoided our Friday lunches and went to the mosque instead, and not the state mosques where our friends go. She began praying all the time. She encouraged us to fast during Ramadan, to observe Islamic holy days. Suddenly, my house was filled with young women I had never known before. They all wore head scarves, long dresses, and thick socks with those clumsy shoes.

"I'll never forget the first time I saw my daughter put on the head scarf. I thought of my mother, of how hard she had fought to take off her veil, to get a job, to have her rights. And here was my own daughter, voluntarily putting on a head scarf. I couldn't help it: I started to cry. But when her friends saw her, they embraced her and cheered: '*Mabrouk!*' Congratulations. And I realized that she was happy, that she had found what she lacked."

So Nadine had tried to understand and not to alienate her only daughter, though it was clear that both she and Karim were terrified that the *mukhabarat* might misinterpret her new Islamic fervor—or perhaps see it correctly—as a form of rebellion. At first, Nadine had hoped her daughter's Islam was just a passing phase. "But when she married one of them," Nadine continued, "I knew it was not. She found her husband herself. Karim and I didn't even know his family! Now they lead what they call Islamic lives: She studies computers at university and teaches part-time. He is a teacher, too, when he's not praying. We don't see them as much as I would like, as much as we would if she weren't —well, the way she is. But I have tried to keep them part of our family—despite our differences. She doesn't enjoy spending time with people who aren't like her."

Everyone in the room clearly sympathized with Nadine. She would never have any of the things a middle-class Syrian mother yearned for: no grand wedding party and traditional white dress with diamond tiara for her daughter, no silver-framed photos of the happy wedding couple in tuxedo and bridal gown on the coffee table and fireplace mantel, no belly dancers wriggling on a stage and champagne that flowed till dawn. Perhaps Nadine's friends, too, had daughters or sons who had rejected them, who secretly despised them for the compromises they had made to win the favor of Assad's cruel and soulless regime. For if the daughter of such pillars of the Damascene bourgeoisie could succumb to the power of Islam, who was immune?

BY THE SPRING of 1994 the Assad regime was in the midst of what its official newspapers called in Arabic "the battle for peace." Despite the lingering hostility of his Arab nationalist intelligentsia and his regime's persistent support for militant Islamic groups that sponsored terrorism in Israel, Assad was pressing ahead with the talks he considered vital to Syria's national interest.

During my previous visits, Assad's expressions of his sincere desire for peace to visiting dignitaries had not been echoed in what he told fellow Syrians. Each concession, including the granting of exit visas to Syria's remaining Jews and the release of more than four thousand political prisoners, some of whom had been held since the early 1970s, had seemed aimed primarily at winning Washington's favor.[48] The unrelenting invective against Israel made me wonder then whether for Syria peace negotiations were merely the continuation of war by other means.

Now the mood in Damascus had shifted. Syria was openly trying to reassure Israelis as well as the United States of its peaceful intentions. Smartly painted billboards throughout the city talked of the need for peace rather than "confrontation." Peace was no longer described as "imposed." "We Work for Peace," declared one popular sign; another improbable billboard depicted Assad in a field of wildflowers with a dove over his shoulder: "Assad, the hero of peace, is waging peace the way he once waged war," the slogan declared. Syrian television provided uninterrupted coverage of Jordan's declaration of peace with Israel, including Rabin's prayer in Hebrew as well as Israel's rapprochement with Morocco and Tunisia. The Syrian press was finally ordered to stop calling Israel the Zionist entity. Syrian cartoons, a favored form of political expression in Arab culture, no longer depicted Jews as evil creatures with hook noses and Nazi uniforms, unlike the cartoons in Egypt. And suddenly Syrian officials were meeting American Jewish leaders they had once shunned and even granting interviews to Israeli reporters to discuss what Assad had called his "peace of the brave" — an interesting reference given its use by de Gaulle to signal France's withdrawal from Algeria in 1962.

But this was not the only stunning change I noticed in 1994. In this most determinedly secular of states, new mosques were being built throughout the country. Assad was increasingly being shown on television meeting with Syria's senior Islamic scholars, men appointed and paid by the state. A State Department expert noted the growing number of allusions to God and Syria's "Islamic" heritage in official speeches, including those by President Assad. Even Rifaat Assad, the "butcher of Tadmor," had supposedly "embraced" Islam. Now sporting sandals and a trim little beard, Rifaat was often found at local mosques, praying and preaching. What was going on?

According to veteran Assad watchers, the Syrian president was demonstrating yet again the political dexterity that Arab and Western diplomats alike had long admired begrudgingly. Assad knew his country, they said. Above all, he knew that while he was feared and respected, Syria's Sunni Muslim majority remained privately bitter about being ruled by "lentils," an Arabic acronym for the vegetable "adis," or a, d, and i, the first letters of the Arabic words for Syria's minority sects: Alawites, Druzes, and Ismailis. A relentless worker and good listener despite his reclusiveness and failing health, Assad sensed that many Syrians were having trouble adjusting to his new world order.

The Arabs had a proverb to describe the way Assad had ruled since Hama: the "hair of Muawiyah." According to legend, the first Umayyad caliph to rule from Damascus had once told his advisers that if the only link between himself and his people were a single strand of hair, the strand would never be broken. Each time the people forcefully tugged at it, Muawiyah would let go; and when the people finally relaxed their grip, he would pull back the strand. Assad, a Jordanian friend had told me, was the modern Arab world's only "Umayyad" ruler.

Assad was proud that he, an Alawite outsider, ruled Damascus, the first capital of a great Sunni Islamic empire outside of Mecca, this ancient citadel of Sunni Islam. While he had repeatedly proved that he was not just another son of an Alawite maid, that it meant death to disobey him or even question his word, he also sensed the political utility of paying homage to Syria's historic preeminence in Arab Islamic history. Before Moscow's collapse and the Gulf war, Assad had championed Arab pride through secular nationalism, cultivating his image as a modern-day Saladin wielding the Arab community's sword in its sacred mission — reclaiming Arab land, along with his nation's dignity and honor. Islam had mattered little in the heyday of radical, secular Arab national-ism. But now that communism and Arab nationalism were dead and military engagement was futile, Assad was trying to bolster his Islamic legitimacy while pressing forward with the American-sponsored peace process. Assad's Islam, of course, was not the resurgent, anti-Shiite brand of the Sunni Muslim Brother-hood, which would defy him again if ever permitted to do so. Nor was it the rebellious Islam promoted by his radical ally Shiite Iran and by Hezbollah in neighboring Lebanon despite similarities between his own Alawi doctrine and Shiism. Assad's Islam was King Fahd's of Saudi Arabia and President Mubarak's of Egypt, the quiescent, order-based Sunni Islam that stressed a Muslim caliph's authority and enjoined believers to obey his every command no matter how distasteful or bitter. Just as Sadat had fallen back on Islam when he embraced America and later made peace with Israel, Assad was now extolling the virtues of Islamic obedience to his own "straight path." The man who had prided himself on his secular credentials and his cold-blooded determination to crush religious militancy whenever and wherever it threatened his regime, the leader who had lectured President Mubarak on the need to crack down harder on his own Islamic militants, was now reaching for Islamic cover.

Assad's goal was not only to fill the void created by the death of the "ism" that Syrians had long espoused but also to co-opt what under some circum-stances might be potentially dangerous opposition. Assad had no fear that his "manipulated" Islam would boomerang, as it did for Sadat: The Egyptian pha-raoh had no Hama in his arsenal. Nor would Assad ever tolerate the proliferation of militant student groups that Sadat had sanctioned. Moreover, Damascus was not complacent. The government intensively monitored every vital sign of the Islamic resurgence taking hold in Syria. In 1992 the government had even considered forming an Islamic party to channel the growing Islamic fervor into a group that could be controlled. But nothing had come of it. The regime concluded it did not need to risk a religious-based party, that its more Islamic veneer was enough. But was it?

•

IT WAS ALMOST SUNSET by the time I arrived at a spacious villa on the outskirts of Damascus for an interview with the man who embodied official Islam in Syria: Sheikh Ahmad Kuftaro, the grand mufti. I was escorted into a vast garden beside the house where Sheikh Kuftaro — Ph.D., his card stated — was seated on a large Oriental carpet under a fruit tree. He was surrounded by a dozen students, bearded men and covered women who, judging from the ecstatic expressions on their young faces, were devouring each sacred word.

The mufti greeted me through a translator and apologized for not rising. He was more than seventy years old; his legs were stiff after lecturing for so long. Though seated, he seemed tall. He had shrewd eyes, a long white beard, and very large ears made to seem larger by his small white skullcap.

While his students looked on, I asked him to explain the cause of the Islamic revival in his region. Arab Muslims, he began, had been living too far from Islam. They had developed and prospered but had not found inner peace. Men who lived in fear and terror could not be happy. Was the grand mufti implicitly criticizing Assad's regime? I wondered.

Despite efforts at development, he continued, Muslims, in general, were backward. But so were Jews, Christians, Buddhists, and others who had wandered too far from their faith. Look at the sophisticated weapons we had produced — evidence of our fear of fellow men and of ourselves. Islam, he said, had always been tolerant of Jews and Christians, the Koranic "Peoples of the Book."

Had Syria been tolerant of its Jews? I asked him. Why, then, had virtually all of them left when Assad finally gave them the chance to do so? Kuftaro eyed me suspiciously. An aide approached our carpet and bowed low as he delivered a bunch of freshly cut flowers from the mufti's lush garden. Kuftaro sniffed them and then gave half to me.

In Syria, he said, Jews, like all citizens, were free. For more than fifteen centuries Jews had lived under Islamic rule. There had been no pressure against them; their rights and property had been protected. They had sought freedom and dignity in the Islamic world when they had been persecuted during the Inquisition in Spain.

Some of what the sheikh said was true but not relevant to my question. "If Syrian Jews chose of their own free will to abandon this country, we have no right to prevent them from leaving," he said. Many would probably return, he predicted, without stating from where. "I hear they are not very happy."

Had the Islamists of Iran been tolerant? I pressed further. Was Iran's persecution of the Baha'i faith in keeping with the tolerance he ascribed to his religion? The Baha'is, after all, were not "Peoples of the Book," but a post-Islamic faith. As such, they were entitled to no Islamic tolerance, and, in Iran, had received none. Kuftaro shifted nervously as another aide delivered more flowers. The sun was setting quickly, and the birds above us were growing ever noisier with the twilight. "Islam gives full freedom of belief to all faiths on one condition: The faithful must not conspire to destroy the structure of Islam." The Baha'is, he declared, "worked against the state, the structure of Islam."

Was there any justification for the forced conversion to Islam and other forms of persecution of Christians in Sudan, another ostensibly Islamic state? I asked. There was no such persecution, Kuftaro insisted, irritated. Reports of such things I had seen firsthand were "malicious propaganda by opponents of Islam."

Was Syria sufficiently Islamic? I continued, dispensing with diplomatic caution. After all, Syria was not ruled by sharia, Islamic law. Kuftaro was now deeply displeased. More flowers arrived. This time he offered me none.

Syria's secularism helped people of all religions. "So all people are happy under this state. The state helps me and all Muslims by building mosques and licensing Koranic academies, by building roads and power plants and working for the general welfare of all Syrians." The state and the church, he said, were "two wings of a bird." They worked together; they were "mutually supportive," he declared, endorsing Islam's traditional role.

This was the role that Assad wanted the mufti to play. He had always supported, and would always support, the state or any regime in power. No wonder his Islam held so little attraction to Nadine's daughter and to other young Muslims who craved justice and economic equality. Kuftaro's Islam was as despised by the Muslim Brotherhood as Assad's secularism. I recalled that Sheikh Kuftaro was grand mufti during the 1982 Hama massacre.

What about Hama? I asked him. Was the massacre justified?

Now Kuftaro was really angry. A student sitting on the edge of the carpet gasped. Even the chattering birds seemed to fall silent.

"Christians were not mistreated in Hama," he said slowly. "And those Muslims — they were wrong to contest the rule of law. Whenever the state and the rule of law are challenged, he who breaks the law must be punished."

But was it ever legitimate to challenge the state? I continued. Militant Islamists argued that true believers had a duty to overthrow a non-Islamic government. When was a Muslim obliged to rebel against the state?

"That is a very political question," he said, rising quickly with the help of his aides. "I thought you came here to discuss religion." His other assistants began collecting the flowers that had fallen from his lap as he rose and were now strewn over the carpet. My interview was over.

INTELLECTUALS AND OTHER diehard Baathists were as disgusted by the mosque building campaign, the encouragement of "Assad Koranic schools," and Syria's new piety as they were by the peace talks with Israel.

"Look around you," said Jamal Atassi, the dissident whose dingy clinic I always visited when in Damascus. "Suddenly we have 'a believing president' who assures us that Syria will be victorious becauses he trusts in God.[49] Is anyone fooled by this?"

In the early 1980s, Atassi complained, he and other Baathists had urged the president to combat militant Islam by broadening participation in his regime. That had not appealed to Assad. "His response was Hama," Atassi said, "and then using the Muslim Brotherhood as a pretext to imprison all opponents, even many of us who had urged dialogue. Some are still in jail!"

Assad's Islam would not persuade young, alienated Syrians who were seeking answers to questions that cynical Baathists had stopped even trying to answer. Would anyone see Rifaat Assad's Islamic fervor as anything other than a ploy to broaden his political constituency beyond the soldiers whose loyalty he retained?

Christians and other minorities, moreover, were also anxious about Syria's new Islamic face. Even with Assad as their champion, many had fled. A decade ago, Kamishli, a town I had visited on the Turkish border, was more than half Christian; by 1994 the Christian sector was deserted.

But the chagrin of intellectuals and Christians mattered little to Assad. He knew that most of them still viewed him as Syria's sole guarantor of stability and its only reliable bulwark against the Islamic militancy they feared even more than another Hama massacre. While few could bring themselves to abandon their secular faith and shift political ground with their president's dazzling flexibility, Assad knew they would never oppose or even criticize him publicly. They had been cowed, and politically they had no place else to go. As I left Atassi's office, I realized that in more than an hour of blistering criticism of the regime, Atassi had never once mentioned Assad by name.

So FAR THE SCOURGE of Islamic militancy had returned only in the form of isolated cells. As late as 1989 the former American ambassador to Damascus, Edward Djerejian, recalled having filed a cable to Washington about an incident that winter in the foothills of Mount Kassyoun, not ten blocks from the American embassy, in the heart of Damascus. On a chilly morning, Syrian police had surrounded a house and through megaphones ordered its inhabitants to surrender. When the anonymous Muslim militants inside refused, the police and army units opened fire, demolishing the house with rocket-propelling grenades and machine-gun fire and presumably its inhabitants—Hama style. Predictably, not a word about the attack had appeared in the press.[50]

Few diplomats or scholars, however, detected a "threat" to the regime from radical Islam. In fact, there were almost no serious calls for political reform of any kind in Syria, said David Waldner, a professor of government who had studied at Damascus University. The only public demand for liberalization—other than from Atassi—came from the Muslim Brethren in Germany and expatriate Syrians in France, a tiny group of aging exiles without an indigenous base of support. Liberalization to date had served mainly to solidify the authoritarian regime's rule by making it slightly more responsive to public needs. Perhaps a future generation of Syrians would demand political inclusion and pluralism—or even Islam—but what most Syrians still seemed to crave was stability.

The regime's political rigidity might encourage greater spirituality and religious fervor among alienated young Syrians, but as long as the trend remained unorganized, Assad's regime had little cause for alarm. Certainly Assad had nothing to fear from sheikhs like Kuftaro, whom he himself had appointed mufti two decades ago. Unlike the ulema of Saudi Arabia, who at least theoretically shared power with the House of Saud and whose Islamic stamp of approval the ruling family required to be truly legitimate in the eyes of its citizens, Syrian religious leaders were the state's creatures; they posed no threat. Indeed, by encouraging traditional, apolitical Islam, the regime seemed to be successfully channeling potentially revolutionary opposition into harmless vessels.

While militant Islam did not threaten Hafiz Assad, Syrians were increasingly worried about what would come after him. Of course, the regime was building mosques, said Jamal Atassi, articulating this concern. What else had Assad built? "Hotels, highways, statues of himself! But in terms of the human spirit, nothing—not democracy, not even real state institutions. Our state has no core. That's why I am afraid," he said. "When he dies, what will happen to us? Anarchy? Civil war? A militant Islamic state?"

Syrians had spirit, genius, creativity, he asserted. But the president had crushed it all. Nothing was left. Another Syrian friend, a painter, had compared art in Syria to masturbation: Both were done secretly, alone in one's home. I also recalled what my friend had told me about the colossal Assad statues at the entrance of Syrian towns; two of the three artists who specialized in making these Stalinesque monuments came from Hama.

Some Syrians hoped that Syria might enjoy democracy after Assad died. Among them was Colette Khoury, a writer and Christian who was elected to Parliament as an independent. Khoury, whose grandfather had been a Syrian prime minister, was an avid Assad champion. Thanks to him, the Islamists would never "roll into Damascus" and take over. "Never! Syria is not Sudan! We are the heart of the Arab world, the beating heart of Arab nationalism." But since no one could ever replace as "gifted and strong" a leader as Assad, she told me, her black eyes twinkling, Syrians might have to fall back on "democracy" when Assad died. Spain's Franco was her model. Perhaps her strongman, too, would lay the groundwork for a pluralistic society. But was that realistic? Syria had even less history of democracy than Spain and no monarch to safeguard what would inevitably be fragile institutions. Very few Syrians seemed to believe that Western-style democracy would stave off chaos or a Muslim Brotherhood victory, given Syria's history. If history and Islamic tradition were any indication, democracy was not a likely successor to Assad.

"He will die at his desk," a Jordanian associate of Assad's had once predicted. And as Assad was dying, my friend told me, he would be asked, as was Alexander the Great, to which of his generals he would leave his kingdom. Assad's reply was bound to be the same as the Greek's, my friend said: "To the strongest among you."

Through Hama, Assad had ensured that in his lifetime a Muslim Brother would never be able to make that claim. No one could know whether his successor would be able or willing to say the same.

Jordan

```
┣┫ ▓▓▓▓▓▓▓▓▓▓▓▓▓▓▓▓▓▓▓▓▓▓▓▓▓▓▓▓▓▓▓▓▓▓▓▓▓▓▓▓▓▓ ┣┫
```

A SALTY WIND blew across the desert from the Gulf of Aqaba. The heat shimmered above the yellow sand. On a temporary stage in the middle of Wadi Arava, a barren border strip between Jordan and Israel, stood King Hussein, a small man in a business suit who appeared even smaller next to the taller men next to him — Prime Minister Yitzhak Rabin of Israel and, the tallest of all, President Bill Clinton.

The noonday sun beat down on the five thousand Jordanians, Israelis, Americans, and Arab dignitaries invited on October 26, 1994, to witness the signing of the peace treaty between Jordan and Israel. Not even the official sun hats — red for Jordanians and their guests, white for Israelis — could protect us from the heat. Bill Clinton's eyes teared, not from emotion but because the tinted sunblock he was wearing for television had dripped into his eyes. Rabin, the only leader wearing a sun hat, shifted uncomfortably in his chair.

Only King Hussein looked truly serene. As he rose from his chair and stepped to the podium, he beamed at the crowd. Many a frustrated adviser had tried to write speeches for him, but Hussein, as usual, spoke without notes. "Friends," he said, gazing out at the euphoric crowd, "this is a day like no other."

The king deserved his reputation for eloquent understatement. But this was no day for understatement. In my twenty-five years of covering the kingdom, I had often hoped for a day like this. But until the Gulf war, I had never expected to see one.

By the fall of 1994 I had attended so many of these incredible events — the October 1991 peace talks in Madrid between Israel and its Arab enemies, the September 1993 accord in Washington between Israel and its archenemy the PLO, and the "end of the belligerency" agreement between Jordan and

Israel in July the following year, again in Washington—that the word "historic" had gone flat. But the ceremony at Wadi Arava was far more poignant for me. For the first time, Arabs and Israelis were signing a peace treaty on their own soil. This was not a truce or the "cold peace" that Egypt had made with Israel in 1979 or even an official peace between states, but as the king called it, a peace "between peoples," an unambivalent peace, at least on the part of those who came to witness it. It was also a peace between two men who had met secretly over many years, two soldier-leaders who respected each other, a peace made by a king who was not embarrassed to be photographed lighting his former enemy's cigarette, a peace without shame.

Finally, it was the first peace on Arab soil that I had ever been able to share with my friend the Israeli journalist Smadar Perry. Smadar was as unsentimental a reporter as I had ever encountered in a region known for such people. But as we stood side by side watching Jordanian and Israeli senior military officers lay down their guns and exchange salutes, and then gifts, I thought I detected tears in her eyes. Realizing that I had been watching her, she pulled her red Jordanian cap down firmly over her long blond hair and pushed back the sunglasses that had slipped down the bridge of her nose. "Dust," she said.

The road to Wadi Arava had often been tortuous. At times, King Hussein had despaired about this elusive peace. But he had always told me that we would live to see such a day. "This is my crowning achievement," he told Smadar and me two days before the ceremony.

How had we gotten to this point? And in a region filled with such irrationality and bitterness, would the peace hold? Could any of us have imagined that only a year after the exhilarating ceremony at Wadi Arava, King Hussein would travel to Jerusalem to eulogize his murdered "brother, colleague, and friend"? That the militant's bullet which Hussein had for so long dreaded would strike Yitzhak Rabin, his "partner in peace," instead? Or that the assassin would not be a frenzied Islamic militant but a middle-class Israeli Jew—a law student— who would echo his zealous Islamic counterpart's conviction that peace was a "betrayal" of his religion and his people?

Within Jordan, an even larger group saw the "king's peace," as they now derided it, as treachery—a sinful betrayal of Islam and Arab history. Would Jordan's militant Islamists or the more mainstream Muslim Brotherhood, until recently King Hussein's tactical allies, wreck what he considered his greatest accomplishment? Would the peace ensure stability in his troubled land?

Even King Hussein could not know. He trusted in God, he told me after Rabin's funeral. For after all, the peace of Wadi Arava in 1994 was but one of several miracles that had taken place in this unpromising strip of land the size of South Carolina, seven-eighths of it desert. Under Hashemite rule, Jordanians had witnessed several miracles, perhaps the greatest of all being the very existence of such a stable, prosperous Jordan in this most barren of lands.

JORDAN'S SPLENDID ANTIQUITIES attest to a time of prosperity and splendor, but they are, indeed, ruins, many of them still buried under eras of sand. Relatively little is known about the land of modern Jordan before the third century B.C., according to Kamal Salibi, the Lebanese historian.[1] But throughout the ages, the land had been a crossroads for all "natural highways" of the Middle East. That made Jordan strategic, which meant being fought on or over.

During the Hellenistic period, a desert people known as the Nabateans built Petra, the ancient trading city hidden deep within a mountainous fold at the edge of the Great Rift Valley not unlike Arizona at the approaches to the Grand Canyon. Petra's awesome classical columns, porticos, cupolas, cavetto moldings, and lintels surrounding caves were carved into the base of towering pastel-colored cliffs three hundred years before Christ's birth.

Strabo, the Roman historian who visited the city in the first century B.C., praised the Nabateans as "a sensible people," merchants "so much inclined to acquire possessions that they publicly fine anyone who has diminished his possessions"—in other words, spiritual ancestors of the commercially minded modern Jordanians and other Levantines. But in 106 C.E., Rome absorbed its territories, with this lucrative trans-Arabian caravan trade, into its "Provincia Arabia." Nabatean civilization gradually declined, and the city "half as old as time" was forgotten about—literally lost until the early nineteenth century, when an eccentric Swiss explorer stumbled upon it while traveling with Bedouins.

Islam rapidly took hold in the seventh century as Muhammad's Arabian tribes swept through the Jordanian highlands. As sea trade between the Indian Ocean and the Mediterranean grew at the expense of the caravan routes, the region's fortunes declined, and the pilgrimage road through Jordan to Arabia became the main source of income along with the meager agricultural and pastoral economy. Once prosperous towns floundered; cities became villages and then desert. In the sixteenth century, Jordan was a remote backwater of the Ottoman empire, but as the great Islamic empire weakened, "Bedouin anarchy" spread, Salibi wrote. The land was rescued from chaos and obscurity by World War I, when a traveler, a Hashemite whose family was destined to stay and rule, crossed into Jordan on the Hijaz railway.

BETWEEN 230,000 AND 300,000 PEOPLE lived in Transjordan in 1920 when Abdullah bin Hussein, the second son of King Hussein ibn Ali of the Hijaz, the "sherif," or religious guardian of Mecca, arrived intent on becoming a king.

Transjordan was a comedown for a family as ambitious as the Hashemites —recognized descendants of the Prophet Muhammad who aspired to re-create and rule a modern Arab empire.

There are two versions of Hashemite history: the family's tragic, idealized account (which is still gospel to Jordanians and many Arabists) in which these first Arab patriots were betrayed by Britain and robbed of what was rightly theirs; and what Fouad Ajami, the scholar, calls the "unsentimental" tale of a minor family of proud lineage from Arabia that overreached and wound up with far less than it desired.

According to official Jordanian history, Abdullah's father, King Hussein (the great grandfather of the present king), led the Great Arab Revolt against the German-allied Ottomans in 1916, a campaign glorified in modern times by David Lean's gorgeous film *Lawrence of Arabia*. In exchange, the British promised him financial aid and arms, the liberation of all the Arab provinces from Ottoman rule, and eventual independence. There is little doubt that Britain reneged on its promises to Hussein. But what Jordanian history omits is that the Great Arab Revolt was less impressive than its name. Most Arab Muslims perceived Hussein as a British lackey and deplored as blasphemous his effort to destroy the Islamic empire in Istanbul on behalf of the West.[2]

However dubious its motives and origins, Kamal Salibi argues, the revolt would not have generated such enormous enthusiasm had it not reflected "genuine national feelings." And whatever its military shortcomings, the Arab Revolt was a political watershed, a demarcation point in modern Middle Eastern history that embodied the longing of Arabs in so many different parts of the Islamic, but non-Arab, Ottoman empire for autonomy and self-expression.

In 1920, two years after Hussein's son Feisal entered Damascus, a Syrian Arab congress proclaimed him king, and Abdullah, Feisal's older brother, king of Iraq. Prince Ali, the eldest of Hussein's sons, would briefly succeed his father as ruler of the Hijaz. But none save Abdullah would endure.

In the landgrab of postwar politics, British promises to the Arabs were broken. In the secret Sykes-Picot agreement of 1916 — approved four months before Hussein launched his Arab revolt — England and France had divided up the Arab Ottoman territories for themselves. Britain got colonial control of Palestine and Iraq, while France took Syria and Lebanon. In 1920, France occupied Damascus and forced "King" Feisal to flee.

To protect against French encroachment of British interests in Palestine, Britain had excluded from Syria the desert and mountainous region east of the River Jordan, the land that became Transjordan. In 1921, Colonial Secretary Winston Churchill carved out the emirate of Transjordan, agreed to finance it with a modest subsidy, and gave it to Abdullah in return for his relinquishing his claim to the Iraqi throne he had been promised. A few months later, Britain created a monarchy in Iraq, which they offered Feisal as consolation for having lost Syria to France.

Hashemite setbacks continued. In 1924, Abdulaziz Ibn Saud, the Great Ibn Saud, aligned with the militant Islamic Wahhabis, drove Sherif Hussein from Arabia. Saudis are fond of telling visitors that when Hussein left Jidda for exile in Cyprus, his ship nearly sank from the weight of the gold on board.

Further losses followed: Feisal's grandson and namesake was killed in a bloody coup in 1958 in Baghdad, ending the Hashemite claim to Iraq and its delusion of a great empire. In less than forty years the family that had ridden British coattails to power had lost Syria, Arabia, and finally Iraq. By the mid-

1950s, all that remained of the grandiose Hashemite vision was an impoverished thoroughfare: Abdullah's Transjordan.

ABDULLAH — AND DESPITE his rarely discussing it, probably Hussein — never stopped pining for an Arab Hashemite empire in "Greater Syria." But even securing his own Transjordan was difficult. Relying on enormous charm, Abdullah slowly built a kingdom and a British-funded and -trained "Arab Legion" to put down the revolt of the Bedouin, who constituted almost a fifth of Transjordan's original inhabitants.

When Jordan was created, it had no real cities or natural resources, few roads, fewer schools, almost no electricity, no hospitals, and a handful of skilled men. Only one of Abdullah's first cabinet was Transjordanian; the others were fellow Hijazis from Arabia or Druze, Palestinians, and Syrians.[3] Abdullah knew he needed the loyalty not only of the Bedouin but also of such minority groups as the Muslim Circassians whom the Ottomans settled in the region after the Russians drove them out of the Caucasus in the 1870s. To this day, the blue-eyed, fair-haired Circassian Muslims, in their tall black fur hats and black woolen military coats, guard the king's palaces. Abdullah also recruited civil servants and businessmen from Palestine. Ambitious young men came to this frontier — Christians, like the Kawars from Nazareth, who arrived in Salt in 1926, opened the country's first pharmacy, and a decade later discovered phosphates, Jordan's largest export.[4] (The Kawars now control much of the country's shipping and tourism.) Although the descendants of these pioneers were Palestinian, they had long been considered "East Bankers" by modern Jordanians, equal in standing and loyalty to the inhabitants of Transjordan when Abdullah arrived. This is but one of the many factors that complicate estimates of Jordan's Palestinian population.

Devout Muslims, too, were attracted by Abdullah's policy of inclusion. According to Sheikh Muhammad Abdel Rahman al-Khalifa, the former Brotherhood comptroller general, Muslim Brotherhood activity in Jordan began as early as 1934, twelve years before Jordan's independence from Britain. But most analysts date the founding of the Jordanian Brethren to 1945, when a wealthy Jordanian merchant who passionately opposed Zionism opened the Brotherhood's first branch in Amman.[5] Abdullah, a shrewd and sophisticated man who had spent his youth in the cosmopolitan world of Mecca and prewar Istanbul, knew that the Brethren could be useful but also dangerous. Secure in his own Islamic credentials, he extended his patronage to the Ikhwan, while stressing at the opening of the Brethren's general offices in 1945 that he expected them to "stick to the mosque and to prayer."[6]

Though Abdullah dreamed of establishing a "Semitic Kingdom" on both banks of the Jordan River where Arabs and Jews would enjoy equality and autonomy under his rule, he knew early on he would have to deal with the Zionists settling in Palestine. As one scholar put it, Abdullah may have underestimated the tenacity of the Zionist movement taking root across the Jordan

River, "but he knew a going concern when he saw one."[7] As early as 1926, Abdullah invited Zionist leaders in Palestine to help him develop his own country. In succeeding years, he made deals with Zionists for electricity, chemicals, and even leased them land. By 1937, he had concluded that the Jews could not be prevented from establishing a state in Palestine.[8]

In 1946, Abdullah and the Jewish leadership agreed informally that Abdullah would not oppose the creation of a Jewish state if the Zionists supported his rule over the Arab parts of Palestine.[9] David Ben-Gurion, the Zionist leader who became Israel's first prime minister, nicknamed the two states "Judea" and "Abdallia."[10]

After war erupted in Palestine between Jews and Arabs in 1948, Abdullah invaded the newborn state of Israel, insisting that Jews accept autonomy under Jordanian sovereignty instead of their own independent state. Ben-Gurion never forgave Abdullah for going back on his word.[11] While Abdullah's Arab Legion respected informal limits, it fought far more effectively than the other Arab forces sent to "save" Palestine.[12] Few Palestinians today acknowledge the debt they owe the Arab Legion: Without Jordanian forces, "Arab Jerusalem" and much of the West Bank would probably have fallen to the new Jewish state.

Abdullah and the Israelis began negotiating even before the fighting stopped. Together they blocked a UN plan to internationalize their Jerusalem. Abdullah, intent on consolidating his hold on Palestine as a first stage of what he hoped would be the eventual recovery of his father's kingdom in Arabia and Syria, tried to make peace — a final settlement with Israel. But his cabinet rejected the deal he had negotiated. Israel, too, preferred the armistice agreements it reached with its neighbors in 1949 to a full peace that would have required substantial Israeli withdrawal from newly acquired territory and other major concessions.[13]

Abdullah's dealings with the Jews enraged his rivals, men like the rigid Palestinian cleric Haj Amin Husseini, the inherited mufti of Jerusalem who admired Hitler and eventually found political refuge in Berlin. But Husseini's impassioned rhetoric could not mask the effective collapse of Palestinian society — the voluntary and Jewish-induced flight of its middle and professional classes — long before the worst of the fighting was over. After blocking an Egyptian plan to make Mufti Husseini responsible for all of Palestine, Abdullah organized impressive gatherings of Palestinians, which included Muslim Brethren, to approve Jordan's annexation of Arab Palestine in 1948, formalized in 1950.[14] Unlike the Arab states that rejected Abdullah's "union" of the Jordan River's East and West Banks, the Brethren, stressing the unity of the Muslim umma and refusing to recognize separate Jordanian and Palestinian nationalisms, supported the annexation.

Abdullah became what one scholar called the natural "scapegoat" for the flight of Palestine's upper and middle classes, the incompetent Arab armies of Syria and Egypt, and the "panic and shame" over the Arab debacle in Palestine.[15] The Arabs preferred to blame Abdullah than themselves for history's devastating verdict. While praying at Al-Aqsa Mosque in Jerusalem in 1951, Abdullah was assassinated by a tailor's apprentice, a Palestinian and former employee of the mufti. His fifteen-year-old grandson, Prince Hussein, was at his side.

IN HIS AUTOBIOGRAPHY, King Hussein, the first Hashemite whose roots were in Jordan, described the hardships of his childhood in the new capital and the political traumas of his youth. Jordan was poor; so was his family. His baby sister died of pneumonia "in the bitter cold of an Amman winter."[16] The family house had no heat and only one bathroom.

The young Hussein was always closer to his grandfather than to his father, Talal, who was afflicted with schizophrenia that became ever more severe. Abdullah's murder forever marked Jordan's future king. Israelis who attended the first secret meeting with Hussein in London in 1963 recalled what one called Hussein's "obsession" with the assassination. Since that day, he has shared Abdullah's emotional commitment to the Arab cause but also a healthy skepticism of his fellow Arab rulers. While Hussein listens to advice from all counselors, he makes his own decisions. And since that day, he has carried a gun or kept one in his car's glove compartment, his desk drawer, or under his pillow — always a short reach away. I must have blanched the first time I saw him strap the revolver into a shoulder holster as he was about to drive me back to my hotel. He smiled reassuringly and told me not to be alarmed. "It's most unlikely that we will need it." But he often did.

The name Hussein is synonymous with assassination attempts. He has given up counting them, he told me. There was the Syrian attempt in 1958 to shoot his plane down as he overflew Syria to Europe; there were poisoned nose drops, a servant who tried to stab him in bed, a cook who tried to poison him, killing several palace cats instead. There was the bomb planted in his prime minister's office on the day of a scheduled visit in 1960 and the numerous coup attempts, beginning with the 1957 revolt organized by the supreme commander of his army, Ali Abu Nuwar. Hussein had pardoned them all. Abu Nuwar, in fact, later served as Jordan's ambassador to Paris and died a senator. No one can remember a political execution in Jordan. Hussein's legendary tolerance was not simply a matter of character: He knew, as did the Al Saud, his historic tribal rivals in Arabia, that mercy had political virtue. Revenge murder in Arab culture triggered blood feuds and, in a country as small and tribal as Jordan, could only mean more violence and discord. Kamal Salibi had an equally plausible explanation for the king's preference for forgiveness: Hussein could afford to pardon former assailants because his opposition was generally as weak and ineffectual as the Senate to which he appointed so many of them.

The king has always relished physical, if not political, danger. As if the extraordinary challenge of sheer survival has not been sufficient, he parachutes, flies stunts in his jets, and races his Porsche and other high-performance cars and motorcycles through the desert. He also savors that most addictive of dangerous Middle East pastimes: smoking. Risk has become second nature to him, he told a journalist—"what water is to fish." [17]

"Those early years were hard for me," King Hussein once told me as I played copilot on a flight to Aqaba. "I was not even seventeen when I became king—far too young. I made so many mistakes. I learned late."

What he learned early was that many of the Arab brothers whose national cause he ostensibly shared considered Jordan an anachronism in their new Middle East. A year after Abdullah's assassination, Gamal Abdel Nasser seized power in Cairo, and a wave of Arab nationalism, of radical socialist and anti-Israeli slogans and passion, engulfed the region, toppling monarchies in Egypt, Libya, and Iraq. The coup in Baghdad particularly unnerved Hussein, for his cousin King Feisal had been gunned down in his palace along with another cousin, whose dismembered body was then dragged through the streets of the capital by a blood-crazed mob, a harbinger of a new, more brutal Arab era. With hysterical mobs manipulated by military men in the name of the Arab nation and its "masses," the Hashemite Kingdom of Jordan, as Transjordan was called after independence in 1946, was a constant target of derision and assault. In such an environment, Muslim Brethren support was particularly welcome.

Surrounded by enemies, Hussein quickly grasped that Jordan could ill afford the progressive measures enacted in the early 1950s or his open reliance on British subsidy and John Bagot Glubb (Glubb Pasha), the British general who had trained his army.

To survive, Hussein made the first of what one American scholar calls the king's "strategic" decisions.[18] In 1957, after firing Glubb Pasha, which temporarily enraged Britain, he abandoned the liberal measures he and his father had adopted, declared martial law, and called out the army against his own people. Once again, the Muslim Brotherhood stood with the young and then vulnerable king, preferring the relatively benevolent "Muslim" protector to the secular radical nationalists ruling in Egypt and threatening other Arab states. Brotherhood ties to the king were further strengthened by Nasser's ban on the Ikhwan in Egypt and Gaza, which Cairo then ruled, and the Egyptian president's imprisonment of more than six thousand Brethren following an assassination attempt on him. Some of those who fled found refuge, as had the Palestinians, in Jordan and the West Bank, which Jordan controlled. So when Hussein was threatened in 1957 by government paralysis and street riots, the Brothers joined Hussein's army in beating up leftists and others who challenged the regime. When the king banned all political parties that same year, only the Muslim Brotherhood, registered as a "charitable" organization, was permitted to continue its political activities.

A year later, however, Hussein did not hesitate to jail many Brethren as part of a general crackdown on political activity when he summoned British troops to protect him. While the Brotherhood continued organizing protests against Britain's presence in Jordan, it did not abandon Hussein. However wanting, a Hashemite descendant of the Prophet was still preferable to the godless nationalists whose secular doctrine was taking hold throughout the Middle East.

As British influence gradually faded in the region, America slowly, and to some extent reluctantly, replaced England as the king's protector.[19] Hussein's relationship with the CIA dates back to 1957, Jordanian and American officials say, when the agency helped foil yet another army coup plot. According to an authoritative source, ties between the CIA and Hussein were cemented in 1958 when American intelligence officials in Washington learned that a coup plot involved Jordanian diplomats in the American capital and warned the king. The conspirators — more than twenty in all — were arrested and, of course, later pardoned by Hussein. The warnings, coupled with monthly checks from the CIA, helped persuade Hussein that America would be a reliable ally. (The payments ended in 1977 when their public disclosure embarrassed Hussein.)[20]

In the summer of 1958, Washington paid the salaries of the Jordanian army that, along with British troops, protected Hussein. It also ferried oil to Amman across Saudi Arabia after Syria and Iraq closed their borders with Jordan. When the Saudis denied permission for the overflights, the vital cargo overflew Israel, an early instance of indirect Israeli assistance to the embattled king. The sale of Hawk missiles to Amman in 1960 reflected the growing importance of Jordan to Washington. During the Jordanian civil war ten years later, Washington prepared to intervene to prevent Syrian and Iraqi forces from entering Jordan on behalf of the beleaguered Palestinians, and also urged Israel to commit air and ground forces as well. As a result, Damascus recalled some 250 Syrian tanks that had crossed into Jordan. By 1971, America had agreed to help rearm the Jordanian military. The Jordanian-American alliance was sealed.

I FIRST MET King Hussein during my first stay in Jordan in the summer of 1971, just as the protracted civil war between the Jordanians and the Palestinians was winding down. Those were desperate days for the country and its king. In 1967 he had lost control of the Palestinian West Bank to Israel through his rash alliance with Nasser's Egypt in the Six-Day War, a disastrous "strategic" decision. The Arabs' crushing defeat had prompted the rise of the PLO, which Egypt created in 1964 to champion Arab efforts to restore Palestine. After 1967, Jordan became the natural base for PLO raids against Israel and as such, the target of Israeli reprisals. Gradually the fedayeen, the PLO guerrillas, came to see Hussein as an obstacle to their struggle. Jordan, the more militant believed, should be led by radical Arab nationalists like those in charge in Cairo, Damascus, Tripoli, and Baghdad. Hussein and the Hashemites were an embarrassing anachronism. PLO chairman Yasir Arafat, the darling of the Left in the Middle East and the West, began challenging Hussein's control.[21]

As the pressure grew, Hussein hesitated. His advisers offered conflicting advice: Some, especially the army, urged him to act before the PLO became too strong; others warned that confronting the PLO would incur Arab wrath and undermine support among Jordanians of Palestinian origin, who even then constituted half of the kingdom. Jordan, unlike other Arab countries, had not only taken in several hundred thousand Palestinian refugees during the 1948 Arab-Israeli war and 380,000 more after the 1967 debacle; it had given them citizenship, passports, and in theory, equal legal standing. Amman had offered the same to all Palestinians in the *ghourba*, in Arabic, the Palestinian diaspora. In fact, almost 40 percent of all Palestinian refugees had found refuge in Jordan, making Amman the world's largest Palestinian city. While the king suspected he could not depend on their loyalty, he was reluctant to resort to action that would split his society.

While Egypt and Syria incited nationalist fervor in Jordan, the Arab media glorified Arafat and the PLO. The king was in despair. In a broadcast to London on the BBC in February 1970, he gave an interview that led many Middle East analysts to conclude he would abdicate. Only once before had the king been as desperate: In 1958, after cousin King Feisal and his family were massacred in Baghdad and a pro-Baathist revolution appeared imminent in Amman, Hussein had begun to seek British and American help in evacuating him and his family from Amman following his abdication.[22] Instead, Hussein decided to dig in and with British help fended off the challenge.

In June 1970, Hussein narrowly escaped death when his car was ambushed. But there were two "last straws," according to senior Jordanians. First was the hijacking to Amman of two U.S. commercial airliners and a Swissair plane by the Popular Front for the Liberation of Palestine (PFLP), the radical Palestinian group headed by George Habash. Denouncing the air piracy as "the shame of the Arabs," Hussein was powerless to affect the fate of the planes or their passengers.[23] The second breaking point came in mid-September when Arafat called for a general strike and gave King Hussein twenty-four hours to leave his own country—an example, one adviser recalled, of what "our neighbors the Jews call 'chutzpah.' "

The decision to call out the military—this time against the Palestinians—was another strategic decision of the king's rule. After days of shelling the refugee camps where some sixty thousand Palestinians lived—henceforth known to Palestinians as Black September—the army finally drove the would-be usurpers out of Jordan into Lebanon. Conservative estimates put Palestinian losses at two thousand. Arafat claimed that Jordan's army had killed as many as twenty thousand.

During this critical test of strength, the Muslim Brotherhood, yet again, supported the king. The Jordanian Brotherhood itself had relatively few Palestinian adherents in those days. While some Palestinians had been attracted by the Brotherhood's universalist Islamist message after the 1967 war, most were drawn to the PLO, which was far more successful in recruiting members in Jordan's sprawling refugee camps. In 1969, Palestinian members of the Brotherhood had established a military training camp in the Jordan Valley, according to Jordanian intelligence officers. But the training began too late to enable the Palestinian Ikhwan to play an active role in the civil war.

The king's war against the PLO gave his Arab nationalist enemies even more ammunition. Sudan's Gaafar al-Nimeiri accused Jordan of conducting a "war of extermination" against Palestinians, and Libya's Qaddafi threatened to send troops to protect the PLO. "The whole civilized world," wrote Italian journalist Oriana Fallaci, was disgusted by Hussein's "bloodbath."

At night, journalists, diplomats, spies, and merchants crowded the bar at the Intercontinental, then Jordan's only first-class hotel, exchanging war stories until dawn. As a young freelance journalist, I was drawn to the strife and intrigue and simultaneously terrified by the smell and sight of it. From that moment on, I was hooked on the Middle East.

Perhaps because I was so new to the region, I did not share the widespread sympathy for the PLO. It seemed natural that the king, or any ruler, would try to survive. Moreover, I had seen the stateless squalor and misery endured by so many Palestinians in the West Bank and Gaza, to say nothing of those in Lebanon and Syria. The king had acted generously toward the Palestinians, it seemed to me. They had not responded in kind. Nor would they later on in Lebanon, where the PLO would soon help spark a second civil war. The Palestinian leadership had not distinguished itself during the fighting in Amman. Arafat fled dressed as a woman, assisted by Egyptian diplomats. "We let him go because, frankly, we couldn't wait to get rid of him," one of the king's advisers later told me. Abu Iyaad, or Salah Khalaf, the PLO's number two, was not so lucky. Caught by the army, he broke down weeping and groveled at the king's feet at Hommar Palace, the official recalled. Hussein, mortified by the humiliating spectacle, ordered Abu Iyaad's immediate expulsion.

While Palestinians in the camps suffered during the civil war, their leadership did not want. The Red Crescent ambulances to Beirut that shuttled Palestinian dead and wounded, the so-called *shaheed*, or martyrs to the cause, were often filled not with the wounded but with cartons of Rothmans and other imported British cigarettes favored by the PLO elite. The smuggling by PLO leaders in these noncombatant vehicles became so common that Jordanians began calling what should have been mercy missions the "Shaheed Rothman" trips.

Hussein had not sought this test of wills. He had done everything possible to avoid it. But after Black September, the king's legitimacy in the East Bank was never again challenged.

Unlike many of my colleagues, I had instantly taken to Amman, a then small city whose seven rolling hills were for the most part unmarred by the ugly concrete high-rises that had ruined so many Arab capitals. Despite the ghastly Arab-Israeli conflict, there was a sense of calm and stability in Jordan, so unusual in the Middle East. The king had built an army, but he had also invested heavily in schools and hospitals and infrastructure. Jordan, which lacked enough educated people in 1921 to staff a government, now had an adult literacy rate of 80 percent, among the region's highest—without oil or natural resources. And it had a thriving middle class, key to any successful modern society. Jordan, in fact, was the most prosperous of poor Arab countries. Roughly 40 percent of its citizens traveled outside Jordan each year. Amman was clean and efficient. Drivers wore seatbelts or risked paying stiff fines. Traffic lights and signals were observed, a rarity in Arab cities. Jordan was governed by a firm but not a heavy hand. The government was not obscenely corrupt. Why were such trappings of "normal" life so unappreciated by so many Palestinians and, less explicably, by my colleagues in the press?

My first interview with Hussein at Nadwa Palace confirmed my instincts. I had never met, much less interviewed, a king before. So I had not known what to expect. Though he looked exhausted and depressed by his long struggle with the PLO and its Arab and Western champions, he could not have been more politely attentive. He called me *sitti,* an Arabic term that loosely translates as "madame," or someone of high station. He lit my cigarette before his own, perhaps because my hand was trembling so visibly that I would have been unable to light it myself. I was so nervous that after I turned on my tape recorder, I couldn't speak. Besides, I had forgotten how to address a king. "Your Highness," I blurted out. "No. I mean, Your Majesty. Or is it Your Excellency?" Hussein laughed, breaking the ice. "Just call me Hussein," he replied. "My friends call me Hussein."

THE 1970S WERE prosperous years for Jordan but politically troubled for Hussein. When we met again in 1974, the king was reeling from the Arab summit conference in Rabat, Morocco, when the Arabs took their revenge for his assault on the PLO—the sacred Arab cause—and for Jordan's abstention from the 1973 war against Israel. (Neither Egypt nor Syria had bothered to include him in plans for their surprise attack, he told me without complaint.) The year before the war, Hussein had proposed the eventual formation of a "United Arab Kingdom," a federation of the East and West Banks after Israel withdrew in which each bank would have its own capital, governor, and institutions and be generally autonomous but under his sovereignty. The plan was remarkably similar to that which his grandfather Abdullah had offered the Jewish leadership in the late 1940s. But Hussein's scheme was rejected not only by Israel but also the PLO. At Rabat, the Arab League punished him by anointing the PLO as the "sole legitimate representative of the Palestinian people," thus denying him the right to negotiate for, or act on behalf of, the Palestinians. Hussein was thunderstruck, particularly by the defection of King Hassan II of Morocco and Egypt's Sadat, who had promised him their support. Since Jordan was more than half Palestinian and had ruled the West Bank between 1948 and 1967, the Arabs had decided, in effect, that Hussein could no longer protect what amounted to his own national interests.[24]

The king appeared equally troubled in 1977 when I visited Jordan. Though the economy was still strong and the country stable, Hussein's wife, Alia, had just died in a tragic helicopter accident.

I had once dined with Alia Toukan, the king's third wife, of Palestinian origin.[25] She was not only beautiful but intelligent, independent, and actively involved in Jordanian affairs. Jordanians of Palestinian origin admired her and saw her marriage to Hussein as assurance of their own equality in Hashemite Jordan. The king adored her and their two children, Prince Ali and Princess Haya.

Hussein's misery was unmistakable. He had grown a short beard and smoked more heavily than usual as he told me about the accident. He blamed himself for her death, he said. He should not have permitted her to fly that night. The weather was awful. But she had promised to visit a school in northern Jordan the following morning and had insisted on going. And Alia was a very determined woman. The king had asked his best pilot, a close friend, to fly the helicopter to set his mind at ease. I knew that the pilot had accompanied Hussein on several of his secret flights to meet Israelis, or as the king called them at the time, "the secret meetings that never were." Hussein had trusted him completely. Now he had lost his wife and a close friend.

Amman had always been a conservative, inbred place, but Alia's death had depressed the entire country and made Palestinians particularly anxious. It made me realize how precariously personal the kingdom was. Perhaps that was inevitable in a monarchy of this size in which the king's every word and mood reverberated so. Such personalization of politics had a price. Rulers, not institutions, mattered in Jordan and throughout the Arab Middle East. And Arab societies had mostly suffered because of it. "Hussein is Jordan and Jordan is Hussein," diplomats were fond of saying. But as a result, Jordanians invested the king's every action, his every whim, with meaning and portent. Palestinians — and for that matter, the well-entrenched Muslim Brotherhood — knew that their continued prosperity in Jordan depended on his benevolence, and most resented it. In such a culture, the accidental death of his wife of Palestinian origin mirrored their own anxieties and would inevitably be suspect. From then on I better understood the craving of Palestinian friends in the West Bank and Gaza for a society that would not be so utterly dependent on one man — even on a kind, well-intentioned ruler. An incompetent or megalomaniac, like Libya's Qaddafi or Iraq's Saddam Hussein, meant a country's ruin. Hussein was enlightened, but would Crown Prince Hassan, Hussein's brother and designated successor, prove as able? The only way to ensure continued prosperity and good governance was to institutionalize government — not easy in a region so accustomed to personal, autocratic rule.

Though I did not realize it at the time, Hussein had come to more or less the same conclusion. In 1979 he had been deeply shocked by Iran's Islamic revolution, which brought the fanatical Ayatollah Ruholla Khomeini to power. He had visited the shah three times in 1978 and had been alarmed by what he had seen in Teheran. Middle Easterners, and their leaders in particular, quickly grasped the awesome implications of Shiite Iran's upheaval even for Arab Sunni Muslim states. Even many members of Jordan's Sunni Muslim Brotherhood had been impressed by the Shiite Islamic upheaval. Hussein had concluded that in addition to institutionalizing power at home, he had to redouble efforts to defuse an important source of religious and secular radicalism in the Middle East—the Arab-Israeli dispute. Though he had broken off his secret meetings with the Israelis in 1977, after Likud's Menachem Begin came to power, he was more determined than ever to end the bitter dispute with the Jews.

SENIOR JORDANIAN OFFICIALS insist that peace between Jordan and Israel could have come much sooner than it did, though few American or Israeli analysts agree. Clearly, it was not the Muslim Brotherhood that prevented the king from making a deal with the Israelis, though the Brethren always ardently opposed any recognition of Israel's right to exist in *Dar al-Islam*, the House or Abode of Islam. Most parties to the protracted conflict acknowledge, however, that there were several "missed opportunities" for peace since 1948.

The only American-sponsored peace plan that King Hussein ever publicly shunned was President Jimmy Carter's Camp David initiative.[26] While many analysts cite Camp David as a major "missed opportunity" for peace, the king said he feared that it would not have required Israel to withdraw from the West Bank and Gaza and hence would have left him politically vulnerable.

King Hussein did reject another American-sponsored initiative whose details were never officially disclosed. Known only to a handful of Americans and Jordanians, the offer was described by a senior Jordanian official as more of a "bribe" than a genuine proposal. The offer came in October 1982, only a month after Jordan had endorsed the ill-fated peace plan outlined by President Reagan and when the administration was attempting to pre-position American equipment overseas for a Rapid Deployment Force. According to authoritative Jordanian sources, two American envoys met with Hussein in Amman to offer Jordan more than $3 billion in economic and military aid if the king would negotiate directly with Israel—without the PLO. In addition to economic assistance, the administration was prepared to sell Jordan two squadrons of F-16s, modern tanks, and to convert its fixed-site missile launchers into fully mobile launchers. In addition, the administration would guarantee Jordan the $1.2 billion it was due under the Baghdad mutual-assistance pact for so-called confrontation Arab states if the Arabs retaliated by suspending their aid.

Though tempted, the king decided that it would be "suicidal" by that time to enter into direct talks with Israel without the Palestinians, a senior adviser later told me, especially since Washington had given Jordan no assurance that Israel, then under Likud leadership, was prepared to withdraw from the occupied territories or Jerusalem.

Gradually, Hussein grew ever more skeptical about America's ability to act as an "honest broker" after what he described as a succession of "disappointments" by Washington. Increasingly, American diplomacy seemed aimed at luring Jordan into open-ended negotiations with an Israel unwilling to relinquish territories and an American broker unwilling to pressure it to do so.[27]

A succession of American presidents, the king's advisers insisted, had refused to provide assurances that Hussein and his throne would be protected if Jordan made peace alone. Moreover, whenever Jordan's interests clashed with those of Israel, the king told me in a memorable interview, Washington's preference for Israel was clear — "indulgence squared." [28]

According to the king, Israel and Jordan never came closer to a deal than in April 1987, when he and then Israeli foreign minister Shimon Peres met secretly in London. Hussein liked Peres, with whom he had been meeting since 1974.[29] The two men agreed that Israel and a joint Jordanian-Palestinian delegation — without the PLO — would enter into direct talks under the umbrella of an international peace conference. Hussein justified leaving Arafat out because the PLO still refused to endorse UN resolutions recognizing Israel's right to exist. Moreover, he knew that Peres, if not Prime Minister Yitzhak Shamir, his coalition partner, was willing to withdraw from most of the territories in exchange for peace. But the so-called London agreement failed when Prime Minister Shamir, unwilling to relinquish occupied land that he considered an inseparable part of "Eretz Israel," the biblical land of Israel, vetoed the conference.

Within months of the agreement's collapse, Palestinians in the West Bank and Gaza rose up against Israeli occupation in what became known as the Intifada, in Arabic the "shaking off" of occupation. The uprising was a rejection not only of Israeli rule but also of Jordan's claim to the territories. Palestinians wanted to control their own political destiny.[30]

By the summer of 1988, with the Likud Party in power and the Intifada still building in the occupied territories, Hussein finally despaired of achieving peace with Israel or reclaiming the West Bank. In July he formally "disengaged" from the West Bank, cutting administrative and legal ties with, and withdrawing funding from, most West Bank groups, except for Islamic institutions, and ceding authority to the PLO. Hussein hoped, one adviser told me, that Arafat would be unable to restore order and that the Palestinians would beg him to return. They did not.

Though some Palestinians wanted to seek Hussein's help in ending Israeli occupation, most did not dare. Anyone who even questioned the Great Uprising of the Streets was considered a traitor. Like the second Great Arab Revolt in Palestine of 1936–38, the Intifada was quickly enveloped in self-serving myth. While the uprising forced Israel to question whether it could occupy the territories forever, it also undermined what remained of Palestine's traditional, indigenous leadership and severely damaged its frail economy. Just as the revolt of the 1930s had led to political exhaustion, hunger, despair, and an infamous "Night of Long Knives" in which Palestinians turned on one another and killed "collaborators" — an "act of self immolation," one scholar had called it — the Intifada, too, triggered debilitating internecine violence.[31] In the name of political purity, black-hooded gangs murdered hundreds of their fellow Palestinians. By the end of 1992 the number of Palestinians slaughtered by these alleged patriots was nearly half the total killed by the Israeli military during the first five years of the uprising.[32]

The Intifada also led to the emergence of radical Islamic Hamas and other militant Islamists in Gaza and the West Bank who rejected the very notion of a Jewish state in Palestine as well as "union" with King Hussein, whom they denounced as a Western lackey. Finally, the uprising prompted the flight to Jordan of more West Bank notables — the traditional middle-class and upper-middle-class professional elite.

Hussein saw the Intifada for what it was: an exercise in collective self-destruction, perhaps unavoidable and even necessary given the unyielding Israeli occupation, but devastating to what remained of Palestine's traditions and social fabric. Yet his decision to cut ties to the West Bank and Gaza did little more than codify political reality. Israeli occupation had been painfully instructive for Palestinians. While they detested Israeli rule, many appreciated what democracy had done for Israel. They had watched the Israelis challenge their own leaders and even change them — unthinkable in most Arab countries, including Jordan. Gradually, they had learned how to use the system to expand the limits of occupation. Once Palestinian nationalism had burst forth in the form of the Intifada, the king was finished in the West Bank, at least temporarily. A Palestinian identity, distinct from Jordan's, had been nurtured by Zionism's example. This "Palestinian Zionism," as Sadiq al-Azm, the Syrian philosopher, audaciously but aptly called the new Palestinian nationalism, could no longer be ignored. There was no going back. The king sensed that. In what an Israeli official described as "schadenfreude," Hussein congratulated Shimon Peres after Israel and the PLO announced their Oslo agreement in 1993, the effective, if temporary, end of Hussein's claim to the West Bank. "Now you will see what it is like to deal with Yasir Arafat and the PLO," the king told Peres. From then on, Israel would have to contend with the PLO chief's childish self-absorption and feudal ways, his unwillingness to trust subordinates or delegate authority, his overweening vanity and personalization of each and every issue, often at the expense of his own people. Peres, an aide confided, would soon have frequent occasion to recall wistfully the king's words.

IN THE 1980s, the Jordanian economy began to deteriorate, long before the Gulf war. The king, alas, had run his economy, as one astute financial writer observed, "as though Jordan were an oil state."[33] Benefiting from its proximity to the Gulf and its educated, skilled workforce, Jordan had enjoyed an average annual rate of growth of 9–10 percent between 1973 and 1981. But two-thirds of that came from foreign aid and remittances of some 300,000 workers employed in the Gulf. Both sources of income peaked in 1981 and then fell. Because Jordan spent heavily on social services as well as on the military and kept the dinar high, export industries were struggling; imports had boomed. So had construction. Remittances financed the proliferation of lavish villas with limestone façades that the king had required to match Jerusalem's building code.

Amman, where the bulk of Palestinians lived, grew so fast during the 1980s that city planners lagged years behind in naming and numbering streets—a failure that, to this day, made visiting friends in Amman what optimists called an adventure and pessimists a nightmare.

In the early 1980s, in an effort to deflect attention from Jordan's worsening economy, Hussein began liberalizing the system and distributing some authority among the country's powerless institutions, laying the groundwork for a constitutional monarchy. In the spring of 1984, Jordan tried to reestablish a political claim to the West Bank, taking advantage of the PLO's weakness after its expulsion from Lebanon. Hussein recalled Parliament and held its first elections in seventeen years. To everyone's surprise, the Islamists scored well: Two Muslim Brethren and another Islamic activist won three of the six seats reserved for Muslims. (Two other seats were reserved for Christians.)

The 1984 by-election, among other factors, emboldened the Islamists, who, like most Jordanians during the boom decade of the 1970s, used the Gulf aid and remittances pouring into Jordan to finance an impressive system of *Da'wa*, schools, clinics, and social centers. Demonstrating new self-confidence, the Ikhwan stepped up calls for an end to corruption and the imposition of sharia, Islamic law in Jordan—appeals that irritated the palace, which viewed the Brethren's veiled criticism of Jordan's political system as an indirect challenge to the king's sovereignty. Hussein wanted to liberalize, but slowly and while firmly in charge—much to the relief of many Jordanians, few of whom wanted the monarchy abolished.

In 1985, Hussein detected an opportunity to discipline the Brotherhood by achieving a diplomatic rapprochement with Syria's Hafiz Assad, who had been battling Islamic militants since 1979 and killing Jordanian diplomats to punish Hussein for Jordan's support of Syria's Muslim Brotherhood. In a rare and public denunciation of the Ikhwan, Hussein blamed the Brethren for the deterioration of relations with Damascus in the past five years. He was shocked, the king said, that the Jordanian Muslim Brotherhood had been training Syrian Brethren in Jordanian-based military camps for missions against Damascus. He had been "deceived" by the "evil designs" of this "criminal" and "rotten" group, he said, issuing a public apology to Syria. Hundreds of Brethren activists were arrested; others were deported to Damascus. The king's prime minister demanded legislation to prevent militant preachers from "sowing seeds of dissension among people," as Hussein had accused the Islamists who had been so useful for so long of doing. It was, by any political standard, a breathtaking policy reversal but one that the king must have decided, for domestic as well as foreign policy reasons, would help him survive.[34]

I saw the king quite often during that period. He was astonishingly relaxed. By then, he had remarried. His present wife, Queen Noor, was a foreigner: Lisa Halaby, the American-born daughter of Najeeb Halaby, a former Federal Aviation Administration chairman and airline executive. The marriage—as well as his crackdown on the Brotherhood—had boosted his spirits. Noor was not only beautiful, she created "good will" for Jordan abroad and was active at home in conservation and efforts to find employment for poor Jordanian women. He began to savor life again despite his mounting economic and diplomatic woes. Whether he was racing his motorcycle through the desert to his weekend palace or waterskiing in Aqaba, waving to Israeli sailors across the bay or camping in the desert valley of Wadi Rum, he exhibited a *joie de vivre* that was rare among Middle Eastern leaders. I could not imagine Hafiz Assad of Syria on water skis. The greatest tests of his rule were behind him, Hussein told me one day. Neither of us realized that Jordan and its king would soon be enmeshed in yet another crisis.

WHEN OIL PRICES collapsed in the mid-1980s and the Gulf states contracted, Jordan's economy plunged. Remittances tumbled in half by 1986, and university graduates could no longer find lucrative jobs in the Gulf. The Gulf states cut foreign aid to Jordan by two-thirds. Yet Amman neither curbed imports nor significantly reduced spending: It borrowed until it could borrow no more.[35] After the International Monetary Fund forced Jordan to increase prices on oil, telephones, electricity, and the holy of holies — cigarettes — rioting erupted in Ma'an, the Hashemite desert stronghold where grandfather Abdullah had first disembarked and where the Muslim Brotherhood and Jordan's powerful tribes were traditionally influential. Since King Hussein was in Washington, Crown Prince Hassan, the heir apparent, traveled south to defuse tension, as his older brother had so often done. But Hassan was not Hussein: Jordanians threw garbage at him. The crown prince was forced to flee — hardly an encouraging omen for Jordan's future. Eight people were killed and more than fifty injured in the weeklong riots.[36]

After the king returned, he fired his prime minister, a boyhood friend, and hired a new one, a cousin. He also tried to deflect attention from economic woes with more freedom. Press rules were liberalized and in November 1989, Jordan held elections for a full new Parliament, its first since 1967. To the king's genuine shock this time, Islamists swept the race, winning thirty-four of the eighty seats in the lower house, or roughly half of those not allotted to Christians and other minorities.[37] Independent Islamists had captured twelve of the thirty-four slots; the Muslim Brotherhood had taken advantage of Jordan's fragmented political field and low secular turn-out and won twenty-two seats.[38]

This was Jordan's situation when Saddam Hussein invaded Kuwait in August 1990 and changed virtually every given in Middle Eastern calculus. Though no one would have predicted it at the time, Saddam's belligerency would inadvertently help reignite prospects for the peace that King Hussein had craved for so long. But first the king had to survive.

WHY DID THE KING tilt toward Saddam Hussein? The answer would always mystify and disappoint me. I would never forget one of my many dinners with Hussein and his family at Nadwa Palace in the mid-1980s. Young Prince Abdullah had just returned from Sandhurst, which he, like his father, had attended. Abdullah was belittling the United States. Britain, he said, was sophisticated and tough-minded. It knew the region and the world. It had triumphed in the Falklands war with Argentina. America, by contrast, was blundering and short-sighted; it shunned conflict and was slow to act.

After a while, an exasperated Hussein could stand no more. "Abdullah," he said sharply, "you don't know what you're talking about." Britain, he said, was a former world power, and today, barely a force in the region. It could take on small conflicts like the Falklands but nothing more. America, by contrast, was a superpower. A vast, diverse nation in which consensus building took time, America had to act slowly. By definition, a superpower was cautious: Rashness would risk inadvertently crushing smaller powers around it. "You are too young to recall how America mobilized in World War II," Hussein lectured his son. "But I will never forget it. Once America, the superpower, mobilizes, the entire world must take note."

Abdullah fell silent. I turned red. Sensing my embarrassment, Hussein changed the subject. While never again in my presence did he so openly acknowledge his respect for American power, I never forgot his esteem for America or his subtle appreciation of its inherent constraints.

Why did a man so aware of American might risk incurring its wrath during the Gulf crisis? I knew the conventional explanations: Iraq supplied almost 90 percent of Jordan's oil—at subsidized rates; Iraq was Jordan's major trading partner, accounting for some $450 million in annual revenues and 40 percent of Jordan's nonphosphate exports, significant numbers in what was then a $4 billion economy.[39] Iraq and Jordan had formed a joint air command, trading military information and supplies during the Iran-Iraq war. And Hussein, like most Arabs from poor countries, bitterly resented the swaggering, spendthrift coupon clippers of the Gulf. The king owed them nothing, he once told me.[40] Jordanians loathed Kuwait in particular. When King Hussein had asked Sheikh Sabah, Kuwait's notoriously profligate ruler, for $1 million to build a university branch, Sabah had dismissed him by saying that a country as poor as Jordan could not afford such luxuries as universities.[41]

But I sensed that there was more than even these factors in the king's complicated relationship with Saddam Hussein. While I normally had no use for pop psychology, it seemed plausible to me, as a close aide had told me, that Hussein had found in Saddam, and in Egypt's Nasser before that, a heroic father figure. Arabs traditionally respect age and position, often more than wisdom or ability. Why should Hussein have been immune? A man as lonely as Hussein, as tired of his solitude, as accustomed to trusting no one but craving a wise and strong adviser, would not be human if he did not yearn to share the tremendous burden of such perilous rule. Just as Hussein had been taken in by Nasser, a towering figure in Middle Eastern politics, so, too, perhaps had he been seduced by Saddam, a cut-rate version of Egypt's ruler.

Stubborn, arrogant, and merciless, Saddam might well have impressed the beleaguered king—as polar opposites so often attract—when they first met at the 1978 Baghdad summit. Though Saddam was not yet Iraq's ruler, Hussein had detected in Saddam "a new Nasser," a forceful leader who could unify the region politically and block Egypt's move toward a separate peace, a senior adviser had told me at the time. Moreover, Saddam had pressed the Gulf states to aid Jordan, a much-appreciated gesture by the perpetually cash-strapped king.

When Iraq invaded Iran in 1980, the king had sided firmly with Saddam, fearing that, as one adviser put it, "again, in the name of Islam, a non-Arab power [a reference to non-Arab Ottoman Turkey, his great grandfather's foe] would rule the Arab world and end his hope of setting up a 'moderate' Arab order."[42] I recalled the king's fear that Iran would export its militant Islamic revolution to Jordan and other Sunni Arab countries, that Teheran might prove perhaps more threatening to the Hashemites than Tel Aviv.

Iraq and Jordan had grown ever closer during the Iran-Iraq war in the 1980s, particularly after the collapse of the 1987 London agreement with Israel's Shimon Peres. Some seventeen thousand Soviet Jews a month were pouring into Israel: a "threat" to the region's stability, the king complained to me at the time. Expansionist forces in Israel might try to annex the West Bank or push even more West Bank Palestinians into Jordan, which would overburden the economy and further upset its demographic balance. While the king did not anticipate reckless behavior from Yitzhak Shamir, could anyone guarantee, he said, that Israel's future prime minister might not be Ariel Sharon? The former Likud defense minister had enraged the king in 1982 by saying that there already was a Palestinian state in the Middle East—Jordan. Hussein increasingly looked to Saddam as insurance in case of Israeli aggression.

During the Iran-Iraq war, Hussein had visited Baghdad more than fifty times. He and Saddam became "friends," the king told me. Theirs was a bond I could not fathom. Saddam was a brutal killer, a thug who had launched his rule with the execution of at least five hundred political opponents and rivals and had continued with an invasion of Iran and the use of poison gas against his own Kurdish citizens. I could not envisage Saddam pardoning men who had tried to kill him. Over dinner at Nadwa Palace shortly before the Gulf war, I asked the king what he and Saddam had in common. What on earth did they talk about?

"Fishing," Hussein replied.

Fishing?

"When he and I went carp fishing," the king said, "we would talk for hours. He's very straightforward, very deep and thoughtful, highly intelligent. We would discuss many things—everything."

Saddam and Hussein had also enjoyed their barbecues together. Saddam was fond of grilling not only the day's catch but mountains of chicken, lamb, and beef kebabs. They were both confirmed night owls whose dinners would invariably last late into the night.

Saddam was "a new phenomenon" in the Middle East, Hussein told me.

Despite eight years of war with Iran, Iraq had emerged well organized and even more powerful. He never had to worry about militant Islamists or any challenge to his rule. "He never goes begging," the king said wistfully, an allusion, no doubt, to his own frequent and humiliating begging-bowl visits to the Gulf.

Saddam had a good sense of humor, the king asserted, though I had never heard anyone accuse the Iraqi leader of that. "When I saw him after the invasion of Kuwait," the king recounted as an example, "he embraced me and said, 'Okay, no more surprises.' "[43]

Some argue that King Hussein supported Iraq because Jordanians had overwhelmingly and enthusiastically supported Saddam's invasion of Kuwait, the oil-rich Gulf sheikhdom that had lorded its wealth over Arab have-nots like Jordan. Saddam, moreover, had repeatedly threatened Israel, the Palestinians' enemy. His occupation of Kuwait was seen by most Jordanians — Palestinian and Jordanian alike — as the beginning of a reassertion of Arab unity, a more equal distribution of Arab wealth, and ultimately, as the adviser put it, "shortening the road to Jerusalem." The amount of food, money, and blood Jordanians donated to Iraq far surpassed what they had collected for the Palestinian Intifada against Israeli occupation of the West Bank and Gaza.[44]

Yet it was hard to believe that Hussein's support of Saddam was based mainly on deference to public opinion, what Western analysts call the Arab "street," though Hussein's stance was clearly affected somewhat by the widespread yearning, especially among Palestinians, for revenge against Israel.[45] But although many Jordanians were sympathetic to Iran in 1980 and blamed Saddam Hussein for starting a war aimed at thwarting Iran's anti-Western, anti-Israeli revolution, King Hussein, cognizant of Jordan's national interests, had staunchly supported Baghdad.[46]

Some American officials argued that Jordanian public opinion was so strongly pro-Saddam that Hussein could not have survived had he not leaned toward Baghdad. Even Israel shared Washington's concern over the king's fate. Despite their ideological differences, Yitzhak Shamir got along well with Hussein, whom he had met secretly shortly before and soon after the Gulf war. The king had been a factor in Shamir's decision to break precedent by not responding to Iraq's Scud attacks against Israeli cities, senior Israelis told me.[47] Bombing Iraq would probably have required overflying Jordan. This, in turn, would almost certainly have forced Jordan to side more openly with Baghdad, as Hussein warned Shamir when they met shortly before the war.[48] As insurance against attack, Israel wanted to send troops to the Jordanian border. But Hussein urged Shamir not to do so: "One nervous young commander could ruin everything," Hussein told Shamir, according to a participant at the meeting. But how did Israel know, Shamir replied, that under Iraqi pressure Jordan would not send its own troops across the Israeli border? "You have my word on that," the king replied.

•

IN THOSE TERRIBLE DAYS before the war, Jordan was a land transformed by passions that terrified me. Each week tens of thousands of Jordanians, and especially Palestinians, decked their homes, offices, cars, T-shirts, and lapel pins with photos of King Hussein and his friend Saddam's mustachioed face. One popular poster showed King Hussein presenting a gun to Saddam. The country I had always thought of as Western, moderate, and pragmatically entrepreneurial was suddenly alien, radical, and hostile — unrecognizable. How could I have so misjudged a country I had visited so often? What furies — envy, guilt, bitterness, and rage — lurked beneath Amman's placidly bourgeois surface? Except for a few of the king's advisers and a precious few intellectuals, virtually all of my Jordanian friends, including those educated in America or Europe, supported Saddam. Those who did not were intimidated into silence — "intellectual terrorism," a Jordanian friend had called it.

Public opinion was so intensely, dogmatically pro-Iraqi that even those who thought that Saddam was a monster remained silent. Like Nasser before him, Saddam had masterfully exploited the despair and impotence so prevalent among so many Arabs. To speak against "Saddam, darling of the people, leader of the Arab nation," as one banner near my hotel proclaimed, was tantamount to disowning one's father, renouncing one's family. Given the prevailing mood and the conformist social pressure in this conservative society, there were few dissenters, and surely none in the press.

Baghdad itself bribed Jordanian journalists whose loyalty could not automatically be assured. I had been working in Arab countries long enough not to be shocked that many Arab journalists would accept such payments. What surprised me was how cheaply some Jordanians could be bought. While a few prominent reporters and editors got Mercedes and other fancy cars, others had settled for little more than a gold Rolex wristwatch. In my prewar visits to Amman, I could not recall reading a single newspaper article expressing unequivocal misgivings about Saddam's aggression.

During the war, cooperation between King Hussein and the Muslim Brotherhood intensified.[49] Like most Islamist movements in the region, the Muslim Brotherhood had initially wavered between siding with its funders in the Gulf, who supported the coalition to rescue Kuwait, and its foot soldiers in the streets, who were wildly pro-Iraq. But once the king signaled his own emotional preference, the statist Brotherhood felt free to embrace the Iraqi dictator. Encouraged by the palace, Islamists gave religious cover to Saddam's repressive regime. In mosques and public rallies, they praised Iraq's opportunistic conversion to "anti-Crusader" Muslim militancy. Saddam Hussein, who had ordered a Koranic inscription to be placed on Iraq's flag, was suddenly the promised "liberator" of holy Jerusalem and historic Palestine. At one Muslim Brotherhood–sponsored rally, some fifteen thousand Saddam supporters urged Saddam to attack Israel: "Use your chemicals, Saddam!" they chanted euphorically. It was always "Saddam," a man who needed no surname.

Prime Minister Mudar Badran gave official credence to a popular conspiracy theory by suggesting in an interview with an Arabic newspaper that American arms companies had engineered the Gulf crisis to create new markets for their sophisticated weapons now that the cold war was over. Jordanian officials openly boasted of their country's military cooperation with Iraq. A combined Iraqi-Jordanian fighter squadron had been formed after the Iran-Iraq war ended, and Iraqi aircraft had become accustomed to flying over Jordanian airspace.[50]

Gradually, the king himself got caught up in the enthusiasm. Stunning several of his closest advisers, he permitted Arab radicals to host a pro-Iraqi conference in Amman in mid-September, and even met with two Palestinian rejectionist leaders — George Habash, of the PFLP, and Nayef Hawatmeh, of the Democratic Front for the Liberation of Palestine — both of whom were banned from Jordan ever since 1970 when they tried to take over his country. Enraged by the king's stance, Saudi Arabia closed its borders to Jordanian goods, cut off oil shipments, and suspended aid.

Jordan was "enjoying its isolation," Hussein told me when I asked him before the war about Riyadh's ominous action. The door to a peaceful settlement of the Gulf crisis was still not closed, he told me in December. Why was America not grateful for his help in persuading Saddam to release the Western hostages he had taken soon after his invasion of Kuwait? No, he said, he would not "press" Saddam to "do anything that would harm Iraq." The king seemed quite agitated; I noticed that he had regrown his beard, a reliable barometer of radical Islamic heat in Amman.

In January, Prime Minister Badran, with the king's blessing, appointed five Muslim Brotherhood members to his cabinet. Shortly after the American-led coalition attacked Iraq, the Jordanian Assembly, the Parliament's lower house in which the Brotherhood had held the largest single bloc since the 1989 elections, approved a resolution that urged "all the Arab and Islamic nations to strike at American interests and the interests of those nations participating in the aggression against Iraq."

Though there were few attacks on Western targets in Amman, the king later told me that he was "embarrassed" by the vote, which did not reflect what he called his "neutrality." But when asked about the resolution soon after its approval, the king replied that the Parliament "had the right to express the people's anger and frustration and despair."[51]

What finally ended American patience was Hussein's emotional twenty-minute speech on February 4, 1991. After witnessing more than three weeks of devastating bombing raids on military targets in Baghdad and other Iraqi military sites, the king heatedly condemned the allied attack on Iraq as "a war against all Arabs and Muslims," a "catastrophe" aimed at "destroying all the achievements of Iraq," returning it to "primitive life," and placing the region under foreign domination. My heart sank as I watched the king's televised tirade in Saudi Arabia. Never once did he mention Saddam by name or his greedy invasion; nor was there a word spoken about the suffering of the Kuwaiti people or the brutality of Saddam's occupation. Instead, Hussein saluted "Iraq, its heroic army, its steadfast people, its glorious women, its brave children, and its aged."

After Iraq's surrender, Jordanians did not want to believe that Iraq had been defeated. They dismissed as "Zionist propaganda" the poignant footage shown on Israeli television — but not on Jordanian television — of Iraqi soldiers on their knees, kissing the sand-covered boots of American soldiers. The images were pathetic: Iraqi soldiers, who Saddam had said would either triumph or die as martyrs, were shown crawling, weeping, and surrendering in droves, even to American journalists, under tattered white flags torn from the robes and head-dresses they had stolen from Kuwaiti homes during their ruthless occupation. On the second day of the war, Prime Minister Badran "congratulated" Iraq on its air strikes against Israel; after the American forces began to move, he told Jordan's Parliament that Iraq's massive retreat was merely "tactical," that Baghdad was winning the war.

No wonder the average Jordanian found Iraq's defeat confusing and incredible. I returned to Amman in March soon after the war, but Iraq's defeat had not yet sunk in. Jordan was in shock. A few Jordanians, mostly East Bankers, told me that they had always mistrusted Saddam Hussein — he had a last name now. They had only "gone along" with the government's line to avoid undermining the king. Most Jordanians had opposed Iraq's occupation of Kuwait, they insisted, but had found the presence of Western forces in Saudi Arabia, sacred Arab soil, even more unpalatable. Like King Hussein, they hoped that the dispute could be settled peacefully, and by Arabs.

Palestinians were particularly grief-stricken. Some friends told me that their children were too upset to attend school. Still others denied reports of Saddam's defeat. A few rationalized the disaster by turning the crushing of Iraq into victory. Saddam was still alive, Samir, a Palestinian friend, told me breathlessly. Saddam had fired missiles at Israel; he had challenged the United States and confronted the West's overwhelming might; he had "brilliantly" withdrawn his forces before they were destroyed; he would live to fight again. Arab honor would be restored. Weeks after the Gulf war had ended, Jordanian newspapers were still running paid notices "congratulating" Saddam on his "steadfastness." Saddam's "mother of all battles" (it sounded better in Arabic) may not have ended in victory, but it did not end in shame.

"You in the West think in terms of win/lose, right/wrong," a senior Jordanian official told me, trying to explain the Jordanian reaction to Saddam's defeat. "But in Arab culture, and particularly in Jordan, where tribes remain the core of our political and social fabric, these distinctions are less important than what is honorable or shameful. Shooting your sister for sleeping with a man may be wrong, but it's honorable; it is her conduct that is shameful. If the brother fails to respond, he is a pimp, an outcast, equally shameful." This was true of Saddam's war, the official asserted. "In the Middle East leaders are judged not by the means they use to fight — poison gas, pillage, massacre — but by their willingness to confront those who challenge them." Therefore, the war in many Arab eyes was not a loss, he said, "because Iraq had stood up to the new Crusaders." Losing was not as shameful as withdrawing or finding a way to avoid a confrontation. "If he lost three hundred thousand, four hundred thousand, however many," the official said, "he still had his honor—as long as his regime survives." And America had let Saddam survive.

Other Jordanians indulged in a favored Arab pastime: shifting blame for what had happened by spinning elaborate conspiracy theories. The United States had "lured" Saddam into invading Kuwait, according to one popular theory, so that Washington would have a "pretext" for smashing Iraq to help its ally Israel and dominate the Saudi oil fields.

Even after Iraq's humiliation, the royal palace continued putting out "explanations" of its position on the war that, while pretending to "clear the air" and end "misinterpretations of Jordan's stance of principle," trotted out every paranoid claim of people accustomed to defining themselves in terms of permanent victimhood. I expected to hear such claptrap in Amman's coffeehouses, but it was a shock to read it from the palace months after the war was over. The palace's "White Paper," its astonishing account of Jordan's actions between August 1990 and March 1991, identified the "main sources of contention" between Iraq and Kuwait as a "dispute about the frontiers" of the states and a quarrel over "the rights to the production of oil from the Rumaila oilfield," which the paper failed to mention belonged to Kuwait before Baghdad seized it. Kuwait, the pseudohistory said, had "a false sense of security" and failed to appreciate the "extreme Iraqi anger" that led to the massing of troops "by both sides." Because Iraq feared "external intervention" and Kuwait was in an "intransigent mood," efforts to resolve the dispute were "doomed to failure." King Hussein believed that underlying the Gulf crisis were "designs on the resources and lands of the Arabs" and a "trap" being set for Iraq "into which it was in danger of falling"—by whom, the paper did not say. A peaceful resolution of the conflict would prove what the king believed: that "Iraq's occupation was an act of self-defense against an inflexible position and not just expansionism or a wish for hegemony." Jordan, an "apologist for peace and not for Iraq," had then been subjected to an "orchestrated campaign" of misrepresentation to sour its relations with Washington. After Kuwait and Iraq, Jordan had "suffered most" from the crisis, but it bore "no grudge" for having to pay for its principled stance.

With some trepidation, I returned to Nadwa to see King Hussein, who received me in his office, not at home as usual. The beard he had worn throughout the crisis was gone. He seemed tired, distracted, in no mood for small talk. I plunged in: Did he regret his stance on the war?

Hussein stared at me, apparently puzzled. "Jordan was neutral," he said. "You of all people should know how hard I tried to prevent this war, to stop it once it had begun."

I felt like a traitor. The previous October, Hussein had given me a detailed, exclusive account of his initial efforts to contain the crisis. The *Times* was thrilled to get the story and even happier a month later when Egyptian president Hosni Mubarak had challenged King Hussein's version and flatly accused him of lying. The king assumed that knowing him as I did, I had believed his version of events. He seemed genuinely shocked that I was questioning his actions now.

"I still cannot understand why my appeal for peace was so misunderstood," he continued.

Perhaps, I suggested, because he had repeatedly characterized Iraq's brutal invasion and occupation of Kuwait as "a dispute between brotherly Arab states" or because he had suggested in his infamous February speech that the Americans had sent forces to the region in an imperialist grab for oil and regional dominance.

"I did not mention the United States in my speech," Hussein said politely but with coldly clipped words.

No, I agreed. He had implicitly referred to America among those "who covet our lands and our resources." He had mentioned only Israel by name.

I could no longer contain my disappointment in a man whom, until the Gulf crisis, I had admired with few reservations. Images of my recent trip to devastated Kuwait flashed through my mind: mothers crying over still-missing sons, their looted homes, the polluted sky. I recalled having stood on a cold, deserted street corner in the slums of Kuwait City, taking notes about a desperate Palestinian family I had just interviewed. I had held my notebook in one hand, a pen and a flashlight in the other. There was no electricity in liberated Kuwait; the air was so black with burning oil that it was impossible to write or even navigate the pitch-black streets without a flashlight. It looked like midnight; it was noon.

I did not think that King Hussein would appreciate hearing about Kuwait's new torture museum, where a Kuwaiti victim of Saddam's interrogation techniques had explained to me the various uses of the instruments on display: baseball bats studded with rusty nails, hooks for hanging people upside down or by the hair, presses imported from China that adjusted to individual finger size to crush joints, sever digits, and leave fingers or toes permanently paralyzed. He would not have wanted to know about the electrical prods of varying sizes that were inserted into vaginas and anuses, or the surgical picks used to pluck out eyes and pierce eardrums. But as King Hussein and I sat in his office staring at each other across his desk, I realized that neither of us would ever fully comprehend the other's position.

Jordan, we both knew, would pay heavily for its Gulf war stance. The suspension of Gulf aid had cost Amman almost a billion dollars a year; the influx of some 300,000 Palestinian refugees from Kuwait and the Gulf had severely strained Jordan's economy. Washington, too, was furious.

But if Hussein had antagonized Washington by tilting toward Saddam, Arafat had become a pariah by having openly embraced the Iraqi leader. The PLO was in even worse shape than Jordan, having lost nearly $100 million in annual contributions from Saudi Arabia and the Gulf, as well as $48 million in annual aid from Baghdad. The PLO was broke, and some Palestinians were demanding Arafat's ouster.

Arafat himself seemed to have become unhinged. The PLO chief was in what I could only describe as a state of "acute denial." "The PLO is at a peak! The peak!" he had shrieked at me in Tunis a few days earlier. He was "more popular than ever before" with the "Arab masses, the Muslim nation, the Third World." He would not step down, he declared, as long as he had "50 percent plus one" of his people's support. He would not give Israel the satisfaction of negotiating with "puppets." Why was America maintaining its double standard? he whined in a familiar refrain. Why had it demanded Iraq's 100 percent withdrawal from Kuwait but permitted Israel to continue occupying Palestine? It was pointless reminding Arafat that Iraq's invasion of Kuwait and Israel's seizure of Arab land in response to repeated Arab aggression were hardly comparable events. Arafat, as usual, was in no mood to listen. He preferred to grouse and squeak demands. If Israel wanted peace, he declared, pounding his pudgy fist on my tape recorder, it would have to withdraw from all Palestinian territories and live with a Palestinian state. There was no other way. He had "no regrets" about his Gulf war stance; he had merely "followed his people." Why were the Americans finding excuses for King Hussein but not for him? Was this America's "new world order"?

King Hussein could have taken advantage of Arafat's weakness—and several advisers urged him to do exactly that—but he would not. Reverting to his prewar caution, Hussein told me he would not substitute for the discredited PLO chief or his crippled organization in peace talks with Israel. Jordan and the "sole representative of the Palestinian people," he said, the Arab slap at him in 1974 still stinging, would have to work together. A "creative solution" would have to be found. He hoped that Amman and Washington would eventually stop "signaling and hooting at each other like ships across a channel in fog." There was so much to do, he said with a sigh, such "opportunities for peace" if only the parties involved would seize them.

THE GOOD WEATHER had nearly ended when I returned to Amman in early November 1993, more than two years after my last disappointing visit. So much had happened since the summer: the Oslo accord between the PLO and Israel in September 1993, the agenda for peace signed the very next day by Jordan and Israel at the State Department.

Most Jordanians were shocked by the developments. By agreeing to make a separate peace with Israel, Arafat had joined Egypt in deserting the Arab cause —and them. Facing political extinction due to soaring debt and the ever-growing popularity in the occupied territories of Islamic militants—particularly the Muslim Brotherhood's Hamas—Arafat had grabbed the life preserver that Israel had thrown him in the secret Oslo talks to salvage what he could for himself, the PLO, and charitably, Palestinians in the West Bank and Gaza. The Washington agreement made no mention of Palestinian refugees in other countries, like Jordan. So many Jordanians of Palestinian origin felt abandoned, politically adrift. Their anxieties were articulated by such Palestinian stars as Edward Said, the American professor of literature at Columbia University and former champion of the PLO, who, from the safety and comfort of his academy in New York, denounced the PLO-Israeli agreement as "an instrument of Palestinian surrender, a Palestinian Versailles."[52]

Within Jordan, both the Arab nationalist Left and the Islamists opposed the accord as well as Jordan's impending peace with Israel. But most Jordanians seemed shaken and confused. The Arabs had endured two traumatic crises in the past quarter century: the 1967 war and the Gulf war, said Amin Mahmoud, a Palestinian friend and the founder of a new women's college in Amman. "But while the '67 war was a defeat for all Arabs, a collective defeat that unified us, if only in misery, the Gulf war defeated only some Arabs. It irrevocably divided us. In the '67 war we lost territory; in the Gulf war we lost hope. Now people no longer believe in anything," he said. "Just money and survival."

Thanks to Saddam, Hussein's Jordan was now more Palestinian than ever. The Gulf war had forced more than 380,000 Palestinians out of Kuwait and other Gulf states. Only Israel and Jordan had taken them in. Israel had accepted 40,000 Palestinians originally from the West Bank or Gaza; Jordan had welcomed the rest of the "returnees," as Amman called the latest wave of exiles, increasing Jordan's population by 10 percent.

Recalling the vast tent camps that stretched across this country only three years earlier, I could hardly believe how rapidly the Palestinians had been absorbed. Official statistics estimated the cost of having accommodated the refugees at more than $4 billion, an enormous burden for a country whose gross national product was then only $2.5 billion more than that. But Jordan's generosity had paid off. While 35 percent of returnee families lived below the poverty line and 44 percent were under the age of fifteen, many others had brought savings and skills with them. Amman was enjoying a construction boom.

I visited the heart of the boom: Abdoun, the suburb that Jordanians called Amman's Beverly Hills. I rode past row upon row of expensive European cars parked near luxury villas—still unnumbered, on unnamed streets, by now a hallowed Jordanian tradition. Nobody who was anybody lived on a street with a name and number. Most villas had satellite dishes and oversized television antennas encased in steel frames in the shape of the Eiffel Tower, another beloved Jordanian custom. The villas' lavish interior courtyards had artificial waterfalls, lush gardens, and swimming pools, much to the king's chagrin, since Jordan was chronically short of water. The newly paved streets were immaculate, split with landscaped dividers of palm trees and native shrubbery and flanked by dozens of new schools and branches of chic European shops.

"Don't be taken in," a banker friend told me over penne à la vodka at Romero's, a favorite haunt of inhabitants of Jebel Amman, the grandest of the capital's seven hills. Most of the houses of Abdoun were built with borrowed money. The deposits of Wahdat were financing them.

Wahdat, or "unity" in Arabic, located in the eastern unchic part of town, was yet another example of why appearances were so often deceiving in Jordan and in much of the Middle East. On paper it was a refugee camp, one of Jordan's ten official and three unofficial camps, with a population of more than a million Palestinians. But it had expanded far beyond the original limits of the makeshift housing units that were hastily thrown up to accommodate Palestinian refugees of 1948. Wahdat throbbed with commercial life. Issa, my banker friend, took me by its vast open-air food market one day. Giant trucks were being loaded with produce that would soon be shipped to all parts of the country and beyond. Such transport accounted for about a fifth of the economy, a sector that had already recovered from Gulf war losses.

"You look at refugee camps like Wahdat or Bakaa," said Issa, a Palestinian born in Jerusalem, "and you say, 'Oh, these poor Palestinians!' But many of them do quite well."

I cringed at the memory of the Bakaa camp on the edge of Amman. Some eighty thousand people were crammed into the tiny concrete boxes, one or two stories high, with corrugated metal roofs and concrete floors. Narrow, unpaved roads of mud and garbage ran like polluted veins through the maze of a camp. Before the Gulf war, I had brought some blankets and food to a Palestinian refugee family that had fled Kuwait and rented one of those semifinished concrete houses without windows or heat. At night, the biting desert air invaded the house, making the cement floor so cold that after a few minutes I could no longer feel my toes. A tiny electric heater, placed amid four paper-thin mattresses on the icy floor, did little to counter the dampness. The al-Seif family, including the wife of a journalist friend who had worked in Kuwait, had no blankets to cover them at night and no chair to sit on during the day. A blue plastic bag held the family's dinner that night: two onions and three small round loaves of bread. All of them were sick.

I reminded Issa about the al-Seifs and the numerous other examples of misery I had seen at Bakaa. "The Gulf crisis was a difficult time," he acknowledged. But many of the refugees in Bakaa could afford to move out to better housing and refused to do so; they wanted to stay with their fellow Palestinians. "It's their way of remaining Palestinian. Others want to continue receiving their UN subsidies. And look at the number of television antennas on top of their houses," he added. "Most Bakaa homes are not like the one you visited."

Many Palestinian families maintained a home inside a camp but lived outside it. "The Palestinians are the life's blood of this economy," my friend insisted. "We built this country, and we're not leaving. We all yearn for Jerusalem, but Amman is the real capital of Palestine. We've earned our place here. They are not doing us any favors."

Statistics confirmed his assessment. East Bankers held 80 percent of all government jobs—military and civil-service posts that were significantly less well paid than jobs in the private sector. Jordan owed its thriving bourgeoisie, its bustling hair salons that specialized in the "big hair" look, its chic boutiques filled with blazers and cashmere sweaters, its many restaurants serving European and Asian cuisine, largely to the "Belgians," as Palestinians were called.

Did he think that given the PLO-Israeli accord, Palestinians might one day be forced to choose between their Jordanian and Palestinian identity? "Not a chance," my friend replied. "We're eighty percent of the business sector in this country. Jordan's economy would collapse without us."

Not all Palestinians were as confident. Adnan Abu Odeh, Jordan's former ambassador to the United Nations and a Palestinian who had served as director of intelligence, was increasingly worried about the growing exclusion of Palestinians from top government posts. Palestinians were now systematically excluded from key jobs in the military and intelligence, Abu Odeh had complained over coffee at his comfortable home that fall. Military conscription was replaced by an all-volunteer army in 1992, which had served to further reduce the proportion of Palestinians in the military. Palestinians now constituted less than 1 percent of the officer corps. The unwillingness to trust Palestinians made people feel alien in their own land. And it made the Muslim Brotherhood all the more attractive to Palestinians. The Ikhwan claimed that it did not distinguish between Jordanians and Palestinians, that all Muslims were equal under Islam. Both Adnan and I knew that this was a false claim, but Adnan was right.

Islamism had enormous appeal in post–Gulf war Jordan, especially at the universities, where the Brotherhood had invested heavily during the boom decade of the 1970s. At the University of Amman, more than two-thirds of the young women now wore head scarves. A professor I knew had scoffed at their fashionable Islamism. The Muslim Brothers paid families forty Jordanian dinars —about a hundred dollars a month—for this demonstration of purity, my professor friend Mustapha had told me. But stories about Islamist pressure at the university abounded: One chemistry student had refused to accept a female lab partner because he would be forced to touch her while they exchanged instruments; other students were demanding prayer hours in school and an end to women's sports. When I interviewed students, many volunteered that Islam gave them a more politically comfortable identity than being "Palestinians in Jordan." And it gave their struggle for national liberation a moral and spiritual dimension. Their faith had also helped them accept a succession of defeats: the loss of their homes in a mythical Palestine they never knew but loved as if they had grown up there, the collapse of the Intifada, and now Saddam's failure to liberate their land. Jordanians of Palestinian origin felt increasingly under siege. East Bankers whispered that soon Palestinians would have their own homeland to return to, that they should leave Jordan or be granted green cards rather than citizenship. Despite the king's repeated endorsement of equality for all Jordanians, the Israeli-PLO peace accord had made them even more insecure and apprehensive.

But King Hussein, a true vector of the pressures of his society, was deceptively relaxed when we dined at his palace, given the past two traumatic years of his rule. Despite our differences over the Gulf war, I was delighted, and relieved, to see him again. In the summer of 1992 the king had discovered he had cancer. Rushed to the Mayo Clinic in Minnesota, Hussein underwent surgery and lost a ureter. Grief-stricken at the news, I had sent the king a fax at Mayo wishing him a speedy recovery. His office had replied, thanking me for my concern and saying that the king hoped we would see each other in Amman.

In September, Hussein had returned to Jordan to a tumultuous welcome. Over a million Jordanians — one-fourth of his kingdom, Jordanian and Palestinian alike — had lined the roads between the airport and the capital to welcome him home, waving banners, pictures, and placards, cheering, chanting, and weeping. They could not imagine their country without Hussein.

But problems abounded. By early 1993, Jordan had run up a foreign debt of $8 billion, $2 billion more than its gross national product. Of that sum, $700 million was owed to the United States. Washington had not restored the aid Congress had cut off in 1991 to punish Hussein for his Gulf war stance. Rescheduling the debt was impossible without American support, and absent American forgiveness of Jordan's debt, no other country was likely to do so. Hussein had begun to repair his relations with Washington.

In May 1993 he had openly broken with Saddam Hussein. Though the king had offered veiled criticism of the Iraqi leader before, his public comments were the final rupture between them. Charging that the Iraqi government had deeply harmed Jordanian interests and the Iraqi people, Hussein declared that he could not "continue to support such policy or such a leadership."

Now in a philosophical mood, he complained about Saddam Hussein and the sorry state of Arab affairs. The Gulf war had been terrible for the Arab world, he told me. He had warned Saddam before the war, at their last meeting, that the American forces would destroy him. He had urged him one last time to withdraw, to let him find an "Arab solution" to the crisis. But Saddam was adamant. "I have God on my side," the king recalled him saying. "So I told him, 'Well, good-bye then,' " Hussein said, recounting their final words at their last face-to-face meeting. "I had a sense of tragedy when I left. I looked at the young men on the tarmac and thought they might soon be dead."

Earlier that day, I had been shown a copy of one of the king's many appeals to Saddam. The letter to Saddam from "Your sincere brother" had begged the Iraqi leader to withdraw from Kuwait "for the sake of Iraq and the whole Arab world."[53] Hussein had never received a reply.

The king's opinion of his former friend had shifted markedly — as had so much in Jordan — since our last discussion after the war. "They say that a million Iraqi children might die of disease and malnutrition" — Hussein sighed — "but he doesn't care. He and his family are fine."

Was this the Arabs' only choice? the king wondered aloud, echoing my own thoughts — "Islamic fundamentalists," a misnomer in his view, or "dictators who think they own the land below and the sky above and everything in between"?

Saddam was not the only depressing menace on the king's mind. Militant

Islamists were a problem once again in Jordan. That summer, the palace had disclosed a plot to overthrow the government and murder Hussein as he presided over the graduation ceremony in June at the Mu'ta military academy, Jordan's West Point. In April the government had arrested six cadets and four senior members of the Islamic Liberation Party, the long-outlawed militant group that had attempted in 1969 to kill the king.[54] Outsiders tended to underplay the importance of the Mu'ta plot, but the king was particularly distressed by it because Mu'ta was the training ground for his army's elite. How had Islamic fanatics infiltrated this college? He still did not believe, he said, that Jordan's Muslim Brotherhood had known about the plot or would have supported it.

How could he be sure? I asked him. President Mubarak had told me that despite the Islamists' denials, Egypt's Muslim Brotherhood maintained links to violent Egyptian Islamic groups.

"Jordan is not Egypt," the king replied firmly. If such ties existed, he would have known. Unlike its Egyptian counterpart, Jordan's Brotherhood posed no threat to the country's stability, the king asserted. In any event, support for the Brotherhood fell far short of a majority of the country.

"We can handle the Brotherhood," Hussein told me as he escorted me to the palace door. I would soon see why the king was so confident.

SOME ISLAMIC GROUPS that had taken root in Jordan had always been hostile to the monarchy, especially the Tahrir, or Liberation Party (Hizb al-Tahrir, in Arabic), which was founded in Jordan in the early 1950s by Sheikh Taqi al-Din al-Nabhani, a Palestinian radical preacher and former Muslim Brother. Nabhani had not only demanded that Jordan be ruled by sharia and that all legislation and methods of rule be Islamized, as did the Brotherhood; he also wanted the Ottoman caliphate restored. The pan-Islamic caliph, Nabhani argued, was the only religiously acceptable ruler, a position that effectively denied the legitimacy of not only the Hashemites but of all modern Arab states established after the collapse of the Ottoman empire. Because of the party's hostility to Hashemite legitimacy, King Hussein had an opportunity to ban Tahrir in 1956 when Sheikh Nabhani was discovered in Beirut with party funds.

For Hussein, however, a thirty-third generation descendant of the Prophet Muhammad, God, king, and country were not inherently contradictory. Godless communism had been the enemy—for him and his allies the Brethren. And for most of Hussein's rule, the Jordanian Muslim Brotherhood had stood with the king during his most desperate tests: the army coup plot of 1957, the defeat by Israel in 1967, and the civil war in 1970.

The tactical alliance, of course, had seen its ups and downs (waves of arrests, crackdowns, and deportations to Syria in 1985). But before the Gulf war, Jordan's Brotherhood had been an accepted part of the country's political life. The palace had permitted the Brethren to recruit widely in towns, schools, and professional associations. Only the military was off-limits.

The Muslim Brotherhood, moreover, had always attracted members from the country's staunchest East Bank families — the middle-class and upper-class elites who helped the king rule. Just as medieval Frenchmen sent one son to the priesthood, another to government, and the third, usually the least promising, to commerce, Jordanian notables usually had at least one sibling in the Brotherhood. ·

"After Hussein became king," said Abdel-Latif Arabiyat, a Muslim Brotherhood leader who had served as Speaker of Jordan's Parliament during the Gulf war, "the first office he visited was the Brotherhood's." Only in Jordan, he noted, was the Brotherhood legal. Because the king was a descendant of the Prophet and came from a religious family, his attitude toward the Ikhwan was "enlightened." Arabiyat himself came from a distinguished Jordanian clan from Salt, a town known for its pro-Hashemite sentiment; his father had opened one of Jordan's first schools.

But now an important rift had grown within the Jordanian Muslim Brotherhood over the Ikhwan's coziness with the Hashemites. Though members were often divided by generations as much as by ethnic origin, East Bank Brothers tended to support the king and favor more moderate policies, while Palestinians — particularly refugees who came from the West Bank and Gaza after the 1967 war or those who were expelled by Israel — championed radical action and greater distance from the throne.

In the 1980s two senior members of the Ikhwan's ruling executive committee, Sheikh Muhammad Abdel Rahman al-Khalifa, an East Banker, and Abdallah Azzam, a Palestinian radical, had vied for leadership on precisely this issue.[55] Khalifa, the Jordanian, had prevailed, thanks to some quiet assistance from Jordan's security agencies. Azzam left Jordan to join the mujahideen, the "holy warriors" fighting the Soviet Union in Afghanistan. After the Soviets withdrew from Afghanistan in 1989, he was killed in Peshāwar, Pakistan, in a mysterious car-bomb explosion whose origins are still unclear. Since his death, Azzam had become a "martyr," a source of inspiration for militant Muslims throughout the Middle East, especially for the "Afghan" radicals attacking their "un-Islamic" secular governments. His picture was everywhere.

Despite this split, the Jordanian Muslim Brotherhood had continued to prosper because of the massive contributions from Saudi Arabia and the Gulf and its efficient social-service network, its reputation for incorruptibility, and the government's helpful ban on all other political organizations. Membership in 1980 stood at nearly three thousand, according to intelligence estimates, and reflected most segments of Jordanian and Palestinian society.

Increasingly, however, success bred audacity. In the mid-1980s the Ikhwan secretly began recruiting within the army. "They crossed the red line," a senior Jordanian official told me.[56]

The government responded by quietly increasing its surveillance of the Brethren. But it hesitated to arrest those who had violated the government's informal ban on army recruitment. "Jailing them would only have created sympathy," a senior intelligence official recounted. Other ways to control the Ikhwan had to be found, and they were.

By 1988, the security services had devised a multipronged strategy for weakening the movement, but after the 1989 riots in Ma'an, the king decided to concentrate instead on political liberalization, or more precisely, electing a new Parliament that would share blame for the economic retrenchment the king knew was inevitable. A few dissenters within Jordan's intelligence community argued that holding elections at this time risked strengthening the Islamist ranks, but the king was adamant. Not until the Brotherhood and independent Islamists swept the elections in 1989 did Hussein conclude that Islamists, particularly the younger Palestinian Brethren, might threaten his throne.

Facing growing radical pressures fueled by the Gulf crisis, the king reappointed Mudar Badran prime minister. Badran knew the Brotherhood well not only because he was related through marriage to leading Islamists but also because he had supervised the training camps for Syrian Brothers in the early 1980s. The palace felt it could rely on him to co-opt leading members of the group, though senior Jordanians later concluded that Badran himself was sympathetic to the Ikhwan's agenda.

In late 1990, in the midst of the Gulf frenzy, Arabiyat, a mainstream Brotherhood figure, was elected Speaker of Parliament, thanks in part to support from leftist, nationalist parliamentarians who, in their anti-Western zeal, had joined forces with the Islamic bloc to support their hero Saddam Hussein. Badran, on the palace's instructions, named five Islamists to his cabinet. While the Brotherhood had long coveted the post of minister of education, the group's radical members vigorously opposed joining the government.[57] The palace, they warned, would blame the Ikhwan for Jordan's growing economic and political crisis and use the ministers to help split the organization.

The radicals proved right. The Muslim Brotherhood "War Cabinet," as it was called, lasted only a few months longer than the war itself.[58] Soon after his appointment, Minister of Education Abdullah al-Akaila became enmeshed in controversy, although the government had taken the precaution of splitting his ministry in two.[59] Akaila outraged many Jordanians by limiting the role of women in the ministry, demanding the segregation of girls and boys in classrooms, and prohibiting fathers from attending their daughters' athletic competitions on grounds that they should not see their daughters' school chums immodestly dressed.

Mainstream Muslims and Christians were soon clamoring for the cabinet's resignation, and in June 1991, King Hussein obliged, happily. Intent on starting peace talks with Israel, Hussein needed to get rid of the loony Islamist cabinet that had been so useful during the Gulf war. Badran was fired, and Islamists were excluded from the new cabinet, much to public acclaim. Whether in Parliament or cabinet, observed Rami G. Khouri, an influential columnist, the Islamists had proved "unable to make the transition from charismatic challengers of government power" to its effective wielders. The Islamists, he said, echoing public sentiment, had turned out to be "weak idea men and lousy administrators." [60]

Meanwhile, Hussein took other steps to end the Brotherhood's monopoly on political action. After the Ma'an riots, the king formed a commission, which included prominent Brotherhood figures, to draft a "national charter," a set of "rules of the game" for political participation in a constitutional monarchy. The king endorsed the draft, a remarkably enlightened document that committed the signatories to political pluralism, democratic rights, and equality of law between men and women—the last in direct contradiction to Islamic sharia. The charter and the law that implemented it also banned foreign funding of Jordan's political parties and assistance from foreign groups—another blow to the internationalist Brotherhood—as well as political organizing within the army and security forces. Finally, the charter barred participation in Jordanian politics to anyone who claimed non-Jordanian nationality or sought "foreign protection." This provision, some analysts maintained, set the legal stage for the day when a Palestinian entity in the West Bank and Gaza might offer citizenship to Jordan's Palestinians. Under the charter, any East Bank Palestinian who accepted such an offer would lose national political rights in Jordan.[61]

The national charter had the desired effect. Whereas the Brotherhood had been the only party to participate in the 1989 elections, some twenty political parties were formed after the national charter became law. Since social welfare and religious groups were prohibited from forming parties, the Muslim Brotherhood was forced to spin off an "Islamic Action Front" as its political wing, another decision that further split the already fractured organization. The Islamic Action Front was eventually led by an Islamist related by marriage to one of the king's daughters and by a former minister, Ishaq Farhan, an American-educated Palestinian from Ein Karim, near Jerusalem, whose family had been in Jordan ever since the 1948 war. Farhan had always been uncompromising toward Israel: The Israeli-Palestinian conflict, he had told me in 1993, was a new "Hundred Years' War" between "modern Crusaders and Palestine's original Arab inhabitants" that could "never" be ended by Arab "surrender to conditions of peace while the enemy is strong." But Farhan was moderate with respect to things Hashemite. The lands of Palestine and Jordan had been unified for thirteen hundred years, he said; their separation was "illegitimate." While the liberation of Palestine was a believer's priority, the use of violence outside of Palestine, especially in Jordan, was "unacceptable," a position that endeared Farhan to Nadwa Palace.

At the same time, the government moved to restrict the spread of Islamist ideas by limiting freedom of the press. Under amendments to the country's media law, newspapers, most of which were wholly or partly government owned, and television, an entirely state-owned enterprise, were prohibited from disseminating news that "offended" the king and his family or insulted Arab, Islamic, or "friendly" heads of state, legally accredited diplomats, or the military and security agencies. In addition, news contrary to "public morals"—whatever that meant—or which "offended the dignity of an individual" or "damaged his reputation" was also barred.

Rather than protest such infringements on freedom of expression, most senior editors endorsed them. Press freedom was "new" to Jordanians and needed to be "nurtured." Irresponsible reporting could inflame Jordanian-Palestinian divisions and ideological disputes that would threaten the nation. "Journalists must learn to be responsible," said Musa Kilani, the editor of the newspaper *Al-Distour*. Kilani was more royalist than the king. Perhaps he had to be: While his brother had been a senior figure in the intelligence service, another relative was a leading Muslim Brother.

In the early 1990s the government also cracked down on Islamic dissidents, or alleged dissidents, to intimidate Islamic radicalism. The government, for example, had arrested more than a hundred young men and accused them of membership in the illegal Jaish Muhammad, or "Muhammad's Army," which one intelligence official had described as a Brotherhood breakaway faction of between seventy-five and a hundred Islamists who had fought in Afghanistan and had returned to Jordan in 1989 to overthrow the government and install an Islamic regime. Ninety of those arrested—they happened to come from prominent families—were released almost immediately. The rest, mostly Palestinians, were tried and convicted, but their sentences were soon commuted by King Hussein.

In early 1994, after two theaters that showed soft-core adult films were bombed and bombs failed to explode at another cinema and a supermarket that sold alcohol, twenty-five men were arrested and accused of the crimes. In December, eighteen of them were convicted, eleven of whom were sentenced to death.[62] While most Jordanians assumed that Hussein would commute the death sentences, as he always had, the speed of the arrests and trials let potential rebels know that Jordan's intelligence network made such violent subversion suicidal.

The government also singled out Laith al-Shubaylat, an independent Islamist who had been the largest single vote getter in the 1989 elections. A genuine eccentric, Shubaylat's independence and erratic political activity had long irritated government officials, among others. In the early 1980s, an Israeli military court had named him in a case involving gunrunning to Islamic radicals in Gaza.

A prominent engineer and son of a former defense minister, Shubaylat had undergone a religious conversion just before the 1967 Arab-Israeli war and had become a popular Islamic thinker. I liked Shubaylat and found him humorously irreverent and original. He fit into no definable category: He was a loner, the rarest of all things in conformist Arab society. An outspoken critic of official corruption, he had exposed high-level kickbacks and bribes on government contracts in his campaign against the prime minister. But he had also infuriated the Brotherhood by assailing what he called the Ikhwan's "appeasement" of the regime. "We're one cozy little municipality here," he once complained to me of Jordan. "There is one ruler and a coterie of servants who hate one another and are easily bought off. Jordan's Parliament settles for taking care of sewage, water, and roads; the Brotherhood looks after souls and hospitals."

In August 1992, Shubaylat and a fellow independent Islamist deputy were arrested and charged with plotting to overthrow the government after their car was stopped and found to contain assorted weapons and explosives. Jordanian officials and intelligence officers swore to me that Shubaylat had, in fact, received money and arms from Iran. But knowing him and his family as I did, I was skeptical. Tried and convicted in a military court—that is, denied basic rights given defendants in civil tribunals—he and his co-Islamist had been sentenced to death. Within forty-eight hours, King Hussein had pardoned them. Shubaylat, who always denied his guilt, told me that while he was "grateful" that Hussein had granted him "justice," he would have preferred to get due process from Jordan's institutions. Those who knew the kingdom well were not surprised by the affair. The king was obviously using such trials to cow the Islamists. We all knew that the king would never countenance Shubaylat's execution, for his brother, a prominent physician, had known King Hussein in the army and was a pillar of Jordanian society. Shubaylat slowly got the message. His trial, coupled with intense family pressure, eventually started to tame him. For several months, he devoted himself to his engineering pursuits. In 1995 the king appointed his brother to the Senate.[63]

By 1993, as Jordanians prepared to vote again in parliamentary elections, the government resorted to a variety of stratagems to assure an anti-Islamist outcome. Much was at stake. The king, having relaunched his secret meetings with Israelis, knew that a peace treaty with Israel was not far off. He needed a Parliament he could count on.

The government adopted a new voting system—from bloc voting to "one-man, one-vote"—that was designed to undermine Islamic candidates. Election rallies were effectively banned. Shortly before the election, King Hussein himself engaged in some unusual campaigning. In an emotional speech, he warned about the grave consequences of repeating "missed opportunities and superficial policies governed by emotions and lack of rationality." He reminded his fellow Jordanians of his family's historical claim to and responsibility for Jerusalem, of the "martyrs" in his family who had paid so dearly for that sacred burden. Finally, he urged them to shun "the few among those who climb the pulpits of the Prophet (blessings and peace be upon him)" to pronounce on "matters that do not concern them." Hussein declared: "Let us leave politics outside the houses of worship." The government, he added, would not act "leniently" toward those who vilified the army officers or intelligence agents—men known for their "piety, scientific aptitude, knowledge, honor, dignity, and high morality," thus tacitly endorsing the methods the government had used to secure the desired election results.

Apparently, even blackmail was not considered off-limits when the nation's future was at stake. A case in point was a longtime veteran of the Ikhwan and senior Brotherhood leader who had been a member of the Jordanian Parliament. According to a senior Jordanian official, Abdullah, as I shall call him, was one of the most influential Brothers — one of the Jordanian branch's "real leaders," as opposed to Sheikh Khalifa, whose age and closeness to the Hashemites made him suspect among younger Islamists. Abdullah, who also had many followers in the United States, which he had visited, was greatly admired by younger Muslim activists for his moral rectitude and for his interest in Islamic education. "But like all men, Islamists like Abdullah had their weaknesses," a senior Jordanian recounted. "And we found them."

In Abdullah's case, the official said, it was women. Though he had more than one wife and many children, Abdullah had other women companions as well, one of whom was "rather young," the official told me. The *mukhabarat*, or intelligence service, had made a tape of him with his friend, which intelligence officials then played for Brotherhood leaders. Akaila, the former education minister to whom Abdullah had been a "guiding light," the official recounted, nearly fainted when he heard the tape. He told the *mukhabarat* that while Abdullah was too senior to be expelled without controversy, he could and would probably be pushed aside. When I asked Akaila about a tape the government had made to pressure Abdullah, he said, "That was a long story. There is no need to talk about it now." The official told me the tape was played repeatedly — whenever the intelligence service needed to shock impressionable young Brethren or threaten recalcitrant radicals.

The official told me the sting accomplished its goal: It not only discredited a leading Brotherhood spokesman and prompted him to step aside in the parliamentary elections; it also let the Brothers know that their organization was thoroughly penetrated, that any member could become the target of such embarrassing personal disclosures.

"You must understand," the official told me without a trace of remorse, "the Islamists' goal — even those you consider 'moderate' — is to overthrow this regime." The danger, he added, came mostly from Palestinians, not Jordanians. The Brethren posed no threat only because they were not strong enough — yet. If they were, they would not hesitate to act. Since they were still weak but smart, they waited. Only extremists, like Muhammad's Army, acted precipitously. Such radicals were not important. As long as the regime made the smart ones wait, as long as the regime understood that the Islamists' goal was its destruction, they would be kept in check. "That is our mission," he told me. "Not to destroy them, but to co-opt those who can be persuaded or bought off and force the others to continue waiting. We know everything they do now. It's just a question of will — if you want to stop them, you can."

I never had the courage to ask King Hussein whether he knew or approved of such tactics, which, of course, were not unknown to America's own FBI. (Only a generation ago, the Bureau had tried to blackmail the civil rights leader Martin Luther King based on information it had acquired through secret surveillance.) But I did visit Abdullah in Amman shortly before the election to ask him why he had withdrawn from the election.

An attractive man with Omar Sharif eyes and a neatly clipped salt-and-pepper beard, Abdullah did not look his age. Did the government perceive the Brotherhood as its enemy? I asked him during an interview at a Jordanian school. "We're neither against the government nor for it," he replied softly. "We're simply for what is right and against what is wrong. Our goal is to promote purity," he said. I suppressed an embarrassed smile.

The government, he continued, was failing the people. The peace talks would yield nothing—at best only 10 percent of Palestine. "We're negotiating about being permitted to be street sweepers, not to run Palestine," he said. I could see why the government feared him. Even in his broken English, Abdullah was an articulate, outspoken opponent of the king's peace talks.

Did I work for the CIA? he suddenly interjected. He had spoken with several alleged American journalists who turned out to be CIA agents, he told me. Under the circumstances, I found it hard to dismiss him as paranoid.

The government allowed the Ikhwan to function, he said. "But they are constantly looking at us. Their projectors are aimed at us. Yes," he said, staring at me with a fractured smile, "they spy on us."

I lost my nerve. I sensed somehow that he knew I had been told about the tape. I could not bring myself to humiliate this man by confronting him with what I had been told—and what other officials had confirmed. Why had he not run in the elections? I asked.

He was sick, he told me, a long-standing health problem, averting his gaze to an empty blackboard. He would not run again for office, but he would continue to write and to protest the government's efforts to reduce the Brotherhood vote.

"Now we are quiet. But one day we shall be strong—strong enough to have an Islamic government. That will take time. But trust me," he declared, "one day Jordan will be Islamic and strong and independent. Islam will prevail."

Could a king like Hussein rule a truly Islamic state? I pressed him. "Why not?" Abdullah replied, now eyeing me suspiciously. "If he is just and wise, why not? I have met him several times," he added. "He's not a bad man. He's better than most leaders."

Perhaps Abdullah was being cautious. Or perhaps he honestly believed what he was saying. I would never know. Nor would I know what Abdullah said to his fellow Muslim Brothers in private. What I sensed was that although he had put up a bold front, the encounter with the security services had broken some of his spirit.

By 1994, the government's strategy seemed to be working. The Ikhwan and the Islamic Action Front were constantly feuding. Those who wanted to boycott the 1993 elections had been forced out of the Islamic Action Front, just as the government had wanted.

Despite all these obstacles and pressures, however, the Islamists still managed to win a sizable share of the vote and nearly 20 percent of the Parliament, less than its previous showing but impressive under the circumstances. The Islamic Front still was the largest single bloc in Parliament. For the moment, however, the government was satisfied. Arabiyat, the most prominent Brother-hood spokesman, had been defeated. So had several other Ikhwan luminaries, most of them Palestinian, whom the palace saw as particularly dangerous. Hus-sein had appointed Arabiyat to the Senate.

For the king, loyalty was what mattered. I thought about the many extreme Islamists I had met who were still welcome in Amman. Hating Jews, inciting violence, and promoting jihad against infidels outside Jordan—all this was permissible provided one did not threaten the throne. Consider the case of Sheikh As'ad Bayyud Tamimi, a former Muslim Brother who in 1980 founded one of the many branches of the Islamic Jihad, the militant Islamic movement whose Palestinian members demanded the eradication of Israel and the creation of an Islamic state in Palestine. His branch of the Islamic Jihad had claimed responsibility for many murderous attacks on Israelis, among the most notorious the January 1990 attack on an Israeli tourist bus near Cairo in which nine Israelis were killed and twelve others injured.

I had interviewed Tamimi at home near his mosque in Amman. I had also read one of his intriguing books, *The Destruction of the State of Israel Is a Koranic Imperative.*[64] Not lacking in humor, Tamimi had given me a copy and inscribed it, in Arabic, as follows: "Mrs. Miller, may you read this book instead of throwing it into the trash bin. Yours sincerely, Sheikh Tamimi, emir (prince) of Islamic Jihad." The book, written, as my translator told me, in exquisite classical Arabic, read like an Arab nationalist tract with bizarre twists. First, it blamed Arab nationalists for the loss of Palestine and the corruption of Arab life. Because the Arab masses had been "betrayed" by secular nationalist leaders, even unity and sacrifice would not liberate them. Only Islam could provide moral and political salvation.

Arab leaders had much to account for, Tamimi wrote. These leaders, "agents of Christians and Jews," had "collaborated" with the West to create the state of Israel. Thus had Palestine been lost to Zionism, an "imperialist national-ist movement." Zionism, he argued, was the result of the persecution of the Jews in Europe. Tamimi had outlined the notorious discrimination against European Jews but then added that Jews had deserved their persecution. They had dominated banks, controlled commerce, and responded to their persecution "by destroying the economies of these states through deception and corruption and creating division and war." Expelled from Europe, the Jews and their Christian allies had conspired with "preachers of nationalism" to destroy the Ottoman caliphate. "Adultery, wine, gambling, and clubs for these things" had been used by corrupt Arab leaders to keep the Muslim masses "in deep slum-ber." But one day they would awaken. The process had begun with the Islamic revolution in Iran, he wrote of the country that had funded the Islamic Jihad until it decided to create its own, more pliable branch.

Tamimi, with his white beard, white turban, white robe, and pale white skin—a veritable study in white—blasted the other Islamic Jihad branches, as well as the Brotherhood, as "Western stooges." The Brotherhood was "still trying to find excuses for inept, corrupt Arab leaders," he told me in Arabic. But eventually, he said, these regimes would crumble, as would America. "We know we are not strong enough to fight you now because you are at your peak," he said. But America's decline had begun. The hurricanes and floods in the south were signs of God's wrath. Twenty percent of Californians were inflicted with AIDS, "more of God's fury!" The American-sponsored peace process was a "farce." The Islamic Jihad would continue its glorious holy war in Palestine. Its martyrs' blood would flow. Eventually, Israel would be destroyed, along with its Arab lackey collaborators.

Did that include Jordan? I asked him. Tamimi's eyes narrowed. Before his expulsion from Jerusalem, Tamimi was the imam, or preacher, at Al-Aqsa Mosque, a Jordanian-appointed post. He owed his very survival to the king. Jordan, he said, was nothing more than a "buffer zone created by the British," but there was nothing incompatible, per se, between Islamic rule and monarchy. King Hussein, he added, was a "good and wise man."

I expected to hear nothing less from Tamimi. His family, which came from Hebron in the West Bank, had been historic allies of the Hashemites. One of his relatives was among King Abdullah's first Palestinian recruits.

As part of his "understanding" with the government of Jordan, he told me, the Islamic Jihad had agreed not to launch its deadly terrorist actions in Palestine from Jordan. Thus, King Hussein had gotten what he wanted from Tamimi: militant Islamic legitimacy for hosting an inspirational leader in the fight for Palestine and acquiescence to his demand that Jordan and the Hashemites be excluded from Islam's theater of action. The holy war would not be brought to, or conducted from, Jordan, at least not by Tamimi.

The king had won out yet again against the Islamists. Because of his own impeccable Islamic credentials and the emphasis in Jordan's political life on Islamic themes, militants had difficulty portraying Jordan as "un-Islamic." The Islamic monarchies, by and large, were better at defusing radical demands for "Islamic" government. Unlike the quasi-secular Arab nationalist states like Egypt, Syria, and Algeria, King Hussein—and the other Middle Eastern kings, Fahd of Saudi Arabia and Hassan II of Morocco—had religious cover.

For the moment, Jordan's monarchy was secure. But some in the palace were still worried. The Brotherhood, an adviser told me over coffee, would not dare challenge King Hussein because he was "too popular and too credible," while the Islamists themselves were still "too divided and weak." They would wait until Hussein was gone and they were stronger. They would bide their time and build their schools and infiltrate Jordanian institutions, hoping that the "king's peace," as they called peace with Israel, would fail to bring prosperity. Jordan's experience did not show that the Brotherhood was "moderate," he said. "It shows they can be patient and pragmatic."

IN MID-OCTOBER 1994, a few days before Israel and Jordan were scheduled to sign their historic peace treaty in Wadi Arava, I received a phone call in New

York from Nadwa Palace in Jordan. His Majesty would be happy to receive me in Amman before the signing ceremony — along with my Israeli friend — the king's adviser told me. A palace car would meet us on the Jordanian side of the Allenby Bridge. Obviously, discretion was important. Mrs. Perry was to tell no one in advance about the interview.

I immediately called Smadar in Tel Aviv. She could not believe that King Hussein had finally agreed to see her, that she would be the first Israeli journalist to interview the man whom she had admired for so long from afar. Being Israeli, she immediately listed all the things that could go wrong. What if the border police would not let her enter Jordan with an Israeli passport? What if the king decided not to make it exclusive? What if news of her meeting leaked in advance in Israel — the only realistic possibility in her list of woes. Don't worry, I consoled her: The palace was very efficient and, unlike her government, enormously discreet.

Journalists, like most people, get obsessions. Arranging this meeting between the Middle Eastern ruler I most admired and my best Israeli friend had become one of mine. While I respected Hussein for his secret diplomacy with Israel and knew how much courage such meetings had required, there was something unseemly after a while about his refusal to meet Israelis openly. An Israeli official who often met with Hussein once confided that at times he felt like a mistress whose boyfriend would never be seen with her in public. For Israelis, whose isolation made public recognition so psychologically crucial, all this scurrying about in semisecret after so many years was demeaning. Hussein's "secret" meetings with Israelis, after all, were about as secret as Israel's nuclear program. Who had not heard an anecdote from one of the king's more than five hundred rendezvous? Was a drive-in movie with Hussein the best that Israel could hope for? When would Hussein take his lover out in public — to a restaurant or a movie?

Granting an interview to an Israeli journalist had become a metaphor to me of Jordan's public acceptance of Israel's existence. Every such concession by the Syrians had to be extracted like an impacted tooth by Washington. Each "favor" — such as permitting Israeli journalists to attend a Clinton-Assad press conference — was tantamount to root canal. Israelis desperately hoped that their relationship with Jordan would be different, that they would be truly welcome in Jordan, that the two peoples would eventually enjoy normal relations. Shaking hands with an Israeli leader was one thing; welcoming an ordinary Israeli journalist in Amman was quite another. So Smadar's interview with King Hussein meant almost as much to me as it did to her.

We drove to the Allenby Bridge together one crisp fall morning, a trip I had so often made alone. I took her picture in the middle of the celebrated rickety wooden bridge — this time, counting the steps. Only twenty-seven steps separated these long-standing neighbors and foes.

An hour later, we were in the capital. Amman's hills and the traffic circles that dissected the city's streets were strewn with Israeli and Jordanian flags, pictures of Hussein, and banners endorsing the peace. "The children of Abraham make peace in the land of peace," one slogan proclaimed in English and Arabic. "With hearts filled with peace, we shall sign the treaty," declared another. The messages were only somewhat undermined by the presence of soldiers fifty feet apart on all major boulevards. If peace was so popular, why was security so tight? I could not help but recall the pictures of Saddam Hussein and the anti-American and anti-Israeli banners that had spanned these same streets only four years ago. Nor could I forget the envy and rage just below Amman's placid surface.

In fact, the mood in Amman was more resigned than euphoric. My friends could not have been more hospitable to Smadar, but few could disguise their discomfort with the pace of events and the prospect of imminent peace with their historical foe. "It's all been a little too fast," said George Hawatmeh, the sophisticated editor of the *Jordan Times*, the only English-language daily in Amman, as we sipped mint tea at his frenetic office. Many of his reporters were hostile to the peace but dared not say so despite the king's liberalization and democratization campaign. I met one of them as I was leaving George's office.

Lamis Andoni, a young and talented Palestinian reporter who was once my newspaper's stringer, offered a tepid smile and even more lukewarm greeting. Like so many Jordanians, Lamis believed that the peace was shameful. She and I had previously quarreled over the Islamic militants, inspired by the Egyptian fanatic Sheikh Omar Abdel Rahman, who had helped blow up New York's World Trade Center. Though Lamis was then studying at the Kennedy School on a prestigious Nieman Fellowship for journalists, she had defended the terrorists. "They were only protesting your government's outrageous foreign policy," she told me, "your one-sided support for Israel and corrupt, reactionary Arab regimes." She sounded like a recording from the 1950s. At least Sheikh Tamimi had condemned the bombing, if only to blame it on "Mossad agents eager to discredit Islam."

Unable to contain my fury, I had lashed out at my former stringer. What had she studied at Harvard? I yelled at her. "Did they teach you ANYTHING about democracy, about how people in democratic societies express disapproval of their government? We vote, Lamis. We get rid of the bastards in power. Maybe we get a new bunch of bastards. But we don't blow up buildings and kill innocent people because we don't like welfare for the poor or aid to Israel. There is no excuse for such violence in a democratic country." She had yelled back, accusing me of a "colonial" mentality. We had spoken infrequently since then. I was devastatingly disappointed in the young woman I had once considered a protégée. If the preservation of tolerance and the building of a democratic tradition depended on young people like Lamis — a secular nationalist with degrees from Moscow and Harvard who had embraced Iraq and then applauded the king's liberalization program — Jordan was in trouble.

At least Lamis had stopped praising Saddam. In fact, no one in Amman talked about Saddam Hussein anymore. They spoke instead about the suffering of the Iraqi people. The store on Jebel Amman that used to sell Saddam watches and pins now had none for sale. But it still had a collection box for the Iraqi "widows and orphans" of the Gulf campaign. The see-through bowl was less than half full.

The Muslim Brotherhood and radical Palestinian groups so well represented in Jordan had called for a general strike — a day of mourning — to protest the peace treaty, the "death of Palestine and Arab dignity." But their appeals had elicited no more enthusiasm than the peace itself. Another Palestinian friend, Leema Nabil, a compassionate but uncompromising journalist, had told me over coffee one morning that the Islamists had debated resigning from Parliament to protest the treaty. The palace had met with them. "Go ahead," they were told. Resign. But the king would not call new elections. He would hold elections only to fill the posts they had vacated. So the Islamists had reconsidered their strategy. Rather than resign, they had decided to boycott the peace ceremony and the parliamentary session that Bill Clinton would address, the first foreign leader to do so.

"The king runs circles around them," Leema reported. Most Jordanians, she told me, had watched the anti-peace-treaty rally that featured my friend Sheikh Tamimi and representatives of Hamas on Israeli television. Jordanian television had refused to broadcast it.

"People are numb," she said, "apathetic and apprehensive. Everyone is just hoping for the best. They are going along not because they like, or approve of, the Israelis, or even because they want peace, but because they trust King Hussein."

For many Jordanians, the peace was begrudging, seen as one of those inevitable natural disasters — like floods or drought. "Like most things, we accept it passively," she said with a sigh.

At least this peace was not like Egypt's cold peace with Israel. In Egypt most ordinary people did not initially oppose the peace; the elite and the court intellectuals did. In Jordan the situation was reversed: The people, overwhelmingly Palestinian, were skeptical about Jordan's initiative; the ruler was for it.

As usual, the king had prevailed. Paradoxically, his stance on the Gulf war, so unpopular abroad, had won him the respect and trust he needed at home to take this audacious step. He hadn't planned it this way, of course, but thanks inadvertently to Saddam, King Hussein was positioned to finish a process his grandfather Abdullah had begun fifty years ago.

If Smadar sensed the ambivalence surrounding her, she gave no hint of it. But since her Arabic was superb, she must have felt it. Perhaps unconsciously she did not wish to acknowledge it. Late that afternoon, a gray Mercedes took us to Nadwa Palace, where we were received by Ali Shukri, a palace official who had been instrumental in arranging Hussein's secret meetings with Israelis. "I know you," Smadar told him in Arabic. His grandfather was Hassan Shukri, the mayor of Haifa. Smadar's grandfather, the chief rabbi of Haifa, had known the elder Shukri well. He had worked with him before the 1948 war. His synagogue was located on Hassan Shukri Street, not far from the Shukri family home, now occupied by Jews, of course. Shukri's mother, Anissa, whose brother was married to a Jew, and Smadar's grandmother had been friends. The families had lived in the same apartment building. Shukri immediately telephoned his mother. She would never believe who was here in the palace with him, he said excitedly: "The granddaughter of Rabbi Baruch Markus!" He gave the phone to Smadar, who chatted happily with Anissa Shukri in Arabic, and even in Hebrew, which Mrs. Shukri had spoken as a child.

For so many years American journalists like me had been the seemingly indispensable brokers between Arabs and Jews. We had explained the Arabs to Israel and vice versa. We had traveled to their mutual forbidden lands. We had made our livelihoods from this conflict—from their misery and suffering. But we were becoming irrelevant. Smadar spoke Arabic better than I ever would; she understood them, and they her, as I never could. True, Israelis were aggressive, and Jordanians passive, by comparison. But this, too, would change. They were, after all, fellow Semites. I would soon be without a virtuous function.

King Hussein smiled broadly as he saw Smadar, a tall and striking blonde, enter his office with me. "So we meet at last!" he said, extending his hand and shaking hers warmly. I could see that my suave friend Smadar was at a loss for words, just as I had been when I first met the king so long ago.

Hussein radiated a serene confidence. The peace treaty with Israel, he told us, would be his "legacy." "I hope future generations will judge me well," he added in typical modesty.

There had been many "disappointments" along the way, Hussein said, not wishing to mar the moment by dwelling on, or assigning blame for, prior failures. He had continued his secret dialogue with Israel, he said, because, despite repeated frustrations, he had wanted to "get to know" his adversary and continue searching for "a way to resolve our differences." He had discovered, he told us, that Israelis were the "mirror image of ourselves," people with the "same worries, same suspicions, the same fears."

Peace was made possible by several factors: First, Egypt had moved separately—a rare public acknowledgment by the king that Sadat, whom he had so often criticized for Camp David, had been courageous. Then the PLO made its own deal, which had freed Jordan to pursue its own peace. Finally, fate had given him a push—his cancer two years earlier. "The prognosis was—well, questionable," he said, staring down at the carpet. He had returned to a welcome he had never expected. "At first I was overwhelmed by the warmth, by the feelings of the people. But then I felt an element of fear—of insecurity—about what might happen if I was not there. So I knew that I had to do everything I could, in whatever time I had left, to achieve peace and make it work."

He was pleased that the peace he and Yitzhak Rabin had crafted along Israel's longest border would not need to be assured by American troops or international police, that it would be a "warm" peace. He and Rabin were "shepherds" of this untried peace.

Who were the "enemies of peace"? I asked Hussein. Only a few "ambitious men who place their own futures above that of the people," he replied. The overwhelming majority of Jordanians wanted peace, he asserted.

But what about the Islamic militants who said that Islam did not permit Muslims to recognize the sovereignty of a Jewish state in *Dar al-Islam*, Islam's abode? The king's eyes widened. He lit a Marlboro Light—his first of the interview. And he lit Smadar's cigarette. For once, I resisted my miserable addiction.

"No one will tell me about my religion," he declared. "I challenge anyone to show me where Islam is for violence and against reconciliation among people." As for Syrian president Assad, he added, Syria's ruler should have "bothered to read the agreement before commenting on it," he said, referring to Assad's denunciation of the treaty as "blasphemy," a view echoed, much to Hussein's astonishment, by Egypt's equally secular president. In any event, he added sharply, "it's our business. I've made this agreement with a clear conscience—and with pride."

There was also just a hint of displeasure with Washington, a remnant of so many disappointments in America, but unusual from a ruler as diplomatic as the king. While he was "grateful" for America's role, Israel and Jordan had done "much of the major work by ourselves."

I could not suppress a smile. Both the king and Rabin had been irritated at the White House's insistence on center stage as the midwife of the Israeli-Jordanian peace. This time, the king and Rabin would have their way: They would sign the peace treaty at Wadi Arava. President Clinton was invited to witness it. When the Americans tried to limit the stage to the three principals, Jordan, again, had balked, insisting that the Russian and Norwegian diplomats share the podium, and the glory, with Clinton.

Was he not risking his life for this peace, as his grandfather Abdullah had done? "No man will frighten me," he said, softening his tone as he sensed my anxiety about the risk he was taking. "I fear no one but God and my conscience. Every life has a beginning—and an end."

IN 1994, THE PALESTINIANS accepted a peace remarkably similar to the Camp David Accords they rejected sixteen years earlier. Some argued that Jordan would have been in a stronger position than it was today had the king grabbed the opportunity to make peace which he, too, had spurned. Had Hussein said yes then, there might not have been 130,000 Israeli settlers in the territories or an Intifada in the West Bank and Gaza that had undermined Jordan's claim to its former territories. Neither the Camp David Accords of 1978 nor the peace treaty Jordan signed in 1994 assured a solution to the dispute's "other fronts"—Syria; neither assured the Palestinians an independent state or a solution to the plight of the refugees; neither decided the fate of Jerusalem.

What had changed in sixteen years? Not the deal, surely, but everything else. Fouad Ajami, an admirer of Hussein's, argued that the king had been able to make peace now only because the definition of what was *haram* and *halal* in

Arab life — impermissible and permissible — had changed beyond all recognition. In 1978, Hussein would have been constrained by all the taboos inherent in the idea of the "Arab nation" that his own Hashemite family had embraced. In 1979, Jordan was too weak and too poor to follow Egypt on its lonely path to peace, too surrounded by Arab purists and hypocrites to ignore the Arabs' designation of the PLO as the "sole legitimate representative of the Palestinian people," too embattled to move alone on the Palestinians' behalf.

The king understood that he was a captive of Arab history and the Hashemite burden of that history. Yes, almost every Middle Eastern state — Sudan, Iran, Iraq, Morocco, Lebanon, Saudi Arabia, and even Syria — had secretly dealt with Israel, but only the Hashemites had been blamed for it. Only King Abdullah was denounced for having taken pride in the effort and killed for refusing to stop. In 1978, Hussein instinctively knew that he could not have survived had he deserted the Arab tribe, as his grandfather had done.

Hussein had taken two "rides with the mob," Ajami called it: joining Nasser in the 1967 war and tilting toward Saddam in 1990. Both had been survival calls. Perhaps Hussein could have survived without bending to popular rage. But what if he had not?

Even now, the king had been able to risk peace only because the Palestinians had settled first. Yasir Arafat had made Jordan's peace with Israel *halal*, permissible. History could not change geography, demography, Jordan's weakness, or its poverty. Hussein's monarchy was fated to reign in a binational state in which his people, the Hashemites and their bedrock East Bank loyalists, were a minority. Because Hussein was not a brutal ruler, he was obliged to accept this reality.

By 1994, the Soviet Union was dead, and so was Arab nationalism. The world, and more importantly, the Arabs, had finally acknowledged the death of their legend. The Arab nation may have existed only in the heated rhetoric of its progenitors, in the dreams of Arab intellectuals, and in its cynical promotion by military autocrats seeking legitimacy, but the Arabs either did not know or had refused to concede as much until the 1967 war. But it took a generation and many more defeats, including the Gulf war, for Hussein to escape the prison of inter-Arab politics, with its mythical solidarity and its confining sense of *aib*, or shame.

Militant Islam, though clearly on the rise in response to the ideological and emotional void created by the death of Arabism, was still too weak in the early 1990s to prevent Hussein from reconciling with his historic foes. Hussein had seized this moment to make peace. The king knew that he still might have to pay for this peace with his life, just as his grandfather King Abdullah and Israel's Prime Minister Rabin had done. What mattered, he told me, was not a life but a legacy. If his own assassination would help ensure that peace would take root, so be it. "When my time comes," he told the mourners at Rabin's funeral in November 1995, "I hope it will be like my grandfather's and like Yitzhak Rabin's."

My friend Smadar praised Hussein's courage and defended his earlier caution. Yes, she told me on our last night together in Amman, of course she had sensed the hostility of so many Jordanians toward peace with her country. Half of this country was Palestinian. How could she blame them? But knowing Arab society as she did, or thought she did, she was encouraged by the strong support for this new peace among the king's men. If the leaders believed in it, she told me, society would eventually follow. That was the Arab way. And that was why the peace with Egypt, as opposed to this new one with Jordan, was so troubling. For in Egypt, the elite had opposed the peace for which the people might have been grateful. But this was Middle Eastern reality. Yes, institutions had to be built, but for the moment wise leaders were what really mattered.

Jordan, in fact, was different from other Arab states — its ruler kinder, more tolerant. Perhaps its Christians, too, were leaving, but at a much lower rate. Most Jordanians were still optimistic about the future. Some attributed such differences to Britain's lengthy stewardship in Jordan. But Whitehall had controlled Cairo and Baghdad with less impressive effect. Glubb Pasha, who had built Jordan's Arab Legion, once credited Jordan's success to its poverty. The new state was "fortunate" in not having had oil, he wrote: For its enemies to seize it "would prove a liability rather than an asset."

The most salient variable was Hussein himself. Were it not for his good temperament and pragmatic leadership, Jordan might well have been another Syria or Lebanon or Libya. What a difference one man made in the Middle East. Of all the Arab countries I had lived and worked in, poor, oilless Jordan had been truly blessed. But would it be so in the long run?

Zaid Rifai, the former prime minister, had laughed at me when I asked him that question on the eve of the peace ceremony at Wadi Arava. "My dear girl," he sighed, "don't you know by now? There is no long run in the Middle East."

ISRAEL

IN A SMALL ROOM at the end of a long white corridor deep within the interrogation wing of the Governor's Building, Israel's highest security prison in the occupied West Bank, Muhammad Abdel-Hamid Salah sat alone, reading his Koran under fluorescent lights.

It was February 11, 1993. Another day of interrogation was about to begin. Though Salah did not know it, I was sitting in an identical room, just down the hall from his, watching him on a television monitor.

Since his arrest by Israeli officials two weeks earlier, Salah had been sitting at a T-shaped Formica table in this spartan room answering questions in Arabic from a man he knew only as Nadav, an Israeli security officer. What Salah told his interrogator had led Israeli authorities to an unsettling conclusion: The United States had become a major base of planning, fund-raising coordination, and even military training — for the Islamic Resistance Movement, better known by its Arabic acronym, Hamas.[1]

To his friends back home in Bridgeview, Illinois, a suburb of Chicago, the forty-two-year-old Salah was a law-abiding citizen, a used-car salesman who was born in a Palestinian refugee camp near Jerusalem and had lived in America since 1970. But Israeli officials knew him by his code name, "Abu Ahmed," or "father of Ahmed," the man who had already confessed to being a senior figure in the clandestine military wing of the U.S.-based command structure of the largest Islamic group, and one of the most violent, operating in Israel and the occupied territories.

Hamas, which means "zeal" in Arabic, was created in late 1987 just after the outbreak of the Intifada, the Palestinian uprising in the territories. Since then, Hamas had rejected the peace accord between Israel and the Palestine Liberation Organization, as well as the PLO's historical status as the "sole legitimate representative of the Palestinian people." It was committed to the annihilation of the Jewish state in Palestine and its replacement by an Islamic government. It had attacked Israeli civilians on both sides of the Green Line, the boundary, drawn literally in green ink by conferees at the 1949 cease-fire negotiations in Rhodes, which designated the land that was to be Israel and that which was to be Palestine.

Before long, Hamas was also the scourge of Palestinians who favored peace with Israel and a two-state solution to the almost century-old Arab-Jewish dispute. The group soon proved more deadly to Palestinians than to Israelis. Between 1987 and Salah's arrest in January 1993, Hamas was blamed not only for the murder of some twenty-six Israelis but also for the deaths of many of the eight hundred Palestinians who were killed for allegedly being Israeli "collaborators."[2] Israeli officials and Palestinian journalists agreed that some two-thirds of the ostensible collaborators had never been Israeli informers at all. Rather, they were women who wore slacks and other "prostitutes," as Hamas called unveiled women; they were alcoholics, drug users, teachers with whom Hamas disagreed, Marxists, atheists, a Darwinist, Freudians, members of the Rotary and Lions Clubs—which Hamas's charter called Jewish spy organizations—and, in particular, supporters of the PLO, Hamas's main rival for power among Palestinians in the Israeli-occupied territories. In December 1992, for example, Hamas had tried but failed to assassinate Faisal Husseini, the unofficial local leader of Palestinians in the West Bank and a member of one of Palestine's most prominent families.

It was Hamas's murder of eight Israeli soldiers in only twelve days and its claims to have kidnapped and killed a border policeman in December 1992 that had led Prime Minister Yitzhak Rabin to incur international as well as domestic opprobrium by deporting to Lebanon 418 Palestinians—many of them doctors, lawyers, teachers, and middle-class professionals from the territories—suspected of links to Hamas and other radical Islamic groups.[3]

Among the most brutal assaults for which Hamas claimed responsibility was the kidnapping and murder of Sgt. Maj. Nissim Toledano, a border policeman and cook in his hometown of Lod, a fifteen-minute drive from Tel Aviv.[4] The militants had warned that they would kill Toledano unless Israel released Sheikh Ahmed Ismail Yasin, Hamas's fifty-nine-year-old founder and spiritual leader who was then serving a life sentence for his role in the murder of alleged Palestinian collaborators. Before the kidnapping, the Israelis had been planning to release the sheikh. A quadriplegic since adolescence and confined to a wheelchair, Yasin was ailing. Israel did not want to help make Yasin a martyr by letting him die in an Israeli jail. But Toledano's kidnapping made the sheikh's release politically impossible.[5]

After Toledano's body was found on the Jerusalem-Jericho highway, the Israeli media reported only that he had been strangled and repeatedly stabbed in the neck and that there were other unspecified "signs of extreme violence." What Israeli reporters knew but did not report,[6] but which all of Israel suspected, was that Toledano had been tortured. Among other things, his eyes had been plucked out.[7]

Sitting alone in his interrogation room, Muhammad Salah did not look like a man who would pluck out another man's eyes. He was serene; he looked like a professor. He was thin; his head was balding, and his pencil mustache and trimmed beard were tinged with gray. He did not seem afraid as his interrogator entered the room, carrying a metal tray with two glasses of Nescafé, milk, and sugar. I wondered whether the coffee was a standard feature of Israeli interrogations or an exception designed to impress me with Israel's treatment of prisoners.

"*Assalam Aleykum,*" Nadav greeted Salah, "peace be with you."

"*Aleykum Salam,*" Salah replied, "and with you."

"You were reading the Koran," Nadav continued in Arabic.

"Yes," said Salah. "A rather interesting Surah."

Only minutes before, Nadav had been sitting next to me. What did I want to know about Salah? Nadav had asked me. What did I want him to ask Salah?

The scene itself was surreal. Israeli security officials were clearly nonplussed by the presence of a journalist, especially a foreigner, in the prison. The government had let me see Salah only because Prime Minister Rabin himself had personally approved it. Rabin was frustrated. Almost no one believed Israel's assertions that the United States had become an important base for Hamas, he told me. Yaakov Perry, then the head of the Shin Bet, Israel's internal security service, had repeatedly warned Washington about growing Hamas activity in the United States, but the Americans had done nothing. Many American officials assumed that Israel was exaggerating the external "terrorist threat" to justify its mass deportations of Palestinians, which the United Nations had condemned.

Soon after Salah's arrest in January, an Israeli journalist had written an opinion article in *The New York Times* describing the alleged Hamas network in America. But if Hamas was operating as blatantly in America as Israel maintained, the Americans responsible for monitoring terrorist links had missed it. So both the FBI and the CIA indignantly denied Israel's assertions.[8]

I believed the Israelis. The prime minister's aides had previously complained to me about Hamas's growing strength in the occupied territories and their difficulty in tracing the deliberately nebulous sources of its funding. Infiltrating Islamic groups was tough: "No booze, no broads, no trips," a senior intelligence official had lamented. Moreover, Israelis had found that all too often their own "infiltrators" began working for the very groups they were supposed to infiltrate after succumbing to the Islamic indoctrination to which new recruits were routinely subjected. The Israelis suspected that Hamas was using the Muslim Brotherhood's *Da'wa*, the impressive network of mosques, schools, clinics, and charitable associations in the territories, and especially abroad, as cover for Hamas agents and to funnel foreign money to militants in the territories. But until Muhammad Salah was arrested, they had almost no evidence that would hold up in court to support their suspicions.

I had come to Tel Aviv to try to verify the American Hamas connection after receiving Rabin's assurances that his government would give me evidence that it had been previously unwilling to disclose. Since the *Times* was skeptical, I had to be sure. Only by seeing Salah myself, by hearing him talk about the Hamas structure in the United States, I told the prime minister, would I be certain about Israel's claims.

Thus, it was a few days later that I found myself face-to-face with Nadav (whose real name I never learned), asking me what I wanted to hear from Salah.[9] His request made me deeply uncomfortable. On the one hand, I wanted to hear Salah repeat what the Israelis insisted he had been telling them. On the other hand, I did not want to become part of an actual interrogation. Where was the line between journalism and participating in an official inquiry, and, for all I knew, torture?

"Ask him to discuss how and why he got involved with Hamas," I suggested tentatively. "Or the material you say you found on him implicating him in military activities in the West Bank and Gaza."

I watched the television anxiously as Nadav began to steer the conversation toward my questions.

Who were the senior people in Hamas in America? Nadav asked.

"There's Mousa Abu Marzook," Salah began slowly.

"And who exactly is Marzook? What are his functions?" Nadav continued.

"I told you. He's political leader in the U.S.," Salah replied.

"What does he do for a living?"

"He has money. He doesn't need a regular job. He owns buildings in the U.S., some in Virginia, I think. He's the highest in the political wing."

"And the military wing?"

"Abu Obeida," he replied. (His real name was Muhammad Qassem Suwalha.) "He's in London.[10] But he travels often to the U.S.—more so these days—and I met him in Washington and Chicago. He consults with Abu Marzook and, of course, with Abu Ahmed."

"Who's Abu Ahmed?"

"Abu Ahmed," he said, was the code name of Ahmed Youssef, a writer and an Islamist sympathizer. He was reputed to have written parts of the group's violently anti-Semitic charter, though Youssef had told me he was not part of Hamas and that he had tried to persuade the group to soften the charter's anti-Jewish rhetoric.

Hamas's political command in the United States, according to Salah, was then based in an ostensible research center called the United Association for Studies and Research (UASR), in Springfield, Virginia, less than a half hour's drive from Washington, D.C.[11] Until recently, Abu Marzook, who had lived in the United States at least since 1981, had been on the board of the UASR, which he helped found. (In July 1995 he was arrested while trying to reenter the United States for being on the U.S. "watch" list for terrorists. Israel had requested his extradition.)

"Abu Ahmed works closely with both Abu Marzook and Muhammad Su-walha," Salah continued. "There are others; I know of about ten people in the U.S., but there are still more in other parts of the country whom I don't know," Salah went on, gradually becoming more talkative. If he was uncomfortable betraying his colleagues, Salah showed no sign of it. He appeared calm. "But the political center is in Virginia. Politically, the base is America. There are also key people in Jordan and in Europe. And don't forget Britain. They all consult with one another."

"How?"

"In meetings and by telephone. They speak in code."

"I've heard this," Nadav said. "Tell me, why do they call military attacks and activity 'positive works'?"

"That's the way they see it," Salah explained, draining his glass of Nescafé. "Killing your enemy is positive. 'Amalat ijabiyah.' It's a code term."

"Do they use these terms when they consult by fax?"

"In America we believe that faxes are more dangerous than telephones. They are too easy to monitor. But we use faxes sometimes. For example, Hamas leaflets written in the territories are faxed to us in America."

"Would local operatives in the territories request permission to stage military attacks?"

"It would be stupid of them to ask that over a phone or a fax. General policy guidance is provided; the rest is up to them."

As a rule, Salah added, Hamas members in Palestine requested American approval for "sensitive" activities. The Hamas commander in Gaza had told Salah that his cell had established a safe house in Rahat, a former Bedouin village in the Negev desert. "They were pleased. It was a good hiding place — inside Israel. But they wanted permission to install a fax to send messages to the U.S. The fax only cost around four hundred dollars. That was no big deal. But they couldn't do it on their own because communications are sensitive. The location, not the cost, had to be approved in the States."

But Salah had also given the Gaza commander money during his most recent trip, he told the Israelis — about $100,000 — and the money was used for something deadlier than fax machines: The five cells under his command had bought M-16s, Kalashnikovs, Uzi submachine guns, and pistols on the Israeli black market. Some of the money was also earmarked for securing at least twenty underground shelters for hiding fugitives and for purchasing equipment to forge student identity cards so that Hamas could smuggle wanted men out of Gaza into neighboring Egypt.

Salah had also given specific instructions about carrying out terrorist operations and some $60,000 in cash to Abdel Ahmed Awadallah, the twenty-five-year-old military commander in Ramallah, a fifteen-minute drive from Jerusalem. This money, too, was for weapons and safe houses. "He asked for $100,000, but I gave him $60,000 and told him to spread it out, little by little," Salah said coolly.

Smaller payments were made to other local Hamas leaders. In less than a week, Salah had disbursed a total of $300,000 in cash. He had been authorized to spend up to $650,000, most of which was transferred into his Chicago bank account, partly by Mousa Abu Marzook.

This, in fact, was Salah's fourth working trip to the territories, Israeli officials said. The first was in 1989, when he accompanied Abu Marzook to the West Bank and Gaza to rebuild the organization's military and political infrastructure after Israel had arrested more than a hundred militants following attacks on Israeli soldiers. Within six months of the American delegation's departure, more than $900,000 in military and humanitarian assistance from America had reached Hamas in the West Bank and Gaza.[12] The trip had been a great success. So was his second visit in August 1992.

Salah's third trip had been ordered by Sheikh Jamal Said, a thirty-eight-year-old militant originally from Jericho who, as of late 1995, was still the preacher at the Bridgeview Mosque in Chicago, which Salah and other Chicago-based Islamic radicals attended. Although Sheikh Said repeatedly denied any links to Hamas, Salah told the Israelis that Said was a high-ranking Muslim Brotherhood activist in America.

"Why did they ask you to do this?" Nadav pressed. "You don't have military experience. Why did they trust you?"

"People just seem to like me," Salah replied modestly. "They had asked around about me in the States. They knew I was a person who could get things done. And I like helping people. Besides, I am an American citizen. That was very important to them. It meant I could move around the territories more freely.

"You hit Hamas every four to eight months or so," Salah told Nadav, pointing his finger at his interrogator. "You bring in all the people and clean the area. Then we have to rebuild. And that teaches us how to rebuild," he added, allowing himself a tiny smile. "So, in fact, you're teaching us."

Was this the tone of a man who feared his interrogator? I wondered, watching Salah taunt Nadav. Was this the behavior of a man who had been tortured into making the confession I was hearing? Earlier, Salah's lawyer had told me that his client had been tortured into confessing in Hebrew, a language he did not understand, by "intense interrogation for three days and nights without sleep" with his hands tied behind his back. It was impossible, of course, for me to know what had happened to Salah before I saw him. But that day, he looked fit and seemed almost jaunty. Israel had finally offered him a mere five years in prison in exchange for information, and he had taken the deal. This was no Palestinian Nathan Hale — five years of his life was more than enough to give for his country.

Nadav seemed intrigued rather than angry at Salah's taunt. "If no money came from the U.S.," he asked him, "would the attacks stop?"

"They would continue, but there would definitely be fewer of them. You know, the people here are broke and tired, very tired," Salah said. "But Hamas doesn't care. We won't ever release any of the land of Palestine. The Intifada will never stop."

Maybe so, I thought, but it would have to carry on without Muhammad Salah and the colleagues he had just betrayed.

AFTER MY OWN ARTICLE on Hamas appeared in the *Times*,[13] I learned that Salah had been an Islamic activist since 1978, when Sheikh Jamal Said had recruited him into the Muslim Brotherhood. He had been active in Hamas in the United States since early 1988, when, parallel to the establishment of Hamas in the occupied territories, Palestinian members of the Brotherhood in America established a U.S.-based group called Filastin (Palestine) to help their militant brothers in the West Bank and Gaza following the outbreak of the Intifada. Hamas had used the United States as a base since early 1988.[14] "Palestine," in effect the Palestinian military wing of the Muslim Brotherhood in America, was headed by Mousa Abu Marzook. And from its inception a key figure in its security branch was the used-car salesman from Chicago, Muhammad Salah.[15]

Only gradually did the Israelis understand how senior a figure Salah was. An important breakthrough came in June 1993, four months after my visit to the Israeli interrogation center, when a twenty-four-year-old Palestinian from Jerusalem named Nasser Issa Jalal al-Hidmi pleaded guilty in an Israeli court to membership in Hamas, a banned organization.[16] Unlike so many other Hamas recruits, Hidmi confessed that he had been trained not in the West Bank or Gaza but in the United States.

Accepted into Hamas in Jerusalem in 1989, Hidmi had been seduced by Hamas's offer to help him finance his stay in America, which he had long dreamed of visiting. On the eve of his departure for Kansas State University in late 1989, he was told to stay in contact with a man from Chicago. In June 1990 his Chicago contact ordered him and twenty-five other Palestinians studying in the United States to attend a "summer camp" near a small lake outside Chicago. Each was given a code number to conceal his identity. Hidmi was "H-3." From Thursday until Sunday, H-3 and the other campers were taught by a Libyan American (a former U.S. Marine) how to assemble bombs, toss grenades, and booby-trap cars. In December 1990, Hidmi attended another series of secret meetings in Kansas City at a conference sponsored by the Islamic Association for Palestine, which has close ties to Hamas and Islamic Jihad, and by the Muslim Arab Youth Association (MAYA), which has served as an unofficial umbrella group for Islamic militants in America and various arms of the Muslim Brotherhood.[17] Once again, he was given a password to enter the closed sessions: "Where is the mosque?" he was asked. "In Al-Aqsa" (the sacred mosque in Jerusalem), he was told to reply.[18] The students were then divided into "committees" that mirrored Hamas's structure in the territories — military, security, culture and education, and political. They also heard lectures from several Hamas leaders about the importance of security and understanding Israeli investigation methods. Mousa Abu Marzook urged the young men to destroy "the outpost of

Western influence" that was "a spearhead in the heart of the Muslim world."[19] These lectures were followed by more lessons on the use of hand grenades, explosives, and bombs. Ibrahim Mahmoud Muzayyin, who introduced himself as the director of the Holy Land Foundation for Relief and Development, a charity to support needy Palestinians in Israel and the territories based in Richardson, Texas, told his students that Hamas had "chosen" them to help escalate the Intifada.[20] Each of them, the man from Chicago concluded, would be expected to wage jihad against Israelis when they returned to Palestine.

In February 1992, his studies finished and his savings gone, Hidmi reluctantly returned to the territories. He was arrested in March 1993 and confessed. Given Hidmi's expression of regret about his actions — "an utterance that is uncommon in this courthouse," the judge stated — Hidmi was given a five-year sentence, only two of which were to be served in prison. (He was subsequently released in the summer of 1994, one of hundreds of Palestinians freed under the PLO-Israel peace agreement.) Because Hidmi had left Hamas before he had killed or hurt anyone, his conviction was not of great interest to most reporters. But it turned out to be important to Israel's case against Salah and the security service's understanding of his role in Hamas, the group's network in the territories, and its structure in America. For the "writ of accusation" filed in Israeli court identified Hidmi's contact in Chicago, the man who had sent him his plane tickets and arranged his participation in the "summer camp," who had organized the lectures in Kansas City and supplied him with orders from Hamas, the man whom the young Palestinians referred to as a key figure in Hamas's military wing in America — Muhammad Salah.

Salah would probably not have taken the risk of operating in the territories himself had Israel's mass deportation of the Palestinians in late 1992 not crippled his group yet again. The situation had become desperate. Someone — preferably a veteran of such missions — had to reconstruct what Israel had destroyed. But the Israelis, having finally penetrated the Hamas group in America, were waiting for him this time. They had followed Salah and his colleague, another Arab American named Muhammad Jarad, a naturalized Palestinian who owned a grocery store in Chicago, as they traveled throughout Israel and the territories.

THE THIRTY-SIX-ARTICLE charter, or covenant, of Hamas clearly identifies the violent group as "a wing of the Muslim Brothers in Palestine" and cites the "blessed memory" of Hassan al-Banna, the Muslim Brotherhood's founder.[21] The Egyptian-based Brotherhood had a long history in the West Bank and Gaza. Banna had sent his own brother to Palestine in 1934 to contact Muslims who were fighting Zionism. Beginning in 1945, the Brotherhood had opened many branches throughout Palestine that railed against Jewish immigration. Many of the Hamas leaders who had emerged during the Intifada had been active in the Brotherhood, particularly in a Brotherhood Islamic group, Al-Mujamma al-Islami, or the Islamic Center, founded in Gaza in 1973. The association, which was licensed by Israel in 1979 as an antidote to the surge in radical Palestinian nationalism in Gaza—a huge mistake, Israeli officials later conceded[22]—was ostensibly devoted to the foundation of mosques, schools—including the Saudi-supported Islamic University of Gaza, with some five thousand students[23]—libraries, and charitable associations. But under the stewardship of Sheikh Yasin, a veteran Brother activist,[24] the Mujamma, in classic Muslim Brotherhood fashion, had used its infrastructure not only to spread its Islamic revival, according to a Palestinian scholar, but also for semiclandestine activity—preaching inflammatory sermons in mosques and distributing incendiary religious and political pamphlets.[25] Until May 1989, when he was rearrested and sentenced to life, Yasin, who had been paralyzed since age sixteen,[26] was the chief spiritual guide of the Brotherhood's militant forces in Gaza.

The Intifada was a turning point for the Islamic movement. Sheikh Yasin had initially argued in typical Muslim Brotherhood tradition that violent jihad against Israel would be counterproductive until Islamic regimes had been established throughout the Muslim realm. But the outbreak of the Intifada changed his mind: Islamic reconquest would have to start rather than end with jihad in Palestine. So stated the Hamas covenant.

In many respects, the covenant reflected Yasin's thinking. Other sections resembled the PLO's charter that had been drafted two decades earlier. But unlike the PLO's controversial covenant, which had been deliberated and debated almost to death and approved by the PLO's "parliament" in exile, that of its Islamic counterpart was presented to Palestinians not for approval but as Hamas's first and final word.

While the PLO charter purportedly criticized Zionism rather than Judaism, the Hamas covenant attacked the Jewish religion itself and accused Jews of slanders lifted from the "Protocols of the Elders of Zion," the nineteenth-century Russian anti-Semitic forgery, and other spurious anti-Jewish tracts.[27] While the PLO charter resonated with the vintage slogans of secular Arab nationalism, Hamas's vocabulary was vibrantly pan-Islamic: Citing passages from the Koran, the charter was purportedly based entirely on Islamic principles. While the PLO charter provided minority rights for what it presumed would be a small Jewish population in the new Palestinian state, Hamas explicitly stated that non-Muslim "Peoples of the Book"—Jewish and Christian Arabs—would be treated according to Islamic law, given "protected" status as second-class citizens in the future Islamic state.

Jihad against the Jews was not a choice but a religious duty for all Muslims, even women, according to the covenant. A Muslim woman's main role, Hamas said, was as "maker of men." Women had to educate the new generation and prepare their sons "for the moral duty of Jihad awaiting them." Righteous mothers also had to manage their homes frugally in the "difficult circumstances surrounding us," the covenant declared. Money saved was "the equivalent of blood."

Intellectuals and artists had to distinguish between art that was "Islamic" and that which was *jahiliyya*, a reference to the pre-Islamic era of barbarity and ignorance before the coming of Muhammad. Islamic works encouraged "ideological mobilization" as well as the "relaxing of the soul." The covenant, of course, did not identify who would distinguish between Islamic art and *jahili* smut or decide whether a work of art relaxed the soul and mobilized Muslims. But the document ordered the artist to err on the side of caution. Holy warriors, the covenant warned, "do not jest."

In its charter the PLO had outlined a distinct governmental structure and institutions for a new Palestine. But Hamas viewed such preoccupations as a waste of time, since the structure of the Islamic system was self-evident: "Allah is its goal, the Prophet its model, the Koran its Constitution, Jihad its path, and death for the sake of Allah its most sublime belief," Article Eight declared. The new Islamic Palestine would probably resemble an even stricter Iran or Saudi Arabia — without oil.

To Hamas, the jihad's enemies were the neo-Crusader Jews, the "Nazi-like enemy," those "merchants of war" who plundered the people's riches, deprived them of "honor," and were forever "scheming." No war erupted anywhere "without their fingerprints on it," Hamas asserted, a charge that even Nazis might have found overstated. Hamas viewed every inch of Palestine as sacred — a *waqf*, property endowed to Islam for the benefit of Muslims that could never be relinquished. All of Jerusalem was the "First Qibla," the holy center to which Muhammad at first had asked Muslims to pray. Hence, sacred Palestine could never be compromised away through peace conferences such as those which had produced the "treacherous" Egyptian-Israeli Camp David Accords. "There is no solution to the Palestinian question except through Jihad," the covenant insisted.

While Hamas paid rhetorical tribute to the PLO as a "father, a brother, a relative, a friend," Islamic militants could not hide their disdain for Yasir Arafat, the PLO chief and his secular, Tunis-based cronies — "pork eaters and wine drinkers," the austere Sheikh Yasin had once called them. The PLO could only be redeemed by embracing Islam.

In fact, the Hamas and PLO leaderships loathed each other. When the Intifada erupted in late 1987 — spontaneously, it seems, and much to the surprise of the Israelis, PLO, and Jordanians alike[28] — the PLO had attempted to gain control of the popular uprising by forming a "Unified National Command." Arafat invited the Muslim Brotherhood and Islamic Jihad, the smaller but older Brotherhood splinter group, to join. But Islamic Jihad refused, and so did Sheikh Yasin, who was certain that the PLO would try to co-opt the Brotherhood or imply that the Brethren had accepted PLO supremacy. Instead, Yasin founded Hamas to claim the leadership of religious Palestinians in the Intifada.[29] Israeli and Palestinian analysts agreed that Yasin had also created Hamas's military branch to protect the Brotherhood's elaborate social-welfare infrastructure from Israeli retaliation. If the Intifada failed, "Hamas would take the blame," an astute Palestinian analyst observed; if it persisted, "the Brotherhood could claim Hamas" as its own, as it later did in the 1988 covenant.[30] Not only did the creation of Hamas enable the Brotherhood to challenge the PLO's claim of exclusive leadership over the uprising; it gave the local Brethren a military presence with which to challenge Islamic Jihad, the rival militant Islamist splinter group that, though small in numbers, was well entrenched in Gaza.[31]

Although Islamic Jihad had almost no social or political program other than holy war, its dramatic terrorist attacks, staged long before the Intifada, had impressed a generation of embittered, powerless Palestinians raised under Israeli occupation. The first Islamic Jihad cells had appeared in Gaza in 1979—the year of Ayatollah Ruholla Khomeini's Islamic takeover in Iran, which had deeply affected the Islamic Jihad's founders.[32] Khomeini's "neo-Shiism," as one scholar called it, his emphasis on action and rejection of the sect's traditional forbearance, proved far more attractive to young Palestinians than the cautious, incrementalist strategy that the Brotherhood had preached ever since it was suppressed in Egypt in the mid-1950s.[33] The Islamic Jihad had also managed to secure Iranian funding, which further endeared Iran to desperate young Palestinians.

Islamic Jihad members shared the Iranian Shiite revolution's reverence not only for jihad but for *shahada* (martyrdom)—a Shiite passion that would soon change the face of terrorism in Israel and its occupied territories. Echoing the Shiite Ayatollah Khomeini, the Islamic Jihad's Sunni Muslim guides said that the Iranian revolution had proved that an elite group of Islamically inspired shock troops—eager for martyrdom—could impose an Islamic order through holy war against a militarily superior power. The Iranian revolution, noted a founder, Sheikh As'ad Tamimi, whom I had interviewed in Amman, had shown that in modern times "Islam was the solution and jihad was the proper means."[34] And the heart of Islam's struggle against the West was Palestine. Had the Iranian revolution not inscribed the word "Jerusalem" on its own flag? Palestine, another Palestinocentric founder agreed, was "the soul of Islam."[35]

In 1987, Israeli security officials estimated that Islamic Jihad had between two thousand and four thousand members, supporters, and sympathizers—many at Gaza's Islamic University, which, despite the financial support it got from the PLO, was the Palestinian Muslim Brethren stronghold.[36] But by mid-1988, Islamic Jihad was in decline. Not only had Israel targeted its cells and deported several of its leaders; the formation of Hamas in December 1987 had ended Islamic Jihad's monopoly on violence among militant Muslim groups. Islamic Jihad's secret and isolated cellular structure, moreover, proved no match for the vast Muslim Brotherhood network of mosques, schools, clinics, and charities that underwrote the Brotherhood's military wing, Hamas. By 1988, Hamas's only serious rival was the PLO.[37]

IN THE FALL of 1990, Fatah, the main PLO group, and Hamas clashed openly in the streets. Eager to avoid charges of dividing the Palestinian resistance, their leaders signed the first of several so-called Pacts of Honor. But fighting continued, especially after Arafat decided that the PLO would attend the American-promoted Madrid peace conference in 1991.

Meanwhile, support for Hamas kept growing at the PLO's expense—

because of local factors and partly because of the Islamic revival under way throughout the region. One factor, though far less influential than others, was the rise within Israel of such radical religious groups as Gush Emunim and other messianic factions that based their claims to the occupied land on religion and spoke openly of "transferring" Arabs from "Judea and Samaria," biblical names for the West Bank that the Israeli government itself had adopted. Such belligerent rhetoric led some terrified Muslims to articulate their own religious defense against Jewish zealotry.[38]

Even before the 1991 Gulf war, the PLO was in trouble. Its expulsion from Jordan in 1970–71 and from Lebanon in 1982 had left the Palestinian secularist standard-bearer without a base near Israel from which to influence the occupied territories. The Gulf war further shifted the balance of power in favor of militant Islam, at least in the territories. Unlike most militant Islamic groups and the PLO—whose chairman had vowed that he and Saddam Hussein would soon "pray together" in Jerusalem's Al-Aqsa Mosque—Hamas had avoided openly embracing Iraq's leader and thus avoided the dramatic decline in financial support from the Gulf states that the PLO suffered after the Gulf war. So Saudi Arabia had quietly shifted some grants and aid earmarked for the PLO to Hamas-affiliated groups and charities in the territories.[39] In addition, Hamas received large contributions from Muslim sympathizers in Arab countries, Europe, and, of course, the United States. Experts on militant Islam asserted that as much as 70–80 percent of $10–$12 million a year that Hamas spent on military activities in the territories originated or came through American channels.[40]

The ailing PLO fought back. Financially squeezed not only by the loss of Gulf aid but also by the expulsion of as many as 400,000 of the 800,000 Palestinians living in the Gulf and from whom the PLO had collected tax,[41] the PLO emphasized its historic legitimacy as the Palestinians' "sole" representative. It denounced the Muslim Brotherhood, Hamas's mother organization, as a "gutless wonder," as one PLO official put it in 1992, a movement that had virtually no tradition of fighting for Palestine.[42] While Hamas boasted of the exploits of Sheikh Izz al-Din al-Qassam, a Syrian-born Islamic militant from Haifa who was killed fighting Zionists and the British in 1935—and had even honored his memory by naming their military squads after him—and while they praised Muslim Brotherhood volunteers from Egypt who had fought so tenaciously against the Jews in the 1948 war, the PLO argued that such examples were exceptions. The Brotherhood's position after the 1967 war was that jihad had to be deferred until Muslims were stronger and ruled by truly Islamic governments. Only the PLO had consistently fought for Palestinian dignity and honor, the PLO asserted.

At the same time, Arafat, like most Arab rulers, was still trying to co-opt the Islamic militants by luring Hamas into membership in the PLO's parliament in exile. But Hamas insisted on more political weight than the PLO chief was willing to relinquish.

In late 1992, Arafat, for the first time, openly criticized Hamas and warned that militant Islamic violence against PLO supporters would lead to unspecified retaliation. There were "limits to our patience," the PLO chief told a reporter.[43] Iranian-funded Hamas squads were killing pro-PLO Palestinians, Arafat told me in a subsequent interview. This was unacceptable. So was aid to his rival from Teheran, which, he charged, had already given Hamas some $30 million—the same figure cited by Israeli prime minister Rabin.[44]

Israel's deportation of Palestinians to Lebanon in 1992 dramatically increased sympathy for Hamas among Palestinians both in the territories and within Israel, much to Arafat's chagrin. Meeting in January 1993 in Khartoum at the invitation of Hassan al-Turabi, the de facto leader of militant Islamic Sudan, Arafat tried again to persuade Hamas to join forces with the PLO. Minutes of the sessions published in a Lebanese newspaper, and later confirmed by participants, revealed how venomous the rivalry had become. Arafat proposed that Hamas become the second-largest group within the PLO, second only to his own group, Fatah.[45] Hamas, represented by its political chief, none other than Mousa Abu Marzook—the former Virginian and frequent visitor to Teheran who would later be arrested in New York—mocked the offer. Hamas, Abu Marzook told Arafat, would not join the PLO until Arafat had suspended his talks with, and renounced his recognition of, Israel. Abu Marzook also accused Arafat of "insulting" Hamas.

"I'll continue to attack you as long as you don't reach an agreement with me," Arafat shouted. "I have prepared a whole dictionary [of names] to call you."

"We didn't come to Khartoum to hear curses," Abu Marzook yelled back.

The communiqué issued by the Sudanese after the meeting could not disguise the failure of Turabi's Islamic mediation.

Meanwhile, the PLO had suspended its negotiations with Israel in Washington to protest Israel's deportations. When the negotiations resumed in April 1993 after a four-month hiatus, they made little progress despite hours of talks at the State Department and the soaring hotel bills of the delegates. I remembered the frustration of my Palestinian friends during trips to Israel and the territories in early 1993. On a shop door in East Jerusalem, I saw graffiti in Arabic that captured the Palestinian mood throughout the territories: "Yes to guns, no to hotels."

The stalled talks also helped Hamas. The PLO, Islamic militants gleefully jeered, was a "spent force," a "defeatist organization." Hamas was sure, Dr. Mahmud al-Zahhar, its spokesman, told me in Gaza in the spring of 1993, that "nothing" would come of the peace talks.

NEWS OF the September 1993 PLO-Israeli peace accord that was laboriously produced in secret meetings in Norway over endless meals of smoked fish and vodka stunned Hamas as much as it did the rest of the world. The Oslo "Declaration of Principles," the agreement between Israel and its long-standing enemy, had, in fact, resulted from Arafat's weakness. What the PLO ultimately accepted at Oslo had repeatedly been rejected by its negotiators in Washington and fell short of what Arafat himself had often described as his minimum demands.[46]

But if Israel was able to make such a favorable deal because it was strong, Prime Minister Rabin, too, had been prompted to do the unthinkable partly by fear of future weakness. The rise of Islamic militancy throughout the region meant that the Palestinian nationalism that Israel had battled as its ultimate demon for more than forty years was no longer the greatest potential threat to the Jewish state. "I came to the conclusion," the prime minister told me on the first anniversary of the accord, "that unless I took the PLO now, there would eventually be no partner among the Palestinians, that extreme Muslims would take over, and there would be no agreement."[47]

Thus, a rising Hamas had inadvertently contributed to the peace by making a deal politically acceptable with the group that Israel had for so long despised. Israel, Rabin concluded, now faced an even greater challenge.[48]

What almost no one predicted at the time was that the peril to Rabin—and to the peace process itself—would come not from Islamic militancy but from its Jewish counterpart.

WHILE THE PLO's decision to attend the 1991 Madrid peace conference had shattered the solidarity of the Islamic movement—causing yet another major split, for instance, within the Islamic Jihad movement[49]—the Oslo peace agreement itself was unanimously condemned by militant Islamists. On the day the accord was signed, in September 1993, Hamas declared in Jerusalem's *Al-Quds* newspaper its "complete rejection" of the peace plan, which called for a staged Israeli withdrawal from unspecified parts of the territories and condemned the PLO's "dangerous concessions" and "outright transgression" of its own principles. In the same newspaper a few days later, Hamas's spiritual guide, Sheikh Yasin, also denounced from his prison cell the "deceptive and ludicrous" accord that would "accomplish nothing for the Palestinian people." Interestingly, however, the sheikh also criticized the agreement on tactical grounds: No accord negotiated "at this time," he said, would be in the Palestinians' interest; "opportunities are not equal when your enemy is in a position of strength and you are not."

Islamic groups that had previously endorsed the Madrid peace conference and, in effect, Arafat's negotiations with Israel now rushed to denounce the Oslo accord. Nadir al-Tamimi, mufti of the Palestinian Liberation Army and a leader of the Islamic Jihad's Jerusalem branch, immediately issued a *fatwa* declaring that "any surrender of even a square foot of Palestinian land may be considered disbelief, *kufr*, and perfidy." Tamimi—the son of Sheikh Tamimi in Amman—also resigned from the PLO's Central Committee, as did most militant Islamists who, two years earlier, had cautiously endorsed Madrid to avoid splitting the Palestinian resistance. Thus, wrote a Palestinian scholar, the PLO lost the "last remnant of Islamic cover."[50]

For Hamas, the accord posed a dual challenge. Not only did it threaten the militant Islamic camp's insistence that no part of sacred Palestine be surrendered to Israel; it also potentially undermined Hamas's support in the newly autonomous Palestinian zones. Hamas had to find a way to continue opposing any agreement with Israel while participating in the institutions created by the peace process in order to preserve its role in Palestinian politics.

Initially, support for the accord among Palestinians in the territories was intense and widespread.[51] So Hamas did what it had previously done when on the defensive: It waited. Eventually, Hamas leaders argued, objective conditions would change, and the popular mood would shift. What that meant, practically, was that Hamas would keep its options open by condemning the peace accord while refusing to rule out working within the new Palestinian Authority, Arafat's government in Gaza and Jericho.

In order to drive a wedge between the PLO leadership and its constituency, Hamas also portrayed the accord as the exclusive work of Arafat and his clique. And while it propagandized against the accord, Hamas prepared to intensify armed resistance—knowing that terrorism in Israel would surely trigger an Israeli security crackdown in the territories that would erode Palestinian confidence in the accord and the PLO.

Hamas sought the moral high ground: It would never condone Arafat's deal with the Jews—a "major sin," its leaders said—but it would not be the cause of *fitna*, civil strife among Palestinians and a sin in Islamic dogma. Thus, Hamas struck yet another Pact of Honor with the PLO, again condemning violence against fellow Palestinians. But that understanding, too, was shattered in late 1994 when fighting between Hamas and the PLO erupted yet again in Gaza.

WHEN ISRAEL BEGAN withdrawing from Gaza and Jericho in the West Bank in May 1994, Muhammad Salah, the Hamas leader from America, was starting to serve his prison sentence. Salah's fellow American courier, Muhammad Jarad, who had a history of heart trouble and had been hospitalized in prison for chest pains, had been released in 1993 after six months in jail. Israeli officials said that Jarad had been a low-level agent but that Salah had ultimately confessed to having recruited and trained young men as Hamas terrorists and also to having suggested that Hamas assassinate Sari Nuseibeh, an influential Palestinian intellectual from Jerusalem who supported peace with Israel.[52] Salah himself had also built more than a dozen timers for bombs.[53]

Meanwhile, American law enforcement officials had increased surveillance of individuals and groups suspected of ties to Hamas and other militant religious groups. The Clinton administration had also stiffened antiterrorism measures, issuing an executive order in January 1995 and introducing legislation that would increase government scrutiny of such individuals and make payments to such groups as Hamas illegal.[54] In April 1995 the CIA director testified that Islamic terrorism posed the "single greatest threat" to U.S. interests. Eager to protect its infrastructure and fund-raising apparatus in the United States, Hamas shifted key military men and missions elsewhere — to England, Jordan, Syria, and Iran.

For its part, Israel had tracked down most of the young men Salah's network had trained and closed some groups that had funneled money to Hamas military operations. Israel had also temporarily closed several Hamas-controlled mosques where the group had stored weapons and propaganda. Preachers, some of whom were installed at Muhammad Salah's orders, were arrested. I had visited a display of captured material in the West Bank headquarters of the Israeli Civil Administration in mid-1993. In these places of worship Israeli soldiers had found guns, knives, chains, Islamic banners and pamphlets, stolen Israeli IDs and uniforms to help Hamas kidnap Israeli soldiers and move about more freely. There were also photographs of Islamic guerrillas as well as of the burned and scarred bodies of Palestinian "collaborators" whom Hamas had "punished" for their alleged crimes. The Hamas torturers, proud of their handiwork, had posted color photos of their mutilated victims on mosque bulletin boards as a warning to others.

By October 1994, Israel had withdrawn from Gaza and Jericho, and neighboring Jordan was about to make its own peace with Israel. On the eve of the Jordanian treaty-signing ceremony, I visited Dr. Zahhar, the Hamas spokesman in Gaza, at his medical office in a dilapidated downtown building that smelled of disinfectant.

Gaza had always been among the most miserable of places I covered. It reminded me of Egypt's poorest slums, but without Egypt's good-humored population. Its oppressive poverty and palpable anguish were even more depressing because of the setting — Gaza had sandy beaches and a serene coastline like that of prosperous northern Israel. I could imagine a string of modern hotels lining its shores. Were it not for the Arab-Israeli conflict and Israel's refusal to permit independent economic development here,[55] Gaza might well have thrived. But within this strip of sand twenty-eight miles long and six miles wide on average, 830,000 people — two-thirds of them children of embittered refugees of the 1948 war and half less than fourteen years old — were crammed into eight squalid refugee camps, four towns, and a few villages. Gaza's rate of annual population growth was 4 percent — among the world's highest. Average per capita GNP was about a thousand dollars a year. There was no economic base.[56]

Yet Gaza had now been spiritually, if not yet economically, transformed by Israel's withdrawal. In the fall of 1994, Palestinian friends who once trembled in their homes under Israeli curfew now strolled, sipped soda, and ate grilled chicken on Gaza's sandy beaches. The PLO, Hamas, and other political groups held public rallies and protests. The once-banned Palestinian flag flew everywhere, and buildings were plastered with photos of Arafat and liberation slogans. Though Israel's repeated closures of Gaza after terrorist attacks in 1993 had inflicted terrible hardship on the 90,000 Gazans among the 130,000 Palestinians who worked in Israel and though living standards, according to one UN official, had "fallen like lead" since the Oslo PLO-Israeli accord,[57] Palestinians in Gaza still seemed jubilant over the end of Israel's twenty-seven-year occupation and grateful to the PLO.

Dr. Zahhar's office that fall evening was crowded with poor Gazans whom he and his interns helped for a pittance, a telling example of *Da'wa*, the social welfare that had won Hamas so many converts in Gaza. A veteran Islamic militant who had helped Sheikh Yasin found his Islamic Center in the 1970s, Zahhar had been among the 418 Palestinians deported to Lebanon in 1992. Though he denied the charge, Israeli and Palestinian journalists had told me that Zahhar was responsible, among other things, for policy regarding the identification and punishment of alleged Palestinian collaborators with Israel, some of whose hideous photos I had seen.

Dr. Zahhar dismissed the many obstacles to his movement's potential growth. He was not concerned, he told me, about the palpable yearning in post-Israeli-occupied Gaza not for Islam but for political freedom; nor did he believe that Hamas's success would be impeded by the Palestinians' strong "secular" tradition, the presence of so many Christian activists and PLO groups in key Palestinian enclaves in East Jerusalem and the territories, or the lack of influential Islamic leaders to compete with Yasir Arafat, "Mr. Palestine," as he was known. Hamas would continue growing even if Sheikh Yasin, Hamas's spiritual leader, remained in prison, he told me.

But I knew that Yasin's charisma and pragmatism had not prevented the Islamic movement from fragmenting over issues of ideology, personality, and money. Hamas had its own extremists who resisted its cooperation with the PLO and their own leadership's agreement with Arafat to limit their jihad against Jews to areas still under Israeli occupation. Moreover, the Saudis, at the request of Israel and the United States, severed overt aid to Islamic groups opposed to the peace process in 1994. Although Hamas had cemented its ties to Iran, which provided alternative funding — some say as much as tens of millions of dollars in aid a year[58] — the group was running short of cash.

Yes, there were challenges, Dr. Zahhar said, eyeing me coldly as he stroked his trimmed graying beard. But the Islamic movement was still gaining ground throughout the Arab world. Given the growing Islamization of the Arab Middle East, he said, Jordan's peace treaty and the PLO-Israeli accord were "temporary" setbacks in a positive trend.[59] Sudan was already Islamic; the oppressive secular regimes in Egypt and Algeria would soon fall. The corrupt PLO would never survive in an Islamic sea.

Was there desperation in Zahhar's bravado? Having the Islamic movement's success depend on an Islamic victory throughout the Middle East or the failure of Arafat's Palestinian Authority to meet local expectations could hardly have been an encouraging prospect for him. But I also knew that if Zahhar had doubts, he would hardly have shared them with me.

"Hamas is not in a hurry," he told me calmly as we said good-bye. "Time is on our side."

•

HAMAS, IN FACT, became increasingly divided and frustrated. Realizing that they could not stop or delay the peace process by defeating Yasir Arafat, the most extreme Hamas militants adopted a new tactic: They would stop the deal with the Jews by destroying Israeli public confidence in the peace and in the Labor government that had made it. Hamas knew that Arafat, as early as May of 1993, had secretly promised Israeli officials at Oslo that he could, and would, stop Hamas terrorism against Israelis. Thus, in the fall of 1994, the radicals launched a series of unprecedentedly deadly suicide bombing attacks against Israelis within Israel and the territories. By September 1995, eighty-nine Israeli civilians and fifty-one soldiers had been killed and hundreds more wounded in raids staged since the signing of the Oslo accord.[60] Defending Israel's new peace became embattled Prime Minister Rabin's foremost political preoccupation.

Arafat, eager to avoid a messy confrontation with Hamas for which the PLO would be blamed, initially hesitated to clamp down on Islamic terrorism launched from his Palestinian Authority. But the suicide attacks slowly persuaded him that he was as much a target of the assaults as Israel. Unless he repressed Hamas and the other militant groups, his aides told me, the peace process — and his own political survival — would be in jeopardy.

Palestinians and Israelis alike agreed that the turning point for Arafat was the October 1994 kidnapping and subsequent murder during a rescue mission of Israeli corporal Nashon Wachsman. Although Wachsman was held in a West Bank town not far from Jerusalem, Hamas had hinted that the Israeli soldier was being held in Gaza, territory under Arafat's ostensible control. The West Bank apartment in which Wachsman had videotaped an emotional appeal for his release had been decorated to look like a typical Gaza dwelling. Hamas wanted the Israelis to believe that Arafat either knew about the abduction or was incapable of finding Wachsman and his captors — which in either case would have destroyed what was left of Israel's confidence in Arafat's stewardship of the territories.

After Wachsman's murder, Arafat quickly increased the Palestinian Authority's security forces from ten thousand to twenty thousand men and his own personal security detachment from twenty-five to seventy. He also began relying on Fatah "Hawks," the militant PLO youth squads that knew the terrain and that of their Hamas rivals far better than the aging policemen whom Arafat had brought with him from Tunis and other Arab capitals. With Israeli cooperation, Palestinian Authority security police hunted down militants and broke up terrorist cells in Gaza and West Bank towns from which Israel would soon withdraw. By early 1995, Arafat felt sufficiently confident to arrest more than a hundred Islamic militants, including boys as young as ten years old whom the police suspected of having been trained as future suicide bombers. In June, Arafat's police detained five Hamas leaders — among them, Dr. Zahhar — and humiliated them by shaving their heads and beards.

Palestinian police increasingly monitored mosques to ensure that parishioners were not incited against the Authority and intensified censorship of the press, closing newspapers and even destroying opposition papers.[61] Palestinian Authority security officers made nighttime raids on suspects' homes, paid Palestinians for information about Islamists, and tortured Palestinians in jail—all of which was denounced not only by the Islamic opposition but by secular Palestinians in the territories and abroad as evidence of Arafat's growing dictatorial tendencies. Arafat was not a ruler but a garbage collector for the Israelis, critics said. The new Palestinian entity resembled Swiss cheese, a Palestinian friend complained, "with Palestinians getting only the holes." Arafat was establishing a "*mukhabarat* state," a police state similar to that of most modern Arab regimes. By accepting Israeli dictates, wrote a prominent Palestinian-American scholar who had initially supported the peace process, Arafat was helping Israel suppress the Palestinian people and "dominate the Arab world." What Israel sought was not reconciliation with Palestinians as a people, he wrote, but "apartheid."[62]

For its part, Israel attempted to assuage the growing Israeli dissatisfaction with the Oslo agreements by cracking down ferociously on suspected Palestinian militants in territories it still controlled, by repeatedly barring Palestinian workers from the West Bank and Gaza from entering Israel to work, and by sealing the family homes of "suicidists" and other Palestinians who staged attacks against Israelis, a practice that had lapsed as the Intifada declined.

An ugly debate erupted over Rabin's decision to permit "tougher" interrogations of Palestinian suspects. Amnesty International and the International Committee of the Red Cross had previously accused Israel of torturing Palestinian prisoners, which Israel had denied. But after the murder of Corporal Wachsman in October 1994, Rabin gruffly dismissed protests in the Knesset over the rough treatment of a Palestinian who was apprehended after having visited the West Bank house in which Wachsman had been held. Israeli commandos had been preparing to raid the house, Rabin told the protesting parliamentarians. The security forces had less than an hour to learn in which room Wachsman was being held and how many men were guarding him. "So we offered him cookies; we asked him if he wanted some coffee," Rabin mocked his challengers. To protect Israeli security, Rabin made clear, the Shin Bet would be free to intensify the abuse of prisoners for which Israel had long been criticized —holding Palestinians in closet-sized cells at low or very high temperatures and in painful, contorted positions, slamming their heads into walls during interrogation, violently shaking, punching, kicking, and choking them, hitting them in the genitals.[63] What had happened to Israel's commitment to be "a light unto the nations"?

IN EARLY 1995, Hamas and the PLO seemed on the verge of civil war. Sheikh Yasin, Hamas's still-imprisoned founding father, denounced Arafat's Palestine Authority as "an arm of Israeli intelligence and the Israeli army." Hamas would fight the PLO as it had the Jews if such "collaboration" continued, he warned. Arafat's peace had legitimized the "usurpation of Palestine." Peace with Israel was "prohibited" by Islamic law; sharia permitted only a ten-year truce "to give the Muslims time to build up enough strength to overcome the Israelis." The jihad against the Jews would never end. He had rejected Israeli offers of release in exchange for a signed pledge of nonviolence, he boasted to his Arab interviewer. "I would rather stay in prison one hundred years than get out in exchange for something," Yasin declared in February.[64]

But something had to be done to protect Hamas's vital institutions — its Muslim Brotherhood–financed Islamic schools and colleges, social service centers, and religious organizations. So Hamas temporarily retreated from terrorist attacks on Israelis in mid-1995.

Then, much to the Islamists' fury, a second Israeli-PLO agreement was signed in September 1995 that mandated Israeli withdrawal from most major West Bank towns and villages. Arafat's popularity soared as Israeli soldiers withdrew from Janeen and other West Bank villages and towns amid jubilant celebrations. Hamas, once again, was on the defensive.

The PLO's new triumph and Arafat's repression of Hamas prompted Hamas to end its assaults on the now hugely popular Arafat, Palestine's "liberator." The Islamists would have to shift political tactics. In October consultations in Sudan, Hamas pragmatists from the territories urged more hard-line colleagues abroad to let them stand for Palestinian elections and, if necessary, to subordinate themselves to the secular PLO in the new Palestinian state.

Dr. Zahhar, whom Arafat had finally released from prison, explained the new political facts of life to Hamas's more extremist cadres: If real peace took hold and the Israeli and Palestinian economies were to prosper, the Islamists would receive no credit for the new prosperity if they shunned the peace and Palestinian government. Time, after all, might not be on Hamas's side.

In November 1995 the still-imprisoned Sheikh Yasin publicly called for an end to terrorist attacks on Israelis. But militants rejected their spiritual guide's counsel. After months of negotiation, Hamas announced in December that while it would field candidates in municipal, trade union, and university elections, it would not seek seats in the new self-governing authority in January 1996. Nor would it abandon military attacks against Israelis, the group declared in Cairo. The pragmatists had lost out to the more militant activists. Rather than split Hamas, they had bowed to the hard-liners. Hamas would survive to fight another day.

ISRAELI CONCERN about the supporters of terrorism was not limited to the West Bank and Gaza. Though the Shin Bet remained what in retrospect was astonishingly oblivious to the implications of growing Jewish militancy, the intelligence service became slowly more alarmed about rising support for Hamas, Islamic Jihad, and other Islamic radicals among Israel's own Arab citizens — "our" Arabs, an intelligence officer called them. "Ask your compatriot Muhammad Salah," he told me.

While the Israeli media had written extensively about the meetings Salah and his traveling companion Muhammad Jarad had held with Hamas contacts in the territories, the American envoys had also met with several prominent Arab citizens of Israel.

According to Israeli officials, Salah and Jarad had met at least twice with Dr. Suleiman Ajbariya, a deputy mayor of Umm al-Fahm, the largest Muslim town in Israel, and once with Sheikh Kamal al-Khatib, the imam of Kafr Kanna, an Arab village near Nazareth in the Galilee, the biblical Cana where Jesus was said to have performed his first miracle, turning water into wine at a wedding feast. Israeli officials told me that these two Israeli Arabs, as well as others being watched, had ties to Hamas. Both were directors of the Arab-Israeli Aid Committee for the Inhabitants of the Territories, a charity registered in Israel that provided money to needy Palestinians under occupation. Each month, Israel's Islamic movement sent to the West Bank and Gaza more than $150,000, which was distributed by Islamic groups in the territories.[65]

Salah had told the Israelis that the committee had received $100,000 from what he identified as one of several Hamas front groups in America — the Holy Land Foundation for Relief and Development, in Texas. The money was supposed to be distributed to families of Hamas men whom Israel had deported in December 1992, but Israeli officials suspected that part of it had financed Islamic military actions in the territories. The committee needed even more money, the Israeli Islamists told their American visitors. The campaign to embarrass Israel by protesting its deportations was costly; the committee's tent outside the prime minister's office had to be manned full-time, and Israeli Arab lawyers for deportee families had to be paid.

Salah and Jarad had told their Israeli Arab interlocutors that Hamas in America would provide money to improve *Sawt al-Haq wal-Hurriya* (the Voice of Right and Freedom), the Israeli Islamic movement's weekly newspaper that was established in 1989. On several occasions, journalists for the paper had been questioned by Israeli security police, and in 1993 the paper's Jerusalem correspondent was convicted of killing Nissim Toledano, the border policeman who had been so brutally tortured. On a second visit, Salah and Jarad had followed Dr. Ajbariya, of Umm al-Fahm, to a meeting of Hamas activists in Gaza.

Sheikh Khatib and Dr. Ajbariya both insisted that their meetings with Salah and Jarad were innocent. Khatib said that he had known Salah since 1990, when they met at an Islamic conference in Kansas City — the same conference where young Nasser Hidmi had been trained in bombs and explosives. "I have nothing to hide," Khatib was quoted as saying after Muhammad Salah's arrest.[66] But Israeli security officials remained skeptical. Hamas activity in the occupied territories was one thing; Hamas-financed and -coordinated activity among Israel's Palestinian citizens was something else. For Hamas's ties to the "good" Arabs, Israel's 900,000 non-Jewish Arab citizens — almost 18 percent of the population — had touched a less frequently articulated Jewish anxiety about people long seen as the potential "enemy within" the Green Line that in time of war or national crisis might side with their fellow Arabs against the Jewish state. Israel had worried about this threat since the 1948 war—Al-Nakba, the Arabs called it, the "catastrophe," the war in which 156,000 Palestinians had refused to leave or were driven out of their historical homeland and who became theoretically equal but minority citizens in their own land, the new Jewish state.

Few visitors to Israel knew that one of the fastest-growing Islamic movements in the Arab Middle East was within Israel. Democracy was a boon to the vibrant young Islamists of Israel, the only Islamic movement in the Middle East to operate within a democratic milieu.

While the majority of Israeli Arabs had once supported Rakah, the Communist Party, or leftist Zionist parties, the loosely structured "Islamic Movement of Israel" was increasingly winning the hearts and votes of young Arab citizens. By the early 1990s it commanded the loyalty of more than a quarter of them. The movement was relatively rich. Israeli security officials estimated that it received about $3 million a year from Muslim communities abroad.

When Islamic candidates first ran for local office in 1984, they won seats on five local village councils and captured the council chairmanship in two of them. In 1989 the Islamic movement won 28 percent of the seats in twelve purely Arab settlements in the fourteen localities in which they competed as well as complete control of five of the fifty-six Israeli Arab villages and townships. Islamists were particularly proud of their showing in Umm al-Fahm, Israel's second-largest Arab town, where Sheikh Ra'id Salah Mahajneh, running under the slogan "Islam Is the Truth, Islam Is the Solution, Islam Is the Alternative," won the mayoralty by defeating a veteran nationalist politician long associated with the Communist Party.[67]

Unlike Hamas, Israel's Islamic Movement endorsed peaceful change. Though Arab Israelis were deeply sympathetic to the plight of their fellow Palestinians in the West Bank and Gaza, most had traditionally observed Israel's "red line" limiting political action: "sympathy yes, violence no," as Sheikh Abdullah Nimr Darwish, a leader of the Islamic Movement, never tired of telling reporters like me and the Jewish audiences he often addressed. As a result, Israel's Islamic Movement was what an Israeli Jewish friend called "vegetarian"—more like Jordan's Muslim Brotherhood than the violent Gama'a Islamiya of Egypt or the Islamic Jihad in the territories.[68]

But would it remain peaceful? How much had Hamas's racism and religious intolerance—and that of Israel's Jewish religious zealots as well—affected Israel's Arabs? And how would Israel's peace with the Palestinians and neighboring Jordan affect Israeli Arabs and Israel's own Islamic Movement? Would it improve the status, alter the identity, or boost the confidence of Israel's non-Jewish citizens?

Many of my Israeli Arab friends argued that peace would dramatically improve their lives. The Jewish majority would no longer have cause to doubt their loyalty or feel threatened by their identification with the PLO and the Palestinians; their "people" would no longer be at war with their "country."

Jews would no longer be able to justify discriminating against them. The issue of what it meant to be a non-Jewish citizen in a Jewish state would have to be reviewed in light of the peace treaties. Israel's Arab minority could be a "bridge" to the Arab world. The most optimistic predicted that peace would create a new, unique "Israeli" identity — neither Western nor Eastern but truly Middle Eastern — in which "Jew" or "Arab" would no longer be stamped on souls or on passports as "nationality." There would be ups and downs, said Mariam Abu Hmeid Mar'i, an Israeli Arab writer and activist from Acre whom I deeply admired. But Mariam was an "opsimist," she said, referring to the word coined by a leading Israeli Arab writer to reflect the skepticism or pessimism inherent in what passed for optimism in Israel.[69]

Other Israeli Arabs were not as confident. Majid Al-Haj, a sociologist from Haifa, argued that Israel's Arabs might be "doubly marginalized" by the peace — increasingly peripheral in Israeli society and equally so within Palestinian and Arab circles. Granting autonomy — and eventual statehood — to Palestinians in the territories might produce among Israeli Arabs a dangerous alienation, a growing frustration, and aggressive, perhaps even violent, demands for cultural and political separation from an Israel that could no longer ignore the inherent contradiction between its commitment to a Jewish state on the one hand and to a democratic one in which all citizens of all religions were theoretically equal on the other.

"National autonomy" for Palestinians in Israel was now being intensely debated by Israeli Arab intellectuals and being promoted not only by secular Palestinians but by Israel's Islamic movement as well. Other questions being raised by Israeli Arabs were also at the core of Israel's identity. What did it mean, in practice, for non-Jewish citizens — and for its Jews as well — to live in a "Jewish state"?

"Israel is at a crossroads," a friend, Elie Rekhess, a Jewish expert on Israel's Arabs, told me. His country had never been forced to confront these controversial issues: The endless Arab-Israeli wars had permitted Israeli Jews to evade questions that might prompt Jewish *fitna* (civil strife) between religious and secular Jews, who had radically different views about the nature and goals of their state and how best to assure Israeli security. Peace meant that such contentious issues could no longer be deferred.

Neither Mariam's "opsimism" nor Majid's fears could be understood without knowing what Israeli Arabs had experienced since 1948. Nor could the prospects of Israel's dynamic Islamic movement be evaluated without appreciating the anger and alienation of so many of Israel's Palestinian citizens. Only gradually did I come to understand such issues during my own travels through the "other" Israel — the Arab villages and towns that most tourists, and even Israeli Jews, seldom, if ever, saw, for example, Dabburiya.

THERE WAS NOTHING unusual about the grave site of Jamal Masalha. Only his name on a small marker distinguished his plot from that of numerous members of his clan who were buried in a cemetery in this village of six thousand Muslims at the base of biblical Mount Tabor. But where and how Jamal Masalha died distinguished his death from the others.

On March 27, 1993, the twenty-year-old Masalha was shot and killed in Tulkarem, in the occupied West Bank, when a Palestinian in the crowded casbah opened fire on his border police unit during a routine patrol.

Prime Minister Rabin had included him among the fifteen Israeli "patriots" who had been killed that year in the "escalation of Palestinian terror" against Israelis. Hebrew newspapers had lauded the "hero" Masalha, the first Muslim volunteer to die serving his nation. Several reported that he had a Koran in his pocket when he was gunned down.

But Masalha was no martyr in his hometown. Because he was the only Arab citizen in this entirely Muslim village ever to have enlisted in the Israeli armed forces, let alone to have been killed policing the occupied territories, Masalha's death evoked intense and divergent emotions.

"I didn't even know that Jamal was in the military," said Asad Azaizeh, Dabburiya's mayor since 1978. "He never wore his uniform when he came home on weekends, so people's first reaction here was astonishment.

"But many were outraged. They wondered what a Muslim from Israel was doing in the territories, oppressing fellow Palestinians, when even many Jews had refused to serve there. Moreover, he was in the border police, known for its ruthlessness in quelling Palestinian protests."

I had traveled to Dabburiya some six weeks after Jamal's death to try to understand the anger in this prosperous Muslim town. I knew that the Islamic movement had little appeal here; the Islamic bloc had won less than 10 percent of the vote in the last municipal elections. So Islamic fervor was probably not the cause. Nor was poverty or even the relative poverty of the Israeli Arab economy. Mayor Azaizeh, now in his third five-year term, was a shrewd politician. Before entering politics, he had been a district officer in Israel's Interior Ministry, which was responsible for internal security; he was experienced, therefore, in operating in a Jewish milieu. As a result, Azaizeh had attracted Jewish investment and secured a greater slice of Israel's budget for his town than had other Israeli Arab mayors.

The mayor tried to explain his constituents' reaction. "You must understand the ambivalence each person in this village feels, all the time, every day, about his identity and status in a Jewish state," the mayor said as we sipped thick Arabic coffee from tiny porcelain cups under an official portrait of Israel's president, Ezer Weizman.

"You will hear this so often that it will become a cliché," he cautioned, "but it remains the core of our problem: We Arab Israelis, Palestinian citizens of Israel, are part of the Arab people, a nation that until recently was at war with our country for more than forty years. For us, it has remained a haunting fact of life. This internal division has torn at us. It has affected everything we say and do. And it obviously affected the way people felt about Jamal's death."

But how could Israeli Arabs expect equal resources and rights with Jews if they did not serve in Israel's military, a key component of Israeli national identity as well as political and economic mobility?

That was just an excuse for not granting Arabs equal rights and resources, the mayor said. "The Druze served in the military," he added, referring to the Muslim sect that broke with Islam in the eleventh century and whose members living in Lebanon I knew so well. "But Druze are not equal, either. In fact, they are the poorest part of the Israeli Arab community. And the Orthodox Jews don't serve at all! No Israeli would think of denying them equality.

"Maybe after there is real peace between the Arabs and Jews, young men in this village will volunteer for military service, if they are permitted to do so," the mayor told me. "But for the moment, many see such service, well, as tantamount to serving in a foreign military."

Azaizeh urged me to talk to Jamal Masalha, the dead Jamal's cousin and namesake who had been close to the young soldier. I found cousin Jamal at Dabburiya's sports and cultural center on top of a hill overlooking the village. The thirty-four-year-old director greeted me in flawless English, which he spoke in addition to French, Hebrew, and his native Arabic.

Jamal, I soon saw, was as exceptional as Dabburiya's mayor. With a master's degree in political science from Haifa University, he had also chosen to be educated in a Jewish high school, a rare choice among Arabs. He believed in the need to promote political dialogue as well as pluralism and democracy. "There is no other way," he insisted, "not for Israel nor any other state in the region."

Jamal had staged many noisy political debates in this five-year-old center, whose floors were damp from the morning scrubbing and smelled of disinfectant. Jews who accepted the stereotype of Israeli Arab villages as filthy and badly run had obviously never visited this place, or Dabburiya itself, which greeted visitors with a brightly painted banner welcoming them in English, Hebrew, and Arabic.

But Jamal's exuberant face deflated when I asked him about his cousin. "I urged him not to join the military, and certainly not to serve in the territories," Jamal told me uneasily.

The Masalhas were among the most important families in the village. But Jamal's branch of the family was neither wealthy nor influential. Because of a heart ailment, Jamal's father could not work; several of his brothers were also unemployed. "And Jamal, well, he was an average student, not exactly a genius," his cousin said with regret. "He never got to the tenth grade." Unable to find a job, Jamal had decided to work for the police. But to qualify, he needed military service. So he enlisted.

The family had a terrible fight after hearing that Jamal had been killed in Tulkarem "in the line of duty," his cousin told me. Jamal's brothers ordered their mother and sisters not to mourn. The family had refused the government's offer of a funeral with full military honors, insisting that Jamal be buried in a simple white shroud, in traditional Islamic fashion, rather than in the blue-and-white Israeli flag that customarily adorned military coffins.

Jamal's service in the Israeli Defense Forces was particularly galling to some villagers given the Masalhas' devotion to the Palestinian cause. Mohammed Masalha, a cousin, had helped lead the infamous 1972 massacre of eleven Israeli athletes by Palestinian gunmen at the Munich Olympic Games. Another cousin, Omar, a physician, had long represented the PLO at the UN Education, Scientific and Cultural Organization in Paris.

A month before his death, "Jamal came home in his military uniform, his Uzi draped over his shoulder," cousin Jamal said, his face clouding as he recalled the village's astonished reaction to this apparition, which Mayor Azaizeh seemed to have forgotten. "I begged him again to find some other work. I told him: 'You are an Israeli. But you are not a Jew. But in the police, you represent them. What are you?'"

His cousin, he said, did not respond. His silence spoke eloquently of the identity crisis that had obsessed the Jewish state's Arab citizens since Israel's creation. It revealed, as did the furor over Jamal's death, the Israeli Arabs' intense identification with Palestine and with the Arab cause despite their Israeli identity cards and citizenship. And it epitomized the quandary Israel had wrestled with since its inception, a dilemma that preoccupied me, too, as I left Dabburiya: Given such alienation and bitterness, could Israel, a self-proclaimed haven for Jews from throughout the world, ever offer its non-Jews, even in peace, truly equal standing?

JUDGING FROM THEIR WRITINGS, many of the founders of modern Zionism barely noticed that Arabs were already living in Palestine when organized Zionist emigration from Europe got under way in the 1880s. Zionism, after all, was nationalism, a European dream promoted by European Jews to rescue not the Jews of the Middle East but the Jews of Central and Eastern Europe from European anti-Semitism. So foreign was the concept of Zionism to Middle Eastern Jews that almost no Sephardic Jews, that is, Jews living in Arab lands, figured prominently in early Zionist history.

Theodor Herzl, the Austrian-born journalist and father of modern Zionism, referred to Palestine in an early speech as "that desolate corner of the Orient." Though much of Palestine was, in fact, desolate and unoccupied, some 500,000 Arabs were living there.[70] Herzl's landmark book *The Jewish State*, which rejected assimilation in Europe and endorsed instead the restoration of a Jewish homeland as the solution to the plight of the Jewish people, said nothing about Palestine's local inhabitants. Herzl, after all, had not yet visited Palestine when he wrote what became Zionism's manifesto.

At first, Herzl and others hoped that Jews would be able to settle in Palestine peacefully because the local Arab population would welcome the inevitable improvement in their living standards. But as Arab hostility to the Jewish settlers — and vice versa — grew steadily along with their numbers,[71] the Zionists concluded that the dream of founding a Jewish state in Palestine would not go unchallenged.

Yet Arab reaction to Zionism was never monolithic. Even within the Palestinian nationalist movement, opinion about the Zionist project was divided. The powerful Husseini family, whose patriarch led the Supreme Muslim Council in Jerusalem, was intensely, inalterably opposed to Jewish immigration and a Jewish state. But the Nashashibis, another preeminent clan, some of whom received money from the Jewish settlement, favored as late as the early 1930s a compromise on Jewish immigration and even the partition of Palestine between Jew and Arab.[72] The violence, assassinations, and blood feuds within the Palestinian community over the response to Zionism would endure to this day.

The growing ferocity of Jewish-Arab violence in the 1930s forced most Zionists to conclude that they would have to fight to establish their state. Fighting erupted in 1947 as soon as Britain announced its intention to withdraw from Palestine. When Ben-Gurion declared the creation of Israel on May 15, 1948, the Arab states sent their armies to help their Palestinian brothers. Hundreds of thousands of native Palestinians, many of whose families had been on the land for centuries, fled in terror. Others were deliberately driven out — and increasingly, the historical record shows, prevented from returning — by Jews who wanted to build an all-Jewish state.

When the war ended, some 758,000 Jews, but only 156,000 Arab Palestinians, remained within Israel's borders. Between 600,000 and 760,000 Palestinian Arabs had become refugees.[73] While historians still debate many aspects of the flight, or expulsion, of the Arabs, one point is not in dispute: Those who fled did not know they were leaving their land forever. During the Arab Revolt of 1936, after all, some forty thousand Arabs had fled, only to return when fighting had ended. Most who fled in 1948 also believed that their exile, too, would be temporary.

FOR MY FRIEND Mariam Abu Hmeid Mar'i, the Israeli Arab writer and activist whose family had lived in the northern Israeli city of Acre for hundreds of years, "temporary" meant an exile of more than five years. For some members of her family, exile continues.

Although she was only eighteen months old in 1948, Mariam knew the story of her family's flight by heart. "My mother was much younger than my father and very frightened," she told me one evening in 1994 over coffee in her villa, whose olive trees and bougainvillea were now encircled by Jewish factories. "We stayed in A'kka [Acre] until the shelling became unbearable," Mariam said, her intense black eyes darting from side to side as she recounted her family's tragic separation.

Mariam's mother's family had been politically active in what she called the "Palestinian Haganah," the Arab resistance, hunted by both the British and the Jews. So her mother's family had fled several weeks earlier to Lebanon.

Remaining in A'kka, her father sent his wife and some of their younger children to friends in a nearby village, where they waited for Arab armies to "liberate" them. "But no one came to our rescue, of course," she said with a sigh. "So our relatives in Lebanon sent a broken-down truck to collect us. I've heard about that trip a thousand times," she said. "How we were loaded onto the back of the open truck with only our mattresses and traveling clothes, how we plodded along in the black of night up those narrow mountain roads, nearly spilling over into a ravine; how we arrived in Lebanon and found the rest of our family in Beirut."

Even then, her father refused to leave his house and land. "He owned houses and shops in A'kka. He had built the city's first mechanized flour mill. He kept telling my mother: 'This is my home and my country. The Turks came and went, and I am still here. The British came and now have left, and I'm still here. And the Jews are coming and will leave. And I shall still be here,'" she said, imitating her father's basso voice.

"It was in this house, at this very table," she said, running her graceful hand along its polished wood, "that what remained of our leadership signed the surrender to the Jews."

Mariam stayed in Beirut until she was seven. She had no love for Lebanon. "We weren't really living. We were passing time, waiting for permission to go home, talking constantly about return. Nobody even tried to get a job. We were living from day to day, being humiliated each day, feeling more helpless each day."

Permission to reunite part of the family was finally granted in 1953. Mariam knows she was lucky. Of the 600,000 to 760,000 Palestinians who became refugees in 1948, only 25,000 were admitted back legally into pre-1967 Israel as a result of family-reunification petitions. An estimated 50,000 more crossed over illegally, but neither these Arabs nor their property claims were recognized by the new state, embittering many Israeli Arabs to this day.

Even being among the Arab "chosen" had its drawbacks. Returning to Israel meant that much of Mariam's family would be separated forever. Permission was granted to her mother and her four unmarried daughters, including Mariam, but not for three of her married sisters. Nor did it include her mother's sons over sixteen. So only one of her brothers could return; three could not. Her father's immediate family had to stay behind. So did all of her uncles and her grandmother.

On her mother's side, no one could return. "My mother was heartbroken," Mariam said, her eyes glistening with tears. "My father told her not to worry, that the rest of the family would eventually be reunited. So my mother came back, hoping he was right. But she missed her mother, her sister, and her own sons terribly.

"Every morning at dawn prayers, at 4:00 A.M., I would wake up and hear her praying quietly for her family. She cried every morning; she would pray for their health and our eventual reunion. It was her own special prayer."

Mariam's mother died in 1994 still murmuring her prayer. "My two older brothers died without our ever seeing them again," she said softly. "So did two of my sisters. Today I have one brother and a sister who live in Lebanon with their children; I have never seen them."

Part of the family was reunited once in 1966 — for ten minutes. "The Jews talk about the Wailing Wall. Well I remember our Wailing Border. The Red Cross had arranged for us all to meet at what was then the Israeli-Jordanian border dividing East [Arab] from West [Israeli] Jerusalem.

"We were so excited. But my father was reluctant to go. We thought he was heartless. How could he not want to see his children! But he turned out to be right. The reunion was like Judgment Day — everyone moving around one another in circles, frantically, aimlessly.

"My family from Lebanon had spent a month in Jordan waiting for the meeting. Then all we had was five minutes. Five minutes! My mother could not stop crying. She kept saying: 'I have only five minutes with my children!'

"An Israeli officer took pity on us and gave us five more minutes. But there was such hysteria — so much screaming and crying and hugging. Then it was over. In an instant. Just like that.

"We cried all the way home. Nobody said a word all the way back to A'kka. It was worse than not having seen one another. I have no memory of their faces — just the tears."

The 1967 war, which reunited the West Bank and Gaza with the rest of Palestine under Israeli sovereignty, gave the Mar'is another opportunity to meet. "After '67, some family members could visit, with special permission. I had a niece in Janeen [the West Bank] whom I saw for the first time. And my brother came to the West Bank and then was permitted to live with us in A'kka."

The Mar'i family's story, so terribly typical of Arab families torn apart by Israel's creation, still has no ending. "There's more realism now. But it pains me to know that the PLO-Israeli accord does not affect more than 350,000 Palestinians in Lebanon or any Palestinians in the diaspora. My family in Lebanon are unwanted 'guests,' without rights or citizenship. Why should a Jew from Latvia have more right to live in A'kka than my brothers and sisters who were born here? Is that just? I want my own 'ingathering' here, a Palestinian right of return. Do you realize that they are only ninety minutes away? From Beirut to A'kka is a ninety-minute drive. Yet our family may never be reunited. What will become of them? If not here, where does the rest of my family belong?"

THE MAR'IS got their home back almost immediately after the war, but they were not permitted to live in it again until 1966, when military rule over Israeli Arabs finally ended, eighteen years after Israel's war for independence and one year before the next Arab-Israeli war. Israeli Arabs do not like to discuss the military rule. But Sabri Jiryis, an Israeli Arab lawyer who was born in 1938 and left his family and Christian village in Galilee in 1970 to join the PLO abroad, remembers almost nothing but that. He meticulously recorded those memories in a book, one of the first serious studies of Israel's Arabs written by an Israeli Arab. Originally published in Hebrew in 1966 (with sections banned by Israeli censors), it was translated and republished in full a decade later.[74]

The defense regulations were unintentionally revealing, Sabri told me when we met for the first time during the civil war in Beirut. Sitting amid his file cabinets and boxes overflowing with documents in what was then the PLO's research center on Sadat Street, Sabri appeared more scholar than terrorist, as Israel insisted on labeling all PLO officials. I couldn't imagine him stabbing an Israeli athlete or opening fire on Jewish schoolchildren with a Kalashnikov.

"But I *am* a terrorist." He laughed dryly. "I rewrite Israel's mythical history. I'm more dangerous than the PLO's guerrillas, our fedayeen!"

He was proud of his scholarship; he detested the "propaganda" that was churned out by both sides in this conflict, he told me. "The truth is awful enough. Why not just tell it without exaggeration or embroidery?"

After Arafat's PLO was expelled from Lebanon, Jiryis reopened his center in Nicosia in July 1983 to continue his research on Israel's "colonial" rule.

"Palestinians were the natives in the new colony, like the 'Redskins' in America," he said. "The regulations gave total authority — literally life-and-death power — to the military governors of the three principal regions in which Arabs in Israel lived: Galilee in the north, where 60 percent of the Arabs reside, the Triangle [connecting three important Arab towns in central Israel, home to some 30 percent], and the Negev in the south," he explained. Article 142 obliterated freedom of expression. Article 109 (I) (d) banned the printing in Israel of any "notice, illustration, placard, advertisement, proclamation, pamphlet or other like document containing matter of political significance" without written authorization. Article 111 gave authorities power to detain Arabs viewed as security risks indefinitely, without trial or charges. Article 124 was used to impose curfews in Arab villages of the Triangle for most of the night for nearly fourteen years.

Under military rule, vast tracts of land — almost half of the land owned by the remaining Arabs of Israel — were expropriated by special order or legislation passed by the Knesset, Israel's Parliament. A generation of Israeli Arabs had grown up under such restrictions.

Always a maverick, even within the PLO, Jiryis was an early and influential proponent of the "two-state solution" to the Arab-Israeli dispute — the creation of a Palestinian state that implicitly recognized Israel's right to exist as a separate state — a position the PLO leadership finally adopted only in 1988.[75]

The collective memory of military rule partly explained why Israel's Arabs so bitterly resented the application of similar laws to fellow Palestinians in the occupied territories. It was also why Israeli Arabs had reacted so emotionally to the 1992 mass deportations of alleged Islamists from the territories. If Israel could flout international law by exiling 418 Palestinians suspected of Islamist sympathies, would Israel's Arab citizens be next?

In 1995, Sabri Jiryis and his files came home. The files went to Arafat's new

Palestinian Authority in Gaza, but Sabri himself, a supporter of the PLO-Israel peace accord, returned to his village in Galilee. Israel quietly restored the citizenship it had taken from him. He now appeared as a commentator on Israel television, appealing for a confederation of Israel, Palestine, and Jordan. But making peace with neighboring Arab states would not end the dilemma of Israel's Palestinian citizens, he warned. "The only real solution to our problem is for the Zionist component of Israel's identity to become less important," he told me, still saying things that most Jews did not want to hear. "Otherwise, Israel's Arabs will remain second-class citizens, non-Jews in a country that defines its essence as a Jewish state."

SEVERAL EVENTS explain the rise of the Islamic movement within Israel. First, Israel's victory in 1967 over the Arabs erased what had been Israel's Green Line border and ended the separation of Israel's quiescent Arab population and the 1.2 million Palestinians living in Gaza under Egyptian rule and in the West Bank as part of Jordan. The Israeli victory brought these very different Palestinian communities into direct contact for the first time since 1948.[76] If the "Six-Day War" humiliated the Arabs — the Arab "holocaust," Sheikh Darwish, the leader of Israel's Islamic movement had called it[77] — the defeat proved particularly unsettling to Israel's Palestinians, many of whom, like Arabs elsewhere, began searching for solace and strength in the Islam that they had abandoned in the heyday of the secular pan-Arabism in the 1950s and 1960s.

The effect of free movement across the old boundaries and the exposure of Israeli Muslims to what one scholar called "the vigorous, well-organized religious life of the West Bank and Gaza Strip" was "startling."[78] Kamal Rayan, who, in 1984, at age twenty-five, became the first Israeli Arab Islamist to win a mayoral election in Kafr Bara, population fifteen hundred, described the impact of his early trips to the West Bank. "We saw their holy books, their mosques, their schools," he told me one day in his small, spare office. "By reminding us that we, too, were Muslims, our brothers in the occupied territories spoke to our hearts. So although we knew almost nothing about our Islamic traditions, though we had almost no Islamic teachers, few mosques, and hardly any Korans, some of us began studying Islam — on our own, in small groups. There was suddenly an insatiable hunger to read, speak, and know everything about Islam."[79]

After 1967, young Israeli Arabs were able to study at Islamic colleges in the territories where Islamism was beginning to vie with nationalism for political preeminence. (Many of the current leaders of Israel's Islamic movement studied at the Islamic Studies Center in Hebron, for example.) In 1978, some Israeli Arabs were also permitted for the first time to go on pilgrimages to Mecca and Medina, further exposing them to the Islamic revival in other Arab countries.[80]

Then came Iran's revolution in 1979. Despite theological and political differences between Sunni Palestinians and Shiite Iranians, young Arabs inside Israel were awed by the Iranian Islamic movement's success in toppling a powerful, non-Arab, Middle Eastern state so closely allied with the United States. Could Tel Aviv be the next Teheran? The notion that a return to Islam's "straight path" might lead to political liberation encouraged the Islamic revival within Israel, as it had within the territories. Even before the outbreak of the Intifada in 1987, mosque construction inside Israel had nearly tripled: from 60 in 1967 to 150 a decade later.[81] By 1993, Israel had 240 mosques.

Within a year of the Iranian revolution, Israeli Islamists had organized an Islamic Jihad group known as Usrat al-Jihad, the "holy war family," with ties to the Muslim Brotherhood in Syria and Jordan. The group conducted sabotage against Jews as well as Muslims — burning down a cinema in the major Muslim town of Umm al-Fahm for showing "pornographic" films and attacking fellow Israeli Muslim "collaborators" with Jews because they defended secularism and other "permissive" trends within Arab society. In 1981, all seventy members were arrested and sentenced to prison, some for terms of up to fifteen years. Among them was a charismatic young Israeli Arab who had abandoned Marxism to become a "born-again" Muslim sheikh — Abdullah Darwish — a future leader of Israel's Islamic movement. Born in 1948 and a graduate of the Islamic Institute in Israeli-occupied Nablus, Darwish would never forget the sobering effect of an Israeli prison or the folly of violently challenging a state as powerful as Israel.

Inadvertently, Israel had helped fuel its own Islamic movement. With responsibility for Arab affairs split among several ministries, a succession of Israeli governments produced an often incoherent, fragmented policy toward Muslims and their institutions. In some respects, Israel's posture toward Islamists had been remarkably similar to that of neighboring Arab states which also faced radical Islamic challenges. Long fearful that Islam would join forces with Palestinian nationalism, the Israeli government's strict controls since 1948 were aimed at preventing the emergence of an independent-minded nationalist Muslim leadership; Arabs widely viewed as "yes-men" had been appointed to official Muslim posts. Islamic education had been discouraged, so much so that by the mid-1960s, Israeli Muslim institutions faced a lack of qualified preachers, qadis (judges), and other Muslim functionaries.[82] Weak and discredited, Israel's official Muslim establishment lacked credibility among Israeli Arabs and hence proved no match for the vibrant young Islamists who sought to fill their community's spiritual vacuum after the 1967 war.

To supplant the Jewish state's co-opted Islamic establishment, the Islamists began creating their own institutions, such as the Islamic College in Umm al-Fahm to train scholars and imams and a National Islamic Association to conduct research into which holy sites and cemeteries had been owned by the Muslim community before 1948. To protect neglected Islamic sites, the Islamists also formed local Islamic associations throughout Israel.[83] And much to the government's chagrin, they rallied considerable popular support for their campaign to regain control of the *waqf*, property endowed to mosques that the Jewish state had controlled since 1948.

The 1987 Intifada intensified Israel's indigenous Islamic trend. Israeli Arabs mobilized as never before to help their brethren under siege. While many Israeli Arabs offered moral support to occupied Palestinians, a few went further: Israeli Arabs in Nazareth, Umm al-Fahm, and small Arab villages in the north secretly printed handbills and leaflets for PLO leaders. And when the Israeli security service blocked international direct-dialing in the territories, making it difficult for Hamas and PLO leaders to receive orders and advice from overseas, Israeli Arabs volunteered the use of their own phones; others even allowed their bank accounts to be used to funnel money to the families of Intifada detainees.[84]

The creation of Hamas in the occupied territories — a by-product of the Intifada — also stimulated Israel's indigenous Islamic movement. *Al-Sirat*, the Islamic monthly from Umm al-Fahm (which stopped publishing in the early 1990s), and *Sawt al-Haq wal-Hurriya*, the weekly from the same town that first appeared in 1989, published detailed accounts of the Intifada and appeals for aid for the families of Palestinian detainees. The papers featured Palestinian poems, essays, and letters that compared Israelis to Nazis, denied the Holocaust, and denounced Israelis as "crusader-like snakes" and "disciples of Satan." Hamas and Islamic Jihad themes and slogans were also picked up by Israel's Islamic press. Among the most popular rhyming slogans was: "Remember Khaybar, oh ye Jews, the Army of Muhammad will surely return." Khaybar was the Arabian oasis where the Prophet Muhammad had massacred Jews who had fled Medina.

After the Islamic Movement of Israel scored its impressive municipal election victories in 1989, editorial demands for jihad against Israel became common in Israel's Islamist papers.[85] But Sheikh Darwish, the Israeli Islamist leader, always carefully stressed that his holy war was a *jihad al-nafs* (jihad of the soul), a struggle between good and evil in the hearts of believers. Nevertheless, as rhetoric intensified, a few Israeli Arabs turned to militant protest. By 1988, acts of sabotage within Israel — Molotov cocktail assaults, stabbings, grenade attacks, and shootings — attributed to Israeli Arabs had tripled from 69 in 1987 to 208.[86]

In February 1992 four Israeli Islamists from the Umm al-Fahm area, the heartland of the Islamic movement, hacked three soldiers to death as they slept in their tents in an army camp in the Galilee. The gruesome murders — for which the four were sentenced to life in prison — turned out to be an isolated act by a tiny band of religious fanatics who had formed an Islamic Jihad cell within Israel proper. But the Galilee murders shocked Jews and increased government suspicion and surveillance of the Islamic movement. To calm Jewish fears, Islamist leaders denounced the murders, declaring that Islam specifically forbade such violence. Sheikh Darwish even issued a *fatwa* commanding believers to shun "racism, provocation and violence" and warning that those who failed to learn the lessons of history were "destined to be deaf, dumb, blind."[87] Darwish and others stressed, moreover, that most Israeli Arabs were conducting an intense but legal struggle against the repression of legitimate Palestinian nationalism in the West Bank and Gaza to improve their own economic standing in Israel.

By and large, the growing militancy in the territories reinforced the Palestinian component of Israeli Arab identity, fostering what analysts commonly called the "Palestinization" of Israeli Arabs. But many Israeli Arabs hesitated to identify themselves as Palestinians or to endorse Palestinian nationalism, for until the 1993 Oslo peace accord, Jews equated the PLO with terrorism and saw any expression of identification with, or sympathy for, the organization as subversive. Since 75 percent of the Israeli Arabs were Muslim, however, defining oneself as "Muslim" not only created the psychological distance from mainstream Jewish society that many Israeli Arabs sought in times of crisis; it did so in a seemingly less provocative way.

The 1990 Gulf crisis further alienated Israel's Jews from its Arab citizens, as support for Saddam Hussein, so widespread within the territories, spread also within the Israeli Arab community.[88] Enthusiasm for Saddam crossed Palestinian class, regional, and religious lines. Even Palestinian Christians, such as Jonathan Kuttab, a human-rights activist in Jerusalem, said that although Saddam was ruthless, the Iraqi leader embodied "something revolutionary and wonderful" that was articulated in the Islamic slogan " 'Allahu Akbar,' . . . the faith in a Great God: Greater than . . . all the might of the 28 states that attacked Iraq."[89]

Israeli Jews were heartsick, of course, when their Palestinian friends in the territories turned on them, though in retrospect they should not have been surprised. How could Palestinians have been anything but euphoric about the prospect—however slight—of ending what Israel called its "benign occupation," which had been humiliating for those occupied as well as brutalizing for the occupiers.[90] But Israeli Jews were even more stunned when Israeli Arabs embraced Iraq—though with somewhat more restraint than their brethren in the territories.[91] Israeli Arab parliamentarians and notables expressed their "disappointment" in Saddam's devastating defeat. Televised pictures of the shoes Iraqi soldiers had discarded in the desert sand "tore at my heart," wrote one Israeli Arab politician, for the images "reinforced the stigma of the Arab as one who runs away. Suddenly I felt as if those shoes belonged to me." Even the normally restrained Sheikh Darwish could not hide his regret. America and its Gulf allies—Saudi King Fahd, Presidents Mubarak of Egypt and Assad of Syria, and the other "pygmies who pretend to be Arabs and Muslims" would soon be "humiliated and swept from the earth's surface by the wrath of the people," Darwish said.[92] But other Israeli Arabs saw that Iraq was defeated not by infidels or imperialists but largely by the failings of Iraq's regime. After the war, many Israeli Arab commentators called for greater democracy and a more critical approach to the ills of Arab society as an antidote to Arab weakness. The Islamic Movement of Israel, however, called for more Islam.

While the 1967 war, the Iranian revolution, and the Intifada undoubtedly spurred the Islamic revival in Israel, they probably would not have had such an intense effect were it not for the gross and growing inequality in living standards between Israeli Jews and Arabs. The abrupt modernization that Israel's Arabs had experienced since 1948 — the "Israelization" of Arab citizens — would have been unsettling in any event. But it was particularly so when combined with a sense of injustice. More than any other factor, economic inequality intensified Arab frustration and alienation and thus enhanced Islam's appeal within Israel. Israeli Arab politics, like all politics, was local.

Poor and besieged by Arab enemies, the new Israeli state had nonetheless done much, Jews maintained, to accommodate its 156,000 stunned and reluctant new citizens — a vanquished, traumatized, leaderless, mostly illiterate population, 70 percent of whom were farmers (as opposed to 7 percent today) and most of whose middle class had fled.[93] Perhaps the heaviest psychological burden initially for Israel's Arabs was their political isolation. At first, Arabs outside the state viewed those who, like Mariam Mar'i's father, had remained not as practitioners of sumud — a "steadfastness" that was eventually respected — but as traitors and collaborators with the Jews. Despised by their neighbors and cut off from their traditional educational, religious, and political centers in Jerusalem, Nablus, and Hebron, the Arabs of Israel were politically and spiritually adrift.

Still, Jewish leaders boasted that the living and educational standards of Israel's Arab minority were higher than those of Arabs in neighboring countries and far higher than their fellow Palestinians in the territories. But Israeli Arabs compared their status and living standards not to those of their Arab neighbors but to those of the Jews. The inequalities were — and remain — breathtaking. Arabs, according to Majid Al-Haj, an expert on Israeli Arab education, lag two decades behind Jews in academic achievement. While in 1992 some 98 percent of Jewish children received some preschool education, only half of Arab children did. In universities, Arabs, who constitute more than 18 percent of the overall population, accounted for only 6 percent of students. Only sixteen of Israel's roughly five thousand full-time university lecturers were Arab. Moreover, college attendance often failed to improve an Arab's job prospects: More than 40 percent of Arabs who graduated from the University of Haifa between 1982 and 1987 were either unemployed or had taken blue-collar jobs.[94] Although 52 percent of Israeli Arabs voted for Zionist parties in 1992, there were no Arab cabinet ministers and only one Arab ambassador. Only one of the more than four thousand directors on the boards of some two hundred government companies was Arab. Even the Department of Muslim Affairs in the Israeli Ministry of Religions was headed by a Jew. For every shekel the government spent on an Arab citizen in 1992, it spent 2.5 on his Jewish counterpart. In 1994 more than half of all Israeli Arabs, as opposed to 11 percent of Jews, lived below the poverty line.[95]

Given such gaps, resentment among Israeli Arabs was bound to grow. And eventually the Arabs' secular leaders were bound to be blamed for failing to deliver. Though Israel's Arabs could not end the discrimination against them, they could change their local leaders — unlike their brethren in Arab countries. And in the municipal elections in 1989 and 1993, that is exactly what many of them did.

•

A SMALL MONUMENT stands in a tiny park at the end of the Street of the Martyrs in the heart of the Israeli Arab town of Kafr Qassem, population eleven thousand. Surrounded by white and red rosebushes, the marble obelisk is engraved in Arabic: "To the eternal souls of the dead heroes who fell through injustice in the aggressive tragedy for which they were not to blame."

Given what had happened in Kafr Qassem, the monument's inscription is restrained. It does not include the word "murdered" to describe the fate of the forty-nine Arabs — including nine women and seven children — who were gunned down or the dozens who were wounded here in 1956.

My friend Smadar Perry, the Israeli journalist, and I had made the twenty-minute car trip from Tel Aviv in the fall of 1993 to cover the election between Ibrahim Sarsur, Kafr Qassem's incumbent Islamic mayor, and his rival, Abdul Rahim Issa, who had been mayor for eleven years before Sarsur's election in 1989 and whose father had ruled here for sixteen years.

"For a long time we didn't dare talk about the massacre," said Fatin Issa, the former mayor's nephew, as the three of us inspected the neat marker. "Now they teach it in my law school as an example of when not to follow orders. But it took years for the trauma to subside. And it took us twenty years to have the courage to erect this monument."[96]

According to Israeli court records, the tragedy began when an Israeli brigadier, Yeshishkar Shadmi, imposed a strict curfew on Kafr Qassem and seven other villages near the Jordanian border on the eve of the 1956 Suez war. To ensure that the area would remain calm, Shadmi was said to have instructed Shmuel Melinki and other officers to shoot any curfew violators.[97] There was to be "no sentimentality" toward anyone working in the fields who might not have heard about the order. Soon after the curfew, the killing began. "The first to be shot . . . were four quarrymen returning on bicycles . . . they were shot from behind at close range," the court records stated. Near the village school, soldiers stopped a truck and demanded that its mostly female passengers disembark. The soldiers "continued firing until 17 of the total of 18 persons were killed. Two girls killed were 12 years old, and two others 14." So it went throughout the night.

After an effort to cover up the massacre failed — thanks to a Jewish reporter who published the story — compensation was offered the families of the dead, and eleven officers and soldiers were tried for carrying out "illegal orders." Two years after the massacre, eight were convicted and given light sentences, which were further reduced by government amnesties. By 1960, the last of those convicted was released, less than four years after the killings. One found guilty was hired that same year as the officer for Arab affairs in the city of Ramle. Melinki eventually got a top security post at Dimona, Israel's nuclear reactor. And Shadmi, whose curfew order Melinki had carried out, was tried belatedly, convicted of a "technical error," and sentenced to a reprimand and a fine of one Israeli piaster, or cent. Ever since then, Sabri Jiryis noted, "Shadmi's piaster" had become proverbial among Israel's Arabs for worthlessness.[98]

The Kafr Qassem massacre was clearly exceptional, but it had scarred Israel's Arabs and implicitly warned them of what they could expect if they ever contemplated redressing their grievances violently: Jews would not hesitate to shoot down their own Arab citizens should "security" require it.

Sheikh Abdullah Darwish, a leading spiritual and political guide of Israel's Islamic movement, came from this town, and so did the movement's national spokesman, Ibrahim Sarsur, Kafr Qassem's young Islamic mayor.

Darwish, who was eight years old when the massacre occurred, had long argued that it had helped create a receptive climate for the Islamic revival. In a speech commemorating the thirtieth anniversary of the massacre in 1986, he had denounced terrorism and violence against innocent people but had then equated the Palestinian exile and suffering to that of the Jews. Unlike the Europeans, Darwish contended, Palestinians had accepted Jews fleeing Europe and therefore did not "deserve" the "pogroms" to which they were submitted. The speech had enraged Israeli Jews, who argued that Palestinians had done everything possible to bar European Jews from Palestine and that Darwish, by calling the massacre in Kafr Qassem a "pogrom," was grossly distorting history.[99]

Seven years after the speech, when we met for the first time, Sheikh Darwish, a chain smoker with a withered left arm and a deep, mesmerizing voice, had not changed his views. Until Israel made peace with the Palestinians and its Arab neighbors, he told me, Israel's Arabs had "no guarantee that we won't be massacred as we were in 1956 and in 1976," referring to Kafr Qassem and to "Land Day," another incident two decades later in which five Israeli Arabs protesting land expropriations were killed and sixty-two were wounded. Israel's Islamic movement favored peace and equality between Arabs and Jews and condemned violence against civilians, he added, but he could not denounce Hamas for its violent campaign to end Israeli occupation of the territories, since violence had long been the Islamists' only resort. Nevertheless, once peace came, Hamas, which was "young," would "evolve," he predicted. When Palestinians in the territories could vote in free and fair elections, Islamists in the West Bank and Gaza would renounce terrorism, just as the PLO had done in 1988.

The Islamic Movement of Israel recognized "the legitimacy of the Israeli Knesset," Darwish stressed. The movement wanted to work democratically for an "Islamic way of life" inside Israel and in Palestine. There was room enough in this troubled land for both peoples, he said firmly. "We are not dreaming of building an Islamic state on the ruins of the Jewish state."

Mayor Sarsur, who was born in 1961, was too young to remember the massacre and hadn't learned about it in school, he told me when we met in his busy office shortly before the city elections. But his family had talked about the killings. His grandfather, after all, had been village chief at the time, and two of his relatives were killed that night. I recalled seeing the names of two Sarsur family members on the monument—along with thirteen members of the Issa clan.

But for Sarsur and his peers, the incident was "ancient history" that had little impact on his own political outlook, he said. "We can forgive, if not forget," he said as he rushed to answer his cellular phone, one of three ringing telephones, and to check the faxes that flooded into his immaculate office in town hall. In his tieless long-sleeved white shirt and black corduroys, the still-slender Sarsur seemed the archetype of the modern Israeli politician — far more worried about the impending election than about his village's tragic past.

This contest, like so many in Israeli politics, was bitter. As in most Arab enclaves, Kafr Qassem was divided among clans, and the two most powerful were the Issas and the Sarsurs. "We had always fought each other," Ibrahim told us as he drove through town pointing out the new schools, clinics, and parks for which his Islamic administration claimed credit. "In fact, until 1989 our elections were purely tribal. Voting was based not on ideology but on family alliance."

The Islamic movement had changed that. "I am a Sarsur, and Sheikh Abdullah comes from the Issa family," he told us, "but under the banner of the Islamic movement, we stood together in the last election. Thanks to the votes of more than three hundred Issa family members, I won."

Since then another "revolution" in Israeli Arab politics was the self-reliance preached by the Islamic movement. Arabs in Kafr Qassem had finally stopped "whining and begging the government for handouts," he said. They had done for themselves — through *zakat*, or Islamic tithing, and contributions of cash and in kind — what the Jews would not do for them. Ibrahim considered this new independence a radical shift in traditional practice — the movement's second-greatest accomplishment.

Like his mentor Sheikh Abdullah Darwish, Sarsur lit one cigarette after another and used little of the mind-numbing Islamic jargon I was so accustomed to hearing from Islamists. Sarsur's background, too, was unusual. Unlike many of his colleagues, this clean-shaven politician had not studied religion in the West Bank or at Egypt's al-Azhar but English literature and linguistics at Bar Ilan University, the center of Israel's Zionist national religious movement and the school attended by Yigal Amir, the Jewish law student who murdered Prime Minister Rabin in November 1995.

Sarsur had been enormously impressed by a Jewish professor, who, having asked his women students to dress modestly despite the summer heat, turned his back on them in his classroom and lectured to the blackboard when they ignored his request.[100] Israel's Arabs, too, he told me, had to "turn their backs" on the temptations of Israel's godless, materialistic society.

But Sarsur was clearly interested mainly in signs of Islamic devotion that might translate into votes — the fact, for instance, that as we left his office and drove through the village most women on the streets of this town so close to cosmopolitan Tel Aviv wore head scarves and ankle-length galabias in the modest Islamic style. His "Islamic Front" never tired of complaining about the "blazers," as they called Issa's supporters, denigrating the clothing his opponents preferred.[101]

Several months earlier, Smadar and I had attended the wedding of a young member of the Issa clan. We had listened to endless complaints from Issa's secular supporters, many of them doctors, lawyers, professionals, and intellectuals, about Sheikh Sarsur's Islamic administration — his inability to repair the city's antiquated sewage system or to develop the planned industrial zone, the fact that a main road had to be repaved because the initial contract had been awarded to a company owned by Sarsur's Islamic cronies rather than a competent firm. The municipality was trying to segregate boys and girls of all ages in school. They also blamed Sarsur for failing to rid Kafr Qassem of drugs, the result, they said, of the town's high youth unemployment rate. They hated the religious "thugs" whom they said Sarsur deployed to break up parties where alcohol was served and to intimidate girls who wore short skirts.

The Issa family wedding had marked the unofficial inauguration of Abdul Rahim Issa's mayoral campaign. More than four hundred people attended the party, where coffee, Coca-Cola, beer, and sodas flowed endlessly and all the wedding guests and prospective voters were invited to a four-course luncheon and an opportunity to chat with the former and perhaps future mayor, who was nattily dressed in a three-piece brown suit, his thinning hair slicked back for the occasion. The electrified rock music and traditional Arab folk songs broadcast throughout the neighborhood had drowned out the muezzins' calls to prayer that hot afternoon.

Smadar's presence had generated enormous excitement — particularly among young Arabs. Village residents were avid fans of Smadar's weekly radio broadcast, which featured news from Arab countries, and her frequent appearances on Israeli television on the Arabic and Hebrew channels made her a celebrity in Kafr Qassem. Smadar, followed by me, was ushered into the bride's family's house to meet the nervous, heavily made up future Mrs. Issa, who wore typically modern Arab dress for the occasion — a floor-length, green-satin-brocade evening gown and a rhinestone tiara that glistened under the fluorescent lights. Blushing with heat and excitement, she welcomed us in Hebrew and Arabic.

Young villagers formed a tight circle around Smadar and grilled her about the peace process and her latest trip to Egypt. Would the Saudis support Arafat despite their anger over the PLO's alliance with Iraq in the Gulf war? What would peace mean for Israel's Arabs?

In their T-shirts, jeans, and loafers, speaking good Hebrew, chewing gum, and singing modern Israeli rock songs, these young Arabs seemed no different from Israeli Jews, and they clearly wanted to be treated no differently. If ever they were truly accepted in Israeli society, the appeal of Sarsur's Islamic puritanism would surely diminish in this suburb of Tel Aviv, Israel's jazzy Mediterranean capital.

Polls supported my hunch. Israeli opinion surveys showed that while Arabs in general were more religious than Jews and while Arabs in towns like Kafr Qassem had experienced a religious revival in the 1980s (as had Israeli Jews and Christians), the long-term trend among Jews and non-Jews alike, due to steady improvement in education, was a steady decline in religious observance.[102] Such well-educated Israeli Islamists as Sheikh Darwish and Ibrahim Sarsur were exceptions to Israel's secular trend.

But true acceptance of Israeli Arabs by Israel's Jewish majority could not be assumed, given the historic hostility and mutual suspicion between the communities—each with its own claim to the land, its own monuments, its own memories, its own fears. Fatin Issa, the mayor's nephew, and his young friends complained about the humiliating discrimination they experienced each day—being stopped and checked at roadblocks simply because their Israeli passports identified their "nationality" as "Arab." At best, Smadar told me, Israeli Jews were indifferent to the well-being of their fellow non-Jewish citizens.[103] When she had proposed a magazine article on the heated election in Kafr Qassem, her editor had shrugged: "Who wants to read about them?"

For their part, Sarsur's supporters had shunned the wedding party with its alcohol, dancing, and Western music—all *haram* to devout Muslims. They mocked Abdul Rahim Issa, their fifty-three-year-old opponent, as the "chronic candidate," reminding voters of the piles of discarded liquor bottles that once littered the city park at the entrance to this hilly town. Islamists also whispered about Abdul Rahim's second wife, Yehudith—a blond, blue-eyed Jew who had fallen in love with the mayor and married him twelve years ago. An Islamic Front leaflet contended that Prime Minister Rabin was Yehudith Issa's uncle.

Sarsur's Islamic movement had also sought a campaign endorsement from an unlikely source—Arafat's secular PLO, whose new peace treaty with Israel was hugely popular among Israeli Arabs. For his part, "Mr. Palestine" wanted the backing of the Israeli Islamists for his peace bid with Israel. Arafat had offered to support Sheikh Darwish's Islamic Front in the municipal elections if the Islamists would endorse the PLO's peace accord and abandon Hamas, which condemned the agreement. The Islamic Movement of Israel, ever pragmatic, had agreed.

Thus, at the annual commemoration of the thirty-seventh anniversary of the Kafr Qassem massacre, only a few days before the election and a month after the 1993 Israeli-PLO peace accord was signed in Washington, Sarsur read aloud a letter he had extracted from the PLO chief. "The blood of the people of Kafr Qassem was not spilled for naught," Sarsur solemnly declared in words that chairman Arafat had supposedly written for the occasion. "The massacre was a sacrifice for peace, part of the great price we paid for the establishment of our national homeland. I pray that Israeli Arabs will help unite the Palestinian people."

The letter from Arafat, the PLO's secular icon, was a triumph for the Islamic Movement of Israel. The massacre of Kafr Qassem had become just another campaign prop. Ibrahim Sarsur was reelected—narrowly—and the Islamic Movement of Israel, thanks to a little help from its godless PLO allies—still had a popular mandate to spread Islam's message in this small part of the Jewish state.

•

ISRAEL'S ISLAMIC MOVEMENT continued to gain political ground, but more slowly, in the 1993 municipal elections. Though the number of Islamic representatives grew from fifty-one to fifty-nine and the number of communities in which the movement won seats increased from fourteen to sixteen, Islamism in Israel, once the fastest-growing political movement within the Green Line, seemed to be reaching a plateau.[104]

Mayor Sarsur soon had difficulty forming a town council in Kafr Qassem. Though he had won reelection, the "tribal" loyalties he had once dismissed as a relic of the past had reemerged. Only after months of negotiations—and concessions to the secular Issa clan and other opponents—was Sarsur able to secure their participation in his "Islamic Alliance."

Meanwhile, in Umm al-Fahm, a city of twenty-eight thousand Muslims nestled on a large, steep hillside overlooking a central valley in Israel, another victor, Sheikh Ra'id Salah Mahajneh, was facing similar problems. In 1989, at age thirty, Sheikh Ra'id, another graduate of the Islamic college in occupied Hebron, had been elected mayor with almost 75 percent of the votes, having unseated the incumbent Communist Party candidate—one of the Mahamids, a rival clan. Some hailed this earnest, soft-spoken young preacher as the future leader of the entire Islamic movement in Israel—a natural successor to, if somewhat more radical than, the current chief, the amiable Sheikh Darwish.

Sheikh Ra'id was widely credited with having lent a sense of dignity and self-reliance to his hometown. He had fulfilled his campaign promise to raise money locally for a huge new $2 million mosque whose glistening gold dome now dominated the town's skyline, to clean up and repave the sloping, narrow streets of this hillside town, and to build new kindergartens, drug centers, and health clinics, which the government resisted funding. Among his first acts as mayor was to donate part of his own small salary to the bankrupt local treasury. His town council had banned alcohol—as had Kafr Qassem and most Islamic-run municipalities—built a segregated high school and gender-segregated bus stops, and opened a new Islamic soccer league whose members wore long trousers and opened each game with a prayer. In a very short time, Umm al-Fahm, which meant "mother of coals," had undergone one of the more remarkable transformations in its six-hundred-year history.

Sheikh Ra'id told me that the Islamic revival in Umm al-Fahm was part of a universal trend among all faiths. Why should the West fear Islam more than it did increased synagogue attendance in America or the rebuilding of churches in Eastern Europe?

Sheikh Ra'id had not always been so tolerant of Jewish revivalism. In October 1989 he had complained to a local Islamic paper about the Jewish conspiracy to destroy Jerusalem's Al-Aqsa Mosque, "the heart which gives us life and unity." He had quoted the "Protocols of the Elders of Zion," saying that the Jewish Third Temple had to be rebuilt on the ruins of Al-Aqsa. The Jews, he said, had built "secret tunnels" under the shrine to blow it up.[105] The sheikh had also parroted Hamas's line on the immorality of a negotiated peace that relinquished Palestinian land. "Historic truth emphasized," he said, that all of Palestine was *waqf*, a religious endowment, which could not be "sold, bought, or granted."[106]

Sheikh Ra'id made no secret of having met Hassan Turabi, Sudan's militant Islamic leader and another arch Israeli foe. Like his Sudanese mentor, Sheikh Ra'id had denigrated the peace talks before the Oslo accord as a "circus." After Oslo, he said little about the peace accord, neither embracing nor denouncing it. But his deputy had met in early 1993 with Muhammad Salah, the American Hamas leader I had seen in prison. Had he known about or approved of the meeting? Sheikh Ra'id would not say. But along with Sheikh Darwish, he was actively involved in trying to mediate and defuse the incipient civil war between Arafat's Palestinian Authority and Hamas.

In the 1989 election Sheikh Ra'id had emphasized his Islamic identity, calling for an end to voting along clan lines. Though technically he belonged to the Mahajnehs, one of the city's four major clans, he had downplayed his family origins, urging all Muslims to unite to improve the city's dismal conditions. But by the 1993 elections Sheikh Ra'id was facing an increasingly demanding constituency. Now he, too, embraced the clan politics he once shunned, emphasizing his "Mahajneh" connection, and won handily.

Thus, while Israel's Islamic movement had instilled in Israeli Muslims new self-reliance and pride, it had not managed to overcome the age-old clan rivalries that were a hallmark of most Arab societies. If the Islamists were going to institutionalize themselves, their movement would have to accommodate itself to, and superimpose itself on, this durable extended-family and clan structure. Israel's democracy had demonstrated, at least for the time being, a striking limitation of the militants' campaign to change politics, and human nature itself, through religious faith.

BY 1995, INTENSE PERSONAL rivalries had emerged within Israel's Muslim *umma*, the community of believers, particularly over Oslo. While Sheikh Abdullah Darwish had warmly endorsed the 1993 PLO-Israeli agreement, more militant Israeli Muslim leaders, like Sheikh Kamal al-Khatib of Kafr Kanna, had denounced the agreement as the desperate act of a failed leader — meaning not Yitzhak Rabin but Yasir Arafat. He called the agreement's deferral of the fate of Jerusalem "an act of treason."[107]

Khatib was the Muslim spiritual leader of a village of twelve thousand Muslims and Christians on the outskirts of Nazareth, Israel's largest Arab-Israeli city, where Arab Christians once played a leading role. I had interviewed him in 1993, and the encounter had not been pleasant. Unlike other Israeli Islamists, the then thirty-year-old sheikh seemed deeply suspicious of non-Muslims. He had immediately asked me whether I was a Muslim. When I told him I was not, he became vague and uncommunicative. He had once told an Israeli interviewer that not only were none of his best friends Jewish; he had never even met an Israeli he liked.[108] But Khatib had no use for Christian Arabs, either. Even Christian radicals like George Habash, leader of the PLO "rejectionist" Popular Front for the Liberation of Palestine, which had always rejected the existence of a Jewish state in Palestine, had no place in the fight for Palestine; Jerusalem, he said, would embrace only Muslims. He had also accused UN Secretary-General Boutros.Boutros-Ghali, a Copt and former Egyptian minister of state, of fostering a "new Crusade" in Palestine by supporting Oslo — sentiments that did not endear him to Israeli Christians.[109]

I was not surprised that Khatib had met with Muhammad Salah, Hamas's American military activist. The sheikh had described the meeting as innocent: No money had exchanged hands, he said; no secret commitments had been made. But the Shin Bet had visited him to inquire about such meetings. In 1995 it also confiscated budget documents from the Umm al-Fahm municipality and an Islamic charity in Nazareth with which Sheikh Kamal was associated.

Israeli Islamists were also increasingly divided over whether their movement should participate in national elections. Sheikh Darwish had long urged his movement to elect candidates to the Knesset, either independently or as part of a united Arab bloc. Citing Islamic tradition and the experience of Islamists in Jordan, Darwish argued that the Islamic movement had much to gain from Knesset membership. Arab municipalities needed Jewish national funding, he argued. While volunteerism and contributions from abroad had enabled the Islamists to improve their towns and villages, the Arabs of Israel now had expectations that only increases in national aid could fulfill. So Sheikh Darwish, and even Sheikh Ra'id of Umm al-Fahm, met often with Rabin's cabinet — particularly with Arye Deri, the then minister of interior and head of Shas, an ultra-Orthodox Jewish party — to lobby for more funding.

For their part, Jewish politicians like "Sheikh Deri," as Jews jokingly called the Israeli minister, wanted Arab votes for their political parties. An Islamic party, after all, did not strike the head of a Jewish religious party as odd or threatening. Shas and the Islamic Movement of Israel, moreover, had their own alternative demons: Shas's main foes were Jewish leftists in the ruling Labor coalition who were trying to eliminate funds for Jewish schools and make Israel more secular; the Islamists considered the atheist Israeli Arab Communists their major enemy.[110]

The Islamic movement's more militant sheikhs, however, had vehemently opposed entering national politics. Serving in the Knesset, after all, meant accepting as legitimate a system based on Jewish-Israeli laws that contradicted sharia, Islamic holy law. How could Islamists pledge allegiance to a flag whose emblem was a Star of David? How could they participate in a secular legislative system when all good Muslims knew that the Koran was the only legitimate constitution and source of divine law? In 1992, Ra'id Salah of Umm al-Fahm had put it bluntly: "The Knesset represents a form of legislation which stands in contradiction to what Allah had ordered and bequeathed upon us."[111]

Ever the politician, Ra'id had told me in 1993 that he opposed participating for different reasons. The only power of Arab Knesset members was "to shout," he said. Because the Islamists could do nothing in Parliament, their credibility would only be eroded, whereas "in our cities we are rulers. We can do more or less what we want."

Kamal Rayan, the Islamist mayor of Kafr Bara, had argued that the movement was not yet strong enough to make an impressive showing in national elections. When the Islamists ran — and he thought they eventually would — they would have to be confident of winning a substantial bloc of seats. "Our aim is to serve the people," he said, "not pretend that we're an Arab government." [112]

But pressure to participate kept building. By mid-1995, even Mayor Salah was having second thoughts about abstaining from national elections. Traveling to Turkey to discuss the issue with prominent Islamists from other countries, he secured a *fatwa* from Sheikh Youssef Qardawi, the militant Egyptian scholar, stating that Muslims had a duty to participate in a non-Muslim government, provided such a government enabled them to practice their faith freely, as Israel's did. But in May 1995, after a fierce internal debate, Israel's Islamic movement decided yet again to abstain from 1996 national elections, unwilling to alienate the many Islamists who still opposed joining the national political fray. As it was for Hamas, fear of *fitna*, or internal divisions, was a key factor in the movement's decision. [113] The Islamic movement reiterated the compromise formula it had adopted for the 1992 elections: While it would not field its own Knesset candidates, it would urge its followers to support the candidates of their choice. [114]

Although the Islamic movement still feared playing national politics by Israel's rules, its choice was its own. Israel, a powerful state with strong institutions, could afford to offer its Islamists the political participation that few Arab countries dared to extend. For in Israel, as in Jordan, both of which had successfully included Islamists in national politics, ultimate power was not at stake. In Israel's democracy, a Jewish majority ensured that an Islamic state would be politically impossible. In Jordan, no parliament had authority to challenge the constitutional supremacy (not to mention the religious legitimacy) of King Hussein. Thus, in neither state — for different reasons — were Islamic militants in a position to take over.

THE 1992 KNESSET elections were a turning point for Israel's Arabs in national politics. To win the election, Yitzhak Rabin's Labor Party had lobbied hard for Arab votes, partly by promising that a right-wing Likud defeat would advance the cause of peace. [115] Despite their antipathy toward Rabin — the former defense minister reputed to have ordered soldiers to "break bones" to prevent Palestinian teenagers from throwing stones during the Intifada — Labor had won 21 percent of the Arab vote, an increase from 17 percent in the 1988 elections. [116]

Arab Knesset members had also played a key role in the formation of Prime Minister Rabin's government. Without them, Rabin would have been unable to consolidate a majority of 61 members in the 120-member Knesset. Although he had refused to include the Arab members in his ruling coalition, Rabin knew that his government would fall if the Arabs stood with Likud on a crucial vote of confidence. From 1992 on, no political party could afford to ignore Arab voters.

After the 1992 parliamentary elections, Arab politicians demanded, and won, commitments for increased funding to close within five years the gap in budgets between Jewish and Arab municipalities as well as other steps to redress socioeconomic inequalities.[117] For the first time, two Arab parliamentarians were also appointed deputy ministers, a symbolic but important gesture.

The new Arab Knesset members and other Israeli Arab activists quickly became involved in efforts to heal internal political rifts among Palestinians in the territories and to pave the way for the Oslo agreement; they visited Arafat in Tunis and Egyptian president Mubarak in Cairo, and after Oslo, Syrian president Assad in Damascus. Ahmed Tibi, an energetic Israeli Arab physician from the village of Taibe, became the unofficial representative of Arafat's PLO, sending messages back and forth, organizing private meetings between Arabs and Jews, and urging compromise by all sides.

In 1994, Abdul Wahab Darawsha, a flamboyant and enduring Israeli Arab parliamentarian, panicked Labor by introducing a resolution that would have changed Israel's definition of citizenship: Israel would no longer be a "Jewish state" but a "state of the Jewish people and all its citizens." This proposal was supported by most of Israel's non-Jewish citizens but was unacceptable to virtually all Jews, even to my liberal friends.

I had visited Darawsha in the Knesset soon after his resolution was shelved in 1994 and following another nasty confrontation on the Knesset floor, which even in its most harmonious moments made the U.S. Senate seem genteel. Goneen Segev, then a member of Tsomet, a right-wing Jewish party, who was now part of the ruling coalition, had accused Labor of "betraying" the Jews by relying for its parliamentary majority on Arab votes. "So what! So what!" Darawsha had yelled, leaping to his feet.

Down came the chairman's gavel. "Mr. Darawsha, you are out of order!" the chairman wailed in Hebrew.

"No government that needs you is legitimate," Segev screamed at Darawsha, disregarding the chairman.

"You're a racist!" Darawsha shouted, shaking his fist at Segev.

"Mr. Darawsha, *shut up!*" the chairman commanded, banging his gavel on his desk. "And Mr. Segev, you shut up, too."

Still yelling, Darawsha was then ejected.

Nattily dressed in a khaki-colored suit and a bold floral tie, Darawsha met me moments later in the Knesset cafeteria. "They need us, but they don't want us as real partners," he told me. "As my colleague Hashem Mahameed said, 'We have them by the balls.' They didn't like hearing that, but it's true. My party is not a Zionist party, but that doesn't make us disloyal. There are non-Zionist Jewish parties, too, but they are distinguished partners in the government coalition. They are not harassed or discriminated against as we are. It all boils down to racism."

As Darawsha and I left the Knesset, he was suddenly surrounded by reporters waving cameras and microphones. He shook his fist at the camera and repeated what he had just told me in what I realized had been a rehearsal for this performance for the media. Then he winked at me and whispered: "The Islamic movement will go crazy tonight! My constituents love this stuff. They may be Islamists, but they vote for me!"

Later that year, Arab political power asserted itself even more dramatically. In an unlikely coalition, the Arab parliamentarians joined forces with Likud — of all parties — to oppose Rabin's plan to confiscate land in East Jerusalem for Jewish housing, an expropriation that all Arab governments had denounced as illegal and inimical to the peace process. Likud had also wanted to build more Jewish housing in Jerusalem, but it wanted to bring Rabin down even more. So it had joined with the Arabs to break Rabin's government. Faced with the prospect of losing a vote of confidence, Rabin had backed down. Darawsha and other Arab parliamentarians rejoiced. "All the Arab states, the Arab League, and the PLO — not one of them succeeded in changing the expropriation decision. Only we did!" said Hashem Mahameed, the leftist Arab parliamentarian.

The showdown had demonstrated how crucial the "marginal" Arab vote could be, given Israel's fragmented political structure and increasingly polarized politics — if only the Arabs could unite as they had over Jerusalem. But Darawsha and his fellow secularists had another reason to gloat: The Islamic movement would receive no credit for having blocked the land confiscation — an intensely emotional issue for all Palestinians, including Israel's Arab citizens. "Since Oslo the Islamists have peaked," he told me confidently.

It was too soon to say whether Darawsha was right or simply exuberant — along with many Jews. The peace process was having a contradictory effect on Israel's Arabs, reinforcing both their "Palestinization" and their "Israelization." But it did seem that "Islamization" was losing political steam.

Darawsha, a seasoned pragmatist, reminded me that Israel's Arabs were not a collective. Nor were they all Muslim. Only about 600,000 of them were Muslims — about 75 percent. Within the Muslim community, there were strong cleavages and rivalries — north versus south, urban versus Bedouin (the fastest-growing segment of Israel's Arab population), to name but two. Almost 9 percent were Druze, non-Muslim Arabs who, unlike other Israeli Arabs, had always insisted on serving in the army and many of whom considered themselves an integral part of Israeli society, though their devotion to the Jewish state was hardly reciprocated.

"My soul and identity are not divided," Naim Araidi, a Druze poet, told me during a recent trip to Israel. "I am not a 'Palestinian in Israel,'" he added, disputing a term popularized by David Grossman in a sensitive book about Israel's Arabs.[118] "I am an Arab culturally — in language, customs, history, and tradition. But I am also an Israeli and a Druze, a persecuted minority within a minority. I served in the army. So when a policeman stops me, I can argue with him. An Arab who is exempted from military service can't." The army, more than anything else, he added, had given him a sense of belonging to the country. "I'm more Israeli than eighty percent of the Jews of Israel! I am a new Israeli — I belong to this new existence, this new identity. I have a doctorate in Hebrew literature, but my poems are in Arabic. For me, there is no contradiction."

For Naim, if not for the Islamists of Israel, exposure to the Palestinians in the West Bank and Gaza after the 1967 war had reinforced his "Israeliness." The Arabs of Israel were so much more "advanced" than Palestinians in the territories. It wasn't just the difference in living standards, he said: "Israeli democracy taught us to think and question." When Egypt and Israel made peace in 1979, Naim had visited Cairo. "A double shock!" he said. "The traditional heart of Arab history and culture was so intellectually primitive in some respects. Our intellectual life was so much richer than theirs." Having seen other Arab societies, what Naim now wanted was not Arab "rights" in Israel but rather expanded opportunity for all Israelis.

Naim, the Druze, had far more in common with my Jewish friend Smadar Perry, and with his Christian Israeli friends, than any of them had with Sheikh Kamal Khatib or Yasir Arafat.

Lufti Mashour, the Christian editor of the Nazareth-based *Al-Sinara* and one of the country's best journalists, reminded me that many Israeli Christians — 14 percent of Israeli Arabs — were also hostile to Islamic parties — yet another limitation on the Islamists' potential strength. But Christians were declining as a percentage of the overall Israeli population — not because they were emigrating, converting, or being driven out, as in other Middle Eastern countries, but because they were being outbred. The Israeli Christian fertility rate was now half that of Israeli Muslims and slightly less than that of the Jews.[119] If the current trend continued, Christians risked all but disappearing from the land where Christ was born.

"Islamists and leftists alike get all hung up on the symbols of the Jewish state," Lutfi complained. "I don't particularly care if Hatikva, our national anthem, speaks about the 'soul of a Jew' longing for Zion. I don't care if the flag has a Jewish star on it. Switzerland's flag has a red cross. So what? Call it Israel. Or Shmisreal. What counts is whether we are integrated and truly accepted here. That could not happen before peace between Arabs and Jews. But now it must happen."

Perhaps part of the solution for all of Israel's citizens was what Naim had called the enhancement of his "Israeliness," the emergence of a new identity. While I considered Smadar almost a sister, she was an Israeli and very different from my American Jewish friends. A majority of her fellow Israeli Jews had been born, or were descendants of Jews who were born, in Arab lands. Her lifestyle — the late nights, her preference for coffee over alcohol, her hospitality, and her sense of humor — was distinctly Middle Eastern, so much like that of my Egyptian friends. Israel's Jews were becoming more Middle Eastern, more "Arabized"—for better or worse—and their Arab neighbors were likely to become, sooner or later, more "Israelized."[120]

I once asked Israel's director general of the Foreign Ministry and a negotiator at Oslo what negotiating with the Palestinian "enemy," the PLO, had been like. "Impossible!" Uri Savir had replied. "They were demanding, stubborn, uncompromising, whining, suspicious of our every suggestion, and often paranoid. In other words"—he smiled—"it was like negotiating with a mirror."

The challenge of making more Israeli "non-Jews" feel as patriotic as Naim and Lutfi did was largely up to the Israelis. So was the question of the Islamic movement's ultimate appeal. Israel was a democracy, imperfect to be sure—an "ethnic democracy," as one Jewish sociologist so aptly put it—yet a democracy nonetheless.[121] But Israel was also a Jewish/Zionist state, a self-declared state of the Jews with a "right of return," which meant ensuring not only that Jews ruled but that they enjoyed special status and legal privileges. Emphasizing the state's democratic nature meant offering non-Jews integration and equal rights. Stressing the state's Jewish identity meant that Jews alone would retain real power. Now that the prolonged war between Jews and Arabs was perhaps ending and security concerns might one day no longer overshadow so much else, Israeli Jews would have to recognize the inherent contradiction in their state's twin identity. What mattered more—being a democracy or a Jewish state? For Ariel Sharon, the former Likud defense minister, the answer was clear: While it was "good" that Israel was a "real democracy," he told the Knesset in May 1993, when he proposed excluding Israel's Arabs from a proposed referendum on the future of the territories, his ancestors had not come to Israel to establish a democracy; they had come "to set up a Jewish state."[122] Likud bluntly stated that while Arab civil rights should be respected, Israel had to do whatever it could to reinforce Jewish domination.

Public opinion polls showed, however, that a majority of Jews felt that while Israel had to remain both Jewish and Zionist, the government should try harder to improve opportunities for Arabs. Nevertheless, only a tiny minority wanted to recast Zionism or to de-Zionize Israel to foster equality for the state's non-Jews. Most Arabs, the majority argued, would still prefer to live in a democratic Israel that granted them some political power than in Arab states that gave them virtually none, despite Israel's Jewish character.[123] They felt that Israel's Arabs would have to accept their symbolic disinheritance, the fact that Israel's symbols and cherished myths might always exclude them. Mariam Mar'i, the Israeli Arab activist whose family had been separated by Israel's creation, and thousands like her would have to acknowledge—as she clearly had—that they might always feel a tug of pain when they celebrated May 15, 1948, the anniversary of Israel's creation, as well as of the war that had divided their families and deprived them of their land. Thousands of Mariams in Israel had accepted this political reality. Those who could not accept it were free to vote against Zionist parties or leave.

In mid-1995, Israeli Jews had reason to be heartened about the prospects for the "Israelization" of their country's Arab citizens: During a conference in Amman, a delegation of Israeli Arabs criticized the Jordanian media for referring to them as "1948 Arabs." They were "Israelis," the delegation leader corrected reporters — and "proud" to be so. A month later, Sheikh Abdullah Nimr Darwish told his Islamic counterparts at an Islamic gathering in Amman that he was not the "leader of the Islamic Movement of Occupied Palestine" but of the "legitimate state of Israel."

In November 1995 tragedy temporarily united Israel's Jewish and Arab citizens, if only in horror and grief. Yitzhak Rabin's assassination — by a militant Jew — traumatized both communities. "I'm still in total shock," Marian Mar'i told me two weeks after the murder. "I never would have anticipated such an intense response from so many Palestinians in Israel — so much sorrow and mourning — just like the Jews. When I saw my daughter crying, I realized that she was an Israeli."

But there was one critical difference, of course: "When I first learned that Rabin had been shot," Mar'i said, "my heart stopped. Maybe it was an Arab, I thought! Then there was a wave of enormous relief, followed by almost inconsolable sorrow for the man, for our loss of a leader who had detested Arafat but still made peace."

But for Israeli Jews, there were only frightening questions: How could a Jew have killed a Jewish leader? And why had the government dismissed Baruch Goldstein's brutal murder of twenty-nine Palestinians as they prayed in a mosque in occupied Hebron in 1994 as an isolated act of a madman? Had no one seen that such brutality was a reflection of a wider fanaticism taking root among some zealous settlers and their radical nationalist supporters within Israel? In their intense introspection, the Israeli Jewish media barely covered Israeli Arab reaction to their national trauma. But even Sheikh Darwish issued an unequivocal condemnation of Rabin's murder on behalf of the Islamic Movement of Israel.

This shared grief and Sheikh Darwish's recent declarations suggested that some of Israel's Islamists, too, might eventually face political facts: Israel was likely to remain a Jewish state. Muslims would not rule in Zion in the foreseeable future. To rebel meant being crushed. But they would continue to be free to practice their faith, live Islamic lives, and dream about the *umma* that might one day replace the Middle East's amazingly durable nation-state system. And if they could overcome their ideological and religious objections to becoming part of the Knesset, they were theoretically capable of changing Israeli policy in important ways — as the rejection of the planned land confiscation in Jerusalem had shown.

It was not the Jews who prevented the emergence of a unified Arab voting bloc of a potential seventeen seats — one that might conceivably be led by Islamists — but the internal divisions and rivalries among Arabs that kept them from exercising what in Israel's democracy was the enormous parliamentary power of swing parties.[124] Arab strength in Israel, moreover, seemed likely to grow. Given current demographic trends, Israel's population would reach 8 million by the year 2025 — 6 million Jews and 2 million Arabs: One out of every four Israeli citizens would be Arab. Today the ratio is one in five.[125] In 1992, the most popular name for a baby boy born in Israel was Muhammad.

Nevertheless, the disdain of so many Israeli Jews toward Arabs had increased Arabs' alienation from Israel — resentment that was reinforced by Israel's 1982 war in Lebanon, the 1987 Palestinian Intifada, and Israeli intransigence in negotiations with the PLO. Such anger might breed, if not overt disloyalty, an inability to feel Israeli or to identify with the nation's institutions and goals. If Israel's Arabs were to lose hope of integration within the Jewish state, what alternative would most have except Islamism — with its cultural and institutional separatism and antipathy toward Jews?

While many secular Israeli Arabs had supported cultural and political autonomy for Arab citizens, they did so as a means to an end — to reduce the economic, social, and educational gaps between Arabs and Jews that prevented Arabs from integrating as equals in mainstream Israeli life. But the Islamists' support for Arab autonomy within Israel had a different aim: to create a permanent separation of the communities, an existential gap that would undermine Israel's social and political cohesion and weaken the Jewish state over time. If Israelis continued to reject Arabs as full partners, Islamism might well become the only "solution" for many frustrated Israeli Arabs. Given Israel's overwhelming strength, few Israelis believed that the Islamists, even if radicalized, would violently confront the state, but even if they did not, suspicion and hostility between Israeli Jews and Arabs would surely grow.

When the state of Israel was created, Uri Lubrani, Ben-Gurion's first adviser on Arab affairs and the son of a Jewish notable from Haifa, devised the formula that would from then on regulate coexistence in the new Jewish state. "We knew they would never love us," Lubrani told me one day. "We only demanded a certain degree of loyalty. Into their hearts we would not look."

Israel was a tiny, endangered state when Lubrani formulated his policy. Today it is powerful and prosperous. Are Israeli Jews and Arabs forever bound, even in peace, to fear what may be in each other's hearts?

Iran

There is no compulsion in religion.

SURAH II, verse 256, the Koran.

MORE THAN A HUNDRED students had filled the hall in June 1995 for Abdolkarim
Sorush's lecture at the University of Shiraz. At first, he didn't spot the thugs in
the crowd of eager young men and women, notebooks in hand. But as he began
speaking, he heard jeers and looked up from his index cards. There they were,
near the front—about a dozen young "Hezbollahis," bearded and angry. "Death
to the enemies of Islam!" they chanted. "Death to enemies of the revolution!"
Then they rushed the podium.

Clutching his glasses and briefcase, Sorush fled. A student led him down a
narrow staircase and into a basement storage room. But the assailants followed,
broke down the door, and cornered him.

"They were ready to kill me right there, but I continued trying to talk to
them, to calm them down—you always have to try," Sorush told me without
emotion three months later. "Yes, they beat me up. It was a pity. But gradually
they started listening. And I kept talking. I tried to make them understand that
I am not an enemy of Islam or the revolution. In the end, I think we parted on
friendlier terms."

He did not want to call his young assailants Nazi "brownshirts," he said.
"It wasn't their own initiative: They were used by others, sinister forces—some
hidden authority." He preferred not to identify this evil force or name names,
he added. "But they thought they were defending God's law."

Sorush told me in September 1995 that he planned to go on speaking. Yes,
he conceded, it would be difficult—and dangerous. Most intellectuals preferred

to keep quiet. It was safer. "But society is ripe for this debate, and it is critical to Iran's future. I may not succeed — the opposition is still very powerful. But I refuse to stop talking and thinking."

A few weeks later, Sorush began lecturing again — this time at the University of Teheran to an even larger audience. And once again, Hezbollahi toughs disrupted the meeting. Shielded by supporters, Sorush fought his way out of the hall, but not before a militant had bashed him in the head with a club. By the time things calmed down, several students had been wounded. Sorush's glasses lay shattered on the classroom floor.

THE ATTACKS on Abdolkarim Sorush, a philosophy professor who argues that Islam is compatible with democracy and pluralism and implicitly, that clerical rule in Iran is a distortion of the faith, suggest how passionately political currents still run as the revolution enters its seventeenth year. Iran remains a nation of crises — uncertain about its economy, its political system, and even its identity, all of which the revolution was supposed to settle.

But while analysts over the years have announced the end of the populist revolution that deposed the shah in 1979, predictions of the Islamic government's collapse, including my own, have so far been wrong. The regime that rules this once oil-rich nation of seventeen nationalities and 65 million people in a land the size of the United States east of the Mississippi has endured, especially among the poor — the "downtrodden," as they are called in Persian, or Farsi, in whose name the revolution was made.

The cost has been enormous. The eight-year war launched by Iraq in 1980, which the Ayatollah Ruholla Khomeini refused to end, is estimated to have claimed more than a million Iranian casualties, though exact figures are unknowable. Almost two decades of economic mismanagement, administrative chaos, state murder, repression, corruption, and unnerving unpredictability have caused many of the most talented to flee and many others who stayed to despair. The pauperization of the middle class and the educated elite continues to alienate young Iranians from the regime, from Islamic government, even from Islam itself.

But perhaps because of these multiple challenges, rarely in modern Iranian history have debates such as those initiated by Abdolkarim Sorush so roiled Iranian society. For implicit in the questions he asks is a questioning of the legitimacy of Islamic government as it has evolved in Iran. Some have gone so far as to challenge the very propriety of "Islamic government" itself. Increasingly, leftist and conservative Iranians alike are openly demanding that the rulers account for their failures and that the system be reformed before it is too late. In September 1995, Iran was in the midst of what some Iranian intellectuals excitedly called an incipient Islamic "Reformation."

Could Iran be capable of such a profound transformation at this time? Having visited Iran twice before this visit in the autumn of 1995, I was well aware of the regime's disgusting human-rights record and its miserable economic performance. During my earlier trips most intellectuals had expressed anxiety about their country's prospects. But now some of my Iranian friends felt that at long last the time for rational reform had come. By the end of my visit I could not help but share some of their hope, if not their optimism. For Iran continues to amaze, confound, disturb, enrage, delight, and surprise while it defies the political laws of gravity. Despite what Iran has endured, it remains a vibrant society—far more than it ever was under the shah and more so than any of its Arab neighbors. How could I explain Iran's infectious zest, its intellectual dynamism and resilience, despite the current economic hardship and political terror and despair?

"ISN'T IT MAGNIFICENT!" said Nahzila Fathi, my twenty-four-year-old translator, as she ran up the ancient steps in the ruins of Persepolis, her head scarf flapping behind her. "Have you ever seen anything like it?"

Our flight had left Teheran for Shiraz at six that morning. From Shiraz we drove forty miles to the ruins of Persia's ancient capital. It was September 29, 1995—a Friday, the Muslim Sabbath and my only free day during my hectic visit. Nahzi had yearned to see this splendid site again. Though it was not yet nine o'clock, the sun was already intense and I was sweating in my black head scarf and heavy "uniform" that women were required to wear at all times in public. Nahzi was more accustomed to her *manteau*, the French word for "coat" that Westernized Iranians used to describe the mid-calf-length coat that city women now prefer to the traditional black chador. I found Persepolis lovely, but I was used to visiting the Egyptian and Syrian ruins in jeans and a T-shirt.

"Well, Nahzi, the Pyramids aren't too shabby," I replied, stopping on the stairs to catch my breath. "You should see Egypt one day."

Nahzi frowned. "But Persepolis is so much older, and, I'm told, much more beautiful!"

Actually, Persepolis wasn't older, but the ruins were spectacular testimony to the fact that a thousand years before the advent of Islam, there was Persia, with its roots in the dynasty of Cyrus the Great, six centuries before the Christian era. Darius, his successor, had built highways and codified laws. Persepolis was his ceremonial capital. We passed through a series of ancient portals. Here Darius's guards had inspected visitors who needed a written permit both to enter and leave the compound. Bureaucracy has a long history in Iran.

In 1971 the shah, Mohammad Reza Pahlavi, had invited world leaders here to a gaudy celebration to mark the 2,500th anniversary of Cyrus the Great's Persian Empire as well as his own thirtieth anniversary on the throne—as if he were a descendant of Cyrus rather than the son of a parvenu army officer who had seized power in 1925. The shah had reportedly spent more than $300 million on the party, flying in food and wine from Maxim's in Paris and even uniforms by the couturier Lanvin for his attendant court when Iran's per capita income averaged five hundred dollars and a famine gripped northern

Iran.[1] No one had denounced this crude self-indulgence more fiercely than Ayatollah Ruholla Khomeini, whom the shah had exiled for opposing him in 1964.

After the Islamic revolution overthrew Pahlavi and forced him into exile, the militants' first impulse was to deface the friezes of Persepolis, a symbol not only of the shah's excesses but of the *jahiliyya*, the time before the Prophet Muhammad. But patriots had prevailed, and Persepolis was spared. The government was now restoring pre-Islamic ruins throughout the country, though officials still played down Iran's pre-Islamic past. Shiraz was only an hour away from this site, but none of the young Iranians whom Nahzi and I had interviewed in the city that morning had ever come here on a school trip.

Nahzi stared at the vast stone reliefs of ancient soldiers — Darius's personal bodyguards, who had numbered ten thousand and were known as the "Immortals," since whenever a man fell in battle, he was immediately replaced from a stable of recruits. The religion practiced by the grand civilization was Zoroastrianism; it was among the first monotheisms. To the Islamic government's annoyance, even devout Muslims continue to observe some of its rituals.

Like most children of Khomeini's revolution, Nahzi knew little of her country's pre-Islamic history. But a clue to Iran's endurance was evident here in these ruins, though they were virtually deserted, even on this Friday, a perfect day for an excursion.

Iran's political culture had always been one of "extremes," of what one scholar described as "sudden swings from revolt to stability, from centralization to decentralization, and from unorthodoxy to orthodoxy."[2] But Iran had always had kings by divine right — twenty-five centuries of absolutist rulers and their descendants, the shahs and finally the Shahanshah, who modestly called himself "King of Kings." Over the centuries, the dictators had accumulated titles: the "Subduer of Climates, Arbitrator of His People, Guardian of the Flock, Protector of the Unfortunate, Conqueror of Lands," and most aptly in modern Iran, the old Islamic title "the Shadow of God."[3]

Although Iran had ruled great empires, scores of invaders had overrun the land. Persepolis itself had been razed in 331 B.C. by Alexander the Great, who had admired and imitated Persian culture. But the Iranians had assimilated the conquerors and their cultures, and taken their revenge by making them Iranian. Even Alexander came to be known as an honorary Iranian in Persian historiography.[4]

In the sixth and seventh centuries, the Persian Sassanids had conducted a seemingly endless war against the Christian West — against Byzantium, the Roman Empire in the East and Persia's Constantinople-based rival.

Perhaps it was this contest between the region's great empires that distracted them from a new threat — a religious upstart named Muhammad from the barbarian oasis towns of Arabia. To this day Iranians seem incredulous that by 650 their empire (and much of Byzantium as well) had been conquered by Islam and the Arabs, a people they viewed, and still do, as primitive. How could

God have spoken Arabic and not Persian? Iran responded by doing what came naturally in adversity or occupation: As Alexander eventually became an honorary Iranian, the new faith of Islam became "Iranianized," imbued with the customs, traditions, and skills of their ancient civilization, destroying the equation "Islam equals Arab."[5] Islam hereafter would include a distinct Persian strain.

Yet relations between Iranians and Arabs were always tense. Early Arab Muslims accused Persian Muslims of incest because of the Sassanid custom of marrying one's mother or sisters; Persians denigrated the Arabs as "lizard eaters."[6]

Iran had become officially Shiite, the minority branch of Islam, only under the Safavids, the sixteenth-century dynasty of Turkish origin that conquered Iran and imposed Shiism as the state religion on what was then a mostly Sunni population. The choice may have been unfortunate, Shiism being the scorned, defeated branch of the faith. Even though it proved to be more skeptical of rulers than the majority Sunni branch, at least in theory, Shiites emphasize this historical dispossession, mourning for their lost imams — Shiism's rightful political and spiritual rulers — as well as Iran's deep sorrow for its own lost empires and grandeur.

Iranians practice "Twelver Shiism," which refers to the twelve divinely designated descendants of the sons of Ali, the prophet's cousin, who were deprived of their right to rule. Persecuted and feared by Sunni Muslims, the later Shiite imams defended themselves and their faith by various stratagems, including *taqiyya*, or dissembling to avoid persecution. According to Twelver Shiite doctrine, God had ordered the Twelfth Imam in 874 to remain on earth in hiding, or "occultation," until he was commanded to manifest himself — to usher in Judgment Day by returning as the Mahdi, the Messiah. The successor to the Prophet Muhammad would possess *walayat*, the ability to interpret the inner mysteries of the Koran and the sharia, the Muslim holy law. Divinely chosen, he would be free of sin and error. As such, he had to be obeyed, a requirement that Khomeini would brilliantly exploit.[7]

About midday, Nahzi and I returned to Shiraz to visit another shrine — the tomb of Hafiz, Persia's great medieval lyric poet who had no problem reconciling his Muslim faith with verses about art, wine, and human beauty. The shrine itself, its dome covered with an intricate turquoise mosaic, was built by the shah's father, the military officer who in 1926 had crowned himself Reza Shah, the Great King. None of Hafiz's verses were on display at the shrine, but they were being sold at exorbitant prices in several editions at a bookstore not far from his tomb. This verse is not untypical:

> Hair disheveled, sweating, laughing-lipped and drunk;
> Shirt torn, singing poems, a cup of wine in hand . . .
> Midnight last night to my pillow he came and sat . . .
> He said: Old love of mine, are you sound asleep?[8]

Hafiz had ridiculed his own Muslim ulema in the fourteenth century, or as he described them, "those preachers who in prayer-arch and pulpit imposingly parade."

> When they to their chamber go — another kind of act perform.
> A problem, Sir! Please ask the assembly's learned man:
> Why do those who command us to repent so seldom themselves
>   repentance make?
> You might say they put no faith in the Day of Judgment
> Since when they act for the "Judge," they employ all this
>   deceit and fraud.

It is no wonder that many contemporary clerics are ambivalent about this national poet. But most Iranians revere him. The park surrounding his shrine was filled with Shirazis, young and old, strolling through the meticulously landscaped walkways, chatting on benches by a small fountain.

Nahzi and I stopped to talk to a young couple holding hands on a park bench — newlyweds. The bride was not yet sixteen. She could not legally have married at so young an age under the shah, but Khomeini had reinstituted child marriage. Aisha, the Prophet's favorite wife, had been only nine when her marriage was consummated. The bride's husband worked in a fruit-and-vegetable market outside Shiraz that exported most of its produce to Germany. Business was awful since the Iranian rial had collapsed. He blamed the currency crisis on the United States, which, in April 1995, had expanded its economic sanctions against Iran, cutting off oil purchases and most other forms of direct American trade and financing. When the rial plunged, the government propped it up. As a result, exports had fallen drastically.

Other Shirazis told us that the U.S. dollar had become Iran's national currency. The rial was now so worthless, a reader complained to a newspaper during my trip, that Khomeini's face should be removed from the currency. "The government has money from oil. But where does it go?" an Iranian tourist from Teheran asked. "Islam means telling the truth. But this deceitful government is not Islamic. Everything in Iran today revolves around money."

Younger Iranians seemed particularly embittered: Shiraz, once known for its fragrant roses, was now bustling with more than a million people. Life in Shiraz was "boring"; the mullahs were corrupt, the government hypocritical, visitors to the shrine told us. "It was better under the shah. We all miss the shah," said one old man. "If there were a free election tomorrow, the shah would win."

THE SHAH DIED in Egypt in July 1980. Concerned about the fate of the American diplomats whom radical students had seized in 1979 and were holding hostage, Washington, his longtime ally, had forced him out of the United States. Egypt's President Sadat granted him refuge after scores of other leaders had refused him entry.[9]

In 1953 the shah had almost lost his throne to a coalition of parties headed by Mohammad Mosaddegh, the nationalist prime minister. Only an army coup, aided by the CIA, restored him to power, an intrusion that led many Iranians, leftists as well as the religious establishment, to hate America.

After his rescue by the CIA, the shah presided over two decades of steady economic growth: He built roads, dams, railroads, power plants, ports, and vast steel and petrochemical complexes. At first, he tried to cultivate the clerics.[10] But in 1963 he launched his "White Revolution," a program of modest land reform that included the confiscation of large land holdings and their distribution to peasants, including land controlled by the clergy as part of religious endowments. He also decreed, without waiting for parliamentary action, that women should vote and promoted other progressive legislation, such as the substitution of the term "holy book" for the Koran in Iran's constitution so that Iranian Jews, Christians, Zoroastrians, Baha'is, and other non-Muslim minorities could enjoy equal legal standing. Alarmed by the surge in the population growth rate from less than 2 percent in the early 1900s to 3 percent in the 1960s, he endorsed family planning in 1970. The independently funded clergy, enraged by such secularizing measures, but particularly, some scholars argue, by the confiscation of its land, denounced the shah. None did so more vehemently than Ayatollah Khomeini, who accused the Pahlavis of trying to destroy Islam in the interests of "Jews, America and Israel." The shah returned the favor, traveling to Qum, the seat of Shia learning, to mock Khomeini and other opposition clerics as "lice-ridden mullahs."

When oil prices soared in the early 1970s, the shah intensified his ambitious, some say megalomaniacal, development schemes. Iranians poured into the cities in search of jobs. Between 1956 and 1976 the urban population nearly tripled, while the rural population increased by just one-third.[11]

Over time, the shah became increasingly capricious and autocratic, surrounding himself with card-playing sycophants, more and more of them from his family. He suppressed political parties, silenced critics, and packed the Parliament with stooges. His own "Immortals," the four-thousand-strong Savak — the secret police, some of whose members were trained by Americans and Israelis — spied on, arrested, and tortured dissidents. When protests over his rule erupted in rioting in the late 1970s, the shah declared martial law, but he hesitated, refusing to let the army retaliate aggressively, which enraged his generals. In the five months that preceded his ouster, some three thousand protesters were killed by the army, but one prominent scholar noted that "we will never know what would have happened if the shah had ordered the army to be brutally repressive" as Syrian President Hafiz al-Assad was in the early 1980s when Islamic militants attempted to overthrow his rule.[12] Whatever his failings, the shah was no Hafiz Assad.

In February 1979 the shah's regime ended with its 400,000-man army still intact. The Iranian regime collapsed, as the Communist states of Eastern Europe would do a decade later, when the shah, secretly ailing from cancer, did not try to subdue a national campaign of civil disobedience. He was brought down not by the disintegration of what was then the world's sixth-largest army, by defeat in war, by a financial crisis, or by a crippling peasant insurrection, but rather by a "loss of legitimacy."[13] No one believed in the shah anymore. As he fled, the triumphant seventy-eight-year-old Khomeini returned from exile in France.

For a brief period after the revolution, Marxist, leftist, and liberal parties competed with the clerics under Mehdi Bazargan, the lay Islamic reformer whom Khomeini had named prime minister. But Bazargan, a self-described enemy of "haste and extremes," resigned in less than a year, and secularists suffered a second blow in June 1981, when the government of Abolhassan Bani-Sadr was overthrown. Purges, political arrests, torture, and executions mounted steadily as the clerics turned on their leftist and liberal partners to transform Iran into an Islamic state. Iran's liberals and secularists now rued their initial enthusiasm for Khomeini — if not the revolution itself — and chastised themselves for not having foreseen that Khomeini would use them to come to power and then crush all non-Islamist forces until only his clerics remained.

Despite its brutality, however, the 1979 revolution had, as one Teherani intellectual put it, "returned Iran to the Iranians." The upheaval also politicized many young people and gave them a sense of independence and access to government officials unimaginable under the shah.

The revolution was not without its accomplishments — especially for the poor — achievements that are particularly visible in the countryside, where 40 percent of Iranians still live. Since the revolution, the government claims to have built more than thirty thousand miles of paved roads, forty thousand schools, and seven thousand libraries and provided electrical power and running water to more than twenty-five thousand of Iran's fifty thousand villages.

But fate was not kind to the revolution. Iranians had barely written their new constitution and elected their first government when Saddam Hussein invaded in 1980. The price of oil that year had also begun its steady decline; a barrel of oil that cost thirty-five dollars in 1980 could be purchased in 1986 for nine. In addition, the Mujahideen-e Khalq, a socialist Islamic group — the Khmer Rouge of Islamic militants — based in enemy Iraq, terrorized the new Islamic state with bombings and assassinations. Although such assaults went largely unreported in the United States, most Iranians loathed these Islamic extremists even more than they did their own revolution's most uncompromising men; they also never forgot that the Mujahideen have lavish offices in Washington. Sayyid Ali Khamenei, the cleric who succeeded Khomeini as Iran's "Leader" in 1989, was nearly killed in 1981 by a Mujahideen mail bomb. He still walks with a cane and can barely move his withered arm.

Iran's population had exploded. Eager for more recruits for the war against Iraq and opposed to birth control on religious grounds, Khomeini's government encouraged Iranians to procreate, with disastrous results. By 1995, Iran's population, some 34 million on the eve of the revolution, was 65 million — 72 percent were under twenty-five; 53 percent were under fifteen. Iran's health minister acknowledged two years earlier that government services could no longer keep pace with the population growth, that 37 percent of children under seven were malnourished, and that homelessness, unemployment, illiteracy, and poverty were increasing despite the government's programs. Half the Iranian population, according to one economist, have monthly incomes of fifty dollars or less, far below the poverty line. Iran needs to produce ten thousand university-educated teachers a year just to educate young Iranians; it has trained only six thousand.[14] Some 48 percent of Iranians are still illiterate.

With low oil prices, a soaring population, and zealous but colossally incompetent clerical administration, Iran's economy staggered. Per capita income in real terms is about a quarter today of what it was before the revolution.[15] About 6 million mostly middle-class Iranians now live outside their country, 1.2 million of them in the United States alone.

ON THE FLIGHT BACK from Shiraz to Teheran in October 1995, Nahzi asked me what life in Iran had been like before Khomeini. But I only knew what I had read in the press and heard from friends. I had refused to visit the country under the shah, and I had been banned when Khomeini came to power. I had written an article for *The New York Times* in December 1978, when Khomeini was still in exile near Paris, about his book *Islamic Government*. Published in Arabic in 1971 and based on lectures Khomeini had given, the book argued that if Iran and Islam were to triumph, the Iranian masses had to be led not just spiritually but politically, by a mystically inspired clerical elite. Khomeini also maintained that monarchy was illegitimate, a view not shared by a majority of Iran's most senior clerics — its grand ayatollahs, or literally "Signs of God," or its *marjas*, the clerics whom Iranians revere and whose piety they try to imitate and to whom they pay their *zakat*, or Islamic taxes. Most leading Shia thinkers did not favor increased political power for the clergy, though they treasured their traditional role as the ruler's spiritual and religious guides. In a dramatic departure from traditional Shiite doctrine, Khomeini was arguing that Muslims should not wait passively for the return of the Twelfth Imam and the establishment of the imamate under the infallible Redeemer but turn immediately to the most enlightened clerics to establish a *walayat al-faqih*, or vice regency, the "guardianship of the jurisconsult," which would rule with the Messiah's authority until his return.[16] He maintained that Iran's leadership could be vested in a "single, outstanding religious figure," the preeminent jurist, whom all Muslims would be religiously bound to obey.

Other demands of *Islamic Government* were not only antidemocratic, I wrote, but ominous for Iran's minorities. Iran's 300,000 Baha'is, Khomeini declared, were apostates. This eighteenth-century sect believed that devout Muslims could contact the hidden imam, a creative force, through a human intermediary, the *Bab*, or door. If it were an apostasy, the faith could not be tolerated; its adherents would have no rights in an Islamic society.[17] Iran's Jews and Christians, the Koranic "Peoples of the Book," Khomeini wrote, would be reduced to *dhimmis*, protected minorities. The book contained numerous references to the perfidious Jews, "they who first established anti-Islamic propaganda," whose treachery continued "down to the present."[18] Finally, Khomeini stressed the importance of freeing Iran from Western control and influence, from America in particular.

Since Khomeini was widely regarded as Iran's next leader, my article outraged proponents of the revolution. "Shaw" Rouhani, then a leading pro-Islamic student activist in Washington, led a delegation to the *Times* bureau in Washington to demand a correction. I was an apologist for the shah's brutal, corrupt regime, the students told my boss. I had "distorted" the thoughts of Khomeini and mistranslated the Arabic.[19]

In 1980, after Khomeini assumed power, I applied for a visa to Teheran. The application was received by a militant who had visited the *Times* to complain about my article and had then been placed in the visa section of the Islamic Republic's embassy in Washington. He returned my unopened application with a note: I had insulted the "Imam Khomeini" — the leader was becoming more godlike by the day. I would never be granted a visa. "As long as the Imam lives," he said, "you will never visit Iran."

IN EARLY 1991, two years after Khomeini's death and eleven years after my first visa application, I made my first trip to Iran. By then, most of the once omnipresent pictures of Khomeini, God's glowering killjoy saint, had been taken down. Nothing had prepared me for Iran's beauty.

Teheran, though congested and smog ridden, was a stunningly beautiful but shabby capital. From my balcony at the Esteghlal Hotel, the former Hilton, which had been confiscated by the government and renamed the Victory, the city of 14 million looked orderly. To the north were the peaks of the snow-capped Elburz Mountains rising ten thousand feet above the city, only a short cable-car ride away. To the south lay desert. But at the city's edge were the miserable slums of south Teheran and, behind them, newer shantytowns to which rural Iranians were still migrating in great numbers. Wealthy Teheranis lived in the north near the Esteghlal, where the air was still crisp and relatively clean. But getting downtown took hours in rush-hour traffic. An Iranian newspaper once calculated that Teheranis wasted 1.2 billion hours a year trapped in traffic jams — one of those arresting, if unverifiable, Iranian "facts."[20]

The Esteghlal had seen better days. The quilted covers of the twin beds were threadbare; the matching curtains, dirty and frayed. The telex service was intermittent. The Esteghlal still used the old Hilton's laundry tags.

The government had given the Hilton and other foreign-licensed "luxury" hotels to the *bunyods*, the supposedly independent foundations that Khomeini created to manage the confiscated assets of the shah and the *taghootis*, his wealthy supporters, who had fled. The Hilton was run by the Bunyod-e Mustazafin, the "Foundation for the Downtrodden," which also controlled the shah's

Pahlavi Foundation, with its massive real estate holdings and assets in the West. The Mustazafin, which employed more than 350,000 people and now owned more than twelve hundred companies, many of them in Europe and the United States, had become one of the richest and most corrupt organizations in Iran — a quasi-government cartel with colossal economic power.[21] One well-informed diplomat estimated its net worth at $10 billion. Mohsen Rafighdoost, its president, was the son of a wealthy *bazaari*, the traditional class of merchants and moneylenders whose long-standing alliance with the clergy of Qum had been critical in ousting the shah. Because he had been given the honor of being Khomeini's driver and bodyguard, he had become even wealthier than he was before. Foundations like these made "off-the-books" payments to important clerics, to secret defense and intelligence projects, and, dependable diplomats told me, to Islamic terrorists throughout the Middle East. Together, one Iranian analyst estimated, these fifteen officially nongovernment foundations controlled as much as 30 percent of Iran's wealth. Their undisclosed financial clout made Iranian bookkeeping an adventure in *taqiyya*, the dissembling that Shiites sanction to protect their faith. The International Monetary Fund had even less faith in Iran's statistics than it did in Egypt's.

One thing was certain: The Mustazafin had not spent much on the Esteghlal. The hotel badly needed refurbishing, and its underpaid, demoralized staff depended on tips to supplement their meager salaries.

In 1991, Iran was still exhausted from its war with Iraq, which Khomeini had finally agreed to end in 1988 by drinking his infamous "poisoned chalice" of peace. Iran had paid heavily for his hubris. The war itself was said to have cost between $60 billion and $70 billion and had left Iran deeply in debt. The human cost was immeasurable: More than 400,000 Iranians were said to have been killed, and twice that number wounded, many of them in the human-wave attacks of 1983 and 1984 that had appalled and terrified the West.[22] Thousands of *basiji*, the 3 million Islamic volunteers in this officially blessed jihad, had died charging across Iraqi minefields with their notorious plastic keys to paradise tied around their necks.

In March 1991, I traveled to Hoveyzeh, a city of more than a million Iranian Arabs in southern Iran to which more then forty thousand Iraqi civilians, fellow Shiite Muslims, had fled when Saddam Hussein crushed the Shiite rebellion in Iraq soon after the end of the Gulf war in 1991. Iran had not invaded Iraq to stop the slaughter or given much military aid to their embattled Iraqi Shiite cousins. But Teheran did organize a well-run relief effort, draining its reserves for the refugees without receiving a penny of international relief aid.

Two things impressed me almost as deeply as the misery of the Iraqi refugees: The first was my Iranian government guide's empathy for the plight of the Iraqi Shiites; the second was her contempt for her fellow Iranian citizens of Arab origin. "Just look at them!" said Nahid, as we drove through the garbage-strewn streets of Hoveyzeh. "They're dirty, and they take many wives. They don't even speak Farsi properly!"

I reminded Nahid that her fellow Iranians spoke the language of the Prophet and the holy Koran, but this did not impress her. The 1 million Arabs of southern Iran were "backward, lazy, and untrustworthy," she continued. They were also "darker" than Persians. Iran's Arabs were among the seventeen nationalities whose tribalism and other "reactionary" attitudes endangered Iran's unity, she told me; only 35 percent of them spoke Farsi as a first language, and only half of her country was of Persian origin. Nahid's suspicion of these minorities and her intense disdain for Arabs, in particular, were not a product of the Islamic Republic. The shah's father had emphasized his nation's "Indo-European" origins in the 1930s and had demanded that the whole world adopt the indigenous name of the country — Iran — instead of Persia, partly to stress his nation's non-Arab, "Aryan" character.

I was also struck by the south's disproportionate suffering during the Iran-Iraq war. It was here that most of the battles had been waged. Hoveyzeh itself had been leveled by Iraqi soldiers, and the city's main boulevards were still lined with pictures of local martyrs. The photographs and posters of hand-drawn likenesses of the lost and the missing stretched for miles in all directions; their black eyes seemed a reproach as we drove in the dusk through this endless memorial to Iranian suffering. A generation of Iranians had been slaughtered, while America, Europe, and even Israel — which officially had no relations with either Iran or Iraq — had watched the war drag on, "tilting" to aid both Baghdad and Teheran to prolong the conflict that conveniently preoccupied the region's superpower bullies.

After Hoveyzeh, I took a far pleasanter trip with a Canadian businessman — Bill, I shall call him. Together we drove from Teheran through spectacular mountains to the Caspian Sea. Along the way, we stopped at towns and villages to chat with shopkeepers while we bought flat, circular *barbari* bread and the succulent *narangi* tangerines then in season. Iranians, unlike many Arabs, were not afraid to criticize their government. Nor were they natural sufferers. "It's just like under the shah," one shop owner near the Caspian complained. "Only now there are more clerics to pay off."

Bill had done business in Iran for three decades and lamented Iran's fate under its Islamic shahs. Iran's economic crisis was largely of its own making, he said. Though many technocrats had returned to Iran to help their country, the clergy continued to monopolize economic policy. Bill had never met a technologically enlightened theologian.

Though we were driving through what was once Iran's most fertile land, the fields were largely deserted and only sparsely planted. I did not see a single tractor. Iran was then importing roughly 65 percent of its food. Despite its ferocious quest for independence, the Islamic Republic could no longer feed itself.

After Khomeini's death in 1989, the pragmatists, led by President Ali Akbar Hashemi Rafsanjani, the clerical son of wealthy pistachio farmers and merchants, had grown stronger at the expense of the "radical" clergy. The "shadow of the tie" was now visible at the Foreign Ministry. Ministers and other officials were no longer addressed as "brother," but "Your Excellency." Rafsanjani was attempting to end his country's diplomatic isolation, in part by helping secure the release of Western hostages long held in Lebanon.

But many clerics were unwilling to relinquish power. They had developed a taste not only for titles but for wealth; the "Mercedes mullahs," Iranians called them. Meanwhile, the Islamic Republic had become less keen on "exporting" its revolution and financially less able to do so. The international Islamic revolution was dead. If Shiism was born thirteen centuries ago with the slaughter of Imam Hussein [the Prophet's grandson] on the battlefield of Karbala, Khomeini's Shiite international revolution had died in modern-day Karbala after the Gulf war, when Iran had done nothing to stop Saddam's slaughter of Iraqi Shiites and the desecration of Shia shrines. Only the grand ayatollahs had protested; Teheran itself was silent.

Increasingly, the revolution had placed Iranian national interests above its Islamic alliances, a choice foreshadowed in the early 1980s when a militant faction of the Syrian Muslim Brotherhood had challenged President Assad. Khomeini supported the secular Syrian leader who had slaughtered as many as thirty thousand of his own militant Islamists in 1982 in the Syrian city of Hama. Defending its policy, Iran argued that the Sunni-dominated Muslim Brotherhood leaders had "gone astray" by attempting to "drive a wedge" between their members and the Iranian revolution. But the real reason for Iran's choice was that Syria, unlike most other Arab countries, had supported Teheran against its Arab brethren in Baghdad during the Iran-Iraq war.[23] More recently, Iran had also supported Armenia against its Shiite brothers in the Republic of Azerbaijan.

Iran was not a traditional dictatorship; power remained decentralized, and the fierce internal quarrels and personal rivalries between Rafsanjani's pragmatists and the Islamic radicals ensured paralysis in Teheran. Only on major foreign policy and national security issues was there consensus. The simplest economic decision took months.

Rafsanjani had tried to curb revolutionary zeal by merging revolutionary and civil organs. Earlier that year, for example, he had merged the komitehs, the state-sanctioned committees of young Islamic zealots who harassed Iranians for "un-Islamic" conduct, into the police force. The Revolutionary Guards, the 150,000-strong paramilitary forces that monitored the military and implemented Islamic principles throughout its ranks, were incorporated into the army.

After Khomeini's death, Rafsanjani had also instituted a serious birth-control program. In 1990, the government proudly announced, some seventy thousand women of childbearing age had been sterilized in state family planning clinics—a most un-Islamic practice. Some 25 million contraceptive pills were imported that month. Yet the population growth rate had eased only slightly, from 3.3 percent in 1988 to about 3 percent in 1990.

But until Rafsanjani secured a pragmatic Parliament, he would be unable to rationalize the economy and push through vital reforms. Khomeini, who was once fond of saying that the revolution was not about the price of watermelons, had learned that the revolution is about the price of melons — and of meat and bread, of housing, education, and transport. And those prices kept rising by more than 60 percent a year, while salaries were constant.

Despite the talk of economic reform, there was still not a single important industry in private hands. Iran imported almost everything, from lightbulbs to matches. And it no longer exported much except pistachios, carpets, and oil — and less oil each year as local consumption grew. Iran's trade deficit stood at about $10 billion. If Iran can't overcome its inertia and develop faster," Bill said sadly, "it will become another Pakistan or Bangladesh in a decade."

IN THE SPRING of 1992, I returned to Iran for a second trip to cover the parliamentary elections that Iranian reformers had been counting on. I was met at Mehrebad airport by Kati Ghazi, a talented Iranian journalist, the *New York Times* stringer in Teheran.

I immediately warmed to Kati, a fellow alumna (1984) of Barnard College in New York. A supporter of the revolution, Kati had returned to Teheran in 1990 because she missed her country. Things were changing in Teheran, she told me confidently. Iran was slowly becoming "normal." The worst excesses of the revolution were over. The pragmatists would win the majlis, or parliamentary, elections because Rafsanjani had won over the Council of Guardians, the octogenarian clerics whom Khomeini had appointed to this important oversight panel that sets election ground rules and approves candidates. After the election, Iran would regain economic momentum, retap the energies of its middle class, and finally achieve the promises of the revolution. Many homesick Iranians who had soured on life abroad were returning.

I sensed Kati was right. Accompanying me on my trip, for instance, was a middle-age technocrat I shall call Mehdi who had worked in the shah's government but who was now an informal adviser to Kamal Kharrazi, the Islamic Republic's ambassador to the United Nations and a Rafsanjani ally. This was Mehdi's first trip back to Teheran since the revolution. Ambassador Kharrazi had asked him to return to assist the many American journalists who had come to Teheran for the elections. Though nervous about his Pahlavi past, Mehdi had reluctantly agreed.

As we left the airport, Kati handed me a *magneh*, a tight black head cover, and a *manteau*, the female "uniform." I had forgotten since my first trip a year earlier how confining psychologically and physically such clothing could be. Although Iranian women — unlike their Saudi counterparts — drove cars and motorcycles, and as recklessly as Iranian men, though they worked in government and business and participated in Parliament and public life, the *hijab* was still a cornerstone of the Islamic Republic. The economy may be bankrupt, the government corrupt, the young without hope, and Iran without a future, but the country would remain "Islamic" as long as it shrouded its women in public. Almost all hotels, restaurants, shops, and offices still displayed stickers reminding the faithful that "Good Hijab Is Purity" and that the "Price of Bad Hijab Is Death." But the stickers were faded along with the government's Islamic fervor.

I had come at a propitious time. Because of the elections, the Ministry of Islamic Guidance had been ordered, by whom it was never clear, to arrange interviews and press conferences for visiting journalists with leading clerics and other powerful figures who normally shunned the press. Among them was Ali Akbar Mohtashami, the hard-line cleric and former interior minister who, from his previous post as Iran's ambassador to Syria, had not only helped found Hezbollah in Lebanon but had also helped carry out the devastating suicide car-bomb attacks in Beirut that killed 241 U.S. Marines and 58 French "peacekeepers" in 1983. The bomb that had destroyed the U.S. Marine compound had been shipped to Lebanon via Damascus, courtesy of Mohtashami's embassy.[24]

Mohtashami had agreed to see several reporters on a Friday night following his lecture—a campaign rally, in fact—at a mosque in the slums of south Teheran. Kati Ghazi and I wore full chador for the occasion.

I was curious about this Islamic extremist who had praised the murder of Westerners in Lebanon. Perhaps his glee was understandable: He had lost most of his left hand and part of his right when a mail bomb sent by Israel in 1985 to the Damascus embassy had exploded in his hands.

Mohtashami was to receive us in the antechamber of the mosque, which was filled with men sitting on carpets in the unheated room. From where we stood, we could see the audience but not the candidate. Some of the younger men still had the three-day stubble and closely shaven heads favored by the *basiji*, the veteran volunteers of the war with Iraq; "jihad chic," a diplomat friend called the look. Others in the audience seemed bored. Most were shabbily dressed. These were clearly Mohtashami's natural constituents, the "dispossessed" who looked to the Islamic state not just for eternal spiritual salvation in paradise but economic salvation on earth.

Mohtashami's voice was surprisingly thin. It reminded me of that of Lebanon's Sheikh Harb, one of Mohtashami's first acolytes, whom I had interviewed almost a decade ago in Jibsheit a few months before he was assassinated by Israeli agents.

Khomeini's death was a "catastrophe" not just for Iran but for all Muslims, he told parishioners, as Kati translated his speech. Some revolutionary leaders had "lost their way" and were "betraying" the "line of the imam." But true believers would "hold fast to the Imam Khomeini's vision." A man in the audience yawned. Several others squirmed. The cleric was losing his audience.

Mohtashami switched topics. "How could the ordinary man afford to live today?" he wailed. Inflation was out of control; prices of bread and "chelo-kebab," the rice and skewered meat that most of his audience could no longer afford, had tripled since Rafsanjani had taken over. Was this Islam? No, this was "capitalist Islam," not "barefoot Islam," the "Islam of the Deprived." Soon the men were murmuring and nodding their heads in agreement. Who were these new "revolutionary rich" — the Islamic *taghootis?* Islam demanded that they vote — against corruption, against the privileged, for the "dispossessed" — that is, for Mohtashami's faction.

Moments after the end of his appeal, which apart from its Islamic jargon was typical of politicians everywhere, the father of Hezbollah entered the anteroom. He was a small man who looked older than his forty-six years. His eyes were almost completely obscured by thick glasses and a large black turban, signifying his descent from the Prophet. The mosque's fluorescent lights exaggerated the bomb scars on his face. Mohtashami smiled at us. We were most welcome in Iran, he said. We would see Islamic democracy in action.

Since non-Islamic groups were not permitted to run for office, was Iran truly democratic? I asked him. "Yes," he replied in Farsi, "even though the elections have been rigged against my group." Mohtashami had either missed my point or more likely preferred to reinterpret it. While some of his colleagues favored boycotting the elections to protest Rafsanjani's campaign manipulations, he told us, Ayatollah Khamenei, whom senior clerics had chosen to succeed the late Imam Khomeini as Iran's Supreme Guide, had urged him to participate. "Don't let yourselves be victimized," Leader Khamenei had advised Mohtashami.

Khamenei was an unimpressive cleric who had been unceremoniously promoted from the rank of *hojatolislam*, meaning "authority on Islam," to that of ayatollah the day Khomeini died. But few devout Iranians considered him a legitimate *marja al-taqlid*, a man to be imitated, since he had not presented a proper *risala*, the book-length thesis required of all great clerics, the grand ayatollahs.[25] Initially, Khamenei had supported Rafsanjani's reforms and was considered fairly pragmatic himself. But as criticism intensified over his lack of religious credentials, Khamenei had veered to the right in search of hard-line clerical allies, among them Mohtashami.

An election victory for his faction did not matter, Mohtashami told us. Whether or not his allies won a majority of the majlis seats, Iran would continue pursuing "the values of Islam" and rejecting Western influence — that is, opposing Rafsanjani's reforms.

Was Islamic government in Iran a failure? I asked. "On the contrary," he replied, still smiling. "We have succeeded. We have defeated efforts by the CIA and other Western agents to destroy us. We've repelled the Mujahideen. And we've survived a war with Iraq launched against us when the revolution was in its infancy."

The Islamic Republic would continue battling Islam's enemies at home and abroad. It had not succumbed to the "satanic temptation" to reestablish relations with the United States and would not do so until Washington abandoned its "despotic" aid to Israel, an illegitimate entity. As long as there were revolutionaries in Teheran, there would be no Americans in Iran. The American-sponsored Madrid peace conference between Arabs and Israelis in October 1991 was a travesty, a position that I knew now made him *persona non grata* in Syria, his former home.

He was proud of his work for Hezbollah and the Palestinians, he said, waving his maimed hand. It was an "honor" to help destroy Israel. Jews created trouble wherever they went. During World War II, he said, some European governments tried to destroy the Zionist empire, and one could not argue too much with their approach or the message. But the Jews had "transferred their pernicious culture to Palestine." The only solution was to destroy the usurper and "send all Jews back to the countries they came from."

Unlike other clerics who denied that Iran had nuclear ambitions, Mohtashami was proud of what one Western diplomat had called Teheran's "shop-till-you-drop" efforts to acquire atomic bombs and other weapons of mass destruction. "Why should the United States have a monopoly on nuclear weapons?" he declared.

It was the spring of 1992. Ramadan, the Muslim holy month of dawn-to-dusk fasting to commemorate God's revelation of the Koran to Muhammad, would coincide with Noruz, the Persian New Year that Iranians mark with two weeks of celebration, including elaborate picnics on the first two days.

Which holiday would most Iranians observe, the Ramadan fast or the joyous Noruz picnics? The answer was obvious: Throughout the city, Iranians were picnicking in the sun, with no sign of government interference. Once again, Iran's Persianness ran deeper than its Islam.

The historic competition between these strands of Iran's identity was a frequent theme of Bahram Beizai, one of Iran's best film directors, whom I visited later that day at his apartment. Iran was marked by dualism, the fifty-four-year-old director told me. His nation was "schizophrenic." Persians loved grand abstractions — the Zoroastrian cosmic struggle between good and evil, for example — but they had a keen eye for the most minute detail, as the ornate inlaid domes of the seventeenth-century mosques of Isfahan attested. Iran was both East and West — perhaps more East than West — but it craved an independent identity. Iranians loved America but hated its power and influence, producing a love-hate attitude toward the United States — an "Americanophobia." Persians detested their isolation but remained xenophobic. They adored stability in a land prone to geological and political earthquakes.

While the clerics had declared war on traditional Persian culture soon after the revolution, Beizai told me, they soon abandoned the futile campaign. "In this land that traced history back seven thousand years, it was impossible to count only the last fourteen hundred!" he said. "Iranians still jump over campfires, as the Zoroastrians did. They no longer even know the origins of these rituals, but they continue to perform them."

The Islamic Republic was now reinventing both ancient and Islamic history, giving them an Iranian Shiite cast. Hussein, the Prophet's grandson, the "hero-martyr" of Shia history," wrote Fouad Ajami, the Lebanese-born Shia scholar, had been turned into a "prototype" of the modern "suicide-driver."[26] Hussein, in fact, had not sought death on the fields of Karbala; he had been trapped there by a more powerful Muslim army. But Khomeini and the militant clerics preferred a history that emphasized the joy of dying for Islam. "Our lives are full of heaven and hell, guilt and fear, atonement and prayer, obedience to authority and punishment for the lack of it. Our stories usually have sad endings," Beizai said. "From childhood on, our festivals turn into mourning ceremonies."

One of Beizai's films, *Mosaferan* (Travelers), which he refused to screen abroad after the government demanded extensive changes to ensure that it conformed to "Islamic values," reflected this theme. In *Mosaferan*, a marriage ceremony becomes a funeral through a string of unfortunate events.

"The government doesn't like my movies because of their Persian themes and also because I give women strong central roles," he said. After four years of work on the film, Beizai was more than thirty thousand dollars in debt.

Iranian directors, artists, and writers repeatedly challenged their government's censors. Mohsen Makhmalbaf, another filmmaker who had been imprisoned under the shah and once had strong Hezbollahi convictions himself, was now making movies critical of his government. The censors had banned two of his films and demanded changes in others, but Makhmalbaf continued making them.[27] In his *Marriage of the Blessed* he presents a savage portrait of the effects of the Iraq-Iran war, a war, critics had noted, in which not a single important cleric's son had died.

Iranian writers and artists paid dearly for their intellectual integrity. Scores of students and teachers had been killed and injured in June 1980 when armed gangs of hooligans loyal to the hard-line clergy assaulted freewheeling political and cultural groups on campus. Iran's thirty-four universities were then closed for two years to produce an Islamic "cultural revolution." The faculty staff was cut in half; more than sixty thousand teachers lost their jobs for political reasons.[28] But the banishment of so many intellectuals to independent publishing companies, small research institutes, and new private universities eventually produced an explosion of political criticism and Iran's Islamic reform movement.[29]

IN APRIL 1992, Rafsanjani got the majlis he wanted but not the bulk of his reforms. In an interview before the elections, Mohsen Adeli, Rafsanjani's energetic, Western-trained central bank director, praised the benefits of privatization, a floating exchange rate, and sound monetary policy. He spoke bravely of instituting reforms pioneered by Milton Friedman, the conservative American economist, such as substituting cash coupons for food stamps and other costly, inefficient state subsidies, and openly invited foreign investors to "consider Iran."[30] But powerful *bazaari* and clerical forces opposed such innovations. Ignoring their denunciations, the government borrowed heavily to finance reconstruction and infrastructure needed to attract foreign investment. But Iran's central bank lost control over international borrowing and was soon unable to service its debt. Gloating radicals blamed the economic mess on Rafsanjani's departure from the "line of Imam." With allies in the majlis and in the office of Supreme Leader Khamenei, the radicals blocked further reform.

I had a hint of the stalemate to come when my friend Mehdi and I tried to leave Iran after the 1992 elections. I had no problem. But Mehdi was stopped at the airport and taken into a small police office near the customs desk. Hours passed, but there was still no Mehdi. My flight was called, but I decided to miss it, reluctant to leave without my friend. Hours after our flight had left, Mehdi emerged from the police office, silent and pale. On the way back to the Esteghlal, he told me that someone — he did not know who — had accused him of smuggling ancient artifacts out of Iran. The charge was ludicrous. Mehdi had made a financial sacrifice to work for the Islamic regime, but the police had told him that he would not be free to leave Iran until the complaint against him was closed. Over the next week, Mehdi's appeals to Ambassador Kharrazi's office in New York seemed to have no effect. But a wealthy friend, a *bazaari* with good clerical contacts and a luxurious villa in north Teheran, began working on Mehdi's "problem" and seemed confident that it could be quickly solved, perhaps, I thought, with a bribe. But finally I could wait no longer; I returned to New York.

A week later, Mehdi also left Teheran. He never learned which ministry, quasi-official agency, or individual had decided to make his life miserable. Like so many things in Teheran, the origins of the campaign against him would remain mysterious, an unsettling example of the regime's legendary unpredictability. Since then, Mehdi had not risked a second visit home.

IN THE FALL OF 1995, I was met at the airport by Nahzi Fathi, my new translator. Nahzi was a friend of Kati Ghazi, who had moved back to New York in late 1995. Kati could no longer endure working in Iran, she told me. The revolution was changing, but too slowly to permit Western-educated Iranians to fulfill their professional aspirations. Though she missed her family and her country, America offered her real job opportunity and political freedom.

Teheran looked much better to me than it had during my earlier visits. Its broad boulevards were now bustling and well landscaped — the result of a "beautification" project launched by Teheran's energetic and controversial mayor, Gholam Hussein Karbaschi. Nahzi, a fan of the forty-two-year-old mayor, recounted his achievements as we drove along the recently repaved Vali Asr Street, the capital's main thoroughfare. Karbaschi had opened a hundred new parks in Teheran and planted more than a thousand trees a year since my last visit. He had also bulldozed apartment and office buildings constructed without his approval and "persuaded" polluting factories to move outside the city by cutting off their electricity and water supply. To reduce traffic gridlock, he had built new roads, bridges, and flyovers and banned all traffic except for cars and motorcycles whose owners paid the city a large fee for permits. Best of all, he had financed his improvements by levying huge taxes on the *bazaaris* and other wealthy shopkeepers and traders. He had also used some of the money to hire additional workers to pick up garbage.

Teheran's streets were now well maintained and clean — in better shape, it seemed to me, than New York's. The once-omnipresent soldiers on the streets were gone. The revolutionary graffiti that used to cover public buildings had been erased: Billboards advertising "Nokios," the latest cellular phones, Kodak, Ray-Ban, Winston, and Xerox were now as ubiquitous as Koranic verses had been only a few years ago. Women still covered their heads, but they tied their scarves more loosely. Their "uniforms" had also changed. Some women, particularly the young, wore pastel *manteaus* and even more brightly colored head scarves, along with obvious makeup. The other day, Nahzi told me, a woman broadcaster had worn a bright pink head scarf on state television! As Nahzi and I window-shopped near the Ministry of Islamic Guidance, I noticed that the *manteaus* in the store windows featured tapered waists and shoulder pads. A few were even embroidered with sequins. What happened to the ban on "Bad Hijab"?

The offices of the Ministry of Islamic Guidance were depressingly unchanged, or so I initially thought. But Ali Reza Haghighi, the young man assigned to assist me with my "program," reminded me that appearances in Iran remain deceiving.

"Iran is moving towards democracy," said the young college graduate, a former *basiji* who had lost many of his friends but not his faith during the Iran-Iraq war. Ali, the son of a poor family from Shiraz, was grateful to the revolution. "I would never have been able to afford university under the shah," he told me. Because he had served in the war, the government sent him to the University of Teheran. There he had discovered a new world — the world of political ideas. He had read all of the "greats," he told me, from the ancient Greeks to Hobbes, Locke, Rousseau, Voltaire, Heidegger, Kant, Hegel, and Marx. He was fascinated by American culture, he said, particularly by the books Americans wrote — such as *One-Dimensional Man*, by Herbert Marcuse — and the films we made between 1945 and 1965, America's "golden age," in Ali's view.

"After World War II, you strove to combine modernization with moral principles, democracy with morality. That is what we are now trying to do. But this nation is deeply Islamic, so our framework must be Islamic. We need to enlist the progressive clergy," he said, "people who can update and reinterpret Islamic principles to assure both effective government and Islamic values."

Ali had prepared a full schedule for my visit — much of what I had requested and more. I was astonished. Since my last visit to Iran I had written two critical articles about Iran's tyrannical regime for *Foreign Affairs*, the American foreign policy journal avidly read by the Iranian elite. Yet despite my denunciation of the Islamic Republic, Iran, unlike Saudi Arabia, which had repeatedly denied me entry after the Gulf war, had given me another visa and itself another chance to make its case. Despite, or perhaps because of, the increased economic and psychological pressure on Teheran by America's expanded sanctions, Iran was reaching out to the West and Westerners, and not just to businessmen. Iran was far shrewder in handling foreign journalists than Saudi Arabia would ever be.

As we started to leave his office, Ali reached into his filing cabinet and removed a videocassette: *Forrest Gump*. A friend of his, one of those progressive clerics whom Ali so admired, was eager to see it. "We love this film here," he told me, sensing my surprise. "It's about faith in God, country, and family — typical Iranian Islamic values!" I suppressed the impulse to tell Ali that the film was also about stupidity.

SINCE I HAD ARRIVED a week before Iran's international trade fair, the Esteghlal was fully booked, and I was lucky to find a room. The hotel had been spruced up slightly since my last visit, but its owner was now in trouble.

In the summer, a multi-billion-dollar corruption scandal reminiscent of those during the shah's last days had rocked the regime. Morteza Rafighdoost, the head of one of Iran's largest banks and the brother of Mohsen, the *bazaari* head of the foundation that owns the Esteghlal, was convicted along with seven other leading government officials of embezzling the equivalent of tens of millions of dollars from state-owned banks. Rafighdoost had been sentenced to life in prison. Though his brother Mohsen, the foundation director, was not directly implicated in the plot, he had been forced to testify at his brother's trial, after which the government launched an investigation into his stewardship of the powerful foundation.

The investigation was stopped by Supreme Leader Khamenei, who controlled the foundations, but these and other financial scandals had further eroded public confidence in the Islamic government. From the holy city of Qum, Ayatollah Ali Akbar Meshkini, the head of the Assembly of Experts, which approves the appointment of the *walayat al-faqih*, the country's Supreme Leader, warned of the banking scandal's implications. Such a betrayal of the republic was "unprecedented," he declared during a Friday sermon. These "heartless people" had "disgraced" Islamic government.[31]

Profiteering within the elite was still rampant. One of Rafsanjani's sons was said to hold a lucrative oil concession and the license for Coca-Cola, Iran's unofficial national beverage. Another son supervised the still-unfinished metro project in Teheran. Still another bought and sold weapons for the government. More distant relatives smuggled cars into Teheran from Iran's free-trade zones, which had become not export centers as intended but opportunities for domestic graft. The late Ahmad Khomeini, the sainted Imam's son, had for a while controlled a portion of Iran's oil trade. The son of Ali Akbar Natiq-Noori, the Speaker of Iran's Parliament and a frontrunner to replace Rafsanjani as president in 1997, ran a lucrative water-skiing school and center near the Karaj Dam — "aqua-turban," Iranians now called him. As in most Middle Eastern countries, family, clan, and tribal interests still took precedence over those of the nation, or Islam.

In one sense, Iran under the mullahs had become more "democratic": Corruption was no longer the exclusive preserve of the rich and well connected. With an inflation rate unofficially pegged at 50–100 percent in 1994, middle-class Iranians were forced to hold two or three jobs to make ends meet. So getting anything done in Teheran—sending a fax, getting garbage collected, paying a traffic ticket, even, I was told, securing an interview with President Rafsanjani—required a gratuity. The morals-enforcing *komitehs* that Rafsanjani had tried to merge into the police force had resurfaced, but mainly for shake-downs. While some eighty-six thousand Iranians had been arrested in 1994 for "social corruption" and another million were warned about "errant behavior," [32] many of these charges had been quietly settled by discreet payoffs. Wealthy Teheranis paid Revolutionary Guards between 100,000 and 500,000 rials—or between $30 and $156—to ignore loud Western music and the consumption of alcohol at weddings and other celebrations. "The bribe is the cheapest part of our parties," a Teherani intellectual confided.

A payment of up to nine hundred dollars—the price of the fine itself—was usually but not always sufficient to protect owners of the more than a quarter of a million satellite dishes in Teheran from nighttime police raids. Earlier this year, the majlis had banned satellite dishes, along with Pepsi and Coca-Cola, to prevent Westoxication. But in south Teheran and other poor neighborhoods, Revolutionary Guards feared disrupting the popular screenings of *Baywatch*, Iran's favorite television show. "Lumpen" Iranians in the capital's slums and surrounding towns may have lived without sewage or adequate health care, but they had satellites. South Teheranis pooled their money to install a dish in their homes and sell tickets to neighbors and friends to watch American serials. Many of these slum dwellers also had powerful protectors among the Hezbollahis and the *komitehs*. For those without connections, a payoff would usually guarantee discretion. This was how the revolution was ending, a veteran diplomat told me, not with a bang or a whimper but a bribe.

The poor, whose buying power was shrinking, were less willing to ignore the Islamic regime's broken promises. Although the government had recently launched an antiprofiteering campaign directed at the *bazaaris* and the revolu-tionary rich, those who made money through exporting oil and importing Coca-Cola, popular discontent frequently erupted in riots. In Qasvin in August 1994 and in Mashhad and the Teheran suburbs of Islamshar and Akbarabad in 1995, thousands of people poured into the streets, burning tires, smashing shop win-dows, and setting banks, gas stations, and government offices on fire. Because local Revolutionary Guards had refused to fire on the crowds in Qasvin, the government had trained new rapid-reaction *basiji* units that did not hesitate to shoot protesters during the later rebellions in Teheran's slums. The repression was merciless, Iranians told me.

For senior clerics, leading politicians, and other revolutionary luminaries, the stakes in the continuation of their regime were high and the internecine quarrels increasingly bitter. Since my last visit, relations had continued to deteri-orate between President Rafsanjani and Supreme Leader Khamenei. One diplo-mat called the relationship a bad marriage: The husband and wife detested each other, but they could not afford to split up. Meanwhile, too open an identifica-tion with either the pragmatic or hard-line camp—categories that grossly oversimplified Iran's diabolically complex, constantly shifting political factions and alliances — could literally prove fatal.

Lately, a series of tragic "accidents" had befallen leading government figures. In 1994 the head of intelligence in Supreme Leader Khamenei's office, along with three of his senior aides, had died in a car crash while returning to Teheran from Mashhad. In 1995, Mansour Satari, the air force chief, and seven of his senior officers were killed when their military jet exploded on takeoff at Isfahan's military airport. A diplomat in Teheran who had investigated the disaster told me he had no doubt that the plane had been sabotaged — why he did not know. But Iranians said that Satari, whose daughter was married to Rafsanjani's son, had been killed by hard-liners, who feared that he was preparing a coup on Rafsanjani's behalf. Finally, Ahmad Khomeini, the sainted Imam's son, a wealthy, hard-line businessman who had become increasingly critical of both Khamenei, his father's successor, and of Rafsanjani, suffered a fatal heart attack. Family members told friends that Ahmad had been poisoned.

In a land awash in rumor and intrigue, the truth about these deaths — unlike the regime's continued assaults and murders on its critics abroad — was unknowable not only to foreigners but even to most Iranians. But gossip about such alleged or real conspiracies kept Iranians psychologically and politically off-balance.

MANY INTELLECTUALS no longer seemed intimidated by the prevailing *javv*, in Farsi the public mood or political "atmosphere," which gave Iranians a sense of what would and would not be tolerated by the most fervent defenders of the Islamic regime. Despite intermittent repression, Islamic Iran, they told me, was far freer and intellectually more resilient than it had been under the shah, especially since Khomeini's death in 1989. In Iran, some 2,777 books were published in 1976, compared with 4,810 in 1987. Although 25 percent of books published since the revolution were religious texts and all were strictly censored for "anti-Islamic" thoughts — including "sorcery" — circulation of most publications had risen sharply.[33]

Iranians were proud of their intellectual heritage. Ideas had always mattered in Iran. The Shia clergy, at least in theory, were the historical champions of *ijtihad*, the continuing interpretation of holy texts by religious scholars. Moreover, the Islamic revolution's own ideology had evolved from the writings not only of clerics but lay Islamic reformers, some, but not all, of them Iranian.[34] Before the revolution, young radicals had devoured the works of Egypt's Sayyid Qutb, the militant Muslim Brotherhood theoretician. Even more influential was a fellow non-Arab thinker, Mawlana Abo'l-Ala Mawdudi, an Indian Muslim journalist with no clerical background or scholarly credentials. Mawdudi, who translated Koranic words and concepts into modern ideas, had declared in 1926 that Islam was a "revolutionary ideology" aimed at "destroying the social order of the world totally and rebuilding it from scratch." Jihad, he wrote, was "revolutionary struggle," and the ancient struggle between good and evil had become a conflict between "Islam and un-Islam," the latter a reference to the *jahiliyya*, the pre-Islamic era of ignorance, an idea that Egypt's Qutb had later developed into one of militant Islam's intellectual cornerstones.[35]

The notion of "Westoxication," omnipresent in the revolutionaries' anti-Western campaign, had been popularized in an essay written by a leftist journalist, Jalal Al-e Ahmad, an Iranian cleric's son. But no single thinker — apart from Khomeini himself — did more to lay the intellectual groundwork for the revolution than Ali Shariati, a French-educated intellectual born in 1933. "Brilliant and naive," as one scholar called him, Shariati blended Marxism's analysis of "suffering and exploitation" with his conviction that "Islam, renewed and reformed, offered the only way out for modern-day Muslims."[36] He detested fellow semi-Westernized Iranians — Iran's "assimilated pseudo-Europeans," he called them — and his "faithless society" in which, between 1956 and 1966, "the consumption of cosmetics had increased 500 percent."[37] Spiritual and political salvation depended on resisting the West by transforming traditional Shiism, his "religion of mourning," into a "religion of martyrdom," which Shariati considered its original, authentic form.

What Shariati would have made of the Islamic revolution he helped nurture is difficult to say. He died in exile in London two years before the event. But I suspect that he might have disapproved. Despite his revolutionary Islam, he mistrusted the clerics and doubted that a government run by them would provide for its citizens. Once, at a lecture in Teheran at a religious meeting hall that now bears his name, a man in the audience asked his friend Shariati whether in existentialism "existence precedes essence or essence precedes existence." Shariati cut him off. He knew that the man was the father of malnourished children from Mashhad, where torrential rains had just washed away the streets linking his neighborhood to the rest of the city. It was more important, Shariati told him, "that the government take care of the asphalt in your street. It precedes both the existence and the essence."[38]

I THOUGHT ABOUT poor Shariati as I stood in front of the modest house in north Teheran where Khomeini had lived after he returned from exile to oversee Iran's Islamic government. Schoolchildren may not have been taken to Persepolis, but they were taken to this shrine. The government had turned Khomeini's tiny salon and bedroom into a museum that stressed the Imam's lack of attachment to worldly possessions.

Unlike so many of his clerical colleagues who had built lavish homes in this neighborhood, Khomeini clearly shunned wealth. Power, not money, was his aim. His bedroom/salon was tiny, attached by a walkway to a "Husseiniyeh," or "place of Hussein," not really a mosque, but a traditional Shiite social and mourning center, from whose balcony Khomeini had given many fiery speeches. In the bedroom where he had sometimes received guests there was a single bed — Khomeini slept alone — a prayer rug rolled up at its foot and a fresh roll of toilet paper on its mantel — though Khomeini had been dead for six years

—a green telephone, a night table with a lamp, a vase of plastic flowers, a clock, and a Koran. There was also a short-wave radio, banned in Iran, and about a dozen books.

Khomeini had gone about building his Islamic government methodically, as he did most things. A journalist friend had told me that each day Khomeini would take three walks lasting exactly twenty minutes.[39] If he found himself at his front door a minute early, he would pace the block in front of his house until precisely twenty minutes had passed. His tiny bedroom/salon reflected this orderliness. Much in Iran mystified me, but of one thing I was sure: Without this extraordinary man, whose charisma was never comprehensible to most Westerners, including me, Iran would not have had an Islamic revolution.

While the ayatollah had depended on men like Shariati to overthrow the shah, he probably would have crushed him as he did thousands of other intellectuals and even clerical critics of his regime. In 1982, for instance, Khomeini had defined the limits of legitimate dissent and established his own authority within the constitutional theocracy by placing under house arrest Grand Ayatollah Shariatmadari, Iran's most influential theologian and a critic of theocratic rule.[40]

Having eliminated a major challenge to his religious and political legitimacy, Khomeini tried to reconcile the unreconcilable, turning what was essentially a partnership between the clerics and the wealthy bazaaris who supported them into a vehicle for bringing prosperity to the "dispossessed." Khomeini himself was perhaps the first to recognize the impossibility of balancing populist pressures from below with the interests of powerful bazaaris and the wealthy private sector in general. So a two-tier economic system evolved—what one scholar called "subsidies for the poor and laissez-faire for the privileged"—in which Khomeini remained the "arbiter of last resort."[41] But Khomeini's conflicting desires to address the needs of the poor while ensuring the sanctity Islam places on private property—the Prophet Muhammad was a merchant, after all—led to inconsistent rulings and a hybrid, jumbled development strategy that failed to achieve its goals. His failure reflected the difficulty inherent in developing a purely "Islamic" economic system.

The longer he ruled, the more Khomeini equated the survival of his own government with that of Islam itself—a belief that fostered ever greater pragmatism, if not moderation, on his part. If Iran had to buy weapons to fight Iraq from the Great Satan, the United States, or even Israel, the "Little Satan," so be it. If Iran had to expose itself to Westoxication to end its isolation and acquire the advanced technology it needed, so be it. If Iran needed a man like Rafsanjani to foster at least the illusion of economic pragmatism and moderation, so be it. And if he, the "armed Imam," had to drink poison to end the war with Iraq that was destroying his revolution, so be it. In 1988 these remarkable shifts were summed up in an extraordinary decree: "Our government has priority over all Islamic tenets," Khomeini ruled, "even over prayer, fasting, and the pilgrimage to Mecca."[42]

Even in this, however, Khomeini was not constant. Shortly before his

death, unable to countenance Rafsanjani's steady progress toward the institu-
tionalization of the revolution and pragmatic reform, Iran's Supreme Leader
issued another *fatwa* aimed at appeasing his country's hard-line revolutionary
clerics and perhaps keeping the outside world at bay. He declared Salman
Rushdie, the Indian-born Muslim writer and British citizen, an apostate for his
Satanic Verses, a book the ayatollah had never read. The *fatwa*, which required
that all believers rid the *umma* of this *murtad*, or apostate, ensured that even
after his death, Khomeini's revolution would continue.

Indeed it had, though I doubted that Khomeini would have approved of its
course. Intellectuals now drew their inspiration not from the Imam, or even
from Shariati, but from Shariati's intellectual descendant, Abdolkarim Sorush,
a leader of the reform movement.

The movement popularized its ideas through some twenty newspapers and
magazines. While there were no truly independent newspapers and journals in
Iran and though censorship remained pervasive and arbitrary, these independent-minded journals and newspapers, which appeared with official authorization, raised daring questions about Islamic government and promoted what they
called a "reformist Islam," which strongly resembled what Western intellectuals
call "secularism."

Among them is *Zanan* (Women), whose feminist editor, Shala Sherkat,
feared that each issue might be her last. The government did not give free paper
to *Zanan*, as it did to other magazines, she complained, which made publication
not only risky but expensive. Yet she and a tiny staff tackled issues at the
heart of the Islamic Republic's discrimination against women, which she called
"un-Islamic." Women's interest in their rights, if not rights themselves, had
increased as a result of the revolution, she told me. Like so many critics, Sherkat
had obviously learned how to articulate her antirevolutionary ideas in politically
acceptable formulations. Perhaps she still believed in the Islamic revolution;
perhaps she no longer did. I would never know.

But her criticism of the government's treatment of women was as scathing
as that of any non-Muslim foreign critic. Her journal and another, *Farzeneh*
(The Clever Woman), were among Iran's leading crusaders for women's rights,
joining more than sixty nongovernmental civic groups — some Islamic, some
not — that shared the goal of ending discrimination against women and govern-
ment-sanctioned privileges for men.

Islam's *hadiths*, the sayings of the Prophet, had been misinterpreted, she
declared, pulling her chador more tightly around her chin; they were not consistent with real Islamic law. Women in Iran were doctors, lawyers, engineers,
newscasters, parliamentarians, scholars, and businesswomen. Where does the
Koran say that women cannot be judges, fighter pilots, or even leaders? Where
does the Koran say that women must wear black? Colors are beautiful, and
beauty is Islamic. Her issue on the topic of "color" sold well, she told me.

So did her issue on wife beating. Islam does not sanction a husband's
physical abuse of his wife, she asserted. In a recent issue, *Zanan* argued that

Iran's toleration of such abuses resulted from a mistranslation of the Koran's Arabic. *Daraba,* or beating, also meant "resting, avoiding, walking, preventing, staying home, changing, having sex with, and sharing a bed."[43] Imam Ali, the article quoted Muhammad's cousin as stating, instructed a man first to "talk and preach to your wife." If she still refused to obey, he should refuse to sleep with her. If disobedience continued, he should "find a judge to settle the dispute between them." But "reactionary" elements in her country had ignored such counsel, sanctioning wife beating, a *jahili,* or pre-Islamic custom.

But beyond problems of mistranslation and misinterpretation, Sherkat added, treading now on dangerous ground, "what made sense in the seventh century may not make sense today." Muhammad was an enlightened man, she argued, a leader who valued women. Since Islam made sense for "all people in all countries in all times," the Prophet himself might not give today the orders he gave then. God's words had to be reinterpreted, updated so that they were applicable to modern life. Iran, for example, permitted citizens to marry at puberty, which it defined as nine for girls and fifteen for boys. "But people died younger in the seventh century. Today these designations are inappropriate."

Despite its circulation of less than ten thousand, *Zanan* was having an impact, Sherkat maintained. Women were being trained in Qum as *mujtahids,* interpreters of Islamic law. Eventually, they would help change the government's policies toward women. The Iranian Parliament, she noted, had recently enacted legislation giving women greater rights in divorce, although women still could not divorce their husbands. And the Judicial Council had recently ruled that women could be "consultants" in court cases — de facto judges. In several cases, their "advice" had been accepted.

A floor above *Zanan* is *Kiyan* (Essence), a quarterly cultural magazine that has published Abdolkarim Sorush's lectures and essays. Mahmud Shams, *Kiyan's* dynamic editor, explained that the journal was founded in 1991 — without government-provided paper — to promote what he called "revisionist Islam," which endorses, among other "Islamic" civil rights, freedom of speech and of the press. "Since we are the children of this revolution, the militants view us as far more dangerous than secularists. For we fight them from an Islamic base."

Shams said that to become a modern nation, Iran must experience a "Reformation" as Christianity did in the West. But since Iran was deeply Islamic, the result would not be secularism, the topic of *Kiyan's* next issue, which he defined as a "rupture between a society and its values." "Islamic revisionism" would provide greater freedom, tolerance and pluralism — "within an Islamic framework." This was Sorush's view as well, he said.[44]

What enhanced Sorush's credibility was his impeccable Islamic credentials. As a former member of the government's senior Cultural Revolution Panel, Sorush had supervised university purges and book burnings in the early 1980s and defended the persecution of leftists. But just as Shariati had argued for revolution to end social injustice through Islam, Sorush was now pressing for tolerance and political pluralism through Islam. No one could claim an exclusive right to interpret the Koran. There could be no "absolute truth" because understanding of Islam was relative. Implicitly, Sorush was arguing for the separation of church and state, though he had refused to confirm this when I had interviewed him. But Shams maintained that Sorush's arguments implied that Islam could not, and should not, be transformed into an ideology. If Islam "ruled," it would be blamed for the failures of temporal rule. Islam had to remain above all that. For such ideas, Shams told me, many called Sorush "Islam's Martin Luther."

This "enlightened, rational" trend would inevitably win, Shams argued, because technology could not be stopped. Satellites, banned as a form of cultural invasion, were installed in every other home. Young Iranians traded jokes and information on the Internet, which the government had also tried and failed to shut down. Iranians would remain fascinated by the West and drawn to Western culture. The government had succeeded only in pushing all that it denounced as "un-Islamic" — promiscuity, alcohol, and satellites — off the streets and indoors. Iran had become not an "Islamic" country but a "twisted" land in which religion was now seen by a majority of younger Iranians not as a "choice" but as a set of onerous "do's and don'ts."

Ramin Jahanbegloo, who helped found *Goft-o-Gu* (Dialogue), a two-year-old reformist quarterly, argued that many young people were now "totally disillusioned" with religious values. The Islamic revolution had succeeded in producing among the young an areligious generation as well as a "James Dean syndrome" — "rebels without a cause" — and a sharp generation gap between young Iran and the aging clerics who made the rules. Teheran's new cultural centers, which the mayor had expanded to attract teenagers, now featured computer and karate classes as well as jazz concerts featuring the music of John Coltrane and Dizzy Gillespie. The concerts were called "popular music of the blacks" to disguise their obviously American origin. Few were fooled, but even fewer knew how Iran could escape the Islamic trap of its own making.

FERMENT WAS NOT confined to Teheran. Some of the most ardent exponents of reform were found in Qum, the Shia theological center where the Islamic revolution had begun some thirty years ago. Qum was only a three-hour drive from Teheran. As Nahzi, Ali Reza Haghighi, of the Ministry of Islamic Guidance, and I drove south, Teheran's rivers and lush greenery were replaced by bleak, vast Iranian desert.

I saw no *manteaus* in Qum. In the dusty, drab streets of this holy city of a million Iranians, one saw almost nothing but black chadors, turbans, and *abas*, the gray or brown robes worn by clerical students and their professors. Qum, the "Vatican of Shiism," trained the nation's future ulema, *faqihs*, or jurists, and *tullab*, its sixty thousand seminarians.[45] But I soon saw that this city, too, was embroiled in the struggle over Iran's future and that opposition to clerical rule now came as much from within the clergy as outside it.

At the University of Golpayagani, a bastion of theological conservatism, clerics in ecclesiastical garb were indexing on computers more than fifteen hundred volumes of Islamic law, creating data banks for other Islamic texts and debating how best to acquire computer scanners for Persian so that their ancient texts could be conserved.

Many mullahs wanted more than modern technology. Hojatolislam Mohsen Khadivar, the head of the Howzeh Islamic Center, called upon Qum's one hundred Islamic research centers to revamp their curricula, only 3–5 percent of which was "of any use in solving contemporary political, economical, and social problems."[46] Khadivar maintained that 98 percent of the more than 100,000 clerics in Iran who were not involved in running the state were now losing legitimacy among the masses because of the ruling clergy's unpopularity. "The clergy does not want its fate to be that of the Marxist parties in the former Communist states," he said.[47]

Nahzi, Ali, and I also visited the five-year-old Al-Moufid University, where Ayatollah Moussavi Ardabilli was also trying to reconcile Islam with modernity. The still-unfinished main building housing the university conference halls, well-lit classrooms, and a cafeteria—for male students—overlooked gardens reminiscent of colleges in Southern California. Its library, we were told, which now housed eighty thousand books in Persian, Arabic, and English, would eventually grow to more than a million volumes.

As I wandered through the stacks, an amazing array of books, some once banned in the Islamic Republic, were on display—works on the origins of the persecuted Baha'i, on Hinduism, Christianity, and Judaism, along with thousands of political-science texts—including those by Islam's modern enemy, Karl Marx, and Jean-Paul Sartre's treatise on existentialism. Bernard Lewis's volume on *Race and Slavery in the Middle East* shared a shelf with *Mein Kampf* as well as works by Karl Popper. The logic of the filing system was unclear to me.

In July 1994, Ayatollah Mohammad Reza Mahdavi-Kani, a former interior minister and secretary-general of the Teheran-based Combatant Clerical Association, the respected liaison between Teheran's clerical apparatchiks and the traditional clergy of Qum, had warned that the Islamic government was losing its legitimacy in the eyes of the poor. Mahdavi-Kani had openly urged the clerics to return to Qum, that is, to resume their traditional advisory role to the rulers. Iran's next president, he declared, should not be a cleric.[48]

Such views, though now labeled "radical," were not new to Qum. Throughout Iranian history, the ulema had cooperated with Iran's shahs more than they had opposed them,[49] though official history now emphasized the clergy's opposition to Iran's tyrannical rulers.

Khomeini, in fact, was one of three ayatollahs who had vied to succeed the late Ayatollah Sayyid Aqa Husayn Burujirdi, who, until his death in 1961, was widely regarded as the *marja al-taqlid*, the one true source of imitation for Shiites throughout the world. Lacking in worldly ambition, Burujirdi of Qum, too, had advocated political neutrality toward the shah, as did Khomeini's rivals for the status of *marja*. Although they were widely regarded as more learned than he, Khomeini was able to triumph largely because his uncompromising hostility to the shah and America had appealed not just to younger clerics but to the influential Communists and other nonclerical proponents of radical change in Iran.[50]

But six years after Khomeini's death, clerics and a new generation of religious dissenters were once again attacking Khomeini's untraditional notion that a *walayat al-faqih* should rule Iran. And now they based their case not just on Islamic theory but on the Islamic Republic's record of failure.

One of the most articulate critics of Khomeini's Islamic dictatorship is Ayatollah Hairi-Yazdi, who lives in Teheran. I visited him as soon as we returned from Qum. In July, Hairi-Yazdi published an essay in an Iranian newspaper that argued that "sovereignty" was not a God-given right of the mullahs but a "contract between citizen and government." Citizens had the right to alter the contract or change the government if it failed to live up to its commitments. The implication was unmistakable: If government was merely the agent for its citizens, there was no place for a Supreme Leader, a *walayat al-faqih*. The article had triggered a furious debate. Radical clerics had denounced Hairi-Yazdi. The aging, American-educated ayatollah was ailing and no longer in command of his senses, some of them had told me. Others maintained that the ayatollah had been misquoted. A philosopher whose father had been Khomeini's teacher, Hairi-Yazdi denied both charges when we met at his villa over tea and Iranian sweets. Yes, he confirmed, he suffered from Parkinson's disease. He walked with a cane, tired easily, and had trouble speaking, but there was nothing wrong with his ability to reason. And no, he had not been misinterpreted: He stood by every word he had written.

Hairi-Yazdi was depressed. Six months before, the government had banned part of his life's work, a small volume entitled *Wisdom and Government*. Based on theory but also on Iran's experiment with Islamic government, he had concluded, sadly, he told me, that the *umma*, an Islamic community, and a "democratic community" were irreconcilable. The regime had obviously concluded that true liberty was not compatible with an Islamic society and had sacrificed the former for the latter. But if a government forced Islam on its citizens, ordering them to pray, to fast, and to make a pilgrimage, it infringed on a man's responsibility for his actions — a distortion of Islam. "A dog can be forced to do such things," he said. The Prophet Muhammad had not forced people to follow him; they had willingly done so. And the Medinans had chosen Muhammad to lead them. A government based on force, no matter what it called itself, was not legitimate. Neither was the concept of *walayat al-faqih*, a religious dictator. Because the Islamic Republic tried to live by Islamic rules and traditions, he would continue obeying it, as his faith commanded. But he would never stop criticizing what he saw as wrong. For these convictions, he told me, "I am ready to die."

•

EVEN IF A LARGE and influential minority of Iranians now agreed with much of what Hairi-Yazdi had written in his banned book and what intellectuals like Sorush were now arguing, it was hard to imagine how the Islamic Republic would reform itself, resecularize its government, and send the clerics back to their pulpits. No one gives up power voluntarily. The government had taken every possible precaution against a coup within the armed forces. In August it had mobilized more than 300,000 *basiji* forces in seventeen cities in military exercises aimed at showing that it could suppress civil uprisings or any other armed challenge.[51] The state itself was much more formidable than it had been under the shah, its bureaucrats more numerous. And though the radical clerics were weakening, their vast intelligence networks, control of the "Hezbollahi" vigilantes, and partnership in Rafsanjani's government enabled them to block measures that would further erode their base.

Mohtashami, the father of Lebanon's Hezbollah, whom I had interviewed during my visit in 1992, was now lying low in Qum, refusing interviews. But he and his allies still terrorized dissident writers by dispatching Hezbollahis to beat them up and burn down bookstores. In August, Morgh Amin, a bookstore, was firebombed and then attacked by a mob for selling a novel accused of offending Islam. Ayatollah Ahmad Jannati, secretary of the Council of Guardians, a senior clerical body, had praised the culprits for having "carried out their duty."[52] In a speech at Friday congregational prayers at Teheran University, Jannati also lauded Hezbollahi thugs for beating up Sorush, which prompted criticism of him by even more senior clerics. But Ayatollah Jannati showed no remorse; his force of some five thousand young vigilantes on motorcycles would be dispatched against those "propagating Western culture and ideas," as he saw fit. Jannati had powerful allies. In November, Supreme Leader Khamenei warned that the Islamic Republic would not "tolerate" anticlerical debates that made "America and the Zionists happy."[53]

Arrests and unreported detentions persisted, not all of them at the behest of the hard-liners. Abbas Abdi, the editor of *Salam*, a radical clerical newspaper, and a former leader of the militant student takeover of the U.S. embassy, also increasingly attacked the government. Abdi had spent three months in prison in 1993, though no charges against him were ever filed. Similarly, *Jahan-e Islam*, a paper published by the brother of Supreme Leader Ali Khamenei, was also shut down in February 1995 on grounds that the paper "created doubts, printed untrue stories and insulted the religious beliefs of the Muslim nation."[54]

Many of the 134 writers who signed a petition in 1994 protesting government censorship had been interrogated, pressured to withdraw their signatures, and warned not to discuss their detentions. Political executions also continued in Iran. In late 1994, Ali Akbar Saidi-Sirjani, a gifted and prolific writer and another leader of the Islamic reform movement whose writing had been banned since 1989, died after months of abuse in jail. The government claimed he had died of "natural" causes.

•

IT WAS TEMPTING to blame Iran's woes on the government's most uncompromising clergy and to place Islamic officials into neat categories labeled "pragmatic"
and "radical." But such labels did not accurately describe the multitude of often
shifting factions vying for power. Iran's complex politics defied such labels, just
as its limits on freedom of expression defied simple definition. It was as impossible to trace censorship to a single source as it was to blame any single trend or
camp for Iran's human-rights abuses at home and its aggressiveness abroad.

The partnership between Leader Khamenei and President Rafsanjani was
often misunderstood, an Iranian analyst told me. Iran's relentless quest for
weapons of mass destruction continued not despite Rafsanjani but with his
blessing. So did assassinations of dissidents abroad and terrorist attacks on Israeli
and Jewish installations, usually in response to Israeli kidnappings or murders
in Lebanon. American intelligence officials had told me there was evidence that
Rafsanjani, often called a "moderate" by the media, had personally approved of
the bombing of the Israeli embassy in Buenos Aires in 1992 as well as the murder
in Paris that same year of former Prime Minister Shapur Bakhtiar. More Iranian
dissidents abroad had been killed during Rafsanjani's first three years than during the ten years of Khomeini's rule.[55]

Only a lack of cash, not disputes between Rafsanjani and Khamenei, had
forced Iran to abandon its plan of spending $10 billion between 1989 and 1994
on sophisticated weapons. While denying that it sought to develop atomic
bombs, Iran still planned to build ten nuclear power plants in the next two
decades despite the relatively lower cost of developing its natural gas.

Yet even when Rafsanjani had tried to moderate his government's policies
and improve its image abroad, he was often unable to do so. While senior
Iranian officials pledged to European governments from whom they were seeking credit and expanded trade that the Iranian government had no intention of
killing Salman Rushdie, the government was unable to provide even these
limited assurances in writing.[56] And the reward offered in 1989 by the Fifteenth
of Khordad Foundation, another of Iran's semiofficial agencies, has twice been
increased, in 1991 from $1 million to $2 million and in 1993 to an "unspecified
amount."[57]

Iran's relentless arms-buying spree and search for weapons of mass destruction, its appalling human-rights record, its continuing financial and logistical
support of terrorism and opposition to the Arab-Israeli peace treaties — coupled
with domestic pressures and intense Israeli lobbying — had led the Clinton
administration to expand sanctions in April 1995.[58] In only ten years, a senior
American defense analyst told me before my trip, Iran would no longer have
sufficient oil to export. What would it do then? Would it invade an oil-rich
Gulf emirate, as Iraq had done? Dying revolutions were dangerous, he said.
Washington intended to do everything possible to change Iranian behavior and
cripple its weapons-buying program before it was too late. Although neither
Europe nor Asia had followed America's lead, the comprehensive sanctions
seemed to have deepened Iran's economic and political crisis.

But even about this Iranian analysts disagreed. Some critics told me that sanctions were economically and psychologically debilitating for Teheran given the Islamic Republic's isolation and obsession with America. Others argued that the sanctions had reinforced the regime's most radical elements. Clinton's cancellation of Iran's $1 billion contract with Conoco, an American operation, to repair neglected Iranian oil fields and develop natural gas was a setback for Rafsanjani, who sought to improve Iranian-American relations. It had also vindicated the radicals' assertion that Washington sought only to topple the Islamic regime.

My own view was that America, too, was not without hubris. Washington would probably only marginally affect the power struggle within Iran. America's record to date suggested that it was inept at playing off Islamic "moderates" against "radicals." On the other hand, I was certain that Iranians fighting for reform — however unlikely their success — would benefit, perhaps only psychologically, from encouragement, if not from the U.S. government, from American groups and individuals that shared their commitment to human rights and pluralism. I, for one, would not abandon my Iranian friends.

IRANIAN REFORMERS disagreed over how best to achieve their aims. For now, most seemed determined to press for free elections and the licensing of Islamic parties opposed to the government, among them Iran's "Freedom Movement," a leading secular liberal party that has been banned for more than a decade. In his elegant home in north Teheran, Ibrahim Yazdi, a former professor of medicine in Texas who was foreign minister during the revolution's first year, was optimistic that his group would be legalized. Iran's many failures, he said, were prompting a "reassessment." If there were a free election today, he told me, "Iranians would vote overwhelmingly against the position of *walayat al-faqih*."

A few days later, I met Yazdi's son-in-law at a small gathering of intellectuals. It was my old friend, Shaw Rouhani, the revolutionary student activist in Washington who had complained so many years ago about my article on Khomeini. Rouhani, who had often been detained since then by the clerics, was now an active Freedom Movement member and a supporter of political pluralism in Iran.

Some Iranians told me that the Freedom Movement would never attract a mass following. Yazdi, though civilized and intelligent, was "a man of the past." The government tolerated his criticism because the clerics knew he did not threaten them. One indication was the funeral last January of Mehdi Bazargan, Iran's first prime minister, the self-described enemy of "haste and extremes" and a founder of the Freedom Party. Sorush had delivered an impassioned oration, praising Bazargan and articulating his view that there is a philosophical religious basis for democracy. While some ten thousand Iranians had gathered to hear Sorush's stirring appeal, the funeral later that year of Ahmad Khomeini, the Imam's hard-line but corrupt son, had attracted almost ten times as many.

"The clerics will only retreat if they are assured a place of importance and respect in this society," said one scholar at a government-supported think tank. "Loose talk about abolishing the *walayat al-faqih* and sending the mullahs back to Qum only reinforces their zealotry and determination to hang on," he told me. Islamic reform was "inevitable," he said, and the reemergence of Iranian nationalism was the best hope for a solution to Iran's current stalemate and political impasse. "The revolution is over," he said. "Those who care about Iran — the vast majority of the country — will want to do what is needed to rebuild Iran and change its image. It will happen."

ON MY LAST DAY in Teheran, Nahzi and I visited the tomb of Khomeini, the Islamic shah of shahs. It was impossible to miss the gigantic gold domes of the Holy Shrine, as his tomb was called. Across the flat plains south of Teheran, it could be seen for miles in all directions. Though the shrine was only twenty miles out of town, it took us more than two hours to drive there Friday, the Muslim day of rest and prayer and the second day of the Iranian weekend. The tomb was a favorite outing for Teheran's poor, those who could afford no other recreation. Friday was also the day that Iranians visit the graves of family members and other lost loved ones at Behesht-e Zahra, or Zahra's Paradise, perhaps the world's largest cemetery. Since the cemetery was near the shrine, Iranians often made a day of it, sharing their Friday picnics near the graves of the dead and ending with a visit to Khomeini's tomb, which is what Nahzi and I decided to do.

Iran had taken the drive-in idea a step further, for this was a drive-through cemetery, with roundabouts featuring maps indicating its many sections and a computerized index for locating lost loved ones: Section A for "martyrs" of the revolution, who were killed trying to end the shah's thirty-eight-year reign; Section B for "martyrs" of the eight-year Iran-Iraq war, and so on. On our way to the Martyrs of the War area, we passed the infamous Fountain of the Martyrs, which once flowed with water dyed red to resemble blood. But after journalists ridiculed this disgusting touch of revolutionary melodrama, the government drained the fountain. Children now climbed on the cracked cement.

Beside one of the graves, a young woman, shrouded in a black chador, wept as if her husband had died yesterday, though the marker showed that he had been killed a decade ago. The war martyrs' section seemed to have no end; thousands of graves stretched toward the horizon.

Not far from the widow's dilapidated car, her young children played soccer on the grass near a blanket covered with food. Such festivity adjacent to their mother's enormous grief shocked me. But this was typical of Iranian society. So much in Iran seemed focused on death: the black chadors worn by devout women, the tombs and shrines throughout the country, the obsession with martyrdom to a succession of religious and political causes. As I stood amid the graves, Iran itself seemed to be in mourning — for its ancient and modern martyrs, its glorious past, and now its own failed revolution that had offered hope to so many only a generation ago. Iran, one of my colleagues said, was as much a necrocracy as a theocracy.[59] "We mourn brilliantly," an Iranian friend and writer had once told me. "And deep down, we are not really religious. We are fanatical."

The Imam's tomb was crowded by the time we arrived. We checked our shoes and entered through the women's side, but once inside this monumental structure, men and women sat and stood together on the shrine's machine-made rugs. This place was the opposite of the mosques of Isfahan, with their delicate, hand-sewn silk carpets, exquisite mosaics, and grand gilded mirrors. This Husseiniyeh had clearly been built for Khomeini's real constituency, the dispossessed, those who would probably never have anything beyond the free kebabs and rice distributed here on Thursday nights. There was nothing holy, or even particularly Islamic, about this place.

The smell of bare feet clung to the carpets. Children shrieked and slid down the slanted marble floors that led to the green cage containing the tombs of Khomeini and his son Ahmad. Their giant portraits hung on the shrine's far wall.

Only slowly did I take in its scale. The huge shrine was air-conditioned, but badly. Its giant, unadorned steel girders stretched hundreds of feet above us, supporting the dome. Its stained-glass windows were shaped like tulips, the symbol of martyrdom, but many of the crudely cut white, red, and green panes were already shattered or cracked. Two giant cut-glass chandeliers, also tulip shaped, hung above us.

The tombs of Khomeini and his son were in the center of the shrine, encased in a green iron cage. Some of the Iranians leaning against the iron frame cried and prayed; others stuck rial notes through thin slots of the cage's interior glass lining. The glass shield was a relatively new feature, one Iranian told me. Some visitors apparently had not shared the widespread reverence for the Imam. Instead of putting rial notes through the cage, some had put in human shit. Hence the shield.

Most of the two hundred visitors that day seemed uninterested in Khomeini's remains. They picnicked on the carpets and chatted softly in small groups while their children played tag near the cage containing Khomeini's earthly remains. Some visitors took pictures; others changed money. The atmosphere was gay.

Outside the shrine, the government was building a new religious college, a vast Islamic hospital, a laundromat, and a hotel-restaurant complex. The "Shrine Bazaar" was doing brisk business. Nahzi and I visited a kiosk that sold chelo-kebab for hungry pilgrims; another sold ice cream and cookies. In the mall there were also a grocery store, a shoe shop, a children's clothing boutique, and a store that specialized in perfume and women's cosmetics. "Cosmetics?" I asked Nahzi. "It's okay," she replied. "They're all made in Iran."

I suddenly thought of poor Shariati, the lay Islamic revolutionary. How sad he would be to find that even under Islam, the masses would still want cosmetics and the mullahs would be happy to provide them, at a profit. Of all the "Islams" that I had encountered during my visits to Iran — "barefoot," "capitalist," "American," "revisionist," and even "Communist," which is what some critics called Khomeini's version — this casual un-Islamic "people's" Islam seemed the most authentic, the most comfortable.

One kiosk specialized in Khomeini souvenirs — Khomeini key chains, prayer beads, desk plaques, as well as Ahmad Khomeini postcards and wooden inlaid, framed photographs of the beloved Imam. I stared in disbelief at a series of photos: Khomeini kissing a child; Khomeini at rest; Khomeini in a family portrait; Khomeini serving tea. Never before had I seen such pictures. For each depicted a grinning Khomeini. Only in death did Khomeini smile.

For followers of the Imam, however, there was little to cheer, I thought as we left the shrine. The Islamic revolution was at an impasse not unlike that of the shah almost twenty years ago. Riots and other evidence of mass discontent could no longer be dismissed as aberrations. Liberal and hard-line intellectuals were at war with their government, if not with the system itself. The middle class was disenchanted, and even many of the poor despised the mullahs and their unfulfilled promises. I noticed that taxi drivers often refused to pick up clerics as passengers. Not since the shah's Peacock Throne had the legitimacy of Iran's government been in such doubt. Rafsanjani may not have seen himself as Iran's Gorbachev, but the "Islamic glasnost" in Iran reminded me most of my visit to the Soviet Union just before communism's collapse. The system might survive; the mullahs might well hang on. But something important was changing in Iran.

Perhaps before his death Khomeini had sensed the inevitable failure of his Islamic experiment. Perhaps he, too, had guessed that no matter what Iran's government called itself, it would inevitably become less and less "Islamic" and more and more pragmatically "Persian." Maybe the armed Imam himself had unintentionally written his revolution's eventual obituary: "This time," he had said, "either Islam triumphs or we disappear."

Conclusions

When I returned from Teheran, I mentioned to several Iranian colleagues the riveting debates about "Islamic government" I had witnessed in Iran. In most of the Middle East, there were no real politics in the Western sense. Only in Israel, Lebanon, and to some extent Jordan did political parties compete for influence in a Parliament with real power as they did in Iran. In Sunni Arab states, discussions about Islamic rule were often hypothetical, perhaps because most of the talk was politically irrelevant. Except for Sudan, militant Islamists rule no country in the Arab Middle East. But Iranian political debate resonated with bold questions about whether the Islamic Republic was truly "Islamic" or whether it had veered from the Koran's "straight path." Could Iran's Islamic system be reformed from within, and if so, how? Such questioning seemed to me desperately serious, for efforts to make the ostensibly Islamic system function effectively were now a matter of political survival for the ruling clerics. Though the regime seemed entrenched, the prospect that the clerics might lose legitimacy or have to slaughter thousands more Iranians to retain power and — of far greater concern to most of the clergy — that Iran's experiment might delegitimize Islam as a framework for governing and undermine the credibility of Islam itself among young adherents has understandably generated enormous ferment.

Yes, agreed Reza Afshari, an Iranian exile who teaches history and human rights in New York. Iranian life has remained vibrant in many respects. But, he told me, had I forgotten that the "lively debate" was made possible only by the "deadly silence" that Islamists had imposed on all non-Islamists, not only secular Iranians but even Islamic groups that did not share the regime's particular Islamic vision?[1] Did I not see that the ruling clerics — by excluding from political life everyone who rejects their brand of Islam, by harassing, arresting, torturing, and executing political dissidents for such preposterous but judicially sanctioned crimes as "apostasy," "warring against God," and "corruption on earth," and by employing improvised, ostensibly Islamic precepts to justify continuing repression and monopoly of power—had failed to institutionalize the revolution's promises in a just or rational way and thus had betrayed the revolution itself?

Of course, now that all serious rivals to clerical rule had been eliminated, the regime could tolerate the publication of articles on Marx and Foucault as well as disagreements in the majlis, Friday sermons, and magazines and newspapers. That many American scholars apologized for the regime by calling debate among the Islamically converted "political pluralism" was an outrage, Afshari argued.

It was wrong to portray tensions among Iran's factions—or within more militant Islamist groups competing for power—as Islamic hard-liners versus Islamic pragmatists or even more inaccurately, moderates. In Afshari's view, the ostensible struggle between the two major factions was more often a division of labor. On human rights, pragmatists were the technocratic "visible" face of the regime that masked the "invisible" clerics who terrorized citizens through the security forces. In today's Iran, a major function of these pragmatic state technocrats—Islamist careerists and other political opportunists—was to protect state torturers from accountability.

If Afshari's critique was accurate—and human-rights groups supported his conclusions—it was unlikely that the clerics would relinquish power and return to Qum.

Yet Iranians, including many clerics, now knew from bitter experience that there was no "Islamic economics" or "Islamic sociology," no "Islamic" way to build a car or stabilize a monetary system, no miraculous, peculiarly "Islamic" path to development as an alternative to the roads followed by the reviled West and East. A country as isolated as Iran, whose government supports Islamic upheaval abroad and repression at home, and often prevents its own citizens from traveling abroad, was probably incapable of nurturing the improvisational, opportunistic economic spirit required by a prosperous modern state. Iran's fanatical image frightened away potential investors. How could the clerics hope to attract scarce capital in an ever more competitive world financial market when in addition to all the other hazards investors face, clerics have added their own "Islamic" disincentives?

Despite what Afshari told me, I found two kinds of progressive Islamic reformers in Iran: There are those who seek to make their system work by gradually opening it up—encouraging free assembly and debate, expanding political participation to include first Islamic dissidents and eventually non-Islamic parties, and slowly reducing the dominance of clerics. This did not seem to me impossible, since Iran's system, though sour and undemocratic, is constitutional and its mechanisms could, in principle, be used to check ruinous abuses of power and perhaps restructure government.[2] A second group, however, wants to abandon theocracy altogether, though few express this goal openly. These Iranians, many of whom are less cynical, I believe, than Afshari suggests, question whether theocracy or any other form of militantly Islamic government is workable in a modern world. "How can a system that is God-given," asks Javad Tabatabai, an Iranian intellectual who still lives in Teheran, "whose basic framework, rules, and parameters cannot be questioned, challenged or be made subject to the will of the people, ever be rational?" Or, put another way, does such a system not invariably face the same problems encountered by any ideological system — that is, communism — when it attempts to deal with the requirements of a modern state?

How can a state compete in an increasingly ferocious global market if it excludes and discourages a large part of its population by adopting as its legal code sharia, which, in the version favored by many militants, denies women and non-Muslim minorities legal and constitutional equality with Muslim male citizens? How can it flourish if young Arab women are valued not for their business or intellectual abilities but for what militant Islamists consider their primary function, as the Hamas charter puts it, as "makers of men"? And why should non-Muslims accept, unless they are forced to, second-class legal status or being forever barred by Koranic imperative from leadership?

Frightened by Islamism's growing appeal, thousands of Christians have been leaving the Arab Middle East. These "canaries in the mine," as an American diplomat in Syria called them, are not only a source of Western culture and values; they also remind the majority that tolerance for those who are different is essential in a modern, civilized society. The Middle East itself will be poorer and less dynamic without them.

A few progressive Islamists argue that given the "universality and centrality" of Islam to Muslims, a secular legal system and Western political institutions cannot take root in the Arab Middle East. Therefore, they argue, since some sort of Islamic rule is inevitable, sharia, and indeed even the Koran itself, should undergo a "modern and revolutionary interpretation." One Sudanese-American scholar, for example, recommends that modern Islamic jurists rely on the Koranic verses Muhammad was given in Mecca, which emphasize universality, noncompulsion, "compassion, fairness, incorruptibility, and good faith" rather than those he received in Medina, where he had to harden Islamic discipline in order to rule.[3] The problem with this approach, as Reza Afshari wrote, is that ever since the rise of Islamist movements, "it has been the more conservative Islamists, in or out of power, who have better succeeded in defining the parameters of the valid version of Islamic politics."[4] In other words, as in any ideological movement, the more ruthless tend to prevail. In addition, traditional ulema are unlikely to accept this unorthodox interpretation of their holy scriptures, to say nothing of those clerics and lay militants who themselves want to impose a strict Islamic culture on their citizenry.

•

WHILE I ENCOUNTERED many "Islams" on my journeys through the Middle East, I found almost as many reasons for Islamic revivalism. As I have tried to show, modern Islamism is the product of many factors: the collapse within the region of Arab nationalism after the 1967 Arab-Israeli war and then of the Soviet Union and the Marxist dream in the late 1980s; a demographic explosion that has strained national resources; and the failure of most Middle Eastern governments to deliver on the ambitious promises they made after independence. The Islamic revival was, of course, also stimulated by Khomeini's populist Islamic revolution in Iran.

My friend Mohammed Sid Ahmed, an independent-minded Egyptian secular writer, all too rare among today's Egyptian intellectuals, also blames the new Islamism on the explosion of petrodollars in the early 1970s, which, in his words, "corrupted politically and intellectually an entire generation and produced, in reaction, a cynical, puritanical Islamic generation." But Saudi Arabia and the Gulf states have reinforced the militant Islamic trend more directly. The United States and its Middle Eastern allies correctly blame Iran for funding extremist Islamic groups and Muslim terrorists throughout the world. But I have concluded that Saudi and Gulf support, though diffuse and often ostensibly donated to cultural and charitable Islamic causes, has been equally, if not more, consequential for Islamist groups. Sheikh Omar Abdel Rahman, after all, convicted in 1995 of conspiring to blow up New York buildings, bridges, and monuments, preached for several years not in Teheran but in Riyadh. And the bombing manual found in the apartment of a World Trade Center bomber was published by the World Assembly of Muslim Youth, a Saudi-funded organization, and was printed in Saudi Arabia.

For decades, Saudi Arabia has provided employment and refuge to many of the same militants who now praise assassinations of secular Arab intellectuals and encourage the terrorist attacks on civilians in and beyond the region. Since the Gulf war, official Saudi assistance to Islamic militants who betrayed Riyadh by supporting Saddam Hussein — such as the Muslim Student Association, a U.S.-based Muslim Brotherhood organization[5] — has sharply declined, but wealthy Saudis and businessmen in the Gulf, including members of the ruling families, still contribute to such groups with quiet, unofficial blessing, some out of fear and others out of sympathy for Islamist goals.[6]

The United States has also contributed to militant Islam. During the cold war, America and its allies mainly saw Islamic groups as insurance against Communist encroachment. Arab nationalism, with its socialist ideology, terrified not only the conservative Arab monarchs but also the West. All were happy to encourage Islamic networks that might prove useful in dampening nationalist fervor. As we have seen, even Israel authorized the Islamic group that became Hamas as a counter to the nationalist PLO.

Starting in 1980, President Carter began sending tens of millions of dollars a year to the mujahideen who were resisting Soviet forces in Afghanistan. By the late 1980s, combined American and Saudi aid to these Afghans came to about $1 billion a year, not counting some $5 billion in weapons sent to the holy warriors between 1986 and 1990 and at least $5.7 billion worth of arms sent to Kabul, a total greater than Iraq's arms imports during the same period.[7] Much of this support went to the faction favored by the Saudis—Hizb-i Islami, led by Gulbuddin Hekmatyar, the most radical of the original Afghan Islamists (who also sided with Saddam Hussein), who then shared these funds with many of the militants whom the United States and Arab countries now accuse of terrorism. Such support for the "good" militant Islamists in Afghanistan seems all the more absurd, since Washington was simultaneously battling the anti-American, "bad" militant Islamists in Iran and Lebanon. Thus, American money helped train thousands of Arab militants in Pakistan who had nowhere to go and nothing to do once the jihad against Moscow was over. Among the Islamic heroes of this last battle of the cold war were some of the immigrants from six Arab countries who detonated the massive truck bomb at the World Trade Center in February 1993, killing six Americans, injuring a thousand, and causing more than half a billion dollars' worth of damage.

Western aid to the anti-Soviet jihad, moreover, did not make allies of the Middle East's militant Muslims. Many of the young Arab Islamists who spread their Islamic slogans on the Internet were trained in the West and live in societies that have already been partially transformed by exposure to the West and the needs of modern technological society.

THOUGH ON MY TRAVELS through the Middle East I witnessed the pervasive persistence of Islamic resurgence, I find it difficult to assess the depth of the trend from country to country and its likelihood of success. Consider the spread of *hijab* among young women, which scholars often cite as quantifiable evidence of growing Islamic fervor. But is it? In fact, I found that Muslim women fancy this style for many reasons, not all of them political. Some women told me they cannot afford weekly trips to the hairdresser or the expensive cosmetics that middle-class Arab women take for granted. In Algeria's Casbah, where families sleep in shifts and share a single bathroom not just with male members of their own families but also with male neighbors and even strangers, *hijab* provides psychological as well as physical protection. The crowded and uncomfortable Middle Eastern cities where I have lived are filled with idle, frustrated young men who have poured into the capitals looking for work. For women in such dense surroundings, *hijab* creates physical and psychological borders which sexually active young men dare not violate. *Hijab* says: This is a devout woman. Leave her alone.

For many poorer women in Iran, where traditional Islamic culture and mores had for generations restricted women to their households, the chador meant mobility and employment for thousands of women. That *hijab* is now also a symbol of state coercion and male oppression, especially for young Iranian women, does not alter the fact that for countless women in the Middle East, *hijab* confers mobility, dignity, and safety.

For many middle-class women, *hijab* is now chic as well as a form of generational rebellion. Many young women in *hijab*, after all, are the grand-daughters of women who defied their own political and social convention by throwing off the veil in the 1920s and 1930s, rejecting not only Western colonial rule but also male domination. The brisk business in expensive silk and hand-embroidered *hijab* — the high-end Islamic couture in the boutiques of Egypt's Heliopolis, Jordan's Shmaisani, and other wealthy Middle Eastern suburbs — suggests that *hijab* can be as much a matter of fashion as of politics.

In other respects, too, the "Islamist" response I saw seems to me a prag-matic response to the problems of modernity — matters of convenience and affordability rather than ideology. Modernity is frightening and disorienting, especially when its cost is likely to exceed its promised benefit. In the Middle East as elsewhere, social roles, values, and traditions are undergoing great changes for which tradition offers psychic protection. It could be a fine thing, perhaps, if the Middle East adapted to modernity in democratic ways, but for many Arabs this choice does not exist in their hierarchical, patriarchal societies.[8]

Just as I found no single Islam, I found no Islamic Comintern, or "Kho-meintern," no vast conspiracy led by Iran and Sudan, no Islamic International issuing orders, guidance, and money to Islamists throughout the Middle East. But I did find a growing interaction — exchanges of ideas, technological exper-tise, experience, and cooperation — particularly among militants in the Islamic diaspora, especially in the Western democracies, where Islamist critics of the West can meet, talk, and work openly without being killed, imprisoned, or spied upon. Hassan al-Turabi's Popular Islamic and Arab Congress in Khartoum in 1991 and a less publicized Nationalist-Islamist Congress in Beirut in October 1994 brought together scores of mostly male Islamist and Arab nationalist leaders in an effort to confront the West, reject peace with Israel, and thwart Arab initiatives to create a new Middle Eastern common market that would include Jews and other non-Arab investors, the idea advocated by Israel's Shimon Peres, among others. But such efforts have so far disappointed Islamists. While Iran, for example, spent an estimated $1 billion in the past decade to create militant Hezbollah, it has not succeeded in making Lebanon an Islamic state. And Hezbollah continues to face competition from other Shiite groups in its effort to mobilize and lead the country's dynamic Shia community.

Such interaction among Islamists nevertheless has consequences, even if subtle, belated, or difficult to trace. Readers of this book may have noticed, for example, the appearance in several chapters of Sheikh Muhammad al-Ghazali, the influential Egyptian Islamic theoretician and onetime Muslim Brother who recently defended the killers of a secular Egyptian writer accused of having abandoned Islam. For years, Ghazali has traveled through Arab lands, proselytiz-ing for his intolerant version of Islam — from Gaza before the Israeli occupation, where he helped establish one of the Brotherhood's first branches, to Algeria, where before his departure in 1989, he helped inspire and influence a vast young audience of educated Islamists who later became leaders of that unhappy country's failed Islamic Salvation Front (FIS). Such men have helped shape

Islamist views about what works—and what does not—in their effort to over-throw their governments and replace them with an "Islamic" order. Gilles Kepel, the French scholar and expert on Egyptian Islamism, argues that it is no accident that Islamic Jihad's campaign against tourists in Egypt began in October 1992, only a few months after Algeria's government refused to accept the Salvation Front's election victory and decided instead to crush the Islamists. Perhaps Egypt's Islamists would have attacked foreign tourists even if Algeria's Islamists had been allowed to govern. But my interviews suggest that Islamist leaders in several Middle Eastern countries learned from the Algerian experi-ence not to count on elections and other nonviolent roads to power, just as many also learned from Islamists' repression in Syria and Egypt that a violent challenge to authority would be met with even greater violence.

Islamists, like most politicians, have made terrible tactical mistakes—for example, the campaign in Egypt against tourism, on which the livelihoods of so many Egyptians depend, or the murder of unveiled women and secular intellec-tuals in Algeria, which alienated the very Algerians whose support the Islamists needed in their struggle for power. But militant Islamists can also be extremely practical. Despite fiery rhetoric about the evils of the West, the impossibility of compromise on issues of Koranic doctrine, the religious "impermissibility" of a Jewish state in Dar al-Islam, they have clearly shown that they can adapt to their political environments in order to survive. Lebanon's Hezbollah has evolved from a group of holy warriors who fight Israel into a political party, however unorthodox, that still fights Israel but which now also controls the largest bloc of seats in Lebanon's Parliament. While denouncing Christian dominance in Lebanon, Hezbollah works closely with some Maronite Christians to thwart growing Sunni Muslim influence. The men who once kidnapped and tortured Western hostages in the Bekaa Valley are now inviting Westerners to return to Baalbek as tourists. Iran's fanatical clerics obtained weapons from the Satans, Big and Little, as did the Afghan resistance. To curry favor with France, Islamic Sudan betrayed Carlos, a secular anti-Western terrorist who was lionized by many young Islamists. Islamist accommodation to political necessity is impres-sive.

As in all politics, moderate and radical are blurred and shifting categories. As we have seen, many an Islamic movement is simultaneously a political group, a militia, and an amalgam of terror cells. Yesterday's terrorist can be today's peacemaker, and vice versa. Such compromises and tactical shifts do not imply that militant Islamists no longer seek to destroy Israel, defy the West, and impose their interpretation of Islam on fellow Arabs or that the militants do not mean what they say. But such flexibility suggests that militant groups should be evalu-ated not only by their words but also by their deeds, and over time.

Despite efforts to avoid fitna, the self-defeating divisions that have long plagued the Muslim community, relations between Islamists and nationalists remain strained,[9] and Islamic movements themselves are increasingly divided by personal rivalries, ideological differences, and disputes over money. Rather than merge into a single coherent stream, Islamists seem ever more susceptible to splits. Hamas resents Islamic Jihad almost as much as it does the PLO. The Syrian Muslim Brotherhood has never overcome the factionalism that gave Assad an opportunity to crush it. The repression in Algeria quickly shattered what was always a fragile, divided Islamic front. R. Hrair Dekmejian, an American political scientist, counts some 175 Islamist groups, 74 percent of them "militant" or "radical," competing in the region.[10] Another scholar finds 45 Islamist groups in Egypt alone.[11]

THE CURRENT WAVE of Islamic militancy seems to me at least to have crested, though a victory in any single Arab state could change that. Most Middle Eastern states have found ways, often illegal and morally repugnant, to contain militant fervor. While some analysts portray Arab states as artificial, fragile creations — "Sand Castles," one writer called them — modern Middle Eastern states have proved remarkably durable. As I have tried to show, modern Arab regimes — with their armies, police, and intelligence forces — are ever more powerful, and they have mobilized to repress or co-opt militant Islamic challengers. The leaders know that once power is lost in such states, retrieving it is difficult.

After a two-year battle, Egypt seems to have crushed its Islamists — for now. By promoting a tamed, official "secular Islam" and through brutal repression — involving the killing of more than eight hundred militants since 1992 and the arrest and torture of thousands of innocent Egyptians — President Mubarak has restored order. Syria's Assad, too, rules, largely through the fear of civil strife within Syria's heterogeneous population and the memory of the savage repression in Hama that few Syrians doubt would be repeated if necessary. Islamists and all other political challengers, not only in Syria but in Iraq and Libya, have been brutally repressed. In Algeria, forty thousand people have died in civil strife, but the military government has prevailed so far. Even Saudi Arabia, which has traditionally shunned violent repression, has increasingly cracked down on its militant critics.

But such repression can probably not be sustained in the long term, especially not by governments that depend on the West — or crave its approval — or by any society with an emerging middle class that cares about its international reputation and demands greater political participation.

Jordan and Israel have been among the boldest in co-opting and marginalizing militant Muslims by offering them political rights and participation. But in neither state do militants stand much chance of ruling. In Israel, the overwhelming Jewish majority will not permit the country's non-Jewish minority, almost a fifth of the population, to challenge Israel's identity or threaten its existence. While King Hussein has relied on his own religious credentials to reinforce the legitimacy of his rule, his repeated repression of violent Islamists, and even of those who reject playing politics by his rules, has persuaded most Islamists that challenging this particular Hashemite is suicidal.

Analysts disagree vehemently about how governments should respond to militant Islam. The debate has become so polarized, so bitter, that some scholars have abandoned their traditional analytic detachment to attack the integrity of colleagues who disagree with them.[12] So-called rejectionists argue that all militant Islamist groups should be repressed and denied political participation on the grounds that they are inherently antidemocratic as well as anti-Western.[13]

Accommodationists, on the other hand, urge Washington to embrace most Islamists, since they represent genuine populist currents that favor social reform and greater economic equality. Though they may not be democrats, the argument goes, the militants could evolve into exponents of pluralism and tolerance. Other analysts want to cultivate Islamists primarily because they believe militant Islam will triumph in the Middle East. Thus, the West alienates such groups at its peril. Still others favor accommodation for an even more cynical reason: Empowering Islamic militants will encourage divisiveness in their ranks and enable ordinary citizens to see, as a Lebanese commentator observed, that "Islam is not the solution."[14] But such Islamic experiments, as Iran and Sudan have shown, may prove terribly expensive for the people of the region. Most failed regimes in the Middle East — secular and Islamic alike — prefer repression to resignation.

The United States has adopted a flexible approach to militant Islam. Careful to stress America's respect for Islam as a religion, the Clinton administration claims to oppose only those militant groups that endorse violence or seek elections only to impose an Islamic order through force — "one man, one vote, one time." In theory, at least, the United States supports those who take "specific steps towards free elections, creating independent judiciaries, promoting the rule of law, reducing restrictions on the press, respecting the rights of minorities and guaranteeing individual rights."[15]

But policy is one thing; national interests are another. In practice, Washington is likely to continue supporting Saudi Arabia, the major source of its oil, and Egypt, the first Arab state to make peace with Israel, no matter how repressive their governments become. Yet the vagueness of America's approach toward militant Islam is, in my opinion, sensible. Evaluating Islamic militant groups one by one, given their diversity, also seems wise.

Equally sensible are efforts to encourage militant Islamists to swear allegiance to democratic rules of political participation. King Hussein's insistence, for example, that political parties sign a national charter committing them to pluralism and respect for equal rights provides some assurance that Islamists will not be permitted to use elections only to disenfranchise the losers. Many opposition Islamist groups have not only provided efficient, low-cost services to Arabs ill served by their own governments; they have enriched political debate and encouraged the development of civil society, that is, groups and institutions that protect individuals against the awesome power of the state. Encouraging such groups toward a pluralistic politics is not without risk, but it seems more likely to work than relentless suppression.

Nevertheless, I have supported Egypt's suppression of violent militant Islamists, but not the torture, emergency military trials, and other illegal means that have become routine features of the government's anti-Islamist campaign. Egypt, given its religious antagonisms between Copts and Muslims, has a sensible ban on all religious parties. And while I share the skepticism of many Egyptian officials about the sincerity of the Muslim Brotherhood's commitment to nonviolence and pluralism, I also believe that Mubarak, by arresting influential Brothers weeks before national elections and refusing to permit them to stand openly in elections, offers Islamists no incentive to renounce violence. Moreover, the government's official Islam, as it crowds out secularism, creates an intellectual climate conducive to Islamism. Mubarak grows more pharaonic by the day and ever more threatened by the notion that Egyptians should one day be trusted to have a say in the choice of those who rule them. Reluctant to rationalize the economy or oppose corruption, the government continues to forgo legitimacy. It is now possible to imagine that an explosion of perhaps biblical proportions may one day shatter "eternal Egypt."

As for Algeria, the government's unwillingness to transfer power to the winners of its cynical national election was clearly unconstitutional and ultimately responsible for the continuing bloodshed. Yet military officials were prepared to sustain what they viewed as a fight to the death because they believed that their very lives, as well as Algeria itself, were at stake. My contacts with Algerian Islamists, the most ruthless of whom oppose pluralism, political tolerance, and equal rights, suggest that sooner or later secular Algerians would have revolted, in turn, against attempts to impose Islam on them. While I can hardly endorse the government's refusal to abide by the election results, I was relieved that it had done so. Apparently the majority of Algerians now agree, for despite the Islamists' demand that patriots and believers boycott the national elections in November 1995, some 75 percent of Algerians voted and overwhelmingly endorsed General Zeroual as their president. The Islamist candidate, a Muslim Brother, received about 25 percent of the vote.

I remain as wary of militant Islamist groups as I am of all groups that claim a monopoly on virtue or truth. A generation ago, when Arab nationalism was the political fashion, Arabs were persuaded, or forced, to sacrifice individual rights for the glory of the "Arab nation." Nasser's "social democracy" argued that bread was more important than freedom. Today Egypt lacks enough of either.

The current version of this fantasy is that individuals should now serve Islam and that in an Islamic democracy justice and authenticity are more important than freedom. As militants have told me in country after country, Islamic justice arises not from democracy, which one Hamas leader recently described as nothing but "an original form of dictatorship."[16] Nor does it arise from an impartial rule of law, free elections, or limited government power but from the rule of a benevolent caliph, or imam, who, with the advice of a majlis or Parliament, will enact sharia in the name of Islamic rule. As for "authenticity," they rarely acknowledge that by itself this is a dubious goal.[17] Foot binding in China was once authentic. So was slavery in much of the Islamic world and my own. As each of my chapters confirms, the persistence of tyrannical government in much of the Middle East is also authentic. The Islamist demand for authenticity is particularly ironic when, as I have tried to show, the authentic Islamic culture that militants advocate often has little genuine basis in their respective societies.

Yet with grossly inadequate jobs, social services, and housing in much of the region and autocratic governments that refuse to relinquish or share power, the appeal of militant Islam seems likely in the long run to grow. Neither the example of Sudan nor of revolutionary Iran nor even of fragmented Afghanistan has deterred young Islamists from trying to impose yet another grandiose new order on their countries. But this time the price of such a historical detour and self-delusion, should the militants succeed, is likely to be even higher than it was fifty years ago.

John Page, the World Bank's chief Middle East economist, believes that the global economy is developing so quickly that nations or regions that fail to make the necessary structural adjustments to compete for market share and capital are now likely to remain permanently poor. In 1960 the average per capita income in the seven most prosperous Arab states was slightly larger than that of the seven East Asian "tigers." By the early 1990s, per capita income of the Arab group was only $3,342, while that of the Asian countries stood at $8,000. In Israel, per capita income is more than $13,000. Today the Middle East attracts only 3 percent of global foreign investment; Asia gets 58 percent.[18] The Middle East's share, despite the new Arab-Israeli peace treaties, continues to decline.

The Arab Middle East and Iran will have to create almost 50 million jobs by the year 2010 simply to provide sufficient work for those who will enter the labor force. Few economists believe this is possible, since no Middle Eastern state except Israel is now creating jobs to match current levels of growth. The region's demographic explosion will continue: The World Bank forecasts that the population of the Middle East will reach 448 million by the year 2000 and 1.17 billion by 2100. Today more than 50 percent of Middle Easterners are under the age of eighteen. Yet Saudi Arabia, Sudan, and Lebanon boycotted the UN Conference on Population and Development in Cairo in 1994, and the Arab Middle East lags behind most developing nations, and far behind East Asia, in every World Bank component of productivity growth — spending on education, worker training, and the number of women in the labor force. Arms purchases, by contrast, remain staggeringly high. The Middle East now buys almost 50 percent of all arms sold to the Third World.

There is no shortage of Arab commentaries on the cause of the Muslim malaise. But as Bernard Lewis, the historian, has observed, the writings fall into two groups. While some analysts ask, "What did we do wrong?" others demand to know: "Who did this to us?" While the first question leads to debate about how to set things right, the second leads only to "delusions and fantasies and conspiracy theories" that intensify feelings of resentment, frustration, and victimization as well as "an endless, useless succession of bigots and tyrants and to a role in world history aptly symbolized by the suicide bomber." [19] Much of the self-critical analysis written by Arabs in Arab countries, alas, falls into the second category.

I believe that responsible Arab intellectuals must raise such painful issues, encourage fellow Arabs to explore the reasons for the persistence of Arab failure, and seek realistic solutions. But in country after country few Middle Eastern thinkers accept this thankless and often dangerous task. Religious fanatics throughout the region have made such inquiry ever more perilous.

If some of my judgments seem harsh, if I seem to have been unrelenting in my scolding, it is because of my love for the region and its people. I do not expect them to conform to my Western ideas of a just society. I am too well aware of the failings of American democracy, free markets, and materialism to promote without reservation my country's model as ideal. But I cannot help but conclude that Islamic militancy is not the "solution" Muslims have been seeking. How sad it would be if after so much suffering the Arabs embraced yet another ideology that seems only likely to compound the obstacles to regaining the prosperity, dynamism, tolerance, and imagination that once characterized their civilization.

Notes

Introduction

1. See Albert Hourani's "Conclusion" in *Islam in the Political Process*, ed. James P. Piscatori (Cambridge, Eng.: Cambridge University Press, 1993), 226–35.

2. Islam is now the world's fastest-growing religion. Gilles Kepel, the French scholar, estimates that by the year 2000 the world will have more Muslims than Catholics.

3. Olivier Roy, *The Failure of Political Islam* (Cambridge, Mass.: Harvard University Press, 1994), 21–27, 35–42. Roy distinguishes further between "Islamists," by which he means militants who want to Islamize society through state power, and "neofundamentalists," who want to do so from the bottom up or through social and political action. I use the terms "Islamist" and "Islamic militants" to include both, especially since militant movements often contain both Islamists and neofundamentalists.

4. Gilles Kepel, *The Revenge of God* (University Park: Pennsylvania State University Press, 1994), 192.

5. Freya Stark, *Letters from Syria* (London: John Murray, 1942), 100.

Egypt

1. Dr. Sayyid 'Uways, a sociologist, has defined ten Egyptian safety valves, including humor, in confronting misfortune or oppression. A discussion of his conclusions is contained in Gilles Kepel, *The Prophet and the Pharaoh* (London: Al-Saqi Books, 1985), 232–34.

2. Afaf Lutfi Al-Sayyid Marsot, *A Short History of Modern Egypt* (Cambridge, Eng.: Cambridge University Press, 1985), 11.

3. P. J. Vatikiotis, *The History of Egypt*, 2d ed. (London: Weidenfeld and Nicolson, 1980), 15.

4. Ibid., 12–29, 467.

5. Daniel Crecelius, "Nonideological Responses of the Egyptian Ulama to Modernization," in *Scholars, Saints, and Sufis: Muslim Religious Institutions in the Middle East Since 1500*, ed. Nikki R. Keddie (Berkeley: University of California Press, 1972), 173–175.

While many scholars credit the ulema with having led a revolt against French rule, Malika Zeghal, a French expert on al-Azhar, agrees with Crecelius that until France made the fatal error of bombing al-Azhar, the seat of Islamic learning, most ulema did not counsel rebellion. Only after a popular rebellion had started did the most influential sheikhs stop urging Egyptians to obey French rule.

6. Interview, Dr. Shawky Karas, American Coptic Association, January 1995. Scholar Fouad Ajami calls the number of Copts one of Egypt's "great riddles." Low estimates start at 2 million; Copts themselves assert they number as many as 10 million. The Egyptian government apparently prefers their demographic weight to remain uncertain. "The Sorrows of Egypt," *Foreign Affairs*, September/October 1995, 78.

7. Edward A. Gargan, "Where Arab Militants Train and Wait," *New York Times*, August 11, 1993.

8. International Institute for Strategic Studies, *The Military Balance, 1994–1995* (London: Brassey's, 1994). The security forces include the paramilitary Central Security Forces, the poorly trained and even more poorly paid tourist police, and the powerful and greatly feared State Security Investigation, known in Arabic as the *mabahas*. The Interior Ministry is also responsible for the care and feeding of the *muhbirun*, the legions of paid and unpaid informants that report on fellow Egyptians.

9. Ehud Ya'ari, "Pederasty in Paradise, Despair on Earth," *Jerusalem Report*, July 30, 1992.

10. Malika Zeghal, *Gardiens de l'Islam: Les Ulamas d'al Azhar dans l'Egypte Contemporaine* (Paris: Presses de la Fondation Nationale des Sciences Politiques, 1995), a forthcoming book. Ms. Zeghal's Ph.D. thesis is widely regarded as the finest new work on the growing political empowerment of al-Azhar. I am indebted to her for sharing it with me.

11. Sara el-Gammal, "Egyptian Who Mocked Fundamentalism Murdered," Reuters Cairo, June 9, 1992.

12. "Egypt: Human Rights Abuses Mount in 1993," Middle East Watch report, vol. 5, no. 8, October 22, 1993, 3.

13. Foreign Broadcast Information Service, NES-93-159, August 19, 1993, "Authorities Arrest 245 'Militants,'." Paris, Agence France-Presse, August 18, 1993; "Al-Alfi Grants Radio Interview," Cairo, Arab Republic of Egypt Radio, in Arabic, August 19, 1993, 9–10.

14. Human Rights Watch/Middle East, "Behind Closed Doors: Torture and Detention in Egypt," U.S.A., July 1992, 3; see also Amnesty International's "Egypt: Ten Years of Torture," October 1991.

15. Human Rights Watch/Middle East, 2.

16. Statement of the Interior Ministry and excerpts from description of attack from *Al Ahram*, the semiofficial Egyptian daily, translated by *Mideast Mirror*, London, August 19, 1993, 12–13.

17. Hisham Mubarak, *Al-Irhabiyuun Qadamoon* (The Terrorists Are Coming) (Cairo: Al Mahrusa, 1995).

18. Among the most noteworthy Egyptians are Sayyid Qutb, author of *Signposts on the Road*; Ahmed Shukri Mustafa, the charismatic young agronomist who founded the militant al-Takfir wa'l Hijra, a cult that kidnapped and killed the minister of Awqaf (religious endowments) in 1977; Sheikh Muhammad al-Ghazali, of al-Azhar; and Sheikh Omar Abdel Rahman, the blind Egyptian religious guide of Gama'a Islamiya, the Islamic Group, who was convicted in 1995 for conspiring to blow up New York landmarks.

19. For a discussion in English of the origins of Egypt's Islamic movement, see

Gilles Kepel, *Muslim Extremism in Egypt: The Prophet and the Pharaoh* (Berkeley, Calif.: University of California Press), first published in French in 1984 and most recently in 1993 in a revised paperback edition, and Barry Rubin, *Islamic Fundamentalism in Egyptian Politics* (London: Macmillan, 1990). Kepel's landmark work explored the origins of the Jihad group that killed Sadat, and Rubin's more updated version explores the varied Islamic political field in Egypt under Mubarak. See also an article by Abdel Azim Ramadan, a professor of modern history at Minūfīya University in Egypt and an editor and writer for the political weekly *October*, entitled "Fundamentalist Influence in Egypt: The Strategies of the Muslim Brotherhood and the Takfir Groups," in *Fundamentalisms and the State*, the third volume of the series on religious fundamentalism issued by the Fundamentalism Project, eds. Martin E. Marty and R. Scott Appleby (Chicago and London: University of Chicago Press, 1993). For a thoughtful discussion of the evolution of modern militant Islamic theology from medieval works, see Emmanuel Sivan, *Radical Islam: Medieval Theology and Modern Politics* (New Haven, Conn., and London: Yale University Press, 1985).

20. There is disagreement within Islamist and academic circles about the origins but not the importance of this group. Hisham Mubarak says that the original al-Jihad was founded in 1960 by a young Egyptian student named Nabil Biri, who, while browsing in a Cairo bookstore in 1958, picked up a book by Ibn Taymiyya. Biri was particularly struck by Ibn Taymiyya's discussion of jihad. According to Mubarak, other activists, like Ayman al-Zawahri, quickly became more powerful within the group. By 1974 members of the original al-Jihad joined forces with Saleh Sirriya, a Palestinian who had migrated to Egypt from Jordan after the PLO-Jordanian clash in 1970. Sirriya, who called the Jihad group the Islamic Liberation Organization, tried to kill Sadat in 1974 by attacking him during a visit to Egypt's Military Technical Academy, a plot that was foiled. Gilles Kepel, the French scholar, argues that the original Jihad sprang from this abortive plot at the military academy in 1974. The latest date given for the creation of al-Jihad comes from Abdel Azim Ramadan, an Egyptian expert, who says that al-Jihad was founded in 1975 in Alexandria, but both Kepel and Mubarak argue convincingly that it existed earlier under other names, with some of the same personalities. In any event, after the academy plot was foiled, Sirriya was executed. Mubarak and Kepel agree that survivors of this group went on to form other militant groups — a spinoff group called the Society of Muslims (Takfir w'al Hijra, or literally, "charging with atheism and emigration"), led by Shukri Mustafa, which, in 1977, kidnapped and murdered the former minister of Awqaf, the department that oversees mosque property. Al-Jihad was reincarnated for a third time in 1979 by Mohammed Abdelsalam Farag, an engineer and radical Islamic theorist. In late 1980, Jihad merged with the Islamic Group, whose spiritual guide was Sheikh Omar Abdel Rahman. In 1981, Jihad and the Gama'a succeeded in killing Sadat. Most of the key leaders were executed, and others were sentenced to lengthy prison terms. Both Nabil Biri and Ayman al-Zawahri were released from jail in 1985 and went to Afghanistan. Zawahri emerged from there as a leader of the New Jihad — in effect, the group's fourth incarnation; the fate of Nabil Biri, says Hisham Mubarak, is not known.

21. Among them was Abbud al-Zumur, who, though he remained in jail, became the titular leader of the neo-Jihad group. In 1987, a daring assassination attempt on a former minister of interior was attributed to the group, whose external branch was said to be headed by Ayman al-Zawahri, a medical doctor who had also spent three years in prison for his role in Sadat's murder. Zawahri had shuttled among Afghanistan, Sudan, and Iran for several years before being given political asylum in Switzerland. Another key New Jihad figure was Muhammad Shawki Islambuli, the brother of Khaled Islambuli, the army lieutenant who had led the raid on Sadat. After his brother's death, Muhammad fled to Peshāwar, in Pakistan, and then to Jalālābād, Afghanistan. In 1992 an Egyptian military court sentenced him in absentia to death.

22. *Al-Hayat*, October 16, 1993, interview with Magdi Salim, leader of the Islamic

Victory Vanguards (part of the al-Jihad group), translated and reprinted by Khalid Duran in his magazine *TransState Islam* 1, no. 1 (Spring 1995).

23. Hisham Mubarak says that the groups clashed over three main points: First, followers of Zumur's al-Jihad believed that the time was not ripe for a violent confrontation with the state, that Islamists should concentrate on infiltrating the security forces and the army, whereas the Gama'a followers of Sheikh Omar Abdel Rahman believed that violent confrontation had to begin immediately and at every level of society. Second, Zumur opposed having Omar Abdel Rahman as the group's *alim* (leader) because the sheikh was blind and clearly not a strategist, unlike Zumur, who had served in the military. Finally, al-Jihad members and followers of the sheikh disagreed over the penalty for failing to carry out Islamic duties. Sheikh Rahman argued that a sinner could be excused if he had failed to do his Islamic duties because he was ignorant or oppressed. Zumur said that such excuses were not legitimate: Heretics, apostates, and others who failed to carry out Islamic obligations should be killed. In sum, Mubarak argues, Zumur's Jihad, if anything, was far more militant and even less tolerant than Omar Abdel Rahman's Gama'a Islamiya.

24. The newspaper was *Al Arabi*, a left-leaning paper critical of the regime. The interview with Zawahri, published in December 1993, was unique: Following its publication, the government banned the press from publishing interviews with outlawed groups.

25. The argument is made in one of the group's manifestos, known in English as *The Philosophy of Confrontation*. I am grateful to Hisham Mubarak for his translation of sections of it.

26. Foreign Broadcast Information Service, NES-93-161, August 23, 1993, "Body of Second 'Terrorist' Identified," Cairo, Middle East News Agency, in Arabic, August 20, 1993.

27. Originally, the police thought that the identity card had been forged on a printing press in Afghanistan known to have been used by other Islamic militants, but detectives eventually discovered that the Christian had reported the theft of his precious card.

28. John Eibner, ed., *Christians in Egypt, Church Under Siege* (Zurich, London, Washington, D.C.: Institute for Religious Minorities in the Islamic World, 1993), 37.

29. Adil Dasuqi, "Special Broadcasting for Extremists in Egypt," *Al-Hayat*, May 18, 1944; cited in Khalid Duran, *TransState Islam* 1, no. 1 (Spring 1995).

30. After considerable negotiation, President Mubarak's office permitted selective quotations from the interview on October 11, 1993, with this author and Chris Hedges, the *Times's* bureau chief in Cairo.

31. *New York Times*, "Nasser's 'True Face of Egypt' Is a Poor, Hard-Working Village," no byline, June 4, 1960. The Cairo bureau chief during that period was Jay Walz, a talented correspondent who died in 1991.

32. In his book *Revolt on the Nile* (London: Allan Wingate Ltd., 1957), Anwar Sadat wrote that after the 1952 coup, King Farouk's most powerful adviser had made a spelling mistake in signing his name to his dismissal letter. A man who had "made and unmade" ministers "hardly knew the Arabic language," Sadat reported with evident disgust.

33. Hedrick Smith, "Watermelon Village Races Against Time," *New York Times Magazine*, August 28, 1966.

34. Timothy M. Phelps, "Village Transformed as Egypt Quickens Pace of Change," *New York Times*, January 11, 1977.

35. Judith Miller, "A Village in Egypt Sits for a Post-Modern Portrait," *New York Times*, November 21, 1985, 2.

36. Four people were killed and dozens injured in the industrial city of Dafr el-Dawaar only a few months later, when some twenty-three thousand workers at the state-owned textile plant tried to stage a peaceful sit-in to protest unfair management

practices and security forces had gone on a rampage. And other Delta towns, such as Edco and Abu Hamad, had exploded in riots in 1992, both in protest of murders of young men in detention, part of the government-ordered crackdown on Islamic militancy. See Gehad Auda, "Rebellion in Egypt: A Civil Society in Question" (paper presented at the Council on Foreign Relations, New York, December 12, 1994).

37. Mohamed Heikal, *Autumn of Fury: The Assassination of Sadat* (London: Andre Deutsch, 1983), 133. Heikal, the prominent Egyptian journalist and Nasser's envoy and confidant, confirms that the government had supported several Islamic groups in Assyut with money and even arms.

38. In one such town — Sanabu, population twenty-five thousand, one-third Christian — sixty-four Christian shops and houses were burned in one month alone in 1992 after Egyptian police shot and killed the local militant Islamic leader. More than fifty Coptic families had fled.

39. A summary of the Egyptian police and prosecutors' interrogations is contained in the new edition of Fouad Ajami's *Arab Predicament* (Cambridge, Eng.: Cambridge University Press, 1992). This differs somewhat from the account presented in Gilles Kepel's book. But Kepel based his version on press accounts of what Sheikh Omar said. Ajami has transcripts of the interrogation sessions. I am grateful for his translation and guidance on Islamic terminology and practices.

40. Although often imprisoned in militant roundups, Abdel Rahman was tried three times and acquitted each time — first because he had been tortured in jail; second, of charges that he conspired to murder Sadat; and in the third case, of leading a 1989 demonstration in his hometown of Fayoum in which a policeman was badly injured.

41. In an interview with Mary Anne Weaver in the *New Yorker*, "The Novelist and the Sheikh," January 30, 1995, Rahman denied that he had issued a *fatwa* declaring Mahfouz an apostate and hence killable. His comments had been "misunderstood," he asserted. What he alleged, he said, was that if "we had punished Naguib Mahfouz for what he wrote in *Children of Gebelaawi* [his prize-winning novel], then Salman Rushdie never would have dared" to write his own heretical work *Satanic Verses*. According to Rahman, his answer to the interviewer was "a reply, an opinion, not a *fatwa*." But Abdel Rahman knows that there is a deliberately vague line between an opinion and a religious ruling, that the listener can interpret the sheikh's opinion as binding or as he sees fit. But there can be no mistake about what Abdel Rahman said, his denials notwithstanding. He declared that in his view Mahfouz was an apostate. Specifically, what he told an interviewer in *Al-Anba*, an Arabic newspaper, on April 13, 1989, is this: "Salman Rushdie harmed Islam and mocked the wives of the Prophet. He said false things about the Koran and this led to the Islamic judgment [against him]. Salman Rushdie and his colleague, Naguib Mahfouz, are apostates. Anyone who speaks like this about Islam is an apostate. The legal Islamic course is to ask him to repent. If he doesn't repent, we have to apply what the Prophet said: 'Kill whoever changes his religion.' Khomeini's *fatwa* is just and correct. You have to kill Salman Rushdie, and if we had applied this to Naguib Mahfouz when he wrote *Children of Gebelaawi*, Salman Rushdie would have been deterred, and no one else would have spoken ill of Islam."

42. An Ottoman-era edict in 1856, known as the Hamayouni Line, required that the ruler personally authorize church construction. That decree is still in force. It was amplified by 1934 Ministry of Interior regulations that outline conditions to be met before a church can be built. Since the overthrow of the monarchy, such presidential decrees have been increasingly difficult to secure, according to Virginia N. Sherry, associate director of Middle East Watch, a division of Human Rights Watch, in New York City. Ms. Sherry is responsible for monitoring Christian rights in Egypt and has written frequently on the topic. See, for example, "The Predicament of Egypt's Christian Minority," *Christian Century*, July 14–21, 1993, 717–20; see also Middle East Watch's report on Coptic Christians issued in December 1994.

43. American and Canadian Coptic Association, "The Copts, Christians of

Egypt," 12, nos. 1 and 2 (June 1985), Jersey City, N.J., 15; see also Human Rights Watch/ Middle East, "Egypt: Violations of Freedom of Religious Belief and Expression of the Christian Minority," 6, no. 2 (November 1994), New York, 11–15. Painting, filling in cracks in decaying cement walls, fixing a leaky roof, or even substituting new church benches requires presidential approval. Between 1973 and 1979, Sadat issued only fifty such permits — eight a year. The government claimed that under Mubarak between 1981 and 1992, some 350 churches were constructed or repaired and that permits had increased further in 1993 and 1994 to an annual average of twenty. But a U.S. State Department report said that while permits for repairs had risen, few new churches were authorized. Even after such permits were given, Copts complained, bureaucratic obstacles often blocked renovation and construction. Since even the simplest repair required a presidential decree, licenses ran woefully behind demand. See Human Rights Watch, "Egypt," and *Country Reports on Human Rights Practices for 1993* (Washington, D.C.: U.S. Department of State, 1994), 1171–72.

44. American and Canadian Coptic Association, "Christians of Egypt," 28.

45. Youssef M. Ibrahim, "Muslims' Fury Falls on Egypt's Christians," *New York Times*, March 15, 1993. The article blamed the violence against Christians not only on Mubarak's regime for showing "increasing deference to Islamic fundamentalists since its beginnings in October 1981" but also on the Coptic church itself for having "turned inward under its leadership, encouraging the faithful to embrace a posture of patience and prayer instead of social and political activism"; see also Eibner, *Christians in Egypt, Church Under Siege.*

46. In 1993, Youssef Boutros-Ghali became minister without portfolio in the prime minister's office, the highest-ranking position held by a Copt. Youssef Boutros-Ghali is the nephew of Boutros Boutros-Ghali, who served as minister of state for foreign affairs under Mubarak and also as acting foreign minister under Sadat. After having enraged many Muslims by visiting Jerusalem and making peace with Israel, Sadat did not dare antagonize them further by appointing this talented Christian his foreign minister. As a measure of how far Coptic fortunes have fallen in Egypt, King Fouad did not hesitate during his reign half a century ago to select Boutros-Ghali Pasha, Ghali's uncle, as Egypt's foreign minister; a century ago Boutros-Ghali's grandfather had served as prime minister. In a preview of the violence to come, Ghali was assassinated by Muslim fanatics in 1910.

47. Consider events in Manshiet Nasser, a farm village near Assyut that is often cited as the spark of the current wave of Islamic terror in Upper Egypt. In May 1992, Muslim militants, carrying knives, pistols, and rifles, marched into the dirt streets of this heavily Christian village and opened fire, killing fourteen people and wounding five children, aged nine to eleven. One of the dead was a Christian teacher who was shot point-blank before horrified children in her local school. Another was a doctor who was stabbed to death in his home. The massacre was described as the deadliest civil clash in Egypt in over a decade. But Coptic friends told me that it might have been prevented had the government acted earlier against the Gama'a Islamiya, which controlled the town and had been provoking violence since 1990. That year, for example, the Islamic Group found workers replacing old floor tiles in a local church without government permission and attacked them. They also smashed the church's windows and doors. The Christians responded by vowing not to cooperate with the Gama'a or do business with its supporters. In December 1991 a Protestant was ambushed and beaten with iron pipes by the Gama'a for failing to pay a $1,000 "fine" after he criticized the group's local leader. His legs and right arm were broken, but the police again took no action against the group. The following March, a fundamentalist leader was killed along with a Christian who was tending his field when the militants opened fire. The survivors identified their assailants, but the police somehow failed to capture them. The Gama'a, however, decided on revenge, which led to the deadly incident in May.

Sectarian tensions were exacerbated further by the social structure of the region. An Egyptian in Upper Egypt — Christian or Muslim — is bound by two sets of social ties: to his *beit* (the household or extended family) and to his *aila* (a clan or group of many households). Given this structure, family or clan vendettas are bound to escalate unless the state quickly intervenes when quarrels among them erupt. But the police did not act, and vengeance killings have become increasingly common. When the government finally intervened, it did so with mass arrests and communal punishment, techniques that only deepened local resentment, mobilized entire clans against the police and their alleged informants, and directed subsequent vendettas against policemen and their families.

48. Interview with Abou Zeid Rageh, housing expert and architect, Cairo, October 25, 1993.

49. Dr. Ibrahim Shahata, World Bank, and Dr. Skaker Shalan, International Monetary Fund (presentations at breakfast for the American University of Cairo, New York, November 11, 1993).

50. Sa'ad Eddin Ibrahim, "Anatomy of Egypt's Militant Islamic Groups," *International Journal of Middle East Studies*, no. 12 (1980).

51. Mustafa Mashur, Muslim Brotherhood leader, *Al-Hayat*, July 1995.

52. Erian denies that he was ever affiliated with the Gama'a, Jihad, or any of the violent student organizations at the University of Cairo, where he studied medicine. But more than one of his fellow classmates assured me in interviews that Erian was not only a member of such a group; he had been its leader.

53. Shimon Shamir, the former director of Israel's Academic Center in Cairo, in *Orbis* (Spring 1986), says that Mubarak's early years provided hope of a political opening. Professor Shamir, who later became Israel's ambassador to Egypt and then Jordan, wrote that from two rather restricted political "platforms" in 1976 the opposition grew to five full-fledged political parties by 1986. The fourteen seats won by opposition parties in the 1976 elections increased to fifty-eight in the elections of May 1984. Most were won by a coalition between the Wafd and the Muslim Brotherhood. In 1987, despite government tampering and district gerrymandering, the Brotherhood, then in a new coalition with the old Socialist Labor Party, a formerly socialist, secular group that was trying to attract Egypt's increasingly Islamically oriented voters, scored even higher. The Muslim Brotherhood–Labor coalition won 60 out of a total of 448 seats. The opposition Wafd, by contrast, won only 35. The opposition failed to convince the government to change the biased election laws. As a result, most opposition parties boycotted the 1990 elections.

54. Richard P. Mitchell, *The Society of the Muslim Brothers* (New York, Oxford: Oxford University Press, 1993), 8. Mitchell's book, first published in 1969, is widely regarded as the most authoritative work on the Brotherhood in English. In Arabic, the best biography — and one that is less sympathetic — is *Hassan al Banna*, by Rifa'at al-Said, published originally in Cairo in 1977.

55. John L. Esposito, *Islam, the Straight Path* (New York, Oxford: Oxford University Press, 1991), 128.

56. Mitchell, *Muslim Brothers*, 236.

57. Saeed Hawwa, *The Muslim Brotherhood*, International Islamic Federation of Student Organizations (Kuwait: Al-Faisal Islamic Press, 1985).

58. Mitchell, *Muslim Brothers*, 297.

59. Kepel, *Muslim Extremism*. When the Brotherhood was legalized again in 1951, the group was ideologically split between those, like its new supreme guide, Hodeiby, who wanted the Brotherhood to remain primarily a religious society as long as it was weak, and others, particularly in the group's secret "apparatus," who favored an activist political role and the use of force, if necessary, to turn Egypt into an Islamic state. My friend Don Peretz, a professor emeritus of Middle Eastern studies in Binghamton, New York, described the fierce internal struggle over this key issue in 1953. In a magazine

article written under the pseudonym Donald Peters, he described his chilling interview with the then head of the secret apparatus and editor of the Brothers' main publication, a man who spoke in "quiet, soft tones, never raising his voice even when making the most violent statements." Assassination, the editor Saleh Ashmawi told him, "occurs only after we have first advised the victim of his errors, then warned him." If this unfriendly advice is ignored, "only then do we shoot him."

60. Kepel, *Muslim Extremism*, 107, citing the Egyptian writer Tariq al-Bishri. This is the best book in French or English — and some of my Arab friends say even in Arabic. My description of Qutb's *Signposts* and some details of his life are drawn from a new paperback edition of this book (Berkeley: University of California Press, 1993), 36–69. I am deeply indebted to Kepel for his help, insights, and friendship.

61. See, for example, Sa'ad Eddin Ibrahim, "Islamic Groups."

62. Kepel, *Muslim Extremism*, 40.

63. *Al-Islam wa-Mushkilat al-Hadara* (Islam and the Problems of Civilization), published in Cairo sometime after 1954 and probably before *Signposts* in 1964. In this work, Qutb quotes from and refers to another of his books, *America As I Saw It*, a journal of his travels in the United States, which was "under publication." According to Gilles Kepel, the journal was never printed in book form. Michael Doran, a scholar at Princeton who translated passages of the book for me, believes that *America As I Saw It* was serialized in a Muslim Brotherhood journal in 1951. I am indebted to Michael Doran not only for his translation but also his guidance on Qutb's writing style and Koranic and literary allusions.

64. Sylvia Haim, "Sayyid Qutb," *Asian and African Studies* 16 (1982): 147–56.

65. Isaac Asimov, *Encyclopedia of Science and Technology* (New York: Doubleday, 1972). I am indebted to Dan Greenberg, the publisher of *Science & Government Report*, in Washington, D.C., for information about Carrel's thinking.

66. In some respects, Qutb's analysis bears a striking resemblance to that of American evangelical Christians — Islam's historic foes — who would, by the 1990s, play an important role in American politics. See Gilles Kepel, *The Revenge of God* (University Park: Pennsylvania State University Press, 1994).

67. Rubin, *Islamic Fundamentalism*, 107.

68. Sivan, *Radical Islam*, 94–107.

69. *The Program for Islamic Action*, the Gama'a guide, said Mubarak, was determinedly vague and lacking in strategy. Its three young authors, who assembled the *Program* under the "supervision" of Sheikh Omar Abdel Rahman, urged a nine-point plan of action that spoke mainly of returning to the tenets of the *salafiya* (the righteous ancestors), through *da'wa* (a call to religion), "commanding what is good," "forbidding the reprehensible," and conducting jihad, that is, fighting those opposed to the "truth" by "correcting them and repressing them." The Gama'a argued that jihad had to begin immediately — at all levels of society. By contrast, al-Jihad's *Philosophy of Confrontation* concentrated on tactics and strategy — how to infiltrate the army and police — and above all, when to move and when to wait. Perhaps this was because its author, Tarek Zumur, was a cousin of Abbud Zumur, who was convicted in the murder plot against Sadat. Zumur had advised against killing the pharaoh in 1981; Egypt, he warned his more zealous colleagues, was not ready for rebellion. Al-Jihad intended to avoid repeating its predecessor's mistakes.

70. I am indebted to Sari Nuseibeh, the Palestinian scholar, for this formulation.

71. Haim, "Sayyid Qutb," 156.

72. Charles J. Hanley, "West Rethinks Islamic 'Threat'; Move Toward Conciliation," *Chicago Tribune*, November 11, 1994.

73. Not all Muslim Brethren share Hodeiby's views on alcohol or other dogma. Mohammed Shawki, the head of the 110,000-strong medical syndicate and a longtime Brethren who now claimed to be a card-carrying member of Mubarak's National Demo-

cratic Party, told me that his Islamic Egypt might permit alcohol to be served in hotel rooms but not in public. Islam was very flexible, he assured me.

74. Rubin, *Islamic Fundamentalism*, 108.

75. Communiqué from the Muslim Brotherhood on the "Gaza-Jericho First Agreement," published in Arabic in *Al-Shaab*, no. 773 (September 7, 1993), translation by Ahmed Mustafa.

76. Al-Mussawar, "The Secret Documents of the Muslim Brethren," June 16, 1994, 20–23. In Arabic. Translated by Khalid Duran. An allusion to the discovery is also contained in an article by Chris Hedges, "Egypt Begins Crackdown on Strongest Opposition Group," *New York Times*, June 12, 1994. Hedges does not mention the name of the company or any specifics about the documents' and disks' contents.

77. *Al-Hayat*, article citing Ayman al-Zawahri, leader of al-Jihad, in *al-Mujahidoun*, the group's publication from Switzerland, *Mideast Mirror*, July 10, 1995, 14.

78. Khalid Duran, ed., *TransState Islam* 1, no. 1 (Spring 1995), 5, citing an interview with Kamal al-Sa'id Habib, described in the Arabic paper *Al-Safir*, published in Beirut, as "one of the founders of the Al-Jihad Organization." Al-Jihad, Sa'id Habib said, "lacks organizational foundations and has no unified leadership. In addition, it received many blows since the assassination of President al-Sadat in 1981." The interviewer does not state the time or place of his interview. Published January 26, 1994.

79. One such broadcast was made by Adel Abdel Baqi in the spring of 1994. Baqi shocked and enthralled Egyptian viewers with tales of wife swapping as a reward for Islamic "virtue" and other acts of sexual immorality within his group, the Shawqiyeen, a Jihad splinter group — more extreme than either al-Jihad or the Gama'a — whose members were heavily influenced by Sayyid Qutb. According to Baqi, he personally helped enlist ten thousand young men into the ranks of the militants — a rather astonishing claim that few Egyptians seemed to question. To finance its activities, his group stole weapons and motorcycles and robbed Christian jewelry stores after it was unable to raise money legally. Appalled by what Baqi called the group's degenerate sexual practices, he defected.

Baqi had supposedly defected in late 1993, but the government did not release the videotape until four months later. And according to a supposedly unedited transcript obtained by an Egyptian magazine, the government had edited the tape. Baqi had supposedly also confessed to having seen a Muslim Brotherhood lawyer give a Jihad leader a check for 250,000 Egyptian pounds, about $75,000, from the *zakat*, Islamic charity funds collected in Saudi Arabia. The money, Baqi said, was intended for the families of terrorists in detention. Baqi also supposedly said that he had personally received the equivalent of almost $600 from a wealthy Muslim Brother in Heliopolis, a middle-class Cairo suburb. While the government might want to avoid offending Saudi Arabia, it was unclear why it would eliminate sections of the tape that supported its hotly disputed claim of linkage between the Brotherhood and the violent Islamic groups. *Civil Society*, the remarkable magazine of the Ibn Khaldoun Center, Cairo, translated and published the broadcast.

80. Interview, Abou Zeid Rageh, Cairo, October 25, 1993.

81. Chris Hedges, "In the Slums, a Tug-of-War for Hearts and Minds," *New York Times*, November 29, 1994.

82. Mamoun Fandy, "The Tensions Behind the Violence in Egypt," *Middle East Policy* 2, no. 1 (1993): 28.

83. Edward T. Pound with Jihan el-Tahri, "Sanctions: The Pluses and Minuses," *U.S. News & World Report*, October 31, 1994.

84. Denis J. Sullivan, *Private Voluntary Organizations in Egypt* (Gainesville: University Press of Florida, 1994), 13.

85. See, for example, Ajami, *Arab Predicament*.

86. Mohamed Amar, interview, October 1993. Dr. Amar, a former Marxist mili-

tant who has become a leading proponent of what he calls "enlightened Islamic government," told me that France under Bonaparte had introduced "belly-dancing and other forms of debauchery" to Egypt and blamed Britain for trying to "undermine Islam" by encouraging in Islamic countries like Egypt the Baha'i faith, a breakaway Shiite Islamic sect regarded by many Muslims as heretical. Dr. Amar, the author of more than two hundred books, has a large following, particularly among young Islamists.

87. The malleability of the Egyptian masses and Egypt's elite was once stressed by Anwar Sadat after Israeli prime minister Menachem Begin visited Egypt after Egypt and Israel made peace. According to Ezer Weizman, now Israel's president and then part of Israel's delegation, Begin told Sadat that he was overwhelmed by the warmth of the greeting he had received. More than a million Egyptians had lined Cairo streets holding placards of welcome and cheering in Arabic for "peace." Sadat, however, was not as moved. "Today they are in the streets cheering for peace because I tell them peace is good for Egypt," he told Begin. "But do not be misled: If I tell them tomorrow to cheer for war, a million people will also do so."

88. Israel's insensitivity to Egyptian fears has exacerbated them. The presence of more than seven hundred Israeli businessmen in Casablanca during a 1994 conference on development was seen by conspiratorial-minded Egyptians as evidence of Zionist ambitions to use the new peace to vanquish the Arabs economically. Arab anxiety was further strengthened in December 1994 when Prime Minister Rabin announced that Israel must once again prepare for yet another Arab-Israeli war "in the 'middle range of time.'" See Amos Elon, "One Foot on the Moon," *New York Review of Books*, April 6, 1995.

89. In a national survey published in late December 1994 in the semiofficial *Al Ahram* newspaper, 71 percent said they did not want to buy Israeli goods. Some 63 percent said they had no desire to visit Israel, and 53 percent said they did not approve of Israelis visiting their country. In mid-January two hundred Egyptian intellectuals signed a petition protesting normalization with Israel and any Arab state. Cited in a newsletter issued by the Elul Group of Israel, Tel Aviv, no. 116, January 1995.

90. Sayed Yassin, the long-serving director of *Al Ahram*'s Center for Political and Strategic Studies, the Cairo think tank created to promote peace and dispassionate inquiry, told me over lunch in Cairo in 1994 that Israel was an "evil nation," a "Hitlerian regime," and that under no circumstances would he ever visit it. Yassin was also among the most vocal proponents of "taming" the Muslim Brotherhood by letting them participate as a political party in national elections. Only in 1995 was he replaced as director.

91. A telling example of such evasion is a harsh critique of Egypt's government delivered at the 1995 Cairo book fair by Mohammed Heikal, Nasser's former adviser and publicist who is still regarded as one of Egypt's most prominent journalists. Rather than acknowledge that Nasser had devastated Egypt's bourgeoisie and aristocracy, crushed liberal critics, closed civic associations, and destroyed individual initiative and enterprise in favor of inept centralized enterprises that would never be able to compete in the international markets of the twenty-first century, Egypt under Nasser, he said, had built "one of the most sophisticated industrial bases in the developing world" and still had an "industrial potential second to none in the region." The trouble with Egypt, he asserted, was Sadat's liberalization and the resultant growth in income disparities, the economic reforms mandated by the International Monetary Fund—which Mubarak himself had once called the International Misery Fund—and the ineptitude and corruption of Mubarak's regime. President Mubarak was a good man, he added quickly, but "poorly advised."

92. Egypt's declining intellectual life has been noted, among others, by John Waterbury, a scholar at Princeton who has written several fine books on Egypt, among them *Egypt: Burdens of the Past, Options for the Future*, Bloomington: American Universities Field Staff (Indiana University Press, 1978), and *The Egypt of Nasser and Sadat* (Princeton, N.J.: Princeton University Press, 1983).

93. Fouad Ajami, "In the Pharaoh's Shadow: Religion and Authority in Egypt," in *Islam in the Political Process*, ed. James P. Piscatori (Cambridge, Eng.: Cambridge University Press, 1983), 31.

94. Crecelius, "Modernization," 183.

95. Ibid., 207.

96. Malika Zeghal reports, based on data from UNESCO — more reliable than those of the Egyptian government — that the number of Azhar-sponsored "preparatory institutes," or primary and secondary schools, doubled under Nasser from twenty-three in 1952 to fifty-seven by 1963. In 1962, sixty-four thousand students were enrolled in them; a decade later, the figure stood at ninety thousand. Their growth has continued under Mubarak. Some 1,273 institutes in 1982 expanded to 3,161 in 1992.

97. "Respect Saudi Laws: Tantawi," *Saudi Gazette*, Riyadh, June 6, 1995.

98. Kepel, *Muslim Extremism*, 80.

99. The sheikh of al-Azhar eventually blessed the population conference held in Cairo in August 1994 at a time when the government was trying to lure tourists frightened of Islamic terrorism back to Egypt. The conference, he said one month after he had demanded (and gotten) changes in the draft document, had succeeded in "preserving the principles of Islam."

100. *Al-Sirat*, August 4, 1989, cited in Raphael Israeli's *Muslim Fundamentalism in Israel* (United Kingdom: Brassey's, 1993), 42.

101. In most cases, banned works such as Foda's essays have been distributed in Egypt, al-Azhar's edicts notwithstanding. But on several occasions Mubarak himself had to intervene to get a book published or a movie shown.

102. Ami Ayalon, "Egypt's Political Order: Continuity and Changes," in *The Politics of Change in the Middle East*, ed. Robert B. Satloff (Boulder, Colo.: Westview Press, 1993, 196; in cooperation with the Washington Institute for Near East Policy.)

103. Yahya M. Sadowski, *Political Vegetables?* (Washington, D.C.: Brookings Institution, 1991), 15. By analyzing Egypt's agricultural sector, this study attributes Egypt's underdevelopment to what Sadowski calls "crony capitalism," cliques of bureaucrats and businessmen who resist reform for fear that it will diminish their power and wealth.

Saudi Arabia

1. "Country Reports on Human Rights for 1994," U.S. Department of State, Washington, D.C., February 1995. See also "Shame in the House of Saud," a 1992 report by the Minnesota Lawyers International Human Rights Committee, which called the kingdom's human-rights record "deplorable."

2. Population statistics, like all official data in the kingdom, are unreliable. The Saudis have long tried to inflate their population figures to downplay their sparse population and potential vulnerability. The first official census was conducted in 1962–63, but the government repudiated the results. In 1974, a second census was conducted, and two years later the government claimed that Saudi Arabia had 7 million people, though the World Bank estimated the population as closer to 5 million, many of whom were foreign workers. In 1989 the government claimed its population stood at 12 million, but the U.S. government and human-rights groups put the figure at 7 million.

3. In the kingdom, the lowercase "al" is the Arabic definite article. When the "a" is capitalized, it means "the house of" or "of the family." So Al Saud means the House of Saud.

4. One of the most popular was dubbed the "Supergun" by Saudi dissidents, a reference to the devastating long-range gun that Saddam Hussein was trying to build. On tape, an unidentified preacher denounces royal princes, ministers, officials, and

military officers for corruption, taking drugs and alcohol, and deviating from "the path of Islam." The government offered substantial rewards for information about the tape's author. According to opposition sources, the preacher was eventually identified and was among those jailed in 1995.

5. One Saudi scholar counts at least ten pejorative references to the Bedouin in the Koran. Histories of the kingdom, moreover, are full of complaints about the Bedouin — "more of a curse than a blessing to any Emir who did rely on them," concluded Sheikh Hafiz Wahba. Most of the legendary "forty" men who joined Ibn Saud in reconquering Riyadh, the new Saudi capital, were apparently *hadari*, not Bedouin. What is viewed as the Bedouin's "last stand" in the kingdom occurred in 1929 when, in the Battle of Sabilah, Ibn Saud routed the Wahhabi Bedouin resistance. See Wahba's *Arabian Days* (London: Arthur Baker Ltd., 1964).

6. Of the biographies in English that try to place Muhammad in political and social context, my favorite is *Mohammed*, by Maxime Rodinson (New York: Pantheon Books, 1971); see also W. Montgomery Watt, *Muhammad, Prophet and Statesman* (Oxford, Eng.: Clarendon Press, 1961) and *Muhammed*, a slender volume by Michael Cook (Oxford, Eng.: Oxford University Press, 1983). One of the three main Arabic biographies is available in English translation: A. Guillaume, *The Life of Muhammad: A Translation of Ibn Is'haq's "Sirat Rasul Allah"* (London: Oxford University Press, 1955); see also Bernard Lewis, *The Arabs in History*, new ed. (Oxford, Eng.: Oxford University Press, 1993).

7. Fatima Mernissi, *Women and Islam* (Oxford, Eng.: Blackwell, 1992), 44. The Muslim scholar was Al-Bukhari, whose editing of the *hadith* in the third Muslim century, *Al Sahih* (Collection of Authentic *Hadith*), is widely regarded as a basic resource work for Muslims. While Muslims have made sustained, scholarly efforts to distinguish false from authentic *hadith*, even the most cautious historians sometimes ended their assessments with the advisory "But God knows best," according to Rodinson, *Mohammed*, 43.

8. Rodinson, *Mohammed*, 293.

9. Cook, *Muhammed*, 15.

10. Historians note that medieval Muslims debated from the eighth to tenth centuries whether the Koran was created and revealed by God or whether it had always existed and was eternal, like God himself. The latter view prevailed.

11. In *Islam and the Arab World* (New York: Knopf, 1976), Bernard Lewis says that the word "Islam" originally conveyed a somewhat different notion — that of "entirety." The Muslim, in this sense, was one who "gave himself entirely to God alone to the exclusion of others, i.e., a monotheist as contrasted with the polytheists among whom the Prophet appeared in 7th century Arabia."

Olivier Roy, *The Failure of Political Islam* (Cambridge, Mass.: Harvard University Press, 1994), also emphasizes the Muslims' preoccupation with "oneness," or in Arabic, *tawhid*, which "extends to the individual, whose practices are considered in the aggregate and not classified according to the area in which they are implemented (the social, private, devotional, political, or economic sphere)." The community's "oneness" under Muhammad, what Roy calls the "paradigm of the original community," rejects any "internal segmentation and derives its unity from a charismatic leader."

12. Rodinson, *Mohammed*, 106–7.

13. Cook, *Muhammed*, 82.

14. Lewis, *Islam*, 38.

15. Rodinson, *Mohammed*, 155.

16. Lewis maintains that the writing of Muslim scholars reflects a certain ambivalence about the veracity of Muhammad's charge against the tribe. Rodinson agrees, noting that most of the Banu Qurayza remained loyal to their defense pact with the Muslims.

17. Rodinson, *Mohammed*, 213.

18. Watt, *Muhammad*, 191.

19. I use the word advisedly. If one uses the word to mean "government of priests," then Muhammad's government was not a theocracy, nor were any Muslim governments until the Islamic Republic of Iran in 1979. But if one uses the word, as does Lewis, to mean a "government of God," just as aristocracy is a "government of the best" and democracy is a "government of the people," then this accurately describes Muhammad's rule, and, indeed, that of any government that claims to be ruled by God's holy law, as opposed to laws made by a sovereign populace. I use the word in this broad sense.

20. For the importance of poets in Arab society during the time of Muhammad, see Watt, *Muhammad*, 50.

21. Rodinson, *Mohammed*, 171.

22. Ibid., 171.

23. Ibid., 261.

24. The Koranic verse says the following: "Men are the protectors and maintainers of women because God has given them more (strength) than the other and because they support them from their means. Therefore the righteous women are devoutly obedient, and guard in (the husband's) absence what God would have them guard. As to those women on whose part ye fear disloyalty and ill conduct, admonish them (first), (next) refuse to share their beds, (and last) beat them (lightly); but if they return to obedience, seek not against them means (of annoyance). For God is most high, great (above you all)." The words in parentheses were added by the translator, Yusuf Ali (*The Holy Quran*, 3d ed. [Washington, D.C.: The American International Printing Co., n.d.]), who may have preferred to believe that a truly wise and merciful God would want errant or disloyal women to be beaten only lightly. Other versions translate the Arabic word *dharaba*, used in the Koran, as "scourge." Some Muslim feminists maintain that the word can also be translated as "strike with a feather." But although the Koran urges in several verses that women be treated gently, the counsel to strike them with a feather seems far-fetched given conditions in seventh-century Arabia.

25. Mernissi argues, for instance, that many of the Prophet's most misogynistic sayings—such as "the dog, the ass, and woman interrupt prayer if they pass in front of the believer"—were, in fact, invented by witnesses such as Abu Hurayra, whom she describes as a hanger-on in the Prophet's entourage who not only hated women but had a "fixation about female cats."

26. Muhammad, she writes, was forced for the sake of his faith and the unity of the community to sacrifice his goal of gender equality, given the implacable hostility of Muslim men to the women's demands for greater sexual and political rights. "Faced with this difficult choice—equality of the sexes or the survival of Islam," Mernissi concludes, "the genius of Muhammad and the greatness of his God shows in the fact that at least at the beginning of the seventh century the question was posed and the community was pushed to reflect about it."

27. Muhammad's problems often reflected those of the community and invariably led to rulings governing their solution.

28. The Ayatollah Khomeini, for instance, legalized child marriage, which the shah had banned.

29. Lewis, *Arabs in History*, 61.

30. Mernissi bitterly claims that the war was named for the camel that Aisha rode into battle rather than for its rider "to avoid linking in the memory of Muslim girls the name of a woman with . . . a battle." It was Aisha's defeat that gave rise to an alleged saying of the Prophet which many Muslim militants use today to oppose women in public life: "No people who place a woman over their affairs will prosper." This might well have amused Khadija, Muhammad's first wife, by whom the Prophet was employed before their marriage and without whom history would have undoubtedly been different.

31. Bernard Lewis notes that the dispute involved economics, not just theology. The Shia drew considerable support from the Mawali, non-Arab converts to Islam who resented the concentration of political, and especially economic, power in exclusively Arab, and particularly Umayyad hands. As the Islamic empire grew, the Mawali merchants and craftsmen in cities conquered by Islam became more numerous and more aggrieved.

32. Shiites, whose origins lay in defeat and, as a result, whose doctrine espoused the virtues of opposition to authority, subsequently split into many factions. Those that have survived include, among others: Imamis, or "Twelver" Shiism, the doctrine espoused by most Iranians; Ismailis, Nusairis, or Alawites, the sect found in modern Syria; and Zaidis, dominant today in Yemen.

33. Edward Mortimer, *Faith and Power* (New York: Vintage, 1982), 43.

34. Abdelwahab El-Affendi, *Who Needs an Islamic State?* (London: Grey Seal, 1991), 26.

35. This was the doctrine widely attributed to Abu Hamid al-Ghazali (1058–1111), sometimes referred to as Islam's St. Augustine. Ghazali argued that all power was legitimate regardless of how it was achieved, provided the ruler implemented the sharia, or holy law. But in his book *Faith and Power*, Edward Mortimer notes that even Ghazali did not counsel that injustice be condoned. Rather, the believer had a moral duty to do whatever he could — short of rebellion — to rebuke the unjust leader and persuade him to reform.

36. After Muhammad's death, for example, Abu Bakr sent his forces to cut off the hands of those he was said to have called the "whores of Hadramut," a town in southern Arabia. The six women's crime was to have celebrated the Prophet's death by playing the tambourine in the streets and painting their hands with henna, which women usually apply for weddings and other happy gatherings. Caliph Umar's record on women was even worse.

37. Wahba, *Arabian Days*, 87.

38. Ibid., 85. Sheikh Wahba, an Arab adviser to King Abdulaziz, saw a "striking parallel" between the lives of Ibn Taymiyya and Luther two centuries later. Both men, he argued, opposed excessive veneration of saints and holy men and their respective clergy's monopoly on scriptural interpretation and understanding. But while Ibn Taymiyya's thirteenth-century reform movement failed because the state's rulers and leading men were against him, Luther succeeded, thanks largely to the support of the elite.

39. See Egypt chapter.

40. The major legal schools are Shafiism, Malikism, Hanafism, and Hanbalism, each named after the interpretation of a leading theologian.

41. The conquest was bloody — shockingly so to much of the Islamic world. Many Muslims, especially the Shia, were outraged when, in 1801, Wahhabi forces stormed Karbala, the sacred Shiite city in neighboring Iraq where Hussein and his forces had been slaughtered centuries earlier. In an "eight-hour orgy of violence," the Wahhabis "massacred some 5,000 people, wrecked Hussein's mosque tomb, looted the city, and then pulled out with 200 camels loaded with treasure." Nadav Safran, *Saudi Arabia: The Ceaseless Quest for Security* (Ithaca, N.Y.: Cornell University Press, 1985 and 1988), 11.

42. Curiously, observes scholar Safran, the Wahhabi religious establishment was studiously neutral during the family's internal power struggles, favoring whoever seemed ascendant at the time, behavior that "contributed little to an orderly resolution of the conflict."

43. Harry St. John Philby, a British adventurer, convert to Islam, and Saudophile, went so far as to compare Ibn Saud to the Prophet Muhammad. Even Sir Percy Cox, the British official who literally drew much of the map of the modern Middle East, said that in the thirty tumultuous years of his reign, Ibn Saud had never made a serious mistake. Sheikh Wahba, the king's adviser, called Abdulaziz the "ablest, the most farsighted, and the most attentive in matters of state" of the Gulf rulers.

44. James P. Piscatori, "Ideological Politics in Sa'udi Arabia," in *Islam in the Political Process*, ed. James P. Piscatori (Cambridge, Eng.: Cambridge University Press, 1983), 57–58.

45. John S. Habib, *Ibn Sa'ud's Warriors of Islam* (Leiden, the Netherlands: E. J. Brill, 1978), 156–61.

46. Safran, *Saudi Arabia*, 16, 56.

47. A female staff member of a powerful congressional committee once had to rouse an American diplomat from bed at midnight when the hotel clerk in Riyadh refused to let her check in without the requisite Saudi stamp of virtue. In 1990, Geraldine Brooks, my colleague from the *Wall Street Journal*, spent most of the night in a Saudi jail because she did not have such a letter. She describes the incident in her sensitive portrait of Arab Muslim women, *Nine Parts of Desire* (New York: Anchor Books, 1995).

48. Saad Abdullah Sowayan, *Nabati Poetry* (Berkeley: University of California Press, 1985), 54–55. I am indebted to Dr. Sowayan, a sociologist at King Saud University, for his help on Saudi culture and traditions.

49. In 1944, when Parker Hart was Washington's vice consul general in Jidda, the Red Sea port, not a single road connected Jidda to Dhahran on the Persian Gulf, the opposite side of the kingdom. The trip, now a two-hour flight, took four days. Hart, interview, June 30, 1995.

50. Adel A. Al-Jubeir, "The Saudi State" (lecture presented at the Smithsonian Institution, Washington, D.C., May 25, 1993); see also *Saudi Arabia*, 12, no. 1 (spring 1995), Information Office of Saudi Arabia, Washington, D.C.

51. United Nations Development Programme, *Human Development Report, 1993* (Oxford, Eng.: Oxford University Press, 1993), 144.

52. "Background Notes," U.S. Department of State, Washington, D.C., August 1994.

53. Saudi Arabia does not permit the worship of any faith except Islam on its own soil. The prohibition was not officially suspended even during the Gulf war. Although Americans were preparing to fight, and perhaps die, for Saudi Arabia, they were not permitted to post pictures of Jesus, Moses, Abraham, or, for some reason, Adam and Eve. According to instructions from the U.S. Army distributed over Christmas shortly before the war, American soldiers were not allowed to display crosses, Jewish stars, or any other non-Islamic religious symbols. They were not permitted to hold Christian or Jewish services on Saudi soil. They were even ordered not to play Christmas carols unless they were instrumental. "Jingle Bells" was "acceptable," the leaflet said.

Though Riyadh has bitterly complained about perceived insults to Islam and discrimination against Muslims in Europe and America, it has financed the construction of mosques throughout the world — even in Rome — and still refuses to permit the worship of any faith except Islam on its soil. The kingdom, moreover, is the only Middle Eastern country that has refused to sign nearly every important human-rights treaty and convention, including the Universal Declaration of Human Rights, which defines basic rights ostensibly for all UN members.

54. The story described, for example, a scandal surrounding gas masks that had failed to reach thousands in those critical days before the Gulf war because Prince Mohammed bin Nayef, the son of the powerful interior minister, was said to have been dissatisfied with his profit on their import. I had also written about the al-Ibrahims, the king's in-laws, and specifically about how a television production company owned by Khaled al-Ibrahim, a brother of King Fahd's favorite wife (he then had two of them), had won a lucrative contract to produce slavishly laudatory minifilms and songs for the kingdom. The king himself had apparently assisted in the final editing of these televised encomiums. Earlier, I had written about the vast commission payments rumored to have been made to Prince Sultan for the Al Yamamah contract with Britain in the mid-1980s, the single largest defense deal in Western history.

55. Sheikh Abdullah had equally orthodox views — in Saudi terms — on women.

For example, he parroted the government's criticism of the forty-seven women who had staged a tiny rebellion shortly before the war by defying the kingdom's then informal ban on women driving. Such women, the sheikh said, were "misguided," echoing Minister of Interior Nayef's charge that they had not been raised in "Islamic homes."

56. David E. Long, "Saudi Arabia: Land of Contradictions," unpublished manuscript. I am grateful to him for sharing with me this well-researched work. He, too, argues that "Muhammad Malthus" is the kingdom's greatest threat.

57. Abdulaziz Bin Baz, "The Ruling on Unveiling, Veiling, and the Marriage of the Unprotected," Riyadh, 1984, in Arabic, translation by Khalid Duran.

58. Frank H. Stewart, *Honor* (Chicago: University of Chicago Press, 1994).

59. According to statistics from the Saudi Health Ministry, enrollment in the kingdom's three medical schools is almost evenly split between men and women. In 1993, 44 percent of the doctors, or 666, were women.

60. *Saudi Gazette*, July 20, 1995. Turki Bin Khlid Al-Sedairi, the chairman of the kingdom's Civil Service Bureau, said that 3,620 "qualified" Saudi women were currently on a waiting list for government jobs and that more than twenty thousand new jobs were available for women graduates "in different parts of the country."

61. In his unusual book *Desert Warrior* (New York: HarperCollins, 1995), Prince Khaled Bin Sultan created a memorable portrait of Princess Munira bint Abd al-Aziz Bin Jiluwi, his determined mother and the wife of Defense Minister Prince Sultan. Prince Khaled, cocommander of the allied forces during the Gulf war, described how Umm Khaled—in keeping with the Arab tradition of being referred to as the mother of one's first son—used to summon her car and demand to be driven past the Defense Ministry each night during the war after Scud missile attacks to ensure that the building, and her son, were intact. "I told her that it wasn't safe on the streets at night—that she might be hit by a Scud, but she ignored me," Khaled told me during an interview after the war. In his own book, the first ever written by a member of the House of Saud, Khaled acknowledged Umm Khaled's enormous influence over him, and one suspects, reading between the lines, within the family. Friends who wanted a favor, he said, frequently visited his mother first, knowing that if Princess Munira were to ask for something, "there is no way I could refuse her." (See p. 56.)

62. "Saudi Arabia: Silent Revolution," *The Economist*, February 4, 1995; see also "Riyadh Boasts Largest Number of Businesswomen in Kingdom," *Saudi Gazette*, June 9, 1995.

63. Interview, Joseph A. Kechichian, Rand Corporation, Washington, D.C., April 27, 1995.

64. "Ulema Submits Follow-Up Reform Document to King," *Al-Quds Al-'Arabi*, London, August 1, 1991; cited in Foreign Broadcast Information Service, NES-91-163, August 22, 1991, 22–26.

65. Judith Caesar, "Liberals and Conservatives Press Riyadh," *New York Times*, July 5, 1991.

66. Piscatori, "Ideological Politics," 62–63.

67. For example, Edward Mortimer notes in his book *Faith and Power* that because the Koran permitted but did not specifically recommend polygamy, Hanbali jurists, unlike experts from other schools, allowed a woman to stipulate in her wedding contract that her husband would not take a second wife.

68. For example, Sheikh Safar al Hawali, a leading dissident and dean of Islamic studies at Mecca's Umm al-Qura University, had previously appealed for the senior ulema's support in a fawning letter to the head of the Senior Ulema Council chairman, the "great scholar Bin Baz," as he called him. Private communication in Arabic to Sheikh Bin Baz. I am grateful to Fouad Ajami for sharing it with me.

69. When it was created in the late 1960s, the Ministry of Justice had no minister or employees and no effective power. Only after the mufti's death was his role as head of

judges, and, in effect, his own supreme court, merged into the Ministry of Justice. A new minister with authority, Muhammad al-Harkan, was also appointed at that time.

70. Joseph Kechichian, "Islamic Revivalism and Change in Saudi Arabia: Juhayman al-Utaybi's 'Letters' to the Saudi People," *Muslim World* 53 (January 1990); see also Mortimer, *Faith and Power*, 181.

71. The family, fearing loss of readers for the kingdom's publications, indirectly established newspapers, radio stations, and television channels in London that, though they were printed and broadcast in the kingdom, were exempted from the restrictions. Saudis point to such deft maneuvers as an indication of the family's political sophistication.

72. According to a Saudi political scientist who requested anonymity, an early example of the ulema's refusal to issue such "political" *fatwas* occurred under Kings Saud and Faisal when the then mufti wanted to issue a *fatwa* branding Egypt's Gamal Abdel Nasser an apostate for his murderous campaign against Egypt's Muslim Brotherhood. The mufti considered the Brethren good Muslims, but the family, reluctant to alienate Egypt, urged him not to issue the *fatwa*. When Nasser began supporting anti-Saudi revolutionaries in Yemen, the family itself asked Sheikh Muhammad Ibn Ibrahim for the *fatwa,* which he then refused to issue on grounds that such a *fatwa* would serve no religious purpose.

73. Mortimer, *Faith and Power*, 182. The same story was later picked up by American writers, among them Edward Said, the Palestinian-American professor who called Bin Baz a "crank" and erred in describing one of his rulings in the March 9, 1995, issue of the *London Review of Books*. Said wrote that Bin Baz had insisted that the world was flat, which, according to Prof. Werne Ende, at the University of Freiburg, a German expert on Bin Baz's *fatwas*, the sheikh never asserted.

74. Neither angels nor people, Bin Baz wrote, quoting a *hadith*, would "enter a house in which there is a dog or a picture." Though few Saudis owned dogs—at least not in the kingdom—Saudis were as fond as most people of displaying family photos on their home bookshelves and coffee tables. The government, too, used photos in its identity cards. So the 1981 *fatwa*, entitled "The Useful Reply to [the question regarding Islam's] Ruling on Photography" (Riyadh, fourth reprint, 1401/1981, in Arabic), was ignored. Bin Baz's deputy, Sheikh Uthaimine, disagreed with his superior and sanctioned photography. But whether or not there had been a dissenting view, the government probably would have ignored Bin Baz. A copy of the *fatwa* was translated by Khalid Duran. I am grateful to Prof. Ende for providing me with several of Bin Baz's *fatwas* and guidance on their interpretation.

75. My interpretation of the relationship between the Al Saud and the ulema is based largely on interviews with Saudi religious scholars, businessmen, and political analysts, virtually all of whom insisted on anonymity in discussing this ultrasensitive issue.

76. Judith Miller, *New York Times*, January 20, 1991. The *fatwa*, published in the Saudi, Arab-language paper *Al Muslimoon*, states: "In the name of God . . . the jihad taking place against the enemy of God Saddam, ruler of Iraq . . . is the legitimate jihad on the part of Muslims and those assisting them in this respect, for he has wrongly transgressed, committed aggression against, and invaded a peaceful country. Therefore it is obligatory to wage jihad against him on the part of the Islamic states to expel him unconditionally from Kuwait, to assist the oppressed, to restore justice, and to deter the oppressor, for Almighty God has commanded the same as well as his Prophet. . . ."

77. Massari described his torture in a telephone interview with me in May 1995 and earlier in a moving cassette, identifying Saud al-Shibrun as his own main tormentor and the official responsible for torturing numerous Saudi dissidents.

Massari, an intellectually impressive man, is obviously a controversial figure in Saudi Arabia. Saudi officials say that the American-educated physics professor embezzled more than $300,000 from the Denver branch of the Saudi Educational Mission, a government office, in the early 1980s. In typical Saudi style, the money that he had diverted to his personal account was quietly replaced by the Saudi embassy in Washington to avoid scandal, and no formal charges were ever filed against him. The Denver office was shut down and Massari was quietly brought back to the kingdom in the mid-1980s. He was then given what officials assumed would be an innocuous teaching post. Massari, an articulate critic, denies impropriety and notes that the Saudi government has consistently refused to provide written proof of its charges.

78. One report, published on March 31, 1995, for instance, accused Prince Bandar Bin Sultan, the Saudi ambassador to Washington, of having met secretly with the CIA at the embassy in London. The purpose of the meeting, the bulletin stated, was to work out the details of a deal in which the Al Saud would recognize Israel in exchange for American assistance in destroying the CDLR and in covering up "crimes committed by the Al Saud both domestically and internationally." The embassy in Washington called the report "ludicrous." At the time of the alleged London meeting, Prince Bandar was in Saudi Arabia, a fact confirmed by several Saudis who had met or dined with him during his visit.

A subsequent bulletin asserted that the U.S. ambassador to Saudi Arabia, Ray Mabus, had ordered King Fahd to resign. Such meetings, the CDLR stated, reflected the "new unholy conspiracy between Al Saud, the Americans and the Zionists."

The CDLR also publicly accused Prince Sultan, the defense minister, of sexual misconduct. Saudi citizens detest public discussions of sexuality and other matters deemed intensely private. Saudi officials never comment on any such charges.

In addition, the CDLR's unrelenting hostility toward the United States, Israel, and the West has made many Western human-rights activists leery of the group. Many of its bulletins contain anti-Jewish and blatantly racist statements. One of its bulletins, for example, called the United Nations an instrument of "Jews and crusaders bent on exterminating the Muslims and confiscating their wealth."

The committee's popularity was further eroded by Dr. Massari's admission, in a telephone interview in May 1995, that he had once been a member of Hizb al-Tahrir al-Islami, the radical Islamic group now based in London that had openly endorsed terror and violence to overthrow "un-Islamic" regimes.

79. "Bin Baz Urges Muslims Not to Read Divisive Bulletins," *Arab News*, Jidda, November 12, 1994.

80. Reliable Saudi sources say that hundreds remain in jail for political crimes. The dissidents, they say, were tried and sentenced in secret by judges who were given special "bonuses" by the ruling family. Massari said in an interview that such payments were often made by the Al Saud to reward loyalty, and that they made a mockery of the judicial proceedings in Saudi eyes. A well-informed Saudi told me that a chief judge in Riyadh was given a bonus worth $4.5 million for his diligence in jailing the regime's opponents and that two associate judges also received bonuses.

81. *Al-Muslimoon*, January 1995, translated by *Mideast Mirror*, London, January 19, 1995, 10–12.

82. *Mideast Mirror*, January 6, 1995, 21–22.

83. *Saudi Gazette*, Riyadh, June 1, 1995. It should be noted that crucifixion in Saudi Arabia's interpretation of Islamic law is inflicted after a criminal has been executed. After he has been killed — either by decapitation or shooting — his body is hung in a public square for a few hours as a deterrent. For Americans, such public displays may seem barbaric. But as an opponent of capital punishment in any form, I find it no more barbaric than electric chairs, gas chambers, or the latest, most "modern" technique, lethal injections by men who claim to be physicians.

84. According to a complaint filed in August 1991 by dissident Saudi ulema and conservatives, for example, the budget of the World Assembly of Muslim Youth, many

of whose young militants had opposed Riyadh's defense by American forces, fell to 5 million riyals from the 6 million it spent when it was founded fifteen years ago. The shrinkage was largely the result of the suspension of Saudi aid.

85. Richard P. Mitchell, *The Society of Muslim Brothers* (New York, Oxford: Oxford University Press, 1993), 241. The Brotherhood, for example, rejected in principle hereditary monarchy as well as the implementation of *hadud* punishments—such as amputations for theft—in a state where, according to Egyptian Sheikh Muhammad al-Ghazali, then a Brother in good standing, "the rulers swim in the gold stolen from the state treasury and the wealth of the people."

86. Roy, *The Failure of Political Islam*, 116–17. His account was confirmed by Egyptian and Saudi officials.

87. In retrospect, a well-placed Saudi official told me, the danger posed by the Muslim Brotherhood should have been obvious. Juhaiman al-Utaibi, for example, a leader of the Saudi Ikhwan who had stormed the Holy Mosque in Mecca in 1979, was a graduate of the Egyptian Ikhwan-dominated Medina University. Utaibi had deeply admired the Muslim Brotherhood movement, he told his interrogators, according to an official privy to the interrogation reports. Most of his coconspirators had also been active in Brotherhood branches in the kingdom or in other militant Islamic movements in their home countries—Yemen, Kuwait, Sudan, and, of course, Egypt. They had come to Saudi Arabia, many on scholarship, to study religion and law with these noted militant Egyptians. Contrary to many published reports, Utaibi was not a descendant of Wahhabi leader Ibn Abd al-Wahhab. Ironically, he came from the branch of the Utaiba tribe that had remained loyal to King Abdulaziz during his battle to suppress the Ikhwan in the late 1920s. So young Utaibi's attack on the Al Saud's stewardship of the kingdom surprised many Saudis. Militants like Utaibi routinely met and traded ideas in Mecca during the annual pilgrimage. While Utaibi was clearly influenced by Egypt's Muslim Brotherhood, Egypt's al-Jihad leaders were also apparently affected by their Saudi counterpart's thinking. American analyst Joseph Kechichian notes, for example, that Khaled al-Islambuli, President Sadat's assassin, had gotten a copy of "Seven Letters," the document in which Utaibi challenged the Saudi regime's Islamic credentials, from his brother Muhammad, who had visited Mecca in late 1979.

88. Interview with senior American official in April 1995. The assassination plot was also confirmed by Saudi officials.

89. Unreported in the press, for example, senior Saudi officials met with Israeli counterparts in Nicosia and elsewhere in the spring of 1995 and even before that permitted Saudi businessmen to travel to Israel on business. In 1991 the Saudis stopped enforcing the Arab League requirement that no visas be granted to visitors with Israeli stamps in their passports—more than a year before Jordan did. Senior Saudi officials held meetings in Riyadh for prominent American Jewish supporters of Israel and Arab-Israeli peace. Saudis lobbied their Syrian counterparts, urging them to come to terms with Israel and thus gain Washington's favor. In September 1994, at America's urging, the kingdom, along with its allies in the Gulf Cooperation Council, lifted the secondary economic boycott of Israel.

90. The equipment was eventually stored in neighboring Kuwait.

91. The freeze in Saudi-Jordanian relations did not thaw, despite repeated reconciliation efforts by Jordan, until August 1995, when King Hussein risked Saddam's wrath by welcoming Iraqi defector Lt. Gen. Hussein Kamel, Saddam's son-in-law, in Amman. King Hussein permitted Prince Turki al-Faisal, the Saudi intelligence chief, to grill Kamel and discuss ways of ousting Saddam during an unannounced visit. Soon after that, King Fahd invited King Hussein to Riyadh.

With respect to U.S.-Saudi relations, there were several more published causes of diplomatic friction. In April 1995, for example, the kingdom violated UN sanctions against Libya by allowing a Libyan plane carrying haj pilgrims to land on Saudi territory, servicing the plane, and permitting it to leave. Two weeks later, American officials confirmed that Riyadh had refused to permit American FBI agents to arrest on Saudi soil America's most wanted terrorist—a Lebanese Shiite leader of Hezbollah sought for more than a decade for his participation in the 1983 bombing of the American marine compound in Beirut in which 241 Americans died. Allowing the FBI to arrest a Shiite terrorist on Saudi soil would surely prompt terrorist retaliation against Saudis in Lebanon and throughout the Middle East, Saudis explained.

92. Kenneth Katzman, "How Stable Are Saudi Arabia and Kuwait?" *Middle East Quarterly*, September 1994.

93. It is widely rumored that when the issue of increases in public utility prices was pressed on the majlis by the king, a council member who was also on the board of an electrical company produced a list of major nonpaying users and advised the government to balance its books by collecting the overdue charges. The nonpaying consumers, it turned out, were government agencies, certain royal family members, and their entourages. While the member's advice was ignored, he succeeded in blocking the council's approval of the surcharges. A few months later, the government began collecting the overdue fees.

94. In fact, Saudi succession calls for Prince Abdullah to follow King Fahd, and then Sultan. But many Saudis believe that if King Fahd continues to rule for some time, succession is likely to skip to Prince Salman, who is more widely respected than the enormously wealthy Sultan, or possibly skip the remaining generation of Al Saud to one of King Abdulaziz's grandsons.

95. The depth of the financial problem first became widely known when *The New York Times* published two front-page stories in the summer of 1993 concluding that Riyadh was engaging in overspending, huge military purchases, and irregular banking practices. Predictably, the Saudi press condemned the articles and similar expressions of American concern. Typically, a Saudi-owned newspaper in London asserted that the "ongoing campaign against the Saudi economy" reflected President Clinton's decision to hand over economic policy, as he had foreign policy, to America's Jews. See "Past and Anticipated Reasons Behind the Campaign Against the Saudi Economy," *Al-Hayat*, London, translated by *Mideast Mirror*, January 23, 1995. *Al-Hayat* is owned by Prince Khaled Bin Sultan, the former cocommander of the Gulf war forces and son of the defense minister.

96. Bandar Bin Sultan, "Challenges to Security in Southwest Asia" (speech delivered in Tampa, Florida, May 20, 1993).

97. Fouad Ajami, the scholar, notes that only for a brief historical moment had Saudi-Arab tensions abated. After the humiliating, Egyptian-led Arab defeat by Israel in 1967 and the explosion of wealth in Arabia in the early 1970s, the same Mohammed Heikal who had propagandized for Nasser proclaimed the dawn of the "Saudi era." If radical nationalism had been the ideological pillar of the now defunct Nasserite order, Islam was its replacement, he maintained. But Heikal's Saudi era did not last long. Riyadh shunned Cairo after Sadat broke Arab ranks and made a separate peace with Israel. See Ajami, *Arab Predicament*, 171.

98. King Fahd's brother-in law, for example, owns the fastest-growing Arabic satellite station. Almost 90 percent of the media, ostensibly run by Lebanese, Egyptian, and other Arab nationals, is Saudi owned and dedicated to serving the Saudi political agenda.

99. Youssef Ibrahim, *New York Times*, June 29, 1992.

Sudan

1. A detailed description of such abuses is contained in *Children of Sudan: Slaves, Street Children, and Child Soldiers* (New York: Human Rights Watch, 1995).

2. *Sudan: A Country Study*, Foreign Area Studies, American University, ed. Harold D. Nelson, Secretary of the Army (Washington, D.C.: U.S. Government Printing Office, 1982), 4.

3. Ibid., 8.

4. Bernard Lewis, *Race and Slavery in the Middle East* (New York: Oxford University Press, 1992), 9.

5. Alan Moorehead, *The White Nile* (New York: Vintage Books, 1983), 79–80.

6. Cited in Edward Hoagland, *African Calliope* (New York: Random House, 1989), 165.

7. The most vivid descriptions of the Mahdi and his rule are those of the several Europeans he held hostage, all but one of whom survived by "converting" to Islam and becoming slaves to the Mahdi or his caliph, Abdullahi. See, for example, Charles Neufeld, *A Prisoner of the Khaleefa* (New York: Putnam, 1899); Father Joseph Ohrwalder, *Ten Years Captivity in the Mahdi's Camp, 1882–1892*, trans. F. R. Wingate (London: Sampson Low, 1892); Sir Rudolf Carl Slatin, *Fire and Sword in the Sudan, 1879–1895*, trans. Maj. F. R. Wingate (London: E. Arnold, 1896); *Colonel Gordon in Central Africa, 1874–1879* (from original letters and documents), ed. George Birkbeck Hill (London: Thos. De La Rue & Co., 1881); and Charles G. Gordon, *General Gordon's Khartoum Journal*, ed. Lord Elton (New York: Vanguard Press, 1956).

For contemporary accounts of the Mahdiya, see Wilfrid Scawen Blunt, *My Diaries*, part 1 (1880–1900) (New York: Knopf, 1922), *Secret History of the English Occupation of Egypt* (New York: Knopf, 1922), and *Gordon at Khartoum* (New York: Stephen Swift, 1911); Winston S. Churchill, *The River War* (London: Eyre & Spottiswoode, 1899); Earl of Cromer, *Modern Egypt*, 2 vols. (New York: Macmillan, 1908); Carl Christian Giegler Pasha, *The Sudan Memoirs of Carl Christian Giegler Pasha, 1873–1883*, ed. Richard Hill (London: Oxford University Press, 1984); Ernest N. Bennett, *The Downfall of the Dervishes* (London: Methuen, 1898); F. R. Wingate, *Mahdiism and the Egyptian Sudan* (London: Macmillan, 1891).

See also secondhand accounts based on the original material: Richard A. Bermann, *The Mahdi of Allah* (New York: Macmillan, 1932); Byron Farwell, *Prisoners of the Mahdi* (New York: Harper & Row, 1967). Finally, for superb scholarly works, see P. M. Holt, *A Modern History of the Sudan* (New York: Grove Press, 1961), and *The Mahdist State in the Sudan, 1881–1898* (London: Oxford University Press, 1958).

8. Farwell, *Prisoners of the Mahdi*, 100.

9. Other estimates put the death toll at 4 million.

10. Bennett, *Downfall of the Dervishes*, 106.

11. Hoagland, *African Calliope*, 78–79, 160.

12. Alexander S. Cudsi, "Islam and Politics in the Sudan," in *Islam in the Political Process*, ed. James P. Piscatori (Cambridge, Eng.: Cambridge University Press, 1983), 45.

13. Interview with Abdullahi An-Naim, director of Human Rights Watch/Africa, New York, June 1994.

14. Interview with Turabi, June 1994, and confirmed by Mohammed Khalil, an opponent now in exile, who was a member of Turabi's committee.

15. Mansour Khalid, *Nimeiri and the Revolution of Dis-May* (New York: Routledge & Kegan Paul, 1985), 271.

16. Some analysts argue that Nimeiri's imposition of sharia triggered the war's renewal, but Col. John Garang, leader of the SPLA, had already declared an end to the truce between north and south three months before Nimeiri unveiled his Islamic code.

There is no doubt, however, that the imposition of Islamic law severely inflamed the southern rebellion and caused Christians and animists to flock to Garang's ranks in record numbers.

17. Interview, December 1984. A similar assertion is contained in Mansour Khalid's *Nimeiri and the Revolution of Dis-May*, cited in an article by Alex de Waal, codirector of Africa Rights, "Turabi's Muslim Brothers: Theocracy in Sudan," *Covert Action* (Summer 1994). Mansour Khalid, who now lives in Nairobi, had served as Nimeiri's foreign minister before becoming disaffected with his regime.

18. Shortly before the coup, Sudan's $9 billion national debt was roughly equal to the gross national product; Sudanese were flocking to Khartoum and overseas in search of jobs as never before. An estimated 1 to 2 million were working overseas, most in Gulf states, among them ten thousand teachers and four thousand of the five thousand doctors who had been trained in the previous decade.

19. For a detailed description of Aissa's punishment and his case, see David Lamb, "Decisive Justice," *Los Angeles Times*, April 19, 1985, and Christopher Dickey, "Sudan's Harsh Law," *Washington Post*, April 22, 1985. Lamb and Dickey conducted the first interviews with Aissa.

20. Among the crimes alleged by Sadiq al-Mahdi, among other Sudanese luminaries, was Nimeiri's "collaboration" with Israel in "Operation Moses" — Israel's secret airlift of some ten thousand Ethiopian Jewish refugees from Khartoum to Tel Aviv between November 1984 and January 1985, when Sudan was still technically in a state of war with the Jewish state. Sadiq had accused Nimeiri of "high treason" for this and for having recognized the Camp David peace treaty.

21. After independence in 1956, Sudan enjoyed only a year of democracy and civilian rule before Gen. Ibrahim Abboud, the army's chief of staff, overthrew the parliamentary government in the first of many coups d'état. But Abboud was no more able to solve Sudan's crushing economic problems or balance its factional interests than the preceding government had been. Strikes, protests, and riots forced him out in 1964, but the civilian coalitions that followed were also unable to overcome a stagnant economy and the political rivalries that had destroyed Sudan's first experiment in democracy. Another burst of popular resentment in 1969 had brought Nimeiri to power.

22. By mid-1995, draft evasion was endemic in the Sudan. The *Saudi Gazette* reported (June 6, 1995) that Sudanese defense minister Hasan Abdel Rahman Ali told Parliament that only eighty-nine people had shown up in response to letters to some ten thousand Sudanese ordering them to report for training. For the past two years the military had been attempting to conscript all males between the ages of eighteen and thirty-three — some 2.5 million men — for a mandatory two-year stint in the military. But so far, only 26,079 men had registered.

23. United Nations, No. E/CN.4/1994/48, February 1, 1994. Response by Sudan: "Letter Dated 22 February, 1994 from the Permanent Representative of the Sudan to the United Nations Addressed to the Secretary-General," Comments of Ali Mohamed Osman Yassin, No. A/49/82, February 24, 1994.

24. Neil Henry, *Washington Post*, May 24, 1990.

25. "Islam, Democracy, the State and the West" (Round Table with Dr. Hassan Turabi, ed. Arthur L. Lowrie, World and Islam Studies Enterprise, May 10, 1992, Florida), 94.

26. In April 1990, a senior State Department official told a skeptical Senate committee that while the Bashir government was supported by "one wing" of the Islamic fundamentalist movement in Sudan, "we do not believe it is correct to say that this is a National Islamic Front government."

27. State Department officials said that the addition of Sudan to the terrorist list was related not to the New York bombing plots but to other intelligence information linking Khartoum to terrorist plots to harm Americans and American interests in Sudan.

28. Farwell, *Prisoners of the Mahdi*, 11.

29. Favored methods, according to the State Department's 1993 annual report on human-rights abuses, include "whipping and clubbing; shackling and suspension by the wrists; the application of electric shocks; burning with hot irons; submersion in hot and cold water; prolonged blindfolding; denial of food, water, sleep, and access to toilet facilities; confinement in overcrowded and unsanitary quarters; and in the case of some female prisoners, sexual abuse." The 1991 report blamed the government—as well as southern rebels—for "the kicking of ribs or kidneys, binding of hands for long periods, blindfolding for days at a time, immersion of hands in boiling water, suspension from ceiling fans, and psychological torture, such as mock executions."

30. "Situation of Human Rights in the Sudan" (interim report prepared by Gaspar Biro, Special Rapporteur of the Commission on Human Rights, as submitted to the General Assembly, New York, November 18, 1993) and a final report, February 1, 1994.

31. "Letter Dated 22 February 1994."

32. Despite their public criticism of the regime in Khartoum, however, both Egypt and Saudi Arabia resisted an effort in mid-1995 to expel Sudan from the International Monetary Fund, which, in the unlikely event that it had succeeded, would have financially crippled the Islamic regime. Egypt's stance reflects a long-standing reluctance to be blamed for undermining Arab "solidarity" by helping to destroy a "brotherly" Arab government, even a rogue state like Sudan. While the Gama'a Islamiya, Egypt's Islamic Group, claimed credit for the failed assassination attempt against Mubarak and denied Sudanese complicity, American officials confirmed that Mubarak's assailants had come from Sudan to Addis Ababa and that two of them were headed back to Khartoum when they were apprehended by the Ethiopian authorities.

33. In the summer of 1994, for instance, Uganda intercepted a shipment of Sudanese arms destined for rebels trying to overthrow the government, according to American officials.

34. Lewis, *Race and Slavery*, 53.

35. Abdelwahab El-Affendi, *Turabi's Revolution* (London: Grey Seal, 1991), 148.

36. Abdelwahab El-Affendi, *Who Needs an Islamic State?* (London: Grey Seal, 1991), and *Turabi's Revolution*, 87–88.

37. This was El-Affendi's version of events. Another comes from Gaafar Idris, an early Muslim Brotherhood leader and ideologist who now lives in Virginia. The Sudanese Brotherhood, he told me, had always been fairly independent of the Cairo organization, so Turabi's "break" was not as dramatic as his champions portrayed it. He also attributed the dispute within the Ikhwan to efforts by Turabi to transform the Muslim Brotherhood from a democratically structured group into one that he could dominate. It was, at heart, a personality dispute, Idris said. "Many of us did not trust Turabi. We felt he was not honest, that he was not truly committed to an Islamic state, that what he really wanted was power." Hard-core Ikhwanis like Idris suspected that Turabi's desire to broaden the Islamic Front to include Umma Party members and others who were only vaguely Islamic was the result of a then secret alliance with his brother-in-law Sadiq al-Mahdi, in whose house Turabi and his wife then lived. They feared that Turabi was trying to neutralize the fledgling Brotherhood as a potential challenger to the Umma, the religiously based party with the broadest appeal that Sadiq headed.

Idris also resented Turabi for changing the Brotherhood's traditional structure. Under the old structure, Brotherhood chapters throughout the country elected representatives to a biannual Congress, which included some three hundred to four hundred members. The Congress then elected a *shura*, or consultative or parliamentary group of sixty people, who, in turn, elected an executive committee of ten members, of which Idris himself had been one. The executive committee elected the national leader. But through a series of parliamentary maneuvers, Turabi reversed the process: The Shura Council elected the leader, who then hand-picked his executive council. Later on, Turabi won approval of another change: The Congress itself would elect the national leader. Since Turabi was a dynamic orator and far better known than most Brotherhood members, these ostensibly procedural changes helped him solidify control of the group.

"Being 'liberal' in religious doctrine did not make you a 'liberal' in politics," Idris concluded. "Some of us wanted more than simply for Islam to be in power; we wanted Islam to succeed."

38. Nathan Gardels, "The Islamic Awakening's Second Wave," interview with Hassan al-Turabi, *New Perspectives Quarterly*, California (Summer 1992). In this article, for instance, Turabi tried to rationalize the N.I.F. government's poor performance, its corruption and abuses of human rights.

When Turabi testified that same year on Capitol Hill, he justified his government's suppression of traditional political parties and any whiff of secular dissent by arguing that the Sudan's traditional parties were little more than ethnic and tribal groupings. Hence, he said, elections were not truly "representative." Yes, he told a magazine editor, the Sudan had detained a few political prisoners, but his impoverished country was fighting for its life because of the civil war and the millions of people who had flooded into the cities to escape war and the famine-ravaged countryside. Sudan was not yet Islam's "ultimate model," he conceded, but this "Islamic state-in-progress" needed to protect itself through measures above and beyond the "ordinary due process of law." Likening Sudan to the United States during World War II, he noted that even Americans had "imprisoned nationals of Japanese descent" during the state of emergency. There might have been some instances of torture soon after the 1989 coup, he acknowledged. But these "transitional features" arose from the tension of "an old order dying and a new one being born."

Asked about the abysmal human-rights record of Iran, Sudan's Islamic ally, Turabi argued that Islam had come to power there through a revolution and hence was a violent and peculiar case. "There were a few excesses," he admitted. "But the Iranian revolution compares reasonably well to the French or Russian examples." And revolution would be the fundamentalists' only resort if other means of securing power were blocked, he warned.

39. "Islam, Democracy, the State and the West," 24.

40. Although the article had not identified Turabi's son by name, all of Sudan had guessed that the anonymous "son" of the "powerful" man in the N.I.F. was Essam, the second eldest son of Turabi's six children by his wife Wassal, Sadiq al-Mahdi's sister.

41. Sudanese journalists had told me a different story. The editor, Mahgoub Erwa, once a senior N.I.F. member, had become disenchanted with N.I.F. rule, they said. In the spring of 1994 he had published a series of articles exposing corruption within the regime. Subjects that had only been whispered about — unauthorized foreign-exchange dealings by the Central Bank, the withholding of medical assistance from Darfur and other needy provinces, the expropriation of cars donated for food aid by the World Bank by army officers and N.I.F. officials, the sale of the country's telephone network at bargain prices to "private" businessmen who just happened to be N.I.F. members — were suddenly front-page articles in a paper long associated with the Brotherhood. The government shut down the paper in April and arrested Erwa as he returned from Saudi Arabia. The "Saudi agent" story stemmed from his efforts to secure Saudi permission to publish his newspaper in the kingdom, where more than a million Sudanese now worked. Erwa's "crime" was to have written a letter to the Saudi Ministry of Information stating that his newspaper was "independent" and another letter in which he told the Saudis that he was critical of the regime, whose factional disputes he described in considerable detail.

42. Ehud Ya'ari, *New York Times* editorial page, January 28, 1993; Judith Miller, *New York Times*, February 17, 1993.

43. Donald Petterson, the U.S. ambassador to Khartoum who delivered what he called the "non-message" or "talking points" to General Bashir and Turabi, confirmed Turabi's description of its contents as well as Turabi's "very angry, very emotional" response to the warning. Though the message did not contain a specific threat of military action against Khartoum, Petterson said in an interview, it did not rule out military action if Americans were hurt in Sudan or as a result of Sudanese-sponsored terrorism abroad. The message, officials in Washington said, was delivered in the fall of 1993, not long after Washington received specific intelligence information that Sudanese agents were planning an action, which, if carried out, would have harmed American officials. In response, Washington ordered the evacuation of all government dependents in the country, drew down the embassy personnel by half, and ordered Petterson to deliver the warning to Bashir and Turabi. In August 1992, Sudanese security forces had seized four Sudanese employees of the U.S. Agency for International Development, along with UN personnel, at a compound in Juba. Sudan subsequently acknowledged that two of the American officials had been killed; the other two have never been seen again. According to Petterson, the U.S. government strongly protested the arrests and executions and says there is evidence that the officials were tortured. In June 1995 the United States rejected the nomination of El Fatih Irwa as Sudan's ambassador to Washington because he had ordered dozens of southern Sudanese killed in early 1992, among them, it believes, the two American government employees.

44. Neufeld, *Prisoner of the Khaleefa*, 137.

ALGERIA

1. See "Algeria Human Rights Practices, 1994," U.S. Department of State, Washington, D.C., February 1995.

2. See "Algeria: Repression and Violence Must End," Amnesty International, New York, October 25, 1994. Also "Human Rights Abuses in Algeria: No One Is Spared," Middle East Watch, U.S.A., January 1994.

3. Abderrahmane Meziane Cherif, minister of interior, speech in Skikda, March 23, 1995, Arabic and French, BBC Summary of World Broadcasts, March 25, 1995. The minister claimed that militants had destroyed more than six hundred schools, but Eric Goldstein, an expert on Algeria at Human Rights Watch, the private human-rights group, said this figure, like so many touted by both sides in the savage conflict, was exaggerated.

4. The Algerian government insisted that the prisoners at Serkadji Prison were killed, along with four guards, only after they took guards hostage in an attempted prison breakout. But human-rights monitors remain skeptical about the government's claims. Such doubts are evident in a joint letter to Algerian president Liamine Zeroual from the American groups Human Rights Watch, the Lawyers Committee for Human Rights, and Physicians for Human Rights. The letter, sent in March 1995, expresses "grave concern" about the disturbances in Serkadji and the "subsequent failure of Algerian authorities to answer some important questions surrounding those events." Specifically, the letter cites the "shockingly high number of fatalities," which is viewed, along with the government's refusal to discuss the affair, as a prima facie indication that "vastly disproportionate force was used by security forces in confronting the prisoners." The groups offered to conduct an "independent investigation" of the incident but have received no response from the Algerian authorities.

5. Alexis de Tocqueville, *Voyages en Angleterre, Irlande, Suisse et Algérie*, Tome V, Oeuvres Complètes (Paris: Gallimard, 1958), 191–217. Author's translation.

6. Raphael Danziger, *Abd al-Qadir and the Algerians* (London: Holmes & Meier, 1977), 14–25.

7. John P. Entelis, *Algeria: The Revolution Institutionalized* (Boulder, Colo.: Westview Press, 1986), 19.

8. Alistair Horne, A *Savage War of Peace: Algeria, 1954–1962* (London: Penguin Books, 1985), 29.

9. John Ruedy, the historian and expert on Algeria, says that between 1830 and 1871 there was only one year — 1861 — in which France did not confront major military resistance in some part of Algeria. Cited in "Continuities and Discontinuities in the Algerian Confrontation with Imperialism," paper prepared for a symposium on "Islamism and Secularism in North Africa," Georgetown University, Washington, D.C., April 1–2, 1993, and later incorporated into *Islamism and Secularism in North Africa* (New York: St. Martin's Press, 1994), an excellent collection of essays edited by him.

10. William B. Quandt, *Revolution and Political Leadership: Algeria, 1954–68* (Cambridge, Mass.: M.I.T. Press, 1969), 5.

11. Horne, *Savage War*, 61.

12. Like his fundamentalist counterparts in Egypt and other Arab states, Ben Badis had been influenced by the great nineteenth-century Muslim reformer Jamal Afghani and his Egyptian disciple Muhammad Abdu, the Egyptian Salafi and reformer. Abdu, in fact, had visited Algeria in 1903 and had deeply impressed Algerian Muslims.

13. The Algerian Muslim nation, he wrote, "is not France; it is not possible that it be France; it does not want to become France, and even if it wished, it could not become France." Cited in Horne, *Savage War*, 41.

14. The group was the Association of Algerian Ulema.

15. Ruedy, *Islamism and Secularism*, 76.

16. Ibid., 77.

17. For an account of Ben Badis, see Ali Merad, *Le Réformisme musulman en Algérie de 1925 à 1940* (Paris: Mouton, 1967).

18. The group he'd led in 1927 was the Paris-based *Etoile Nord-Africaine*, the North African Star, and in 1937 a successor mass-based group called *Parti Progressiste Algérien*. This, too, was banned and reformed in 1954 as the *Mouvement pour le Triomphe des Libertés Democratiques*.

19. Entelis, *Algeria*, 49, and Ruedy, *Islamism and Secularism*, 9.

20. Quandt, *Revolution*, 14–15.

21. According to Quandt's perceptive, still highly relevant book, this debilitating pattern persisted long after the French left Algeria. Algerian "revolutionaries," symbolized by Ahmed Ben Bella, the country's first president, were replaced by the "military," even tougher men whose leader was Houari Boumédienne, the general who overthrew Ben Bella in a 1965 military coup after the latter failed to inspire public confidence. Finally, "intellectuals," or what today we call socialist "technocrats," backed by the military, of course, came to the fore and have continued to dominate Algerian politics.

22. Abderrazak Chentouf, cited in Quandt, *Revolution*, 265, and Horne, *Savage War*, 50.

23. Ruedy, *Islamism and Secularism*, 78. Ruedy notes, for example, that within FLN military cells, genders were strictly separated. Persons caught in illicit sexual encounters were sometimes executed. Prayers were routinely performed, and the Ramadan fast was vigorously enforced.

24. A spiritual leader of this tendency was Sheikh Abdel Latif Soltani, who became disenchanted with reform after his experience with the state-sanctioned Al-Qiyam. After violent student protests at the University of Algiers, Soltani was placed under house arrest. His funeral in 1984 turned into a demonstration against the state that attracted several thousand people.

25. Severine Labat, "Islamism and Islamists: The Emergence of New Types of Politico-Religious Militants," in Ruedy, *Islamism and Secularism*, 103–23. Ms. Labat, a

young French scholar, is widely regarded as one of the most knowledgeable experts on the Algerian Islamists.

26. Entelis, *Algeria*, 81.

27. Historian John Entelis, who did research in Algiers in the 1970s, recalls that Boumédienne imported as many as twenty thousand Egyptian schoolteachers, many of them Muslim Brethren, who were already teaching in Algerian schools during his work there.

28. Interview, Hussein Amin (an Egyptian diplomat in Algiers in the late 1980s), May 1995.

29. Five interviews (in Arabic) with Rabah Kebir, president of the FIS Executive Committee Abroad, Al-Wassat, June 14, June 21, June 28, July 5, July 12, by Jamal Khashoggi, a Saudi journalist and expert on militant Islamic groups. Translation by L. Abu-Odeh.

30. Abderrahmane Bensid, "Democratization in the Arab World." Speech delivered at the 25th Anniversary Convention of the Association of Arab American University Graduates, Washington, D.C., November 14, 1992.

31. Francis Ghiles, "Algeria: A Time for Boldness — The Economy," *Financial Times*, January 28, 1991. This is but one of Ghiles's meticulous articles on Algeria, a country he knows perhaps better than any other English-speaking journalist.

32. Fouad Ajami, "The Battle of Algiers: A Referendum on the Postcolonial State," *New Republic*, July 9, 1990.

33. The delegation of Islamists whom Chadli received on October 10, 1988, included, among others, Abbassi Madani, Ali Benhadj, Mohamed Sahnoun, and Mafoudh Nahnah. The group presented a list of grievances. See M. Al-Ahnaf, B. Botiveau, and F. Fregosi, *L'Algérie par ses Islamistes* (Paris: Karthala, 1991), 312. This volume and an earlier one, *Les frères et la mosquée*, by Ahmed Rouadjia (Paris: Karthala, 1990), both in French, are indispensable in understanding the development of Algeria's modern Islamic movement. They have not been translated into English. The translations are mine.

34. According to a former senior Algerian official, President Chadli was meeting with his advisers in 1990 when he was told that the erratic Libyan leader was circling the capital in his private plane and requesting permission to land. Chadli, accustomed to such bizarre behavior from his neighbor, agreed, and Qaddafi soon joined Chadli and his men. "Qaddafi was in quite a state," the official recalled. The Libyan leader had learned of Chadli's decision to recognize the FIS and permit the Islamic party to compete in elections. He argued heatedly that such a decision would threaten not only Algeria's political stability but all of North Africa's. "We all dismissed him as crazy," the adviser recalled. "But in retrospect, Qaddafi may well have been mad, but he was not wrong about the consequences of the course Chadli had chosen." After the coup, Qaddafi continued helping the military against the Islamists. Both his and Egypt's security forces have given Algeria advice and assistance.

35. Roberts noted in an interview that, unlike the Egyptian government, which was unable to respond to the massive earthquake in Cairo because of the president's absence, the Algerian government was capable of offering such relief but refrained from doing so. As evidence, he cites the sustained, highly effective relief effort mounted by the government in the aftermath of previous earthquakes.

36. Saudi Arabia, at least before the Gulf war, had endorsed Chadli's decision to try to coexist with the Islamist FIS. According to Hussein Amin, King Fahd himself had fostered "reconciliation" between the FLN and the FIS by inviting Abbassi Madani, the FIS coleader who was then a guest in the kingdom, to his own meeting with Chadli at Jidda airport. While Hussein Amin is an ardent foe of the FIS, the story was confirmed by diplomatic sources in Algiers and in Paris.

37. Algerians, like their French colonizers, were sticklers for law. Only fully

constructed mosques were technically subject to government regulation. So Islamists exploited the technicality by leaving new mosques unfinished, thus evading government supervision. Several ministers had urged Chadli to stop this practice, but according to interviews with leading officials, Chadli ignored them.

38. John Entelis, an American expert on Algeria, said in an interview, for example, that "in retrospect," both Chadli and Abbassi Madani, an FIS leader, had "what they perceived to be congruent interests."

39. The fifteen-point *"Plate-forme"* published by the FIS (*El-Mounqid*, no. 16) mentioned the need for economic reform only once. Specifically, the platform called for the "urgent need to end the worrying increase in unemployment, the emigration of skilled workers and the resulting loss of know-how and the stupefying spread of criminality in all forms" (author's translation). M. Al-Ahnaf et al., *L'Algérie*, 49–50.

40. Interview with Sheikh Hachemi Sahnouni, Algiers, February 1993. According to Sahnouni, a blind thirty-five-year-old imam in Algiers who was among the original FIS founders, he and Benhadj had discussed calling the group the Front Islamique Uni, the FIU, or the United Islamic Front. It was Abbassi who insisted on including the term "salvation" in the title, which resulted in the "FIS" abbreviation.

41. Hugh Roberts, "From Radical Mission to Equivocal Ambition: The Expansion and Manipulation of Algerian Islamism, 1979–1992," in *Accounting for Fundamentalisms*, eds. Martin E. Marty and R. Scott Appleby (Chicago: University of Chicago Press, 1994), 428–29.

42. M. Al-Ahnaf et al., *L'Algérie*, 71, 72, and Kim Murphy, "Islam Fundamentalism Sweeps Over Algeria Like Desert Wind," *Los Angeles Times*, June 16, 1990.

43. The following analysis and quotations from Benhadj's cassettes come from Emmanuel Sivan, the Israeli scholar and expert on Islam, who has analyzed the political philosophy of militant Islamists as expressed in the cassettes of thirty of the region's leading militant preachers. Sivan's thesis is that what these men tell their parishioners is different from what they tell foreigners and more reflective of their real views. See Emmanuel Sivan, "Eavesdropping on Radical Islam," *Middle East Quarterly* 2, no. 1 (March 1995): 13–24. I am grateful to Professor Sivan for discussing his guidance on Islamic history and theology.

44. M. Al-Ahnaf et al., *L'Algérie*, 70.

45. Sivan, "Radical Islam," 17. Sivan notes that Benhadj, like most Islamists, attributed the despotism of Arab regimes not to Islamic or Arab history and tradition but to their adoption of imported "isms" — socialism, communism, atheism. Efforts by Egypt and other Arab countries to save their illegitimate governments by attracting Western tourism and investment, as Sadat had tried through his *infitah*, his economic liberalization, had resulted in "a further loss of self-confidence and even looser morality." According to Benhadj, Algeria's FLN combined the worst aspects of Nasser's and Sadat's rule — political despotism, economic anarchy, and subservience to the West.

46. Pierre Devoluy and Mireille Duteil, *La Poudrière Algérienne* (Paris: Calmann-Levy, 1994). In their account of the coup, the senior official sent to recruit Boudiaf was Ali Haroun. In addition, Sid Ahmed Ghozali, the French-educated technocrat who became prime minister, told me in a 1993 interview that he had also secretly gone to Morocco to persuade Boudiaf to return.

47. For example, voting districts in rural areas, where FLN bosses still exercised control and patronage, had as many seats as the FIS strongholds, the overcrowded cities in which 75 percent of Algerians lived.

48. This account, provided by a senior government official and confirmed in part by interviews with other officials, is further supported by Hugh Roberts, who reports that prior to the strike, Abbassi and Chadli's aides had agreed on the public squares that the FIS would be permitted to occupy during its protest. See Roberts, *Fundamentalisms*, 469.

49. Surveys conducted by the government showed that the FIS would probably win between 23 and 34 percent of the vote, officials said.

50. Roberts, *Fundamentalisms*, 429. Roberts argues that FLN notables in many parts of the country, disaffected from their own party, deliberately refused to mobilize FLN votes and in some districts even mobilized votes for the FIS.

51. A public reference to the FIS's willingness to let Chadli stay on as president provided he implement the Islamists' agenda can be found in a news conference with Hachani in December 1991 that was carried on Algerian television and radio. According to a chronology of key events in the crisis prepared by the FIS, Hachani stressed the need for "cooperation and solidarity between all the sons of the this [sic] Muslim people, in a climate of brotherhood, a climate of love, in order to take the country out of its various crises in the framework of Islamic principles." Hachani also stated that if there were "firm guarantees" that Parliament and the government would be able to implement their program, "then the FIS consultative council could re-examine the question of calling for early presidential elections." The FIS document also states that on January 6, 1992, "sources at the Presidency" denied reports in the local press that President Chadli had received Sheikh Hachani or "any other FIS member." See "Democracy Hijacked: A Chronological Account of the Betrayal of Democracy in Algeria," in English, 16 pp. (no place or date of publication).

52. Horne, *Savage War*, 537–38.

53. See Saadi Nouredine, *La femme et la loi en Algérie* (Casablanca: U.N.U.-Wider, Éditions Le Frennec, 1991).

54. Frantz Fanon, *A Dying Colonialism*, trans. Haakon Chevalier (New York: Grove Press, 1967).

55. Peter R. Knauss, "Algerian Women Since Independence," in *State and Society in Algeria*, eds. John P. Entelis and Phillip C. Naylor (Boulder, Colo.: Westview Press, 1992), 151–90.

56. Susan Slyomovics, "Hassiba Ben Bouali, If You Could See Our Algeria," *Middle East Report*, Washington, D.C., no. 192 (January–February 1995): 8–18.

57. Such suspicions were reinforced by a government inquiry into the assassination that strongly suggested that Boudiaf was killed as the result of a conspiracy involving government officials. The six-member commission, several of whom were friends of the late president, concluded that Lembarek Boumaarafi, a twenty-six-year-old second lieutenant charged with the crime, "did not act alone," that he did not have "the profile of a kamikaze," and that the "complicity of Islamic fundamentalists in the murder is far from evident."

In fact, several commission members believed, as did many of my colleagues in the press, that the army conspired in Boudiaf's murder, suspecting that he might crack down on corruption that sustained many in this privileged sector. See *The New York Times*'s account of the commission report, which was never published in full, by Youssef Ibrahim, July 28, 1992.

58. The FIS issued several statements denying involvement in this murder as well as a subsequent "criminal" bombing at Algiers airport in which nine Algerians were killed and more than 128 wounded. See, for example, Communiqué No. 1, *Front Islamique du Salut*, signed by Rabah Kebir, spokesman of the FIS, October 11, 1992. While the FIS stood to gain from the death of Boudiaf—which eliminated the last of Algeria's historic, charismatic FLN founders—the FIS was eager to distance itself from such events that it feared would diminish its popularity.

59. Among them were two traditional leaders of the Islamic community—Sheikh Mahfoud Nahnah, who has ties to the Egyptian Muslim Brotherhood, and Sheikh Abdallah Djaballah, a lawyer by training. In interviews, Sheikh Nahnah, who, in December 1990, formed his own group called Hamas (no relation to the Palestinian rejectionists in the West Bank and Gaza), told me that he never approved of the FIS's operating style

or its tactics, that he, in fact, favored the creation of a pluralist, democratic Islamic state in stages, through legal and nonviolent means. Nahnah took a much more neutral stance than the FIS during the Gulf war, which may account in part for its lack of success at the polls. In addition, many hardline Islamists hated Nahnah, accusing him of having given the police information about the whereabouts of Mustafa Bouyali, the Islamic warrior, which enabled the police in 1987 to ambush and kill him.

Djaballah, who had also formed a group called Nahda, opposed the government's liberal reforms and its privatization at the expense of the public sector, attempting to stake out his own turf on the left of the Islamic movement.

Many analysts believe that both men were motivated partly by personal ambition. Each a leading Islamic figure in his own right, neither sheikh wanted a lesser status than that of Abbassi Madani, who was not a formally trained "alim," or the young, radical preacher Ali Benhadj, who lacked Islamic stature and had not been trained in a great Muslim center. Personal rivalries were probably just as important a factor in their decisions to reject the FIS as political considerations.

60. According to Severine Labat, the "cradle" of Djaz'ara was the Central Faculty of Algiers University, where, in 1968, French-speaking students founded a mosque and began publishing a review. They were quickly joined by Arabic-speaking Islamic activists. In 1973, after a fire in the mosque, Islamists and leftists fought each other at the Central Faculty. As tension mounted, the government closed the mosque. Three leading Islamists, including Abbassi Madani, organized a protest and issued in November 1982 a fourteen-point petition calling for concessions to Islam — the Arabization of education, banning alcohol, segregation of classes by gender, and the like. The "fourteen points" are considered a benchmark in the growth of the Islamic movement.

61. Gueshi asserts, and other FIS founders confirmed in interviews, that Ali Benhadj pushed Abbassi toward an ever more pro-Saddam stance. Gueshi, hostile to Iraq's secular regime, wanted the FIS to remain neutral. Whatever the case, Abbassi's ardent rhetorical support for Saddam Hussein soured his ties to the Saudi government. Saudi businessmen, however, continued their support of Abbassi and the FIS. In fact, according to a senior Arab official, a wealthy Saudi car importer had paid more than a million dollars in legal fees for Abbassi's defense after his arrest.

62. Abbassi was denounced by three leading FIS majlis members — Sheikh Ahmed Merani, who called his behavior "dictatorial"; Sheikh Hachemi Sahnouni, who told me that the strike was "the real end of the FIS"; and Bechir Fkih. All three men said in interviews that they considered the strike the turning point of their movement but also the moment in which they first understood Abbassi's "authoritarian" tendencies. Each man, curiously, also expressed continued goodwill toward Ali Benhadj, who has been portrayed in most press accounts as far more militant and unyielding than Abbassi.

63. In his letter of resignation, dated May 19, 1990 — a copy of which he shared with me — Gueshi said he was resigning for "health, personal, and other reasons." The "other" reasons, he told me, were his view that the FIS's stance during the Gulf war was "an abortion" of Islamic ideals and the strike "suicidal." The letter itself makes no explicit reference to these views.

64. Among those whose FIS membership was "frozen" by the Batna conference were two men who later became leading fighters in the Armed Islamic Group, the militants who have carried out many of the most violent Islamist attacks in Algeria and, starting in 1995, in Paris.

65. In June 1992 the government charged Abbassi Madani's sons with having formed this group. But most foreign experts are dubious about this claim and argue that Fidèles au Serment did little but issue communiqués.

66. Its leader, Mansouri Meliani, who was eventually caught and tried for his attacks, confessed to having formed the GIA in the summer of 1991. Having admitted his group's responsibility for the attack on the Admiralty, he was convicted and executed.

The identity of those responsible for the deadly attack in the Place des Martyrs has never been established.

67. Yossef Bodansky, "Algeria, Under Pressure from Iranian-Backed Extremist Groups, Faces Government Collapse," *Defense & Foreign Affairs Strategic Policy*, August 31, 1994.

68. The other groups are the Shawiyas of eastern Algeria, the Mozabites, and the Tuareg nomads of the south in the Algerian Sahara. Scholar John Entelis notes that these subcultures have little in common with one another except that their dialects are derived from a common root. Since Algerian Arabs and Berbers are descendants of the same tribal peoples, however, they do not represent rigid, or exclusive, ethnic blocs. See Entelis, *Algeria*, 4–5.

69. In January 1995, the FFS was one of seven Algerian opposition parties that met in Rome and joined the FIS in signing a platform that called for dialogue, democracy, and a negotiated end to the bloody civil strife. The government denounced the effort, but many Western diplomats hoped that the Rome platform, as it became known, might have served as the starting point for a dialogue between the military and the Islamists.

70. Khaled Bouzeraa was killed in February 1995 in the uprising at Serkadji Prison in Algiers, according to Selima Ghezali. In an interview in October 1995, Selima told me that three of her former students were among the dead in the prison revolt.

71. Hugh Roberts, the English expert on Algeria, argues that this is a misleading division. The army, he maintains, is really divided between "nationalists," officers who favor true independence from France, and officers who are "pro-French." Most, but not all, of the *éradicateurs* are pro-French, having been trained by and having served in the French army. But Zeroual is said to be a "nationalist" as well as a *réconciliateur*. Roberts maintains that his strength is growing within the military, which makes him somewhat more optimistic than other analysts that a negotiated settlement is possible. If one accepts his characterization of the split within the military, then the current struggle can also legitimately be seen to some extent as an extension of the FLN's war for independence against the French.

72. Michael Field, *Inside the Arab World* (London: John Murray, 1994), 142.

73. Haddam is also the nephew of the former rector of the Paris Mosque in France, one of the five men who served on the High State Council created by the military after the coup as civilian window dressing for military rule. Haddam has never been willing to discuss his family with journalists.

74. In an interview in Arabic and French in 1993, Kebir refused to be pinned down on what or who constituted a legitimate target of the Islamists' jihad against the state. Pressed as to whether it was "legitimate" to kill intellectuals and other civilians who were not involved in the political struggle, Kebir replied: "We support jihad by all means against the powers that be *(le pouvoir)*. We know this diminishes our popular support, but we have no choice." Kebir also stated that despite the appearance of chaos and lack of coordination among Islamic groups, different groups were still acting in a coordinated fashion. "There is still an Islamic front," he said.

75. "Human Rights Abuses in Algeria: No One Is Spared," Middle East Watch, U.S.A., January 1994, 58. U.S. officials apparently concluded in early 1995 that Haddam was not, in fact, a moderate and stopped their dialogue with him. But Washington has continued informal contacts with other FIS representatives in the United States and abroad. One official told me that the Clinton administration wanted the dialogue to continue in case the FIS eventually succeeded in coming to power and also in order to protect the several hundred American citizens in Algeria. Several government officials noted that so far even the GIA has not targeted Americans, as it has the French and other foreigners in Algeria.

76. After the unexpected FIS landslide in December 1991, several prominent FIS

leaders vowed to transform Algerian society, changing not only how Algerians dressed but what they ate for dinner. They also began saying more openly that democracy had to be subordinated to sharia. Such statements led many secular Algerians to support the military coup they might have otherwise opposed.

LIBYA

1. John L. Esposito, *The Islamic Threat: Myth or Reality?* (New York: Oxford University Press, 1992), 80. Esposito also asserted that the *Green Book* "heralded a universal, revolutionary ideology . . . for the creation of a new political and social order — a third alternative to the two great modern options of capitalism and Marxism." Qaddafi, he wrote in 1992, long after Qaddafi's support for repression at home and support for international terrorism abroad were well documented, was the Middle East's Mao Zedong, an "innovative" leader who had "boldly" challenged his society's conservatism and traditional Islam (see pp. 81 and 83).

2. Mohammed Heikal, *The Road to Ramadan* (London: Collins, 1975).

3. Ruth First, *Libya: The Elusive Revolution* (New York: Africana Publishing Company, 1975), 35. Ms. First was a Marxist South African scholar who visited the country several times soon after Qaddafi took over. An outspoken critic of the South African regime, she was murdered, allegedly by South African agents, several years ago. Her book remains invaluable in understanding Qaddafi's rule.

4. Majid Khadduri, *Modern Libya: A Study in Political Development* (Baltimore, Md.: Johns Hopkins University Press, 1963), v.

5. John L. Wright, *Libya: A Modern History* (Baltimore, Md.: Johns Hopkins University Press, 1982), 12.

6. A mystical movement that arose early in Islam's history in response to disappointment with the Umayyad caliphs and their increasingly rigid ulema, the religious scholars, Sufis were the Islamic counterpart of the "ascetic and monastic tradition within Christianity." See Marshall G. S. Hodgson, *The Venture of Islam*, vol. 1 (Chicago: University of Chicago Press, 1974), 238, 393–409.

7. For a closer look at the Sanusi origins and credo, see E. E. Evans-Pritchard, *The Sanusi of Cyrenaica* (Oxford: Clarendon Press, 1949); Nicola A. Ziadeh, *Sanusiyah* (Leiden: E. J. Brill, 1958); Edward Mortimer, *Faith and Power* (New York: Vintage, 1982).

8. Wright, *Libya*, 13.

9. Ibid., 21.

10. In 1883, Sayyid al-Mahdi, the Grand Sanusi's son and then head of the order, sent a representative to Sudan at the Mahdi's invitation to meet the man who claimed to be the fulfillment of Islam's prophecies. The envoy arrived in El Obeid, a town that the Mahdi's dervishes had just captured after a lengthy siege. What he found appalled him: children, servants, and slaves who had been tortured into revealing the hiding places of family treasures; men hacked to death by dervish swords; houses razed for spite. The envoy quickly returned to his native land without even attempting to see the self-declared Mahdi. Whoever had sanctioned such purposeless slaughter could not possibly be the expected one, he was said to have told the Sanusi chief. Though many of Sayyid al-Mahdi's followers believed that their chief was, in fact, the true Mahdi, Sayyid al-Mahdi repeatedly denied this and emphasized his view — as opposed to that of the Wahhabis and Sudan's self-proclaimed "Mahdi" — that Islam had to be spread and reformed "through peaceful means and not bloodshed." The only legitimate jihad, in other words, was defensive. See Mortimer, *Faith and Power*, 75.

11. The Frenchman was Gentil Lamotte. Cited in John K. Cooley, *Libyan Sandstorm* (New York: Holt, Rinehart and Winston, 1982), 29.

12. Wright, *Libya*, 42.

13. Cooley, 34.

14. Dirk Vandewalle, "Libya: The Unfinished Revolution, Part Two: Creating a Kingdom" (Institute of Current World Affairs, DJV-31, Hanover, New Hampshire, September 1989). According to Vandewalle, by the end of the struggle, 80–90 percent of all the province's livestock had been killed, and the desert oases, with their complex irrigation systems and delicate palm groves, obliterated.

Vandewalle, who teaches at Dartmouth, was kind enough to share with me this and other "Letters to Peter" published by the institute during his research for the institute in Libya between 1986 and 1988. They paint a vivid portrait of Libyan life.

15. Lisa Anderson, "Qaddafi's Islam," in *Voices of Resurgent Islam*, ed. John Esposito (Oxford: Oxford University Press, 1983), 134–49. This excellent article traces the evolution of Qaddafi's use of Islam for political legitimacy.

16. Wright, *Libya*, 38, 43. Freya Stark, the British writer and Arabist who visited Benghazi soon after World War II, was appalled by the "family phalanxes" of colonial Italians strolling at leisure after work who had managed to obliterate "the raucous Arab voice of the Levant." Beneath the surface of "this gay little town," she felt "a deadening substratum of fear." See *The Coast of Incense* (London: John Murray, 1953), 162. Also cited in First, *Revolution*, 56.

17. Vandewalle, "Creating a Kingdom."

18. Anderson, "Islam," 137.

19. Dirk Vandewalle, interview, April 1994.

20. Qaddafi's coup changed not only how Libya was ruled but by whom. One scholar described his rebellion as the "oases and the interior" against the traditional, powerful families of the coast and the dominant tribes of the interior, a coup made by the country's "second-class" citizens, the "children of nomads or lowly cultivators" — children like Qaddafi — who had gone to military academy, as they had in Egypt and Syria, for want of better opportunities. See First, *Revolution*, 115.

21. The withdrawal agreements were negotiated under the monarchy.

22. Anderson, "Islam," 140.

23. Interview with Lisa Anderson.

24. Cited in First, *Revolution*, 135.

25. In an interview in August 1995, Lisa Anderson, a scholar and expert on Qaddafi's Islam, said: "The Sanusi tradition enabled Qaddafi to be more creative in his interpretations of Islam than orthodox Islamic tradition would have permitted him to be." Thanks to the Sanusi legacy, she said, "a self-confidence in religious interpretation persists that is peculiar to Libya."

26. For an excellent analysis of the regime's laws and approach to Islam, see Ann Elizabeth Mayer, "In Search of Sacred Law: The Meandering Course of Qaddafi's Legal Policy," in *Qadhafi's Libya, 1969–1994*, ed. Dirk Vandewalle (New York: St. Martin's Press, 1995).

27. Ibid.

28. Anderson, "Islam," 142.

29. First, *Revolution*, 138.

30. Anderson, "Islam," 143.

31. Mortimer, *Faith and Power*, 281.

32. Mayer, "Sacred Law."

33. Anderson, "Islam," 145.

34. "Gadaffi Turns His Pipedream into Reality," *Financial Times*, London, August 29, 1991.

35. Qaddafi speech, Al-Khadra Square, Tripoli, marking the eighth anniversary of "Revenge Day," the day of eviction of Italians from Libya, October 7, 1978.

36. Schuler's account is not supported by most other Libya experts. Dirk Vande-

walle, among many others, argues that the CIA never had such grandiose hopes or schemes in mind for Qaddafi.

37. Gerald F. Seib and Robert S. Greenberger, *Wall Street Journal*, May 1992.

38. Seymour Hersh, "Exposing the Libyan Link," *New York Times Magazine*, June 21, 1981. Wilson is currently in a high-security prison after being convicted in connection with his Libyan activities in an American court. As of late 1995, Terpil was in Cuba.

39. David Blundy and Andrew Lycett, *Qaddafi and the Libyan Revolution* (London: Weidenfeld and Nicolson, 1987), 151.

40. Estimates of Libyan funding for terrorist operations vary wildly. The lowest estimate comes from John Wright, whose *Libya: A Modern History* reports that Qaddafi contributed a total of about $250 million to terrorist groups. Israel estimated the contribution in an intelligence document at about $1 billion. Blundy and Lycett, in their *Qaddafi and the Libyan Revolution*, concluded that "the truth probably lies somewhere between these last two figures." The U.S. State Department estimated in 1985, the year before the American raid, that Libya had given $100 million in that year alone to terrorist groups. Maj. Abdel-Salam Jalloud, Qaddafi's second in command, boasted in 1990 that Libya spent 22 percent of its national income, or more than $1 billion a year, on support for national "liberation" movements. This boast, however, like most official Libyan statements, cannot be taken at face value.

41. First, *Revolution*, 155.

42. Qaddafi asserted that Libya had spent this amount on arms in a speech given in November 1992. Several experts and diplomats who had covered Libya said it was a reasonable estimate.

43. Qaddafi's first marriage, to the daughter of a well-to-do Libyan businessman, who had resisted the union of his daughter with the then provincial, ill-educated soldier with seemingly so few prospects, did not last long.

44. Muammar Al Qathafi, *Green Book*, World Center for the Study and Research of the Green Book (Tripoli: Jamahiriya, no date of publication), 93, 94, 98. Mayer notes that Article 20 of Qaddafi's Great Green Charter of Human Rights, approved by the Parliament in 1988, requires women to breast-feed and provide for their children's early care at home. In addition to omitting any reference to women's equality, the charter also fails to provide for "freedom of conscience or religion," according to Mayer, and contains no right of peaceful assembly, no freedom of expression or association, no prohibition of torture, no guarantee against arbitrary arrest and detention, and no presumption of innocence for an accused or right of appeal.

45. See, for example, Mayer, "Sacred Law."

46. David Shipler, *New York Times*, April 12, 1987.

47. George Lardner, Jr., and John M. Goshko, *Washington Post*, February 27, 1992.

48. Kim Murphy, *Los Angeles Times*, September 15, 1991.

49. Interviews, American and Arab officials.

50. Foreign Minister Omar Montasser told me in an interview in the fall of 1994 in New York that more than $500 million a year of oil revenue was now being distributed directly to Libyans, as Qaddafi had ordered. Montasser also asserted that the River Project made "economic sense."

51. "Leader's Dialogue with the Experts of Economy, Oil, and Solar Energy," article from *Al-Fajr Al-Jadid*, Zahra Office for Legal Translation, Tripoli, March 11, 1993 (Proceedings of meeting held February 28, 1993).

52. Mayer, "Sacred Law."

53. Judith Miller, *International Herald Tribune*, April 16, 1973, and *New Republic*, May 31, 1993.

54. The trip itself was financed not by Fellah or Qaddafi but by Yaacov Nimrodi,

an Israeli arms merchant and occasional business partner of Adnan Khashoggi, a Saudi financier and businessman who was also promoting Libyan-Western rapprochement.

55. America, Dirk Vandewalle had argued, paraphrasing an Arabic proverb, had "put on boxing gloves to milk an ant."

LEBANON

1. Mahmoud Darweesh, *Sand and Other Poems* (London: KPI, 1986).

2. Vivid, conflicting descriptions of Bashir Gemayel are contained in two excellent books about Lebanon's civil war. *Going All the Way*, Jonathan C. Randal's passionate account of the war, contains a highly negative portrait of Bashir (New York: Vintage Books, paperback ed., 1994), 1–5, 11–12, 115–18, 141–42. For a more enthusiastic portrayal, see David Kimche, the former director general of the Israeli Foreign Ministry, *The Last Option: After Nasser, Arafat, and Saddam Hussein* (New York: Charles Scribner's Sons, 1991), 125–83.

3. Thomas L. Friedman, *From Beirut to Jerusalem* (New York: Anchor Books, 1990).

4. See by Kamal Salibi, among others: *Modern History of Lebanon* (London: Weidenfeld and Nicolson, 1965), and also *A House of Many Mansions* (Berkeley: University of California Press, 1988).

5. Salibi, *Lebanon*, 80, 106. Regarding Druze casualties, Salibi notes that the Druze had also lost "a number of dead," but, he adds, "otherwise their triumph had been amazing."

6. T. G. Appleton, *Syrian Sunshine* (Boston: Roberts Brothers, 1877), preface, 261.

7. The famine inspired a young Lebanese Christian immigrant in New York, Khalil Gibran, to compose an emotional poem on behalf of his beleaguered countrymen: "My people died of hunger," he wrote, "and he who did not perish from starvation was butchered with the sword; . . . They perished from hunger in a land rich with milk and honey. They died because the monsters of Hell arose and destroyed all that their fields grew. . . . They died because the vipers and the Sons of vipers spat out poison into the space where the Holy Cedars and the roses and the jasmine breathe their fragrance." Gibran, then unknown, went on to become the world-famous writer of *The Prophet*, a popular inspirational best-seller. Khalil Gibran, *The Treasured Writings of Khalil Gibran* (New York: Castle Books, 1981).

8. By the 1940s, Emil Edde, Lebanon's president between 1936 and 1941, was so worried about the impending Muslim majority in Lebanon that he tried to persuade Zionist leaders to incorporate southern Lebanon and its mostly Shiite Muslim population into its own national homeland, an offer Weizmann graciously but insistently refused. See Itamar Rabinovich, *The War for Lebanon, 1970–1985* (Ithaca: Cornell University Press, 1985), 22.

More than a decade after the Arab-Israeli war in 1967, Camille Chamoun, Lebanon's Christian president, warned Israel's Prime Minister Menachem Begin not to make the mistake "we made in the Lebanon," namely, annexing territories that were heavily populated by Muslims. See Kimche, *Last Option*, 125.

9. Israel, in fact, faced precisely the same trade-off after 1967, when the resounding Arab defeat more than doubled territory under Israeli rule. While most Israelis were initially delirious at the thought of controlling so much land, Abba Eban, the Israeli statesman, had offered Lebanon as a cautionary tale. More land would invariably come at the cost of communal solidarity and homogeneity. After 1967, Israel decided not to annex much of the West Bank partly because it feared the consequences of incorporating so many non-Jewish Palestinians into Israel; and in 1993, Israel decided to discard the

land — and its troublesome inhabitants — partly to maintain a Jewish majority within Israel as well as to secure peace with the Arabs.

10. Fouad Ajami, *The Arab Predicament* (New York: Cambridge University Press, 1992), 192.

11. In addition, the Lebanese Parliament and all public offices agreed to respect an unwritten rule that there should be six Christian posts for every five posts for Muslims.

12. The distribution of power was based on a census conducted in 1932. Christians refused to permit the Census Bureau (headed, of course, by a Maronite) to carry out another after that. Such a reckoning would have undoubtedly revealed that Lebanon's Christian population was already shrinking and that the Muslims, especially the traditionally underrepresented Shiites, were rapidly growing.

13. The Palestinians were themselves something of a "biting gift" from the Arabs to weak, quarrelsome Lebanon. In 1969 the Arab League had met in Cairo and forced the Lebanese government to accept the PLO, which wanted to use Lebanon as a base for its struggle against Israel. King Hussein of Jordan, who was preparing to move against the PLO in his own country, wanted a dumping ground for his unwanted, troublesome Palestinians. And Egypt's President Nasser was searching for another, non-Egyptian venue from which to continue his war against the Jews. Lebanon, despite its reservations, was to be that battlefield.

14. Fouad Ajami and Eli Reed, *Beirut, City of Regrets* (New York: Norton, 1988), 31. See also Fouad Ajami, *The Vanished Imam: Musa al Sadr and the Shia of Lebanon* (Ithaca: Cornell University Press, 1986).

15. Ibid., 146.

16. There had been seventy attacks or attempted attacks in which five Israelis had been killed and twenty-two injured since September 4, when Israel had redeployed its forces from the Shuf Mountains near Beirut to positions along the Awali River in the south.

17. Clinton Bailey, "Lebanon's Shiites After the 1982 War," Tel Aviv University, December 1984, 18. For a prescient account of the rise of the Shia in Lebanon as a result of the civil war, see Fouad Ajami, "Lebanon: The Prospects," *Foreign Affairs*, Spring 1985.

18. Saudi Arabia's special envoy to the Taif peace negotiations was Rafic Hariri, who was then still living in Riyadh. According to one of his aides, Hariri paid the hotel bills in Paris of Lebanese delegates to the Taif conference who had been forced to flee Lebanon after signing the controversial accords in 1989 that had officially ended the war. "Few could afford to spend months in Paris until the threats against them in Lebanon subsided," the Hariri adviser told me. "So he helped them out." What Hariri's aides call charity could not have hurt when he sought their support to become prime minister three years later.

19. I am indebted to Jamil Mroue, a Lebanese journalist who has returned to Beirut to publish a new newspaper, for the term and many insights into his complicated country.

20. David Ignatius, "The Vanished Imam: Musa al-Sadr and the Shia of Lebanon," *Atlantic Monthly*, June 1986.

21. After Hezbollah had repeatedly shelled Israeli kibbutzim in northern Israel, Israel had bombed the south for seven days — the most intensive attack since its 1982 invasion. The goal of Operation Accountability was to pressure the Lebanese government and its Syrian patrons into disarming Hezbollah or, at the very least, to stop them from firing Katyusha rockets into Israel. The offensive, which, according to foreign journalists, killed fewer than 10 Hezbollah fighters, left at least 127 Lebanese civilians dead, 500 wounded, and an estimated 150,000 residents of the south displaced. Journalists who traveled south with the Lebanese army heard firsthand the Shiites' complaints about the arrogant young Hezbollah militiamen who were making their lives miserable.

22. For an account of the struggle between them, see Julie Flint's "Construction Companies Wage Battle for Influence in Lebanon," *Guardian* (London), August 7, 1993, and reporting by Marie Colvin of the *Times* (London).

23. Holy War Construction was well prepared for its mission. Established in 1987, the office had grown out of a car-bomb attack in October 1985 on a Beirut mosque that had killed more than a hundred and devastated two blocks of apartments. The goal of the attack, a Saudi-financed operation that used rogue CIA-trained Lebanese, was to kill Sheikh Fadlallah, who was not in the mosque when the bomb went off. Neither the CIA nor the U.S. government has ever acknowledged a role in the deadly operation. But for a persuasive discussion of the CIA's involvement in the disastrous car-bomb attack, see Bob Woodward's account in *Veil* (New York: Simon & Schuster, 1987), 396–98.

24. When President Assad's son Basil was killed in a car crash in early 1994, for example, Lebanese politicians of all religions competed to display their grief in supplication to Damascus. Lebanon declared a national day of mourning; radio stations switched to classical music and Koranic verses; the Lebanese Parliament closed for five days. Politicians lauded the fallen "martyr." In fact, most Lebanese politicians couldn't stand Assad or his horse-loving yuppie son.

25. Seeking foreign support in domestic quarrels, after all, was as old as Lebanon itself; no, older. I was reminded of an ancient Lebanese prince of Byblos, Rib-Addi, who, in 1370 B.C., had begged Amenhotep IV of Egypt to send forty archers to help him defend his city against an attack by his brother. "Beneath the feet of the king, my Lord, seven times, and seven times I fall," the prince had pleaded in time-honored groveling. "Let the king hear the words of his servant . . . and let the king not restrain himself at the deed of this dog [Rib-Addi's brother]. Let my lord know that I would die for him." James B. Pritchard, ed., *Ancient Near Eastern Texts (Relating to the Old Testament)* (Princeton, N.J.: Princeton University Press, 1969), 483–90. I am indebted to Jamil Mroue for calling my attention to the letters.

26. Wilbur Crane Eveland, a former CIA agent, wrote in his book *Ropes of Sand* (London and New York: W. W. Norton and Company, 1980) that the agency had paid $25,000 in campaign expenses to help get Charles Malik, Habib's father, elected to Parliament in the late 1950s. My colleague John Randal also had little use for Malik, whom he dismissed as "more Maronite than the Maronites when it came to obstinacy." But many Christians continued to see Habib's father as a philosopher-politician who represented the best in Western values and traditions.

27. Other similarities abound. The Jews were those whom God had "chosen"; the Maronites were Pope Leo's "rose among the thorns." Both had an implicit mission. Zion had its "law of return," the right of anyone of Jewish blood to come back to the land his ancestors had inhabited thousands of years ago; the Maronites dreamed of a spiritual return to a pre-Arab, pre-Islamic time in which the Phoenicians, the non-Arab cosmopolitan traders and seafarers, had ruled the land. Some also envisaged a physical return: A Maronite patriarch in the early 1900s had urged France to create in Lebanon, according to Fouad Ajami, a "refuge for all the Christians of the Orient." Ajami and Reed, *Beirut, City of Regrets*, 19.

28. Two key officials of the Jewish Agency, the organization that prepared the ground in Palestine for Israel's birth in 1948, had met throughout the 1930s with leading Maronites. These Zionists were Eliahu Sasson, a Damascus-born Jew and onetime supporter of Arab nationalism, and Eliahu Elath, a Russian Jew who eventually became a prominent Israeli diplomat and president of Hebrew University.

Their diaries contain many references to Maronite enthusiasm about the creation of a Jewish state. Elath, for example, met often with Emil Edde, the Maronite aristocrat who was Lebanon's president between 1936 and 1941. The Zionists and their wish for a Jewish homeland were "natural allies of Christian Lebanon," Elath quoted Edde as saying, and would be "quite helpful in liberating Christian Lebanon" from its deplorable dependence on Syria and the Arab world. "We found in him the notion that a Jewish state would offer natural protection for Lebanon in that it would help prevent the absorption of Lebanon into Greater Syria," the then popular goal among many Lebanese Sunni Muslims, Elath wrote. Lebanon, Edde had said, was a "Christian island in this Islamic sea." Beirut was like "the cities of southern France" where one felt "thousands of miles from Damascus." Edde wanted to ensure that Mount Lebanon remained "a fortress" for the Maronites and that Maronites would always be "the synthesis of Hellenic thought" in the region. He had described the Christian group, Phoenician Youth, as "the Zionists of Lebanon" and had told Elath that he wanted Maronites throughout the world to "dream of return to Lebanon."

Elath also recorded the "emotional meeting" in Paris in 1937 between Edde and Chaim Weizmann, the Zionist leader, soon after Britain's Peel Commission had recommended that Palestine be partitioned and a Jewish homeland created. Edde had congratulated Weizmann on the "historic decision," the prospective restoration of "the Jewish people to their homeland which they had lost two thousand years ago." Weizmann in response had called Edde a "true friend, a loyal friend," adding that the "friendship between Lebanon and a Jewish state was a way of ensuring that Western culture would have a natural base in the Middle East."

Bishara al Khoury, the Maronite who became Lebanon's first president after independence in 1943, had gone further. According to a prophetic entry in Sasson's diary, Khoury had urged the Jewish Agency to help him remove an "obstacle" and "danger to both our countries" — the Shiite Muslims of Jabal Amil, the Shia stronghold in what is now southern Lebanon. During the Arab Revolt against British occupation and Jewish immigration to Palestine between 1936 and 1939, Khoury told Sasson, the Shia had smuggled men and weapons into Palestine to help the vehemently anti-Zionist Mufti of Jerusalem. Khoury suggested that the Jewish Agency lend the Maronite Patriarch "a substantial sum" so that Maronites in America could be settled in Jabal Amil. The Shia could then be expelled so there would be "common borders between Christian Lebanon and Jewish Palestine."

In 1937, Elath sailed from Alexandria to Venice on the same ship as the then patriarch, Antoine Arida. Under pressure for having praised the Jews in a Beirut synagogue as "brothers in destiny," Arida told Elath that he was determined to continue contacts with Zionists, provided, of course, they were discreet. While he wanted to avoid giving Muslims more "ammunition" against Christians, the patriarch remained committed to everything that would "sabotage Islamic and Arab goals," Elath reported.

Despite the patriarch's emphasis on discretion, the history of Zionist-Maronite contacts became intellectual "ammunition" for Lebanon's Muslims some fifty years later during the civil war. Until then the diaries of Sasson and Elath were available in Hebrew. Excerpts from them were first published in Arabic in Beirut in 1982, translated by Badr al-Haj, a scholar who apparently sought to brand the Christians as historic traitors to the Arab cause, as the title of his book suggests: *The Historic Roots of the Zionist Project in Lebanon.* The book, only available in Arabic, was published in Beirut by Dar Masbah al-Fikr in 1982. The scholar relies heavily on the Sasson and Elath diaries in Hebrew. I am grateful to Fouad Ajami for translating portions of this work for me.

29. Randal, *Going All the Way.* See also Kimche, *Last Option*, 130–31. According to Kimche, a former director general of Israel's Foreign Ministry and former Mossad agent, two schools of thought prevailed in Israel regarding relations with Lebanon's Christians. Israeli founders like Ben-Gurion and Moshe Dayan believed that "Israel should support any minority in the Middle East," preferring a region comprised of "different peoples and religions rather than a Sunni Arab region in which Israel herself would be an isolated minority." But others, such as Prime Minister Moshe Sharett, maintained that Israel "would have to make her peace and learn to live with the Sunni Muslim Arabs and not with a mixed multitude of minorities."

Menachem Begin was deeply moved in 1975, Kimche argues, when Israeli embassies abroad were suddenly deluged with Lebanese Christian requests for arms, training, and help in its civil war two years before Sadat made his historic visit to Jerusalem. In the atmosphere of "near-hermetic isolation" in which Israel had existed since its creation, "such pleas for help from neighbors were little short of intoxicating," Kimche observed.

30. Farid Al-Khazen, "Kamal Jumblatt, the Uncrowned Druse Prince of the Left," *Middle Eastern Studies* 24 (April 1988): 178–206.

31. Called Druze after Muhammad ibn Ismail al-Darazi, a founder of the sect who had preached in Syria, members of this secret cult were driven out by the Muslims and sought refuge from religious persecution in Mount Lebanon, like the Christian Maronites. Because the Druze had sided with the Muslims against the first Crusader invasion in Syria, these clannish mountain peasants were trusted by the Sunni establishment in Istanbul and selected to rule Mount Lebanon in its name.

32. Al-Khazen, "Kamal Jumblatt," 191. I am indebted to Farid Al-Khazen for many insights not only about the Druze but Lebanon's confessionalism.

33. There are two vivid descriptions of the Shia from nineteenth-century British travelers. David Urquhart called the Metuali, as the Shia were then known, an "unclassifiable" race, "hated by the Persians as Arab, and by the Turks and Arabs as Shiites." Centuries of persecution had bred into them, he wrote, "dignity of manners, and pride of descent with ferocity and lawlessness of disposition." See David Urquhart, *The Lebanon (Mount Souria): A History and a Diary* (London: Thomas Cautley Newby, 1860), 135.

A harsher appraisal came from Gertrude Bell, the British Arabist who eventually helped British colonialists draw the lines in the sand that became the Middle East's modern boundaries. During one of her trips to Baalbek in the early 1900s, a Shiite resident of what was then Syria had tried to steal Kurt, Ms. Bell's beloved dog. Kurt was eventually recovered, but the "regrettable occurrence" provoked a searing indictment of all Shia: "I have, therefore, the pleasure to record that the Metawileh are as dishonest a sect as rumour would have them to be," she wrote in her 1907 travel memoir. However, she added happily, "their machinations can be brought to nought by vigilant Christians." Gertrude Lowthian Bell, *Syria: The Desert and the Sown* (London: Heinemann, 1907), 168.

34. Ajami, "Lebanon: The Prospects."

35. An excellent profile of Abbas Musawi is Martin Kramer's article in the *New Republic*, "Musawi's Game: The Hezbollah's Late Leader," March 23, 1992.

36. Obeid, who was thirty years old when Israelis kidnapped him from his home, had also been a member of Hezbollah's ruling *shura* council and had helped guide its military campaign against Israel and its proxy, the thousand-man-strong South Lebanese Army. According to Israeli intelligence officials, Lt. Col. William Higgins, an American and a senior UN officer who was abducted in early 1988 and subsequently killed, was initially held prisoner in Sheikh Obeid's house.

37. Among the dead were Mohammed Saad, a Shiite radical from Amal, and Khalil Jaradi, of Hezbollah. For an account of the bombing, see Ihsan Hijazi, "Blast in Lebanon Kills 15 in Mosque," *New York Times*, March 5, 1985.

38. I am indebted to Mike Wallace, Lowell Bergman, and Don Hewitt of CBS's *60 Minutes* for sharing with me the transcript of Wallace's interviews with Musawi and other Hezbollah leaders in January 1994. Segments of the interviews, but not this part, appeared in the *60 Minutes* broadcast of January 16, 1994.

39. The head of Amal, Nabih Berri, had decided that Amal should join a coalition of Lebanese leaders created to deal with the repercussions of Israel's invasion. Musawi, an early, fervent advocate of the Ayatollah Khomeini's hard line, had opposed Amal's participation and sought Teheran's mediation. When Berri joined the coalition anyway, Musawi resigned from Amal and set up his rival group, "Islamic" Amal, which,

as its name implied, was to mobilize and fight according to "Islamic principles." Although Musawi and most Muslims were allergic to the splits and disunity that had historically weakened Arabs and Muslims, Berri's decision to join the coalition had forced his hand, Musawi told me. For the coalition included Bashir Gemayel, the Christian Phalangist leader and Israel's ally. Amal had betrayed Islam when it had joined forces with the likes of Bashir, Musawi asserted.

40. For an excellent analysis of the various radical Islamic groups founded during the Lebanon war, see Marius Deeb's "Militant Islamic Movements in Lebanon: Origins, Social Basis, and Ideology," Georgetown University's Center for Contemporary Arab Studies, Occasional Papers Series, Washington, D.C., November 1986. See also As'ad Abukhalil's article, "Ideology and Practice of Hizballah in Lebanon," *Middle Eastern Studies* (July 1991). Both papers cite an article in Arabic by Sharif Al-Husayni in *Ash-Shira*, Beirut, March 17, 1986, based in large part on information supplied by Hezbollah's leaders.

The structure of Islamic Amal has long been in dispute. Musawi told me in our interview that although the groups still maintained separate *shura* councils, Islamic Amal now operated independently of Hezbollah only in the realm of information.

41. Martin Kramer, "The Oracle of Hizbullah: Sayyid Muhammad Husayn Fadlallah," in the forthcoming *Spokesmen for the Despised: Fundamentalist Leaders of the Middle East*, ed. R. Scott Appleby (Chicago: University of Chicago Press, 1996).

42. "Some say we are Muslim Lebanese. No!" Musawi had told an Iranian journal in 1986. "We are Muslims of the world and we have close links with other Muslims of the world." Lebanon, Sheikh Fadlallah had said a year earlier, "was created by great powers in artificial borders as the result of a political deal." The citations are found in an excellent discussion of Hezbollah's shift in views contained in Kramer's chapter on Sheikh Fadlallah in the *Fundamentalism* series, and in an earlier work, "Hezbollah's Vision of the West," Washington Institute, Policy Papers, no. 16, Washington, D.C., 1989, 26–27.

43. Kramer, "The Oracle."

44. Syria, after all, was ruled by Alawites, a despised heretical minority long dependent on Sunni Muslim acquiescence within Syria. Syrian Alawites and Lebanese Shiites had long been mutually sympathetic to the other's historical marginality. In 1973, Lebanon's Musa Sadr had shrewdly embraced the neighboring Alawites as allies and won President Assad's patronage by issuing a *fatwa* designating the Alawites as "honorary" Shia. This was a rather important favor to Hafiz al-Assad: The Syrian constitution required that Syria's president be a Muslim. And until Musa Sadr's ruling, few in Syria considered Alawites Muslim. See Ajami, *Vanished Imam*, 174. A similar version of this, from a Syrian standpoint, appears in Patrick Seale, *Asad* (Berkeley: University of California Press, 1989), 173.

45. While Assad found Hezbollah's war against Israel useful, he feared the possibility of broader Shia encirclement. If the Shiite population of Iraq, Syria's traditional rival, ever came to power in Baghdad and if Iran, Syria's ally to the east, remained an increasingly well-armed, radical Shiite state, the last thing Damascus wanted was another Shiite state on its western border. For an analysis of Syria's goals in Lebanon, see Rabinovich, *The War for Lebanon*, and Kamal Salibi's many works on the origins of the civil war.

46. In an interview in *Middle East Insight* 4, no. 2 (June/July 1985), Fadlallah talks about bringing about political change through education and "enlightening the people from within the social and political institutions." He returns frequently to this theme in subsequent interviews, some of the few interviews available in English, in *Middle East Insight*. I am grateful to George Nader, editor of *Middle East Insight*, for providing the transcripts.

47. Abukhalil, "Hizballah," 401.

48. Almost a year before Israel and the PLO signed their historic accord in 1993 on the White House lawn, Fadlallah was quoted as saying that the "battle which will begin after reconciliation with Israel will be the battle against the subjugation of the Arab and Muslim person to Israel in politics, culture, economics, and security. . . . The Islamists must deploy their Quranic and Islamic legal culture to combat normalization. Fatwas should be issued against Israeli goods and receiving the Israelis. The Islamists may not enjoy complete success, because not all Muslims are committed to Islam. But this will hamper much of the effort by Israel to encircle the region and become a natural member of it." Martin Kramer, "The Strategy of Hezbollah," Washington Institute, "Policy Watch," no. 59, Washington, D.C., July 30, 1993.

49. Ajami, *Vanished Imam,* 214–16.

50. Brazil is home to South America's largest Shiite Lebanese community. The frequent visits of Hezbollah dignitaries and agents to the country were cited by Israeli analysts as part of the circumstantial evidence linking Hezbollah to the devastating bombing of the Jewish community in Buenos Aires in 1994. But American and Israeli analysts agree that there is no direct evidence of Hezbollah's involvement in this latest blast.

51. Most of the Fadlallah quotes I cite come from Martin Kramer's essay "The Oracle" and a lecture he gave at Johns Hopkins School for Advanced International Studies in Washington, D.C., on January 31, 1994. I am indebted to Kramer for providing me with a copy of his lecture notes, along with his essay on Fadlallah that is being published in the forthcoming *Spokesman for the Despised.*

52. Ajami, "Lebanon: The Prospects."

53. Ajami, *Vanished Imam,* 127–28.

54. Deeb, "Militant Islamic Movements," 13. I learned in the Bekaa that one of Musawi's cousins had shot him in the leg after an argument; Musawi had responded by shooting and killing his cousin. Years later, the feud had been patched up by other family members. Hussein Musawi was now free to return to Nabishit.

55. "Islamic Execution in Lebanon Raises the Question: Who's in Charge Here?" *Middle East Mirror,* February 7, 1994, 11.

56. Many scholars have argued that Hezbollah had evolved out of Islamic Amal, but while the group had housed and helped the Iranian revolutionaries, Sheikh Fadlallah insisted that Hezbollah had links to an earlier militant group, Islamic *Da'wa,* a Shiite organization originally based in Iraq that had established branches in Lebanon in the 1970s. Shehabi confirms this as well.

57. Much of Hezbollah's history as recounted by Hikmat Shehabi is consistent with what Marius Deeb, a Lebanese scholar in Washington, D.C., has written. I am grateful to Professor Deeb for his insights and guidance on Hezbollah's complex history.

58. The school was the Imam al-Mahdi Religious Seminary in Baalbek. Abbas Musawi himself had volunteered for one of the guards' first military courses in the Bekaa —sessions that, according to Martin Kramer, the Israeli scholar, had deeply impressed him. "When I sat with the brethren in the first course they gave in the Bekaa," Musawi was quoted as saying, "I felt I had truly penetrated genuine Islam." Kramer, "Musawi's Game."

59. Robin Wright, *In the Name of God: The Khomeini Decade* (New York: Simon & Schuster, 1989), 120–23.
I interviewed Mohtashami in Teheran in 1992, long after he had lost half his hand to a mail bomb while serving in Damascus. He had boasted of his critical role in establishing the Party of God in Lebanon. Iran's Revolutionary Guards minister had openly declared in the late 1980s that Iran had trained the young Shiite who had driven the suicide truck bomb into the U.S. Marine compound in Beirut in 1983; the bomb itself had been transported to Lebanon through Syria, presumably with the help of the Iranian embassy in Damascus.

60. Shehabi's information is consistent with an account of relations among Iranian militants, Lebanese Shia, and the PLO contained in a book entitled *Beyrouth: Les Soldats de l'Islam* by Gilles Delafon, a French journalist who had worked in Lebanon, published by Stock, in Paris, in 1989. The estimate of Iranians trained was confirmed by Hani el-Hassan, a senior PLO official who was the PLO's first ambassador to Teheran, in an interview in Tunis in 1992.

According to Delafon and Shehabi, an Iranian militant named Moustapha Chamran, an engineer by training, had sought refuge in Lebanon in 1971. The man who in 1980 would become the Iranian Islamic Republic's defense minister (and be killed a year later in a plane crash) had worked out the arrangement with Yasir Arafat. By 1975, hundreds of Iranian militants who hoped to overthrow the Shah were being trained at PLO camps in Lebanon.

61. The Musawi quote appears in Martin Kramer's profile of him in the *New Republic*. The description of the Iranian Revolutionary Guard activities and bases of operation in the early 1980s is based on interviews with Lebanese and Iranian officials. See also an early account of the growth of Islamic Amal and Hezbollah in the *Washington Post*, January 9, 1984, by David B. Ottaway, datelined Baalbek.

62. The compound was taken by Hezbollah without a fight. According to Shehabi, the Islamists sent women wearing chadors to the barracks who demanded entry in order to pray. It seems that the compound was near the hut of an early Shiite martyr. "The women carried Kalashnikovs under their cloaks. After they had entered the compound, they took out their guns and said: 'This belongs to Islam,'" Shehabi said. The army had left without firing a single shot.

63. Marius Deeb argues that the economic devastation of Lebanon increased Shia frustration and made it easier for Hezbollah to recruit and mobilize in the Bekaa. By the end of August 1982, direct and indirect losses attributable to Israel's invasion alone, Deeb estimates, stood at $4 billion, almost half the country's gross national product the previous year.

64. Fouad Ajami, interview, August 1995.

SYRIA

1. Article in unidentified newspaper, 1948. Cited in Wilhelm Dietl, *Holy War* (New York: Macmillan, 1984), 39.

2. Perhaps not even Bashar himself. On July 31, 1995, *Al-Muharrer*, an Arabic newspaper, quoted Bashar as saying: "I am not a candidate for the presidency." Bashar's reticence about politics, however, cannot be taken at face value. The young Assad would undoubtedly be persuaded to accept a "draft" for the presidency if his father willed it.

Syrian experts note that initially Basil Assad seemingly had little interest in, or aptitude for, politics when his father gave him his first important post. By the time of his death, however, Basil was widely viewed in Syria as Assad's "natural" successor, and not only within Syria. So intent was Syria's ally Egypt on currying favor with the Assad family that Ibrahim Nafie, head of Egypt's leading semiofficial journal *Al-Ahram*, and the influential press syndicate, wrote a glowing introduction to a panegyric published in Arabic soon after young Assad's death entitled "Basil in the Eyes of the Egyptians."

3. Patrick Seale, *Asad of Syria: The Struggle for the Middle East* (Berkeley: University of California Press, 1989), 331.

4. The lower casualty estimates come from Seale and other writers who tend to be sympathetic to Assad's regime. The higher estimate is cited in Daniel Pipes, *Greater Syria* (New York: Oxford University Press, 1990). Pipes is a staunch critic.

5. Fred Barnes, "Brushed Assad," *New Republic*, December 26, 1994.

6. Thomas L. Friedman, *From Beirut to Jerusalem* (New York: Anchor Books, 1990), 76–105.

7. *Hama: The Tragedy of Our Times* (Cairo: Dar al-I'tisam, 1984). There are many accounts of the Hama uprising. Among the best in English is Thomas Friedman's *From Beirut to Jerusalem*, 76–87. *See also report from Amnesty International to the government of the Syrian Arab Republic, U.S.A., November 1983.*

8. *Interview with Tammam M. al-Barazi, an expert on the Syrian Muslim Brotherhood, Washington, D.C., October 1994.*

9. *William Wright, An Account of Palmyra and Zenobia* (New York: Nelson, 1895), 163.

10. *Syria: Torture by the Security Forces* (New York: Amnesty International Publications, 1987), 2.

11. Charles Glass, *Tribes with Flags* (New York: Atlantic Monthly Press, 1990), 167.

12. John Bagot Glubb, *Syria, Lebanon, and Jordan* (New York: Walker, 1967), 17.

13. Philip K. Hitti, *Syria: A Short History* (New York: Macmillan, 1959), 115.

14. Ibid., 117.

15. The era of the de facto separation of the spiritual and the temporal in Islamic rule is much debated, but almost all scholars agree with James Piscatori, a New York–based Islamic scholar, that the separation occurred early in the Islamic empire — in fact, soon after the Prophet's death. Bernard Lewis maintains that it occurred later on during the Abbasid empire. But Hitti argues that this landmark in Islamic governance should more accurately be credited to the Umayyads.

16. Glubb, *Syria, Lebanon, and Jordan.*

17. Mark Sykes, *Dar-ul-Islam* (London: Bickers & Son, 1904), 54.

18. The Sykes-Picot treaty of 1916 divided up the Ottoman Empire provinces between France and Britain. Approved by the French and British cabinets in February 1916, neither the existence of such a treaty nor its contents were made public until two years after its approval. The Arabs have remained understandably furious about the secret deal that redrew the map of the Middle East and placed their own leaders, promised independence after the war, under European rule.

19. Hama's population stood at only thirty thousand when the Rev. J. L. Porter visited Hama in 1896. Even then he was struck by the fanaticism of the city's Sunni Muslim aristocrats. "I once met a distinguished member of this proud race at the house of a learned and liberal Moslem friend," Porter wrote in his memoir. The conversation turned to the scientific and artistic accomplishments of Western Europe, including the printing press. The Hamaite had "listened with perfect calmness and indifference," Porter recounted, until a "beautiful copy of the Koran, a gem of the Leipzig press, was put into his hand. . . . 'It is printed,' he exclaimed, throwing it from him and wiping his fingers as if the very touch was pollution." See J. L. Porter, *The Giant Cities of Bashan and Syria's Other Holy Places*, 1896, cited in Glass, *Tribes with Flags*, 169–70.

The 1932 *Blue Guide* described Hama as the Syrian town "least touched by the West" and warned that its inhabitants "border on the fanatic." See Ross Burns, *The Monuments of Syria: An Historical Guide* (London: I. B. Tauris & Co. Ltd., 1992), 124. Burns, a former Australian ambassador to Damascus, has included extensive historical information in his excellent new guide to Syria. The book avoids the misleading, slavishly pro-Syrian commentary that fills so many other popular guidebooks.

20. The families are the Azms, Barazis, Kaylanis, and Tayfurs.

21. Specifically Ibn Taymiyya accused them of having helped the Crusaders seize the Syrian coast (even though many Nusayris were killed when the Crusaders swept through Syria in 1097) and of having helped the dreaded Mongols sack Syrian cities and turn Arab castles over to the "enemies of Islam." See Matti Moosa, *Extremist Shiites* (Syracuse, N.Y.: Syracuse University Press, 1988), 269–70.

22. Ibid., 287–88, and also Pipes, *Greater Syria*, 167. Pipes cites the original source as well: Document 3547, dated June 15, 1936, Ministère des Affaires Etrangères.

23. Dietl, *Holy War*, 37–41. According to Dietl's early account of militant Islamic politics, Mustafa al-Sibai, founder of the Syrian Brotherhood, was born in 1915, the son of a well-known Sunni preacher from Homs, north of Damascus. As did so many Islamic revivalists, Sibai studied at Egypt's al-Azhar, and was repeatedly jailed there, and later in Syria, for his anticolonial activities. In 1946, Sibai was elected leader of the Syrian Ikhwan, which was subordinate to Cairo and to Egyptian Supreme Guide Hassan al-Banna. In the summer of 1957 he became the head of the executive committee of the entire organization. Issam al-Attar, the Syrian culture minister's brother who has been in exile in West Germany since the early 1960s, then became the head of the Syrian Brotherhood. The Syrian Ikhwan, several experts note, is famous for its internal feuding and ideological quarrels. The current head of the Syrian Brotherhood lives in West Germany.

24. David Pryce-Jones, *The Closed Circle: An Interpretation of the Arabs* (New York: Harper & Row, 1991), 330.

25. Olivier Carré and Gérard Michaud [Michel Seurat], *Les Frères Musulmans, 1928-1982* (Paris: Collection Archive, 1983), 135.

26. Seale, *Asad*, 325.

27. "Syrian Troops Massacre Scores of Assad's Foes," *Washington Post*, June 25, 1981, no byline. See also "Human Rights in Syria," Human Rights Watch, New York, September 1990, p. 21.

28. Normally, the *Times* insists on the accuracy of bylines and datelines. But Abe Rosenthal made rare exceptions when he felt that a reporter's safety was endangered, as he did in this case.

29. "Syria Said to Face Split Among Elite Over Succession," no byline, Washington, *New York Times*, March 7, 1984.

30. Israeli officials sensed a shift in Syria as early as 1989 — more than a year before the Gulf war — when Assad decided to restore diplomatic relations with Egypt. Assad never forgave Egypt's Sadat for abandoning Syria and shattering any remaining illusion of Arab solidarity by making peace with Israel; he had vowed to isolate Egypt as long as the Israeli flag flew over Cairo. But in December 1989, Assad stood next to President Hosni Mubarak at Abdoun Palace, less than a mile away from the hated Israeli embassy. In January 1990, Israel's Ambassador Rabinovich emphasized the importance of Assad's rapprochement with Egypt in an article in *The New York Times*. If Syria was willing to mend fences with Egypt, perhaps Washington should "explore the possibility of generating Syrian-Israeli negotiations."

31. According to a senior Saudi official, King Fahd had sent Prince Bandar Bin Sultan to seek Assad's help soon after Iraq's invasion of Kuwait in August 1990. Assad had asked only three questions, the official told me. "Are the Americans serious about stopping the Iraqis? Will they finish the job by going all the way? And do you trust them?" When Bandar replied affirmatively, Assad pledged his help. Daniel Pipes notes that Assad didn't announce his "snap" decision for forty days.

32. Occasionally, Assad balked. Syria, for instance, supported Iran rather than Saudi-backed Iraq in the Iran-Iraq war, and Assad risked Saudi anger by torpedoing an early effort by then Crown Prince Fahd to extend feelers to Israel regarding Arab recognition.

33. The warning, reported in several newspapers soon after the Gulf war, was confirmed by an American intelligence official in Washington in January 1992.

34. Estimate made by Syrian Vice President Abd al-Halim Khaddam in an interview in March 1992.

35. Raymond A. Hinnebusch argues in "Syria: The Politics of Peace and Regime Survival," *Middle East Policy* 4 (April 1995), that Assad's "presidential monarchy" rests

on four pillars: the army, his Alawi sect, the Baath Party, and a "state-dependent bourgeoi-sie." Assad's regime, he concludes, is quasi-"Sultanism," wherein the monarch can make and break any of his political or financial barons.

36. Syria has a well-documented record of direct support for international terror-ism until 1986 and indirect support as of the publication of this book, which has pre-vented its removal from the American terrorism list despite intense Syrian lobbying.

Two terrorist incidents that I covered stand out. The first occurred in 1986, when a Syrian agent of Palestinian origin planted a bomb containing 1.5 kilograms of Semtex, a powerful plastic explosive, in the false bottom of a suitcase belonging to a pregnant Irish woman, his unwitting "fiancée" who thought she was flying to Israel on an El Al jet from London allegedly to meet her future in-laws. The bomb was detected, an Israeli official told me months later, only after an Israeli security agent became suspicious when the woman said that she would stay at the Hilton Hotel in Jericho. Fortunately, the agent knew there was no Hilton anywhere in the occupied territories. He tore apart her suitcase and found the bomb. The Syrian agent, Nizar Hindawi, fled the airport when the plot was uncovered and went straight to Ambassador Lutfallah Heidar at the Syrian embassy. Heidar was a cousin of Mohammed Heidar, the Alawite Baath official whom I had interviewed years earlier in Damascus. Seale, in his 1988 Assad biography and in a book on Abu Nidal, the Palestinian terrorist based in Damascus until 1987, when Syria was pressured into expelling him, admits there was "convincing" evidence that Syria's air force intelligence was deeply involved in the bomb plot. (The agency, for example, had sent Abu Nidal's bomb to London in a Syrian diplomatic pouch.)

While Syria's complicity could not be denied, Seale accepted Assad's denial of per-sonal involvement in the Hindawi affair as well as the Syrian president's assertion that the El Al bombing had been planned by Israel to "exploit it for political ends," according to Seale. Fearing that this perverse logic might not persuade objective readers, Seale added wistfully that "random atrocities were not in Asad's style," implying, presumably, that Assad preferred deliberate atrocities like Hama.

Britain, persuaded of high-level Syrian government involvement, cut most trade and diplomatic ties with Damascus, which were not restored until November 1990, and only after considerable American prodding to reward Assad for his support of the campaign against Iraq. See Patrick Seale, *Abu Nidal: A Gun for Hire* (New York: Random House, 1992), 248.

The second example of Syrian assistance to a deadly terrorist act remains controversial. Until 1991, Washington and London believed that Ahmed Jabril, the Damascus-based chief of a radical Palestinian rejectionist group, had blown up Pan American Flight 103 over Lockerbie, Scotland, in 1988. But in 1991, not long after Assad agreed to join the American-led coalition in Kuwait, new evidence was discovered implicating Libya, not Syria, in the disaster. Despite this, several friends in intelligence continue to argue that Syria was somehow involved. The Bush administration had "clear information," ac-cording to L. Paul Bremer III, a former ambassador for counterterrorism in the Reagan administration, that Iran had contracted with the Damascus-based Jabril group to blow up U.S. airliners. Only after its operation was uncovered in Germany did it hand over the Lockerbie mission to the Libyans, whose agents, in fact, blew up the plane. But despite the Jabril group's attacks on Americans and American targets, Syria has refused to expel the group, which Damascus has often praised for its struggle to liberate Palestine. For a survey article on Syrian terrorism, see Daniel Pipes, "Terrorism: The Syrian Connection," *National Interest*, Spring 1989, 15–25.

37. Interview, October 1994.

38. In an interview broadcast on the *MacNeil/Lehrer NewsHour* on October 1, 1993, Assad said that "many mix terrorism and legitimate struggle, which mankind has exercised since time immemorial." Assad defined terrorism as follows: "A terrorist is a criminal who kills for the sake of stealing, plundering, blackmailing, and in general, for

evil personal reasons." Arab violence against Israelis, therefore, was not terrorism but "a struggle against occupiers." Transcript provided by the *NewsHour* and Foreign Broadcast Information Service (FBIS) Daily Report: Near East and South Asia, October 4, 1993, 46–50, and also *Middle East Quarterly* 1, no. 1 (March 1994): 81–85.

39. "No one should expect us to wax enthusiastic over a secret agreement concluded behind our backs," Assad told the *MacNeil/Lehrer NewsHour* in October 1993. Speaking of Arafat, Assad said: "He did a disservice to himself and the parties with which, and under whose shadow, he marched for a long time." FBIS and *Middle East Quarterly*.

40. Daniel Pipes, "The Mind of Hafez Assad," *Washington Post*, October 9, 1994.

41. Pryce-Jones, *The Closed Circle*, 4.

42. Aflaq's main works include *Fi Sabil al-Baath* (For the Baath), published in Arabic in Beirut in 1959, and a recycled Baathism in *Nuqtat al Bidaya*, also published in Arabic in Beirut in 1971. For a discussion of what he calls Aflaq's "vague metaphysics," see Fouad Ajami, *The Arab Predicament* (Cambridge, Eng.: Cambridge University Press, 1992).

43. Itamar Rabinovich, *Syria Under the Ba'th 1963–66* (Jerusalem: Israel Universities Press, 1972), 212–13. The origins of his book are intriguing and in some ways quintessentially Middle Eastern. As a young officer in the army in 1967, Rabinovich found himself on the Golan Heights in possession of a cabinet filled with Baath Party documents and memoranda that the retreating Syrians left behind. The contents ultimately provided this Arabic-speaking scholar with the raw material for his Ph.D. dissertation and this book, his first. See also his later book about early Arab-Israeli negotiations, *The Road Not Taken* (Oxford, Eng.: Oxford University Press, 1991).

44. Muslim Students Association NEWS, KCWD/Kaleidoscope, September 16, 1994, Country: Syria. Vital statistics.

45. David Waldner, "Politics and Power in Syria in the 1990s" (Paper prepared for a seminar on Syria and the peace process, University of Virginia, May 23, 1994). I am grateful to Waldner for sharing the paper with me, along with his thoughts on the Assad regime.

46. These reports are based on conversations with Syrian businessmen who, for obvious reasons, asked not to be identified.

47. Waldner, "Politics and Power in Syria," 32.

48. During the Madrid conference in October 1991, for example, Syrian television never showed a single picture of an Israeli delegate, and the government jammed Jordanian television, only two hours away from Damascus, which provided detailed coverage of the proceedings.

49. See, for example, Assad's speech to Islamic clerics in Damascus, February 27, 1995, as reported by the official Syrian news agency SANA. Translation by *Mideast Mirror*, February 28, 1995.

50. Interview, Wye, Maryland, June 20, 1995.

JORDAN

1. Kamal Salibi, *The Modern History of Jordan* (London: I. B. Tauris & Co Ltd., 1993). Unfortunately, this is most readily available in Amman, where the Jordan Book Centre has domestic rights to its sale.

2. David Fromkin, *A Peace to End All Peace* (New York: Avon Books, 1990), 218–23.

3. Salibi, *Jordan*, 95.

4. Interview, Tawfiq Kawar, Amman, August 1993.

5. Beverley Milton-Edwards, "Temporary Alliance with the Crown: The Islamic

Response in Jordan," in *Islamic Fundamentalism and the Gulf Crisis*, ed. James Piscatori (Chicago: American Academy of Arts and Sciences, 1991), 89. For an exploration of the relations between the Hashemites and the Muslim Brotherhood, see also Lawrence Tal, "Co-opting Islamists," in *Survival*, Autumn 1995; Sabah el-Said, "Between Pragmatism and Ideology: The Muslim Brotherhood in Jordan, 1989–1994" (Policy Papers, no. 39, Washington Institute for Near East Policy, Washington, D.C., 1995), and Robert B. Satloff, *Troubles on the East Bank* (New York: Praeger, 1986).

According to Murawi Tal, a Jordanian expert on Islam, and Marion J. Boulby, a Ph.D. candidate at the University of Toronto whose thesis concerns the ideology and social base of the Jordanian Muslim Brotherhood, the Ikhwan's "founding father" in Jordan was Abdelatif Abu Qura, a wealthy, poorly educated merchant, philanthropist, and Islamic activist whose family came to Jordan from Syria in the nineteenth century. In 1945, Abu Qura founded a Brotherhood chapter in Amman and with it a Young Men's Muslim Association, a "Boy Scout–like group," according to Boulby, that recruited young members and offered mostly Koran readings and other recreational activities. Abu Qura, who remained the Jordanian Brotherhood's leader until the early 1950s, passionately opposed the creation of a Jewish state in neighboring Palestine and in the mid-1940s went to Palestine to fight the Zionists. His main preoccupation in founding the Jordanian Brotherhood was to fight Zionism, which gave the movement, from its inception, an obsession with Palestine's fate. The Brotherhood sought and received an official blessing from King Abdullah on the condition that it remain strictly a religious, social, and charitable organization that did not engage in political activity. When Khalifa became the Brotherhood leader, Boulby says, he began recruiting younger, better-educated members who expanded the group's agenda and gave it a more overtly political cast.

6. Tal, "Co-opting Islamists"; also interview, Tariq Tal, London, November 1995.

7. Fouad Ajami, review of *Collusion Across the Jordan: King Abdullah, the Zionist Movement and the Partition of Palestine* by Avi Shlaim, *New Republic*, April 10, 1989.

8. In a letter, Abdullah attributed the inevitable success of Zionism to three "pillars": Britain's Balfour Declaration, Europe's expulsion of the Jews from their own states, and "those partisans of the Arabs who will accept no solution but are content with weeping and wailing and calling for help to those who cannot aid them. Thus," Abdullah wrote, accurately as things turned out, "is Palestine giving up the ghost." See King Abdullah of Jordan, *My Memoirs Completed, Al-Takmilah* (London: Longman Group Ltd., 1978), 87.

9. For a detailed look at the relationship between Abdullah and the Zionists, see Avi Shlaim, *Collusion Across the Jordan: King Abdullah, the Zionist Movement, and the Partition of Palestine* (New York: Columbia University Press, 1988); Mary C. Wilson, *King Abdullah, Britain and the Making of Jordan* (Cambridge, Eng.: Cambridge University Press, 1987); and Robert B. Satloff, *From Abdullah to Hussein: Jordan in Transition* (New York: Oxford University Press, 1994). Finally, for an assessment of their conclusions based on recently released archives, see Itamar Rabinovich, *The Road Not Taken* (New York: Oxford University Press, 1991).

10. Ajami, review of *Collusion*.

11. Rabinovich, *The Road Not Taken*, 46.

12. Ajami, review of *Collusion*.

13. Benny Morris, "A Second Look at the 'Missed Peace,'" *Journal of Palestine Studies*, Winter 1994.

14. Tal, "Co-opting Islamists," 141.

15. Ajami, review of *Collusion*.

16. King Hussein, *Uneasy Lies the Head* (London: Heinemann, 1962).

17. Oriana Fallaci, *Interview with History* (Boston: Houghton Mifflin, 1976), 150.

18. Robert B. Satloff, *Abdullah*, and interviews. I am indebted to Satloff for his generous guidance on the king's tactics and strategic alliances.

19. Robert B. Satloff, "The Jekyll and Hyde Origins of the U.S.–Jordanian Strategic Relationship," in *The Middle East and the United States: A Historical and Political Reassessment*, ed. David W. Lesch (Boulder, Colo.: Westview, 1996). I thank Rob Satloff for sharing his manuscript with me.

20. Bob Woodward, *Veil* (New York: Simon & Schuster, 1987), 218, 381.

21. The fedayeen, for example, stopped members of the royal family — even the king's wife — at impromptu checkpoints. They ignored Jordan's laws, carried weapons in the streets, and issued communiqués as if they were, in fact, the government.

22. Satloff, *Abdullah*, 15.

23. James Lunt, *Hussein of Jordan* (London: Macmillan, 1989), 132. The PFLP eventually released passengers but demolished the planes in a spectacular explosion.

24. For Hussein, the Arab summit decision was an unmitigated disaster. Kenneth Stein, a Middle East analyst and historian who worked in the Carter administration, saw Rabat as an extraordinary obstacle to American efforts to negotiate Arab-Israeli peace. "Rabat not only complicated Hussein's domestic situation," he said; "it tied the diplomatic cord in knots."

25. Alia Toukan, the daughter of a prominent Palestinian diplomat from Nablus who had settled in Salt, was the king's third wife. His first marriage to Dina Abdul Hamid, a Cambridge intellectual and an older distant cousin, had ended after only eighteen months. Hussein and Dina, a lively and independent woman who found sleepy Amman unbearably dull, had one child — a daughter — but they had little else in common. Though they parted amicably, she later married a Palestinian commando who had taken part in the 1970 uprising against Hussein — perhaps, I thought, an unsubtle act of revenge. But if Hussein resented the union, he did not show it. I met Dina and her husband years later in Amman, where they were clearly welcome. The king's second wife, utterly different from Dina, was Toni Avril Gardiner, whom the king named Muna, or in Arabic, "my wish." The shy daughter of an English colonel in the British embassy, Muna had little interest in politics and refused to accept the title of queen. She and Hussein had four children. She was fond of settled life, especially of cooking him dinner at home. The marriage appeared happy until Hussein fell in love with Alia, whom he subsequently married. Muna still has a house in Amman.

26. For the most complete account of the peace process since 1967, see William B. Quandt, *Peace Process: American Diplomacy and the Arab-Israeli Conflict Since 1967* (Washington, D.C.: Brookings Institution, University of California Press, 1993). The king's willingness under certain conditions to make a separate peace was supported by interviews with several State Department officials, who requested anonymity, and also by a profile of the king written by John Newhouse, "Monarch," *The New Yorker*, September 19, 1983. The article cites a former State Department official as saying, "He sent us a telegram saying that he'd decided to take a chance and make peace by himself. He wanted the United States to back him up. We told him that it was his decision — that he was on his own."

27. One major "disappointment" occurred in 1980, senior Jordanians said, when American negotiator Philip Habib offered Amman $150 million in aid in connection with the construction of a so-called Unity Dam. The project was to provide Syria, Jordan, and Israel water from Lake Tiberias. All Jordan had to do, Habib told the king, was negotiate the dam's "technicalities" with Israel. But what Habib failed to mention was that neither the PLO nor Syria had agreed to participate in such a joint venture. Jordan insisted that Syria signal its participation before any "technical" talks with Israel were held and Habib left empty-handed.

28. Judith Miller, "Hussein Rules Out Talks with Israel and Bars U.S. Role, *New York Times*, March 15, 1984.

29. Shimon Peres, *Battling for Peace* (New York: Random House, 1995), 269. Much of his description of the London meeting was confirmed by senior Jordanian officials.

30. Perhaps the king's intermittent efforts to ensure Jordanian influence in the West Bank would have failed even without the Intifada. As early as 1986, public opinion polls in the West Bank showed that Palestinians who had grown up under Israeli rule had no loyalty to a monarch they had seen only on television. One poll showed that only 3 percent of the Palestinians who responded favored Hussein as their leader. See Stanley Reed, "Jordan and the Gulf Crisis," *Foreign Affairs* 69, no. 5 (winter 1990–91), 21–35. The poll cited by Reed was conducted by ABC News and *Newsday* and published in September 1986, more than a year before the Intifada erupted.

31. Ajami, review of *Collusion*.

32. Don Peretz, *Palestinians, Refugees, and the Middle East Peace Process* (Washington, D.C.: United States Institute of Peace Press, 1993), 33.

33. Reed, "Gulf Crisis," 26.

34. Satloff, *East Bank*, 55–58; Tal, "Co-opting Islamists," 143.

35. Reed, "Gulf Crisis," 27. Hussein was clearly unprepared for the depth of public anger. When that fury was reported in the media, Hussein, blaming the messenger for the message, wrote an open letter that signaled an impending crackdown on the press. Hussein complained about "our newspaper writers" who attack "social institutions, our customs, and our values." Such promotion of a "downtrend to frustration" was unhealthy, the king said. Clearly, Hussein's devotion to his democratic experiment had its limits.

36. Senior Jordanian officials remain persuaded to this day that Saudi Arabia, the Hashemite family's historic religious and political rival, helped foment the unrest in Ma'an through its tribal and Muslim Brotherhood allies, then the recipients of generous financial support from Riyadh.

37. Adnan Abu Odeh, a former head of intelligence who served until 1995 as Jordan's ambassador to the United Nations, was then a palace adviser. He later conceded that the palace had calculated that the Islamists would win twelve seats, fifteen at most. The underestimation of Islamist strength, he told a conference in 1992 at the U.S. Institute of Peace in Washington, D.C., was a "major intelligence failure" in a country that could ill afford such miscalculations. "We were really surprised," he said.

38. Tal, "Co-opting Islamists," 143–44.

39. Reed, "Gulf Crisis," 24.

40. According to King Hussein, the wealthier members of the Arab League had pledged at the Baghdad summit of 1978 to give Jordan and the other "confrontation" states surrounding Israel $10 billion a year. But Algeria had made only one payment; Libya never paid a penny; and Qatar and Abu Dhabi had stopped paying Jordan in 1983.

41. Interview, King Hussein, Amman, April 1991.

42. Mustapha Hamarneh, "The Gulf Crisis and Jordan" (Paper prepared by a history professor who worked in the Royal Court during the Gulf crisis with the encouragement of the palace). I am grateful to Dr. Hamarneh for sharing it with me.

43. Interview, Nadwa Palace, October 1990. King Hussein even gave credence to Saddam Hussein's absurd contention that he was descended from the Prophet. The king, a genuine descendant of Islam's first family, takes enormous pride in his heritage, so I expected him to be skeptical about Saddam's politically expedient claim. But much to my surprise, when I asked the king whether he believed Saddam's claim, he replied: "Well, it's possible. It is a large family."

44. Hamarneh, "The Gulf Crisis."

45. David Pollock, "'The Arab Street'? Public Opinion in the Arab World" (Policy Papers, no. 32, Washington Institute for Near East Policy, Washington, D.C., 1992). In this lively and informative essay, Pollock, a public opinion expert, shows that there was a "rough congruence" between the policies of Arab governments during the Gulf war and public opinion in their respective states and that, in general, public opinion often matters more to Arab governments than many analysts believe.

46. Satloff, *East Bank*, 41.

47. President Bush also pleaded with Shamir not to retaliate, fearful that Israel's entry into the war would play into Saddam's hands and shatter the Arab coalition against Iraq.

48. The Palestinians would "rip up his palace," Hussein told Shamir, if Jordan failed to retaliate against Israeli overflights. See *U.S. News & World Report* Staff, *Triumph Without Victory: The Unreported History of the Persian Gulf Conflict* (New York: Times Books, 1992), 248.

49. Milton-Edwards, "Alliance," 93.

50. Moshe Arens, *Broken Covenant* (New York: Simon & Schuster, 1995), 149.

51. Cited in Scott MacLeod, "In the Wake of Desert Storm," *New York Review of Books*, March 7, 1991.

52. Edward W. Said, "Palestinian Versailles," *Progressive Magazine*, December 1993, 22.

53. The letter, dated September 22, 1990, was one of five appeals that the king sent to Iraq's leader about the crisis. "We want Iraq to progress under your leadership," the king wrote. "You know, my brother, how committed we are to the inadmissibility of the acquisition of territory by force." Iraq's occupation, he continued, was "a major dangerous precedent from which Israel will benefit." "There is no way that anyone can remain silent about such an action." The superpowers would retaliate militarily, he warned, which would be "the beginning of a chaotic world." For these reasons, he wrote, "we hope Iraq will withdraw from Kuwait." Failure to withdraw risked "the destruction of Iraq under the pretext of supporting the legitimate rights of Kuwait." Such a war "would be a very severe blow to all we had hoped to create and in our peoples' confidence in us. . . . We're racing against time to avoid a catastrophe."

54. Satloff, *East Bank*, 37.

55. Glenn Robinson, "Dilemmas of States: Islamicism, Liberalization and the Arab-Israeli End Game. The Case of Jordan" (draft paper prepared for the Middle East Studies Association Annual Conference, Phoenix, Arizona, November 1994).

56. This account of the Jordanian government's relationship with the Brotherhood and other militant Islamic groups is based in large part on interviews conducted in late 1993 and 1994 with Jordanian officials and intelligence officers who insisted on anonymity.

57. Whether or not to participate in government has long been one of the most divisive issues within the Brotherhood. In a series of articles in Arabic, Ziad Abu Ghanimah, a former Brotherhood parliamentarian, described the debate in detail, which he says dates back to the late 1960s when Ishaq Farhan secured the Ikhwan's approval to become a minister in Prime Minister Wasfi Tal's cabinet. See *Al-Aswaq* newspaper, Amman, July 10, 1995–September 6, 1995.

58. Michael Collins Dunn, "Islamist Parties in Democratizing States: A Look at Jordan and Yemen," *Middle East Policy* 2, no. 2 (Washington, D.C.), 20.

59. The government had created a special post for "Minister of Higher Education" before Akaila assumed the portfolio.

60. Rami G. Khouri, "Jordan's Islamists—A Growing Force or a Fading Footnote?" *Jordan Times*, November 16, 1993.

61. Robinson, "Dilemmas," 8.

62. Among those convicted in absentia and sentenced to hang were Muhammad al-Khalifa, a brother-in-law of Usama bin Laden, a Saudi financier of Muslim radical groups throughout the Middle East who had been expelled by Riyadh and had taken refuge in Khartoum. The Sudanese Islamic government used Bin Laden to fund and assist a wide variety of violent actions in the region. Khalifa managed to secure an American visa in 1994 and sought shelter in California. Jordan requested his extradition. Khalifa was deported in 1995, retried in Jordan, and acquitted.

63. In December 1995, Shubayat was arrested again for his unrelenting tirades against peace with Israel and Jordan's policies.

64. Sheikh As'ad Tamimi, *The Destruction of the State of Israel Is a Koranic Imperative* (Jerusalem: Supporters of the Islamic Revolution in Palestine, 1988). Translation by Lama Abu Odeh. The book was originally published in Beirut sometime in the early 1980s. The edition Tamimi gave me contained an updated "author's note" in which the sheikh took account of recent developments since its first printing.

ISRAEL

1. The Arabic name is Harakat al Muqawama al-Islamiyya.

2. Interview, Israeli security official, February 11, 1993. See also "Statement to the Security Council" by Gad Yaacobi, Israel's ambassador to the United Nations, December 18, 1992. Even B'Tselem, an Israeli human-rights group that has repeatedly criticized Israeli violations of Palestinian human rights, concluded in a January 1994 report that Palestinian political leaders were responsible for the murder of 750–950 Arabs in the territories accused, falsely in most cases, of collaborating with Israel. The report also concluded that the situation had not improved much since the September 1993 Israeli-PLO peace accord.

3. In an interview in Tel Aviv in October 1995, an Israeli official acknowledged that from a security standpoint, the deportations were "stupid." Only half of those deported turned out to have been affiliated with Hamas or other militant Islamic groups, he said. But as a result of the deportations, all of them became more sympathetic to Hamas. Moreover, the deportees in Lebanon received military training and religious indoctrination from the Iranian-trained Shiite Hezbollah, which reinforced Hamas's military capabilities and the deportees' ideological commitment to ousting Israel and creating an Islamic state in Palestine after the Israeli government finally relented and permitted them to return. Several former deportees were subsequently apprehended in deadly assaults on Israeli settlers and civilians, among them those involved in the deadly attack on Bus No. 5 in Tel Aviv in October 1994. The official called the deportation decision "political," that is, one that was aimed at restoring Israeli public confidence in the peace process before the Oslo accords and in Rabin's stewardship.

4. The four Palestinians later convicted of murdering Toledano were not yet members of Hamas when they kidnapped him. According to several sources, the Hamas spokesman in Jordan, for example, did not even know who precisely had staged the assault when he and other Hamas leaders claimed credit for the kidnapping and began negotiating with Israel as if they were in charge. After Toledano's murder, the four militants were formally recruited into Hamas, trained, and sent out on other missions. In 1993 they killed two Israeli policemen who were sleeping in their car on guard duty near the Israeli town of Hadera.

5. Interview, Israeli security official, New York, January 7, 1993.

6. Israeli reporters, and non-Israeli reporters based in Israel as well, are required to submit stories affecting national security to the government for censorship. In this case, a senior Israeli official told me, the government suppressed details of Toledano's death to prevent enraged Israeli citizens from staging revenge attacks against either Arab Israelis or Palestinians in the territories.

7. Interview, Israeli security official, Tel Aviv, February 10, 1993.

8. The story was initially broken in the United States in early January by Ehud Ya'ari, an Israeli reporter. See *The New York Times*, January 27, 1993. For FBI and CIA denials, see *Time*, February 15, 1993, and *The New York Times*, February 4, 1993. In the *Times*, an unnamed official is quoted as saying that fund-raising for Hamas in the United

States involved "a very small amount of money, and a very small number of people." Several administration officials agreed that Hamas was only "raising money for political, welfare and religious activities" and that there was a "clear distinction between Hamas's welfare and military wings."

9. Substantial portions of the interviews "Nadav" and other Israeli security officials conducted with Muhammad Salah became public in October 1995, when Israel sent nearly a thousand pages of documents, including excerpts of transcripts of several taped interrogation sessions, to a U.S. Federal District Court in Manhattan in support of its request to extradite Mousa Abu Marzook, the head of Hamas's Political Bureau, who was arrested in New York in mid-1995 as he tried to reenter the country. The sworn affidavit of "Nadav," whose real name Israel does not reveal due to what it says is the dangerous nature of his work, is consistent with this account of Muhammad Salah's actions on behalf of Hamas.

10. Much of what Salah initially told Israeli interrogators during his early sessions turned out to be disinformation. For example, while Abu Obeida (Muhammad Suwalha) was, in fact, a Hamas activist, he knew virtually nothing of Hamas's military activities. In affidavits filed in New York Federal District Court in connection with the Abu Marzook case, Israel disclosed that it had tricked Salah into revealing information about Hamas by recruiting as informants prisoners in his jail cell who pretended to be Hamas recruits. In prison, Salah told them that he was deceiving the Israelis and revealed the real identities of many of his contacts in America and the territories. His fellow inmates, according to the affidavits, persuaded Salah to put much of the real story in writing. Salah was then confronted with this second written account and began to confess in earnest. Failing to do so would have resulted in an extended prison sentence.

11. The UASR has repeatedly denied any connection to Hamas. It has worked assiduously to ingratiate itself with the American academic community. It lists, for example, as "advisory editors" of its flagship publication *Middle East Journal* several prominent scholars regarded as sympathetic to the Islamic resurgence. Among them are John Esposito, director of Georgetown University's Center for Muslim-Christian Understanding; Yvonne Haddad, of the University of Massachusetts; Dr. Robert Crane, of the American Muslim Council; Louis Cantori, of the University of Maryland; and John Entelis, of Fordham University. Most of the professors said in interviews that while they had agreed to serve as advisers to the UASR's publication, they had no relationship with the UASR itself. But Haddad said that the UASR had listed her despite her refusal to join the advisory board. After she protested a second time, the UASR agreed to remove her name from its list of advisers.

12. This figure and other details in Salah's account are consistent with those in *Hamas: From Belief in Allah to Routes of Terror*, by Israeli journalists Aviva Shabi and Roni Shaked (Jerusalem: Keter Publishing House, 1994). Their description of the Hamas organization and its activities is in Hebrew and not yet available in English. I am indebted to Tamar Kaplan for translating portions of the book and to Roni Shaked, who provided additional material and insights.

13. Judith Miller, *New York Times*, February 17, 1993. The front-page article, which concluded that Hamas had drawn "critical financial support and political and military guidance from agents in the United States," was greeted with skepticism until the bombing of the World Trade Center on February 26, after which the U.S. government no longer denied the danger posed by militant Islamic networks operating in America.

14. Much of the following is also contained in Israeli court documents in the extradition case of Mousa Abu Marzook in New York Federal District Court. See, in particular, affidavit by "Nadav, Head of Investigations Unit in Ramallah Area" and "Translation of Material Written by Muhammad Salah during interview conducted in June, 1993," August 21, 1995.

15. See Shabi and Shaked, *Hamas*, and "Nadav" affidavit in Federal District Court in Manhattan, the case of Mousa Abu Marzook.

16. Israeli court report: "June 23, 1993, Defendant: Issa Al-Hidmi," in Hebrew, translation by Tamar Kaplan.

17. American law enforcement officials say that MAYA, founded in 1974 in Plainfield, Indiana, is an Arab-American youth group with links to the Muslim Brotherhood. Its annual conferences, as well as those of the Islamic Students of North America (ISNA), usually held around Christmas, which discourages non-Muslims from attending, have hosted some leading representatives of groups now on the State Department's terrorist list. In the *New Republic* (June 12, 1995), Steve Emerson, an investigative journalist, quotes MAYA's "constitution" as stating: "In the heart of America, in the depths of corruption and ruin and moral deprivation, an elite of Muslim youth is holding fast to the teachings of Allah."

18. Interview, Roni Shaked, Jerusalem, October 1994.

19. Emerson, *New Republic*, 28.

20. Ibid. In March 23, 1995, Shukri A. Baker, executive director of the Holy Land Foundation, stated in a letter to me that the fund supports only charities and institutions in Israel and the territories licensed by Israel. "To the best of my knowledge," the letter states, "none of these entities has been involved in any illegal activities or is being investigated by the Israelis for security threats to society." This assertion is inconsistent with Hidmi's testimony and evidence collected by Israeli security services. According to Steve Emerson and U.S. law enforcement officials, Shukri Abu Baker is a Hamas activist. As of late 1995, his foundation was still collecting money and holding conferences in the United States.

21. "The Covenant of the Islamic Resistance Movement," August 18, 1988 (in English).

22. Two senior Israeli officials formerly responsible for Israel's administration of the West Bank and Gaza, Benjamin Ben Eliezer, former coordinator of West Bank and Gaza and currently minister of housing, and Ephraim Sneh, also a former coordinator and currently minister of health, confirmed in interviews in October 1994 that Israel had approved and licensed the Mujamma in Gaza. Both agreed that in retrospect the decision was extremely unwise.

23. Ziad Abu-Amr, *Islamic Fundamentalism in the West Bank and Gaza* (Bloomington: Indiana University Press, 1994), 140. In this excellent account, Abu-Amr reports that the Saudi-based Islamic Development Fund, established during King Faisal's reign, gave the university $150,000 to start building the campus.

24. Ibid., 4–22. Abu-Amr notes that before it was banned by Egypt in 1954, the Muslim Brotherhood was Gaza's largest organization. But when the mother organization in Egypt was persecuted, the Gaza organization, which in 1954 had 1,011 branches in the Strip, also suffered. After Brethren in Egypt tried to seize power in 1965, among the Gaza members arrested by Egypt was Sheikh Yasin.

25. Ibid., 16–17. For an Israeli view, see "Hamas–The Islamic Resistance Movement" (Background paper, IDF Spokesman, January 1993).

26. Ziad Abu-Amr, "In the Right Place at the Right Times: Shaykh Ahmad Yasin and the Origins of Hamas," in *Spokesmen for the Despised: Fundamentalist Leaders of the Middle East*, ed. Scott Appleby (Chicago: University of Chicago Press, 1996). According to Abu-Amr, Yasin, who was born in 1936, fell and broke his back while playing on the beach in 1952. As is often the case for those who endure a cataclysmic illness or accident, Yasin turned to religion. Men who are blind or handicapped are often spiritual leaders of militant Islamic movements, for men who have overcome physical disabilities are highly respected in Arab society. Although neither Abu-Amr nor many of the other objective Palestinian political scientists consider Yasin a brilliant writer or Islamic thinker, almost all express admiration for his energy, stamina, and success in having overcome such a debilitating handicap.

27. This was not new. Bernard Lewis, the historian, notes in *The Jews of Islam* (Princeton, N.J.: Princeton University Press, 1984), 185, that the specific campaign against

Jews in the Middle East first appeared among Christian (Greek Orthodox) Arabs in the nineteenth century and then spread to Arab Muslims in the next century. The first anti-Semitic tracts in Arabic were translated from French and written mostly by Arab Christians. The "Protocols" was first published in Cairo in 1927 (see p. 185).

28. Prominent Israeli and Palestinian sources agree on this. See, for example, Abu-Amr, *Islamic Fundamentalism*, 59, and Ze'ev Schiff and Ehud Ya'ari, *Intifada: The Palestinian Uprising* (New York: Simon & Schuster, 1990), 17–50.

29. Interviews, Hamas spokesmen in Gaza and Amman, April 1993. See also Schiff and Ya'ari, *Intifada*, 188–219; and Abu-Amr, *Islamic Fundamentalism*, 63–89.

30. Abu-Amr, *Islamic Fundamentalism*, 68.

31. Schiff and Ya'ari, and Abu-Amr, noted that a few weeks before the eruption of the Intifada, the Islamic Jihad managed to draw thousands of Palestinians into the streets for unprecedented demonstrations and that Israel's decision to arrest and subsequently deport the group's spiritual leader, Sheikh Abd al-Aziz Odeh, prompted two thousand people to attack the police station in Gaza's Jebalya camp in November 1987.

32. Some of the founders include Sheikh Odeh, a fiery preacher and lecturer at the Gaza branch of Egypt's al-Azhar who was deported in 1988; Fathi Abd al-Aziz Shikaki, a physician who was killed by Israeli agents in Malta in October 1995; and Sheikh As'ad al-Tamimi, the former resident of Hebron deported to Jordan in 1970 whom I had interviewed in Amman. Though both Shikaki and Odeh had studied at Egypt's Zagazig University, a center of Islamic radicalism, their own writing and statements suggest that it was Iran's revolution that convinced them that an Islamic movement could defeat a stronger secular power. Israeli and Palestinian sources said that Sheikh Tamimi was largely responsible for securing Iranian funding.

33. Elie Rekhess, "The Iranian Impact on the Islamic Jihad Movement in the Gaza Strip," in *The Iranian Revolution and the Muslim World*, ed. David Menashri (Boulder, Colo.: Westview Press, 1990), 191.

34. Interview, *Al-Mukhtar al Islami*, June 1987, cited in Rekhess, *Iranian Revolution*, 193. Tamimi said he still held that view when I interviewed him in Amman in late 1993. The Islamic Jihad's reverence for Iran is atypical of Sunni militant groups, most of which have disdain for things Shia, even Khomeini's "Islamic" upheaval. Tamimi himself is no longer supported by Iran, he told me, since Jordan made it clear that while he was welcome in Amman, his group could conduct no military activities against Israel or Israeli targets in the territories from Amman.

35. Fathi Abd al-Aziz Shikaki, "Al-Khomeini, al-Hall al-Islami wal-Badil," Cairo, 1979, cited by Rekhess, *Iranian Revolution*, 195.

36. Interview, Ahmed Abu Halabiya, acting president of the Islamic University, Gaza, July 1993. Abu Halabiya also told me that the PLO had repeatedly tried to "secularize" the university, without success.

37. Hamas-PLO rivalry increased in the fall of 1988 after the Palestinian quasi-Parliament adopted a resolution in Algiers calling for an end to the war with Israel in exchange for the partitioning of land between Israel and Palestine.

38. Many analysts discount the importance of the rise of the religious Right within Israel on militant Palestinian Islamism. But Abu-Amr concludes in *Islamic Fundamentalism*, xvi, that "increased Israeli intransigence (represented in the positions of the right-wing Israeli political parties and Jewish fundamentalists)" helped attract many Palestinians to the Islamic movement.

On the growth of Jewish fundamentalism within Israel, see Ian Lustick, *For the Land and the Lord: Jewish Fundamentalism in Israel* (New York: Council on Foreign Relations, 1988), and Ehud Sprinzak, *The Ascendance of Israel's Radical Right* (New York: Oxford University Press, 1991).

39. Jean-François Legrain, "A Defining Moment: Palestinian Islamic Fundamentalism," in *Islamic Fundamentalism and the Gulf Crisis*, ed. James Piscatori (Chicago: The Fundamentalism Project, 1991).

40. The estimate on Hamas funding is contained in an affidavit filed in supporting documentation for Abu Marzook's extradition. See "Ministry of Justice, Deposition of Yaacov Amidror (Head of Analysis and Assessment Division of Israeli Defense Forces Intelligence, August 1995)"; see also Abu-Amr, *Islamic Fundamentalism,* 87.

In an interview in July 1995, Steve Emerson, the investigative journalist, said that the peak year of American Hamas fund-raising was 1990–91, when it raised more than $5 million. He estimated that American charities have transferred $10–$20 million to the territories since its creation. Israeli sources said that the total Hamas budget was between $50 and $80 million a year.

41. Gen. Daniel Rothschild, former coordinator of the Civil Administration in the Occupied Territories and member of the Israeli delegation to the Palestinian-Israeli peace talks, estimated in 1993 that the West Bank and Gaza lost between $250 and $350 million a year due to the suspension of Gulf aid to the PLO and another $450 million a year due to the expulsion of Palestinians from the Gulf after the Gulf war—a total loss each year of between $700 and $800 million.

In *The Gaza Strip* (Washington, D.C.: Institute for Palestine Studies, 1995), 13–26, Sara Roy, an independent researcher, estimates Gulf remittances to the West Bank and Gaza at $250 million, or 10 percent of the territories' GNP, plus $70 million in annual aid to local institutions in the territories. In addition, she estimates that the PLO lost $480 million in direct aid from Gulf sources, a large percentage of which was funneled into the territories. Both Rothschild and Roy agree that as a result of the war, the PLO was virtually bankrupt and that many local institutions in the territories were forced to shut down.

42. Interview, Bassam Abu Sharif, Arafat's political adviser and troubleshooter, PLO, Tunis, February 1992.

43. *Al-Hayat,* London, December 17, 1995, translation by Michael Doran, Princeton University.

44. The U.S. State Department's Office of Counterterrorism supports allegations by Israel and the PLO of Iranian funding for Hamas. In the office's "Patterns of Global Terrorism: 1993," the State Department noted that both Hamas and Islamic Jihad received aid from Iran. And in testimony in January 1995 outgoing CIA director James Woolsey told the Senate Intelligence Committee that Iran had provided more than $100 million to Hamas, without stating over how long a period the aid was given. For its part, Islamic Jihad has not denied its obvious financial and political links to Teheran.

45. *Al-Safir,* February 2, 1993, in Arabic. A translation by Ehud Ya'ari appeared in English in *Jerusalem Report,* March 25, 1993, from which my account is drawn.

46. For an early attack by a secular intellectual, see Edward Said, *The Politics of Dispossession: The Struggle for Palestinian Self-Determination* (New York: Pantheon, 1994). See also "Symbols Versus Substance: A Year after the Declaration of Principles," *Journal of Palestine Studies* 24, no. 2 (Winter 1995). For an Israeli view, see David Makovsky, *Making Peace with the PLO* (Boulder, Colo.: Westview Press, 1996). I thank Makovsky for sharing the manuscript with me before its publication.

47. Makovsky, *Making Peace,* adds that Rabin's fear that his coalition government might fall as a result of a corruption scandal unrelated to the peace process compelled him to conclude the first Oslo agreement with the PLO more quickly than he would have preferred.

48. After Rabin's shocking murder, much was made of his conversion to the peace camp and the alleged warming of his relations with PLO chief Yasir Arafat. But Rabin never forgave Arafat for the "Jewish blood on his hands," his closest friends told me. Rabin insisted, for example, that families of the victims of PLO assaults be present at every peace accord he signed with the Palestinians, and he never failed to mention them and their loss in his speeches.

Rabin did not have a change of heart about Arafat. He grew to trust Arafat, but never to like him. Rather, he had made a hardheaded recalculation of how Israel's security could best be guaranteed. After the Gulf war, he had concluded that the occupied territories alone — "strategic depth," as military men called it — would not protect Israelis against the dangers inherent in the spread of Islamic militancy in the region. Soon not only Iran but also such zealous groups as Islamic Jihad might secure chemical and biological agents and other weapons of mass destruction, he had often told me. The territories, after all, had not protected Israel from Saddam Hussein's Scud missiles, nor, for that matter, had the United States. Israel had to make peace now, while its military strength was at a peak, with those Arab "enemies" willing to recognize Israel's right to exist. For Rabin, a blunt man of few words, safeguarding the security of the Jewish people remained his overriding objective. Making peace was not a favor he did for Arafat or the Palestinian people. For Rabin, relinquishing territory for peace was a way of neutralizing Israel's neighbors and eliminating a cause of Islamic militancy and hence vital to his nation's security interests. Because of this constancy and his reputation for intense suspicion of the Arabs' political goals and motives, and even of the peace whose terms he himself had shaped, many Israelis trusted him sufficiently to overcome their own anxieties and hostility toward Arabs and support the peace accords Israel had signed.

49. Israeli experts say that the split within Islamic Jihad and Sheikh Tamimi's expulsion were caused more by a dispute over money than by policy disagreements. But according to Ali al-Jarbawi, a Palestinian political scientist from the West Bank's Bir Zeit University, Sheikh Tamimi was expelled for agreeing to attend the twentieth session of the PLO's National Council to decide whether to participate in Madrid. Tamimi then founded a new Islamic Jihad branch — Islamic Jihad Movement Bayt al Maqdis. Most Islamic Jihad members had sided with Fathi Shikaki, the secretary-general of the Islamic Jihad who was deported in 1987 from the territories and who opposed Madrid unconditionally. As he wrote in an open letter marking the fifth anniversary of the Intifada (December 1992), "This 'favor' of being allowed to participate in the funereal conference held for the burial of our people and their cause is an accursed 'favor,' particularly when the participants of the conference see you as a national minority that will have to live in the shadow of a Jewish majority waiting for the right moment to banish you from your homeland and from the sacred city of Jerusalem." In October 1995, Shikaki was killed by Mossad agents in Malta on his return to Damascus from Libya.

I have relied heavily on Abu-Amr and Jarbawi in analyzing the Islamic movement's reaction to peace with Israel. See Jarbawi's "The Position of Palestinian Islamists on the Palestine-Israel Accord," *Muslim World* 84, no. 1–2 (January–April 1994): 129–34.

50. Ibid., 134.

51. Just before the 1993 signing ceremony, nearly 65 percent of Palestinians in the territories said they approved of the peace agreement, and almost three-quarters said they expected it to improve their economic conditions. See Survey Research Unit, Center for Palestine Research and Studies (CPRS), Nablus (poll on attitudes toward peace conducted on September 10–11, 1993). The second poll focused on political support for various parties and groups, November 5–8, 1993. Polling in the territories has traditionally presented a tremendous challenge, given the fear and suspicion bred by Israel's more than twenty-five-year occupation and, prior to that, of strict Egyptian rule of Gaza and Jordanian rule of the West Bank since 1950.

52. According to the court documents filed in Abu Marzook's extradition case, Salah had discussed with Abu Marzook in 1992 the possibility of killing Sari Nusseibeh, whom he identified as the "brains of the peace process." According to an affidavit based on Salah's confession, Abu Marzook was said to have replied: "They should really kill him." The murder was not carried out, the Israelis claim, because Salah "lost contact" with the Hamas activist in the territories who had proposed killing Nusseibeh: Israel had arrested him.

53. See *Mideast Mirror*, October 22, 1993, 6, and Steve Emerson, "The Other Fundamentalists," *New Republic*, June 12, 1995.

54. The executive order issued on January 24, 1995, blocks the American assets of twelve "terrorist organizations which threaten to disrupt the Middle East peace process," including Hamas, the Islamic Jihad, and Hezbollah, as well as the Jewish radical groups Kach and Kahane Chai. The Omnibus Counterterrorism Act, which was still stalled in Congress in late 1995, would grant the FBI new power to monitor and infiltrate suspected terrorist groups and would add a thousand new federal posts for counterterrorism.

55. Israel denies that this was its policy in Gaza, but Sara Roy, in *The Gaza Strip*, presents a compelling case to the contrary.

56. Roy, *The Gaza Strip*, 13–26 and 295.

57. Interview, October 1994, Terje Larsen, UN Under-Secretary-General for Palestinian Affairs. Larsen, a Norwegian who helped set up the secret talks in Oslo that led to the 1993 peace accord, said that unemployment in Gaza had soared to 60 percent, that rents had doubled, and that the value of all goods and services sold in the Strip had fallen by 15 percent since the PLO-Israeli accord in September 1993. See also Roy, *The Gaza Strip*, 309–16.

58. Assessments of alleged Iranian financial support for militant Islamic groups are unreliable. My assertion is based on interviews with Arab officials in several capitals. See also Abu Amr, *Islamic Fundamentalism*, 87–88, and Kenneth Katzman, "Hamas's Foreign Benefactors," *Middle East Quarterly* 2, no. 2 (June 1995). For an Israeli view, see Elie Rekhess, "The Terrorist Connection — Iran, Islamic Jihad, and Hamas," *Justice* 5 (May 1995).

59. For additional comments by Zahhar, see Hussein Hijazi, of *Al-Hayat*, "Hamas: Waiting for Secular Nationalism to Self-Destruct," *Journal of Palestine Studies* 24, no. 3 (Spring 1995): 81–88.

60. "Fatal Terrorist Attacks in Israel Since the Signing of the Declaration of Principles," Israel Foreign Ministry, September 6, 1995.

61. On May 3, 1995, the offices of *Al-Umma*, an East Jerusalem Arabic weekly affiliated with the leftist, secular opposition to Arafat's Palestinian Authority, were set on fire and gutted by plainclothes members of the Palestinian security police, according to *Jerusalem Report*, Jerusalem, June 15, 1995. Also in May, *Al-Watan*, a Hamas-run Gaza weekly, was closed down for three months. Sayed Abu Masameh, its editor and a leading Hamas member, was tried in a secret security court and given three years in jail for publishing an article on torture in Palestinian prisons.

62. "Opening Remarks," Hisham Sharabi, in *The Palestine National Authority: A Critical Appraisal* (Washington, D.C.: Center for Policy Analysis on Palestine, 1995). My Washington-based friend Sharabi, a Muslim nationalist and longtime supporter of the PLO, wrote that his initial support of the Oslo agreement was "tragically mistaken." The Islamic resistance movement, he wrote, was not composed of "bearded religious fanatics" but "militants of the Intifada now come of age, and of former members of the secular organizations who had given up on the PLO and its leadership." He also accused the American media of presenting a "stereotype" of Islamic militants. In his short essay, Sharabi, in fact, seemed to blame Israel, America, and the Western media for the admittedly sorry state of affairs in the new Palestinian autonomous entity — everyone except the Palestinians themselves, who, one would think, have at least some responsibility for the failings of the new Palestinian government.

63. In addition, the Israeli military commander in the occupied West Bank revealed in April 1995 that his soldiers had been ordered to kill fugitive Palestinians rather than arrest them. See "Israeli General Says Soldiers Must Kill Wanted Militants," *New York Times*, April 29, 1995.

64. *Mideast Mirror*, February 23, 1995, interview with Sheikh Yasin by Jamal Khashoggi.

65. Steve Rodan and Jacob Dallal, "A Fundamental Gamble," *Jerusalem Post Magazine*, August 19, 1994.

66. Ibid.

67. "Resurgent Islam in Israel" (Paper by Elie Rekhess presented at a conference on "The Arab Minority in Israel," Tel Aviv University, June 3–4, 1991); and Raphael Israeli, *Muslim Fundamentalism in Israel* (United Kingdom: Brassey's, 1993).

68. The term was coined by Elie Rekhess. I am indebted to him for his insights.

69. The word was coined by Emile Habiby, a leading Arabic writer and the recipient of Israel's first-ever prize for Arabic literature in 1992. In November 1993 Habiby defined opsimism as a mental state in which "I expect the worst and see the not-so-bad as an achievement."

70. *Zionist Writings, Essays and Addresses, Teodor Herzl*, vol. 2 (New York: Herzl Press, 1975), 19.

71. Anita Shapira, an Israeli historian, argues that there was a distinct shift in Zionist attitudes toward the indigenous Arabs between the first and second waves of Jewish immigration. The thirty-five thousand Jews who came to Palestine mainly from Russia and Eastern Europe in what the Israelis call the second *aliya*, between 1904 and 1914, had a decidedly more combative attitude toward Arabs than their predecessors. These immigrants, veterans of anti-Jewish riots, pogroms, and the revolution of 1905 in Russia, were idealistic young socialists who opposed what some of them saw as the earlier Jewish immigrants' "colonial" exploitation of the Arabs who tilled Jewish land. Keen on "self-defense," they did not want to remain a supplicant minority in their new land. "Attitudes acquired in the Diaspora were transferred to the realities of Palestine," she wrote. Anita Shapira, *Land and Power: The Zionist Resort to Force* (New York, Oxford: Oxford University Press, 1992), 29.

72. For a Palestinian account of the tensions between the Nashashibis and the Husseinis, see Nasser Eddin Nashashibi, *Jerusalem's Other Voice: Ragheb Nashashibi and Moderation in Palestinian Politics, 1920–1948* (Exeter: Ithaca Press, 1990), 55–57, 67, 87, 96, 100–101. For a somewhat sympathetic portrait of Mufti Husseini, see Philip Mattar, *The Mufti of Jerusalem*, rev. ed. (New York: Columbia University Press, 1991).

73. Danny Rubinstein, *The People of Nowhere: The Palestinian Vision of Home* (New York: Times Books, 1991), 9. Rubinstein attributes the estimate of destroyed settlements to Dr. Sharif Kana'ne of Bir Zeit University and to Mustafa Murad Dabbagh. Benny Morris, in his groundbreaking book *The Birth of the Palestine Refugee Problem, 1947–1949* (Cambridge: Cambridge University Press, 1988), counts 369 "abandoned" villages. Whether the Arabs "fled" or were systematically pushed out of Israel by the Jews is among the more controversial issues in Israel to this day.

74. Sabri Jiryis, *The Arabs in Israel* (New York and London: Monthly Review Press, 1976).

75. Among the first Arab citizens of Israel to graduate from Hebrew University with a law degree, Jiryis was an early member of the al-Ard, or "The Land" movement. Created in the late 1950s, al-Ard was a nationalist, anti-Zionist movement that fought for equal rights for Arabs in Israel. Strongly influenced by the pan-Arabism and socialism of Egypt's Nasser, the group endorsed the creation of a Palestinian and an Israeli state. Its suggestion that Galilee be annexed to a neighboring Arab state infuriated Israelis, and in 1964 the Israeli Supreme Court banned the group.

76. See, for instance, Sammy Smooha's *Arab and Jews in Israel*, vol. 2 (Boulder, Colo.: Westview Press, 1992), 13.

77. Interview, Kafr Qassem, Israel, May 1993.

78. Elie Rekhess, "Resurgent Islam in Israel" (Paper presented at a conference at Tel Aviv University's Moshe Dayan Center for Middle Eastern and African Studies, June 3–4, 1991).

79. Interview, Kafr Bara, July 1993.

80. Israel eventually placed restrictions on the haj. After gathering evidence that young Palestinians were being recruited into violent Islamic groups during the pilgrim-

age, according to Israeli intelligence officers, the government denied exit permits for pilgrimage to men between the ages of eighteen and twenty-five. Within Israel, Muslim men had to be at least thirty years old.

81. Rekhess, "Resurgent Islam," 7.

82. Alisa Rubin Peled, "Debating Islam in the Jewish State: Formative Moments in the Development of Muslim Communal Institutions in Israel," Center for Middle Eastern Studies, Harvard University, 1995, 252. Ms. Peled's doctoral dissertation is being published in 1996 by Cambridge University Press. See also her essay "The Islamic Movement in Israel," in *Islam, Muslims, and the Muslim States*, ed. Hussein Mutalib and Taj al-Islam Hashmi (London: Macmillan, 1994), 278–97.

83. Peled, "Debating Islam," 237–38.

84. Schiff and Ya'ari, *Intifada*, 171.

85. Israeli, *Muslim Fundamentalism*, 41. Israeli notes that the Islamic press's more militant tone was evident as early as November 1988, when an *Al-Sirat* editorial said that the "Palestinian people have hoisted the banner of Jihad to die for the sake of Allah." A November 1989 edition featured a photograph of Al-Aqsa Mosque in Jerusalem along with the following caption: "Oh fighter of Jihad! Awake! Acre and its shores are calling you!"

86. Elie Rekhess, "Arabs in a Jewish State: Images vs. Realities," *Middle East Insight* (January/February 1990).

87. *Fatwa*, March 3, 1992, in Hebrew. Translation by Tamar Kaplan.

88. Arabic newspapers in Jerusalem, for example, published phony pictures of King Fahd of Saudi Arabia with a giant cross on his chest; another wrote of the Saudi king's secret conversion to Christianity at the behest of Queen Elizabeth. Radical Palestinian Islamists, such as Islamic Jihad's Sheikh Tamimi, accepted Saddam's timely return to Islam. From exile in Amman, he called it "a high point in the Islamic awakening" of the 1980s. Kanan Makiya, *Cruelty and Silence* (New York: W. W. Norton & Company, 1993), 251.

89. Ibid., 244.

90. Since 1967, more than 500,000 Palestinians had been arrested or detained, 30,000 of them since the outbreak of the 1987 Intifada, according to a July 1994 report by Amnesty International. Al Haq, a Palestinian human-rights group, reported that some 564 houses of terrorism suspects had been demolished and 475 others sealed, not counting those destroyed for having been built illegally. And from the start of the Intifada until the end of 1994, some 1,258 Palestinians had been killed by Israelis, 11 percent of them after the 1993 Oslo peace accord, according to a report issued by B'Tselem, an Israeli human-rights group. During the same period, some 251 Israeli soldiers and civilians were killed by Palestinians, 91 of them (36 percent) since Oslo. *B'Tselem* 3, no. 1 (Spring 1995).

91. The following quotes come from "The Palestinians in Israel Debate Democracy in a Self-Critical Mood," Report No. 87, 1991, by Israel Shahak, a well-known leftist Jewish critic.

92. Ibid., 6.

93. Most Israeli Jews defend their treatment of the country's non-Jewish minority. Given what historian Howard M. Sachar termed the "remorselessness of Arab hostility," the successive wars, the guerrilla raids across their borders, and the general insecurity of the newfound and bankrupt state, many Israeli Jews felt that Israel could not realistically have been expected to honor its prewar promises of full and equal civil rights for its Arab minority. But Israel's Arabs were immediately given the right to vote — including Arab women for the first time — and to become members of Israel's Parliament, the Knesset. Israel's first 120-member Knesset, in fact, had three Arab members. Despite what must have been deeply ambivalent feelings at best about the Jewish state, Arab turnout in early Knesset elections was usually proportionately higher than that of the Jews.

Arabs had the right to establish their own political parties (though, practically, Israel made it difficult to do so) and to publish their own newspapers and magazines, albeit under heavy censorship. They sent their children to their own schools in their own language, and because Jewish compulsory education laws applied to Arabs as well, many Arab children received elementary school education for the first time. Sachar notes that although the Arab population of young Israel was far smaller than it had been under the British mandate, the number of Arab primary schools rose from 59 in 1948 to 114 by 1956, the number of teachers from 250 to 846, and the number of students from 10,000 to 26,500. See Howard M. Sachar, *A History of Israel* (New York: Knopf, 1979), 382–89.

94. Majid Al-Haj, *Education, Empowerment, and Control* (New York: State University of New York Press, 1995), 24–25.

95. See Jacob M. Landau, *The Arab Minority in Israel, 1967–1991* (Oxford: Clarendon Press, 1994); and a 1993 annual report by "Sikkui," Hebrew for "chance," which updates efforts by the Rabin government to redress basic inequalities but concludes that far more needs to be done.

96. The obelisk itself was erected in 1976 soon after another tragedy known in Israel as "Land Day," an annual Israeli Arab commemoration of five Arabs who were killed and sixty-two who were wounded when Israeli police opened fire in Nazareth that year on Israeli Arab citizens protesting Israel's expropriation of five thousand more acres of their land in Galilee.

97. This account of the court records is contained in Sabri Jiryis's book *The Arabs in Israel*, 140–53, and is confirmed by Uri Avnery, a leftist Jew who helped publicize the massacre. Interview, Tel Aviv, October 1994.

98. In October 1993, I interviewed Shadmi about the tragedy. He attributed the massacre to "unfortunate coincidences" and blamed his junior officer, Melinki, whom he called a "frustrated and cruel lieutenant" who had "misinterpreted" his orders. But he accepted "indirect responsibility" for the slaughter. "I was in charge. I can't say that I wasn't." Almost forty years after the events, Shadmi is still troubled by the massacre. "It was a tragedy for Israel, a young country then, so soon after the Holocaust, seeking acceptance in the world community, in the midst of war," he said. The one-piaster fine showed that the court believed that his guilt was limited to a "bureaucratic mixup" and that, as the court held, his major error was in not specifically telling Melinki and the border guard that no curfew violator was to be shot unless all other means to remove him from the village streets had been exhausted. He also noted that families of victims were compensated for the deaths of relatives — in accordance with "Arab tradition," a reference to the blood money often paid in Muslim countries as compensation to families whose kin have been injured or murdered. He and his family, he says, had visited Kafr Qassem to try to explain to young Israeli Arabs what happened. "As an Israeli, I'm still ashamed that such a thing happened. But I don't feel personally responsible." Shadmi, who is now in the real estate business, lives in a villa in Tel Baruch, an upper-middle-class suburb of Tel Aviv.

99. Raphael Israeli, *Muslim Fundamentalism*, 56. Israeli goes on to note that the speech so enraged Gen. Ehud Barak, Israel's foreign minister, who was then the chief of Israel's Central Command, that relying on British emergency rules, Barak had confined Darwish to his village and ordered him to report every morning to the district police for six months.

100. A similar version of this story appears in Israeli's *Muslim Fundamentalism*.

101. Smadar Perry, "Candidates Battle in Kafr Qassem Municipal Elections," *Yediot Ahronot*, October 29, 1993. Translation by Yafitte Bendory, consulate general of Israel, New York.

102. Smooha, 38–43. In a 1976 poll, for instance, the percentage of Arabs who identified themselves as "religious or very religious" stood at 46.5 percent. That percentage dropped to 38.2 percent by 1980, and to 31.8 percent by 1988. The percentage of Jews who had so identified themselves stood at 17.6 percent in 1980, a percentage that had

dropped to 13 by 1988. Smooha found an inverse correlation between religious devotion and educational levels.

103. The lack of interest in Arabs and Arabic culture in general is affirmed by another poll in Smooha's book. According to a 1988 survey, three-quarters of Israeli Arabs spoke fluent Hebrew, and 67 percent said they could speak, read, and write in both languages. Some 53 percent of all Arabs said they read Hebrew newspapers, as did 74 percent of Arabs who were literate in Arabic. Only 31 percent of Hebrew-speaking Jews, however, could speak Arabic, and most of those came from Arab countries. Almost none read Arabic newspapers.

104. Rekhess, "Resurgent Islam," 189–206.

105. Israeli, *Muslim Fundamentalism*, 45, 106. Israeli adds that the "secret tunnels" were, in fact, archeological excavations around the Temple Mount. The work was largely completed by early 1990. "No substantial damage is known to have occurred to the Muslim holy sites," Israeli notes.

106. *Al-Sirat*, March 1988, cited by Rekhess in "Resurgent Islam," 203.

Hamas's interpretation, however, may be no less self-serving than the Israeli categorization of some Israeli Arabs as "present absentees" whose land is forfeit to the state, according to Danny Rubinstein, in *People of Nowhere*. According to Israeli law, this category includes Palestinians who were displaced from or were not in their actual places of residence when the state was created. In 1949, they totaled about eighty thousand people in some four hundred Arab villages and about 750,000 acres of land, as well as twenty-five thousand homes in cities. In addition, Israel does not recognize fifty-one other Arab settlements, for other reasons.

In his book on Israeli Arabs, *Sleeping on a Wire: Conversations with Palestinians in Israel* (New York: Farrar, Straus and Giroux, 1993), 83, David Grossman calls the term "present absentees" oxymoronic. Imagine, he writes, "the shiver of delight that must have run through the entrails of the bureaucratic octopus when the term was first ejaculated in clerical ink."

107. Elie Rekhess, "Israel's Arab Citizens and the Peace Process," in *Israel Under Rabin*, ed. Robert Freedman (Boulder, Colo.: Westview Press, 1995), 190.

108. Orit Galili, *Ha'aretz*, July 29, 1988, cited in Israeli, *Muslim Fundamentalism*, 71.

109. *Al-Sirat*, no. 7, November 1987, cited in Israeli, *Muslim Fundamentalism*, 96–97.

110. For example, Ibrahim Sarsur, of Kafr Qassem, had once declared that even if the Israeli Arab Communists managed to liberate all of Palestine, he would still reject an alliance with them, for communism was "against human nature." Cited in Israeli, *Muslim Fundamentalism*, 53.

111. Peled, "Debating Islam," 233. Also Elie Rekhess, cited in "Islamic Activism in Israel: Municipal vs. Parliamentary Politics" (Lecture delivered at the Moshe Dayan Center, Tel Aviv University, May 26–27, 1992).

112. Interview, Kafr Bara, July 1993.

113. According to Rekhess, 37 percent of Islamic delegates to the general congress in 1995 supported boycotting the Knesset elections and were against running either independently or on a united Arab list; 25 percent were in favor of running as part of such a list; 5 percent wanted to run independently, and 33 percent thought that the movement's supporters should be allowed to vote as they saw fit.

114. The low voter turnout in the 1992 elections in some Islamist-run towns and villages suggests that at least some of the mayors might have quietly urged their constituents not to vote. In Umm al-Fahm, for instance, only 55 percent of eligible voters cast ballots, as opposed to 70 percent of Arabs nationally.

115. Shimon Peres had traveled to Umm al-Fahm and other Arab towns to campaign. So did the future labor minister Ora Namir, who said that she had won from

Sheikh Darwish himself a personal commitment to urge fellow Islamists to vote against Likud. Interviews, January 1994.

116. Nearly 9 percent of the Arabs supported Likud in the 1992 elections, but the star of the Arab-Israeli political scene was Shas, whose support rose from 1 percent in 1988 to 5 percent four years later. While the Communist Party (ICP) still received the largest proportion of Arab votes, its share fell dramatically from 33 percent in 1988 to 22 percent in 1992.

117. The Sikkui annual report for 1993 states that government spending in the Arab sector more than doubled in 1993, from about $60 million in 1992 to $140 million. In 1994, Arabs became eligible for monthly child-care payments, which until then had been granted only to those who had served in the military.

118. Grossman, *Sleeping on a Wire*.

119. Majid Al-Haq, *Education*, 19.

120. "Jews and Arabs in Israel, Common Values and Reciprocal Images," published by Sikkui in 1995, highlights the striking similarities in attitudes and perceptions among Israel's Jews and Arabs. The survey of more than 1,000 Jews and 530 Arabs between November 1993 and February 1994 — after the Oslo accord — showed "considerable similarity in patterns of daily life and leisure" and attitudes toward government, for example. Both groups, the report found, were "committed to living their lives in Israel, though the "desire for co-existence" was twice as high among the Arabs as among the Jews.

121. Smooha, *Arabs and Jews*, 271.

122. Cited in Rekhess, "Israel's Arab Citizens," 195.

123. An even more divisive question in Israel is the definition of a Jewish state — that is, to what extent religion and state should be separated and what constitutes an appropriate role of religion in the state, which is not the subject of this book. Personally, however, I share Herzl's view, articulated in *The Jewish State* in 1896: "Shall we end by having a theocracy? No, indeed. We shall keep our priests within the confines of their temples in the same way as we shall keep our professional army within the confines of their barracks. . . . They must not interfere in the administration of the state. . . . And if it should occur that men of other creeds and different nationalities come to live amongst us, we should accord them honorable protection and equality before the law."

124. In 1995, there were nine Israeli Arabs in the Knesset, but only five belonged to Zionist parties: Three are members of Labor; one is with the conservative Likud; one is with left-wing Meretz. Four others belong to the non-Zionist parties, two with the Arab Democratic Party and two with Haddash, a Jewish-Arab left-wing coalition. The Israeli Arabs have often tried to form an Arab bloc to maximize their leverage, but ideology and personality disputes have doomed such efforts.

125. "Jews and Arabs in Israel in an Era of Peace: Towards Accommodation or Alienation?" (panel discussion at Tel Aviv University, October 31, 1994, Konrad-Adenauer-Stiftung, Jerusalem), 11.

IRAN

1. William Shawcross, *The Shah's Last Ride* (New York: Simon & Schuster, 1988), 38–48.

2. *Religion and Politics in Iran*, ed. Nikki R. Keddie (New Haven: Yale University Press, 1983).

3. *Iran: A Country Study*, Area Handbook Series (Washington, D.C.: American University, 1978), 47.

4. Ibid., 19.

5. See Richard Frye, including his *Golden Age of Persia* (London: Weidenfeld and Nicolson, 1975); *The Cambridge History of Iran* vol. 4 (Cambridge, Eng.: Cambridge University Press, 1975).

6. Roy Mottahedeh, "The Shuubiyah Controversy and the Social History of Early Islamic Iran," *International Journal of Middle East Studies*, London, no. 2 (April 1976): 161–82.

7. Shiites reject not only the Sunni Muslim caliphs but the title itself, for caliph has a temporal connotation, while Shiites believe — much to the advantage of Ayatollah Khomeini — that their leader, or imam, is a divinely ordained figure, not unlike the Catholic church's king and pontiff before the Reformation. For differences between Sunni and Shiite theories of rule in Egypt and Iran, see Shahrough Akhavi, "The Clergy's Concepts of Rule in Egypt and Iran" and "Political Islam," *Annals of the American Academy of Political and Social Science* (November 1992).

8. This and the following verse are cited in Roy Mottahedeh's marvelous *The Mantle of the Prophet* (England: Penguin, 1985), 163, 180.

9. Mohammad Reza Pahlavi, *Answer to History* (New York: Stein & Day, 1980). The shah's bitter book about his rule and exile was published in French shortly before his death.

10. Several excellent works focus on the background of the Iranian revolution and, in particular, on the growing antagonism between the shah and the clerics. See, for example, Shaul Bakhash, *The Reign of the Ayatollahs*, rev. ed. (New York: Basic Books, 1990); Ervand Abrahamian, *Iran Between Two Revolutions* (Princeton, N.J.: Princeton University Press, 1982); Marvin Zonis, "Iran: A Theory of Revolution from the Accounts of the Revolution," *World Politics*, July 1983; Nikki R. Keddie, *Roots of Revolution* (New Haven: Yale University Press, 1981); Said Amir Arjomand, *The Turban for the Crown* (New York: Oxford University Press, 1988); and Edward Mortimer, *Faith and Power* (New York: Vintage, 1982).

11. Arjomand, *Turban for the Crown*, 91.

12. Ibid., 190.

13. Ibid., 191.

14. *Financial Times*, Special Supplement, February 8, 1993, "Crisis Looms," vi.

15. Patrick Clawson, "Iran's Challenge to the West: How, When, and Why" (Policy Papers, no. 33, Washington Institute for Near East Policy, Washington, 1993), 26. The same statistic appears in another Clawson study published in 1995, "Business as Usual?" American Jewish Committee, New York.

16. See Hamid Enayat, "Iran: Khumayni's Concept of the 'Guardianship of the Jurisconsult,'" in *Islam in the Political Process*, ed. James P. Piscatori (Cambridge, Eng.: Cambridge University Press, 1983), 160–81; Daniel Brumberg, "Khomeini's Legacy: Islamic Rule and Social Justice," in *Spokesmen for the Despised: Fundamentalist Leaders of the Middle East*, ed. Scott Appleby (Chicago: University of Chicago Press, 1996).

17. Khomeini was true to his word. After coming to power, his Islamic government relentlessly persecuted the Baha'is. Some two hundred have been executed and thousands arrested since the reign of the ayatollahs. As late as 1993, the government approved a secret blueprint that denies employment and education to members of this faith. The code was obtained and publicized by Reynaldo Galindo Pohl, the United Nations' special envoy to Iran, who scored this and other human-rights abuses in his reports. Some eighty thousand Christians remain in Iran. In 1994 they were subjected to what Human Rights Watch called "a fierce campaign," which included shutting down churches and the arrests of scores of young Christians, many of them converts from Islam. In almost no other Middle Eastern country has there been a pattern of conversions to Christianity. The phenomenon indicates the extent of the alienation of young Muslims from Islam in its ruling form. As for Iran's Jews, this once-sixty-thousand-strong

community has dwindled in the face of political pressure. But some thirty thousand Jews remain in Iran, legally free to practice their religion but subject also to harassment and police scrutiny.

18. Brumberg, "Khomeini's Legacy," 87.

19. The text, in fact, was translated by a Princeton professor who wishes to remain anonymous.

20. *Reselaat* newspaper, cited in *Los Angeles Times*, June 20, 1995, by Robin Wright.

21. According to Iranians, the foundation owns or represents in Iran, among numerous other companies and ventures, the Mercedes dealerships, General Motors, Pepsi, Procter & Gamble, the former Hilton, Inter-Continental, and Hyatt hotels, Yamaha, and Mars.

22. Dr. Assad Homayoun, interview, Washington, D.C., September 1995. I am grateful to Dr. Homayoun for giving me copies of his excellent newsletter "Focus on Iran."

23. Jamal Khashoggi, "Iran and Islamic Movements," *Mideast Mirror*, December 19, 1994. The Iranian policy paper, entitled "The Islamic Revolution and Leadership in the Muslim Brotherhood Movement," was published in Arabic. I am grateful to Khashoggi for sharing it with me. Khashoggi notes that the Muslim Brotherhood's bitterness toward Teheran was exacerbated by the Iranians' disclosure of the names of Brotherhood leaders around the world. The policy paper accuses Brotherhood leaders of a "hostile" and sometimes "childish" attitude toward Iran's Islamic revolution. As a result, it adds, the Brotherhood is "biased towards the West," and some of its factions are "client/agents of the Iraqi and Jordanian regimes."

24. Mohsen Rafighdoost, the head of the Foundation for the Oppressed, admitted that Iran had trained the Shiite militant who carried out the bombing. See Robin Wright, *In the Name of God: The Khomeini Decade* (New York: Simon & Schuster, 1989), 120–23.

25. Emmanuel Sivan, "The Enclave Culture," in *Fundamentalisms Comprehended*, eds. Martin E. Marty and R. Scott Appleby (Chicago: University of Chicago Press, 1995), 54. Sivan and other scholars have noted that non-Shia scholars opposed Iran's recent effort to impose Khamenei as the *marja al-taqlid* for Shiites living outside of Iran. Among the most vehement is Sheikh Sayyid Muhammad Hussein Fadlallah, the spiritual leader of Hezbollah in Lebanon. In an interview in 1994, Fadlallah stressed his political independence from Teheran and made clear that his supporters consider him a senior ayatollah who is worthy of *marja* status. To further bolster his already impressive collection of scholarly works, Fadlallah published in Arabic a hefty compendium of his *fatwas*, a move that Sivan viewed as a reflection of his desire to be recognized as a source of imitation for Arab Shia outside Iran. While Fadlallah does not specifically reject the concept of *walayat al-faqih*, he has rejected the idea that Lebanon can be an Islamic state in the near future, given its religious and sectarian diversity. Based on my reporting in the Middle East, Fadlallah commands far more respect among Shia theologians for his mastery of Islamic thought and law than does Khamenei.

26. Fouad Ajami, "Iran: The Impossible Revolution," *Foreign Affairs*, 1988–1989, America and the World.

27. "Guardians of Thought: Limits on Freedom of Expression in Iran," A Middle East Watch Report, Human Rights Watch, New York, August 1993.

28. *Iran Times*, February 22, 1991, cited in "Guardians of Thought," 117.

29. Interview, Richard W. Bulliet, New York, November 1995.

30. Interview, Teheran, April 1992.

31. "Iran — Tearing Itself Apart?" *Jane's Intelligence Review* 7, no. 10 (October 1, 1995).

32. Robin Wright, *Los Angeles Times*, June 27, 1995.

33. The average number of print runs for a book was now around three thousand, as compared to one to two thousand before 1979. "Guardians of Thought," Middle East Watch, 69.

34. Arjomand, *Turban for the Crown*, 96–99.

35. Ibid., 104.

36. Fouad Ajami, "The Impossible Life of Moslem Liberalism," *New Republic*, June 2, 1986.

37. Ibid.

38. Ibid.

39. Wright, *In the Name of God*, 45.

40. Edward G. Shirley, "The Iran Policy Trap," *Foreign Policy*, no. 96 (Fall 1994). Shirley is the pseudonym of a former CIA specialist on Iran. He remains one of this country's most subtle analysts of the Iranian political scene. I am grateful to Shirley for his encouragement and insights.

41. Ajami, "Impossible Revolution."

42. Ibid., and Sivan, "Enclave Culture," 54.

43. *Zanan*, no. 19, Teheran. Translation by Nahzila Fathi.

44. In issues 11 and 21 (1994–1995) of *Kiyan*, Sorush defends democracy on Islamic grounds. "The first criterion of democracy is to tolerate other people's ideas and to be patient with them, to respect an opinion you consider completely false," Sorush writes. Referring by implication to the *fatwa* against Salman Rushdie, Sorush says: "It is not right [in the name of banning blasphemy] to repress opinion-makers and free thinkers, to discard scientific thinking about religion, and to replace serious doubts with emulated beliefs just to keep up appearances." If a system of government is "above the law," he writes, no matter what the pretext or rationale, "it is against democracy." As for democracy, its results "are not pre-determined, nor is the choice of the [*hakim*] leader of the Muslims. The leader needs to be determined with a vote of and choice by the people. It is not only the right, but the Islamic responsibility of religious people to select their [*hakim*] leader in a fair manner and to determine his responsibility in a way that will prompt him to make fewer errors. If he does transgress, his errors should be corrected in a democratic way." From "Coping and the Management of the Faithful: A Discourse on the Relations Between Religion and Democracy."

45. Eric Rouleau, "The Islamic Republic of Iran: Paradoxes and Contradictions in a Changing Society," *Middle East Insight* 11, no. 5, special ed., Iran (1995). Rouleau's article was among the first to describe in detail Iran's "silent revolution," as he called the Islamic reform movement.

46. Transcript of interview, Qum, October 1993, Ministry of Islamic Guidance.

47. Rouleau, "Islamic Republic."

48. Edward G. Shirley, "Is Iran's Present Algeria's Future?" *Foreign Affairs* 74, no. 3 (May/June 1995).

49. Nikki R. Keddie, "Religion and Rule in Iran: An Historical Perspective," *Middle East Insight*, special ed., Iran, July–August 1995.

50. Hamid Algar, "The Oppositional Role of the Ulama in Twentieth-Century Iran," in *Scholar, Saints and Sufis*, ed. Nikki R. Keddie (Berkeley: University of California Press, 1972), 245–55.

51. Amir Taheri, *Asharq al-Awsat* newspaper, London, in *Mideast Mirror*, August 10, 1995.

52. Letter of protest to Ali-Mohammad Besharati, minister of interior, from Human Rights Watch/Middle East, September 14, 1995.

53. Xinhua News Agency, November 1, 1995.

54. *New York Times*, May 30, 1995.

55. Patrick Clawson, "Iran's Challenge to the West: How, When, and Why (Washington, D.C.: Washington Institute Policy Papers, no. 33, 1993): xi.

56. Patrick Clawson, "Business as Usual?" *International Perspectives* 33, American Jewish Committee, 1995.

57. "Guardians of Thought," 89.

58. Iran is accused of supporting numerous groups that the State Deparment has labeled terrorist organizations as well as countries known to host such terrorist groups, like Sudan. Since late 1991, American officials say, Iran, for example, has given Hamas, the Palestinian militants who oppose the Arab-Israeli peace process, an estimated $20 million a year. Islamic Jihad has an office in Teheran, as do several other militant Islamic organizations. Many Palestinians, however, deny that Iran has actually provided the assistance it has pledged. They often complain that the Islamic Republic, perpetually short of cash, has failed to live up to its financial commitments to its fellow militants throughout the Middle East.

59. Robert Fisk, *Independent* (London), May 22, 1995.

Conclusions

1. Reza Afshari, "An Essay on Scholarship, Human Rights, and State Legitimacy: The Case of the Islamic Republic of Iran." I am grateful to Afshari for sharing his manuscript with me, which is being published in *Human Rights Quarterly* (May 1996). My discussion with Afshari is based on the argument he presents in this essay, from which I have quoted.

2. Several Iranian clerics and lay reformers, for example, mentioned the authority of the Hobregan, the clerical "Council of Experts," which appoints the Leader and has the authority to remove him and, in theory, to restructure his post and responsibilities as well.

3. Abdullahi Ahmed An-Na'im, *Toward an Islamic Reformation* (New York: Syracuse University Press, 1990), 19–21. An-Na'im, a human-rights activist and legal scholar, proposes that this reinterpretation be accomplished through the Islamic principle of *naskh*, the abrogation, or repeal, of the legal efficacy of certain verses of the Koran in favor of other verses.

4. Reza Afshari, "An Essay on Islamic Cultural Relativism in the Discourse of Human Rights," *Human Rights Quarterly* 16, no. 2 (May 1994), 270.

5. Olivier Roy, *The Failure of Political Islam* (Cambridge, Mass.: Harvard University Press, 1994), 121.

6. Ghassan Salamé, "Islam and the West," *Foreign Policy*, no. 90 (Spring 1993): 29.

7. Barnett R. Rubin, *The Fragmentation of Afghanistan* (New Haven and London: Yale University Press, 1995), 179.

8. Hisham Sharabi, a Palestinian-born professor and longtime friend who lives in Washington, D.C., has presented an anguished but savagely honest portrait of contemporary Arab society that he calls "neopatriarchy"—a modern sultanism that mixes modernity with traditional patriarchy and winds up both distorting development and corrupting tradition. See *Neopatriarchy* (New York: Oxford University Press, 1988).

9. Emmanuel Sivan, "Arab Nationalism in the Age of Islamic Resurgence," to be published in *Rethinking Arab Nationalism*, eds. J. Jankovsky and I. Gershuni (New York: Columbia University Press, 1996).

10. R. Hrair Dekmejian, *Islam in Revolution*, 2d ed. (New York: Syracuse University Press, 1995), 57.

11. Sana Abed-Kotob, "The Accommodationists Speak: Goals and Strategies of the Muslim Brotherhood of Egypt," *International Journal of Middle East Studies* 27 (August 1995): 322.

12. Those anxious about the implications of rising religious militancy for nascent

civil society in the Middle East and for terrorism within the United States have been denounced for alleged expressions of "cultural superiority at its most arrogant" and accused of complicity in a Zionist-led conspiracy against Islam itself. Not even the bombing of the World Trade Center has given these defenders of Islamic militancy pause.

One egregious example is a recent article in *Middle East Policy* 4 (September 1995) by Arthur L. Lowrie, an adjunct professor at the University of South Florida. Lowrie misrepresents the published views of several critics of Islamic militancy; he also defends institutions — including his own — against charges that they have employed a violent Islamic radical and supporters of such extremists. As I write these words, law enforcement officials are investigating links between Islamic Jihad, the Palestinian terrorist group, and the Tampa-based World and Islam Studies Enterprise (WISE), an Islamic think tank that until June 1995 had a three-year affiliation with the University of South Florida. The university finally severed ties to WISE only after its administrative director, Ramadan Abdullah Shallah, who also taught Middle East politics at the university in 1994 and 1995, moved to Damascus and announced that he was the new leader of Islamic Jihad, which claims credit for murdering dozens of Israelis in suicide attacks. Steve Emerson, an investigative journalist, had made serious allegations about WISE as early as November 1994. In May 1995, the *Tampa Tribune* ran a series of articles by Michael Fechter documenting the connections of WISE and its personnel with groups and individuals that praise terrorist attacks against Israelis and oppose peace between Arabs and Israelis. Both Fechter, who met with university officials, and Emerson confirm that the university repeatedly failed to respond to such allegations and expressions of concern. The university suspended its relations with WISE in the fall of 1995 as part of a review of all its contracts with outside groups. It finally dissociated itself from WISE only after Abdullah Shallah surfaced in Syria as head of Islamic Jihad and called for revenge against Israel and America for the murder of Islamic Jihad's former chief.

In a subsequent article, Lowrie expressed "shock" but did not say that he may have been wrong to embrace Abdullah, whom he called "a devout Muslim" and a "strong family man" who enjoyed USF basketball games. "Behind the Mask of Islam," *Tallahassee Democrat*, November 12, 1995.

13. Martin Kramer, an American-born Israeli scholar, has discussed the range of reaction to Islamism in several essays, including "The Mismeasure of Political Islam" (Annual Goldman Lecture, Georgetown University, Washington, D.C., April 11, 1995). I am indebted to Kramer, who counts himself in the "modified rejectionist" camp, for his insights on the militant Islamic trend.

14. Ghassan Salamé, *Democracy Without Democrats?* (New York: St. Martin's Press, 1994).

15. Edward Djerejian, assistant secretary of state for Middle East and Near Eastern affairs (speech at Meridian House, Washington D.C., June 1992).

16. Mahmud al-Zahhar, interview in *Muslim World* (Spring 1995).

17. Afshari, "Islamic Cultural Relativism," 255.

18. "Claiming the Future," The World Bank, October 1995; "Will Arab Workers Prosper or Be Left Out in the Twenty-first Century?," The World Bank, August 1995.

19. Bernard Lewis, "The Middle East Crisis in Historical Perspective," *American Scholar* (Winter 1992).

Acknowledgments

BOOKS, LIKE JOURNALISM, are joint ventures. While errors of fact or omission are my fault, many friends, scholars, and even critics tried to prevent me from making too many of them. I would like to thank, first of all, the Twentieth Century Fund—Richard Leone and his able staff, especially Carol Starmack, Laurie Ahlrich, and Tomasin Whitaker—for giving me such a wonderful place to work and for providing financial support while I was on leave from the *Times*. Ellen Chesler and David Callahan listened patiently to many of my ideas and challenged them. I am grateful for the fund's support during these two years.

The New York Times gave me a much appreciated leave, for which I would like to thank Joe Lelyveld, who knows firsthand how hard it is to write a book and work at daily journalism, as well as others who helped me—Linda Lake, Walt Baranger, Warren Hoge, Marty Arnold, Geri Fabrikant, Arthur Gelb, Abe Rosenthal, Bill Safire, Bernie Gwertzman, Steve Weisman, Jim McKinley, and Kati Ghazi.

Throughout this book, I thanked many of the people whose ideas I borrowed, but I owe a special debt to Fouad Ajami and his wife, Michelle, for their friendship and guidance. Bernard Lewis read and corrected my version of Islamic history, as did Gilles Kepel, Peter Awn, and Emmanuel Sivan, superb analysts of Islam. Fareed Zakaria at the Council on Foreign Relations edited some of my articles in *Foreign Affairs*. Jim Hoge made several trips possible by publishing my work in *Foreign Affairs*. Les Gelb provided encouragement, wisdom, and humor.

Don Peretz read and commented on several chapters, and I received considerable help from several other able scholars: Dirk Vandewalle, Robert Satloff, Malika Zeghal, Ray Hinnebusch, John Entelis, Shimon Shamir, Martin Kramer, Abdullahi An-Na'im, Lisa Anderson, Daniel Pipes, and Abdelwahab El-Affendi, an Islamist himself, whom even I might vote for if ever he sought political office rather than a life of contemplation. I must also thank my late friend Selim Issa for introducing me to a Middle East that I would otherwise never have known. He was also loved by my dear friend Smadar Perry, to whom my gratitude is immeasurable.

Itamar Rabinovich helped me understand not only his native Israel but Syria. So did my friend Patrick Seale, a learned journalist. In Israel, Elie Rekhess, Dan Rothschild, Majid Al-Haj, Mariam Mar'i, Uri Lubrani, and Eitan Haber deserve special mention. Raghida Dergham, Odeh Aburdene, and Marius Deeb made excellent suggestions on Lebanon, along with Habeeb Malek and Jamil Mroue. Professor Werner Ende, in Germany, helped me on Saudi Arabia, along with Barbara G. B. Ferguson. In Jordan, a special thanks to Lucy Aslou, Metri Twal, Leema Nabil, Tammy Qassem, and Salameh Neamat. My chapter on Egypt benefited from J. C. Hurewitz's guidance and Tahseen Bashir's great wisdom and skeptical eye. My dear friends Lea and Boutros Boutros-Ghali, Nadia and Zuheir Farid, Amy Matouk, and Daisy and Ahmad Baha'edin have been my teachers ever since my first encounter with Egypt many years ago.

In Washington, D.C., Roscoe Suddarth, of the Middle East Institute, and Christine Rourke helped me find books I couldn't locate. Robert Kaplan, Steve Emerson, and Joseph Braude encouraged and advised me, as did Harold Rhode, Karin Lissakers, Martin Mayer, Juliet Gal, Frances Cook, Assad Homayoun, and Marilyn Melkonian.

Many of the works cited in this book would not have appeared without those who translated Arabic texts for me: Lama Abu Odeh, Michael Doran, and Khalid Duran. I am indebted in particular to Khalid, who possesses an encyclopedic knowledge of Islamic militants in Europe and elsewhere. Tamar Kaplan translated several works in Hebrew, even a Hebrew *fatwa*, an Islamic ruling.

I also thank Rita Hauser for her friendship, her library, and her constant concern that I see the latest reports from the region as well as all points of view.

Ricky Goldstein, Virginia Sherry, Elahe Hicks, Andrew Whitley, Susan Osnos, and others at Human Rights Watch either read chapters or provided me with invaluable material.

In London, Mai Qassoub helped with friendship and her marvelous bookstore. In Paris, Safa Haeri, Ghassan Salamé, and others who asked not to be identified provided valuable guidance. Chris Dickey, Susan Grant, and Larry Maisel encouraged not only my last two books but this one as well.

The Society Library in New York and the librarians at John Jermain Memorial Library in Sag Harbor, New York, found several obscure works for me.

Several friends in New York read chapters for me to see if this book—or parts of it—made sense to them: I am grateful to Caroline Seely, Bob Denison, David Harris, and Joy de Menil in particular.

There are many Arabs—too many, in fact—who live in countries where they would be endangered if I thanked them by name. But they know who they are, and I hope that the future will be better and freer for them and their children.

In America, Gary Press made valiant efforts to keep me solvent during this project, and Stanley Mirsky is a doctor no foreign correspondent would want to be without. Sam Piekarski and Fay Weiss got me safely to and from odd places throughout the region.

At Simon & Schuster, there are so many people to thank. But above all, I owe this book to Alice Mayhew, my friend and incomparable editor, and Roger Labrie, who made me refine so many important points and put up with my intermittent smoking binges. And many thanks to Steve Messina, who oversaw the copyediting of the book, with its many Arabic and Persian terms.

Finally, I want to thank Jason Epstein, for all the reasons he knows and for far too many to list: The book is already too long.

Index